David Hume, William Strahan, George Birkbeck Norman Hill

Letters of David Hume to William Strahan

David Hume, William Strahan, George Birkbeck Norman Hill

Letters of David Hume to William Strahan

ISBN/EAN: 9783744687522

Printed in Europe, USA, Canada, Australia, Japan

Cover: Foto ©Thomas Meinert / pixelio.de

More available books at **www.hansebooks.com**

LETTERS

OF

DAVID HUME

TO

WILLIAM STRAHAN

NOW FIRST EDITED

WITH NOTES, INDEX, ETC.

BY

G. BIRKBECK HILL, D.C.L.

PEMBROKE COLLEGE

Oxford

AT THE CLARENDON PRESS

1888

TO

THE RIGHT HONOURABLE

ARCHIBALD PHILIP

FIFTH EARL OF ROSEBERY

IN GRATEFUL ACKNOWLEDGMENT

OF THE SERVICES WHICH HE HAS RENDERED

TO LITERATURE

BY SAVING THESE LETTERS

FROM DISPERSION

THIS WORK IS DEDICATED.

PREFACE.

In the summer of last year I was allowed to examine this series of Letters[1]. The interest with which I read them made me long to save them from dispersion. Were they once scattered by auction, their fate would be the fate of the leaves of the Sibyl—

> Numquam deinde cavo volitantia prendere saxo,
> Nec revocare situs, aut jungere carmina curat.

The price that was asked for them, though large in itself, was moderate when the importance of the collection was considered. Yet for some weeks I almost despaired of finding a purchaser. The funds at the disposal of the Bodleian Library were altogether inadequate. At the British Museum I should probably have met with success, had not its grant been lately curtailed. By the happy suggestion of the Master of Balliol College I applied to the Earl of Rosebery. His lordship at once consented to buy the whole collection. The obligation under which he has thereby laid men of letters will, I feel sure, be by them gratefully acknowledged. Unfortunately

---

[1] They belonged to Mr. F. Barker, of 43, Rowan Road, Brook Green, a dealer in autographs, to whom I have expressed my acknowledgments in my edition of *Boswell's Life of Johnson*, for the permission which he gave me to print some of Johnson's letters that were in his possession. I may add that he has lent me also a large and curious collection of letters written to William and Andrew Strahan, by men of letters and publishers, chiefly Scottish. Of these I have made some use in my notes to the present work. It would be a great pity if the dispersion which threatens them were not averted.

the series is not quite perfect, for a few of the letters had been sold separately by a previous owner. My efforts to get copies of these have been so far fruitless.

In preparing my notes I have made use of the collection of Hume Papers in the possession of the Royal Society of Edinburgh[1]. I had hoped to find among them the other side of the correspondence, but in this I was disappointed. Only a few of Strahan's letters have been preserved. Of one letter that was missing he happily had kept a copy. Hume, with a levity which is only found in a man who is indifferent to strict truthfulness, had charged him with deception. The answer which was sent must have startled that ease-loving philosopher from his complacency, and taught him a lesson which it was a disgrace to him not to have learnt long before[2].

In my notes my aim has been not only to make every letter clear, but also to bring before my readers the thoughts and the feelings of Hume's contemporaries in regard to the subjects which he discusses. 'Every book,' he says, 'should be as complete as possible within itself, and should never refer for anything material to other books[3].' If this rule is just, I could not but let my notes swell under my hand, so varied and so interesting are the matters touched on in his letters. On his quarrel with Rousseau I dwell at considerable length. The, rank which the two men held in the republic of letters was so high, the interest which their strife excited was so great, and the spectators of the contest were so eminent, that even at this distance of time it deserves to be carefully studied. My endeavour has been not only to examine the conduct of the two men[4], but also to exhibit the opinions which were entertained by all who were in

[1] My extracts from these papers are marked *M. S. R. S. E.*
[2] *Post*, p. 266.   [3] *History of England*, ed. 1802, ii. 101.
[4] *Post*, pp. 76-84.

any way concerned[1]. The violence of Hume's feelings towards the English which is shown in many of his letters[2] is curious enough to justify a long note[3]. It was due it is clear partly to a deep sense of slighted merit, and partly to anger at what he describes as 'the mad and wicked rage against the Scots[4].' Violent as he was towards Englishmen in general, still more violent was he towards the most famous Englishman of his time[5]. Why Lord Chatham roused his anger I have attempted to explain[6]. The confidence of Hume's belief that the country was on the eve of bankruptcy[7], is one more proof how fallible may be the judgment of even the first historian and the first economist of his age[8]. His no less confident expectations about the war with our American colonies were however speedily justified by the event. From the outset he saw that conquest was impossible[9]. It will be seen that a few months after his death some of these letters were shown to George III[10]. We may wonder whether the king's obstinacy was for a moment shaken, when he read the lines in which his highly-pensioned Tory historian proved that only 'the oppressive arm of arbitrary power' could crush the rebels[11]. How much it were to be wished that he had seen also that other letter where Hume tells how he had found the First Lord of the Admiralty, with some loose associates, fishing for trout 'with incredible satisfaction, at a time when the fate of the British Empire was in dependence, and in dependence on him[12].'

If these Letters exhibit, as they too often do, Hume's

[1] *Post*, pp. 86–92.   [2] *Post*, pp. 114, 151, 247, 248, 255.
[3] *Post*, pp. 50–58.   [4] *Post*, pp. 49, 58–63.
[5] *Post*, pp. 113, 134, 185, 289.   [6] *Post*, p. 195, *n.* 29.
[7] *Post*, pp. 114, 161, 173, 185, 201, 217.
[8] *The Decline and Fall of the Roman Empire* and *The Wealth of Nations* were not published till the last year of Hume's life (*post*, p. 314).
[9] *Post*, pp. 174, 288, 308.   [10] *Post*, p. 367.
[11] *Post*, p. 289.   [12] *Post*, p. 324.

'distempered, discontented thoughts,' his moral cowardice, his vanity, and his unmanly complaints of the neglect of the world, they show at the same time the noble industry of the scholar. If from a love of 'ignoble ease' he suppressed Essays and Dialogues[1], yet it was not into 'peaceful sloth' that he sank. He more than once quotes 'a saying of Rousseau's, that one half of a man's life is too little to write a book and the other half to correct it[2].' In truth, he never wearied of the attempt to bring his works as near to perfection as possible, and it was from his death-bed that his last corrections were sent[3].

Hume's spelling I have retained, for it is interesting both in its peculiarities and its blunders. That he had his own views about orthography is shown hereafter[4].

His brief *Autobiography*, which I have reprinted, will be a convenient introduction to the study of his Letters.

In the letters from Adam Smith, one of which is new[5], and from Hume's brother and nephew, some account is given of the publication of the manuscripts which he left behind him.

I should treat the memory of an eminent man of letters with injustice did I not express my great obligations to Dr. Burton's *Life of David Hume*. I have also to thank Sir James Fitzjames Stephen for his permission to print an interesting letter on post-office franks[6]; Dr. Andrews for information about the Ohio Scheme[7]; Mr. James Gordon, M.A., the learned Librarian of the Royal Society of Edinburgh ; and Mr. G. K. Fortescue, of the British Museum, who has helped me in many difficulties which from time to time I encountered in editing these Letters.

G. B. H.

[1] *Post*, pp. 230, 233, 330–2, 346.
[3] *Post*, p. 342.   [4] *Post*, p. 27.
[6] *Post*, p. 189.

[2] *Post*, p. 200.
[5] *Post*, p. 351.
[7] *Post*, p. 163.

TABLE OF CONTENTS.

CONTENTS.

THE LIFE OF DAVID HUME, Esq.

WRITTEN BY HIMSELF.

MY OWN LIFE.

It is difficult for a man to speak long of himself without vanity, therefore I shall be short. It may be thought an instance of vanity that I pretend at all to write my life ; but this narrative shall contain little more than the history of my writings, as indeed almost all my life has been spent in literary pursuits and occupations. The first success of most of my writings was not such as to be an object of vanity.

I was born the twenty-sixth of April, 1711, old style, at Edinburgh. I was of a good family, both by father and mother. My father's family is a branch of the earl of Home's or Hume's[1]; and my ancestors had been proprietors of the estate which my brother possesses for several generations[2]. My mother was daughter of Sir David Falconer, President of the College of Justice : the title of Lord Halkerton came by succession to her brother.

My family, however, was not rich ; and, being myself a younger brother, my patrimony, according to the mode of my country, was of course very slender. My father, who passed for a man of parts, died when I was an infant, leaving me with

---

[1] Hume showed his family pride by selecting the Earl of Home as one of the two witnesses to his will. For the spelling of the name see *post*, p. 9, *n.* 10.

[2] The estate, which lay very near Berwick, bore the name of Ninewells. ' It is so named from a cluster of springs of that number. They burst forth from a gentle declivity in front of the mansion, which has on each side a semicircular rising bank, covered with fine timber, and fall, after a short time, into the bed of the river Whitewater, which forms a boundary in the front.' Burton's *Life of Hume*, i. 8.

b

an elder brother and sister, under the care of our mother, a woman of singular merit : who, though young and handsome, devoted herself entirely to the rearing and educating of her children [1]. I passed through the ordinary course of education with success, and was seized very early with a passion for literature, which has been the ruling passion [2] of my life, and the great source of my enjoyments. My studious disposition, my sobriety, and my industry, gave my family a notion that the law was a proper profession for me ; but I found an unsurmountable aversion to every thing but the pursuits of philosophy and general learning ; and, while they fancied I was poring upon Voet [3] and Vinnius [4], Cicero and Virgil were the authors which I was secretly devouring [5].

[1] Dr. Alexander Carlyle records the following anecdote, which he had from one of 'Hume's most intimate friends, the Honourable Patrick Boyle.' ' When David and he were both in London, at the period when David's mother died, Mr. Boyle found him in the deepest affliction, and in a flood of tears. He said to him, " My friend, you owe this uncommon grief to your having thrown off the principles of religion ; for if you had not, you would have been consoled by the firm belief that the good lady, who was not only the best of mothers, but the most pious of Christians, was now completely happy in the realms of the just." To which David replied, " Though I threw out my speculations to entertain and employ the learned and metaphysical world, yet in other things I do not think so differently from the rest of mankind as you may imagine." ' Dr. A. Carlyle's *Autobiography*, p. 273. With this anecdote we may contrast the following : Lord Charlemont ' hinted ' to Hume, shortly after his return to England in 1766, ' that he was convinced he must be perfectly happy in his new friend Rousseau, as their sentiments were, he believed, nearly similar. " Why no, man," said he ; " in that you are mistaken ; Rousseau is not what you think him ; he has a hankering after the Bible, and indeed is little better than a Christian in a way of his own." ' *Memoirs of the Earl of Charlemont*, ed. 1812, i. 230.

[2] The ' ruling passion ' comes from Pope's *Moral Essays*, i. 174 :—
  ' Search then the ruling passion : there alone
      The wild are constant, and the cunning known.'
Johnson speaks of this as Pope's ' favourite theory,' and adds :—' Of any passion, thus innate and irresistible, the existence may reasonably be doubted.' Johnson's *Works*, ed. 1825, viii. 293.

[3] Paul Voet, born 1619, died 1677, a Dutch jurisconsult, published among other works *Commentarius in Institutiones imperiales*. His son John, born 1647, died 1714, published *Commentarius ad Pandectas*. *Nouv. Biog. Gén.* xlvi. 335.

[4] Arnold Vinnen, born 1588, died 1657. Francis Horner, in the plan which he laid down for the study of the Scotch law in 1797, says :—' I must study both Heineccius and Vinnius.' *Life of Horner*, ed. 1843, i. 52.

[5] Hume, in a statement of his health which he drew up for a physician in the year 1734, says :—' Every one who is acquainted either with the philosophers or critics knows that there is nothing yet established in either of these two sciences,

My very slender fortune, however, being unsuitable to this plan of life, and my health being a little broken by my ardent application, I was tempted, or rather forced, to make a very feeble trial for entering into a more active scene of life [1]. In 1734, I went to Bristol, with recommendations to eminent merchants; but in a few months found that scene totally unsuitable to me [2]. I went over to France with a view of prosecuting my studies in a country retreat; and I there laid that plan of life which I have steadily and successfully pursued. I resolved to make a very rigid frugality supply my deficiency of fortune,

and that they contain little more than endless disputes, even in the most fundamental articles. Upon examination of these, I found a certain boldness of temper growing in me, which was not inclined to submit to any authority in these subjects, but led me to seek out some new medium by which truth might be established. After much study and reflection on this, at last, when I was about eighteen years of age, there seemed to be opened up to me a new scene of thought, which transported me beyond measure, and made me, with an ardour natural to young men, throw up every other pleasure or business to apply entirely to it. The law, which was the business I designed to follow, appeared nauseous to me, and I could think of no other way of pushing my fortune in the world, but that of a scholar and philosopher.' Burton's *Hume*, i. 31.

[1] In this same statement, after describing a weakness of spirits into which he had fallen, which hindered him from 'following out any train of thought by one continued stretch of view,' he continues :—' I found that as there are two things very bad for this distemper, study and idleness, so there are two things very good, business and diversion ; and that my whole time was spent betwixt the bad, with little or no share of the good. For this reason I resolved to seek out a more active life, and though I could not quit my pretensions in learning but with my last breath, to lay them aside for some time in order the more effectually to resume them.' *Ib.* p. 37. It is a curious coincidence that Hume and Johnson were first attacked by melancholy at the same time. 'About the beginning of September, 1729,' says Hume, ' all my ardour seemed to be in a moment extinguished.' *Ib.* p. 31. 'While Johnson was at Lichfield,' writes Boswell, ' in the college vacation of the year 1729, he felt himself overwhelmed with an horrible hypochondria.' Boswell's *Life of Johnson*, Clarendon Press edition, i. 63. We may compare with both these cases the melancholy into which John Stuart Mill sank at about the same age, in the autumn of 1826. Mill's *Autobiography*, ed. 1873, p. 133.

[2] In the *Memoirs of Hannah More*, i. 16, it is stated that ' she was much indebted for her critical knowledge to a linen-draper of Bristol, of the name of Peach. He had been the friend of Hume, who had shown his confidence in his judgment by entrusting to him the correction of his *History*, in which he used to say he had discovered more than two hundred Scotticisms.' He told her that ' Hume was dismissed from the merchant's counting-house on account of the promptitude of his pen in correction of the letters entrusted to him to copy.' The narrative is not free from error, as it is stated in it that Hume resided two years in Bristol.

to maintain unimpaired my independency, and to regard every object as contemptible, except the improvement of my talents in literature.

During my retreat in France, first at Rheims, but chiefly at La Fleche, in Anjou, I composed my *Treatise of Human Nature.* After passing three years very agreeably in that country, I came over to London in 1737. In the end of 1738, I published my treatise [1], and immediately went down to my mother and my brother, who lived at his country-house, and was employing himself very judiciously and successfully in the improvement of his fortune.

Never literary attempt was more unfortunate than my *Treatise of Human Nature.* It fell *dead-born from the press* [2] without reaching such distinction as even to excite a murmur among the zealots. But being naturally of a cheerful and sanguine temper, I very soon recovered the blow, and prosecuted with great ardour my studies in the country. In 1742, I printed at Edinburgh the first part of my *Essays,* the work was favourably received, and soon made me entirely forget my former disappointment [3]. I continued with my mother and brother in the

---

[1] The publisher, John Noone, gave Hume £50, and twelve bound copies of the book for right to publish an edition of the first two volumes, of one thousand copies. Dr. Burton, after praising Noone's 'discernment and liberality,' continues :—' It may be questioned whether in this age, when knowledge has spread so much wider, and money is so much less valuable, it would be easy to find a bookseller, who, on the ground of its internal merits, would give £50 for an edition of a new metaphysical work, by an unknown and young author.' Burton's *Hume,* i. 66. The book had become so scarce by the time of Hume's death, that the reviewer of his *Life* in the *Annual Register* for 1776, ii. 28, thinks it needful, he says, to give some account of it.

[2]   ' All, all but truth, drops dead-born from the press,
          Like the last Gazette, or the last Address.'
                              Pope, Epil. Sat. ii. 226.

[3] Hume not only published these Essays anonymously, but feigned that they were the work of a new author. Burton's *Hume,* i. 136. On June 13, 1742, he wrote to Henry Home (afterwards Lord Kames) :—' The Essays are all sold in London, as I am informed by two letters from English gentlemen of my acquaintance. There is a demand for them ; and, as one of them tells me, Innys, the great bookseller in Paul's Churchyard, wonders there is not a new edition, for that he cannot find copies for his customers. I am also told that Dr. Butler [the author of the *Analogy*] has everywhere recommended them.' *Ib.* p. 143. The first volume was published in 1741. They are mentioned in the list of books for March, 1742, in the *Gent. Mag.,* but are not reviewed. *The Treatise of Human Nature* was not even mentioned.

country, and in that time recovered the knowledge of the Greek language, which I had too much neglected in my early youth[1]. In 1745, I received a letter from the Marquis of Annandale, inviting me to come and live with him in England; I found also that the friends and family of that young nobleman were desirous of putting him under my care and direction, for the state of his mind and health required it. I lived with him a twelvemonth. My appointments during that time made a considerable accession to my small fortune[2]. I then received an invitation from general St Clair, to attend him as secretary to his expedition, which was at first meant against Canada, but ended in an incursion on the coast of France[3]. Next year,

[1] Hume, in a letter dated Feb. 19, 1751, speaks of 'having read over almost all the classics both Greek and Latin.' Burton's *Hume*, i. 326. See *post*, p. 322, *n*. 2, for an instance of his inaccuracy as a Greek scholar.

[2] 'On March 5, 1748, the Marquis was found, on an inquest from the Court of Chancery in England, to be a lunatic, incapable of governing himself, and managing his own affairs, and to have been so since Dec 12, 1744.' Burton's *Hume*, i. 171. 'He appears to have been haunted by a spirit of literary ambition.' He wrote a novel 'of which,' says Hume, ' we were obliged to print off thirty copies, to make him believe that we had printed a thousand, and that they were to be dispersed all over the Kingdom.' *Ib.* p. 173. Hume was treated with great insolence by a Captain Vincent, a cousin of the Marchioness-Dowager, whom he suspected of evil designs about the property. He was suddenly dismissed, and he was robbed of a quarter's salary of £75, which was clearly due to him. So late as the year 1761 he was still urging his claim, by which time the accumulated savings of the Annandale property amounted to £400,000. Whether he was paid or not is not known. *Ib.* p. 205. Dr. Thomas Murray, who in 1841 edited *Letters of David Hume*, says (p. 80) 'that his claim was only resisted because the agents for the estates did not regard themselves safe in making any payments, unless the debt was established by legal evidence.' So early as July 7, 1742, Horace Walpole had written :—' Lord Annandale is at last mad in all the forms; he has long been an out-pensioner of Bedlam College.' *Letters*, i. 185.

[3] The incursion on the coast of France in 1746 was devised in the vain hope of saving the Ministry from disgrace, who had delayed the departure of the expedition against Canada till it was too late in the year. An attempt was first made against Port L'Orient; that disgracefully failing, a second was made against the peninsula of Quiberon. A ship of war was destroyed, a small fort was dismantled, and two little islands were held by our sailors for at least a fortnight. Lord Charlemont was told by General St. Clair (Sinclair), that he had earnestly requested from the War Office a set of accurate maps, as he was wholly unacquainted with the country which he was to invade. When he unpacked them, 'they proved to be sea-charts!' *Memoirs of Charlemont*, i. 16. Hume wrote to his brother :—' The general and admiral were totally unacquainted with every part of the coast, without pilots, guides, or intelligence of any kind.' Burton's *Hume*, i. 213.

to wit 1747, I received an invitation from the general, to attend him in the same station in his military embassy to the courts of Vienna and Turin. I then wore the uniform of an officer, and was introduced at these courts as aid-de-camp to the general, along with Sir Harry Erskine, and Captain Grant, now General Grant[1]. These two years were almost the only interruptions which my studies have received during the course of my life: I passed them agreeably, and in good company; and my appointments, with my frugality, had made me reach a fortune which I called independent, though most of my friends were inclined to smile when I said so: in short, I was now master of near a thousand pounds.

I had always entertained a notion that my want of success in publishing the *Treatise of Human Nature*, had proceeded more from the manner than the matter, and that I had been guilty of a very usual indiscretion, in going to the press too early[2]. I therefore cast the first part of that work anew in the *Enquiry concerning Human Understanding*, which was published while I was at Turin[3]. But this piece was at first little more successful than the *Treatise of Human Nature*. On my return from Italy, I had the mortification to find all England in a ferment, on account of Dr Middleton's *Free Enquiry*[4], while my performance

[1] Lord Charlemont, who met Hume at Turin, thus describes him:—'Nature, I believe, never formed any man more unlike his real character than David Hume. . . . His face was broad and fat, his mouth wide, and without any other expression than that of imbecility. His eyes vacant and spiritless, and the corpulence of his whole person was far better fitted to communicate the idea of a turtle-eating alderman than of a refined philosopher. His speech in English was rendered ridiculous by the broadest Scotch accent, and his French was, if possible, still more laughable. . . . His wearing an uniform added greatly to his natural awkwardness, for he wore it like a grocer of the trained bands. Sinclair was sent to the Courts of Vienna and Turin as a military envoy, to see that their quota of troops was furnished by the Austrians and Piedmontese. It was therefore thought necessary that his Secretary should appear to be an officer, and Hume was accordingly disguised in scarlet.' *Memoirs of Charlemont*, i. 15. Horace Walpole, writing of Sinclair's appointment, says:—'He is Scotchissime, in all the latitude of the word, and not very able.' *Letters*, ii. 100.

[2] See *post*, p. 302, *n.* 21.

[3] This work, which was published anonymously, and at first under the title of *Philosophical Essays on Human Understanding*, is included in the list of books for April in the *Gent. Mag.* for 1748. It is not reviewed. Hume's publishers put a very moderate price on his philosophical works. This book was sold for three shillings, and his *Essays Moral and Political* for half-a-crown. *Ib.* 1742, p. 168.

[4] *A Free Enquiry into the miraculous powers which are supposed to have sub-*

was entirely overlooked and neglected. A new edition, which had been published at London of my *Essays, moral and political,* met not with a much better reception [1].

Such is the force[2] of natural temper, that these disappointments made little or no impression on me. I went down in 1749, and lived two years with my brother, at his country-house, for my mother was now dead. I there composed the second part of my essay, which I called *Political Discourses,* and also my *Enquiry concerning the Principles of Morals,* which is another part of my treatise that I cast anew. Meanwhile my bookseller, A. Millar[3], informed me that my former publications (all

sisted in the Christian Church from the earliest ages through several successive centuries. Gent. Mag., December, 1748. Gibbon, describing how, in the year 1753, in his undergraduate days at Oxford, 'he bewildered himself in the errors of the Church of Rome,' says:—' It was not long since Dr. Middleton's *Free Enquiry* had sounded an alarm in the theological world: much ink and much gall had been spilt in the defence of the primitive miracles; and the two dullest of their champions were crowned with academic honours by the University of Oxford. The name of Middleton was unpopular; and his proscription very naturally led me to peruse his writings, and those of his antagonists. His bold criticism, which approaches the precipice of infidelity, produced on my mind a singular effect; and had I persevered in the communion of Rome, I should now apply to my own fortune the prediction of the Sybil,

Via prima salutis,
Quod minime reris, Graia pandetur ab urbe[1].

The elegance of style and freedom of argument were repelled by a shield of prejudice. I still revered the character, or rather the names of the saints and fathers whom Dr. Middleton exposes; nor could he destroy my implicit belief, that the gift of miraculous powers was continued in the Church during the first four or five centuries of Christianity. But I was unable to resist the weight of historical evidence, that within the same period most of the leading doctrines of Popery were already introduced in theory and practice: nor was my conclusion absurd, that miracles are the test of truth, and that the Church must be orthodox and pure, which was so often approved by the visible interposition of the Deity.' Gibbon's *Misc. Works,* ed. 1814, i. 60. In his *Vindication* Gibbon says:—' A theological barometer might be formed, of which Cardinal Baronius and our countryman, Dr. Middleton, should constitute the opposite and remote extremities, as the former sunk to the lowest degree of credulity which was compatible with learning, and the latter rose to the highest pitch of scepticism in anywise consistent with religion.' *Ib.* iv. 588.

[1] It was the third edition. With three editions in seven years Hume might have been contented.   [2] In the first edition, *source.*

[3] 'Mr. Andrew Millar, bookseller in the Strand, took the principal charge of conducting the publication of Johnson's *Dictionary.* . . . When the messenger who carried the last sheet to Millar returned, Johnson asked him, "Well, what did he

[1] *Æneid,* vi. 96.

but the unfortunate treatise) were beginning to be the subject of conversation; that the sale of them was gradually increasing, and that new editions were demanded. Answers by Reverends and Right Reverends came out two or three in a year [1]; and I found, by Dr Warburton's railing, that the books were beginning to be esteemed in good company. However, I had fixed a resolution, which I inflexibly maintained, never to reply to any body [2]; and not being very irascible in my temper,

---

say?" "Sir (answered the messenger) he said, thank God, I have done with him." "I am glad (replied Johnson with a smile) that he thanks God for any thing." . . . Johnson said of him, "I respect Millar, Sir; he has raised the price of literature."' Boswell's *Johnson*, i. 287. 'Talking one day of the patronage the great sometimes affect to give to literature and literary men, "Andrew Millar," says Johnson, "is the Mæcenas of the age."' Johnson's *Works* (1787), xi. 200. Mr. Croker says that Millar was the bookseller described by Johnson on April 24, 1779, as 'so habitually and equably drunk that his most intimate friends never perceived that he was more sober at one time than another.' Croker's *Boswell*, 8vo. ed. p. 630. Drunkenness such as this seems inconsistent with 'the consummate industry' which Nichols praised in him. Nichols adds :—' He was *not extravagant;* but contented himself with an occasional regale of humble port at an opposite tavern ; so that his wealth accumulated rapidly.' Nichols, *Lit. Anec.* iii. 387. By his italicising ' not extravagant,' he implies no doubt that he was somewhat near. In a note on Millar in my edition of *Boswell*, i. 287, I have made an absurd blunder in quoting, as if serious, a letter written by Hume in a spirit of wild extravagance. See *post*, p. 149, *n.* 10, for the marriage of Millar's widow.

[1] One of the answers was by Johnson's friend, Dr. William Adams. When Johnson and Boswell called on him in March 1776, at Pembroke College, of which he was then Master, 'he told me,' says Boswell, 'he had once dined in company with Hume in London; that Hume shook hands with him, and said, "You have treated me much better than I deserve"; and that they exchanged visits. I took the liberty to object to treating an infidel writer with smooth civility. . . . Johnson coincided with me, and said, "When a man voluntarily engages in an important controversy, he is to do all he can to lessen his antagonist, because authority from personal respect has much weight with most people, and often more than reasoning. If my antagonist writes bad language, though that may not be essential to the question, I will attack him for his bad language." ADAMS. "You would not jostle a chimney-sweeper." JOHNSON. "Yes, Sir, if it were necessary to jostle him *down*."' Boswell's *Johnson*, ii. 441.

[2] Hume forgets his reply to Rousseau (*post*, p. 84), and his note in his *History* on ' a person that has written an *Enquiry historical and critical into the Evidence against Mary Queen of Scots ;* and has attempted to refute the foregoing narrative. It is in this note that he makes his famous assertion :—' There are, indeed, three events in our history which may be regarded as touchstones of party-men. An English Whig, who asserts the reality of the Popish Plot, an Irish Catholic, who denies the massacre in 1641, and a Scotch Jacobite, who maintains the innocence of Queen Mary, must be considered as men beyond the reach of argument or reason, and must be left to their prejudices.' *History of England*, ed. 1802, v. 504.

I have easily kept myself clear of all literary squabbles. These symptoms of a rising reputation gave me encouragement, as I was ever more disposed to see the favourable than unfavourable side of things; a turn of mind which it is more happy to possess, than to be born to an estate of ten thousand a year. In 1751, I removed from the country to the town, the true scene for a man of letters[1]. In 1752, were published at Edinburgh, where I then lived, my *Political Discourses*, the only work of mine that was successful on the first publication. It was well received abroad and at home[2]. In the same year was published at London, my *Enquiry concerning the Principles of Morals*[3]; which, in my own opinion, (who ought not to judge on that subject,) is of all my writings, historical, philosophical, or

The 'person' was the Scotch Jacobite, Patrick Lord Elibank, to whom Hume wrote a very bitter letter. Burton's *Hume*, ii. 252.

[1] 'I have the strangest reluctance to change places,' wrote Hume from London on Jan. 25, 1759. Burton's *Hume*, ii. 50. This reluctance he expresses on other occasions. He might have remained at Ninewells had not his brother 'plucked up a resolution' and got married. Writing on March 19, 1751, he says :—'Since my brother's departure, Katty [his sister] and I have been computing in our turn, and the result of our deliberation is, that we are to take up house in Berwick ; where, if arithmetic and frugality don't deceive us (and they are pretty certain arts), we shall be able, after providing for hunger, warmth, and cleanliness, to keep a stock in reserve, which we may afterwards turn to the purposes of hoarding, luxury, or charity.' Burton's *Hume*, i. 338. On June 22 he wrote from Ninewells :—'While interest remains as at present, I have £50 a year, a hundred pounds worth of books, great store of linens and fine clothes, and near £100 in my pocket; along with order, frugality, a strong spirit of independency, good health, a contented humour, and an unabating love of study. In these circumstances, I must esteem myself one of the happy and fortunate; and so far from being willing to draw my ticket over again in the lottery of life, there are very few prizes with which I would make an exchange. After some deliberation, I am resolved to settle in Edinburgh. . . . Besides other reasons which determine me to this resolution, I would not go too far away from my sister, who thinks she will soon follow me. . . . And as she can join £30 to my stock, and brings an equal love of order and frugality, we doubt not to make our revenues answer.' *Ib.* p. 342. At the end of the year he was a candidate for the Chair of Logic in the University of Glasgow, which was vacated by Adam Smith's transference to the Chair of Moral Philosophy. He had, it is said, Edmund Burke for his competitor, but to both of them was preferred one Mr. Clow. *Ib.* p. 350. Adam Smith wrote to Dr. William Cullen :—'Edin. Tuesday. November 1751. . . . I should prefer David Hume to any man for a colleague ; but I am afraid the public would not be of my opinion ; and the interest of the society will oblige us to have some regard to the opinion of the public.' Thomson's *Life of Cullen*, i. 606.

[2] It is in the list of books in the *Gent. Mag.* for Feb. 1752, but is not reviewed.

[3] It was published in Dec. 1751. *Gent. Mag.* 1751, p. 574.

literary, incomparably the best. It came unnoticed and un-observed into the world [1].

In 1752, the Faculty of Advocates chose me their librarian; an office from which I received little or no emolument, but which gave me the command of a large library [2]. I then formed the plan of writing the *History of England*, but being frightened with the notion of continuing a narrative through a period of 1700 years, I commenced with the accession of the house of Stuart, an epoch when I thought the misrepre-sentations of faction began chiefly to take place [3]. I was, I own, sanguine in my expectations of the success of this work. I thought that I was the only historian that had at once neglected present power, interest, and authority, and the cry of popular prejudices; and, as the subject was suited to every capacity, I expected proportional applause. But miserable was my disap-pointment: I was assailed by one cry of reproach, disapproba-tion, and even detestation: English, Scotch, and Irish, Whig and Tory, churchman and sectary, freethinker and religionist, patriot and courtier, united in their rage against the man who had presumed to shed a generous tear for the fate of Charles I [4]

[1] It is not even mentioned in the *Gent. Mag*.

[2] In this post Hume succeeded Thomas Ruddiman, the learned grammarian of Scotland; 'whose farewell letter to the Faculty of Advocates, when he resigned the office of their Librarian, should,' said Johnson, 'have been in Latin.' Boswell's *Johnson*, ii. 216. Hume describes the post as 'a petty office of forty or fifty guineas a year.' He calls it also 'a genteel office.' Burton's *Hume*, i. 370. In 1754 he was censured by three of the curators—James Burnet (Lord Monboddo), Sir David Dalrymple (Lord Hailes), and another—for buying three French books, which they described as 'indecent, and unworthy of a place in a learned library.' Writing about this to Adam Smith, he says:—'Being equally unwilling to lose the use of the books, and to bear an indignity, I retain the office, but have given Blacklock, our blind poet, a bond of annuity for the salary. I have now put it out of these malicious fellows' power to offer me any indignity, while my motive for remaining in this office is so apparent.' *Ib*. p. 393. See *post*, p. 352, *n*. 4. In January, 1757, he resigned his office in the curtest of letters. *Ib*. ii. 18.

[3] 'David Hume used to say that he did not find it an irksome task to him to go through a great many dull books when writing his *History*. "I then read," said he, "not for pleasure, but in order to find out facts." He compared it to a sportsman seeking hares, who does not mind what sort of ground it is that he goes over further than as he may find hares in it. From himself.' *Boswelliana*, p. 263.

[4] Hume writing to his friend William Mure about the first volume of his *History* says:—'The first quality of an historian is to be true and impartial. The next to be interesting. If you do not say that I have done both parties justice, and if Mrs. Mure be not sorry for poor King Charles, I shall burn all my papers and return to philosophy.' Burton's *Hume*, i. 409.

and the Earl of Strafford; and after the first ebullitions of their fury were over, what was still more mortifying, the book seemed to sink into oblivion. Mr. Millar told me, that in a twelvemonth he sold only forty-five copies of it [1]. I scarcely, indeed, heard of one man in the three kingdoms, considerable for rank or letters, that could endure the book [2]. I must only except the primate of England, Dr Herring [3], and the primate of Ireland, Dr Stone [4], which seem two odd exceptions. These dignified prelates separately sent me messages not to be discouraged.

[1] It is in the list of books in the *Gent. Mag.* for November, 1754, but is not reviewed; Hume wrote to the Earl of Balcarres from Edinburgh, on Dec. 17 :— ' My *History* has been very much canvassed and read here in town, as I am told ; and it has full as many inveterate enemies as partial defenders. The misfortune of a book, says Boileau, is not the being ill spoke of, but the not being spoken of at all. The sale has been very considerable here, about 450 copies in five weeks. How it has succeeded in London, I cannot precisely tell ; only I observe that some of the weekly papers have been busy with me.—I am as great an Atheist as Bolingbroke ; as great a Jacobite as Carte ; I cannot write English, &c.' Burton's *Hume*, i. 412. Hume seems at one time to have attributed the smallness of the London sale to the fault of his Edinburgh bookseller, Baillie Hamilton. He wrote to Millar on April 12, 1755 :—' I think the London booksellers have had a sufficient triumph over him, when a book, which was much expected and was calculated to be popular, has had so small a sale in his hands. To make the triumph more complete I wish you would take what remains into your hands, and dispose of it in a few months.' *MS., R. S. E.*

[2] Horace Walpole. writing of it on March 27, 1755, speaks of it as 'a book, which though more decried than ever book was, and certainly with faults, I cannot help liking much. It is called Jacobite, but in my opinion is only not *George-Abite* ; where others abuse the Stuarts, he laughs at them : I am sure he does not spare their ministers. Harding [the Clerk of the House of Commons], who has the History of England at the ends of his parliament fingers, says that the Journals will contradict most of his facts. If it is so, I am sorry ; for his style, which is the best we have in history, and his manner, imitated from Voltaire, are very pleasing.' *Letters*, ii. 428. Johnson called Hume 'an echo of Voltaire.' Boswell's *Johnson*, ii. 53.

[3] Horace Walpole, writing on Oct. 4, 1745, in the midst of the alarm caused by the Young Pretender's victory at Preston-Pans, says :—' The nobility are raising regiments, and everybody else is—being raised. Dr. Herring, the Archbishop of York, has set an example that would rouse the most indifferent : in two days after the news arrived at York of Cope's defeat, and when they every moment expected the victorious rebels at their gates, the Bishop made a speech to the assembled county, that had as much true spirit, honesty, and bravery in it as ever was penned by an historian for an ancient hero.' *Letters*, i. 394. Herring was made Archbishop of Canterbury in 1747.

[4] Horace Walpole says that Stone, ' with no pretensions in the world but by being attached to the House of Dorset, and by being brother of Mr. Stone [subgovernor to the Prince of Wales, afterwards George III], had been hurried through

I was, however, I confess, discouraged; and, had not the war at that time been breaking out between France and England, I had certainly retired to some provincial town of the former kingdom, have changed my name, and never more have returned to my native country[1]; but as this scheme was not now practicable, and the subsequent volume was considerably advanced, I resolved to pick up courage and to persevere.

In this interval, I published at London my *Natural History of Religion*, along with some other small pieces[2]: its public entry was rather obscure, except only that Dr Hurd wrote a pamphlet against it, with all the illiberal petulance, arrogance, and scurrility, which distinguish the Warburtonian school[3]. This pamphlet gave me some consolation for the otherwise indifferent reception of my performance.

In 1756, two years after the fall of the first volume, was published the second volume of my *History, containing the period from the death of Charles I till the Revolution.* This performance happened to give less displeasure to the Whigs, and was better received. It not only rose itself, but helped to buoy up its unfortunate brother[4].

two or three Irish bishoprics up to the very primacy of the kingdom, not only unwarrantably young, but without even the graver excuses of learning or sanctimony.' *Memoirs of George II*, ed. 1822, i. 244.

[1] Hume wrote to a friend on April 20, 1756:—'Were I to change my habitation, I would retire to some provincial town in France, to trifle out my old age, near a warm sun in a good climate, a pleasant country, and amidst a sociable people. My stock would then maintain me in some opulence; for I have the satisfaction to tell you, dear Doctor, that on reviewing my affairs I find that I am worth £1600 sterling, which, at five per cent., makes near 1800 livres a year—that is, the pay of two French captains.' Burton's *Hume*, i. 437. Horace Walpole, writing on March 28, 1777, says:—'Have you read Hume's *Life*, and did you observe that he thought of retiring to France, and changing his name, because his works had not got him a name? Lord Bute called himself Sir John Stuart in Italy to shroud the beams of a title too gorgeous; but it is new to conceal a name that nobody had heard of.' *Letters*, vi. 423.

[2] For some Essays which he suppressed at this time see *post*, pp. 230-3, and p. 346, *n*. 2.

[3] See *post*, pp. 20, 200. Gibbon in his *Decline and Fall*, ed. 1807, iv. 86, thus mentions 'the Warburtonian school':—'The secret intentions of Julian are revealed by the late Bishop of Gloucester, the learned and dogmatic Warburton; who, with the authority of a theologian, prescribes the motives and conduct of the Supreme Being. The discourse entitled *Julian* is strongly marked with all the peculiarities which are imputed to the Warburtonian school.'

[4] See *post*, pp. 2, 4.

But though I had been taught by experience that the Whig party were in possession of bestowing all places, both in the state and in literature, I was so little inclined to yield to their senseless clamour, that in above a hundred alterations, which further study, reading, or reflection, engaged me to make in the reigns of the two first Stuarts, I have made all of them invariably to the Tory side [1]. It is ridiculous to consider the English constitution before that period as a regular plan of liberty.

In 1759, I published my *History of the House of Tudor.* The clamour against this performance was almost equal to that against the *History of the two first Stuarts.* The reign of Elizabeth was particularly obnoxious [2]. But I was now callous against the impressions of public folly, and continued very peaceably and contentedly in my retreat at Edinburgh, to finish, in two volumes, the more early part of *The English History,* which I gave to the public in 1761, with tolerable, and but tolerable, success [3].

[1] See *post,* p. 75, *n.* 4, for his complaint in his last illness of the design of the Whigs to ruin him as an author. He forgets to point out that only four years after the publication of his second volume, by the accession of George III, the Tory writers were in a far more favourable position than the Whigs. See his *Philosophical Works,* ed. 1854, iii. 74, for a long passage on Whigs and Tories, which he suppressed in the later editions of his *Essays.* In it, speaking of the Tories, he had said :—' There are few men of knowledge or learning, at least few philosophers since Mr. Locke has wrote, who would not be ashamed to be thought of that party.'

[2] Hume wrote to Dr. Robertson on Jan. 25, 1759 :—' You will see what light and force this History of the Tudors bestows on that of the Stuarts. Had I been prudent, I should have begun with it. I care not to boast, but I will venture to say that I have now effectually stopped the mouths of all those villainous Whigs who railed at me.' Dugald Stewart's *Life of Robertson,* ed. 1811, p. 342. Horace Walpole wrote of it on March 15 :—' I have not advanced far in it, but it appears an inaccurate and careless, as it certainly has been a very hasty performance.' *Letters,* iii. 216. It was brought out almost at the same time as Robertson's *History of Scotland,* Voltaire's *Candide,* and Johnson's *Rasselas.*

[3] Dugald Stewart says :—' Adam Smith observed to me, not long before his death, that after all his practice in writing he composed as slowly and with as great difficulty as at first. He added that Mr. Hume had acquired so great a facility, that the last volumes of his *History* were printed from his original copy, with a few marginal corrections. When Mr. Smith was composing, he generally walked up and down his apartment, dictating to a secretary. All Mr. Hume's works (I have been assured) were written with his own hand. A critical reader may, I think, perceive in the different styles of these two classical writers the effects of their different modes of study.' *Life of Adam Smith,* ed. 1811, p. 107.

' Horne Tooke said that Hume wrote his *History* as witches say their prayers—backwards.' *Table-Talk of Samuel Rogers,* p. 123.

But, notwithstanding this variety of winds and seasons to which my writings had been exposed, they had still been making such advances, that the copy-money given me by the booksellers much exceeded any thing formerly known in England[1]. I was become not only independent, but opulent, I retired to my native country of Scotland, determined never more to set my foot out of it; and retaining the satisfaction of never having preferred a request to one great man, or even making advances of friendship to any of them. As I was now turned of fifty, I thought of passing all the rest of my life in this philosophical manner[2], when I received, in 1763, an invitation from the Earl of Hertford, with whom I was not in the least acquainted, to attend him on his embassy to Paris, with a near prospect of being appointed secretary to the embassy; and, in the mean while, of performing the functions of that office[3]. This offer, however inviting, I at first declined, both because I was reluctant to begin connections with the great,

[1] See *post*, p. 33, *n.* 2. In 1767 writing to a friend he says :—'Some push me to continue my *History*. Millar offers me any price.' Burton's *Hume*, ii. 39ɔ.

[2] 'When Mr. David Hume began first to be known in the world as a philosopher, Mr. Thomas White, a decent rich merchant of London, said to him, "I am surprised, Mr. Hume, that a man of your good sense should think of being a philosopher. Why, I now took it into my head to be a philosopher for some time, but tired of it most confoundedly, and very soon gave it up." "Pray, Sir," said Mr. Hume, "in what branch of philosophy did you employ your researches? What books did you read?" "Books?" said Mr. White; "nay, Sir, I read no books, but I used to sit you whole forenoons a-yawning and poking the fire."' *Boswelliana*, p. 221. See Burton's *Hume*, ii. 392, where Hume speaks of his pleasure in 'idleness, and sauntering and society.' In reporting to a friend Lord Hertford's invitation he said, 'he rouses me from a state of indolence and sloth, which I falsely dignified with the name of philosophy.' Hume's *Private Corres.* p. 70.

[3] Hume wrote to a friend on Jan. 9, 1764:—'When I came up to London, I found that Mr. [afterwards Sir Charles] Bunbury, a gentleman of considerable fortune, and married to the Duke of Richmond's sister, had already been appointed Secretary; but was so disagreeable to the ambassador that he was resolved never to see, or do business with his secretary, and therefore desired I should attend him, in order to perform the functions.' Burton's *Hume*, ii. 183. In another letter he adds:—'The King gave me a pension of £200 a year for life, to engage me to attend his Lordship. My Lord is very impatient to have me Secretary to the Embassy; and writes very earnest letters to that purpose to the Ministers. . . . Mr. Bunbury has great interest. . . . The appointments of this office are above £1000 a year, and the expense attending it nothing.' *Ib.* p. 188. See *post*, pp. 40, 69, *n.* 1.

and because I was afraid that the civilities and gay company of
Paris would prove disagreeable to a person of my age and
humour; but on his lordship's repeating the invitation, I
accepted of it. I have every reason, both of pleasure and
interest, to think myself happy in my connections with that
nobleman, as well as afterwards with his brother, General
Conway[1].

Those who have not seen the strange effects of modes will
never imagine the strange reception I met with at Paris, from
men and women of all ranks and stations[2]. The more I re-
siled[3] from their excessive civilities, the more I was loaded with
them. There is, however, a real satisfaction in living at Paris,
from the great number of sensible, knowing, and polite company
with which the city abounds above all places in the universe.
I thought once of settling there for life.

I was appointed secretary to the embassy; and in summer
1765, Lord Hertford left me, being appointed Lord Lieutenant
of Ireland[4]. I was *chargé d'affaires* till the arrival of the Duke
of Richmond, towards the end of the year. In the beginning of
1766 I left Paris[5], and next summer went to Edinburgh[6], with
the same view as formerly, of burying myself in a philosophical
retreat. I returned to that place not richer, but with much
more money, and a much larger income, by means of Lord
Hertford's friendship, than I left it[7]; and I was desirous of
trying what superfluity could produce, as I had formerly made
an experiment of a competency. But in 1767 I received from
Mr Conway an invitation to be under-secretary; and this invitation both the character of the person, and my connections
with Lord Hertford, prevented me from declining[8]. I returned
to Edinburgh in 1769 very opulent, (for I possessed a revenue

[1] See *post*, p. 69, *n.* 1; 103, *n.* 1.
[2] See *post*, p. 50, *n.* 3.
[3] Johnson in his *Dictionary* gives *resilience*, and *resiliency*, but not *resile*.
[4] See *post*, p. 69, *n.* 1.
[5] He passes over in silence his quarrel with Rousseau which took place in this year (*post*, p. 74).
[6] See *post*, p. 86, *n.* 1.
[7] Hume, I conjecture, means to say that his invested property was not larger, but that by the addition to his pension, which he owed to Lord Hertford's friendship (*post*, p. 55), he had a much larger income. He had also a much larger stock of uninvested money.
[8] See *post*, p. 103, *n.* 1.

of one thousand pounds a year[1],) healthy, and though somewhat stricken in years, with the prospect of enjoying long my
ease, and of seeing the increase of my reputation[2].

In spring, 1775, I was struck with a disorder in my bowels[3],
which at first gave me no alarm, but has since, as I apprehend
it, become mortal and incurable. I now reckon upon a speedy
dissolution. I have suffered very little pain from my disorder ;
and, what is more strange, have, notwithstanding the great
decline of my person[4], never suffered a moment's abatement of
my spirits ; insomuch that were I to name a period of my life
which I should most choose to pass over again, I might be
tempted to point to this later period[5]. I possess the same
ardour as ever in study, and the same gaiety in company. I
consider, besides, that a man at sixty-five, by dying, cuts off
only a few years of infirmities ; and though I see many symptoms of my literary reputation's breaking out at last with
additional lustre[6], I knew that I could have but very few years
to enjoy it. It is difficult to be more detached from life than I
am at present.

[1] On Oct. 6, 1767, he wrote to his brother :—' My income will be above £1100
a year, of which I shall not spend much above the half.' *MS., R. S. E.*

[2] Gibbon, only 'twenty hours before his death, happened to fall into a conversation, not uncommon with him, on the probable duration of his life. He said
that he thought himself a good life for ten, twelve, or perhaps twenty years.'
Gibbon's *Misc. Works*, ed. 1814, i. 422.

[3] See *post*, p. 322, *n.* 2.

[4] Six months before his death he had lost five stones' weight. *Post*, p. 312, *n.* 1.

[5] Gibbon in his fifty-second year wrote :—' I shall soon enter into the period
which, as the most agreeable of his long life, was selected by the judgment and
experience of the sage Fontenelle. His choice is approved by the eloquent historian of nature [Buffon], who fixes our moral happiness to the mature season in
which our passions are supposed to be calmed, our duties fulfilled, our ambition
satisfied, our fame and fortune established on a solid basis. In private conversation that great and amiable man added the weight of his own experience ; and this
autumnal felicity might be exemplified in the lives of Voltaire, Hume, and many
other men of letters. I am far more inclined to embrace than to dispute this comfortable doctrine. I will not suppose any premature decay of the mind or body;
but I must reluctantly observe that two causes, the abbreviation of time and the
failure of hope, will always tinge with a browner shade the evening of life.'
Gibbon's *Misc. Works*, i. 275.

[6] See *post*, p. 55, *n.* 7, and p. 329. In an interesti¹ g review of his *Life and
Writings* in the *Annual Register* for 1776, ii. 31, it is said that by the time his
History was finished, 'his reputation was complete. He was considered as the
greatest writer of the age : his most insignificant performances were sought after
with avidity.'

To conclude historically with my own character. I am, or rather was (for that is the style I must now use in speaking of myself, which emboldens me the more to speak my sentiments) I was, I say, a man of mild disposition, of command of temper, of an open, social, and cheerful humour [1], capable of attachment, but little susceptible of enmity, and of great moderation in all my passions. Even my love of literary fame, my ruling passion, never soured my temper, notwithstanding my frequent disappointments [2]. My company was not unacceptable to the young and careless, as well as to the studious and literary; and as I took a particular pleasure in the company of modest women, I had no reason to be displeased with the reception I met with from them. In a word, though most men, anywise

[1] 'Dr. Robertson used frequently to say that in Mr. Hume's gaiety there was something which approached to *infantine.*' Stewart's *Life of Robertson,* ed. 1811, p 211. Dr. Blair, in a letter to Hume's nephew dated Nov. 20, 1797, speaks of 'that amiable naiveté and sprightly gaiety for which his uncle was so distinguished.' *M.S., R.S.E.* Gray, writing to Dr. Beattie on July 2, 1770, asks :—' Is not that *naiveté* and good-humour, which Hume's admirers celebrate in him, owing to this, that he has continued all his days an infant, but one that unhappily has been taught to read and write ?' Mason's *Gray,* ed. 1807, ii. 298. Dr. Burton tells how at the beginning of Hume's last illness a woman called on him 'with the information that she had been intrusted with a message to him from on High. "This is a very important matter, Madam," said the philosopher ; "we must take it with deliberation ;—perhaps you had better get a little temporal refreshment before you begin. Lassie, bring this good lady a glass of wine." While she was preparing for the attack he entered good-humouredly into conversation with her ; and discovering that her husband was a chandler, announced that he stood very much in want at that time of some temporal lights, and intrusted his guest with a very large order. This unexpected stroke of business at once absorbed all the good woman's thoughts ; and forgetting her important mission she immediately trotted home to acquaint her husband with the good news.' Burton's *Hume,* ii. 457. See *post,* p. 320.

[2] Goldsmith admitted to Walpole that he envied Shakespeare. Walpole's *Letters,* vi. 379. Hume, in like manner, was jealous of Thomas à Becket. After mentioning the thousands of pilgrims to his tomb, he continues :—' It is indeed a mortifying reflection to those who are actuated by the love of fame, so justly denominated the last infirmity of noble minds [1], that the wisest legislator and most exalted genius that ever reformed or enlightened the world can never expect such tributes of praise as are lavished on the memory of pretended saints, whose whole conduct was probably to the last degree odious or contemptible, and whose industry was entirely directed to the pursuit of objects pernicious to mankind.' *Hist. of Eng.,* ed. 1802, i. 422.

[1] 'That last infirmity of noble mind.'
Milton's *Lycidas,* l. 71.

eminent, have found reason to complain of calumny, I never was touched, or even attacked, by her baleful tooth ; and though I wantonly exposed myself to the rage of both civil and religious factions, they seemed to be disarmed in my behalf of their wonted fury. My friends never had occasion to vindicate any one circumstance of my character and conduct: not but that the zealots, we may well suppose, would have been glad to invent and propagate any story to my disadvantage, but they could never find any which they thought would wear the face of probability [1]. I cannot say there is no vanity in making this funeral oration of myself; but I hope it is not a misplaced one; and this is a matter of fact which is easily cleared and ascertained.

April 18, 1776.

LETTER from ADAM SMITH, LL.D. to WILLIAM STRAHAN, Esq. [2]

Kirkaldy, Fifeshire,
Nov. 9, 1776.

Dear Sir,

It is with a real, though a very melancholy pleasure, that I sit down to give you some account of the behaviour of our late excellent friend, Mr Hume, during his last illness.

Though in his own judgment his disease was mortal and incurable, yet he allowed himself to be prevailed upon, by the entreaty of his friends, to try what might be the effects of a long journey [3]. A few days before he set out he wrote that account of his own life, which, together with his other papers, he has left to your care. My account, therefore, shall begin where his ends.

He set out for London towards the end of April, and at Morpeth met with Mr John Home and myself, who had both come down from London on purpose to see him, expecting to have found him at Edinburgh [4]. Mr Home returned with him, and attended him, during the whole of his stay in England, with that care and attention which might be expected from a temper so perfectly friendly and affectionate. As I had written to my mother that she might expect me in Scotland, I was under the necessity of continuing my journey. His disease seemed to yield to exercise and change of air ; and, when he

---

[1] Lord Cockburn, in his *Memoirs,* ed. 1856, p. 201, gives a curious instance how thirty years after Hume's death the zealots of Edinburgh made use of the prejudices entertained against him to persecute Professor John Leslie.

[2] See *post,* pp. 346, 348. [3] See *post,* p. 319, *n.* 2. [4] See *post, ib.*

arrived in London, he was apparently in much better health than when he left Edinburgh[1]. He was advised to go to Bath to drink the waters, which appeared for some time to have so good an effect upon him, that even he himself began to entertain, what he was not apt to do, a better opinion of his own health[2]. His symptoms however soon returned with their usual violence, and from that moment he gave up all thoughts of recovery, but submitted with the utmost cheerfulness and the most perfect complacency and resignation. Upon his return to Edinburgh, though he found himself much weaker, yet his cheerfulness never abated, and he continued to divert himself, as usual, with correcting his own works for a new edition, with reading books of amusement, with the conversation of his friends ; and sometimes in the evening with a party at his favourite game of whist. His cheerfulness was so great, and his conversation and amusements ran so much in their usual strain, that notwithstanding all bad symptoms, many people could not believe he was dying. ‘ I shall tell your friend colonel Edmondstone[3],’ said doctor Dundas to him one day, ‘ that I left you much better, and in a fair way of recovery.’ ‘ Doctor,’ said he, ‘ as I believe you would not choose to tell any thing but the truth, you had better tell him I am dying as fast as my enemies, if I have any, could wish, and as easily and cheerfully as my best friends could desire.’ Colonel Edmondstone soon afterwards came to see him, and take leave of him ; and on his way home he could not forbear writing him a letter, bidding him once more an eternal adieu, and applying to him, as to a dying man, the beautiful French verses in which the Abbé Chaulieu, in expectation of his own death, laments his approaching separation from his friend the Marquis de la Fare[4]. Mr Hume’s magnanimity and firmness were such, that his most

[1] See *post*, p. 321.
[2] See *post*, p. 323.
[3] Colonel Edmondstoune of Newton had served in the Expedition against France in 1746, when most likely he had become acquainted with Hume. Burton's *Hume*, i. 212. On Aug. 6, 1776, Hume wrote to John Home the poet:—‘ Poor Edmondstoune and I parted to-day with a plentiful effusion of tears ; all those Belzebubians [1] have not hearts of iron.’ Mackenzie's *Life of John Home*, i. 65.
[4] ‘ Colonel Edmondstoune’s letter has been preserved, and is as follows :—

“ Linlithgow, Wednesday.

“ My Dear, Dear David,—My heart is very full. I could not see you this morning. I thought it was better for us both. You can't die, you must live in the memory of all your friends and acquaintances[2], and your works will render you immortal. I could never conceive that it was possible for any one to dislike you

[1] ‘ Edmondstoune was a member of what was called the Ruffian Club ; men whose hearts were milder than their manners, and their principles more correct than their habits of life.’
[2] See *post*, p. 9.

affectionate friends knew that they hazarded nothing in talking and writing to him as to a dying man ; and that so far from being hurt by this frankness, he was rather pleased and flattered by it. I happened to come into his room while he was reading this letter, which he had just received, and which he immediately showed me. I told him, that though I was sensible how very much he was weakened, and that appearances were in many respects very bad, yet his cheerfulness was still so great, the spirit of life seemed still to be so very strong in him, that I could not help entertaining some faint hopes. He answered, ' Your hopes are groundless. An habitual diarrhœa of more than a year's standing would be a very bad disease at any age ; at my age it is a mortal one. When I lie down in the evening I feel myself weaker than when I rose in the morning ; and when I rise in the morning weaker than when I lay down in the evening. I am sensible, besides, that some of my vital parts are affected, so that I must soon die.' ' Well,' said I, ' if it must be so, you have at least the satisfaction of leaving all your friends, your brother's family in particular, in great prosperity.' He said that he felt that satisfaction so sensibly, that when he was reading, a few days before, Lucian's *Dialogues of the Dead*, among all the excuses which are alleged to Charon for not entering readily into his boat, he could not find one that fitted him : he had no house to finish, he had no daughter to provide for, he had no enemies upon whom he wished to revenge himself. ' I could not well imagine,' said he, ' what excuse I could make to Charon, in order to obtain a little delay. I have done every thing of consequence which I ever meant to do, and I could at no time expect to leave my relations and friends in a better situation than that in which I am now likely to leave them : I therefore have all reason to die contented.' He then diverted himself with inventing several

or hate you. IIe must be more than savage who could be an enemy to a man of the best head and heart [1], and of the most amiable manners.

> O toi, qui de mon âme es la chère moitié ;
> Toi, qui joins la délicatesse
> Des sentimens d'une maitresse
> À la solidité d'une sûre amitié,
> *David,* il faut bientôt que la Parque cruelle
> Vienne rompre de si doux nœuds,
> Et malgré nos cris et nos vœux
> Bientôt nous essuierons une absence éternel'e.
> Adieu! Adieu !" *M.S., R. S. E.'*
>
> Burton's *Hume,* ii. 510.

These lines were written seventeen years before Chaulieu's death. They are entitled *Épître à M. Le Marquis De La Fare, qui m'avait demandé mon portrait, en* 1703. They were incorrectly quoted by Colonel Edmondstoune, but I have corrected them in accordance with the text of the edition of 1774 of *Les Œuvres de Chaulieu,* tome i. p. 220. For *David* we find of course La Fare.

---

[1] ' Dr. Johnson added *"something much too rough,"* both as to Mr. Hume's head and heart, which I suppress.' Boswell's *Life of Johnson,* v. 30.

jocular excuses, which he supposed he might make to Charon, and with imagining the very surly answers which it might suit the character of Charon to return to them. ' Upon further consideration,' said he, ' I thought I might say to him, " Good Charon, I have been correcting my works for a new edition. Allow me a little time that I may see how the public receives the alterations '." But Charon would answer, " When you have seen the effect of these, you will be for making other alterations. There will be no end of such excuses ; so, honest friend, please step into the boat." But I might still urge, " Have a little patience, good Charon, I have been endeavouring to open the eyes of the public. If I live a few years longer, I may have the satisfaction of seeing the downfall of some of the prevailing systems of superstition." But Charon would then lose all temper and decency. " You loitering rogue, that will not happen these many hundred years. Do you fancy I will grant you a lease for so long a term ? Get into the boat this instant, you lazy loitering rogue." '

But though Mr Hume always talked of his approaching dissolution with great cheerfulness, he never affected to make any parade of his great magnanimity. He never mentioned the subject but when the conversation naturally led to it, and never dwelt longer upon it than the course of the conversation happened to require ; it was a subject indeed which occurred pretty frequently, in consequence of the in- quiries which his friends, who came to see him, naturally made con- cerning the state of his health. The conversation which I mentioned above, and which passed on Thursday the 8th of August, was the last, except one, that I ever had with him. He had now become so very weak that the company of his most intimate friends fatigued him ; for his cheerfulness was still so great, his complaisance and social dis- position were still so entire, that when any friend was with him he could not help talking more, and with greater exertion, than suited the weakness of his body. At his own desire, therefore, I agreed to leave Edinburgh, where I was staying partly upon his account, and re- turned to my mother's house here at Kirkaldy, upon condition that he would send for me whenever he wished to see me [2]; the physician who saw him most frequently, doctor Black [3], undertaking, in the mean time, to write me occasionally an account of the state of his health.

On the twenty-second of August, the doctor wrote me the following letter :—

' Since my last Mr Hume has passed his time pretty easily, but is much weaker. He sits up, goes down stairs once a day, and amuses himself with reading, but seldom sees any body. He finds that even

---

[1] Hume's final corrections were sent only thirteen days before his death (*post*, p. 342).

[2] See *post*, p. 344, *n.* 3, for Hume's thrift, in the case of a letter which he sent to Adam Smith.

[3] See *post*, p. 343, *n.* 2.

the conversation of his most intimate friends fatigues and oppresses him, and it is happy that he does not need it ; for he is quite free from anxiety, impatience, or low spirits, and passes his time very well with the assistance of amusing books.'

I received, the day after, a letter from Mr Hume himself, of which the following is an extract :—

' My dearest friend,   *' Edinburgh, August* 23, 1776.

'I am obliged to make use of my nephew's hand in writing to you, as I do not rise to-day.

[There is no man in whom I have a greater confidence than Mr. Strahan, yet have I left the property of that Manuscript to my nephew David, in case by any accident it should not be published within three years after my decease. The only accident I could foresee was one to Mr. Strahan's life, and without this clause my nephew would have had no right to publish it. Be so good as to inform Mr. Strahan of this circumstance.

You are too good in thinking any trifles that concern me are so much worth your attention, but I give you entire liberty to make what additions you please to the account of my life.]

I go very fast to decline, and last night had a small fever, which I hoped might put a quicker period to this tedious illness ; but unluckily, it has in a great measure gone off. I cannot submit to your coming over here on my account, as it is possible for me to see you so small a part of the day ; but Dr Black can better inform you concerning the degree of strength which may from time to time remain with me. Adieu.'

[My Dearest Friend,

DAVID HUME.

P.S. It was a strange blunder to send your letter by the carrier.] [1]

Three days after I received the following letter from Dr Black :—

' Dear Sir,   *' Edinburgh, Monday, August* 26, 1776.

'Yesterday, about four o'clock, afternoon, Mr Hume expired. The near approach of his death became evident in the night between Thursday and Friday, when his disease became excessive, and soon weakened him so much, that he could no longer rise out of his bed.' He continued to the last perfectly sensible, and free from much pain or feelings of distress. He never dropt the smallest expression of impatience ; but when he had occasion to speak to the people about him, always did it with affection and tenderness. I thought it improper to write to bring you over, especially as I had heard that he had dictated a letter to you, desiring you not to come. When he

---

[1] The passages enclosed in brackets, which were not in the letter as published by Adam Smith, are taken from the original in the possession of the Royal Society of Edinburgh.

became very weak it cost him an effort to speak, and he died in such a happy composure of mind that nothing could exceed it [1].'

Thus died our most excellent, and never-to-be-forgotten friend; concerning whose philosophical opinions men will no doubt judge variously, every one approving or condemning them according as they happen to coincide, or disagree with his own; but concerning whose character and conduct there can scarce be a difference of opinion. His temper, indeed, seemed to be more happily balanced, if I may be allowed such an expression, than that perhaps of any other man I have ever known. Even in the lowest state of his fortune, his great and necessary frugality never hindered him from exercising, upon proper occasions, acts both of charity and generosity. It was a frugality founded not upon avarice, but upon the love of independency. The extreme gentleness of his nature never weakened either the firmness of his mind, or the steadiness of his resolutions.

[1] Dr. W. Cullen wrote to Dr. Hunter on Sept. 17, 1776:—'You desire an account of Mr. Hume's last days, and I give it you with some pleasure, for though I could not look upon him in his last illness without much concern, yet the tranquillity and pleasantry which he constantly discovered did even then give me satisfaction, and now that the curtain is dropped allows me to indulge the less alloyed reflection. It was truly an example "des grands hommes qui sont morts en plaisantant [1];" and to me who have been so often shocked with the horrors of the superstitious on such occasions, the reflection on such a death is truly agreeable. For many weeks before his death he was very sensible of his gradual decay, and his answer to inquiries after his health was several times that he was going as fast as his enemies could wish, and as easily as his friends could desire. He was not however without a frequent recurrence of pain and uneasiness, but he passed most part of the day in his drawing-room, admitted the visits of his friends, and with his usual spirit conversed with them upon literature, politics, or whatever else was accidentally started. In conversation he seemed to be perfectly at ease, and to the last abounded with that pleasantry, and those curious and entertaining anecdotes which ever distinguished him. This however I always considered rather as an effort to be agreeable, and he at length acknowledged that it became too much for his strength. For a few days before his death he became more averse to receive visits; speaking became more and more difficult for him; and for twelve hours before his death his speech failed altogether. His senses and judgment did not fail till the last hour of his life. He constantly discovered a strong sensibility to the attention and care of his friends, and amidst great uneasiness and languor never betrayed any peevishness or impatience.' After recounting the anecdote about Lucian and the codicil to his will (*post*, p. 9, *n.* 10), Dr. Cullen continues:—'These are a few particulars, which may perhaps appear trifling, but to me no particulars seem trifling that relate to so great a man. It is perhaps from trifles that we can best distinguish the tranquillity and cheerfulness of the philosopher, at a time when the most part of mankind are under disquiet, anxiety, and sometimes even horror. I consider the sacrifice of the cock as a more certain evidence of the tranquillity of Socrates than his *Discourse on Immortality.*' Thomson's *Life of Dr. Cullen*, i. 607.

[1] 'In reference to a work so entitled, published at Amsterdam in 1732.'

THE LIFE OF DAVID HUME.

His constant pleasantry was the genuine effusion of good-nature and good-humour, tempered with delicacy and modesty, and without even the slightest tincture of malignity, so frequently the disagreeable source of what is called wit in other men. It never was the meaning of his raillery to mortify ; and therefore, far from offending, it seldom failed to please and delight even those who were the objects of it. To his friends, who were frequently the objects of it, there was not perhaps any one of all his great and amiable qualities which contributed more to endear his conversation. And that gaiety of temper, so agreeable in society, but which is so often accompanied with frivolous and superficial qualities, was in him certainly attended with the most severe application, the most extensive learning, the greatest depth of thought, and a capacity in every respect the most comprehensive. Upon the whole, I have always considered him, both in his lifetime, and since his death, as approaching as nearly to the idea of a perfectly wise and virtuous man, as perhaps the nature of human frailty will admit[1].

I am ever, dear Sir,   .

Most affectionately yours,

ADAM SMITH.

[1] Dr. Blair, in a letter to Strahan dated April 10, 1778, said:—'Poor David! what an irreparable blank does he make amongst us here. Taking him all in all, we shall never see the like'. Indeed, I cannot but agree with what Adam Smith says of him in the last sentence of his printed letter to you.' *Rosebery MS.*
Boswell records on Sept. 16, 1777:—'I mentioned to Dr. Johnson that David Hume's persisting in his infidelity when he was dying shocked me much. JOHNSON. "Why should it shock you, Sir? Hume owned he had never read the New Testament with attention. Here then was a man who had been at no pains to inquire into the truth of religion, and had continually turned his mind the other way. It was not to be expected that the prospect of death would alter his way of thinking, unless God should send an angel to set him right." I said I had reason to believe that the thought of annihilation gave Hume no pain. JOHNSON. "It was not so, Sir. He had a vanity in being thought easy. It is more probable that he should assume an appearance of ease, than that so very improbable a thing should be, as a man not afraid of going (as, in spite of his delusive theory, he cannot be sure but he may go) into an unknown state, and not being uneasy at leaving all he knew. And you are to consider that upon his own principle of annihilation he had no motive to speak the truth."' Boswell's *Johnson,* iii. 153.
Boswell had suggested to Johnson on July 9 of the same year that he should 'knock Hume's and Smith's heads together, and make vain and ostentatious infidelity exceedingly ridiculous.' *Ib.* iii. 119. See *ib.* v. 30, *n.* 3, for Dr. Horne's *Letter to Adam Smith, LL.D., On the Life, Death and Philosophy of his Friend, David Hume, Esq. By one of the People called Christians.*

[1] 'He was a man, take him for all in all,
I shall not look upon his like again.'

Hamlet, Act i. Sc. 2.

CHIEF EVENTS OF THE LIFE OF
DAVID HUME.

A BRIEF ACCOUNT OF

WILLIAM STRAHAN.

———••———

WILLIAM STRAHAN, Hume's correspondent, was born in Edinburgh in the year 1715. 'His father, who had a small appointment in the Customs, gave his son the education which every lad of decent rank then received in a country where the avenues to learning were easy, and open to men of the most moderate circumstances[1].' After having served his apprenticeship in his native town, he was enchanted, like so many of his countrymen, by 'the noblest prospect which a Scotchman ever sees,' and took 'the high road that leads to England[2].' There he carried on his trade with great success and rose to a position of importance and affluence. 'I remember,' wrote to him his friend Dr. Franklin, 'your observing once to me, as we sat together in the House of Commons, that no two journeymen printers within your knowledge had met with such success in the world as ourselves[3].' It was in his coach that Dr. Johnson, Boswell and blind Mrs. Williams, were one day carried to a dinner at his brother-in-law's house in Kensington. 'A printer having acquired a fortune sufficient to keep his coach was a good topic for the credit of literature. Mrs. Williams said that another printer, Mr. Hamilton, had not waited so long as Mr. Strahan, but had kept his coach several years sooner. JOHNSON. "He was in the right. Life is short. The sooner that a man begins to enjoy his wealth the better[4]."' In 1770 Strahan purchased from Mr. George Eyre 'a share of the patent for King's Printer[5].' In the general election of 1774 he was returned to Parliament for the borough of Malmesbury, and had the honour of having Charles Fox for his colleague.

[1] Nichols's *Lit. Anec.*, iii. 391. [2] Boswell's *Life of Johnson*, i. 425.
[3] *Post*, p. 64, *n.* 11. [4] Boswell's *Johnson*, ii. 226. [5] Nichols's *Lit. Anec.*, iii. 392.

In the succeeding Parliament he sat for Wooton Basset; but having supported the Coalition Ministry he lost his seat at the general election of 1784[1]. He outlived his friend David Hume nearly nine years, and died on July 9, 1785.

That he was a man not only of great worth but of a strong and cultivated understanding is shown by the men whom he had made his friends and by the services which he rendered to some of them. Garrick, it is true, thought that he 'was rather an *obtuse* man'—one not likely to be 'a good judge of an epigram.' To which Johnson replied, 'Why, Sir, he may not be a judge of an epigram; but you see he is a judge of what is *not* an epigram[2].' That he was a good judge in general of the merits of a book cannot be doubted. First in partnership with Andrew Millar, 'the Mæcenas of the age,' the man whom 'Johnson respected for raising the price of literature[3],' and then in partnership with Thomas Cadell, he published some of the most important works of his time. When Elmsly, the bookseller, 'declined the perilous adventure' of bringing out the *Decline and Fall of the Roman Empire*, it was Strahan and Cadell who 'undertook the risk of the publication.' It was by Strahan's 'prophetic taste,' writes Gibbon, that the number of the impression was doubled[4]. 'There will no books of reputation now be printed in London,' wrote Hume to him, 'but through your hands and Mr. Cadell's[5].' Though in this statement there is somewhat of Hume's flattery, yet it is true that they were the publishers of works not only of Gibbon and of Hume, but of Johnson, Robertson, Adam Smith, Blackstone, and Blair. Hume and Robertson availed themselves moreover of his knowledge of English in the correction of their proofs. 'He was,' writes Dr. Beattie, 'eminently skilled in composition[6].' His services in this respect Hume more than once gratefully acknowledges[7]. He ranks him indeed among the learned printers, who, since the days of Aldus and Stephens, had not been seen on the earth[8]. He made him his literary executor[9]. The long correspondence which he maintained with him shows the value that he set on his letters. 'I have

---

[1] Nichols's *Lit. Anec.*, iii. 393.   [2] Boswell's *Johnson*, iii. 258.   [3] *Ib.* i. 287.
[4] Gibbon's *Misc. Works*, ed. 1814, i. 222.   [5] *Post*, p. 314.   [6] Forbes's *Life of Beattie*, ed. 1824, p. 341.   [7] *Post*, pp. 214, 224, 231.   [8] *Post*, p. 235.
[9] *Post*, p. 335, *n.* 14.

always said without flattery,' he wrote to him, 'that you may give instructions to statesmen [1].' A denial of flattery, it is true, means as little in Hume's mouth as it would have done in the mouth of any of those French philosophers or men of letters in whose society he so much delighted. Nevertheless the length of many of his answers is a proof that he thought highly of his correspondent's understanding and knowledge of public affairs. 'Mr. Strahan loved much,' wrote Boswell, 'to be employed in political negotiation [2].'

He must have had an unusual breadth of character, for he was the friend of men so unlike as Johnson and Hume, as Franklin and Robertson. It was at his house that Johnson and Adam Smith met when 'they did not take to each other [3].' He tried to get Johnson a seat in the House of Commons [4], and was 'his friendly agent in receiving his pension for him, and his banker in supplying him with money when he wanted it [5].' When Johnson wrote to Scotland, 'I employ Strahan,' he said, 'to frank my letters, that he may have the consequence of appearing a Parliament-man among his countrymen [6].' There was a difference between the two men which kept them apart for a few months, when it was healed by a letter from Johnson and a friendly call from Strahan [7]. The warmth of the friendship that existed between him and other eminent men of letters is shown by their letters. Adam Smith writing to him signs himself, 'Most affectionately yours [8],' and so does Robertson [9]. Beattie and Blair are scarcely less warm [10]. Johnson indeed, when among the Aberdeen professors, mocked at his intimacy with Bishop Warburton. 'Why, Sir, he has printed some of his works, and perhaps bought the property of some of them. The intimacy is such as one of the professors here may have with one of the carpenters who is repairing the college [11].' But Beattie who had seen the correspondence that had passed between the two men said that 'they were very particularly acquainted [12].' The manly indignation of his answer to Hume, who had accused him of deception [13], is not the letter of a man

[1] *Post*, p. 145.   [2] Boswell's *Johnson*, ii. 137.   [3] *Ib.* iii. 331.
[4] *Ib.* ii. 137.   [5] *Ib.* ii. 137.   [6] *Ib* iii. 364.   [7] *Ib* iii. 364.
[8] *Post.* p. 352.   [9] Letter dated Dec. 21, 1780, *Barker MSS.*   [10] *Barker MSS*   [11] Boswell's *Johnson*, v. 92.   [12] Forbes's *Life of Beattie*, p. 341.   [13] *Post*, p. 266.

who was intimate with any one on unworthy terms. The earnestness of the apology which Hume at once made to him is a sure proof of the high value which he set on his friendship.

His portrait was painted by Sir Joshua Reynolds in those troubled days when London was still under the scare of the Gordon riots. During the week when the disorder was at its height Sir Joshua's note-book records that he had sittings fixed, among others, for Mr. Strahan. ' No wonder the appointments between Monday and Thursday have a pen drawn through them[1].' Even if the great painter had had the calmness to go on with his work in the midst of such confusion, the eminent printer would not have kept the appointments. 'He had been insulted,' writes Johnson, 'and spoke to Lord Mansfield of the licentiousness of the populace ; and his Lordship treated it as a very slight irregularity. . . . He got a garrison into his house, and maintained them a fortnight ; he was so frighted that he removed part of his goods[2].'

[1] Leslie and Taylor's *Life of Reynolds*, ed. 1865, ii. 302.
[2] Boswell's *Johnson*, iv. 428, 435.

ERRATUM.

Page 94, note 8. I failed to notice that Hume's Letter of May 15, 1759, quoted in this note, was written in a humorous strain. Dr. Warburton was the last man in the world whose compliments he would have transmitted.

LETTERS OF HUME

LETTERS OF DAVID HUME.

LETTER I.

The History of England under the Stuarts.

D^R S^{IR}

I am entirely of your opinion, that Mr. Balfour's ill humor on this Occasion has no manner of Foundation. Mr. Millar seems to me to have all along us'd him very well; Only, I thought the Price offerd for the large Paper Copies a little too low; and I see you have rais'd it. He has disoblig'd me very much at present, by spreading about a Story, that, when we made our Bargain for the first Volume, I had promis'd he shoud have the second at the same Price. This was demanded, and positively refus'd by me: I only said, that I was not accustomd lightly to change the People whom I dealt with; but that I woud not bind myself. Accordingly, when all the Articles of our Bargain, even the most trivial, were written over, I woud not allow this to be inserted. Baillie[1] Hamilton, who is a very honest Man, remembers and acknowleges this Fact. Indeed, it was very lucky I had that Precaution: For if I had entangled myself in such a Bargain, I never shoud have wrote a second Volume which I coud not hope ever to see succeed in their Management[2]. I am very well pleas'd with the State of the Sale; and hope it is the Prognostic of good Success. I certainly deserve the Approbation of the Public, from my Care and Disinterestedness, however deficient in other

B

Particulars. I shall regard myself as much oblig'd to you, if you inform me of all the Objections, which you hear made by Men of Sense, who are impartial, or even who are not: For it is good to hear what is said on all Sides. It was unlucky, that I did not publish the two Volumes together: Fools will be apt to say, that I am become more whiggish in this Volume: As if the Cause of Charles the 1 and James the 2 were the same, because they were of the same Family[3]. But such Remarks as these, every one, who ventures on the Public, must be contented to endure[4]. Truth will prevail at last; and if I have been able to embellish her with any Degree of Eloquence, it will not be long before she prevail.

I am Dr S^{ir} Your most obedient Servant

DAVID HUME.

EDINBURGH, 30 *of November*, [1756].

P.S.—It is easy for me to see, that Mr. Millar has certainly offerd to take from Baillie Hamilton 900 copies at nine Shillings[5]. He never woud have offerd seven at the beginning. It was a strange Infatuation in the Baillie to refuse it.

Note 1. ' Baillie, Bailie. A magistrate second in rank, in a royal borough ; an alderman.' Jamieson's *Dict. of the Scottish Language.*

Note 2. In November 1754 he published *The History of Great Britain. Volume I. Containing the reigns of James I, and Charles I.* quarto. Price 14*s.* in boards ; in November 1756 the second volume from the death of Charles I, to the Revolution ; in March 1759 *The History of England under the House of Tudor.* 2 vols. quarto. Price £1 in boards ; and in November 1761 *The History of England from the invasion of Julius Cæsar to the accession of Henry VII.* 2 vols. quarto. He had at one time intended to carry down the first instalment of his work beyond the Revolution. In a letter written in 1753 he says :—' My work divides into three very moderate volumes : one to end with the death of Charles the First ; the second at the Revolution ; the third at the Accession ; for I dare come no nearer the present times.' Burton's *Hume*, i. 378. The following curious letter in my possession, written by Gavin Hamilton, of the firm of Hamilton, Balfour & Neill, Edinburgh booksellers, shews that a year later Hume intended to make the Treaty of Utrecht the conclusion of his work. No doubt he resolved to stop there to avoid the necessity of describing the

Jacobite plot which was formed by some of Anne's ministers, and was baffled by her sudden death.   Such a matter was of too delicate a nature to have much attraction for a man whose love of tranquillity grew far more rapidly even than his years.

'EDINBR., 29 *Janry*, 1754.

'MY DEAR WILLIE,

'in any important step I make, in bussines, I should rekon my self very much out of my duty to you as on of my sincerest freinds if I did not un bosome my self, lett this serve for preamble to what I am going to say.

'I have within these ten days concluded a bargain that is rekoned very bold by every body that hears of it, and some think it rash, because they never heard of the like pass here ; tho' at the same time I remain very well content with my bargain.

'John Balfour and I have agread to pay 1200£ sterling of coppy money, for a single impression of a book, 'tis the history of great britain composed by David Hume our scots authour.   I print 2000 and have right to print no more, the calcul will stand thus, to print 3 quarto volls which it will make, will cost with advertisements and incidents about 320 per voll : the book will sell at 15/ bound or ten shillings to Bk. Sellers in sheets, but lett us rekon the London coppies only producing 9 shilling, then 2000 coppies will yeald about 920£ sterling per voll after deducing 320£ for printing and 400£ to the authour which is not payable very soon, there remains of proffit for our selves about 200£ per voll, which we are content to putt up with as we are perswaded that this first impression will be short while in hands, and this is the next question, how do you know that? all I can say to you in the bounds of a very short letter is that we have been at due pains to inform our selves of the merit of the work and are well satis- fyed one that head that it is the prittyest thing ever was attempted in the English History, the three volls contians three grand periods, the first from the union of the Crowns to the death of the king, the 2ᵈ voll from the death of the king to the Revolution, and the last till the treaty of Utrecht, the facts are well vouched and thrown together into a light as to give the treu character of the times, it is neither whig nor tory but truely imparshal.

'I am with sincerity, yours

'GAVIN HAMILTON.'

'To Mr. William Strachan
   Printer in New street near Fleet street London.'

Whether this bookseller was related to Burns's Gavin Hamilton I have not been able to ascertain.

It is clear from Hume's letter to Strahan that the bargain, as described by Hamilton, was never completed.   To the Edinburgh firm he sold only the right of publishing the first edition of the first volume.   The second volume was brought out by Andrew Millar, the great London bookseller, who became at length the owner of the entire copyright of the whole *History*. Writing to Millar on April 12, 1755, Hume had said :—' Baillie Hamilton is a very honest Man, and far from being interested. But he is passionate and even wrong-headed to a degree.' On May 27, 1756, he wrote :—' I agree that the edition be 1750.' *M. S. R. S. E.*

Note 3. In his letter to Millar of April 12, 1755 he had said :—' I have always said to all my acquaintaince that if the first Volume bore a little of a Tory aspect, the second wou'd probably be as grateful to the opposite Party. The two first Princes of the House of Stuart were certainly more excusable than the two second. The constitution was in their time very ambiguous and undetermin'd, and their Parliaments were, in many respects, refractory and obstinate : But Charles the 2nd knew, that he had succeeded to a very limited Monarchy : His long Parliament was indulgent to him, and even consisted almost entirely of Royalists ; yet he could not be quiet, nor contented with a legal Authority. I need not mention the Oppressions in Scotland nor the absurd conduct of K. James the 2nd. These are obvious and glaring Points. Upon the whole, I wish the two Volumes had been published together. Neither one Party nor the other would, in that Case, have had the least Pretext of reproaching me with Partiality.'— *M. S. R. S. E.*

Note 4. Both in his *Autobiography* and in his correspondence he shews that he had but little of this kind of endurance.

Note 5. These must have been the unsold copies of the first volume.

LETTER II.

On the Reception of Vol. II of the History.

DEAR SIR,

Your Letter gave me a great deal of Satisfaction ; and I am much oblig'd to you for it. I must own, that, in my private Judgement, the first volume of my History is by far the best[1] ; The Subject was more noble, and admitted both of greater Ornaments of Eloquence, and nicer Distinctions of Reasoning. However, if the Public is so capricious as to prefer the second, I am very well pleas'd ; and hope the Prepossession in my Favor will operate backwards, and remove even the Prejudices formerly contracted[2].

I assure you, that, tho' Mr. Millar has probably had

an Intention of writing me to the Purpose he told you, yet he never did it, and his Memory has fail'd him in this Particular.   On the contrary, he said to me, that he in-tended to put this Volume of my philosophical Writings[3] into the same hands with the Dissertations[4], which are soon to be publish'd, who is, I think, one Bowyer[5].   I did not oppose him, because I thought, that was a Matter, which it did not belong me to meddle with.   However you will see by the enclos'd, which I have left open, what woud be my Choice in such a Case; and I hope hence-forth he will never think of any but you, wherever any of my Writings are concern'd.

I cannot think of troubling you so far in this new Edition as I did in my History; but I woud be extremely oblig'd to you, as you go along to mark any Doubts that occur to you, either with regard to Style[6] or Argument.   Mr. Millar thinks of making very soon another Edition in Twelves[7], and these Observations woud then serve me in good Stead. These Writings have already undergone several Editions, and have been very accurately examind every Impres-sion[8]; yet I can never esteem them sufficiently correct.

You will see by my Letter to Mr. Millar that I mention a Dedication, which may perhaps surprize you, as I never dealt in such servile Addresses[9]; But I hope it will not surprize you, when you hear it is only to a Presbyterian Minister, my Friend, Mr. Hume, the Author of Douglas[10]. I was resolv'd to do what lay in my Power to enable a Youth[11] of Genius to surmount the unaccountable Obstacles, which were thrown in his Way[12].   You will probably see it publishd in a few Days.   I hope the Goodness of the Intention will apologize for the Singularity of the undetaking [sic].

I am Dear Sir Your most obedient Servant

DAVID HUME.

Note 1. The first volume contained the Reigns of James I, and Charles I. Hume wrote to William Mure in 1757 (the exact date is not given) :—'I must own that I think my first volume a great deal better than the second. The subject admitted of more eloquence and of greater nicety of reasoning and more acute distinctions.' Burton's *Hume*, ii. 20.

Note 2. In his *Autobiography* he says of the second volume :— 'This performance happened to give less displeasure to the Whigs, and was better received. It not only rose itself, but helped to buoy up its unfortunate brother.' On the fly-leaf of the copy in the Bodleian of vol. i. of the first edition I have found in the hand-writing of the Rev. Charles Godwyn, Fellow of Balliol College, and a great benefactor to the Bodleian Library, the following entry, interesting as shewing the opinion formed of Hume at this time in England : —'I have heard much of Mr. Hume from persons who know him well, and think him to be one of the oddest characters in the world. Consider him as an historian and in private life there is not a better man living. No man has more generous sentiments of social virtue. He has great candour and humanity and the utmost regard for truth. Consider him as a philosopher in his speculative capacity, there is not a grain of virtue or religion in him. . . . I am informed that he has a great regard for the Church of England, and that if he was disposed to make choice of a religion, he would give this the preference. Written in the year 1757.'

Note 3. Hume refers, I believe, to the edition of his *Essays and Treatises* which was published in one quarto volume in 1758 (perhaps in the late autumn of 1757). He wrote to Millar on Dec. 4, 1756 :—'I am extremely desirous to have these four volumes [of *Philosophical Writings*], with that which you will publish this winter, brought into a quarto volume.' Burton's *Hume*, ii. 4.

Note 4. See *post*, p. 18.

Note 5. 'One Bowyer' was William Bowyer, 'confessedly the most learned printer of the eighteenth century.' Nichols's *Lit. Anec.* i. 2. Johnson wrote to Nichols on Oct. 20, 1784 :—'At Ashbourne, where I had very little company, I had the luck to borrow *Mr. Bowyer's Life*; a book, so full of contemporary history that a literary man must find some of his old friends.' Boswell's *Johnson*, iv. 369.

Note 6. Hume, Scot of Scots though he was, spared no pains to clear his style from Scotticisms. He laments 'his misfortune to write in the language of the most stupid and factious barbarians in the world' (*post*, Letter of Oct. 25, 1769); but none the less does he rebuke Gibbon for composing his first work in French. 'Let the French,' he writes, 'triumph in the present diffusion of their tongue. Our solid and increasing establishments in America, where we need less dread the inundation of barbarians, promise a superior stability and duration to the English language.' Gibbon's *Misc. Works*, i. 204. Though he never, like Mallet, 'cleared his tongue from his native pronunciation' (Johnson's *Works*, viii. 464), but always spoke 'in a broad Scotch

tone,' yet his words were always English. ' He never used Scotch '
said one who as a young man had known him well. Burton's *Hume*,
ii. 440. Like most of the Scotch literary men of his day he had
studied English almost as laboriously as if it were wholly a foreign
tongue. Beattie (*Life* by Forbes, ed. 1824, p. 243) wrote on Jan. 5, 1778 :—
' We who live in Scotland are obliged to study English from books,
like a dead language, which we understand but cannot speak.' He
adds :—'I have spent some years in labouring to acquire the art of
giving a vernacular cast to the English we write.' Johnson accused
Hume of Gallicisms. ' Why, Sir, his style is not English ; the structure of his sentences is French.' Boswell's *Johnson*, i. 439. Lord
Mansfield told Dr. A. Carlyle that ' when he was reading Hume and
Robertson's books, he did not think he was reading English.' Carlyle's
Auto. p. 516. Hume in the fourth chapter of his *History of England*,
expresses his deliberate preference for the foreign element in our
language. He speaks of ' that mixture of French which is at present
to be found in the English tongue, and which composes the greatest
and best part of our language.' Ed. 1802, i. 259. Francis Horner, in
his student days at Edinburgh, making ' a very rigid examination of
the style of Mr. Hume in his *History*,' says, ' I am astonished to find it
abound so much both in inaccuracies and inelegancies.' *Memoirs of
Horner*, i. 11. Mackintosh, speaking of Hume's philosophical works,
says :—' In clearness and vivacity he surpassed all English specula-
tors. . . . It must be owned that he not only copied the liveliness and
perspicuity of French writers, but the structure of their sentences ;
that he has frequently violated the rules of English syntax ; and what
is a more serious offence, that his style exhibits little of the idiom and
genius of the language ; it too often betrays a Scotchman whose
literary habits were formed in France.' Of the *History* he says :—
'.The negligences of style, which are too frequent in this noble work,
may be left to the petty grammarian.' *Life of Mackintosh*, ii. 168.
Horace Walpole, on the other hand, speaking of the first volume of
the *History*, when it was as yet in its first unrevised edition, says that
' his style which is the best we have in history . . . is very pleasing.'
Letters, ii. 429. Gibbon (*Misc. Works*, i. 122) writing after Hume's
death, records how in ' the repeated perusals ' of his *History*, ' the
careless inimitable beauties often forced me to close the volume with
a mixed sensation of delight and despair.' Hume sought the aid of
writers far inferior to himself in general powers in his eagerness to
refine his style. Mallet, Johnson's 'beggarly Scotchman,' treated him
with the insolence of a superior. Hume writing to Millar in 1756
about the second volume of his *History* says :—' Notwithstanding Mr.
Mallet's impertinence in not answering my letter (for it deserves no
better a name), if you can engage him from yourself to mark on the
perusal such slips of language as he thinks I have fallen into in this
volume it will be a great obligation to me ; I mean that I shall lie
under an obligation to you ; for I would not willingly owe any to him.'

Burton's *Hume*, ii. 3. Six or seven years later Mallet wrote to Hume about the last two volumes of the *History* :—' I have done at last what nothing but the greatest regard for the writer and the truest friendship for the man could have made me submit to ; I have gone over both your volumes again with the eye and attention of a mere grammarian. The task of looking after verbal mistakes or errors against the idiom of a tongue, though not unnecessary, is trivial and disgusting in the greatest degree ; but your work and you deserved it of me.' *Ib.* p. 142. So early as 1754, Hume sending Wilkes a copy of the *History* 'asks his advice as to language, and says :—" Notwithstanding all the pains I have taken in the study of the English language, I am still jealous of my pen."' *Historical MSS. Com.* 4th Report, p. 401. As late as 1775, in the last year of his life, he set two young Scotch lads, fresh from an English school, the task of detecting the Scotticisms in his account of Harold. *Caldwell Papers,* i. 39. The following from a letter to a Scotch doctor settled in London, is an instance of the points on which he sought assistance :—' You know that the word *enough* or *enuff*, as it is pronounced by the English, we commonly in Scotland, when it is applied to number, pronounce *enow.* Thus we would say :—" Such a one has books enow for study, but not leisure enuff." Now I want to know whether the English make the same distinction.' Burton's *Hume*, i. 384. It will be seen hereafter how grateful he was to Strahan for the assistance which he gave him in correcting his style. 'Strahan,' says Dr. Beattie, 'was eminently skilled in composition, and had corrected (as he told me himself) the phraseology of both Mr. Hume and Dr. Robertson.' Forbes's *Beattie,* p. 341. Dr. Burton gives instances of the corrections in the second edition of the *History*. *Life of Hume,* ii. 79. See *ante,* Adam Smith's letter for the humorous way in which Hume a few days before his death joked about his love of making corrections. He was ready in his turn to help others in refining their style. Dr. Franklin wrote to him from Coventry, on Sept. 27, 1760 :— ' I thank you for your friendly Admonition relating to unusual Words in the Pamphlet. It will be of service to me. The *pejorate* and the *colonize*, since they are not in common use here, I give up as bad.' Franklin goes on to regret that we cannot 'make new words when we want them by composition of old ones whose meanings are already well understood,' as *uncomeatable* for *inaccessible*.' *M.S.R.S.E.* Hume was shewn in manuscript Reid's *Inquiry into the Human Mind.* Though it was an attack on his own philosophy, yet in reading it 'he kept,' he says, 'a watchful eye all along over the style,' so that he might point out any Scotticisms. Burton's *Hume*, ii. 154. When Boswell told Johnson that ' David Hume had made a short collection of Scotticisms, " I wonder," said Johnson, "that *he* should find them."' Boswell's *Johnson,* ii. 72. In this list (given in Hume's *Phil. Works,* ed. 1854, i. cxii) some expressions were included which were good English at the time, and others which pass current now, as :—

Scotch.	*English.*
Friends and acquaintances.	Friends and acquaintance.
Incarcerate.	Imprison.
Tear to pieces.	Tear in pieces [1].
In the long run.	At long run.
'Tis a question if.	'Tis a question whether.
Simply impossible.	Absolutely impossible.
Nothing else.	No other thing.
There, where.	Thither, whither.
Defunct.	Deceased.
Adduce a proof.	Produce a proof.
In no event.	In no case.
Common soldiers.	Private men.
To open up.	To open, or lay open.
On a sudden.	Of a sudden.

It was this laborious study of English by Scotch authors that explains Churchill's lines on Dr. Armstrong's *Day* :

> ' Where all but barren labour was forgot,
> And the vain stiffness of a *Letter'd* Scot.'
>
> Churchill's *Poems*, ed. 1766, ii. 330.

A passage in Dugald Stewart's *Life of Robertson,* which was published in 1801, places in the strongest, and I may add the strangest light the difficulties under which a Scotch writer still laboured, ' The influence,' he says, ' of Scottish associations, so far as it is favourable to antiquity, is confined to Scotchmen alone, and furnishes no resources to the writer who aspires to a place among the English classics. Nay, such is the effect of that provincial situation to which Scotland is now reduced, that the transactions of former ages are apt to convey to our-selves exaggerated conceptions of barbarism from the uncouth and degraded dialect in which they are recorded.' Within four years after this was written Scott was to publish his *Lay of the Last Minstrel,* and within thirteen years his *Waverley.*

Note 7. In duodecimo.

Note 8. *Impression* is defined by Johnson as *Edition; number printed at once; one course of printing.*

Note 9. Johnson was like Hume in this. 'The loftiness of his mind prevented him from ever dedicating.' Boswell's *Johnson,* ii. 1. Boswell on the contrary dedicated his chief works. ' For my own part,' he wrote, 'I own I am proud enough. But I do not relish the stateli-ness of not dedicating at all.' *Ib. n. 2.*

Note 10. The author of *Douglas* signed himself John Home, as did most of that name. 'The practice of writing Hume,' says David Hume, 'is by far the most ancient and most general till about the Restoration, when it became common to spell Home contrary to the pronunciation.' Burton's *Hume,* i. 7. Sir Walter Scott, in a review of Home's *Works,* says :—' The word is uniformly, in Scotland,

[1] ' Tear him to pieces; he's a conspirator.' *Julius Cæsar,* iii. 2.

pronounced *Hume*; and in ancient documents we have seen it written Heume, Hewme, and Hoome.' *Quarterly Review*, No. 71, p. 170. He should have added that a Scotchman's pronunciation of *Hume* is not the same as an Englishman's.

The historian was not able to persuade his elder brother, the Laird of Ninewells, to adopt his mode of spelling. To the poet 'he at one time jocularly proposed that they should determine the controversy by casting lots. "Nay," says John, "this is a most extraordinary proposal, Mr. Philosopher; for if you lose, you take your own name, and if I lose, I take another man's."' Home's *Works*, i. 164. Hume went on joking with him to the last about the spelling. When, accompanied by Home, he was returning to Edinburgh to die, after his fruitless journey to Bath, he sent a card of invitation to Dr. Blair which began:—'Mr. John Hume, alias Home, alias The Home.' To his will he added as a codicil:— 'I leave to my friend Mr. John Home of Kilduff ten dozen of my old claret, at his choice, and one single bottle of that other liquor called port. I also leave to him six dozen of port, provided that he attests under his hand, signed John *Hume*, that he has himself alone finished that bottle at two sittings. By this concession he will at once terminate the only two differences that ever arose between us concerning temporal matters.' *Ib.* p. 163. Home, like almost all Scotchmen, drank claret. 'On the enforcement of the high duty on French wine' in Scotland, he made the following epigram :—

'Firm and erect the Caledonian stood,
Old was his mutton and his claret good.
"Let him drink port," an English statesman cried—
He drank the poison, and his spirit died.' *Ib.* p. 164.

Wilkes in *The North Briton*, No. 12 (date of Aug. 22, 1762) makes no distinction between the names, no doubt intentionally. He writes:—'There is one Scottish pension I have been told of which afforded me real pleasure. It is Mr. Hume's; for I am satisfied that it must be given to Mr. David Hume, whose writings have been justly admired both abroad and at home, and not to Mr. John Hume, who has endeavoured to bring the name into contempt by putting it to two insipid tragedies and other trash in the *Scottish Miscellanies*.' Hume's pension was not given till 1764. Burton's *Hume*, ii. 191. For Home's pension see below, *n.* 12. Johnson in his *Life of Collins* writes Home's name Hume. *Works*, viii. 403.

Note 11. Home was thirty-four years old.

Note 12. Home's tragedy was finished in 1754. In the first sketch of the play Young Norval was Young Forman. 'Even after the first representations [at Edinburgh] the name Randolph was substituted for Barnet, which had struck some of the English part of the audience as producing a bad effect from its being the same with that of the village near London.' Home's *Works*, i. 36, 101. Hume writing about the play to Spence on Oct. 15 of that year, says:—'As you are a Lover of Letters, I shall inform you of a Piece of News which will be agreeable to you : We may hope to see good Tragedies in the English Language. A young man called Hume, a clergyman of this Country, discovers a very fine Genius for that Species of Composition.' Spence's *Anecdotes*, p. 452. To Adam Smith he wrote :—'When it shall be printed (which will be soon) I am persuaded it will be esteemed the best, and by French critics the only tragedy of our language.' Burton's *Hume*, ii. 17. It was in this same year, 1754, that in the Appendix to the Reign of James I, writing of Shakespeare, he says :—' His total ignorance of all theatrical art and conduct, however material a defect, yet, as it affects the spectator rather than the reader, we can more easily excuse, than that want of taste which often prevails in his productions, and which gives way only by intervals to the irradiations of genius.' Adam Smith was not inferior to his friend in perversity of taste. He regretted that in comedy the English writers had not followed the model of the French school in the use of rhyme. Dugald Stewart's *Life of Adam Smith*, p. 71. Wordsworth had some justification for describing Adam Smith as 'the worst critic, David Hume not excepted, that Scotland, a soil to which this sort of weed seems natural, has produced.' Wordsworth's *Works*, ed. 1857, vi. 367. H. C. Robinson (*Diary*, i. 311) records, though evidently with imperfect recollection, a saying of Coleridge about Hume's preference of the French tragedians to Shakespeare :— 'Hume comprehended as much of Shakespeare as an apothecary's phial would, placed under the falls of Niagara.' Burns however was no better than Hume or Smith. In one of his *Prologues* he says of Scotland :—

    ' Here Douglas forms wild Shakespeare into plan.'

Douglas was refused by Garrick to whom it was first offered. '.After reading it, he returned it with an opinion that it was totally unfit for the stage.' Dr. A. Carlyle's *Auto.* p. 304. It was brought out in Edinburgh in the end of 1756, and met with the greatest success. Among the clergy however a flame was kindled, for not only was the author a minister, but at the performance several ministers were present. The Presbytery of Edinburgh published a paper ' lamenting the extraordinary and unprecedented countenance given of late to the playhouse in that city.' The Presbytery of Glasgow, on Feb. 2. 1757, the day after the date of Hume's letter in the text, supported their brothers in Edinburgh in the following manner :— ' Having good reason to believe that this paper refers to the following melancholy but notorious facts, that one who is a minister of the Church of Scotland did himself write and compose a stage-play, entitled *The Tragedy of Douglas*, and got it to be acted on the theatre at Edinburgh ; and that he, with several other ministers of this church were present, and some of them oftener than once, at the acting of the said play before a numerous audience : The Presbytery being deeply affected with this new and strange appearance do think it their duty,' etc. *Gent. Mag.* 1757, p. 89. One of these ministers was punished by a six weeks' suspension, 'owing a mitigated sentence to his plea that, though he attended, he concealed himself as well as he could to avoid giving offence.' Dr. A. Carlyle's *Auto.* p. 315. Dr. Carlyle writing of himself says:—' I had attended the play-house, not on the first or second, but on the third night of the performance, being well aware that all the fanatics and some other enemies would be on the watch, and make all the advantage they possibly could against me. But six or seven friends of the author, clergymen from the Merse [Home's country] having attended reproached me for my cowardice ; and above all the author himself and some female friends of his having heated me by their upbraidings I went on the third night, and having taken charge of the ladies I drew on myself all the clamours of tongues and violence of persecution which I afterwards underwent.' *Ib.* p. 314. Home, who was threatened with an ecclesiastical prosecution, 'gave in a demission of his office on the following 7th of June, and withdrew from the Church.' *Ib.* p. 325. Some years before he had been introduced to Archibald, Duke of Argyle, who said to him :—' Mr. Home, I am now too old to hope for an opportunity of doing you any material service myself; but I will do you the greatest favour in my power by presenting you to my nephew, the Earl of Bute.' Home's *Works*, i. 33. The value of Lord Bute's friendship was now seen. Home from this time 'lived very much with him, and was in habits of intimacy with his young pupil, the Prince of Wales [afterwards George III].' *Ib.* p. 50. A few days before he left the Church he had received a pension of £100 a year from the Princess Dowager of Wales. Walpole's *Letters*, iii. 78. Four years later George III in the very beginning of his reign 'settled on him a pension of £300 per annum from his privy purse.' Not long afterwards he gave him a post worth the same sum. Home's *Works*, i. 58.

Churchill in *The Prophecy of Famine (Poems*, ed. 1766, i. 103) introduces, among the Scotch who flocked to London,

'Home, disbanded from the sons of prayer
   For loving plays.'

He continues :—

'Thence simple bards, by simple prudence taught,
   To this wise town by simple patrons brought,
   In simple manner utter simple lays,
   And take with simple pensions simple praise.' *Ib.* p. 103.

Home made a generous use of his money. ' " His house," said Dr. Adam Ferguson, "was always as full of his friends as it could hold, fuller than in modern manners it could be made to hold." Hume told Ferguson he should lecture his friend on his want of attention to money-matters. "I am afraid I should do so with little effect," he answered ; "and to tell you the truth, I am not sure if I don't like

him the better for this foible."' Home's *Works*, i. 59. It was a foible
from which Hume, who in early life had had to practise 'very rigid
frugality' (*ante*, Hume's *Auto.*), remained singularly free. When Lord
Elibank, who was somewhat parsimonious, heard of the pension, he
said, ' It is a very laudable grant, and I rejoice at it; but it is no more
in the power of the King to make Adam Ferguson or John Home
rich than to make me poor.' *Ib.* p. 54.

Some years before Hume dedicated his *Dissertations* to Home,
Collins had inscribed to him his *Ode on the Superstitions of the Highlands.*

> ' Home, thou return'st from Thames, whose naiads long
>   Have seen thee lingering with a fond delay,
> 'Mid those soft friends, whose hearts, some future day,
>   Shall melt, perhaps, to hear thy tragic song.'

In 1760 Voltaire brought out his comedy *L'Écossaise* under the
veil of a translation of a piece by John Home. In the preface he
says :—' La comédie dont nous présentons la traduction aux amateurs
de la littérature est de M. Hume, pasteur de l'église d'Édimbourg,
déjà connu par deux belles tragédies jouées à Londres : il est parent
et ami de ce célèbre philosophe M. Hume qui a creusé avec tant
de hardiesse et de sagacité les fondemens de la métaphysique et de
la morale. Ces deux philosophes font également honneur à l'Écosse,
leur patrie.' *Œuvres de Voltaire*, ed. 1819. v. 12.

LETTER III.

Bargaining with Millar the bookseller.

Dear Sir,

I have wrote apart a Letter, which you may send to
Mr. Millar: I shall here add a Word to Yourself; and
ask a little of your Advice. Some time ago, I wrote
to Mr. Millar, that if he was inclin'd to purchase the full
Property of these two Volumes of History, I wou'd part
with it, if he wou'd make me a proper Offer. He desir'd
me to name my Terms. I ask'd 8oo Guineas[1]; but have
not yet receiv'd an answer from him. I own to you, that
the Demand may appear large; but if Mr. Millar and
I reason upon the same Principles it will not appear
unreasonable. I think History the most popular kind
of writing of any[2], the Period I treat of the most in-

teresting, and my Performance will I hope rise in Credit every day. We have so little, or rather nothing of this kind that has the least Appearance either of Impartiality [3] or Eloquence, that I cannot doubt but in the long run it will have a considerable Success. Now I was offerd 800 Pounds for the first Edition alone by Baillie Hamilton ; and he propos'd to have reasonable Profits after paying me that Sum : I cannot think but all the subsequent Editions must be at least equal in Value to the first alone. This is the View in which the Affair appeard to me : If it appears to you in the same Light, I doubt not but you will express your Mind to him. If you think my Demand unreasonable, I shall be oblig'd to you for telling me so, and for giving me your Reasons. For tho' it is not probable, that I shall fall much, if any thing, of that Demand : Yet if I see it impracticable for me to obtain it, I shall endeavor to contrive some other Method, by which I may adjust Matters with Mr. Millar in case of a second Edition. It is chiefly in order to avoid the Trouble and Perplexity of such Schemes that I desire at once to part with all the Property.

I am Dear S[ir] Your most obedient humble Servant

DAVID HUME.

15 *Feby.*, 1757.

P.S.—You will certainly like my Friend's Play [4]. It was acted here with vast Success. And reads as well as it acts. Mr. Millar woud tell you the Accident, which occasiond many copies of the Dissertations to be sold without the Dedication [5]. It has given me some Vexation. However there is no Remedy.

Note 1. Hume, as I have shewn (*ante*, p. 3), had sold only the copyright of the first edition of the first volume to the Edinburgh booksellers. The first edition of the second volume he had sold to Millar, for £700, it seems. Writing to him on Sept. 3 of this year about the *History of England under the Tudors*, which at that time he thought would be comprised in one somewhat bulky volume, he

says :—' I am willing to engage with you for the same price, *viz.*
seven hundred pounds, payable three months after the publication.'
Burton's *Hume*, ii. 37. What he now wishes to sell is the copyright
of the first two volumes of the *House of Stuart.* As Hamilton and
Balfour had agreed to pay £1200 for three volumes it may be assumed
that they paid £400 for one. For the second volume, if my supposition is right, Hume received £700. If he was paid 800 guineas, i. e.
£840 for the entire property in the two volumes, his total payment
for the *House of Stuart* amounted to £1940. Robertson was offered by
Hamilton and Balfour £500 for one edition of his *History of Scotland.*
Burton's *Hume*, ii. 42. For his *Charles V* he was to receive from
Cadell and Strahan £3400, with £400 more in case of a second
edition. Robertson to Strahan, May 27, 1768. *Barker MSS.* See
post, Letter of June 21, 1770, for Hume's complaint of Hamilton's
extravagance.

Note 2. Addison, Bolingbroke, and Johnson had pointed out the
inferiority of English historians. Hume wrote in 1753 :—' You know
that there is no post of honour in the English Parnassus more
vacant than that of history.' Burton's *Hume*, i. 378. Gibbon (*Misc.
Works*, i. 122) writing of the year 1759 says :—' The old reproach
that no British altars had been raised to the Muse of history was
recently disproved by the first performances of Robertson and Hume.'
Though Hume complained of the slow sale of his own *History*, yet
he wrote in 1769 :—' People now heed the theatre almost as little as
the pulpit. History now is the favourite reading, and our friend
[Robertson] the favourite historian.' Burton's *Hume*, ii. 421. Robertson's *History of Scotland* went through fourteen editions in thirty-
four years. Stewart's *Life of Robertson*, p. 326. ' The first impression of Gibbon's *Decline and Fall* was exhausted in a few days ; a
second and third edition were scarcely adequate to the demand.'
Gibbon's *Works*, i. 223. See *post*, Letter of Aug. 1770, where Hume
says:—' I believe this is the historical age and this the historical nation.'

Note 3. Horace Walpole, Whig though he was, wrote of Hume's
first volume (*Letters*, ii. 428) :—' It is called Jacobite, but in my opinion
is only not *George-Abite*: where others abuse the Stuarts he laughs
at them : I am sure he does not spare their ministers.' This was
before Hume had made, as he tells us in his *Autobiography*, ' above a
hundred alterations in the reigns of the two first Stuarts, all of them
invariably to the Tory side.' Rousseau wrote in August, 1762 :—' M.
Hume est le plus vrai philosophe que je connaisse, et le seul
historien qui jamais ait écrit avec impartialité. Il n'a pas plus aimé
la vérité que moi, j'ose le croire ; mais j'ai mis quelquefois de la
passion dans mes recherches, et lui n'a mis dans les siennes que
ses lumières et son beau génie.' Hume's *Private Corres.* p. 25. Voltaire
begins a brief notice of Hume's *History* by saying :—' Jamais le
public n'a mieux senti qu'il n'appartient qu'aux philosophes d'écrire
l'histoire.' He continues :—' M. Hume, dans son histoire, ne paraît

ni parlementaire, ni royaliste, ni anglican, ni presbytérien ; on ne découvre en lui que l'homme équitable.' He ends :—' La fureur des partis a long-temps privé l'Angleterre d'une bonne histoire comme d'un bon gouvernement. Ce qu'un tory écrivait était nié par les whigs, démentis à leur tour par les torys. . . . dans le nouvel historien on découvre un esprit supérieur à sa matière, qui parle des faiblesses, des erreurs et des barbaries, comme un médecin parle des maladies épidémiques.' *Œuvres de Voltaire*, ed. 1819–25, xxv. 517.

Note 4. *Douglas.* ' The play had unbounded success for a great many nights in Edinburgh. . . . The town was in an uproar of exultation that a Scotchman had written a tragedy of the first rate, and that its merit was first submitted to their judgment.' Dr. A. Carlyle's *Auto.* p. 311.

Note 5. Hume wrote to Millar on Jan. 20, 1757, that some of the poet's friends ' were seized with an apprehension that the dedication of my *Dissertations* to him would hurt that party in the Church with which he had always been connected, and would involve him, and them of consequence, in the suspicion of infidelity.' ' Burton's *Hume*, ii. 18. A little later he wrote to Mr. Mure:—' Pray whether do you pity or blame me most with regard to this dedication of my *Dissertations* to my friend, the poet ? I am sure I never executed anything which was either more elegant in the composition or more generous in the intention ; yet such an alarm seized some fools here (men of very good sense, but fools in that particular), that they assailed both him and me with the utmost violence, and engaged us to change our intention. I wrote to Millar to suppress that dedication ; two posts after I retracted that order. Can anything be more unlucky than that in the interval of these four days he should have opened his sale, and disposed of 800 copies without that dedication, whence I imagined my friend would reap some advantage, and myself so much honour ?' *Ib.* ii. 21. In the Dedication Hume addressing Home says :—' You possess the true theatric Genius of Shakespeare and Otway, refined from the unhappy Barbarism of the one and Licentiousness of the other.'

LETTER IV.

The Quarto Edition of the Essays.

Sɪʀ

I suppose you have now begun, and are somewhat advanc'd in the Quarto Edition of my Essays. I intend to make an Index to it [1], and for this Reason have desir'd that the corrected Sheets may be sent me by the Post. I must also desire you to send them from time to time, as they are printed off; that, if there be any Mistakes in the Press (and some are unavoidable) I may be able to make a more full Errata. Please send under a Cover as many as a Frank will admit[2]: And if you want Franks, either Mr. Millar or you may send Covers directed to me to Mr. Mure[3], Mr. Oswald[4], Mr. Elliot[5] or S[ir] Harry Erskine[6]. You may chuse either of them whose House lye most convenient. I fancy Mr. Mure may have most Leizure.

I am S[ir] Your most humble Serv[t]

DAVID HUME.

Note 1. On Dec. 18, 1759, Hume writing to Millar about the *History of the Tudors*, says :—' I think that an Index will be very proper, and am glad that you free me from the Trouble of undertaking that Task, for which I know myself to be very unfit.' *M. S. R. S. E.*

Note 2. See *post*, note on Letter of March 25, 1771.

Note 3. William Mure of Caldwell, one of Hume's correspondents, who was in 1761 made a Baron of the Exchequer in Scotland. Burton's *Hume*, i. 152. He was at this time Member for Renfrewshire. *Parl. Hist.* xv. 321.

Note 4. James Oswald, Member for the Kirkaldy Burghs, at this time a Commissioner of Trade and Plantations. *Ib.* p. 322. Horace Walpole, writing of an important division in Parliament just before Sir Robert Walpole's fall, says of the Opposition :—' They have turned the Scotch to the best account. There is a young Oswald, who had engaged to Sir R. but has voted against us. Sir R. sent a friend to reproach him ; the moment the gentleman who had engaged for him came into the room, Oswald said, " You had like to have led me into a fine error ! did you not tell me that Sir R. would have the majority?" ' *Letters*, i. 121. He was one of Hume's closest friends. See Burton's *Hume*, i. 156.

Note 5. Gilbert Elliot of Minto, Member for Selkirkshire, afterwards third baronet of that name, and father of the First Earl of Minto. See *post*, Letter of March 13, 1770.

Note 6. Sir Henry Erskine was Member for the Crail Boroughs. Horace Walpole, writing on March 13, 1751, says that ' Erskine, who had just come into Parliament, was laying a foundation for the next reign by attacking the Mutiny Bill.' *Letters*, ii. 242. In Jan. 1756 he was dismissed the army (*ib.* p. 498) ; but a few days after the accession of George III, Walpole, calling him ' the favourite of the favourite,' —that is to say of Lord Bute—says that he is to be rewarded with the command of a regiment. *Ib.* iii. 359. He and Hume had attended General St. Clair in his military embassy to the Courts of Vienna and Turin. *Ante* Hume's *Autobiography.* Hume describes him paying court to his constituents in 1754. 'I was lately told that one day last winter he went to pay a visit to a deacon's wife, who happened in that very instant to be gutting fish. He came up to her with open arms, and said he hoped madam was well, and that the young ladies her daughters were in good health. "Oh, come not near me," cried she, " Sir Harry ; I am in a sad pickle, as nasty as a beast." " Not at all, Madam," replied he ; " you are in a very agreeable négligé." " Well," said she, " I shall never be able to understand your fine English." " I mean, Madam," returned he, " that you are drest in a very genteel deshabillé." ' Burton's *Hume,* i. 397.

LETTER V.

The Bargain with Millar concluded.

S^{IR}

    I have receiv'd the two first Sheets of the Quarto Edition of my philosophical Writings ; and am very well satisfy'd with it. Please only to tell the Compositor, that he always employ a Capital after the Colons. Here follow a few Alterations, which I desire you to make on the last published Volume or four Dissertations which are to be inserted in different Places of the Quarto Volume.

[These alterations, as they are minute and can only be understood by a reference to the printed volume, I think it needless to print.]

    Please to get a Copy of the Dissertations from Mr. Millar and make these Alterations. Observe also that the two Dissertations, which are to be inserted among the Essays, are to be entitled Essays. The other two are to be inserted in the Places as directed[1].

    I am very well pleas'd to finish the Bargain with Mr. Millar. I hope we shall both find our Account in it. I believe his Offer may be reckond very reasonable and even frank and generous. We have only a small Difference about the time of Payment, which I hope will easily be adjusted. If it be not convenient for him to pay the Money in May next, I wou'd delay it till the 2nd of August, which is our Lambas term[2], and woud endeavour to get his Bill discounted, tho' that Practice be not very common in Scotland[3].

I hope the Douglas has had a good Success in London[4]. The Public will certainly at first be divided. That Simplicity both of Fable and Style are Novelties on the English Stage, and will no doubt meet with Opposition; but they must prevail, I think, at last[5].

I am Sir Your most obedient Servant

DAVID HUME.

NINEWELLS[6] NEAR BERWICK, 18 *April*, 1757.

P.S.—I return to Edinburgh in a few days.

Note 1. In Feb. 1757, Hume published the four *Dissertations*, entitled *The Natural History of Religion*; *Of the Passions*; *Of Tragedy*; *Of the Standard of Taste*, separately in a duodecimo volume, price three shillings. *Gent. Mag.* 1757, p. 94. He included them in the quarto edition of his *Essays and Treatises* which was published either at the end of that year or the beginning of the next. It was the latter two of the *Dissertations* that were inserted among the *Essays*. See *post*, Letters of Jan. 25 and Feb. 7, 1772, for the two Essays which Hume had suppressed.

Note 2. 'Lammas, a name for August 1. Anglo-Saxon, *hláf-mæsse*, literally, 'loaf-mass.' A loaf was on this day offered as a first-fruits of harvest.' Skeat's *Etym. Dict.*

Note 3. Adam Smith in his *Wealth of Nations*, published in 1776, describes the great change caused in Scotland 'within these five-and-twenty or thirty years by the erection of new banking companies in almost every considerable town, and even in some country villages.' After explaining the Scotch system of 'cash accounts' he goes on to say:—'The facility of discounting bills of exchange, it may be thought, indeed gives the English merchants a conveniency equivalent to the cash accounts of the Scotch merchants. But the Scotch merchants, it must be remembered, can discount their bills of exchange as easily as the English merchants; and have besides the additional conveniency of their cash accounts.' Ed. 1811, ii. 32, 38. Hume in his Essay *Of the Balance of Trade* describes the same system under the name of a Bank-Credit.

Note 4. In the *Gent. Mag.* for March 1757 nearly seven columns are given to an abstract of the story of the tragedy. Dr. A. Carlyle (*Auto.* p. 325) says that 'it was acted in Covent Garden (for Garrick, though now the author's friend, could not possibly let it be performed in his theatre [Drury Lane] after having pronounced it unfit for the stage), where it had great success. It still maintains its ground, [written about the year 1800,] has been more frequently acted, and is more popular than any tragedy in the English language.' The speech in it that begins 'My name is Norval,' is perhaps all of it that is now remembered.

Note 5. Hume, writing of Home's earlier tragedy *Agis*, said:— 'The author, I thought, had corrupted his taste by the imitation of Shakespeare, whom he ought only to have admired.' He continues:—'But the same author has composed a new tragedy [*Douglas*] on a subject of invention; and here he appears a true disciple of Sophocles and Racine. I hope in time he will vindicate the English stage from the reproach of barbarism.' Burton's *Hume*, i. 392.

Note 6. Ninewells was the estate of which 'Hume's ancestors had been proprietors for several generations.' It was now held by his elder brother, John Home. It lies so close to Berwick, that Hume may be said to have missed being an Englishman by only a mile or two. Yet, according to Ramsay of Ochtertyre, before the Rebellion of 1745 'the people of Northumberland and the Merse, who spoke dialects of the same language, and were only separated by a river, had little more intercourse than those of Kent and Normandy.' *Scotland and Scotsmen in the Eighteenth Century*, ii. 213. Ninewells takes its name 'from a cluster of nine springs, that burst forth from a gentle declivity in front of the mansion, which has on each side a semi-circular rising bank, covered with fine timber, and fall, after a short time, into the bed of the River Whitewater, which forms a boundary in the front.' Burton's *Hume*, i. 8.

LETTER VI.
Dr. Hurd's Artifices.

[EDINBURGH, 1757.]

Dᴿ Sɪʀ

I am positive not to reply a single Word to Dr. Hurd; and I also beg of you not to think of it. His Artifices or Forgeries, call them which you please, are such common things in all Controversy that a man woud be ridiculous who woud pretend to complain of them; and the Parsons in particular have got a Licence to practice them. I therefore beg of you again to let the Matter pass over in Silence [1]. I have deliverd to Mr. Becket a Volume of Essays [2].

I am yours D. H.

Note 1. *Remarks on Mr. David Hume's Essay on the Natural History of Religion,* by a Gentleman of Cambridge, in a Letter to the Rev. Dr. W., is advertised in the list of books for May 1757. *Gent. Mag.* 1757, p. 243. The book was written by Warburton and Hurd. On Feb. 7 of this year Warburton, writing to Hurd about Hume's *Essay,* says :—' I will trim the rogue's jacket, at least sit upon his skirts, as you will see when you come hither, and find his margins scribbled over. . . . They say this man has several moral qualities. It may be so. But there are vices of the mind as well as body ; and a wickeder heart, and more determined to do public mischief, I think I never knew.' *Letters from a late Eminent Prelate to one of his Friends,* p. 239. In a second letter he writes that he is ' beating out of the mass ' an answer to Hume, to which Hurd is ' to give the elegance of form and splendour of polish. . . . I propose it to bear something like this title, *Remarks on Mr. Hume's late Essay, called the Natural History of Religion, by a Gentleman of Cambridge, in a Letter to the Rev. Dr. W.* I propose the address should be with the dryness and reserve of a stranger. . . . The address will remove it from me ; the author, a *Gentleman of Cambridge,* from you ; and the secrecy in printing from us both.' *Ib.* p. 241.

The publication of Hume's *Autobiography* was at once followed by a republication of the *Remarks.* Speaking in it of his *Natural History of Religion,* Hume had said :—' Its public entry was rather obscure, except only that Dr. Hurd wrote a pamphlet against it, with all the illiberal petulance, arrogance and scurrility which distinguish the Warburtonian school. This pamphlet gave me some consolation for the otherwise indifferent reception of my performance.' To the new edition of the *Remarks* was prefixed ' the following Advertisement from the bookseller to the reader :

' " The following is supposed to be the pamphlet referred to by the late Mr. David Hume *as being written by* Dr. Hurd. Upon my applying to the Bishop of Litchfield and Coventry [Hurd] for his permission to republish it, he very readily gave me his consent. His Lordship only added, he was sorry he could not take himself the WHOLE infamy of the charge brought against him ; but that he should hereafter, if he thought it worth his while, explain himself more particularly on that subject.

" T. CADELL."'

Annual Register, 1777, ii. 9.

Strand, *March,* 1777.

Hume at once suspected that Warburton had had a hand in the pamphlet. On Sept. 3 he wrote to Millar :—' I am positively assured that Dr. Warburton wrote that letter to himself, which you sent me ; and indeed the style discovers him sufficiently. I should answer him ; but he attacks so small a corner of my building, that I can abandon it without drawing great consequences after it.' At the end of the letter Hume adds :—' I should not be displeased that you read to Dr. Warburton the paragraph in the first page with regard to himself. The hopes of getting an answer might probably engage him to give us something farther of the same kind; which at least saves you the expense of advertising. I see the Doctor likes a literary squabble.' Burton's *Hume*, ii. 35. On July 28, 1759, in a letter to Adam Smith, mentioning some more 'abuse' by Hurd, he says :— 'He is of the Warburtonian school; and consequently very insolent and very scurrilous; but I shall never reply a word to him.' *Ib.* p. 60. Johnson shews why even Warburton might be left unanswered by those whom he attacked. 'When I read Warburton first, and observed his force and his contempt of mankind, I thought he had driven the world before him; but I soon found that was not the case; for Warburton by extending his abuse rendered it ineffectual.' Boswell's *Johnson*, v. 93. Speaking of his controversy with Lowth he said :—'I do not know which of them calls names best.' *Ib.* ii. 37.

On the publication of Hume's *Autobiography*, Horace Walpole wrote to Mason :—'It is a nothing, a brief account of his disappointments on his irreligious works making no noise at first, and his historic making some. He boasts that in the latter he dared to revive the cause of despotism—a great honour truly to a philosopher; and he speaks of your friend, Bishop Hurd, with a freedom that I dare to say the whole Court will profess to his Lordship they think monstrous rudeness. My Lord H[ertford], whose piety could swallow Hume's infidelity, will be shocked now that he should have employed such a brute.' *Letters*, vi. 420. See *ante* in Hume's *Autobiography*, his 'fixed resolution never to reply to any body,' and *post*, Letter of June 25, 1771 for a fresh attack on 'Warburton and his gang.'

Note 2. Perhaps a corrected copy of his *Essays and Treatises on Several Subjects*, of which a new edition was published in the following year. 'Mr. Becket' is probably Thomas Becket, the bookseller, who had been, and perhaps still was, one of Millar's assistants. See Nichols's *Lit. Anec.* iii. 387. He had apparently some connection with the Scotch, for he published Macpherson's *Ossian*. He may at this time have been on a visit to Edinburgh.

LETTER VII.

Errata in the Essays.

Sᴵᴿ

I hereby send you the Index, Title-Page, and all the Preface, which I intend; being only a short Advertisement, to be inserted in any Corner: For I do not think it deserves a Page to itself[1]. The Errata are many of them small Alterations, which I coud not forbear making myself in the Style.

There are only two Errata which are material, those in page 455 and 459, where your Compositor has made me say the direct contrary to my meaning. I know, that such Mistakes are altogether unavoidable; but yet, if it were not too much Trouble, I coud wish, that they were corrected with the Pen, before publication [2].

I am so sensible of your great Care in this Edition, that I have desird Mr. Millar to give you one of the Copies, which he delivers to me on every Edition, and I beg of you to accept it as a small Testimony of my Regard.

I am Sir Your most obedient Servant

DAVID HUME.

EDINBURGH, 3 *Sept.*, 1757.

Note 1. The Advertisement or Preface is as follows:—' Some Alterations are made on the Titles of the Treatises, contained in the following Volume. What in former Editions was called *Essays moral and political*, is here entitled *Essays, moral, political, and literary*, Part I. The *political Discourses* form the *second Part.* What in former Editions was called, *Philosophical Essays concerning human Understanding*, is here entitled *An Enquiry concerning human Understanding*. The *four Dissertations* lately published are dispersed thro' different Parts of this Volume.'

Note 2. The mistakes occur in the following passages in Sections viii and ix of *An Enquiry concerning the Principles of Morals* :—

'The most profound metaphysics, indeed, might be employed in explaining the various kinds and species of wit; and many classes of it, which are now received on the sole testimony of taste and sentiment, might, perhaps, be resolved into more general principles. But this is sufficient for our present purpose, that it does *not* affect taste and sentiment, and bestowing an immediate enjoyment, is a sure source of approbation and affection.' The word *not* that I have italicised should be omitted.

''Tis sufficient for our present purpose, if it be allowed, what surely without the greatest absurdity cannot be disputed, that there is some benevolence, however small, infused into our bosom; some spark of friendship for human kind; some particle of the dove, kneaded into our frame, together with the elements of the wolf and serpent. Let these generous sentiments be supposed ever so weak; let them be *sufficient* to move even a hand or finger of our body; they must still direct the determinations of our mind, and where everything else is equal, produce a cool preference of what is useful and serviceable to mankind, above what is pernicious and dangerous.' *Sufficient* is a misprint for *insufficient.* In the copy in the British Museum the corrections with the pen have not been made.

LETTER VIII.
Millar suspected of Extortion.

EDINBURGH, 15 *Octr.*, 1757.

DEAR S[IR]

I have sent you a Letter of mine to Mr. Millar open, because I desire you to peruse it, and to give me your Opinion, as a Friend, of the Contents of it. Mr. Millar departs somewhat from an Offer he made me last Spring for a new Volume of History[1]. If the Reason be just which he assigns, the slow Sale of the former Volumes, I own I shoud be extremely discouragd to proceed. But tho' I have never had any Reason to complain of him, some People in my Situation woud be apt to suspect, that, after I had gone some Length in composing the Work, he intends to extort it from me at somewhat a lower Price; which is so ungenteel a Method of Proceeding that I cannot allow myself to believe it, and it woud much discourage me from dealing with him. Your general Character and the Instances, which I have receivd of your Friendship, assure me of your Candor, and make me have recourse to you on this Occasion. Can I believe, that he has any real Reason for coming down of the Offer which he formerly made me?

I have sent you along with this, an ostensible Letter, of the Nature of those you desird me to write. I hope Mr. Millar did not forget to deliver you the Copy of my last Volume, as I desird him. I need not put you in mind to put a Wafer in my Letter to Mr. Millar.

I am D[r] S[ir] Your most obedient Servant

DAVID HUME.

Note 1. Hume had written to Millar on Sept. 3:—'I am pretty certain that I shall be able to deliver to you the manuscript [of the *History of England under the Tudors*] about a twelvemonth hence ... You seemed desirous that we should mutually enter into articles about this volume; which I declined, till I should be so much advanced as to be sure of my resolution of executing it, and could judge with some certainty of the bulk.' He goes on to ask for £700. Burton's *Hume*, ii. 37.

LETTER IX.

Second Edition of the History of England under the Stuarts.

Dear Sir

I am oblig'd to you for the Letter with which you favord me. I fancy, you woud have found part of it answerd, before I receivd it. This day three Weeks, I sent up the second Volume of my History [1] by the Stage Coach to Mr. Millar, which is probably put into your hands by this time. The Alterations I make on this Volume are not very considerable; those I make on the first Volume are more so, particularly in the Reign of James, which requires to be changd in many Places, in order to adjust it to this previous Volume [2], which I am now composing, and which is nearly finishd. It is for this Reason, I coud wish Mr. Millar woud make a new Edition of both at once, and I have told him my Sentiments on that head. His Resolution will probably depend on the Number of Copies, which remain of the first Volume [3]; but as there were only 250 thrown off more than of the Second, I fancy there cannot be many on hand, after all the second are sold off. For there is always a considerable Defalcation in the Sale of second Volumes [4].

I am really concernd for what you tell me of Mr. Millar's being Ill, tho I hope his Ailment will only be slight. I know few who woud make a greater Loss to this Country, especially to the young Men of Letters in it [5].   I propose to see you about the Autumn, when I hope to commence a personal Acquaintance with you.

I am D[r] S[ir] Your most obedient humble Servant

DAVID HUME.

EDIN[R]., 12 *June*, 1758.

Note 1.   *The History of Great Britain under the Stuarts*, of which Hume was preparing a second edition.   The first volume, requiring as it did more alterations, was not sent up till six weeks later (*post*, p. 28).

Note 2.   By 'this previous volume' he means the second volume of *The History of England under the Tudors*.   The *History of the Reign of James I* having been published before the *History of the Reign of Elizabeth* was begun had now to be so altered that one volume might be 'adjusted' to the other.

Note 3.   Millar had bought from Hamilton and Balfour the unsold copies of the first volume.

Note 4.   Hume says that when the two volumes of a work are brought out at different times not so many copies are taken of the second as of the first.

Note 5.   For Johnson's praise of Millar, see *ante*, note on Hume's *Autobiography*.

LETTER X.

The new Method of Spelling.

[*June or July*, 1758.]

DEAR S[IR]

I am glad to find that Mr. Millar and I have agreed about reprinting the first Volume of my History [1].   I shall soon send you up a corrected Copy of it; and in the mean time you may proceed in printing the second Volume. The Title of it will be *History of Great Britain under the House of Stuart, in two Volumes* [2].   As the Title of the other Volume will be *History of England under the House of Tudor.*   By this Means they will be different Works; and some few Repetitions which will be unavoidable in this Method of composing them, will be the more excusable.

X.]
    THE NEW METHOD OF SPELLING.
    27

I had once an Intention of changing the Orthography in some particulars: But on Reflection I find, that this new Method of Spelling (which is certainly the best and most conformable to Analogy) has been followd in the Quarto Volume of my philosophical Writings lately publishd; and therefore I think it will be better for you to continue the Spelling as it is [3].

I woud not give you the Trouble of sending me the Sheets. I shall see you in London before the Publication; and shall then be able to correct any Errata that may have escapd you.

I am Dr Sr Your most humble Servant

DAVID HUME.

Note 1.   Millar, as was seen in the last letter, was hesitating about reprinting the first volume of the *History of the Stuarts*, of which more copies had been printed than of the second volume.

Note 2.   The original title of the first published portion of his work had been *The History of Great Britain, Volume I. Containing the reigns of James I and Charles I.*

Note 3.   Hume writing to Millar on June 20, 1758 about a volume of *Sketches and Essays* that Dr. Armstrong published anonymously, says:—'I find the ingenious author, whoever he be, ridicules the new method of spelling, as he calls it; but that method of spelling *honor*, instead of *honour*, was Lord Bolingbroke's, Dr. Middleton's, and Mr. Pope's; besides many other eminent writers.   However, to tell truth, I hate to be any way particular in a trifle; and therefore if Mr. Strahan has not printed off above ten or twelve sheets, I should not be displeased if you told him to follow the usual, that is, his own way of spelling throughout.'   Burton's *Hume*, ii. 43.   Bolingbroke and Pope certainly did not always follow the new spelling. In the Patriot King, ed. 1750, I find indeed *splendor*, but also *honour* and *favour*.   In the second edition of *The Dunciad*, Pope follows the old spelling, as also in the first edition of *Seventeen Hundred and Thirty Eight*.   He spells however *again, agen*.   In turning over a page or two of the first volume of the first edition of Hume's *History* I came on such spelling as *tho', thro'-out, knowlege, spred, ardor, splendor, favor, rigor, labored*.   Boswell in the Preface to his *Tour to Corsica*, published in 1767, writes:—'Of late it has become the fashion to render our language more neat and trim by leaving out *k* after *c*, and *u* in the last syllable of words which used to end in *our*.'

LETTER XI.

The History of England under the Tudors completed.

DEAR SⁱR

I sent off last Tuesday by the Stage Coach a corrected Copy of the first Volume of my History directed to you, and it will probably be with you as soon as this. There is only a small Correction more, which you will please to make. At Page 100. Line 16; Add this Note. *Rushworth Vol. 1. p. 82.*

On Tuesday come Sennight the 15 of this Month, the Manuscript Copy of my new Volume [1] will be put into the Stage Coach, in two white Iron Boxes, directed to you. As there are in the same Boxes a few Papers on private Business, you will please to leave the Boxes unopened till I come to London, which will probably be about the End of this Month or beginning of the next. I go up on Horseback [2], which is the Reason why I send the Manuscript before me.

I shall be sure to see you as soon as I arrive, and hope then to commence a personal Acquaintance with you, and to return you thanks for the many Instances, which I have receivd of your Attention and Friendship.

I am Dʳ Sⁱr Your most obedient humble Servant

DAVID HUME.

EDINBURGH, 5 *of August,* 1758.

———————

Note 1.   *The History of England under the House of Tudor.*   It was published in two volumes quarto early in the following year.   See *Gent. Mag.* 1759, p. 133.

Note 2.   Dr. A. Carlyle (*Auto.* p. 302) tells how John Home three years earlier started on the same journey on horse-back, with his 'tragedy in one pocket of his great coat and his clean shirt and night cap in the other.'   His friends, alarmed lest the tragedy should be lost, persuaded him to buy a pair of leather bags.   In the spring of 1758 Carlyle accompanied his eldest sister to London.   'It is to be noted,' he writes, 'that we could get no four-wheeled chaise till we came to Durham.   Turnpike roads were only in their commencement in the north.'   *Ib.* p. 331.   'The first toll,' says Hume, 'we read of in

England for mending the highways was imposed in the reign of Edward III. It was that for repairing the road between St. Giles's and Temple-bar.' Ed. 1802, ii. 496. 'The morning of the Perthshire election in 1761 I heard James, Duke of Athole, say that in 1713, when he was chosen member of Parliament, there was a great meeting, yet his father's coach was the only carriage there.' *Scotland and Scotsmen*, ii. 88.

LETTER XII.

Dr. Robertson's History of Scotland.

[*Jan. or Feb.* 1759.] [1]

DEAR SIR

On the Conclusion of this Work, I thank you for your Care, Exactness, Diligence and Dispatch; and have put my angry Letter into the Fire, where, partly by its own heat, partly by that of the burning Coals, it was immediately consumd to Ashes.

I had a Letter from Dr. Robertson, who is very earnest with me to have a Copy of my Volume as soon as possible, promising not to show it to a mortal, till publication. I have obtain'd Mr. Millar's Consent [2]; and therefore desire you to bind in boards a Volume of large Paper as soon as possible, and send it to the Stage Coach, directed to Mr. Robertson Minister of the Gospel at Edinburgh, near the head of the Cowgate [3]. The Stage Coach sets up near you [4]; so I must beg you to take this Trouble.

Mr. Andrew Reid [5] was so good as to look over some Sheets for me, but has so blotted them with Corrections that he has renderd it useless for me. I must therefore beg of you to bind in boards another compleat Copy of small Paper, and to send it to my House as soon as it is ready.

I am yours

DAVID HUME.

Friday.

Note 1. This letter, I have little doubt, was written on the conclusion of the *History of England under the House of Tudor*. That it was written, not in Edinburgh, but in London, is clear from the letter

itself. Hume had gone thither towards the end of 1758, to see this
portion of his work through the press. Robertson, who was on the
eve of publishing his *History of Scotland*, would be most eager to see
how his friend had dealt with that period in which the affairs of
England and Scotland became so much involved. Here there was
some danger of a rivalry between the two friends. ' I was exceedingly
sorry,' wrote Hume to Robertson on Jan. 25, 1759, ' not to be able to
comply with your desire, when you expressed your wish that I should
not write this period.' Stewart's *Robertson*, p. 341. In the same
letter he says :—' I am nearly printed out, and shall be sure to send
you a copy by the stage-coach, or some other conveyance.' The only
ground of hesitation I had in fixing the date is that Hume speaks of
' my volume,' whereas the *History of the Tudors* was in two volumes.
In the last letter, however, he speaks of it as ' my new volume.' He
cannot be speaking of his *History of the Stuarts* which was indeed
published a volume at a time, for he was in Edinburgh when both
volumes were brought out. Dr. Burton is in error when he states
(*Life of Hume*, ii. 65) that Hume on his return to Scotland about the
beginning of November, 1759, left behind him the *History of the Tudors*
for publication. It had already been shewn (*ib.* p. 52) that the book
was published in the previous spring.

Hume wrote to Robertson about the beginning of March :—' Next
week I am published, and then I expect a constant comparison will
be made between Dr. Robertson and Mr. Hume. I shall tell you in a
few weeks which of these Heroes is likely to prevail. Meanwhile I
can inform both of them for their comforts, that their combat is not
likely to make half as much noise as that between Broughton and the
one-eyed coachman.' Stewart's *Robertson*, p. 345. In the concluding
volumes of his *History* he pays Robertson the compliment of speaking
of him as ' an elegant historian.' Ed. 1802, ii. 486.

Note 2. Millar, no doubt, without obtaining Hume's consent, had
shewn a copy also to his old assailant Warburton ; who wrote to
Hurd on March 3 of this year :—' Hume has out-done himself in this
new *History* in showing his contempt of Religion. . . . If his history
be ,well received, I shall conclude that there is even an end of all
pretence to religion. But I should think it will not ; because I fancy
the good reception of Robertson's proceeded from the decency of it.'
Letters from a late Eminent Prelate, p. 282.

Note 3. Dr. A. Carlyle, writing of September, 1759, says that ' he
supped one night with the celebrated Dr. Franklin at Dr. Robertson's
house, then at the head of the Cowgate, where he had come at Whit-
sunday, after his being translated to Edinburgh. Dr. Franklin had
his son with him ; and there were David Hume, Adam Smith, and
two or three more.' ' Franklin,' he adds, ' was a silent man ;' but
' his son was open and communicative, and pleased the company
better than his father.' Carlyle's *Auto.* p. 394. Sir Walter Scott's
father had married the year before, and had taken a house at the

head of the College Wynd which led up from the Cowgate to the
College. Here Scott was born on Aug. 15, 1771. Lockhart's *Scott*,
ed. 1839, i. 19. Robertson was not made Principal of the College till
1762.

Note 4. Boswell writing in May, 1775, about his departure from
London for Scotland says :—' Dr. Johnson went with me to the inn in
Holborn, where the Newcastle fly sets out.' *Letters of Boswell*, p. 196.
New Street, in which Strahan lived, is close to Holborn.

Note 5. 'Andrew Reid, a man not without considerable abilities,
and not unacquainted with letters or with life, undertook to persuade
Lyttelton, as he had persuaded himself, that he was master of the
secret of punctuation ; and as fear begets credulity he was employed,
I know not at what price, to point the pages of *Henry the Second*.'
Lyttelton's fear was of hostile critics. He published his book 'with
such anxiety as only vanity can dictate.' Johnson's *Works*, viii. 492.

LETTER XIII.

The early History, and the Accession of George III.

[*November or December*, 1760.][1]

DEAR S[IR]

You gave me a sensible Satisfaction by writing
to me ; and tho I am a little lazy myself in writing (I mean,
Letters : For as to other kinds of writing, your Press can
witness for me, that I am not lazy) there is nothing gives
me greater Pleasure than hearing from my Friends, among
whom I shall be always fond of ranking Mr. Strahan. You
have probably heard from Mr. Millar, that I am wholly
engrossd in finishing my History[2] ; and have been so
above a twelvemonth. If I keep my Health, which is very
good and equal to any Fatigue, I shall be able to visit you
in eight or nine Months ; and then you may expect to
have a very troublesome Dun upon you, in making
Demands of a regular Visit of your Devil[3] ; and I shall be
able to cure you of some Indolence, which as our Friend
opposite Catherine Street in the Strand[4] complains to me,
is growing upon you. If this Indolence comes from Riches,
I hope also to cure it another way, by gaining your
Money at Whist ; tho' really the Person abovementiond

is a Proof that Indolence is no immediate or necessary
Effect of Riches: So that I fancy it is born with you; and
that there is no hopes of curing you. However, it will
give me some Satisfaction to come to you in case of any
Negligence, and first scold you and then gain your Money,
in order to punish you.

I am sorry, both on your Account and Mr. Rose's [5], for
whom I have a great Regard, that it shoud be absolutely
impossible for me, till my present Undertaking is finishd,
to have any hand in what he proposes to me. If I had
leizure, I shoud certainly comply with his Request: He only
disobliges me in mentioning any other Acknowlegement,
than his being sensible of my Inclination to oblige him.

Is this new Reign to be the Augustan Age [6]? or have
the Parsons got entire Possession of the young Prince [7]?
I hear that they brag much of their Acquisition; but
he seems by his Speech to be a great Admirer of his
Cousin of Prussia [8], who surely is no Favourer or Favourite
of theirs [9]. I wonder how Kings dare be so free: They
ought to leave that to their Betters; to Men who have
no Dependance on the Mob, or the Leaders of the Mob.
As to poor Kings they are obligd sometimes to retract and
to deny their Writings.

I was glad to observe what our King says, that Faction
is at an End and Party Distinctions abolish'd [10]. You
may infer from this, that I think I have kept clear
of Party in my History; that I think I have been much
injurd when any thing of that Nature has been imputed to
me, and that I now hope the public Ear will be more open
to Truth: But it will be a long time first; and I despair of
ever seeing it [11].

I beg my compliments to Mrs. Strahan, and all your
Family, and am Dear Sir with great Sincerity,

Your most obedient Servant

DAVID HUME.

Note 1. The reference below to the King's Speech shows that this letter was written shortly after Nov. 18, 1760.

Note 2. Hume was finishing the last part of his History, the first as it now stands—*The History of England from the Invasion of Julius Cæsar to the Accession of Henry VII.* On July 28, 1759, he had written to Adam Smith :—'I signed yesterday an agreement with Mr. Millar, where I mention that I proposed to write *The History of England* from the beginning till the accession of Henry VII ; and he engages to give me £1400 for the copy. This is the first previous agreement ever I made with a bookseller. I shall execute this work at leisure, without fatiguing myself by such ardent application as I have hitherto employed.' Burton's *Hume*, ii. 60. Francis Horner records :—'I have heard from very good authority that when Hume was engaged in the composition of his History, he generally worked thirteen hours a day.' Horner's *Memoirs*, i. 175. It was published at the end of 1761. 'The copy-money given me by the booksellers,' writes Hume in his *Autobiography*, 'much exceeded anything formerly known in England. I was become not only independent, but opulent.' Horace Walpole wrote of these volumes on Dec. 8, 1761 (*Letters*, iii. 465) :—'I not only know what has been written, but what would be written. Our story is so exhausted that, to make it new, they really *make* it *new*. Mr. Hume has exalted Edward the Second and depressed Edward the Third. The next historian, I suppose, will make James the First a hero and geld Charles the Second.'

Note 3. On June 29 of the following year, 1761, Hume wrote from Ninewells that he was 'so far on his road to London.' Burton's *Hume*, ii. 90. That he was in London as late as Sept. 2 is shown by a letter in his *Private Correspondence*, p. 4. He went up, no doubt, to carry his two new volumes through the press. The Devil was the printer's devil, or messenger who would bring the proofs. See Boswell's *Johnson*, iv. 99, for 'a very respectable author who married a printer's devil.'

Note 4. Our friend was Andrew Millar. His first shop, when he started business in a very small way, was close to St. Clement's Church. Nichols, *Lit. Anec.* vi. 443. He had afterwards moved to the shop that had been occupied by ' Jacob Tonson, the friend and bookseller of Dryden, at " Shakspeare's Head, over against Catherine Street in the Strand," now No. 141 (since rebuilt). Millar was a Scotchman, and distinguished his house by the sign of " Buchanan's Head."' Cunningham's *Hand-Book of London*, ed. 1850, p. 475.

Note 5. Perhaps Dr. William Rose, of Chiswick, 'the eminent schoolmaster and critic, and one of Andrew Millar's literary counsellors. He was largely concerned in the *Monthly Review.*' Nichols, *Lit. Anec.* iii. 386.

Note 6. George III began to reign on Oct. 25, 1760. 'The accession of George the Third to the throne of these Kingdoms,' wrote Boswell, 'opened a new and brighter prospect to men of literary

merit, who had been honoured with no mark of royal favour in
the preceding reign.' Boswell's *Johnson*, i. 372. For Hume it was
indeed the Augustan age. In 1765 he was appointed Secretary
to the Embassy at Paris, having for nearly two years performed the
duties of that office (*ante*, *Auto.*), and in 1767 he was made one of the
Under-Secretaries of State. In 1765 a pension of £400 a year was
settled on him. Burton's *Hume*, ii. 289. In 1751 his income was
only £50 a year, while he had 'a hundred pounds' worth of books,
great store of linens and fine clothes, and near £100 in his pocket.'
Ib. i. 342. ' In 1769 I returned to Edinburgh,' he writes, 'very opulent,
for I possessed a revenue of £1000 a year.' *Ante, Auto.* Johnson
received a pension of £300 a year, Beattie of £200, and Home of
£300 with an appointment. Adam Smith was made a Commissioner
of Customs, and Robert Burns a gauger. The hack-partisan, Sheb-
beare, who had written himself into the pillory under George II,
wrote himself into a pension under George III.' Boswell's *Johnson*,
ii. 112, *n.* 3. Gray, Goldsmith, Shenstone, Smollett, Sterne and Cowper
lived and died unpensioned.

Note 7. ' Nov. 4, 1760. The Archbishop [Secker] has such hopes
of the young King that he is never out of the circle. He trod upon
the Duke's [Duke of Cumberland] foot on Sunday in the haste of his
zeal ; the Duke said to him, "My Lord, if your Grace is in such
a hurry to make your court that is the way."' Walpole's *Letters*,
iii. 359. ' Nov. 24, 1760. The Archbishop, who is never out of the
drawing-room, has great hopes from the King's goodness that he shall
make something of him, that is something bad of him.' *Ib.* p. 365.

Note 8. ' My good brother and ally the King of Prussia [Frederick
the Great], although surrounded with numerous armies of enemies,
has with a magnanimity and perseverance almost beyond example
not only withstood their various attacks, but has obtained very considerable victories over them.' King's Speech on opening Parliament,
Nov. 18, 1760. *Parl. Hist.* xv. 983. Horace Walpole, writing six
days later about his forthcoming *Anecdotes of Painting*, says (*Letters*,
iii. 365) :—' It neither flatters the King of Prussia nor Prince Fer-
dinand . . . ; how should it please ?'

Note 9. Johnson, writing in 1756 of the general toleration of
religion granted by Frederick, says :—' It is the great taint of his
character that he has given reason to doubt whether this toleration is
the effect of charity or indifference, whether he means to support
good men of every religion, or considers all religions as equally
good.' Johnson's *Works*, vi. 443. Voltaire, describing the life at
Potsdam, says :—Il n'entrait jamais dans le palais ni femmes ni
prêtres. En un mot Frédéric vivait sans cour, sans conseil, et sans
culte.' *Œuvres de Voltaire*, ed. 1819-25, lxiv. 210. In *La Loi Natu-
relle* (written about 1751) Voltaire writes :—

    ' Nous le lui rendons bien : nous damnons à la fois
      Le peuple circoncis, vainqueur de tant de rois,

Londres, Berlin, Stockholm, et Genève; et vous-même,
Vous êtes, ô grand roi! compris dans l'anathème.
En vain par des bienfaits signalant vos beaux jours,
A l'humaine raison vous donnez des secours,
Aux beaux-arts des palais, aux pauvres des asiles,
Vous peuplez les déserts, vous les rendez fertiles;
De fort savans esprits jurent sur leur salut
Que vous êtes sur terre un fils de Belzébuth.'
Ib. x. 97.

Note 10. 'That happy extinction of divisions and that union and good harmony which continue to prevail amongst my subjects afford me the most agreeable prospects.' *Parl. Hist.* xv. 985. Horace Walpole, writing three weeks later, says :—'I have a maxim that "the extinction of party is the origin of faction."' *Letters,* iii. 370. In 1783 Boswell and Johnson were discussing how it was that 'this has been a very factious reign.' Boswell's *Johnson,* iv. 200.

Note 11. In 1756 Hume wrote to Dr. Clephane :—'With regard to politics and the character of princes and great men I think I am very moderate. My views of *things* are more conformable to Whig principles, my representations of *persons* to Tory prejudices. Nothing can so much prove that men commonly regard more persons than things as to find that I am commonly numbered among the Tories.' Burton's *Hume,* ii. 11. On May 15, 1761, he wrote to the Countess De Boufflers :—'The spirit of faction which prevails in this country, and which is a natural attendant on civil liberty, carries everything to extremes on the one side as well as on the other; and I have the satisfaction to find that my performance has alternately given displeasure to both parties.' *Priv. Corresp.* p. 2. See *ante* in his *Autobiography* for the alterations made by him in his *History of the Stuarts* 'invariably to the Tory side.' The student who reflects on the light that has of late years been thrown on the history of England under the Stuarts will smile at Hume's self-complacency when he writes :— 'I have been very busy in adding the Authorities to the Volumes of the Stuarts. . . . I fancy that I shall be able to put my account of that Period of English History beyond controversy.' Letter of Dec. 18, 1759. *M. S. R. S. E.* In his *Autobiography,* written shortly before his death, he says :—'I see many symptoms of my literary reputation's breaking out at last with additional lustre.'

LETTER XIV.

James Macpherson introduced to Mr. Strahan.

DEAR SIR,

I cannot give you a better Return for your obliging Letter than by introducing to your Acquaintance, the

Bearer, Mr. M^cpherson, who translated some Fragments of Highland Poetry, which have been extremely well receivd by the Public, and have probably come to your Hands. He has also translated a larger Work, a narrative Poem of great Antiquity, which lay in Obscurity, & woud probably have been bury'd in oblivion, if he had not retrievd it. He proposes to print it by Subscription, and his Friends here are already very busy in procuring him Encouragement. He goes up to London with the same Intention; and you may readily believe, that I advis'd him to think of nobody but our Friend, Mr. Millar, in disposing of the Copy. He will probably need your Advice in several Particulars, and as he is an entire Stranger in London, you will naturally of yourself be inclind to assist him. He is also very worthy of your Friendship; being a sensible, modest young Fellow, a very good Scholar, and of unexceptionable Morals. I have advis'd him to be at first on a Footing of Confidence with you; and hope you will receive him as one who merits your Friendship [1].

I am Dear S^{ir} Your most obedient Servant

DAVID HUME.

EDINBURGH [2], 9 *Feby.* 1761.

Note 1. James Macpherson, in the summer of 1760, published *Fragments of Ancient Poetry collected in the Highlands.* Gray, who had seen some of them in manuscript, wrote :—' I am gone mad about them; they are said to be translations (literal and in prose) from the Erse tongue, done by one Macpherson, a young clergyman in the Highlands. . . . I was so struck with their beauty that I writ into Scotland to make a thousand inquiries; the letters I have in return are ill-wrote, ill-reasoned, unsatisfactory, calculated (one would imagine) to deceive, and yet not cunning enough to do it cleverly. In short the whole external evidence would make one believe these fragments counterfeit; but the internal is so strong on the other side that I am resolved to believe them genuine spite of the Devil and the Kirk. . . . In short this man is the very demon of poetry, or he has lighted on a treasure hid for ages.' Mason's *Gray,* ed. 1807, ii. 163. He reproached Mason with 'the affectation of not admiring,' who says in a note :—' It was rather a want of credulity than admiration that Mr. Gray should have laid to my charge.' *Ib.*

p. 170. Hume, in a letter dated Aug. 16, 1760, which was shown to Gray, says :—'Certain it is that these poems are in every body's mouth in the Highlands, have been handed down from father to son, and are of an age beyond all memory and tradition ... Everybody in Edinburgh is so convinced of this truth, that we have endeavoured to put Mr. Macpherson on a way of procuring us more of these wild flowers. He is a modest, sensible, young man, not settled in any living.... We have therefore set about a subscription of a guinea or two guineas a-piece, in order to enable him to undertake a mission into the Highlands, where he hopes to recover more of these fragments.' Burton's *Hume*, i. 463. Dr. A. Carlyle (*Auto*, p. 276) told Hume that he had met but two people in Scotland who doubted their authenticity. Gibbon even so late as 1776 quotes *Ossian* in the first volume of the *Decline and Fall*, ch. vi, though he admits that 'something of a doubtful mist still hangs over these Highland traditions.' Horace Walpole at first was a believer. On April 14, 1761, he wrote :—'My doubts of the genuineness are all vanished.' *Letters*, iii. 395. Eight months later, when the first volume of *Ossian* was published, his doubts returned as convictions :—'*Fingal* is come out; I have not yet got through it; not but it is very fine—yet I cannot at once compass an epic poem now. It tires me to death to read how many ways a warrior is like the moon, or the sun, or a rock, or a lion, or the ocean. *Fingal* is a brave collection of similes, and will serve all the boys at Eton and Westminster for these twenty years. I will trust you with a secret, but you must not disclose it ; I should be ruined with my Scotch friends ; in short I cannot believe it genuine.' *Ib.* p. 466. In a long review of this volume in the *Annual Register* for 1761, ii. 276, we are told that 'the venerable author and his elegant translator have mutually conferred immortality on each other.' The reviewer perhaps was Burke. The following passage is not unworthy of his pen. 'The editor has recovered from the obscurity of barbarism, the rust of fifteen hundred years, and *the last breath of a dying language*, these inestimable relics of the genuine spirit of poetry.' Johnson from the first scorned them as forgeries and as froth. 'Sir,' he said, 'a man might write such stuff for ever, if he would *abandon* his mind to it.' Boswell's *Johnson*, i. 396, *n.* 3. To Macpherson, who had threatened him in 'a foolish and impudent letter,' he wrote :—'I hope I shall never be deterred from detecting what I think a cheat by the menaces of a ruffian.' *Ib.* ii. 298. Blair foolishly flattered himself at one time that he had convinced Johnson. He wrote to Hume on July 1, 1765 :—'Have not I silenced all infidelity and even scepticism concerning Fingal in the Appendix to my Dissertation ... I have converted even that barbarian Sam. Johnson by it, who as L[ord] Elibank tells me owns himself now convinced. Will you still have any scruples?' *M.S.R.S.E.*

Hume in time changed his opinion both of Macpherson and his poems. 'I have scarce ever known,' he wrote in 1763, 'a man more

perverse and unamiable.' Burton's *Hume,* i. 470. Dr. A. Carlyle
says that ' Hume at first gloried in Ossian's poems, but on going to
London he went over to the other side, and loudly affirmed them to
be inventions of Macpherson.' Dr. A. Carlyle's *Auto.* p. 276. From
London, Hume wrote to Dr. Blair on Sept. 19, 1763 :—' I often hear
them totally rejected with disdain and indignation, as a palpable and
most impudent forgery. This opinion has indeed become very
prevalent among the men of letters in London.' Burton's *Hume,*
i. 465. He wrote an *Essay on the Authenticity of Ossian's Poems,*
though he never published it, perhaps out of regard for his friend
Dr. Blair, who stood forth as Macpherson's champion, perhaps from
his unwillingness to expose a Scotchman. In it he says :—' I think
the fate of this production the most curious effect of prejudice, where
superstition had no share, that ever was in the world. A tiresome,
insipid performance, which, if it had been presented in its real form
as the work of a contemporary, an obscure Highlander, no man
could ever have had the patience to have once perused, has, by
passing for the poetry of a royal bard who flourished fifteen centuries
ago, been universally read, has been pretty generally admired, and
has been translated in prose and verse into several languages of
Europe. Even the style of the supposed English translation has
been admired, though harsh and absurd in the highest degree ;
jumping perpetually from verse to prose, and from prose to verse ;
and running, most of it, in the light cadence and measure of *Molly
Mog.* Such is the Erse epic which has been puffed with a zeal
and enthusiasm that has drawn a ridicule on my countrymen.' *Ib.*
i. 471.

Macpherson flourished by his roguery. He had a pension which
Horace Walpole in one place puts at £600 a year and in another
place at £800, for ' supervising the newspapers ' (*Journal of the Reign
of George III,* ii. 17, 483) ; he sat for a time in Parliament (Wheatley's
Wraxall's Memoirs, v. 218), and he was buried in Westminster
Abbey (Stanley's *Westminster Abbey,* ed. 1868, p. 298).

Note 2. A MS. letter of Hume of this time that I have seen is
dated ' Edinburgh, Jacksland, 1st Jany. 1761.' ' Jack's Land,' says
Dr. Burton, ' was a tenement in the Canongate, right opposite to
a house in which Smollett occasionally resided with his sister. The
term "Land" applied to one of those edifices—some of them ten
or twelve stories high—in which the citizens of Edinburgh, pressed
upwards as it were by the increase of the population within a narrow
circuit of walls, made stair-cases supply the place of streets, and
erected perpendicular thoroughfares. A single floor was a century
ago [written in 1846] sufficient to accommodate the family of a
Scottish nobleman.' *Life of Hume,* i. 343.

LETTER XV.

On ' accommodating' the different Parts of the History.

[*March*, 1762.]

Dᴿ Sɪʀ,

I return you thanks for the favourable Sentiments you express, in which I am sensible there is great Partiality; a Circumstance, however, which renders them the more obliging. I do not expect ever to live and see the Completion of your Prophecy[1].

I send you the second Volume of the Stuarts[2]. Mr. Millar tells me, that he intends to throw off a small Number of 250 to compleat the Sets; and at the same time a larger number of 750, on Medium paper, which he intends likewise for a new Edition of the Tudors and this antient History. Now I am going to propose to you an Improvement, if it be practicable. I always intended, that the whole six Volumes shoud be printed and shoud read as one continued Work, and that the Chapters shoud go on without Interruption from beginning to end. In that Case, the first Chapter of James I, is the forty fifth of the whole. Could you not therefore without any difficulty alter the Types for the last 750 Copies, so as to accommodate the Work to this Alteration. There needs only to change the beginning of the Chapter & the marginal Title, which may be done without Trouble. Unless this be done at present, I do not know when we shall be able to bring them to an Uniformity[3].

I am Dear Sɪʳ Yours sincerely

Dᴀᴠɪᴅ Hᴜᴍᴇ.

Note 1. What was the nature of the prophecy I have not been able to ascertain.

Note 2. Hume wrote to Millar on March 15, 1762:—' I am running over both the ancient history and the Tudors, and shall send you them up by the wagon as soon as they are corrected. Please tell Mr. Strahan to keep carefully this copy I send up, as well as that which I left of the Stuarts; for if you intend to print an octavo edition next summer, it will be better to do it from these copies which are corrected than from the new edition, where there will necessarily be some errors of the press.' Burton's *Hume*, ii. 130. The copy which he tells Millar he is sending up is no doubt 'the second volume of the Stuarts' mentioned in the letter to Strahan. It is not 'the ancient history' or 'the Tudors,' for both of these he is correcting, nor one of the volumes of 'the Stuarts,' which he had left in London corrected on his visit in 1761. It must therefore be the second volume, and the letter must have been written at the same time as the one to Millar.

Note 3. Hume wrote to Millar on March 18, 1764 :—'I shoud be glad to know how your new Method of publishing Volume by Volume has succeeded.' *M. S. R. S. E.* Whether he is speaking of the edition of his own History in eight volumes published in 1763, or of some other book, I do not know.

The first uniform edition of the *History* was that of 1763 in 8 vols. octavo ; in 1770 a quarto edition was published, also in 8 vols.

LETTER XVI.

Hume's Departure for France.

Mr. Hume's Compliments to Mr. Strahan: He sets out Morrow for France[1]; but wishes to put Mr. Strahan in Mind, of what he promisd, to correspond with him at Paris. His Direction is under Cover to Lord Hertford, Northumberland House in the Strand.

Wednesday.

Mr. Worral[2] had a Laws of Jamaca[3].

Oct. 14, 1763.

Note 1. Hume wrote from Edinburgh to Adam Smith on Aug. 9, 1763 :—' I have got an invitation, accompanied with great prospects and expectations, from Lord Hertford, if I would accompany him, though at first without any character, in his embassy to Paris. I hesitated much on the acceptance of this offer, though in appearance very inviting; and I thought it ridiculous at my years to be entering on a new scene, and to put myself in the lists as a candidate of fortune. But I reflected that I had in a manner abjured all literary occupations; that I resolved to give up my future life entirely to amusements; that there could not be a better pastime than such a journey, especially with a man of Lord Hertford's character; and that it would be easy to prevent my acceptance from having the least appearance of dependance.' Burton's *Hume*, ii. 157. Writing from London on Sept. 13, after mentioning all the advantages of the position, he continues:—' But notwithstanding all these consider- ations, shall I tell you the truth? I repine at my loss of ease and leisure and retirement and independence; and it is not without a sigh I look backwards, nor without reluctance that I cast my eye forwards.' *Ib.* p. 161. On Nov. 9 he wrote from Fontainebleau:— ' I am sensible that I set out too late and that I am misplaced; and I wish twice or thrice a-day for my easy chair and my retreat in James's Court. Never think, dear Ferguson, that as long as you are master of your own fireside and your own time you can be unhappy, or that any other circumstance can make an addition to your enjoyment.' *Ib.* p. 173. In an undated letter he says:—' Thus you see my present plan of life sketched out, but it is unsuitable to my age and temper; and I am determined to retrench and to abandon the fine folks before they abandon me.' *Ib.* p. 181.

Note 2. John Worrall kept a book shop in Bell Yard, Temple Bar; and his brother Thomas one at Temple Bar. Nichols, *Lit. Anec.* iii. 739.

Note 3. In the list of books in the *Gent. Mag.* for November 1739, p. 608, is entered *The Jamaica Laws from* 1681 *to* 1737. Printed by J. Basket. Folio, price £1 1s.

LETTER XVII.

French Works for Translation into English.

DEAR SIR,

I have long expected to hear from you and to learn your Sentiments of English Politics[1], according to the Promise you made me on parting: Perhaps, you have as long expected to hear from me; and thus while we stand upon Ceremony, our Correspondence is never likely to begin. But I have now broke the Ice, and it will be your Fault, if our Commerce of Letters does not continue.

I have been on the Watch this Winter for any publica- tion, which might answer in an English Translation, and have even fix'd a Correspondence with one of the Licencers of the Press to give me early Intelligence; but there has nothing appeard, which I thought woud answer, except

Voltaire's Treatise of Toleration, of which only a very few stolen copies came here, and it was impossible for me to procure one [2].

Are you acquainted with the Merit of Madame Riccoboni's Novels? She is the Author of Lady Juliette Catesby, and others which have been very well receivd both in France and England; and are indeed wrote with great Elegance and Decency [3]. She has just now in the Press a Novel [4], wrote upon English Manners, from which great Success is expected. Woud you think it worthy of being translated? I coud get from her some Sheets of it, which I woud send you by a Courier [5], and which woud secure you the Property: The rest I woud send by any Traveller, of whom Numbers set out every day [6].

As she is a Woman of Merit, but poor, any small Present, proportiond to the Success of the Work, I shall only mention in general, and shall leave the Amount of it to your own Discretion afterwards.

Please to direct to me, under Cover to the Earl of Hertford, and send your Letters to Northumberland House in the Strand.

I am Dear Sir

Your affectionate Friend and humble Servant

DAVID HUME.

PARIS, 20 *March*, 1764.

P.S.—Pray inform me, if you can, of the Reason of this continued low Price of Stocks [7]: They say, that Money is as scarce in private Transactions. But what is the Reason of that, after the Peace has been establishd for above a twelve month?

Since I wrote the above, I have procurd the two first printed Sheets, from Mad^e Riccoboni. They will secure you the Property, if you think proper to have them translated, which I think they very much deserve. The whole will make two small Volumes.

These are the proof Sheets corrected. The Translator must follow the Corrections on the Margins. What do you think of a French Edition also of the Original?

Note 1. Two days earlier Hume, writing to Millar, had asked him to send to him 'a copy of this new Book burnd by Order of the House of Commons.' *M.S.R.S.E.* Very likely he had heard of the book from the Earl of Hertford, to whom Horace Walpole had written on Feb. 24 :—'The events of the week have been a complaint made by Lord Lyttelton in your House of a book called *Droit le Roy*; a tract written in the highest strain of prerogative, and drawn from all the old obsolete law-books on that question. The ministers met this complaint with much affected indignation, and even, on the complaint being communicated to us, took it up themselves; and both Houses have ordered the book to be burned by the hangman.' *Letters,* iv. 198.

Note 2. Voltaire's *Traité sur la Tolérance à l'Occasion de la Mort de Jean Calas* was published at the end of 1763. Voltaire, in his letters written in December of that year, tells of the difficulties he had in getting it introduced from Switzerland into France. On Dec. 13 he wrote to D'Alembert :—'Vous ne savez pas combien il est difficile de faire parvenir de gros paquets par la poste. . . . L'éditeur a pris, pour envoyer à Paris ses ballots, une route si détournée et si longue, qu'ils n'arriveront pas à Paris cette année.' In a postscript he adds :—'Les pauvres Cramer [his publishers at Geneva] ont été obligés de faire faire à leurs paquets le tour de l'Europe, pour arriver à Paris.' *Œuvres de Voltaire,* ed. 1819-25, lxii. 252-4. On Dec. 31 he writes:—'Deux paquets adressés à M. Damilaville sont restés entre les griffes des vautours. Il faut que le vôtre n'ait point échappé à leur barbarie, puisque je n'ai aucune nouvelle de vous; tout cela m'embarrasse. Je vois qu'on ne tolère ni *la Tolérance* ni les tolérans.' *Ib.* p. 259. On Feb. 13, 1764, he writes:—'Le petit livret de *la Tolérance* a déjà fait au moins quelque bien. Il a tiré un pauvre diable des galères, et un autre de prison. Leur crime était d'avoir entendu en plein champ la parole de Dieu prêchée par un ministre huguenot. Ils ont bien promis de n'entendre de sermon de leur vie.' *Ib.* p. 270. Later on he described the treatise as 'le catéchisme de quiconque a du bon sens et de l'équité.' *Ib.* lxiv. 315.

In 1757, when there was war with France, Hume was forced to seek a round-about mode of communication. He directs Millar to send three copies of his *History* and three of his *Dissertations* to Mons. De La Rouvière at Rotterdam, who 'is to send them as presents to Paris.' *M.S.R.S.E.*

Note 3. Mme. Riccoboni was born in 1714 and died in 1792. She belonged to a family of good position which was ruined by sharing in Law's speculations. For a short time she was on the stage, where she met with but moderate success. Her husband who died in 1772 was an actor, and belonged to a family of actors. Among her novels were *Les lettres de Fanny Butler, Les lettres de Julie Catesby*, and *L'histoire de Miss Jenny.* Her last days were passed in great poverty. *Nouv. Biog. Gén.* xlii. 153. She was a correspondent of Garrick. Writing to him on May 15, 1765, she says :—'J'ai reçu hier par un libraire de Paris des compliments très-honnêtes d'une Madame Broock ou Brock, je ne m'en souviens plus. C'est la traductrice de Milady Catesby : elle écrit qu'elle en est à la quatrième édition. Cela est fort différent de Monsieur Becket, qui s'est ruiné avec Miss Jenny. Cette dame me fait demander *la permission* de m'envoyer ses ouvrages. J'avais dessein de lui faire tenir les miens ; mais Monsieur Hume ne la connaissait point, et s'avisa de donner cette malheureuse Jenny à Monsieur Becket, qui en a fait un garde-boutique, un fond de magasin pour ses arrière-neveux.' *Garrick Corresp.* ii. 436. In the list of books in the *Gent. Mag.* for April and May 1760, p. 251, I find ' *Letters from Lady Catesby to Lady Henrietta Campley.* From the French. Price three shillings. Dodsley.' According to the *Dict. of Nat. Biog.* vi. 420, this book soon reached a sixth edition. Mrs. Frances Brooke, the translator, was the author of *The Siege of Sinope.* She pressed Johnson to look over this play till at last he told her that she must correct it herself. ' " But, Sir," said she, " I have no time. I have already so many irons in the fire." " Why, then, Madam," said he, " the best thing I can advise you to do is to put your tragedy along with your irons." ' Hannah More's *Memoirs*, i. 200.

Note 4. *L'histoire de Miss Jenny Revel, écrite et envoyée par elle à Milady Comtesse de Roscommon.* In the translation, *The History of Miss Jenny Salisbury, addressed to the Countess of Roscommon.*

Note 5. No doubt one of the couriers or messengers going between the French Embassy and London. See *post*, p. 45.

Note 6. Horace Walpole, writing from Paris on Sept. 22, 1765, says (*Letters*, iv. 407) :—' There are swarms of English here, but most of them are going to my great satisfaction.'

Note 7. Hume wrote to Millar on April 8, 1762 :—' I was extremely obliged to you for advancing the money in order to enable me to take part in the last subscription. I shall certainly keep it till the Peace, which seems now to be in a tolerable good way ; and then I shall be a considerable gainer.' *M. S. R. S. E.* On Aug. 30 of the same year Robert Wood, the author of *The Ruins of Palmyra* and for some time an Under-Secretary of State, wrote to Hume :—' Shan't we see you next winter with a pair of quartos? You must make haste to put them into the funds, for scrip rises fast. Ramsay and little Hall talk of nothing else but their paper riches. We consider every shilling we put in as eighteen-pence the moment it goes to the Alley ' ['Change Alley]. *Letters of Eminent Persons to David Hume*, p. 263. On Nov. 22 following, Hume wrote from Edinburgh to Millar :—' The Stocks are now very high ; but I suppose will not come to their full height this twelvemonth, and till then I fancy you will not think it prudent in me to sell out.' Burton's *Hume*, ii. 140. On Sept. 3, 1764, he wrote to Millar from Paris :—' The lowness of stocks surely proceeds not from any apprehension of war ; never was a general peace established in Europe with more likelihood of its continuance ; but I fancy your stocks are become at last too weighty, to the conviction of all the world. What must happen if we go on at the same rate during another war ?' *Ib.* p. 232. Millar replied early in 1765 :—' It is generally believed that Mr. Grenville is a good manager of the finances and in general means well ; as a proof of it, our stocks have been creeping up daily, and it is now generally believed that 3 per cent. will soon come to par if affairs continue peaceable.' *Ib.* p. 265. In Feb. 1762, the 3 per cent. consols were as low as 62, *Gent. Mag.* 1762, p. 96 : by November they had risen to 86. *Ib.* p. 554. On March 20, 1764, the day on which Hume wrote, they were at 85. *Ib.* 1764, p. 148. In March 1737, during the long peace of Walpole's ministry, Sir John Barnard in a motion for the reduction of interest said :—' Every one knows that even those public securities which bear an interest of 3 per cent. only now sell at a premium in 'Change Alley.' *Parl. Hist.* x. 74.

LETTER XVIII.

Madame Riccoboni's Novel.

Mr. Hume's Compliments to Mr. Strahan. He sent him the two first Sheets of this Work, which he hopes Mr. Strahan receivd. In case he has not, Mr. Hume recommends it to Mr. Strahan to be translated into English. It is a work of Mad⁰ de Riccoboni, so well known by the Letters of Lady Juliette Catesby. Mr. Hume will send over the other Sheets as they come from the Press. He desires Mr. Strahan to write to him. His Direction is under Cover to Lord Hertford at Northumberland House in the Strand.

PARIS, 1 *of April*, 1764.

This Sheet may come to Mr. Strahan's hand before the two others : As this goes by a Messenger [1] ; the other by General Clerk [2].

Note 1. Messenger. See *ante*, p. 44, *n.* 5.
Note 2. Hume, writing on April 26 of this year, says :—' It is

almost out of the memory of man that any British has been here on a
footing of familiarity with the good company except my Lord Holderness. . . . I may add General Clarke, who was liked and esteemed by
several people of merit, which he owed to his great cleverness and
ingenuity, and to his surprising courage in introducing himself.'
Burton's *Hume*, ii. 194. Dr. A. Carlyle, who met Clarke at Harrogate
in 1764, gives a ,very different account of him (*Auto.* p. 451) :—'He
was a very singular man, of a very ingenious and active intellect,
though he had broke short in his education by entering at an early age
into the army; and having by nature a copious elocution, he threw
out his notions, which were often new, with a force and rapidity
which stunned you more than they convinced. He applied his warlike ideas to colloquial intercourse, and attacked your opinions as he
would do a redoubt or a castle, not by sap and mine, but by open
storm. I must confess that of all the men who had so much understanding he was the most disagreeable person to converse with
whom I ever knew. . . . You must contradict him and wrangle with
him, or you had no peace.'

LETTER XIX.

*The Printing-Presses in London: Medicine for the Dutch
Ambassador.*

DEAR S^{IR}

I receivd Yours, for which I am much obligd to
you: It gave me great Insight into the Affairs you
mention.

I am desird by some People here to enquire how many
Presses there may be in London. I suppose it must be an
Affair more of Conjecture than of exact Calculation [1].

I send you over three other Sheets. The Work seems
tó be very fine. The Author cannot exactly tell how many
Pages each Volume will contain; but two Volumes of such
large Print in 12°, must make but a small Book.

I am Yours sincerely

D. H.

PARIS, 18 *April*, 1764.

P.S.—Since I wrote the above, I have again seen Madame
Riccoboni, who tells me that she is now near a Certainty
with regard to the Size of her Work. It will be 4 Volumes

in twelves of about 240 pages each. The Dutch Ambassador has desird me to procure him the enclosd Medicine. The whole must not be bought nor sent at a time. Send only so many as may make a small Packet, which a Courier may carry. Pack them up carefully under Cover to Lord Hertford, and send them to Northumberland House in the Strand. Pardon this Trouble.

Note 1.   Strahan replied on July 10:—' It is not easy to say how many presses there are in London, but as near as I can guess they are from 150 to 200—150 is pretty near the truth, I mean such as [are] constantly employed.' *M. S. R. S. E.*   He adds :—' At present, and indeed ever since Wilkes's affair was finished, we have been in a state of most profound tranquillity.   The Names of *Pitt* and *Wilkes* and *Liberty* and *Privilege* are heard no more. . . .   Lord Bute still holds his usual Influence at Court and is very likely to do so long ; for the King (if I may use the expression) doats upon him.   Certain it is, he does nothing without his Advice and Approbation.'   Wilkes, on Feb. 21 of this year had been convicted of re-publishing No. 45 of the *North Briton,* and of printing and publishing an *Essay on Woman.*   As he did not appear to receive judgment he was outlawed and was at this time in Paris.

LETTER XX.

Madame Riccoboni's Novel.

DEAR SIR,

I see sometimes Mad° Riccoboni, who is extremely surpriz'd, that Mr. Becket answers none of her Letters, sends her none of the Copies which she bespoke, informs her nothing of the Success of her Book, and in short takes no manner of Notice of her[1]. I beseech you make him write, or write yourself for him, if he continues obstinately negligent. I owe Mr. Becket three Pounds, which I shall either pay him in London, or pay M° Riccoboni for him, in case the Success of her Book has been such, as to entitle her to any Recompence. You or Becket may write her in English. Her Direction is *Rue Poissoniere au dela*

le boulevard. I am somewhat in a hurry, which will
apologize for the Shortness of my Letter. I am always
much oblig'd to you, when you have Leizure to write
to me [2] ; being very sincerely Dear Sir

Your most obedient Servant

DAVID HUME.

PARIS, 28 *of Decr.* 1764.

Note 1. T. Becket was the publisher of the translation of Mme.
Riccoboni's new novel. On Aug. 31, 1765 she wrote to Garrick :—
'J'ai remis à Mr. Foley la petite somme dont j'étais redevable à Mr.
Becket. Remerciez-le bien pour moi, I charge you. Je ne lui écris
point, dans la crainte qu'il ne se fasse lire ma lettre par son traducteur,
qui y trouverait une foule de malédictions contre lui. Jenny est
pitoyable ; une traduction lâche, froide, pleine de contresens, de
répétitions, de plates épithètes, *snowy hands, the fountain of love,* fy,
eh, fy ! rien de plus long, de plus maussade, ce n'est ni mon style ni
mes idées.' *Garrick Corresp.* ii. 457. In 'fy, eh, fy' she is imitating
Garrick. Boswell describes him as saying on one occasion :—'You
are, perhaps, the worst—eh, eh !' Boswell's *Johnson,* ii. 83 ; and on
another occasion :—'What! eh! is Strahan a good judge of an epigram?' *Ib.* iii. 258.

Note 2. On Jan. 11, 1765 Strahan replied :—'Mme. Riccoboni's
book does not sell at all. Of course we must be losers. . . . We have
been all this summer in a state of profound tranquillity . . . Wilkes's
last letter hath made very little impression, and serves only to bolt
the door against himself, and seal his expulsion from his country.'
M. S. R. S. E. Wilkes's letter was addressed to the Electors of
Aylesbury, dated Oct. 22, 1764, and first printed in Paris. Almon's
Wilkes, iii. 85.

LETTER XXI.

Session of 1765 : *Rage against the Scots.*

PARIS, 26 *of Jany.* 1765.

DEAR S^{IR},

I receivd both your Letters, which gave me great
Satisfaction. Your Accounts of things are the fullest and
most candid I meet with ; and if your Leizure allowd you,
you coud not do me a greater Satisfaction, than to continue
them, when any thing remarkable occurs. I think there is

all the Probability that this will prove a quiet Session[1];
and there is a general Tranquillity establishd in Europe[2];
so that we have nothing to do but cultivate Letters: There
appears here a much greater Zeal of that kind than in
England[3]; but the best & most taking works of the French
are generally publishd in Geneva or Holland, and are in
London before they are in Paris[4]: So that I cannot have
an Opportunity of serving you in the way I coud wish. I
am sorry, that the last Publication[5] has not been success-
full. I only saw the Beginning and judged from the
Authors Character. The Beginning is much the best
of the Work. I have not lost view of continuing my
History[6]. But as to the Point of my rising in Reputation,
I doubt much of it[7]: The mad and wicked Rage against
the Scots, I am told, continues and encreases, and the
English are such a mobbish People as never to distinguish.
Happily their Opinion gives me no great Concern[8]. I see
in your Chronicle[9] an Abridgement of a Treatise on the
Constitution[10]; which Treatise seems to be nothing but an
Abridgement of my History; yet I shall engage, that the
Author has not nam'd me from the beginning to the end of
his Performance. On the whole, I can have no Motive of
Ambition or Love of Fame to continue my History:
Money in my present Circumstances is no Temptation: If
I execute that Work, as is probable, it must be for Amuse-
ment to myself, after I am tir'd of Idleness. My Health
and Spirits are as good at present as when I was five and
twenty. Believe me, Dear S[ir], with great Sincerity,
      Your affectionate Friend and humble Servant
                              DAVID HUME.
My Compliments to D[r]. Franklin[11].

Note 1. Sir Gilbert Elliot wrote to Hume on March 25, 1765:—
'Our business here draws to a close. To-morrow Mr. Grenville opens[1]

[1] In the *Parl. Hist.* xvii. 164, we read:—'April 10, 1771. Lord North opened
his budget.'

the budget, as it is usually called.' *M.S.R.S.E.* So quiet indeed
was the Session that it closed as early as May 25. The King in his
speech on that day said :—'The dispatch which you have given with
so much zeal and wisdom to the public business enables me now to
put a period to this Session of Parliament. . . . I have seen with the
most perfect approbation that you have employed this season of tranquillity in promoting those objects which I have recommended to your
attention ; and in framing such regulations as may best enforce the just
authority of the legislature, and at the same time secure and extend
the commerce, and unite the interests of every part of my dominions.'
Parl. Hist. xvi. 78. It was in this quiet Session that the American
Stamp Act was carried. Burke, in his *Speech on American Taxation*,
in 1774, answering the statement that the opposition shown to it in
Parliament had encouraged the Americans, said :—' As to the fact of
a strenuous opposition to the Stamp Act, I sat as a stranger in your
gallery when the Act was under consideration. Far from anything
inflammatory, I never heard a more languid debate in this House. No
more than two or three gentlemen, as I remember, spoke against the
Act, and that with great reserve and remarkable temper. There was
but one division in the whole progress of the Bill; and the minority
did not reach to more than 39 or 40. In the House of Lords I do not
recollect that there was any debate or division at all.' Payne's *Select
Works of Burke*, i. 140.

The House of Lords was not however careless of the tranquillity of
America. On March 6 of this year the keeper of the Sun Tavern, in
the Strand, was summoned to their bar, and examined about an
exhibition in his house of two Indian Warriors. He assured their
Lordships 'that they had their meals regularly and drank nothing
stronger than small beer.' The House resolved : ' That the bringing
from America any of the Indians who are under his Majesty's protection, without proper authority for so doing, may tend to give great dissatisfaction to the Indian nations, and be of dangerous consequence to
his Majesty's subjects residing in the Colonies.' *Parl. Hist.* xvi. p. 51.

Note 2. Horace Walpole wrote to Sir Horace Mann on March 26
of this year :—' I don't remember the day when I was reduced to complain in winter and Parliament-tide of having nothing to say. Yet it
is this kind of nothing that has occasioned my long silence. There
has not been an event, from a debate to a wedding, capable of making
a paragraph. Such calms often forerun storms.' *Letters*, iv. 337.
Though he was in Parliament at the time, yet he only once mentions
the debates on the Stamp Act. On Feb. 12, he wrote :—'There has
been nothing of note in Parliament but one slight day on the American
taxes.' *Ib.* p. 322.

. Note 3. Hume wrote to Blair on April 6 of this year :—'There is a
very remarkable difference between London and Paris, of which I
gave warning to Helvétius when he went over lately to England, and
of which he told me on his return he was fully sensible. If a man

have the misfortune in the former place to attach himself to letters, even if he succeeds, I know not with whom he is to live, nor how he is to pass his time in a suitable society. The little company there that is worth conversing with are cold and unsociable; or are warmed only by faction and cabal; so that a man who plays no part in public affairs becomes altogether insignificant; and if he is not rich he becomes even contemptible.   Hence that nation are relapsing fast into the deepest stupidity and ignorance. But in Paris a man that distinguishes himself in letters meets immediately with regard and attention.' Burton's *Hume,* ii. 268. When he was in London in 1767, while thanking Dr. Blair for offering to introduce him to Dr. Percy, he says:—'It would be impracticable for me to cultivate his friendship, as men of letters here have no place of rendezvous; and are indeed sunk and forgot in the general torrent of the world.' *Ib.* p. 385.

Grimm, writing on Jan. 1, 1766, on the eve of Hume's return to England, says :—'M. Hume doit aimer la France; il y a reçu l'accueil le plus distingué et le plus flatteur. Paris et la cour se sont disputé l'honneur de se surpasser. . . . Ce qu'il y a encore de plaisant, c'est que toutes les jolies femmes se le sont arraché, et que le gros philosophe écossais s'est plu dans leur société. C'est un excellent homme que David Hume; il est naturellement serein, il entend finement, il dit quelquefois avec sel, quoiqu'il parle peu; mais il est lourd, il n'a ni chaleur, ni grace, ni agrément dans l'esprit, ni rien qui soit propre à s'allier au ramage de ces charmantes petites machines qu'on appelle jolies femmes.' *Corresp. Lit.* v. 3.

Goldsmith wrote in 1759 in *The Present State of Polite Learning,* ch. vii :—'The fair sex in France have also not a little contributed to prevent the decline of taste and literature, by expecting such qualifications in their admirers. A man of fashion at Paris, however contemptible we may think him here, must be acquainted with the reigning modes of philosophy as well as of dress to be able to entertain his mistress agreeably. The sprightly pedants are not to be caught by dumb show, by the squeeze of a hand, or the ogling of a broad eye; but must be pursued at once through all the labyrinths of the Newtonian system, or the metaphysics of Locke.' Dr. Moore, in his *View of Society and Manners in France,* 1779 (i. 24), says :—'Many of the eminent men of letters are received at the houses of the first nobility on the most liberal footing. You can scarcely believe the influence which this body of men have in the gay and dissipated city of Paris. Their opinions not only determine the merit of works of taste and science, but they have considerable weight on the manners and sentiments of people of rank, of the public in general, and consequently are not without effect on the measures of government.' He points out the influence of the fashionable world on the men of letters, 'whose air, behaviour and conversation are equally purified from the awkward timidity contracted in retirement, and the disgusting arrogance inspired by university honours or church dignities. At Paris the pedants of Moliere are to be seen on the stage only.' *Ib.* p. 26.

Mrs. Barbauld says:—'I believe it is true that in England genius and learning obtain less personal notice than in most other parts of Europe.' She censures 'the contemptuous manner in which Lady Wortley Montagu mentioned Richardson :—'The doors of the Great,' she says, 'were never opened to him.' *Richardson Corresp.* i. clxxiv. Horace Walpole wrote from Paris on Sept. 22, 1765 :—' For literature, it is very amusing when one has nothing else to do. I think it rather pedantic in society; tiresome when displayed professedly; and besides in this country one is sure it is only the fashion of the day. Their taste in it is worst of all : could one believe that when they read our authors Richardson and Mr. Hume should be their favourites? The latter is treated here with perfect veneration. His *History*, so falsified in many points, so partial in many, so very unequal in its parts, is thought the standard of writing.' *Letters*, iv. 408. 'The veneration' with which he was received Hume describes to Robertson, on Dec. 1, 1763 :—'Do you ask me about my course of life? I can only say, that I eat nothing but ambrosia, drink nothing but nectar, breathe nothing but incense, and tread on nothing but flowers. Every man I meet, and still more every lady, would think they were wanting in the most indispensable duty, if they did not make to me a long and elaborate harangue in my praise. What happened last week, when I had the honour of being presented to the D[auphi]n's children at Versailles, is one of the most curious scenes I have yet passed through. The Duc de B[erri] the eldest [afterwards Lewis XVI] a boy of ten years old, stepped forth, and told me how many friends and admirers I had in this country, and that he reckoned himself in the number from the pleasure he had received from the reading of many passages in my works. When he had finished, his brother, the Count de P[rovence], [afterwards Lewis XVIII] who is two years younger, began his discourse, and informed me that I had been long and impatiently expected in France; and that he himself expected soon to have great satisfaction from the reading of my fine *History*. But what is more curious; when I was carried thence to the Count d'A[rtois] [afterwards Charles X], who is but four years of age [1], I heard him mumble something, which, though he had forgot it in the way, I conjectured from some scattered words to have been also a panegyric dictated to him.' Stewart's *Robertson*, p. 353.

The Marquis of Tavistock wrote to the Duke of Bedford from Paris on April 6, 1764 :—' I have lived so much with French people that it's a wonder I have not yet seen the *illustre Hume*, for there is nobody so *fêté* by the fine ladies as he is.' *Correspondence of John, Duke of Bedford*, iii. 261. The esteem in which Richardson was held at this time is shown by a letter of the Marquis de Mirabeau, the author of

[1] The three princes were nine, eight, and six years old.

L'ami des Hommes, to Hume, dated Aug. 3, 1763. He writes :—' Je vous avoue que le plus digne des hommes selon moi, Richardson seul m'aurait souvent fait regreter de ne savoir pas l'anglais.' *M.S.R.S.E.*

Lord Charlemont, after stating that ' no man from his manners was surely less formed for French society than Hume,' attributes his reception to the fact that 'free thinking and English frocks were the fashion, and the *Anglomanie* was the *ton du pays*.' He tells the following anecdote of the first Lord Holland who about this time visited Paris. 'The French concluded that an Englishman of his reputation must be a philosopher, and must be admired. It was customary with him to doze after dinner, and one day at a great entertainment he happened to fall asleep. "Le voilà !" says a Marquis, pulling his neighbour by the sleeve, "Le voilà qui pense!"' He adds that, though Hume's conversation could give little pleasure to French men, still less to French women, 'yet no lady's toilette was complete without Hume's attendance. At the Opera his broad unmeaning face was usually seen *entre deux jolis minois*.' *Memoirs of the Earl of Charlemont*, i. 234.

In one respect Hume had owned that authors were far better off here than on the other side of the Channel. After describing to Elliot in 1762 his comfortable flat in James's Court, for which he had paid £500, he continues :—'On comparing my situation with poor Rousseau's, I cannot but reflect how much better book-sellers we have in this country than they in France.' Stewart's *Robertson*, p. 360. Voltaire, in his review of *Julia Mandeville*, says :— ' Pour peu qu'un roman, une tragédie, une comédie ait de succès à Londres, on en fait trois et quatre éditions en peu de mois ; c'est que l'état mitoyen est plus riche et plus instruit en Angleterre qu'en France, &c.' *Œuvres de Voltaire*, xliii. 364.

. Little more than a year before Hume wrote that 'the little company in London that is worth conversing with are cold and unsociable,' Reynolds and Johnson had founded their famous club. Boswell's *Johnson*, i. 477. Nearly ninety years after he had complained of the want of zeal in England for the cultivation of letters, Darwin was lamenting the indifference to science. Writing in 1854 about an unsolicited grant by the Colonial Government of Tasmania towards the expenses of Sir. J. Hooker's *Flora of Tasmania*, he says :—' It is really a very singular and delightful fact, contrasted with the slight appreciation of science in the old country.' *Life of Darwin*, i. 394.

Note 4. See *ante*, p. 43, *n.* 2, for an explanation of this.

Note 5. Mme. Riccoboni's novel.

Note 6. Hume's *History* closes with the Revolution. The following extracts from his letters show that a continuation of it was for some years in his thoughts.

' Edinburgh, March 10, 1763. I am in a good measure idle at present ; but if I tire of this way of Life, as is probable, I shall certainly continue my *History*, and have no Thoughts of any other

work. But in this State of Affairs, I suppose your People of Rank and
Quality woud throw the Door in my Face because I am a Scotsman.'
M. S. R. S. E.

'Edinburgh, 12 March, 1763. I am engaged in no work at present;
but if I tire of idleness, or more properly speaking, of reading for my
amusement, I may probably continue my *History*. My only discouragement is that I cannot hope to finish this work in my closet, but
must apply to the great for papers and intelligence, a thing I mortally
abhor.' Burton's *Hume*, ii. 146.

'Edinburgh, 28 March, 1763. I may perhaps very soon gather silently
together the books which will enable me to sketch out the reigns of
King William and Queen Anne, and shall finish them afterwards, together with that of George I, in London. But to tell you the truth, I
have an aversion to appear in that capital till I see that more justice
is done to me with regard to the preceding volumes. The languishing
sale of this edition makes me conjecture that the time is not yet come;
and the general rage against the Scots is an additional discouragement.'
Ib. ii. 147. (Seven weeks after this letter was written Boswell, on
being introduced to Johnson, said :—'I do indeed come from Scotland,
but I cannot help it.' Boswell's *Johnson*, i. 392.)

'Paris, 14 Jany. 1765. I am now in a situation to have access to all
the families which have papers relative to public affairs transacted in
the end of the last and beginning of this century. . . . The rage and
prejudice of parties frighten me; and above all, this rage against the
Scots, which is so dishonourable, and indeed so infamous to the English
nation. We hear that it increases every day without the least appearance of provocation on our part. It has frequently made me
resolve never in my life to set foot on English ground. I dread if I
should undertake a more modern history the impertinence and ill
manners, to which it would expose me.' Burton's *Hume*, ii. 264.

'[1766.] Some push me to continue my History. Millar offers me
any price. All the Marlborough papers are offered me; and I believe
nobody would venture to refuse me. But *cui bono?* Why should I
forego idleness and sauntering and society, and expose myself again
to the clamours of a stupid factious public?' *Ib.* ii. 392. (The
Marlborough papers had been in Mallet's possession. For more than
twenty years 'he had a pension from the late Duke of Marlborough
to promote his industry,' in publishing them. On his death in
1765 it was found that he had not even touched them. Boswell's
Johnson, v. 175.)

'Oct. 6, 1767. When Mr. Conway was on the point of resigning,
I desird him to propose to the King that I might afterwards have the
liberty of inspecting all the public Offices for such Papers as might
serve to my purpose. His Majesty said that he was glad I had that
object in my Eye; and I should certainly have all the Assistance in his
Power.' David Hume to John Home of Ninewells. *M. S. R. S. E.*

'8 Oct. 1766. I shall probably do as you advise, and sketch out the outlines of the two or three subsequent reigns, which I may finish at London.' Burton's *Hume*, ii. 393.

'London, 27 Nov. 1767. The king himself has been pleased to order that all the records and public offices shall be open to me, and has even sent for some papers from Hanover, which he thought would be useful.' *Private Corresp.* p. 250.

'London, 26 April, 1768. Lord Hertford told me that he and his brother [General Conway] had made a point with the King and the ministers, that in consideration of my services I should have some further provision made for me, which was immediately assented to, only loaded with this condition by the King, that I should seriously apply myself to the consummation of my *History.*' *Ib.* p. 257.

'London, 24 May, 1768. The King has given me a considerable augmentation of my pension, expressing at the same time his expectation that I am to continue my *History*. This motive, with my habits of application, will probably engage me in this undertaking, and occupy me for some years.' *Ib.* p. 261.

Strahan wrote to Sir A. Mitchell on April 1, 1768:—'Mr. D. Hume dined with me to-day. He is now applying in good earnest to the continuation of his History, having collected very considerable materials.' *M. S. R. S. E.* On May 14, 1768, Boswell, whom Hume had lately visited, wrote:—'David is going to give us two more volumes of *History*, down to George II. I wish he may not mire himself in the Brunswick sands. Pactolus is there.' *Letters of Boswell*, p. 151. On Dec. 9, writing from Edinburgh, Boswell says:—'Mr. Hume is not to go to Paris; he is busy with the continuance of his *History.*' *Ib.* p. 159. Hume relapses once more into indolence. He writes to Strahan on May 22, 1770:—'I am fully determined never to continue my History, and have indeed put it entirely out of my power by retiring to this country for the rest of my life.' Two years later his determination is not quite so strong. 'If I find my time lie heavy on my hands, I may, for my amusement, undertake a reign or two after the Revolution. But I believe, in case of my composing any more, I had better write something that has no Reference to the affairs of these factious Barbarians.' *Post*, Letter of March 5, 1772. His amusement apparently does not require any fresh composition, for at the beginning of the next year he writes:—'Considering the treatment I have met with, it would have been very silly for me at my years to continue writing any more, and still more blamable to warp my principles and sentiments in conformity to the prejudices of a stupid, factious nation, with whom I am heartily disgusted.' *Post*, Letter of Jan. 30, 1773.

Note 7. Dr. J. H. Burton, writing of the years 1765-6, says:— 'Allusion has occasionally been made to the difficulty of satisfying Hume with any amount of literary success. His correspondence with Millar is a long grumble about the prejudices he has had to encounter, and their influence on the circulation of his works; while the bookseller, by the most glowing pictures of their popularity, is only able to elicit a partial gleam of content.' Burton's *Hume*, ii. 263. It is shown hereafter (Letter of March 13, 1770) that Millar's pictures were more glowing than correct. Nevertheless, Hume's success as a writer was so great that 'Millar offered him any price' for the continuation of his *History*. At the close of his life he wrote in his *Autobiography*:—'I see many symptoms of my literary reputation's breaking out at last with additional lustre.'

Note 8. The violence of Hume's feelings towards the English is not seen in his earlier correspondence. He had even at one time thought of settling in London. On Jan. 25, 1759, he wrote:— 'I used every expedient to evade this journey to London; yet it is now uncertain whether I shall ever leave it.' Burton's *Hume*, ii. 50. On July 28 in the same year he wrote:—'I am in doubt whether I shall stay here and execute the work; or return to Scotland, and only come up here to consult the manuscripts. I have several inducements on both sides. Scotland suits my fortune best, and is the seat of my principal friendships; but it is too narrow a place for me.' *Ib.* p. 61. (Boswell in like manner 'complained to Johnson that he felt himself discontented in Scotland, as too narrow a sphere.' Boswell's *Johnson*, iii. 176.)

A great change was wrought in Hume by the storm of abuse which burst on his countrymen when the new King put himself and the nation in the leading-strings of the Earl of Bute. Though he had written the *History of England*, he never seemed to understand for one moment the anger that was stirred up in a proud people, when their Great Commoner had to yield to the favourite of a Palace, with his vile system of 'King's friends' and secret 'influence.' Some indulgence must be extended to him as a man, though not perhaps as a philosopher, on account of the disappointment which he himself had suffered through his origin. As will be seen (*post*, p. 58) he was refused the high office of Secretary to the Lord Lieutenant of Ireland merely because he was born north of the Tweed. His return from France, which followed close on this humiliation, still further embittered his feelings. In that country his genius had been recognised to the full. 'Few people,' wrote Dr. Blair to him, 'have been more fortunate than you; you have enjoyed in France the full blaze of your reputation and fame; you have tasted all the pleasures of a court and of public life; and after receiving every tribute due to letters and to merit, you retire before it was too late to your own philosophic ease and tranquillity.' Blair to Hume, Oct. 8, 1765. *M. S. R. S. E.* Philosophic ease was not by any means enough. His ruling passion, as he himself owned in his *Autobiography*, was 'love of literary fame.' To him might be applied, though not in all its extent, what Johnson said of Richardson:—'He could not be contented to sail quietly down the stream of reputation, without longing to taste the froth from every stroke of the oar.' (Piozzi's

Anecdotes, p. 184.) He returned to our shores one of the most famous men in Europe, and he at once passed from 'the full blaze' to that dim and uncertain glimmer which was all that genius could throw round itself here. Had he been content with the company of men of letters, his love of fame might perhaps have been satisfied; but he was used to the homage of men and women of rank and fashion in the most famous drawing-rooms of Paris. Princes no longer made him addresses, nor did fine ladies 'believe him implicitly,' (Walpole's *Letters*, iv. 426). His vanity, I believe, was wounded just as was Rousseau's, when that philosopher found how quickly a great writer sinks into insignificance in London. Both men were wanting in that humour which 'holds the world but as the world,' and in the midst of disappointments and neglect smiles at them and at itself.

In the extracts from his letters given in Note 3 the bitterness of his feelings has been seen. The following passages show that it did not lessen with growing years :—

'Paris, 1 Dec. 1763. It is probable that this place will long. be my home. I feel little inclination to the factious barbarians of London.' Burton's *Hume*, ii. 178.

'Paris, 27 March, 1764. I have been accustomed to meet with nothing but insults and indignities from my native country[1].' *Ib.* p. 191.

'Paris, 26 April, 1764. The taste for literature is neither decayed nor depraved here, as with the barbarians who inhabit the banks of the Thames.' *Ib.* p. 196.

'Paris, 22 Sept. 1764. From what human motive or consideration can I prefer living in England than in foreign countries? I believe, taking the continent of Europe from Petersburgh to Lisbon and from Bergen to Naples, there is not one who ever heard of my name, who has not heard of it with advantage, both in point of morals and genius. I do not believe there is one Englishman in fifty who, if he heard I had broke my neck to-night, would be sorry. Some, because I am not a Whig; some because I am not a Christian; and all because I am a Scotsman. Can you seriously talk of my continuing an Englishman[2]? Am I, or are you, an Englishman? Do they not treat with derision our pretensions to that name, and with hatred our just pretensions to surpass and govern them?' *Ib.* p. 238.

'Paris, 14 Jany. 1765. The rage and prejudice of parties frighten me; and above all this rage against the Scots, which is so dishonourable, and indeed so infamous to the English nation. We hear that it increases every day without the least appearance of provocation on

---

[1] By native country he means Great Britain, as distinguished from France.

[2] His correspondent, Sir Gilbert Elliot of Minto, had written to him:—'Love the French as much as you will; but above all continue still an Englishman.' *Ib.* p. 235.

our part. It has frequently made me resolve never in my life to set foot on English ground.' *Ib.* p. 265.

'Paris, Aug. 23, 1765. I have a reluctance to think of living among the factious barbarians of London ; who will hate me because I am a Scotsman, and am not a Whig, and despise me because I am a man of letters. . . . Lord Hertford, on his arrival in London, found great difficulty of executing his intentions in my favour [1]. The cry is loud against the Scots ; and the present ministry [2] are unwilling to support any of our countrymen, lest they bear the reproach of being connected with Lord Bute.' *Ib.* p. 290.

'Paris, Nov. 5, 1765. London is the capital of my own country ; but it never pleased me much. Letters are there held in no honour ; Scotsmen are hated ; superstition and ignorance gain ground daily.' *Ib.* p. 292.

It was my duty, as editor of Boswell's *Life of Johnson*, to gather in a Concordance Johnson's sayings against the Scotch. I shall feel more confidence among my friends of that race, when I show them that Hume in his abuse of the English as much surpassed Johnson in violence as he was inferior to him in wit. On one occasion, and on one alone, do I find him writing as an Englishman. In a letter to the Abbé Morellet, dated London, July 10, 1769, he says:—'The Abbé Galliani goes to Naples ; he does well to leave Paris before I come thither ; for I should certainly put him to death for all the ill he has spoken of England. But it has happened, as was foretold by his friend Caraccioli, who said that the Abbé would remain two months in this country, would speak all himself, would not allow an Englishman to utter a syllable, and after returning would give the character of the nation during the rest of his life as if he were perfectly well acquainted with them.' Burton's *Hume*, ii. 428.

He urges indeed his brother to give his eldest son an English education, so that he may not, by staying in Scotland, 'acquire such an accent as he will never be able to cure of.' *Ib.* p. 403. In his *History* moreover he recognises the advantage of a union of the two nations. So early as the reign of Edward I. he speaks of it as 'a project so favourable to the happiness and grandeur of both Kingdoms.' He describes that King's attempt to seize the Scottish crown, as a 'great object, very advantageous to England, perhaps in the end no less beneficial to Scotland, but extremely unjust and iniquitous in itself.' Ed. 1802, ii. 246, 250.

I do not find that Hume's friends among his countrymen shared in the violence of his dislike. On the contrary some of them remonstrated with him. Sir Gilbert Elliot wrote to him in the autumn of 1764 :—' Notwithstanding all you say, we are both Englishmen ; that

---

[1] He had intended to take Hume to Ireland as his Secretary, in his post of Lord Lieutenant.

[2] The Rockingham Ministry.

is, true British subjects, entitled to every emolument and advantage that our happy constitution can bestow. Do not you speak and write and publish what you please? and though attacking favourite and popular opinions, are you not in the confidential friendship of Lord Hertford, and intrusted with the most important national concerns? Am not I a member of Parliament. . . . ? Had it not been for the clamour of *a Scott*, perhaps indeed I might have been in some more active, but not more honourable or lucrative situation. This clamour we all know is merely artificial and occasional. It will in time give way to some other equally absurd and ill-founded, when you, if you will, may become a bishop and I a minister.' Burton's *Hume*, ii. 240. In the same month Millar sent him the following extract from a letter which he had received from Adam Smith, who was at Paris:—'Though I am very happy here, I long passionately to rejoin my old friends, and if I had once got fairly to your side of the water, I think I should never cross it again. Recommend the same sober way of thinking to Hume. He is light-headed, tell him, when he talks of coming to spend the remainder of his days here or in France. Remember me to him most affectionately.' *M. S. R. S. E.*

On Feb. 25 of the following year (1765) Millar wrote :—'You are totally mistaken about any prejudice against the Scots in general here. I find no difference of respect to particulars. The cry was raised and is continued only with a view to distress Lord Bute whom they heartily hate, and it would have been happy for his Country he had never been born ; his particular friendship being placed on weak or designing men is a misfortune and the certain [?] affectation and manner is disgusting.' *Ib.* John Crawfurd wrote to Hume on Jan. 20, 1767 :—'What you say of your being detested as a Scotsman, and despised as a man of letters is melancholy nonsense.' *Ib.* Boswell, 'a very universal man ' as he was, we find associating with Churchill only two or three months after that scurrilous but most vigorous writer had bitterly assailed Scotland in his *Prophecy of Famine.* It was by 'the witty sallies' of him and of a libeller equally gross, John Wilkes, that the young Scotchman 'was enlivened' on the morning on which he first called on Johnson. Boswell's *Johnson*, i. 395. On the other hand, Boswell's friend, George Dempster, a Member of Parliament well known in his day, writing to him in 1775 about Johnson's *Journey to the Western Islands*, shows how strong the English antipathy was. He says :—'I hope the book will induce many of Dr. Johnson's countrymen to make the same jaunt, and help to intermix the more liberal part of them still more with us, and perhaps abate somewhat of that virulent antipathy which many of them entertain against the Scotch ; who certainly would never have formed those *combinations* which he takes notice of, more than their ancestors, had they not been necessary for their mutual safety, at least for their success, in a country where they are treated as foreigners.' *Ib.* v. 408. Nevertheless the great popularity of the Scotch authors, Blair, Beattie, Robert-

son, and Hume himself; the 'extraordinary applause' that was given
to Beattie in the Theatre at Oxford, when on July 9, 1773 he received
his degree of Doctor of Laws, show that, however strong may have
been the general feeling against the race, it did not necessarily extend
in all its force to individuals.

That the provocation was very great that Hume as a Scotchman
received cannot be denied. That much of the attack was provoked,
as I have said, by the favour shown to his countrymen by the King's
Scotch favourite, is equally true. Johnson, who was disposed to
think well of the Earl of Bute, from whom as Prime Minister he had
received his pension, said of him :—' Lord Bute showed an undue
partiality to Scotchmen. He turned out Dr. Nichols, a very eminent
man, from being physician to the King, to make room for one of his
countrymen, a man very low in his profession. He had Wedderburne and Home to go on errands for him. He had occasion for people
to go on errands for him ; but he should not have had Scotchmen ; and
certainly he should not have suffered them to have access to him
before the first people in England.' Boswell's *Johnson*, ii. 354. There
was however another and a less worthy ground for the general ill-will
of the English towards the North Britons. There was a jealousy of
the success which the Scotch were fairly winning in almost every
path of life. The knowledge which they had gained in their schools
and universities, 'countenanced in general,' to use Johnson's words,
'by a national combination so invidious that their friends cannot
defend it, and actuated in particulars by a spirit of enterprise so vigorous
that their enemies are constrained to praise it, enabled them to find,
or to make their way to employment, riches, and distinction.' Johnson's
Works, ix. 158.

The following anecdote, recorded by Jefferson in his *Diary*, illustrates this Scotch occupation of England :—' The confederation of the
States, while on the carpet before the old Congress, was strenuously
opposed by the smaller States, which feared being swallowed up by
the larger ones. We were long engaged in the discussion ; it produced great heats, much ill-humour, & intemperate declarations from
some members. Dr. Franklin at length brought the debate to a close
with one of his little apologues. He observed that "at the time of the
Union of England and Scotland the Duke of Argyle was most violently
opposed to that measure, and among other things predicted that, as the
whale had swallowed Jonah, so Scotland would be swallowed by
England. However (said the Doctor) when Lord Bute came into the
Government, he soon brought into its administration so many of his
countrymen, that it was found in the event that Jonah swallowed the
whale." This little story produced a general laugh, and restored good
humour, and the article of difficulty was passed.' *Life of Franklin*, ed.
by J. Bigelow, 1879, iii. 299.

Having shown Hume's rage against the English, I will now give a
few instances of 'the mad and wicked rage against the Scots.' Wilkes,

in the *North Briton*, No. xiii. (Aug. 28, 1762), in a passage which he
says comes from Howell, writes :—

'As for fruit for their grandsire Adam's sake they [the Scotch]
never planted any; and for other trees, had Christ been betrayed
in this country (as doubtless he should, had he come as a stranger)
Judas had sooner found the grace of repentance than a tree to hang
himself on.' This attack he follows up with such abuse as the following :—'Jany. 22, 1763. A Scot hath no more right to preferment in
England than a Hanoverian or a Hottentot.' *Ib.* No. 34.

'April 2, 1763. The restless and turbulent disposition of the Scottish
nation before the Union, with their constant attachment to France and
declared enmity to England, their repeated perfidies and rebellions
since that period, with their servile behaviour in times of need
and overbearing insolence in power, have justly rendered the very
name *Scot* hateful to every true Englishman.' Wilkes goes on to
attack Lord Bute for 'his gross partiality to his own *beggarly* countrymen[1].' *Ib.* No. 44.

Churchill's *Prophecy of Famine*, published in 1763, is full of scurrilous
passages such as :—

> 'Oft have I heard thee mourn the wretched lot
> Of the poor, mean, despis'd, insulted Scot.'
>
> > *Works*, ed. 1766, i. 105.

> 'Jockey, whose manly high-bon'd cheeks to crown
> With freckles spotted flam'd the golden down,
> With mikle art could on the bagpipes play,
> E'en from the rising to the setting day;
> Sawney as long without remorse could bawl
> Home's madrigals and ditties from Fingal.
> Oft at his strains, all natural tho' rude,
> The Highland Lass forgot her want of food,
> And whilst she scratch'd her lover into rest
> Sunk pleas'd, though hungry, on her Sawney's breast.'
>
> > *Ib.* i. 111.

In his last poem, written in 1764, on his departure from England, he
says, speaking of the Muses :—

> 'If fashionable grown, and fond of pow'r
> With hum'rous Scots let them disport their hour;
> Let them dance fairy-like, round Ossian's tomb;
> Let them forge lies and histories for Hume;
> Let them with Home, the very Prince of verse,
> Make something like a tragedy in Erse.'
>
> > *Ib.* ii. 328.

F. Greville, writing to Hume from Brussels on Sept. 24, 1764, about
'that wretch Churchill,' says :—'My own heart glowed at the honest

---

[1] Johnson in 1754 had said that Bolingbroke 'left half a crown to a beggarly
Scotchman to draw the trigger after his death.' Boswell's *Johnson*, i. 268.

indignation he seems to have excited in your breast, and you flatter
me very much in pouring it out so freely before me.' *M.S.R.S.E.*
Walpole wrote on Nov. 15 of the same year :—' Churchill, the poet, *is*
dead—to the great joy of the Ministry and the Scotch.' *Letters*, iv.
291. Beattie, in some lines written shortly after Churchill's death,
did what he could to pay back the poet's insults. They end :—
   ' Sacred from vengeance shall his memory rest ?
   Judas, though dead, though damned, we still detest.'
   The ' rage ' continued for years after Bute's retirement from office,
for the secret 'influence' was still suspected. Dr. A. Carlyle (*Auto.*
p. 509) says that in 1769 Garrick, who was bringing out a new play by
John Home, 'justly alarmed at the jealousy and dislike which prevailed at that time against Lord Bute and the Scotch, had advised the
author to change the title of *Rivine* into that of *The Fatal Discovery*, and
had provided a student of Oxford who appeared at the rehearsals as
the author, and wished Home of all things to remain concealed till the
play had its run. But John, whose vanity was too sanguine to admit
of any fear or caution, and whose appetite for praise rebelled against
the counsel that would deprive him for a moment of his fame, too
soon discovered the secret, and though the play survived its nine
nights, yet the house evidently slackened after the town heard that
John was the author.' Murphy, in his *Life of Garrick*, p. 295, says of
Home's play:—' The names of the persons of the piece are grating to
an English ear. *Kastreel, Dunton, Connon*, and the like are exotics
beneath the dignity of tragedy. The play might as well be written in
Erse.' Dr. Blair, on the other hand, as became the champion of
Ossian, writing to Hume on March 11, 1769, says :—' I have this morning received *The Fatal Discovery* by post. I sit down to read it with
great greediness. What made Home give it such a foolish *Novel* kind
of name ? *Rivine* ought to have been the name of the play.'
M.S.R.S.E. We may pause a moment to reflect on the vast
change in sentiment that has been wrought since the days when a
Highland name was thought sufficient to damn a play. Now, not
only Lowlanders, but even Englishmen, when they go to 'the mountains of the North' are proud to disguise themselves in a dress which
their forefathers in Edinburgh or in London, in the days of David
Hume and John Home, would have looked on with a feeling of
scorn not altogether unmingled with fear. Perhaps by the end
of the twentieth century the descendants of the Orangemen of
Belfast and Londonderry, and people of rank and fortune from
England, when they go to shoot and fish in the wilds of Kerry and
Connemara, will hope in their long frieze coats, their knee breeches,
and their worsted stockings, to be taken for the children of the soil.
Johnson, when he was surrounded by the M'Craas with their 'very
savage wildness of aspect and manner,' and felt that ' it was much
the same as being with a tribe of Indians,' if any one had told him that
in another hundred years English gentlemen would be proud to be

mistaken for Highlanders, in all probability would have replied : —
' Sir, you lie, and you know that you lie.' It was less than twenty
years before the date of Hume's letter that Ray, in his *History of the
Rebellion of* 1745 (p. vii), describes the Young Pretender's army as
' the barbarians that over-run the country.'

To return from this digression to the main subject of this note.
Smollett in *Humphry Clinker*, published in 1771, (Letter of July 13),
describes how ' from Doncaster northwards all the windows of all the
inns are scrawled with doggrel rhymes in abuse of the Scottish nation.'
Lord Shelburne wrote :—' I can scarce conceive a Scotchman capable
of liberality, and capable of impartiality.' Fitzmaurice's *Shelburne*, iii.
441. Of Lord Mansfield he wrote that ' like the generality of Scotch
he had no regard to truth whatever.' *Ib.* i. 89. Horace Walpole was,
in his old age, as violent against the Scotch as Hume against the
English. ' June 14, 1780. What a nation is Scotland ; in every reign
engendering traitors to the State, and false and pernicious to the
Kings that favour it the most ! National prejudices, I know, are very
vulgar ; but, if there are national characteristics, can one but dislike
the soils and climates that concur to produce them ?' *Letters*, vii. 400.
' Feb. 5, 1781. Pray look into the last *Critical Review* but one ; there
you will find that David Hume in a saucy blockheadly note calls
Locke, Algernon Sidney, and Bishop Hoadly *despicable writers.* I
believe that ere long the Scotch will call the English *lousy* ! and that
Goody Hunter will broach the assertion in an Anatomic lecture. Not
content with debasing and disgracing us as a nation by losing
America, destroying our Empire, and making us the scorn and prey
of Europe, the Scotch would annihilate our patriots, martyrs, heroes
and geniuses. Algernon Sidney, Lord Russell, King William, the
Duke of Marlborough, Locke, are to be traduced and levelled, and with
the aid of their fellow-labourer Johnson, who spits at them while he
tugs at the same oar, Milton, Addison, Prior and Gray are to make way
for the dull forgeries of Ossian, and such wights as Davy and Johnny
Home, Lord Kames, Lord Monboddo, and Adam Smith !—Oh ! if you
[Mason the Poet] have a drop of English ink in your veins, rouse and
revenge your country ! Do not let us be run down and brazened out
of all our virtue, genius, sense and taste by Laplanders and Bœotians,
who never produced one original writer in verse or prose.' *Ib.* p. 511.

A curious contrast to the violence of Walpole's attack is afforded
by a passage in a letter written in the spring of 1759, in which Hume
informs Robertson of the great popularity of the *History of Scotland.*
' Mr. Walpole,' he says, ' triumphs in the success of his favourites, the
Scotch.' Stewart's *Life of Robertson*, p. 180. A justification for Hume's
statement is found in Walpole's own letters ; for on March 25 of
this year he wrote to Sir David Dalrymple :—' I could not help
smiling, Sir, at being taxed with insincerity for my encomiums on
Scotland. They were given in a manner a little too serious to
admit of irony, and (as partialities cannot be supposed entirely

ceased) with too much risk of disapprobation in this part of the
world, not to flow from my heart. My friends have long known my
opinion on this point, and it is too much formed on fact for me to
retract it, if I were so disposed.' *Letters*, iii. 217. This was written, be
it observed, while George II was King, and the Earl of Bute nothing
more than the favourite of the Princess Dowager of Wales.

See post, *Letters* of Oct. 25, 1769; March 5, 1772; Jan. 30, 1773.

Note 9. In 1756 Johnson 'accepted of a guinea for writing the introduction to *The London Chronicle*, an evening newspaper. . . . This
Chronicle still subsists,' continues Boswell, 'and from what I observed,
when I was abroad, has a more extensive circulation upon the Conti-
nent than any of the English newspapers. It was constantly read by
Johnson himself.' Boswell's *Johnson*, i. 317. Boswell wrote to
Johnson on March 12, 1778 :—'The alarm of your late illness dis-
tressed me but a few hours ; for I found it contradicted in *The London
Chronicle*, which I could depend upon as authentic concerning you,
Mr. Strahan being the printer of it.' *Ib*. iii. 221.

Note 10. '*An Essay on the Constitution of England*, price 1s. 6d. T.
Becket and P. de Hondt, London ': *London Chronicle*, Jan. 5, 1765. In
the number for Jan. 10 three columns of extracts are given.

Note 11. Franklin had met Hume when he visited Edinburgh in
1759. Dr. A. Carlyle's *Auto.* p. 395. Later on he stayed in his house
in James's Court for several weeks. *Ib.* p. 437. Dr. Carlyle does not
mention the year of his second visit, but I have little doubt that it was
in 1771. See *post*, Letter of Nov. 12, 1771. Franklin's friendship with
his brother-printer Strahan, which had been long and close, was
broken by the American War. Strahan, who was a strong supporter
of Lord North's ministry, received from his old friend the following
letter :—

'Philadᵃ. July 5, 1775.

'MR. STRAHAN,

'You are a Member of Parliament, and one of that Majority which
has doomed my Country to Destruction.—You have begun to burn
our Towns, and murder our People,—Look upon your Hands !—They
are stained with the Blood of your Relations ! You and I were long
friends.—You are now my Enemy,—and

'I am, yours,

'B. FRANKLIN.'

[Franklin's *Memoirs*, ed. 1818, iii. i.]

Their friendship was renewed when peace was made between the
two countries. Franklin wrote to Strahan in 1784 :—'I remember
your observing once to me, as we sat together in the House of
Commons, that no two journeymen printers within your knowledge
had met with such success in the world as ourselves. You were then
at the head of your profession, and soon afterwards became a
Member of Parliament. I was an agent for a few provinces, and now
act for them.' *Ib.* p. 172.

LETTER XXII.

The King's Birth-day kept in Paris.

DEAR Sᴵᴿᴿ

There have some Transactions pass'd with you
of late[1], which much excite our Curiosity at a Distance ;
but I do not wish that you woud write me your Opinion
freely about them, unless you can get a private hand, by
whom you can send your Letter[2].

I shall be much obligd to you, if you will be so good as
to insert the following Article in the Chronicle[3], and give
it about to the other Papers.

'Paris.   On Tuesday the fourth of June, being the
Anniversary of his Majesty's Birth day, the Earl of Hertford, Ambassador from England, invited all the English of
Rank and Condition in this Place, to the Number of
seventy Persons, who dind with him and celebrated that
Solemnity.   The Company appeard very Splendid, being
almost all drest in new and rich Cloaths on this Occasion ;
the Entertainment was magnificent, and the usual Healths
were drunk with great Loyalty and Alacrity by all
present[4].'

I am sorry it is not allowd me to communicate to you any
more interesting Intelligence ; but be assurd of my Regard,
and excuse my abrupt Conclusion, as I write in a Hurry.

I am Dear Sir Yours most sincerely

DAVID HUME.

PARIS, *6th of June,* 1765.

Note 1.   The Grenville Ministry which had been formed on April
16, 1763, was succeeded by the Rockingham Ministry on July 13,
1765.   The nature of the transactions which excited Hume's curiosity
at a distance can be seen in the following extracts :—

'May 25, 1765.   My last, I think, was of the 16th.   Since that we
have had events of almost every sort.   A whole administration
dismissed, taken again, suspended, confirmed ; an insurrection ; and
we have been at the eve of a civil war.   Many thousand weavers

F

rose on a bill for their relief being thrown out of the House of Lords by the Duke of Bedford. For four days they were suffered to march about the town with colours displayed, petitioning the King, surrounding the House of Lords, mobbing and wounding the Duke of Bedford, and at last besieging his house, which with his family was narrowly saved from destruction. At last it grew a regular siege and blockade; but by garrisoning it with horse and foot literally, and calling in several regiments the tumult is appeased. Lord Bute rashly taking advantage of this unpopularity of his enemies, advised the King to notify to his Ministers that he intended to dismiss them, —and by this step, no succedaneum being prepared, reduced his Majesty to the alternative of laying his crown at the foot of Mr. Pitt or of the Duke of Bedford; and as it proved at last, of both. The Duke of Cumberland was sent for, and was sent to Mr. Pitt, from whom, though offering almost *carte blanche*, he received a peremptory refusal. The next measure was to form a Ministry from the Opposition. Willing were they, but timid. Without Mr. Pitt nobody would engage. The King was forced to desire his old Ministers to stay where they were.... Here are all the great and opulent noble families engaged on one side or the other. Here is the King insulted and prisoner, his Mother stigmatised, his Uncle affronted, his Favourite persecuted. It is again a scene of Bohuns, Montforts and Plantagenets.... When I recollect all I have seen and known, I seem to be as old as Methuselah; indeed I was born in politics,— but I hope not to die in them. With all my experience, these last five weeks have taught me more than any other ten years.' Walpole to Mann. *Letters*, iv. 370-2.

'June 26, 1765. You have known your country in more perilous situations, but you never knew it in a more distracted one in time of peace than it is at present. Nor had I ever more difficulty to describe its position to you. Times of party have their great outlines which even such historians as Hollingshed or Smollett can seize. But a season of faction is another guess thing. It depends on personal characters, intrigues and minute circumstances, which make little noise and escape the eyes of the generality. The details are as much too numerous for a letter as, when the moment is past, they become too trifling and uninteresting for history.' *Ib.* p. 377.

Burke, writing on May 18 to Henry Flood, said :—' Nothing but an intractable temper in your friend Pitt can prevent a most admirable and lasting system from being put together; and this crisis will shew whether pride or patriotism be predominant in his character; for you may be assured that he has it now in his power to come into the service of his country upon any plan of politics he may choose to dictate, with great and honourable terms to himself and to every friend he has in the world; and with such a stretch of power as will be equal to everything but absolute despotism over the King and kingdom. A few days will shew whether he will take this part, or that of continuing on his back at Hayes, talking fustian, excluded from all ministerial, and incapable of all parliamentary service ; for his gout is worse than ever, but his pride may disable him more than his gout.   These matters so fill our imaginations here that with our mob of six or seven thousand weavers who pursue the Ministry, and do not leave them quiet or safety in their houses, we have little to think of other things.'   Burke's *Private Corres.* i. 80.

Dr. Blair wrote to Hume in Paris on July 1 [1765] :—' Our Political Revolutions here would amaze you. . . . All that seems to be certain is that L. B. [Lord Bute] is worsted and —— [the King] made a prisoner.   If the present Establishment take any root, it will probably end in his relapsing altogether into the condition of a private man and amusing himself with his Wife and his Children ; now that they have found the ways of subduing him.'   *M. S. R. S. E.*

Macaulay, in his second *Essay on the Earl of Chatham* (ed. 1874, iv. 318), describing his conduct at this time says :—' And now began a long series of errors on the part of the illustrious statesman, errors which involved his country in difficulties and distresses more serious even than those from which his genius had formerly rescued her. His language was haughty, unreasonable, almost unintelligible.   The only thing which could be discerned, through a cloud of vague and not very gracious phrases, was that he would not at that moment take office.'

Note 2.   In the letter writers of this age distrust is very often shewn of the Post Office.   Such passages as the following are not unfrequently met with :—' London, April 19, 1748.   I know that most letters from and to me are opened.'   Lord Chesterfield to Mr. Dayrolles.   Chesterfield's *Misc. Works*, iv. 47.

'London, June 8, 1757.   The public, perhaps at the moment I write this, is at the crisis of its fate[1].   But I say no more.   For at the Post Office, it is said, they use a liberty without licence (just the contrary of what is done everywhere else, where they use licence without liberty) to open people's letters.'   Warburton to Hurd.   *Letters from a late Eminent Prelate,* ed. 1809, p. 244.

'London, June 26, 1765.   You know, my dear Sir, I never expect you to answer me on these delicate subjects [a threatened change of Ministry].   I even send this by a safe conveyance to Lord Hertford at Paris, as I did a former one which I hope you received.'   Horace Walpole to Mann.   *Letters,* iv. 378.

'London, Aug. 29, 1766.   I am told there is a great fracas at the Post Office about a letter from the Duke of Bedford to the Duke of Grafton [the Prime Minister] having been opened.   Mr. Saxby is named as the person doing it, and is under strict examination, I hear, to name who set him on to do it. . . .   Sept. 2.   Saxby is turned out of an office of £1200 a year for opening the Duke of Bedford's letter,

---

[1] The Pitt and Newcastle Ministry was forming.

it is said, to the Duke of Grafton.' Mr. Lloyd to Mr. Grenville. *Grenville Papers*, iii. 311. The editor quotes a Private Memorial to Mr. Grenville, when Prime Minister, from Mr. Anthony Todd, the Secretary to the General Post Office, dated August 1763, containing an account of £5810 Secret Service Money applied to the payment of the allowances on the Secret List for one year. A request was made that the allowance of one Mr. Bode might be increased, 'for engraving the many seals we are obliged to make use of.' On this Secret List Mr. Todd's name is entered for £750, with £25 added, 'for distributing these allowances.' His regular salary was only £200 (*Court and City Register* for 1765, p. 129). It must have been raised later on, for on June 17, 1783, Mr. Pitt in the Debate on his Bill for Reform of Abuses in the Public Offices, 'speaking of fees mentioned the place of the Secretary of the Post Office, who with a salary of five or six hundred pounds made an annual income of upwards of three thousand. Mr. Pitt stated this to arise from his having two and a half per cent. on all packets [packet-boats]; and in the last year of the war he said £140,000 had been expended in packets, so many were either lost at sea or taken.' *Parl. Hist.* xxiii. 951. I was puzzled at finding in the Secret List the Bishop of Bath and Wells as the recipient of £500 a year; but after some search I solved the mystery by discovering the following mention of him by Horace Walpole in 1741:—'Old Weston of Exeter is dead. Dr. Clarke, the Dean, Dr. Willes, the decipherer, and Dr. Gilbert of Llandaff are candidates to succeed him. Sir R[obert Walpole, the Prime-Minister] is for Willes, who, he says, knows so many secrets that he might insist upon being made Archbishop.' *Letters*, i. 116. His death is thus mentioned in the *Gent. Mag.* for Dec. 1773, p. 582:—'In Hill Street, Berkeley Square, aged 80, Dr. Edward Willes, Lord Bishop of Bath and Wells, and joint Decipherer (with his son Edward Willes, Esq.) to the King. He was consecrated Bishop of St. David's in 1742, and translated to the see of Bath and Wells in 1743.' Edward Willes is entered on the Secret List as receiving £500, and Thomas Willes £300.

'Dublin, May 19, 1769. To avoid the impertinence of a post-office I take the opportunity of sending this by a private hand.' Earl of Charlemont to Burke. *Burke Corres.* i. 167.

'Gregories, July 9, 1769. Might I presume to suggest that just at this time he [the Duke of Richmond] may possibly expect to hear from your lordship by the first safe conveyance. If the letter be given to his porter it will be sent by the coach to Goodwood.' Burke to the Marquis of Rockingham. *Ib.* p. 176.

If we may trust Hume the correspondence of private life was safe. He wrote to the Countess de Boufflers in 1775:—'No private letters are ever opened here.' Hume's *Private Corres.* p. 282.

At this time the posts to France left London on Tuesday and Friday in every week, and arrived in London from France on Monday and Friday. Their punctual arrival must of course have depended on a favourable wind. *Court and City Register for* 1765, p. 132.

Note 3. It was inserted in the *Chronicle* of June 13.

Note 4. On June 5 of the previous year Wilkes wrote from Paris, where he was living in exile :—'Lord Hertford gave yesterday a grand dinner to all the English here except *one*, and to the true Irish Whigs ; nor, like a good courtier, did he omit the new converts, the Scotch. . . . I am the single Englishman not invited by the ambassador of my country on the only day I can at Paris shew my attachment to my Sovereign, as if I was disaffected to the present establishment. . . . To say the truth, I passed the day much more to my satisfaction than I should have done in a set of mixed or suspicious company ; a fulsome dull dinner ; two hours of mighty grave conversation to be purchased (in all civility) by six more of Pharaoh— which I detest as well as every other kind of gaming.' Almon's *Memoirs of Wilkes*, iii. 124-7.

LETTER XXIII.

Faction in England.

COMPEIGNE, 4 *of Augt.*, 1765.

DEAR SIR

Your Letter is the most satisfactory and most impartial Account of the present Transactions, which I have met with from any hand. I give you thanks for it. I had long entertain'd Hopes, that, being here in a foreign Employment, we lay much out of the Road of Faction ; and that your Ministry in England might toss and tumble over one another, without affecting us ; but I see we are now involvd to a certain degree, and must run the Fate of the rest. It is probable I shall be soon in England when I shall have an Opportunity of conversing with you and thanking you more fully[1]. I am glad to hear better Accounts of Mr. Millar.

Yours

D. H.

Note 1. On July 13, 1765, Hume received his commission under the Great Seal as Secretary to the Embassy at Paris. On June 3, on hearing of the appointment, he had written to Elliot :—' In spite of

Atheism and Deism, of Whiggism and Toryism, of Scotticism and
Philosophy, I am now possessed of an office of credit, and of £1200 a
year.' Burton's *Hume*, ii. 281. The fall of the Grenville Ministry made
a great change in his fortune. His patron, the Earl of Hertford, was
offered by the Marquis of Rockingham the post of Lord Lieutenant of
Ireland. For some time the Earl hesitated between Ireland and
Paris. 'He takes the former,' wrote Walpole on July 30 (*Letters*, iv.
388), 'not very gladly, but to accommodate his brother, and his
nephew, Grafton.' His brother, General Conway, and the Duke of
Grafton were the two Secretaries of State in the new Ministry.
Hume was left to represent the Ambassador till the arrival of the
Duke of Richmond, Lord Hertford's successor, in November, 1765.
Horace Walpole, who visited Paris in the interval, wrote on Sept. 26
(*Ib.* p. 409) :—'Lady Hertford is gone and the Duke of Richmond not
come ; consequently I am as *isolé* as I can wish to be.' He lodged in
the same hotel as Hume, and often met him ; yet he makes very
little mention of him in his letters. The two men had but little in
common.

For some time it seemed that Hume was to have a still higher
office. 'Lord Hertford had assured him that he would not accept of
the Lord-Lieutenancy unless he were allowed the naming of the
Secretary.' He had now heard that 'the office was destined for himself in conjunction with Lord Hertford's son, Lord Beauchamp.'
Burton's *Hume*, ii. 287. On Aug. 4, Hume wrote to his brother from
Compiègne :—' My Sallary [as Secretary to the Lord Lieutenant] will
be about 2000 a year. . . . This is an office of Credit and Dignity, and
the Secretary has always an unquestioned Claim, whenever his Term
expires, of being provided for in a handsome Manner. Thus you see
a splendid Fortune awaits me ; yet you cannot imagine with what
Regret I leave this Country. It is like Stepping out of Light into
Darkness to exchange Paris for Dublin. . . . I shall probably have it
in my Power to do Service to my Friends, particularly to your young
Folks. For as to you and myself it is long since we thought our
Fortunes entirely made. . . . I shall remain all the Winter and
Spring in Ireland ; and no more for two Years.' *M. S. R. S. E.*

Before the end of the month he learnt that the office was not for
him. He wrote to his brother :—' Lord Hertford, on his arrival in
London, found great difficulty of executing his intentions in my
favour. The cry is loud against the Scots ; and the present Ministry
are unwilling to support any of our countrymen, lest they bear the
reproach of being connected with Lord Bute. For this reason Lord
Hertford departed from his project ; which he did the more readily,
as he knew I had a great reluctance to the office of Secretary for
Ireland, which requires a talent for speaking in public to which I was
never accustomed. I must also have kept a kind of open house, and
have drunk and caroused with the Irish, a course of living to which
I am as little accustomed.' Burton's *Hume*, ii. 290.

In a letter to Adam Smith, dated Nov. 5, after mentioning 'the Rage against the Scots,' he adds : — ' Perhaps the Zeal against Deists entered for a share.' In the same letter he describes the office as one ' of great Dignity, as the Secretary is in a manner prime Minister of that Kingdom.' *M. S. R. S. E.*

Two years later we find Junius mocking at 'a Scotch secretary teaching the Irish people the true pronunciation of the English language.' In a note it is stated that it was Sir Gilbert Elliot, Hume's friend, who was meant. *Letters of Junius,* ed. 1812, ii. 474.

When the Earl of Chesterfield was made Lord Lieutenant in the year 1745, he chose for his Secretary ' one " who was," he said, " a very genteel pretty young fellow, but not a man of business." On the first visit his Secretary paid him, he told him, " Sir, you will receive the emoluments of your place ; but I will do the business myself, being determined to have no first Minister." ' Chesterfield's *Misc. Works,* i. 255. We may wonder whether Hume, if he had been appointed, would, like Windham, have felt ' some modest and virtuous doubts, whether he could bring himself to practise those arts which it is supposed a person in that situation has occasion to employ. " Don't be afraid, Sir (said Johnson, with a pleasant smile,) you will soon make a very pretty rascal." ' Boswell's *Johnson,* iv. 200. Among the Hume Papers belonging to the Royal Society of Edinburgh, I found the following letter written to him the year before by one Mr. O'Conor.

LONDON, *February* 10*th,* 1764.

' SIR !

' The Author of the annexed printed Letter, is an *Irish* Gentleman, who is highly concerned, that so great a Man as Mr. Hume should be ranked among the Foes of IRELAND. He Observes, that you mention the Irish with Scorn and Contempt, whenever they fall in your way, not only in your history, but even in your Miscellanies. Prejudices against this or that Nation, are prejudices unworthy of a philosopher, who knows that all men are formed by NATURE of the same materials, and who ought to be the *Common* friend and protector of his Species.

The Author's intention was, that his friend in London should present you this letter in Manuscript, but his Friend being informed, that you did not reside in London, published [it] in the Gentlemen's Musæum [1] for April and May of the year '63.

' How far the reasonings contained in the annexed Letter, will contribute to change your Opinion, with respect to the Conduct of the Irish ever since they were reduced under the Yoke of England, I cannot determine. But I HOPE these reasonings will have a favorable Effect. Mr. Hume is not only a great man, but he is a good man, but he is an upright man. He will therefore expunge from his History,

---

[1] *The Universal Museum, or Gentleman's and Ladies' Polite Magazine of History, Politicks and Literature.* Vol. i. was published in 1762.

the ill-grounded Censures, which he has thrown upon the unfortunate Irish. He will cure the Wounds, that he has inflicted upon this most distressed Nation under the Sun.

'Grant, Sir, by way of Supposition, that the Charge you bring in your History against the Irish is false. On this hypothesis what has not Mr. Hume to account for?—the Roman Catholic Irish have been for seventy years past, the Continual Objects of political Calumny. Hence it is that all the Batteries of Law are perpetually playing against them. Hence it is that Penal Laws are enacted to beggar them, to corrupt them, to divide them, to force them to become Apostates, perjurers and Informers, for THE DESTRUCTION OF EACH OTHER.

'To consider the present Roman Catholic Irish in a proper Light, you must consider them, Sir, as a people half murthered, chained to the ground, and constantly trod upon in this situation, by a troop of wanton Oppressors. Shall the illustrious Mr. Hume join in the horrid Cruelty by propagating and swelling the political Lie that has always been, and continues to be, the Cause of it? If a Reparation of Honour be due to a Private Person who is injured by a false imputation, how much more sacred does this Debt become, when a whole Nation is Calumniated, when Thousands yet unborn are destined to feel the effects of the Slander.

'The Case between you, Sir, and Ireland stands thus : you have fastened the Chains, you have widened the wounds of an expiring people, upon the authority of some English historians who thought themselves interested in robbing the Irish of their reputation, as well as of their lands.

'Had the Account which you give come from an inferior Hand—it would do little hurt—but coming from the hands of Mr. Hume, one of the first Geniuses of the Age he lives in, it arms not only the Prejudices of England, but the Prejudices of the whole Human Race, against the forlorn Irish.

'For the justness and force of the reasoning contained in the annexed Letter, the Author appeals to your own bosom. You will therefore, Sir, it is hoped, do something to repair the Injury you have done a Nation that never did, that never could offend you. Your bookseller, A. Millar, is on the point of giving a new edition of your History. Something by way of Appendix may be added to atone for the Mistakes that have crept into the first Editions, and to prevent the growing Mischiefs of a popular Error, which has obtained the sanction of the [*sic*] great Name.

'I expect, Sir, that you will honour me with an Answer, which I shall transmit to the Irish Gentleman who wrote the annexed Letter. You will please to address it to Mr. Daniel O'Conor, At the Bull and Gate, in Holborn, London.

'I am with the greatest Respect and Attachment Sir
'Your most obedient and most humble Servant
'DANIEL O'CONOR.'

LETTER XXIV.

The Arrival of Hume and Rousseau in London.

[LONDON, early in 1766.]

DEAR STRAHAN

Is it not strange that you and I have not yet met[1]? I have been so hurry'd both with my own Affairs and with Mon^r Rousseau's, that I can excuse myself: But I own that I hopd your Leizure woud allow you to come hither. I go out of town to morrow and Sunday[2]: As soon as I come back I propose to beat up your Quarters. My Compliments to Mrs. Strahan.

Yours sincerely

DAVID HUME.

Buckingham Street, York Buildings[3],
Mrs. Adams's.   Friday.

Note 1. Grimm, writing on Jany. 1, 1766, says that Rousseau came to Paris on Dec. 17, and was to leave for England with Hume on Jany. 4. *Corres. Lit.* v. 3. The travellers were detained some days at Calais by contrary winds. They arrived in London on the 14th. In the *London Chronicle* the following notices are given of their arrival. 'Jan. 14. Yesterday [Monday] David Hume Esq., arrived in London from Paris.' p. 48. 'Jan. 16. Monday last arrived in town the celebrated Jean Jacques Rousseau.' p. 50. It seems highly probable, as Strahan the printer of the paper was Hume's friend, that it was by Hume's own wish that it was not made known that they came together.

Rousseau, speaking of his arrival in England, says:—'J'y apportais l'estime universelle et le respect même de mes ennemis.' *Œuvres de Rousseau*, ed. 1782, xxiv. 328. It was on Feb. 15 of this same year that Johnson said of him:—'I think him one of the worst of men; a rascal who ought to be hunted out of society, as he has been. Three or four nations have expelled him; and it is a shame that he is protected in this country. . . . Rousseau, Sir, is a very bad man. I would sooner sign a sentence for his transportation than that of any felon who has gone from the Old Bailey these many years. Yes, I should like to have him work in the plantations."' Boswell's *Johnson*, ii. 11.

Note 2. Perhaps Hume paid the visit which he thus describes :— 'I had accompanied Mr. Rousseau into a very pleasant part of the county of Surrey, where he spent two days at Colonel Webb's; Mr.

Rousseau seeming to me highly delighted with the natural and solitary beauties of the place. Through the means of Mr. Stewart therefore I entered into treaty with Colonel Webb for the purchasing the house, with a little estate adjoining, in order to make a settlement for Mr. Rousseau.' *A Concise Account of the Dispute between Mr. Hume and Mr. Rousseau,* p. 11.

Note 3. 'York Buildings, in the Strand, so denominated from the Archbishop of York's house there, purchased by Nicholas Heath the Archbishop, about the year 1556, of the Bishop of Norwich; but afterwards coming to John, Duke of Buckingham, he demised the house and garden to several builders, and they erected there several handsome streets and alleys, in which his name and title are recorded, *viz.,* John Street, Villars Street, Duke Street, Off (? Of) Alley, and Buckingham Street. However these streets together are still denominated York Buildings.' Dodsley's *London and its Environs,* ed. 1761, vi. 369.

LETTER XXV.

Hume's Quarrel with Rousseau.

[LONDON, *July* 15, 1766.]

All I can say of S[ir] David Dalrymple is that he is now a Lord of the Session, and passes by the Name of Lord Hales or New-hales, I know not which[1]. He is a godly Man; feareth the Lord and escheweth Evil, And works out his Salvation with Fear and Trembling[2]. None of the Books Sir David publishes are of his writing: They are all historical Manuscripts, of little or no Consequence[3]. I go to Woburn[4] for three or four days.

I have got a Letter from Rousseau, which woud make a good eighteen penny Pamphlet. I fancy he intends to publish it[5]. It is perfect Frenzy[6]; consequently sets my Mind quite at Ease[7].

Yours

D. H.

Note 1. The fifteen Scotch Judges, or Lords of Session, 'have,' writes Boswell, 'both in and out of Court the title of Lords from the name of their estates.' Boswell's *Johnson,* ii. 291, *n.* 6. Lord Cockburn, writing in 1852, says :—' This assumption of two names, one

official and one personal, and being addressed by the one and sub-
scribing by the other, is wearing out, and will soon disappear.' Cockburn's *Jeffrey*, i. 365. Dalrymple took the title of Lord Hailes. His
grandfather, who had bought the family mansion, then lately erected,
had given it the name of New Hailes, to distinguish it, no doubt, from
some older house. See *Scotland and Scotsmen*, i. 411 note. Boswell
informed Johnson of ' Sir David's eminent character for learning and
religion.' Johnson thereupon 'drank a bumper to him, " as a man of
worth, a scholar, and a wit." " I have," said he, " never heard of him
except from you ; but let him know my opinion of him ; for as he
does not shew himself much in the world, he should have the praise
of the few who hear of him."' Boswell's *Johnson*, i. 432, 451.
When Johnson visited Scotland he met Dalrymple and was highly
pleased with him. *Ib.* v. 48. Later on he revised at his request the
proofs of his *Annals of Scotland*, which he described as ' a new mode
of history. . . . The exactness of his dates raises my wonder.' *Ib.* ii.
383.

Note 2. Hume, in his Scriptural phrases, apparently has in mind
Job ii. 3, and *Philippians* ii. 12. Dalrymple was one of 'the malicious
fellows,' who, as Curators of the Advocates' Library, had ' struck
out of the catalogue, and removed from the shelves as indecent
books, and unworthy of a place in a learned library,' three French
works which Hume, when Librarian, had purchased. See *ante*,
my note on Hume's *Autobiography*.

Note 3. ' Dr. Johnson had last night [Aug. 15, 1773] looked into
Lord Hailes's *Remarks on the History of Scotland*. Dr. Robertson and
I said it was a pity Lord Hailes did not write greater things. His
Lordship had not then published his *Annals of Scotland*.' Boswell's
Johnson, v. 38. Hume wrote from London to Sir Gilbert Elliot, on
July 5, 1768 :—' I have seen a book newly printed at Edinburgh,
called *Philosophical Essays*; it has no manner of sense in it, but is
wrote with tolerable neatness of style ; whence I conjecture it to be
our friend, Sir David's.' Burton's *Hume*, ii. 414. Elliot having
informed him that James Balfour was the author, Hume replied :—' I
thought Sir David had been the only Christian that could write
English on the other side of the Tweed.' *Ib.* p. 418.

Note 4. Hume wrote to Dr. Blair on July 15, 1766 :—' I go in a few
hours to Woburn' [the seat of the Duke of Bedford]. Burton's
Hume, ii. 345. He had been introduced by the Countess de Boufflers
to the Duke and Duchess, 'who have,' he wrote, 'been essentially
obliged to her in their family concerns. She wrote the Duke about a
fortnight ago that the time was now come, and the only time that probably ever would come, of his shewing his friendship to her by assist-
ing me in my applications [to be made Secretary to the Embassy] ; and
she would rest on this sole circumstance all his professions of regard
to her. He received her letter while in the country, but he wrote her
back that he would immediately hasten to town, and if he had any

credit with the King or Ministry, her solicitations should be complied with.' *Ib.* p. 279. Hume, in his last illness, complained to John Home of the design of the Whigs to ruin him as an author. 'Amongst many instances of this he told me one which was new to me'. The Duke of Bedford (who afterwards conceived a great affection for him) by the suggestions of some of his party friends ordered his son, Lord Tavistock, not to read his *History of England.' Ib.* ii. 500.

Note 5. So early as the summer of 1762, Hume touched with pity for Rousseau, 'who was obliged to fly France on account of some passages in his *Emile*, had offered him a retreat in his own house, so long as he should please to partake of it.' At the same time he tried to procure him a pension from George III. ' It would,' he wrote to Gilbert Elliot, 'be a signal victory over the French worth a hundred of our Mindens[1], to protect and encourage a man of genius whom they had persecuted[2].' At this same time Rousseau was writing to the Countess de Boufflers :—'Ainsi successivement on me refusera partout l'air et l'eau. . . . Dans l'état où je suis, il ne me reste qu'à me laisser chasser de frontière en frontière, jusqu'à ce que je ne puisse plus aller. Alors le dernier fera de moi ce qu'il lui plaira[3].' To Hume he wrote on Feb. 19, 1763 from Motiers Travers, where he was under the protection of the exiled Earl Marischal of Scotland :— ' Que ne puis-je espérer de nous voir un jour rassemblés avec Milord dans votre commune patrie, qui deviendrait la mienne ! Je bénirais dans une société si douce les malheurs par lesquels j'y fus conduit, et je croirais n'avoir commencé de vivre que du jour qu'elle aurait commencé. Puissé-je voir cet heureux jour plus désiré qu'espéré ! Avec quel transport je m'écrierais, en touchant l'heureuse terre où sont nés *David Hume* et le *Maréchal d'Écosse,*

" Salve fatis mihi debita tellus !
Hic domus, hæc patria est[4]." '

No further correspondence passed between the two philosophers till the middle of the year 1765, when Hume who was at Paris was informed that Rousseau wished to seek under his protection an asylum in England. ' I could not,' writes Hume, ' reject a proposal made to me under such circumstances by a man so celebrated for his genius and misfortunes[5].' He brought him over to England, and treated him with the greatest kindness. ' I must own,' he wrote, ' I felt an emotion of pity mixed with indignation, to think a man of letters of such eminent merit should be reduced, in spite of the simplicity of his manner

---

[1] The French were beaten at Minden by the English and Hanoverian army on Aug. 1, 1759. ' All we know is,' wrote Horace Walpole on the 9th, ' that not one Englishman is killed, nor one Frenchman left alive.' *Letters,* iii. 244.

[2] *A Concise Account*, p. 2, and Stewart's *Robertson*, p. 359.

[3] Hume's *Private Corres.* p. 11.

[4] *Ib.* p. 59. The quotation is from the *Æneid*, vii. 120-2.

[5] *A Concise Account*, p. 5.

of living, to such extreme indigence; and that this unhappy state should be rendered more intolerable by sickness, by the approach of old age, and the implacable rage of persecution. I knew that many persons imputed the wretchedness of Mr. Rousseau to his excessive pride, which induced him to refuse the assistance of his friends; but I thought this fault, if it were a fault, was a very respectable one. Too many men of letters have debased their character in stooping so low as to solicit the assistance of persons of wealth or power, unworthy of affording them protection ; and I conceived that a noble pride, even though carried to excess, merited some indulgence in a man of genius, who, borne up by a sense of his own superiority and a love of independence, should have braved the storms of fortune and the insults of mankind[1].'

Hume was generous and even delicate in more than one scheme which he formed to help his friend. But while he was still planning, Mr. Davenport, 'a gentleman of family, fortune, and worth,' offered his house at Wooton in the County of Derby. That Rousseau's dignity might be saved, he consented to receive thirty pounds a year for his board and that of his housekeeper[2].

Through Hume's intercession, the King moreover agreed to grant him a pension on condition that it should not be made public. To this Rousseau at first willingly assented[3]. But all the while the black clouds of suspicion were once more gathering in his mind. In the *St. James's Chronicle* was published a letter, as malicious as it was witty, addressed to him in the name of Frederick the Great, but really written by Horace Walpole. The Prussian King is made to offer him a shelter, and to conclude :—'Si vous persistez à vous creuser l'esprit pour trouver de nouveaux malheurs, choisissez les tels que vous voudrez. Je suis roi, je puis vous en procurer au gré de vos souhaits : et ce qui sûrement ne vous arrivera pas vis-à-vis de vos ennemis, je cesserai de vous persécuter quand vous cesserez de mettre votre gloire à l'être[4].' Rousseau suspected Hume of having had a hand in its publication. He became sullen even before he left London for Wooton. In a letter dated April 3, Hume describes a curious scene with him ' which proves,' he says, ' his extreme sensibility and good heart.' Rousseau had charged him with sharing in a good-natured contrivance, by which Mr. Davenport hoped to save him part of the expense of the journey to Derbyshire. Hume in vain protested his ignorance. 'Upon which M. Rousseau sat down in a very sullen humour, and all attempts which I could make to revive the conversation and turn it on other subjects were in vain. After near an hour, he rose up, and walked a little about the room. Judge of my surprise when, all of a sudden, he sat down upon my knee, threw his

---

[1] *A Concise Account*, p. 9.

[2] *Ib.* p. 13, and *Private Corres.* p. 161.

[3] *A Concise Account*, p. 18.

[4] Walpole's *Letters*, iv. 463. A translation is given in the *London Chronicle* of April 5, 1766.

arms about my neck, kissed me with the greatest ardour, and bedewed all my face with tears ! " Ah ! my dear friend," exclaimed he, "is it possible you can ever forgive my folly? This ill-humour is the return I make you for all the instances of your kindness towards me. But notwithstanding all my faults and follies, I have a heart worthy of your friendship, because it knows both to love and esteem you [1]." '

Hume referring to this outburst of feeling in a letter to Rousseau says :—'I was very much affected, I own ; and, I believe, there passed a very tender scene between us. You added, by way of compliment, that though I had many better titles to recommend me to posterity, yet perhaps my uncommon attachment and friendship to a poor unhappy persecuted man would not altogether be overlooked [2].'

The following day Rousseau went to Wooton, while Hume, who remained in London, went on busying himself about the pension. Rousseau had suddenly objected to its being kept secret, and had written a letter to General Conway in which he seemed to decline it altogether. To Hume's letters he returned no answers. ' I thought,' said the complacent philosopher, ' that my friend, conscious of having treated me ill in this affair, was ashamed to write to me [3].' What were the feelings which up to this time he had entertained of Rousseau, is shewn in the following extracts from his correspondence.

Hume to the Countess de Boufflers.

' Edinburgh, July 1, 1762.' After speaking of ' my esteem, I had almost said veneration, for the virtue and genius of M. Rousseau,' he continues :—' I assure your Ladyship there is no man in Europe of whom I have entertained a higher idea, and whom I would be prouder to serve ; . . . I revere his greatness of mind, which makes him fly obligations and dependance ; and I have the vanity to think, that through the course of my life I have endeavoured to resemble him in those maxims [4].'

Hume to Elliot.

' Edinburgh, July 5, 1762.' Speaking of Rousseau's writings he says :—' For my part, though I see some tincture of extravagance in all of them, I also think I see so much eloquence and force of imagination, such an energy of expression and such a boldness of conception, as entitles him to a place among the first writers of the age [5].'

Hume to the Countess de Boufflers.

' Edinburgh, Jan. 22, 1763.' After pointing out some faults in Rousseau's *Treatise of Education*, he continues :—' However it carries still the stamp of a great genius ; and what enhances its beauty, the stamp of a very particular genius. The noble pride and spleen and indignation of the author bursts out with freedom in a hundred places, and serves fully to characterize the lofty spirit of the man [6].'

[1] *Private Corres.* p. 151.   [2] *A Concise Account*, p. 85.

[3] *Ib.* p. 26.   [4] *Private Corres.* p. 8.

[5] Stewart's *Robertson*, p. 358.   [6] *Private Corres.* p. 56.

Hume to the Countess de Boufflers.

'London, Jan. 19, 1766.   My companion is very amiable, always polite, gay often, commonly sociable.   He does not know himself when he thinks he is made for entire solitude. . . . He has an excellent warm heart; and in conversation kindles often to a degree of heat which looks like inspiration.   I love him much, and hope that I have some share in his affections [1].'

Hume to the Marchioness de Barbantane.

'Feb. 16, 1766.   M. Rousseau's enemies have sometimes made you doubt of his sincerity, and you have been pleased to ask my opinion on this head.   After having lived so long with him, and seen him in a variety of lights, I am now better enabled to judge; and I declare to you that I have never known a man more amiable and more virtuous than he appears to me : he is mild, gentle, modest, affectionate, disinterested; and above all, endowed with a sensibility of heart in a supreme degree.   Were I to seek for his faults, I should say that they consisted in a little hasty impatience, which, as I am told, inclines him sometimes to say disobliging things to people that trouble him : he is also too delicate in the commerce of life : he is apt to entertain groundless suspicions of his best friends; and his lively imagination working upon them feigns chimeras, and pushes him to great extremes.   I have seen no instances of this disposition, but I cannot otherwise account for the violent animosities which have arisen between him and several men of merit, with whom he was once intimately acquainted; and some who love him much have told me that it is difficult to live much with him and preserve his friendship; but for my part, I think I could pass all my life in his company without any danger of our quarrelling [2].'

Hume to his brother John Home.

'Lisle Street, March 22, 1766.   Rousseau left me four days ago. . . . Surely he is one of the most singular of all human Beings, and one of the most unhappy.   His extreme Sensibility of Temper is his Torment; as he is much more susceptible of Pain than Pleasure. His Aversion to Society is not Affectation as is commonly believd. When in it, he is commonly very amiable, but often very unhappy. And tho' he be also unhappy in Solitude, he prefers that Species of suffering to the other.   He is surely a very fine Genius.   And of all the Writers that are or ever were in Europe, he is the Man who has acquird the most enthusiastic and most passionate Admirers.   I have seen many extraordinary Scenes of this Nature [3].'

Hume to the Countess de Boufflers.

'Lisle Street, April 3, 1766.   The chief circumstance which hinders me from repenting of my journey is the use I have been to poor Rousseau, the most singular, and often the most amiable man in the world. . . . Never was man who so well deserves happiness so

---

[1] *Private Corres.* p. 125.   [2] *Ib.* p. 142.   [3] *M. S. R. S. E.*

little calculated by nature to attain it. The extreme sensibility of his character is one great cause; but still more the frequent and violent fits of spleen and discontent and impatience, to which, either from the constitution of his mind or body, he is so subject. He is commonly, however, the best company in the world, when he will submit to live with men. . . . For my part I never saw a man, and very few women, of a more agreeable commerce. . . . It is one of his weaknesses that he likes to complain. The truth is, he is unhappy, and he is better pleased to throw the reason on his health and circumstances and misfortunes than on his melancholy humour and disposition [1].'

Hume to M.——. (A French friend.)

' Lisle Street, ce 2 de Mai, 1766. Il a un peu la faiblesse de vouloir se rendre intéressant, en se plaignant de sa pauvreté et de sa mauvaise santé; mais j'ai découvert par hasard qu'il a quelques ressources d'argent, petites à la vérité, mais qu'il nous a cachées, quand il nous a rendu compte de ses biens. Pour ce qui regarde sa santé, elle me paraît plutôt robuste qu'infirme, à moins que vous ne vouliez compter les accès de mélancolie et de *spleen* auxquels il est sujet. C'est grand dommage: il est fort aimable par ses manières; il est d'un cœur honnête et sensible; mais ces accès l'éloignent de la société, le remplissent d'humeur, et donnent quelquefois à sa conduite un air de bizarrerie et de violence, qualités qui ne lui sont pas naturelles [2].'

Hume to the Countess de Boufflers.

' Lisle Street, May 16, 1766. I am afraid, my dear Madam, that notwithstanding our friendship and our enthusiasm for this philosopher, he has been guilty of an extravagance the most unaccountable and most blamable that is possible to be imagined.' After describing Rousseau's letter to General Conway, in which he declined to receive a pension unless it were made public, Hume continues:—' Was ever anything in the world so unaccountable? For the purposes of life and conduct and society a little good sense is surely better than all this genius, and a little good humour than this extreme sensibility [3].'

Not a whit discouraged by Rousseau's extravagance and sullen silence, he went on doing his best to overcome the only difficulty that remained about the pension, by getting the condition of secrecy removed [4]. In the midst of his self-complacency, while he was, no doubt, flattering himself with the thought that he had attained the highest degree of merit which can be bestowed on any human creature, by possessing ' the sentiment of benevolence in an eminent degree [5],' the fat good-humoured Epicurean of the North received, one day in June, a ruder shock than has perhaps ever tried a

---

[1] *Private Corres.* pp. 148–153.   [2] *Ib.* p. 161.   [3] *Ib.* p. 169.
[4] *A Concise Account*, p. 28.   [5] Hume's *Phil. Works*, ed. 1854, iv. 243.

philosopher's philosophy. A letter was brought to him from Rousseau. The postage, in spite of his early training in 'a very rigid frugality[1],' he paid no doubt with cheerfulness and even with alacrity. His friend's prolonged silence 'he still accounted for by supposing him ashamed to write to him[2].' That feeling of shame must surely at last have given way to an outburst of gratitude, when he had learnt of the generous efforts which had been made, and successfully made, in his behalf. 'Je vous connais, Monsieur,' wrote his brother philosopher, 'et vous ne l'ignorez pas ... Touché de votre générosité, je me jette entre vos bras; vous m'amenez en Angleterre, en apparence pour m'y procurer un asyle, et en effet pour m'y déshonorer. Vous vous appliquez à cette noble œuvre avec un zèle digne de votre cœur, et avec un art digne de vos talens. Il n'en fallait pas tant pour réussir; vous vivez dans le grand monde, et moi dans la retraite ; le public aime à être trompé et vous êtes fait pour le tromper. Je connais pourtant un homme que vous ne tromperez pas, c'est vous-même[3].'

Hume, startled from his pleasing dreams, replied in a letter of manly indignation. 'You say that I myself know that I have been false to you; but I say it loudly, and will say it to the whole world, that I know the contrary, that I know my friendship towards you has been unbounded and uninterrupted, and that though instances of it have been very generally remarked both in France and England, the smallest part of it only has as yet come to the knowledge of the public. I demand that you will produce me the man who will assert the contrary; and above all, I demand that he will mention any one particular in which I have been wanting to you. You owe this to me; you owe it to yourself; you owe it to truth and honour and justice, and to everything that can be deemed sacred among men[4].' Rousseau took three weeks to rejoin, and then sent Hume his justification in an 'enormous letter[5].' He thus describes 'the very tender scene' that had passed between them[6]. 'Après le souper, gardant tous deux le silence au coin de son feu, je m'aperçois qu'il me fixe, comme il lui arrivait souvent, et d'une manière dont l'idée est difficile à rendre. Pour cette fois, son regard sec, ardent, moqueur, et prolongé devint plus qu'inquiétant. Pour m'en débarrasser, j'essayai de le fixer à mon tour; mais en arrêtant mes yeux sur les siens, je sens un frémissement inexplicable, et bientôt je suis forcé de les baisser. La physionomie et le ton du bon David sont d'un bon homme, mais où, grand Dieu ! ce bon homme emprunte-t-il les yeux dont il fixe ses amis? L'impression de ce regard me reste et m'agite ; mon trouble augmente jusqu'au saisissement: si l'épanchement n'eût succédé, j'étouffais. Bientôt un violent remords me gagne ; je m'indigne de moi-même ; enfin dans un

[1] *Ante, Autobiography.*
[2] *A Concise Account,* p. 26.
[3] *Œuvres de Rousseau,* ed. 1782, xxiv. 337.
[4] *A Concise Account,* p. 31.
[5] *A Concise Account,* p. 33.
[6] *Ante,* p. 77.

transport que je me rappelle encore avec délices, je m'élance à son cou, je le serre étroitement; suffoqué de sanglots, inondé de larmes, je m'écrie d'une voix entrecoupée : *Non, non, David Hume n'est pas un traître; s'il n'était le meilleur des hommes, il faudrait qu'il en fût le plus noir.* David Hume me rend poliment mes embrassemens, et tout en me frappant de petits coups sur le dos, me répète plusieurs fois d'un ton tranquille : *Quoi, mon cher Monsieur! Eh, mon cher Monsieur! Quoi donc, mon cher Monsieur!* Il ne me dit rien de plus; je sens que mon cœur se resserre; nous allons nous coucher, et je pars le lendemain pour la province [1].'

Hume, in that he had brought him to England, had been, Rousseau says, in some sort his protector and his patron. How he treated this patron, when once he had seen through his malicious tricks, he next shews. In this part of his narrative he closes each paragraph with words which Marmontel justly describes as 'Cette tournure de raillerie qui est le sublime de l'insolence [2].'

'Premier soufflet sur la joue de mon patron. Il n'en sent rien.'

'Second soufflet sur la joue de mon patron. Il n'en sent rien.'

'Troisième soufflet sur la joue de mon patron, et pour celui-là, s'il ne le sent pas, c'est assurément sa faute; il n'en sent rien [3].'

Voltaire in *Les honnêtetés littéraires*, published in 1767, thus ridicules this passage :—'Ah! Jean-Jacques! trois soufflets pour une pension! c'est trop!

"Tudieu, l'ami, sans nous rien dire,
    Comme vous baillez des soufflets." '

(*Amphitryon*, acte Ier.)

'Un Génevois qui donne trois soufflets à un Écossais! cela fait trembler pour les suites. Si le roi d'Angleterre avait donné la pension, sa majesté aurait eu le quatrième soufflet. C'est un homme terrible que ce Jean-Jacques [4].'

It seems astonishing to us, perhaps because we have the key to Rousseau's character, that Hume did not see that this narrative, if it bore the marks of genius, bore quite as much the marks of madness. He should have remembered old Bentley's saying :—'Depend upon it, no man was ever written down but by himself [5].' 'Que craindriez-vous?' wrote to him the Countess de Boufflers. 'Ni Rousseau, ni personne ne peut vous nuire. Vous êtes invulnérable, si vous ne vous blessez pas vous-même [6].' But Hume was wanting in that happy humour which enables a man, in the midst of the most violent attacks, to laugh at the malicious rage of his adversary. It was the same want of humour which made him take so much to heart the coarse abuse which Lord Bute's ministry brought upon the Scotch.

---

[1] *Œuvres de Rousseau*, xxiv. 354.

[2] *Œuvres de Marmontel*, ed. 1807, iii. 12.

[3] *Œuvres de Rousseau*, xxiv. 365, 367.

[4] *Œuvres de Voltaire*, ed. 1819-25, xxv. 92.

[5] Boswell's *Johnson*, v. 274.   [6] *Private Corres.* p. 194.

Johnson with half a dozen strong words would have rent the fine but flimsy web of suspicion which Rousseau had woven; and would never have troubled his head about it again. But Hume was too much troubled by his 'love of literary fame—his ruling passion,' as he himself avowed it. He and his enemy were in the very front rank of European writers; Voltaire perhaps alone equalled them in fame. Rousseau, in the days of their friendship, had addressed him as 'le plus illustre de mes contemporains dont la bonté surpasse la gloire[1].' And now, to use the words of Hume's champions, 'the news of this dispute had spread itself over Europe[2].' There was a fresh terror added. Rousseau, he says, 'who had first flattered him indirectly with the figure he was to make in his *Memoirs*, now threatened him with it.' 'A work of this nature,' Hume continues, 'both from the celebrity of the person, and the strokes of eloquence interspersed, would certainly attract the attention of the world; and it might be published either after my death, or after that of the author. In the former case, there would be nobody who could tell the story, or justify my memory. In the latter, my apology, wrote in opposition to a dead person, would lose a great deal of its authenticity[3].' The Apology was accordingly published. The justification was complete, but the end was missed. For Hume's memory, which would have proved invulnerable to the attack, has suffered from the vanity which prompted the defence. In the brief memoir which he has left us of his life we observe without surprise that he passes over in silence his quarrel with Rousseau. It may be that he was unwilling to give his enemy a chance of escaping that 'perpetual neglect and oblivion' to which he maintained that he had been consigned[4]. It is far more probable however that, like some other conquerors, he grew to be ashamed of the quarrel into which he had entered, and of the victory which he had won.

Note 6. Hume writing to Blair on July 15, 1766, expresses himself in almost the same words. He writes:—'To-day I received a letter from Rousseau, which is perfect frenzy. It would make a good eighteen-penny pamphlet; and I fancy he intends to publish it. . . . I own that I was very anxious about this affair, but this letter has totally relieved me.' Burton's *Hume*, ii. 345-6. Rousseau thus describes his letter to Lord Marischal :—'Je voudrais vous envoyer copie des lettres, mais c'est un livre pour la grosseur.' *Œuvres de Rousseau*, xxiv. 382.

Note 7. How little his mind was at ease is shewn by the very

---

[1] *Œuvres de Rousseau*, xxiv. 317.   [2] *A Concise Account*, p. vii.

[3] *Ib.* p. 92.

[4] Hume wrote to Adam Smith on Oct. 8, 1767 :—'Thus Rousseau has had the satisfaction during a time of being much talked of for his late transactions; the thing in the world he most desires; but it has been at the expense of being consigned to perpetual neglect and oblivion.' Burton's *Hume*, ii. 378.

long account of the affair which he wrote on this same 15th of July to the Countess De Boufflers. In it he says :—'I must now, my dear friend, apply to you for consolation and advice in this affair, which both distresses and perplexes me. . . . It is extremely dangerous for me to be entirely silent. He is at present composing a book, in which it is very likely he may fall on me with some atrocious lie. . . . My present intention therefore is to write a narrative of the whole affair. . . . But is it not very hard that I should be put to all this trouble, and undergo all this vexation, merely on account of my singular friendship and attention to this most atrocious scélérat ? . . . I know that I shall have Mme. de Barbantane's sympathy and compassion if she be at Paris.' Hume's *Private Corres.* p. 181.

LETTER XXVI.

Hume's Account of his Quarrel with Rousseau.

[EDINBURGH, *Oct.* 1766[1].]

DEAR S[IR],

My Friends at Paris have thought it absolutely necessary to publish an Account which I sent them, of my Transactions with Rousseau, together with the original Papers : The Affair had made a great Noise every where, and he had been such a Fool, as to write Defiances against me to all parts of Europe ; so that the Justification of my Character they thought requir'd a Publication, which, however, is very much against my Will, coud it have been prevented[2]. The whole will compose a pretty large Pamphlet, which, I fancy, the Curiosity of the Public will make tolerably saleable. I desire you to take upon you the printing and publishing of it ; and if any Profit result from it to you, I shall be very happy ; reserving the after property and Disposal of the Pamphlet to myself. You will take in what Bookseller you please[3] ; Becket[4] or Caddel[5] or any other : For Mr. Millar woud not think such a Trifle worthy of his Attention.

I shall immediatly send you up a Copy of the original

Manuscript, which is partly English, partly French; but more of the latter Language, which must be translated. I shall employ Mr. Coutt's Cover[6]. The Method the Translator must proceed is this [7]: My Friends at Paris are to send me over in a Parcel ten Copies, which will be deliverd to Miss Elliot[8]. I have desird her to send them to you; open the Parcel and take out one Copy for your own Use. Get a discreet and careful Translator[9]: Let him compare exactly the French Narration with my English: Where they agree, let him insert my English: Where they differ, let him follow the French and translate it: The Reason of this is, that I allowd my Friends at Paris to make what alterations they thought proper[10]; and I am desirous of following exactly the Paris Edition. All my Letters must be printed verbatim, conformable to the Manuscript I send you.

My Parisian Friends are to add a Preface of their own composing, which must be translated: Add, by way of Nota bene, that the Original Letters will all be deposited in the Musæum[11]. The Reason of this is, that Rousseau has been so audacious as to write, that I dare not publish his Letters without falsifying them[12].

If you think, that a Republication of the French Edition will answer the Expence, I am also willing you should do it[13].

Of the remaining nine Copies, send one to Lord Hertford, lower Grosvenor Street, another to Mr. Secretary Conway, another to Horace Walpole, Arlington Street[14], another to Lady Hervey[15], St. James Place. Send the remaining five to me by any private hand or by the Waggon.

Mr. Kincaid[16] tells me, that two Years ago he sent enclosd in a Parcel of Yours a corrected Quarto Copy of my History to be deliverd to Mr. Millar. Yet Mr. Millar told me in London that he had never seen any such thing. I suppose he has forgot and will be able to find it upon Search. Try, if you can recollect and put him in mind of it [17].

I am Dear S[r] Your most obedient humble Servant

David Hume.

Note 1. Hume returned to Edinburgh late in this summer. Millar writing to him from Kew Green, on Oct. 4, says :—'I could scold you most heartily if you were here, and so could Mrs. Millar, for breaking your appointment with friends that love you sincerely, when they had provided a turtle, and a fine haunch of forest venison for your entertainment, and to be disappointed of you and Geo. Scott two such heroes was too much, though we had tolerable heroes : both your losses was very mortifying, and I am sure to more cordial friends you could not go, though perhaps to more powerful.' Hume replied from Edinburgh, on Oct. 21 :—'I hope to be often merry with you and Mrs. Millar in your House in Pall Mall ; and I wish both of you much Health and Satisfaction in enjoying it.' *M.S.R.S.E.*

A son of Hume's friend, Baron Mure, gives the following description of the historian and Sir James Stewart on their return to Edinburgh. 'They came home from Paris about the same time. I remember, as a boy of five or six years old, being much struck with the French cut of their laced coats and bags [1], and especially with the philosopher's ponderous uncouth person equipped in a bright yellow coat spotted with black.' *Caldwell Papers*, i. 38.

Note 2. The following extracts shew the opinions formed by Hume and others as to the expediency of publication :—

Hume to Blair.

'London, July 1, 1766. I know you will pity me when I tell you that I am afraid I must publish this to the world in a pamphlet, which must contain an account of the whole transaction between us. My only comfort is that the matter will be so clear as not to leave to any mortal the smallest possibility of doubt. You know how dangerous any controversy on a disputable point would be with a man of his talents. I know not where the miscreant will now retire to, in order to hide his head from this infamy.' Burton's *Hume*, ii. 344.

Adam Smith to Hume.

'Paris, July 6. I am thoroughly convinced that Rousseau is as great a rascal as you and as every man here believes him to be ; yet let me beg of you not to think of publishing anything to the world. . . . Expose his brutal letter, but without giving it out of your own hand, so that it may never be printed ; and if you can, laugh at yourself, and I shall pawn my life that before three weeks are at an end this little affair, which at present gives you so much uneasiness, shall be understood to do you as much honour as any-

---

[1] Johnson defines *Bag* as *An ornamental purse of silk tied to men's hair.*

thing that has ever happened to you. . . . M. Turgot and I are both afraid that you are surrounded with evil counsellors, and that the advice of your English *literati*, who are themselves accustomed to publish all their little gossiping stories in newspapers, may have too much influence upon you.' *Ib.* p. 350.

Hume to the Countess de Boufflers.

'Lisle Street, July 15. This is a deliberate and a cool plan to stab me. . . . Should I give the whole account to the public, as I am advised by several of my friends, particularly Lord Hertford and General Conway, I utterly ruin this unhappy man. . . . Notwithstanding his monstrous offences towards me, I cannot resolve to commit such a piece of cruelty even against a man who has but too long deceived a great part of mankind. But on the other hand it is extremely dangerous for me to be entirely silent. He is at present composing a book in which it is very likely he may fall on me with some atrocious lie. I know that he is writing his memoirs, in which I am sure to make a fine figure. . . . My present intention is to write a narrative of the whole affair . . . to make several copies . . . to send a copy to Rousseau, and tell him in what hands the other copies are consigned; that if he can contradict any one fact he may have it in his power.' Hume ends by calling him 'this most atrocious *scélérat.*' *Private Corres.* p. 180.

D'Alembert to Voltaire.

'[Paris] 16 de juillet. Il [Hume] se prépare à donner toute cette histoire au public. Que de sottises vont dire à cette occasion tous les ennemis de la raison et des lettres ! les voilà bien à leur aise ; car ils déchireront infailliblement ou Rousseau, ou M. Hume, et peut-être tous les deux. Pour moi, je rirai, comme je fais de tout, et je tâcherai que rien ne trouble mon repos et mon bonheur.' *Œuvres de Voltaire* (ed. 1819-25), lxii. 383.

D'Alembert to Hume.

'Paris, July 21. [D'Alembert sends Hume the opinion of Turgot, Morellet, Marmontel and other friends who had met at the house of Mlle. de l'Espinasse.] 'Tous unanimement, ainsi que Mlle. de l'Espinasse et moi, sommes d'avis que vous devez donner cette histoire au public avec toutes ses circonstances.' Burton's *Hume*, ii. 354.

Horace Walpole.

'Then [towards the middle of July] arrived Rousseau's long absurd letter to Mr. Hume, which most people in England, and I amongst the rest, thought was such an answer to itself that Mr. Hume had no occasion to vindicate himself from the imputations contained in it. The *gens de lettres* at Paris, who aim at being an *order*, and who in default of parts raise a dust by their squabbles, were of a different opinion, and pressed Mr. Hume to publish on the occasion. Mr. Hume however declared he was convinced by the arguments of his friends in England, and would not engage in a controversy. Lord

Mansfield told me he was glad to hear I was of his opinion, and had dissuaded Mr. Hume from publishing.' Walpole's *Works*, ed. 1798, iv. 253.

Favart to Garrick.

'Paris, Ce 24 juillet. Tout le monde littéraire se déchaine contre le philosophe de Genève.' *Garrick Corres.* ii. 484.

The Countess de Boufflers to Hume.

'Ce 25 [Juillet] à Paris. Votre douceur, votre bonté, l'indulgence que vous avez naturellement, font attendre et désirer de vous des efforts de modération qui passent le pouvoir des hommes ordinaires. Pourquoi se hâter de divulguer les premiers mouvements d'un cœur grièvement blessé, que la raison n'a pu encore dompter? . . . Mais vous, au lieu de vous irriter contre un malheureux qui ne peut vous nuire, et qui se ruine entièrement lui-même, que n'avez-vous laissé agir cette pitié généreuse, dont vous êtes si susceptible? Vous eussiez évité un éclat qui scandalise, qui divise les esprits, qui flatte la malignité, qui amuse aux dépens de tous deux les gens oisifs et inconsidérés, qui fait faire des réflexions injurieuses, et renouvelle les clameurs contre les philosophes et la philosophie. . . . Vous ne serez pas son délateur après avoir été son protecteur. De semblables examens doivent précéder les liaisons, et non suivre les ruptures.' Hume's *Private Corres.* pp. 188–194.

Horace Walpole to Hume.

'London, July 26. Your set of literary friends are what a set of literary men are apt to be, exceedingly absurd. They hold a consistory to consult how to argue with a madman; and they think it very necessary for your character to give them the pleasure of seeing Rousseau exposed, not because he has provoked you, but them. If Rousseau prints you must; but I certainly would not till he does.' Walpole's *Works*, ed. 1798, iv. 258, and *Letters*, v. 7.

Mme. Riccoboni to Garrick.

'Paris, Ce 10 Août. La rupture de M. Hume et de Jean-Jacques a fait un bruit terrible ici. Les gens de lettres sont pour M. Hume ; et les personnes sensées ne le soupçonnent point d'avoir tort.' *Garrick Corres.* ii. 488.

Hume to the Abbé Le Blanc.

'Lisle Street, Leicester Fields, 12 of Aug. 1766. I am as great a Lover of Peace as he [Fontenelle], and have kept myself as free from all literary Quarrels : But surely, neither he nor any other Person was ever engaged in a Controversy with a Man of so much Malice, of such a profligate Disposition to Lyes, and such great Talents. It is nothing to dispute my style or my Abilities as an Historian or a Philosopher : My Books ought to answer for themselves, or they are not worth the defending. To fifty Writers, who have attacked me on this head, I never made the least Reply : But this is a different Case : Imputations are here thrown on my Morals and my Conduct; and tho' my Case is so clear as not to admit of the least Controversy, yet

it is only clear to those who know it.' *Morrison Autographs,* ii.
318.

Lord Marischal to Hume.

'Potsdam, Aug. 15. You did all in your power to serve him; his
écart afflicts me on his account more than yours, who have, I am sure,
nothing to reproach yourself with. It will be good and humane in
you, and like *Le Bon David,* not to answer.' Burton's *Hume,* ii. 354.

Hume to Adam Smith.

[No date, probably London, about the middle of August.] 'I shall
not publish them unless forced, which you will own to be a very great
degree of self-denial. My conduct in this affair would do me a great
deal of honour, and his would blast him for ever, and blast his writings at the same time; for, as these have been exalted much above
their merit, when his personal character falls they would of course
fall below their merit. I am however apprehensive that in the end I
shall be obliged to publish.' *Ib.* ii. 349.

Hume to the Marchioness de Barbantane.

'Lisle Street, Aug. 29, 1766. You will see that the only possible
alleviation of this man's crime is that he is entirely mad; and even
then he will be allowed a dangerous and pernicious madman, and of
the blackest and most atrocious mind. The King and Queen of
England expressed a strong desire to see these papers, and I was
obliged to put them into their hand. They read them with avidity,
and entertain the same sentiments that must strike every one.
The king's opinion confirms me in the resolution not to give them to
the public, unless I be forced to it by some attack on the side of my
adversary, which it will therefore be wisdom in him to avoid.' *Private
Corres.* p. 210.

Rousseau to Lord Marischal.

'[Wooton] 7 Septembre. Il [Hume] a marché jusqu'ici dans les
ténèbres, il s'est caché, mais maintenant il se montre à découvert.
Il a rempli l'Angleterre, la France, les gazettes, l'Europe entière,
de cris auxquels je ne sais que répondre, et d'injures dont je me
croirais digne si je daignais les repousser.' *Œuvres de Rousseau,*
xxiv. 393.

Voltaire to Damilaville.

'[Ferney] 15 Octobre. Il [Hume] prouve que Jean-Jacques est un
maître fou, et un ingrat pétri d'un sot orgueil; mais je ne crois pas
que ces vérités méritent d'être publiées; il faut que les choses soient
ou bien plaisantes, ou bien intéressantes pour que la presse s'en mêle.
. . . Je pense que la publicité de cette querelle ne servirait qu'à faire
tort à la philosophie. J'aurais donné une partie de mon bien pour
que Rousseau eût été un homme sage; mais cela n'est pas dans sa
nature; il n'y a pas moyen de faire un aigle d'un papillon: c'est
assez, ce me semble, que tous les gens de lettres lui rendent justice,
et d'ailleurs sa plus grande punition est d'être oublié.' *Œuvres de
Voltaire,* liii. 492.

Baron Grimm.

'Paris, 15 Octobre, 1766. Il y a environ trois mois qu'on reçut à Paris les premières nouvelles de la brouillerie de J.-J. Rousseau avec M. Hume. Excellente pâture pour les oisifs! Aussi une déclaration de guerre entre deux grandes puissances de l'Europe n'aurait pu faire plus de bruit que cette querelle. Je dis à Paris; car à Londres, où il y a des acteurs plus importans à siffler, on sut à peine la rupture survenue entre l'ex-citoyen de Genève et le philosophe d'Écosse; et les Anglais furent assez sots pour s'occuper moins de cette grande affaire que de la formation du nouveau ministère et du changement du grand nom de Pitt en celui de Comte de Chatam (sic).' *Correspondance Littéraire de Grimm et de Diderot,* ed. 1829, v. 191. (Grimm adds that several of Hume's friends in France wrote to him for no other purpose but to dissuade him from making the quarrel public. *Ib.* p. 193.)

Voltaire to Hume.

'Ferney, 24 Octobre. A dire vrai, monsieur, toutes ces petites misères ne méritent pas qu'on s'en occupe deux minutes; tout cela tombe bientôt dans un éternel oubli. . . . Il y a des sottises et des querelles dans toutes les conditions de la vie. . . . Tout passe rapidement comme les figures grotesques de la lanterne magique. . . . Les détails des guerres les plus sanglantes périssent avec les soldats qui en ont été les victimes. Les critiques mêmes des pièces de théâtre nouvelles, et surtout leurs éloges sont ensevelis le lendemain dans le néant avec elles et avec les feuilles périodiques qui en parlent. Il n'y a que les dragées du sieur Kaiser qui se soient un peu soutenues.' *Œuvres de Voltaire,* liii. 503.

Hume to Horace Walpole.

'Edinburgh, Nov. 4. I would give anything to prevent a publication in London (for surely the whole affair will appear perfectly ridiculous); but I am afraid that a book printed at Paris will be translated in London, if there be hopes of selling a hundred copies of it. For this reason, I fancy it will be better for me to take care that a proper edition be published.' Walpole's *Works,* iv. 262.

Horace Walpole to Hume.

'[London] Nov. 6. You say your Parisian friends *extorted* your consent to this publication. I believe so. Your good sense could not approve what your good heart could not refuse. You add, that they told you *Rousseau had sent letters of defiance against you all over Europe.* Good God! my dear Sir, could you pay any regard to such fustian? All Europe laughs at being dragged every day into these idle quarrels, with which Europe only [the rest of the sentence is too coarse for quotation]. Your friends talk as loftily as of a challenge between Charles the Fifth and Francis the First. What are become of all the controversies since the days of Scaliger and Scioppius of Billingsgate memory? Why they sleep in oblivion, till some Bayle drags them out of their dust, and takes mighty pains to ascertain the date of each author's death, which is of no more consequence to the world than the

day of his birth.   Many a country squire quarrels with his neighbour
about game and manors, yet they never print their wrangles, though
as much abuse passes between them as if they could quote all the
Philippics of the learned [1].'   Walpole's *Letters*, v. 23.

Bishop Warburton to Hurd.

'Prior Park, Nov. 15, 1766.   As to Rousseau I entirely agree with
you that his long letter to his brother philosopher, Hume, shews him
to be a frank lunatic.   His passion of tears—his suspicion of his
friends in the midst of their services—and his incapacity of being set
right, all consign him to Monro [2].   You give the true cause too of this
excess of frenzy, which breaks out on all occasions, the honest neglect
of our countrymen in their tribute to his importance. . . . The merits
of the two philosophers are soon adjusted.   There is an immense
distance between their natural genius; none at all in their excessive
vanity. . . . However the *contestation* is very amusing; and I shall be
very sorry if it stops now it is in so good a train.   I should be well
pleased particularly to see so seraphic a madman attack so insuffer-
able a coxcomb as Walpole; and I think they are only fit for one
another.'   *Letters from a late Eminent Prelate*, p. 385.

Hume to Horace Walpole.

'Edinburgh, Nov. 20.   I readily agree with you that it is a great
misfortune to be reduced to the necessity of consenting to this publication; but it had certainly become necessary.   Even those who at
first joined me in rejecting all idea of it wrote to me and represented
that this strange man's defiances had made such impression, that I
should pass universally for the guilty person, if I suppressed the
story. . . . I never consented to anything with greater reluctance in
my life.   Had I found one man of my opinion I should have persevered in my refusal. . . . I am as sensible as you are of the ridicule
to which men of letters have exposed themselves by running every
moment to the public with all their private squabbles and alterca-
tions; but surely there has been something very unexpected and
peculiar in this affair.   My antagonist by his genius, his singularities,
his quackery, his misfortunes and his adventures, had become more
the subject of general conversation in Europe (for I venture again on
the word) than any person in it.   I do not even except Voltaire, much

---

[1] Walpole, writing from Paris on Nov. 21, 1765, had spoken with scorn both of
Hume and Rousseau.   ' I desire,' he says, ' to die when I have nobody left to laugh
with me.   I have never yet seen or heard anything serious that was not ridiculous.
Jesuits, Methodists, philosophers, politicians, the hypocrite Rousseau, the scoffer
Voltaire, the encyclopedists, the Humes, the Lytteltons, the Grenvilles, the atheist
tyrant of Prussia, and the mountebank of history, Mr. Pitt, all are to me impostors
in their various ways.'   Walpole's *Letters*, iv. 441.

[2]   ' Sure I should want the care of ten Monroes.'

Pope, *Imitations of Horace*, 2 Epist. ii. 70.
Monroe was Physician to Bedlam Hospital.

less the King of Prussia and Mr. Pitt.' Walpole's *Works* (ed. 1798), iv. 266.

Hume to the Countess de Boufflers.

'Edinburgh, Dec. 2. It was with infinite reluctance I consented to the last publication. I lay my account that many people will condemn me for it, and will question the propriety or necessity of it; but, if I had not published, many people would have condemned me as a calumniator and as a treacherous and false friend. There is no comparison between these species of blame; and I underwent the one to save me from the other.' *Private Corres.* p. 229.

Note 3. Strahan, I think, had no shop. His chief business was that of a printer, but he was also a publisher. In that capacity he would need to 'take in a Bookseller' as his partner in the venture. Thus Johnson's *Political Tracts* bear at the foot of the title page :— 'Printed for W. Strahan; and T. Cadell in the Strand.' While Cadell's address is given, Strahan's is not.

Note 4. It was published by Becket and his partner under the following title :—*A Concise and Genuine Account of the Dispute between Mr. Hume and Mr. Rousseau; with the Letters that passed between them during their Controversy. As also the Letters of the Hon. Mr. Walpole and Mr. D'Alembert, relative to this extraordinary Affair. Translated from the French. London. Printed for T. Becket and P. A. De Hondt, near Surry-street, in the Strand. MDCCLXVI.* Becket was the publisher of *Ossian*, and, it should seem, not over-scrupulous. 'What does Becket mean,' wrote Boswell, 'by the *Originals* of Fingal and other poems of Ossian, which he advertises to have lain in his shop?' Boswell's *Johnson*, ii. 294.

Note 5. Thomas Cadell was born at Bristol in 1742. In 1758 he was apprenticed to Andrew Millar. In 1765 he became his partner, and in 1767 his successor. In conjunction with Strahan he published the *Histories* of Robertson and Gibbon, the later editions of Hume's *Works*, and some of the later *Works* of Johnson. They were part proprietors also of Blackstone's *Commentaries*. Gibbon described him as 'that honest and liberal bookseller.' Stewart's *Robertson*, p. 366. It was at his house that the dinner was given, at which Hume, by his own request, met 'as many of the persons who had written against him as could be collected.' Rogers's *Table Talk*, p. 106. In 1793 he retired, 'leaving the business which he had established, as the first in Great Britain,' to his son Thomas, and to William Davies. In 1798 he was elected Alderman of Walbrook Ward. He died on Dec. 27, 1802. See Nichols's *Lit. Anec.* iii. 388, 696; vi. 441; and *Dict. of Nat. Biog.* viii. 179. He was not related to Scott's publisher, Robert Cadell of Edinburgh, though it was 'from the respectable house of Cadell and Davies in the Strand, that appeared in the course of January 1802, the first two volumes of the *Minstrelsy*, which may be said to have first introduced

Scott as an original writer to the English public.' Lockhart's *Scott*,
ed. 1839, ii. 79.

Note 6. James Coutts, a banker in the Strand, was member for
Edinburgh City (*Parl. Hist.* xv. 1099), and so could frank letters. He
wrote to Hume, probably soon after his election in 1762, a modest
letter in which he complains of his unfitness for his new position.
He says :—'With all pleasures there are great mixtures of mortification, and every instant my limited education stares me more and
more in the face. I have hardly lookt on any but Manuscript folios
since I was 14. You'll say from idleness or want of taste. I say no,
but from too much business and bad health. My constitution will
probably be always unfit for deep study ; but pray is there no
remedying this great defect a little without much study, for rather
as (*sic*) suffer such mortifications I had better continue a Banker
still, which I'm convinced would enable me better to purchase Merse
Acres. But seriously I wish you would give me some advice on this
head, what abridgements to read, &c.' In another letter to Hume
(also undated) he writes :—'Coll. Graeme and Mr. Drummond Blair
are candidates for Perthshire ; the former will carry it unless the
Pretender dies, and leaves some old fools at liberty to take the oaths.'
M.S.R.S.E.

Note 7. Hume sent Strahan a copy of the manuscript which he
had placed in the hands of his French friends for publication in
France. It contained his own narrative, and such part of his correspondence with Rousseau as he had preserved. Rousseau's letters
to him were in French, and his to Rousseau in English. Each of the
translators therefore had but a portion of the document to translate.
The French editors, however, had his leave to make whatever
alterations in his account they pleased. All these alterations are,
he says, to be adopted, and his own narrative in such passages is
not to be followed. In his next letter he gives contrary directions ;
for by that time he had seen the Paris editions and been displeased
with some of the changes. His French translator was Suard, who
translated Robertson's *Charles V* (Stewart's *Robertson*, p. 218).
Gibbon, writing in 1776 about the first volume of his *Decline and Fall*,
which had lately appeared, says :—'To-morrow I write to Suard,
a very skilful translator of Paris, who was here in the spring with
the Neckers, to get him (if not too late) to undertake it.' Gibbon's
Misc. Works, ii. 176. It was, no doubt, at this visit to London that
'Suard at Reynolds's saw Burke for the first time, when Johnson
touched him on the shoulder, and said, "Le grand Burke."' Boswell's *Johnson*, iv. 20, *n.* 1. When in 1774 he was admitted into the
French Academy, Voltaire wrote to him :—'Je vais relire votre
Discours pour la quatrième fois.' *Œuvres de Voltaire*, lvi. 387. It
was to him that Mrs. Montagu made her clever reply, when Voltaire's
'invective' against Shakespeare was read at the Academy. He said
to her :—'Je crois, Madame, que vous êtes un peu fâchée de ce que

vous venez d'entendre.' She replied, 'Moi, Monsieur, point du tout!
Je ne suis pas amie de M. Voltaire.' Walpole's *Letters*, vi. 394.

Note 8. 'I shall lodge in Miss Elliot's, Lisle Street, Leicester
Fields,' Hume wrote on June 29, 1761. Burton's *Hume*, ii. 90. She
was, I fancy, the lady for whose creature comforts he wished to
provide in a letter written from London on May 15, 1759. 'If you
pass by Edinburgh, please bring me two pounds of rapee, such
as Peggy Elliot uses to take. You will get it at Gillespy's near
the Cross.' The letter which thus begins with Peggy Elliot and her
snuff ends with compliments to Adam Smith, and from Dr. Warburton. *Ib.* p. 62. She is again mentioned in an amusing letter
dated July 6 of the same year, in which Hume shows his imagination
in inventing extravagant news. 'Miss Elliot,' he writes, 'yesterday
morning declared her Marriage with Dr. Armstrong [the Poet]; but
we were surprised in the afternoon to find Mr. Short, the Optician,
come in and challenge her for his Wife. It seems she has been
married privately for some time to both of them.' *M.S.R.S.E.*
No doubt she was a decent elderly body, the last person to give
grounds for any scandal.

Note 9. The English translator was scarcely up to his work, as
the following passages show.

'Comme tout est mêlé d'inconvéniens dans la vie, celui d'être trop
bien est un de ceux qui se tolèrent le plus aisément.' *Œuvres de
Rousseau*, xxiv. 323.

'As there is nothing in life without its inconvenience, that of being
too good is one. of those which is the most tolerable.' *A Concise
Account*, p. 15.

'Peu de temps après notre arrivée à Londres, j'y remarquai dans
les esprits à mon égard un changement sourd qui bientôt devint
très-sensible.' *Œuvres de Rousseau*, xxiv. 348.

'A very short time after our arrival in London I observed an
absurd change in the minds of the people regarding me, which soon
became very apparent.' *A Concise Account.* p. 42.

Note 10. With some of these alterations Hume was displeased.
Writing to Horace Walpole he says:—'Several passages in my
narrative in which I mention you are all altered in the translation,
and rendered much less obliging than I wrote them.' He suspected
D'Alembert of having had this done through malevolence towards
Walpole. Walpole's *Works*, ed. 1798, iv. 262, 7.

Note 11. Hume wrote to the Librarian of the British Museum on
Jany. 23, 1767:—'I was obliged to say in my Preface that the
originals would be consigned in the Museum. I hope you have
no objection to the receiving them. I send them by my friend
Mr. Ramsay. Be so good as to give them the corner of any drawer.
I fancy few people will trouble you by desiring a sight of them.'
The Trustees refused to accept them. Dr. Maty wrote to Hume
on April 22 :—'I longed to have some conversation with you on the

subject of the papers, which were remitted to me by the hands of Mr. Ramsay, and, as our Trustees did not think proper to receive them, to restore them into yours.' They are in the possession of the Royal Society of Edinburgh. Burton's *Hume*, ii. 359–360. Dr. Maty was Under-Librarian of the Museum. He became Principal Librarian in 1772. Knight's *Eng. Cyclo. of Biog.* iv. 153. Perhaps the refusal to receive the papers was due to idleness. The Librarian may have dreaded troublesome visitors. How badly the Museum was managed eighteen years later is shown by W. Hutton in his *Journey to London*, p. 114. He paid two shillings for a ticket of admission, and was then 'hackneyed through the rooms with violence,' being allowed just thirty minutes to see everything.

Note 12. 'Wooton, le 2 Août. M. Hume écrit, dit-on, qu'il veut publier toutes les pièces relatives à cette affaire. C'est, j'en réponds, ce qu'il se gardera de faire, ou ce qu'il se gardera bien au moins de faire fidèlement. . . . Plus je pense à la publication promise par M. Hume, moins je puis concevoir qu'il l'exécute. S'il l'ose faire, à moins d'énormes falsifications, je prédis hardiment, que malgré son extrême adresse et celle de ses amis, sans même que je m'en mêle, M. Hume est un homme démasqué. Rousseau to M. Guy. *Œuvres de Rousseau*, ed. 1782, xxiv. 387.

The following is the note which was added to the translation of the pamphlet :—' The original letters of both parties will be lodged in the British Museum ; on account of the above-mentioned defiance of Mr. Rousseau, and his subsequent insinuation that if they should be published they would be falsified.' *A Concise Account*, p. viii.

Note 13. It was published under the title of *Exposé succinct de la contestacion qui s'est élevée entre M. Hume et M. Rousseau, avec les pièces justificatives*. Londres, 1766, 12°. *British Museum Catalogue*.

Note 14. 'I was born,' writes Horace Walpole, 'in Arlington Street, near St. James's, London, September 24, 1717, O. S.' *Letters*, i. lxi. Writing on Dec. 1, 1768, he says :—'From my earliest memory Arlington Street has been the ministerial street. The Duke of Grafton is actually coming into the house of Mr. Pelham, which my Lord President is quitting, and which occupies too the ground on which my father lived ; and Lord Weymouth has just taken the Duke of Dorset's.' *Ib.* v. 136. On Nov. 6, 1766, having received Hume's pamphlet, he wrote to him :—'You have, I own, surprised me by suffering your quarrel with Rousseau to be printed, contrary to your determination when you left London, and against the advice of all your best friends here ; I may add, contrary to your own nature, which has always inclined you to despise literary squabbles, the jest and scorn of all men of sense. . . . You have acted, as I should have expected if you *would* print, with sense, temper, and decency ; and, what is still more uncommon, with your usual modesty. I cannot say so much for your editors. But editors and commentators are seldom modest. Even to this day that race ape the dictatorial tone of commentators at the restoration of learning, when the mob thought that Greek and Latin could give men the sense which they wanted in their native languages. But *Europe*[1] is grown a little wiser, and holds these magnificent pretensions now in proper contempt.' *Ib.* v. 23.

Note 15. Lady Hervey was the widow of John, Lord Hervey, whom Pope, in the *Prologue to the Satires* (l. 305), attacked as Sporus with a brutality that defeated itself. Her brother-in-law was 'Harry Hervey,' of whom Johnson said :—'He was a vicious man, but very kind to me. If you call a dog Hervey I shall love him.' Boswell's *Johnson*, i. 106. She was the Mary Lepell whom Pope introduces in his *Answer to the Question of Mrs. Howe, What is prudery ?*

> ''Tis an ugly envious shrew,
> That rails at dear Lepell and you.'
>
> Elwin and Courthorpe's *Pope*, iv. 447.

Mr. Croker (*Memoirs of Lord Hervey*, i. xxiv.) quotes the following verse from a ballad on her :—

> 'For Venus had never seen bedded
> So perfect a beau and a belle,
> As when *Hervey the handsome* was wedded
> To the beautiful *Molly Lepell.*'

Swift wrote to Arbuthnot on Nov. 8, 1726 :—'I gave your service to Lady Harvey. She is in a little sort of a miff about a ballad that was writ on her to the tune of *Molly Mogg*, and sent to her in the name of a begging poet.' Swift's *Works*, ed. 1803, xvii. 97.

Horace Walpole, writing to her from Paris on Sept. 14, 1765, says :—'Mr. Hume, that is *the Mode*, asked much about your Ladyship.' *Letters*, iv. 405. It was Hume very likely who lent her Home's tragedy over which she wept, as Scott tells us in his review of that poet's *Works* :—'We have the evidence of the accomplished Earl of Haddington, that he remembers the celebrated Lady Hervey (the beautiful Molly Lapelle of Pope and Gay) weeping like an infant over the manuscript of *Douglas.*' *Quarterly Review*, lxxi. 204. On Sept. 22, 1768, Walpole mentioning her death, says :—'She is a great loss to several persons ; her house was one of the most agreeable in London ; and her own friendliness, good breeding and amiable temper had attached all that knew her. Her sufferings with the gout and rheumatism were terrible, and yet never could affect her patience or divert her attention to her friends.' *Letters*, v. 129.

Note 16. Alexander Kincaid, Printer and Stationer to his Majesty for Scotland, died on Jany. 21, 1777, in his year of office as Lord Provost of Edinburgh. *Gent. Mag.* 1777, p. 48. Dr. Blair wrote to Strahan on Jany. 28, 1777 :—'I am just come from the burials of our

---

[1] Walpole in italicising *Europe* refers to Hume's statement that 'Rousseau had sent letters of defiance all over Europe.' *Ante*, pp. 90, 91.

friend poor Kincaid. He was interred with all the public honours which could be given him; and his funeral was indeed the most numerous and magnificent procession I ever saw here. The whole inhabitants were either attendants or spectators.' *Barker MSS.*

Sir Alexander Dick, writing to Joseph Spence in 1762, says that Kincaid, who had been dining at his house, 'mentioned freely that the bulk of the clergy of this country [Scotland] buy few books, except what they have absolute necessity for.' Spence's *Anecdotes*, ed. 1820, p. 463. This is some confirmation of Johnson's attack on 'the ignorance of the Scotch clergy.' Boswell's *Johnson*, v. 251.

Note 17. Hume, writing to Millar from Paris on April 23, 1764, about a new edition of his *History*, says :—' You were in the wrong to make any edition without informing me ; because I left in Scotland a copy very fully corrected with a few alterations, which ought to have been followed. I shall write to my sister to send it to you.' Burton's *Hume*, ii. 201. On Oct. 21, 1766, he wrote to him :— 'Kincaid sent you the corrected copy in a parcel of Strahan's. This circumstance is entered by Kincaid in his minute book of 16 of Oct. 1764. When in London I asked you about this copy, and you told me that you had never heard of it. I suppose this is only a defect of memory. . . . If you recover it, be so good as to send it me by the wagon.' *M.S.R.S.E.* Hume seems to imply that Millar was not telling the truth. Later on he learnt that on another matter he had lied to him (*post*, Letter of March 19, 1773). On Nov. 2 Millar replied that he had the corrected copy. *M.S.R.S.E.*

LETTER XXVII.

Further Directions about printing the Pamphlet.

DEAR SⁱR

I have receiv'd by the Post a Copy of the Paris Edition of the Pamphlet I mention'd to you. I wish it were possible not to print an Edition in London, because the whole Affair will appear perfectly ridiculous[1] to the English : But as I am afraid this is impossible, I believe it is better for me to take care, that a true Edition be printed. I committ that matter to your Care.

Contrary to my former Directions, I now desire you not to follow the Paris Edition in my Narrative ; but exactly the English Copy which I sent you in Manuscript[2]. There is

only one Passage, where I desire a Sentence to be inserted :
It is a little before the Copy of the King of Prussia's letter
to Rousseau[3].   I there say, 'But I little expected, at the
Distance of 150 Miles[4] and employing myself constantly in
his Service, to be the Victim of his Rage and Malevolence.'
Add, 'An Incident happened about this time, which set
this Disposition of M. Rousseau in a full Light.   There
had been a feigned Letter of the King of Prussias,' etc.[5]

There is a very material Note, ommitted by the Editors
of the Paris Edition, which I desire you to insert.   I send
you a Copy of it, with Directions for inserting it[6].   I
suppose all along, that you have receivd the Paris Edition
by this time :   Otherwise I woud have sent it you.

I am D[r] S[ir] Yours sincerely

DAVID HUME.

EDINBURGH, 4 *of Nov.*, 1766.

P.S.—I need not tell you that Rousseau's long Letter to
me is to be translated from the Paris Edition with all the
Notes.   The other Letters may be translated indifferently
either from that Edition or from my Manuscript.

Note 1.   He used the same words in the letter that he wrote to
Horace Walpole on the same day.   See *ante*, p. 90.

Note 2.   He apologises to Walpole for the omission in the Paris
edition of a compliment to his 'usual politeness and humanity.'   He
continues :—'I have wrote to Becket the bookseller to restore this
passage, which is so conformable to my real sentiments; but whether
my orders have come in time, I do not know as yet.'   Walpole's
Works, iv. 267.

Note 3.   See *ante*, p. 77.

Note 4.   Hume was at that time in London, and Rousseau at
Wooton in Derbyshire.

Note 5.   This insertion was not made.

Note 6.   Rousseau had charged Hume with opening his letters.
Œuvres de Rousseau, xxiv. 354.   Hume, in a note on this, says :—'The
story of M. Rousseau's letters is as follows.   He had often been
complaining to me, and with reason, that he was ruined by postage
at Neuf-chatel, which commonly cost him twenty-five or twenty-six
louis d'ors a year, and all for letters which were of no significance,
being wrote, some of them by people who took that opportunity of

abusing him, and most of them by persons unknown to him.   He was therefore resolved, he said, in England to receive no letters which came by the post. . . . When he went to Chiswick the postman brought his letters to me.   I carried him out a cargo of them.   He exclaimed, desired me to return the letters and recover the price of postage.   I told him that, in that case, the clerks of the Post Office were entire masters of his letters.   He said he was indifferent, they might do with them what they pleased.   I added that he would by that means be cut off from all correspondence with all his friends. He replied, that he would give a particular direction to such as he desired to correspond with.   But till his instructions for that purpose could arrive, what could I do more friendly than to save at my own expense his letters from the curiosity and indiscretion of the clerks of the Post Office?   I am indeed ashamed to find myself obliged to discover such petty circumstances.'   *A Concise Account*, p. 51.   In the French translation, instead of this note the following is given :—' Ces imputations d'indiscrétion et d'infidélité sont si odieuses, et les preuves en sont si ridicules, que je me crois dispensé d'y répondre.' P. 68.

LETTER XXVIII.

Millar's Complaint of Neglect.

DEAR Sᴵᴿ

I had a Letter from Mr. Millar, complaining of my giving to any other besides him the Publication of my Account of this ridiculous Affair, between Rousseau and me[1].   I am certainly in the wrong, not to have conjoind him, if I coud have imagind, that he woud have thought it worthy of his Attention.   I wish you may find it worth while; but I fancy 500 Copies will be more than sufficient to gratify the Curiosity of the Public[2].   It is necessity, not choice, that forces me on this Publication.

If it be not too late, add the following short Note to Page 59 of the Paris Edition, at these words: Des ce moment les imprimés ne parlerent plus de moi que d'une maniere equivoque ou malhonnete.   *So then, I find I am to answer for every Article of every Magazine and Newspaper printed in England*[3]:   *I assure Mr. Rousseau I woud rather answer for every Robbery committed on the high way; and I*

am entirely as innocent of the one as the other.   If you have
already printed the Page to which this Note refers, print
the Note apart, as an Ommission or Erratum[4].   I doubt
not but you have already got the Paris Edition otherwise
I coud send it you.

I am Yours etc.

D. H.

_____

Note 1.   Millar wrote to Hume on Nov. 2 :—'I will tell you honestly
that I was much hurt yesterday with yours to Mr. Strahan which he
showed me when in Town about Messrs. Beckett or Cadell being
employed by you in publishing this absurd dispute of Rousseau with
you, as you imagined it would not be worth my *while*.   Can you
imagine anything however so trifling in which your name is concerned
not worth my while?   Surely [?] I never did.   Dr. Lowth thought
differently in a more delicate affair and even one less in point of
value[1].   In truth the money that will be got I do not value but in the
the eye of the World where I have so cordial a friendship, to see
others names and not mine looks as you were offended.'

Hume sent the following reply; misdating it Oct. 8; it is endorsed
by Millar, 'David Hume's 8 Nov. 1766':—

'Your letter gave me a great deal of Uneasyness, by letting me see,
that I had, innocently and undesignedly given you Uneasyness.   I
assure you, that I believe I have made a very trifling Present to Mr.
Strahan and what will scarce be worth his Acceptance.   I fancy, that
500 Copies of the Account of that ridiculous Affair between Rousseau
and me will be more than sufficient to satisfy the Curiosity of the
Public at London.   The Pamphlet will not appear as coming from my
hand but as a Translation of the Paris Edition; and as Becket has
commonly the first Copies of French Books, it will be thought quite
natural to come from his Press.   If I had imagin'd, that it woud have
given you the least satisfaction to be the Publisher it shoud never
have been sent to any other hand.'

On Nov. 22, Millar wrote that he 'had asked Strahan to have his
namé put to the translation of the pamphlet, as people thought that
there was some difference between himself and Hume.   Strahan
agreed, but Becket refused.'   He adds that 3000 copies of the *History*
had been sold in the last three years, and 'between 20 and 30 sets
this and last week.'   *M.S.R.S.E.*

Note 2.   The pamphlet is in the list of books published in November
of this year, *Gent. Mag.* 1766, p. 545.   I cannot find that it reached a
second edition.

Note 3.   Rousseau, after describing how well he had been received

_____

[1] Millar published for Lowth in 1759 *An Answer to an Anonymous Letter to
Dr. Lowth, concerning the Late Election of a Warden of Winchester College.*

on his arrival in England, continues :—' Tout-à-coup, et sans aucune cause assignable, ce ton change, mais si fort et si vite que dans tous les caprices du public, on n'en voit guères de plus étonnant.   Le signal fut donné dans un certain *Magasin*, aussi plein d'inepties que de mensonges, où l'Auteur bien instruit, ou feignant de l'être, me donnait pour fils de Musicien.   Dès ce moment les imprimés ne parlèrent plus de moi que d'une manière équivoque ou malhonnête.' He goes on to hint that the change was due to Hume. *Œuvres de Rousseau*, xxiv. 348. According to Lord Charlemont the change was due to a very simple and natural cause :—' When Rousseau first arrived in London, he and his Armenian dress were followed by crowds, and as long as this species of admiration lasted he was contented and happy.   But in London such sights are only the wonder of the day, and in a very short time he was suffered to walk where he pleased, unattended, unobserved.   From that instant his discontent may be dated.' *Memoirs of the Earl of Charlemont*, i. 230.

Note 4.   It was printed as an erratum.

LETTER XXIX.

Further Directions about Printing the Pamphlet.

DEAR SIR

As I have not heard from you ; I suspect that you have not yet got the Paris Edition of my Pamphlet.   I have therefore sent you the Manuscript of Rousseau's long Letter with all the Notes such as I wish them to be printed ; excepting the Note which I sent you in a Paper apart, and which must be inserted.   Mr. Rousseau's Notes must be printed in Italics to distinguish them from mine [1] ; and you must advertise the Reader of this Precaution, in order to prevent Confusion.   Even tho' you shoud have got the Paris Edition rather follow the Manuscript, if it be not too late.   The Paris Editors have added a Preface and a Declaration of M. D'Alembert [2], and a Latin Motto [3] at the End.   You must not publish the Pamphlet without these.   If you have not got that Edition I shall send it you ; tho' I wish you coud rather get it in London.

I am Dear Sᵣ Yours sincerely

DAVID HUME.

13 *Novr.*, 1766.

Note 1.   They were distinguished, not by italics, but by the author's name at the end of each note.

Note 2.   Rousseau had accused D'Alembert of being the author of the letter from the King of Prussia and of maintaining a secret correspondence with Hume.   D'Alembert denied both one and the other.   *A Concise Account*, p. 94.

Note 3.   'Perdidi beneficium.   Numquid quae consecravimus perdidisse nos dicimus?   Inter consecrata beneficium est; etiamsi male respondit, bene collocatum.   Non est ille qualem speravimus; simus nos quales fuimus ei dissimiles.'   Seneca, *De Beneficiis*, lib. vii. cap. 19.   *Ib.* p. 93.

LETTER XXX.

Complaints of Strahan's Negligence.

Nothing coud more surprize me, Dear Strahan, than your Negligence with regard to this silly Pamphlet I sent you.   You have never been at the Pains once to answer one of my Letters with regard to it; tho' certainly I intended you a Friendship by sending it to you: You never informd me, that Becket had got over a Copy from Paris: You have never conveyd any of my Directions to the English Translator; but the greatest Enormity of all, and what covers me with Shame and Confusion, is your printing the Name of two Ladies, who had expressly forbid it; and that under Pretence, that the same Reason did not hold for concealing them in London as in Paris: As if it were impossible, that any Piece of Intelligence coud pass from the one Place to the other.   How your Compositor came so much as to know the Name of Md^e de Boufflers I cannot so much as imagine: He has surely read it thro my Razure and so has inserted it.   What do you think of that Practice?   I have scarce met with anything that has given me more Displeasure [1].

I am Dear Sir Your most obedient Servant

DAVID HUME.

EDINBURGH, 25 *of Nov.*, 1766.

Note 1. Rousseau in his letter of Dec. 4, 1765, quoted in Hume's narrative, says :—'It is the advice also of Madam . . . .' On which there is the following footnote :—'The person here mentioned desired her name might be suppressed. *French editor.* As the motive to the suppression of the lady's name can hardly be supposed to extend to this country, the *English translator* takes the liberty to mention the name of the Marchioness de Verdelin.' *A Concise Account,* p. 6. Mde. de Boufflers is mentioned on p. 86 as one of Hume's correspondents. Writing to her on Dec. 2, 1766, he says :— 'I had erased your name ; but it seems not so but that it was legible ; and it is accordingly printed. The bookseller, the printer, and the compositor all throw the blame on each other for this accident.' *Private Corres.* p. 230.

Grimm writing on Oct. 15, 1766 says :—'Les personnes dont les noms sont supprimés dans ce procès sont madame la comtesse de Boufflers et madame la marquise de Verdelin.' *Corres. Lit.* v. 197.

LETTER XXXI.

Hume's Occupations as Under Secretary.

[Spring of 1767.]

DEAR SIR

I was sorry not to be at home, when you did me the Favour to call on me the other day : My occupations [1] prevent my calling on you : But if you be any day at this End of the Town, the best way is to call on me at Mr. Conway's House, where I am every forenoon [2], and commonly between 10 and 3 : It is in little Warwick Street [3] : You'll do me a Pleasure in allowing me at any time half an hour's Conversation with you.

I am Dear Sir Yours sincerely

DAVID HUME.

Friday, Forenoon [4].

Note 1. Hume wrote to the Countess de Boufflers from London on March 1, 1767 :—'There has happened, dear Madam, a small change in my situation and fortune since I wrote to you. I was then very deeply immersed in study, and thought of nothing but of retreat and indolence for the rest of my life, when I was surprised with a letter from Lord Hertford, urging me to come to London, and accept of the office of Depute-Secretary of State under his brother [General

Conway]. As my Lord knew that this step was contrary to the maxims which I had laid down to myself, he engaged my Lady Hertford to write me at the same time, and to inform me how much she and my Lord desired my compliance. I sat down once or twice to excuse myself; but I own, I could not find terms to express my refusal of a request made by persons to whose friendship I had been so much obliged. . . . I do not suspect myself at my years, and after such established habits of retreat, of being ensnared by this glimpse of Court favour to commence a new course of life, and relinquish my literary ambition for the pursuit of riches and honours in the state. On the contrary, I feel myself at present like a banished man in a strange country; I mean, not as I was while with you at Paris, but as I should be in Westphalia or Lithuania or any place the least to my fancy in the world.' *Private Corres.* p. 235. Horace Walpole writes in his *Memoirs of the Reign of George III*, ii. 414 :—' It happened at this period [Feb. 1767] that Mr. Conway, who talked of nothing but resigning, became in want of a secretary, William Burke quitting his service to follow his cousin Edmund into Opposition. My surprise was very great when Mr. Conway declared his resolution of making David Hume, the historian, who had served his brother, Lord Hertford, in the same capacity at Paris, his secretary. [Walpole's surprise was not so much at the appointment of Hume, as at the indication it gave that Conway had no intention to resign.] . . . I was pleased with the designation of Hume, as it would give jealousy to the Rockinghams, who had not acted wisely in letting Burke detach himself from Mr. Conway; and I prevailed on Lady Hertford to write a second letter, more pressing than her lord's, to Mr. Hume to accept. The philosopher did not want much entreaty.'

Hume in a letter to Blair dated April 1, 1767, thus describes his occupations :—' My way of life here is very uniform, and by no means disagreeable. I pass all the forenoon in the Secretary's house from ten till three, where there arrive from time to time messengers that bring me all the secrets of the Kingdom, and indeed of Europe, Asia, Africa and America. I am seldom hurried; but have leisure at intervals to take up a book, or write a private letter, or converse with any friend that may call for me ; and from dinner to bed-time is all my own. If you add to this that the person [General Conway] with whom I have the chief, if not only transactions, is the most reasonable, equal-tempered, and gentleman-like man imaginable, and Lady Aylesbury [the General's wife] the same, you will certainly think I have no reason to complain ; and I am far from complaining. I only shall not regret when my duty is over, because to me the situation can lead to nothing, at least in all probability; and reading and sauntering and lounging and dosing, which I call thinking, is my supreme happiness. I mean my full contentment.' Burton's *Hume*, ii. 384. The cup of his philosophic happiness was never destined to be full. Like ordinary men he had his unsatisfied longings. His 'full contentment,' should have come in the following year, when he was consoled for the loss of the easy dignity and the emoluments of an English Under-Secretary of State by a handsome pension conferred by the English King, and paid by the English people. It was then that his 'lounging and dosing, which he called thinking,' his 'supreme happiness,' thus found expression. '22nd July, 1768. There are fine doings in America. O! how I long to see America and the East Indies revolted, totally and finally,—the revenue reduced to half,—public credit fully discredited by bankruptcy,—the third of London in ruins, and the rascally mob subdued! I think I am not too old to despair of being witness to all these blessings.' Burton's *Hume*, ii. 417.

Note 2. Boswell, who was careful to clear his writings of Scotticisms, in the third edition of his *Life of Johnson* in at least four places changed *forenoon* into *morning*. Boswell's *Johnson*, ii. 283, *n.* 3. Hume in one of his early letters says :—' I last summer undertook a very laborious task which was to travel eight miles every morning, and as many in the forenoon to and from a mineral well.' Burton's *Hume*, i. 34.

Note 3. Little Warwick Street opened out of Cockspur Street, Pall Mall.

Note 4. This letter must have been written soon after Hume's arrival in London, at the end of February, 1767. Adam Smith, writing to him on the following June 7, addresses his letter :—' To David Hume Esq. Under Secretary for the Northern Department, at Mr. Secretary Conway's house, London.' *M. S. R. S. E.* In the *Court and City Register* for 1765, p. 108, is a list of Ambassadors and Ministers which shews how the business with foreign countries was divided between the two Secretaries of State :—

Southern Province.	*Northern Province.*
France.	Vienna.
Spain.	Copenhagen.
Sardinia.	Poland.
Constantinople.	Prussia.
Naples.	Hague.
Florence.	Russia.
Venice.	Hamburg, Bremen and Lubeck.
Swiss Cantons.	Diet of the Empire at Ratisbon.
Portugal.	Brussels.
	Elector of Cologne and Circle of Westphalia.
	Stockholm.

LETTER XXXII.

An Appointment sought for Strahan.

[Spring of 1767.]

DEAR SⁱR

I spoke to Lord Hertford on Sunday Evening: I know not if what I said woud have any Influence; but he seemd to think, that the Determination of that Question woud depend on the Lords who had been active in conducting the Affair, viz: Marchmont[1], Sandes[2] and Bautitout[3]: I know not by what means you can have Access to them.

I send you a Volume of Olivet's Cicero[4] at Mr. Millar's Desire, who proposes instantly to begin an Edition of my Essays in that Form, as a Forerunner to the like Edition of my History[5]. Let us see a Sample of your English Press: I do not believe you can make such a Book; and I give you a Defiance. Pray return the Book carefully, after you have carefully survey'd it.

If Becket has a few Copies to spare of the French Edition of my Controversy with Rousseau, I shoud be glad to have three or four of them.

There was a good pleasant Paper, inserted, I believe in your Chronicle[6], about three months ago. It containd Rousseau's Articles of Charge against me, and then some good humourd Raillery against him and Voltaire and me[7]. I shoud be glad to have two or three Copies of it, if you can readily find them.

I know not if Becket printed Voltaire's Letter to me[8], but if he did he may perhaps have two or three Copies to spare, which woud oblige me.

I am Dʳ Sⁱʳ Yours sincerely

D. H.

Note 1. Hugh, third Earl of Marchmont, the friend and executor of Pope. He is the 'Polwarth' in Pope's *Seventeen Hundred and*

Thirty Eight (ii. 130), and the 'Marchmont' of his *Grotto.* 'Were there no other memorials,' writes Boswell, 'he will be immortalised by that line of Pope in the verses on his *Grotto*:—
"And the bright flame was shot through Marchmont's soul."'
Life of Johnson, iv. 51. See *ib.* iii. 392 for Johnson's interview with him. He was at this time Keeper of the Great Seal for Scotland. *Court and City Register*, 1765, p. 140. Boswell recommends his pronunciation of English as a proper model for a Scotch gentleman. 'His Lordship told me,' he says, 'with great good humour that the master of a shop in London, where he was not known, said to him, "I suppose, Sir, you are an American." "Why so, Sir?" said his Lordship. "Because, Sir," replied the shopkeeper, "you speak neither English nor Scotch, but something different from both, which I conclude is the language of America."' *Ib.* ii. 160. Boswell's recommendation contrasts oddly with Colonel Barré's 'ridiculous description' of Marchmont's pronunciation. In a debate on Dec. 13, 1770, on a difference between the two Houses, the Members of the House of Commons having been turned out of the House of Lords, Barré said :—'It seemed as if the mob had broke in ; and they certainly acted in a very extraordinary manner. One of the heads of this mob—for there were two—was a Scotchman. I heard him call out several times, "Clear the Hoose! Clear the Hoose." The face of the other was hardly human ; for he had contrived to put on a nose of an enormous size, that disfigured him completely, and his eyes started out of his head in so frightful a way, that he seemed to be undergoing the operation of being strangled.' The Scotchman was the Earl of Marchmont and the other peer the Earl of Denbigh. *Cavendish Debates*, ii. 162. See also *Chatham Corres.* iv. 58. For Lord Denbigh see *post*, Letter of May 10, 1776.

Note 2. Samuel Sandys, first Baron Sandys, who was known in his House of Commons days as 'the Motion-maker.' Smollett's *History of England*, ed. 1800, iii. 16. Horace Walpole describes him as 'a republican, raised on the fall of Sir Robert Walpole to be Chancellor of the Exchequer, then degraded to a peer and cofferer', and soon afterwards laid aside.' *Letters*, i. 104. Sir Denis Le Marchant, in a note on Walpole's *Memoirs of George III*, iv. 119, says that Sandys 'had been placed at the Board of Trade in 1760. He seems to have regarded the post as a sinecure—as indeed it in a great measure became by the withdrawal of the West Indies from the department.'

Note 3. Norborne Berkeley, Lord Bottetourt. Horace Walpole, writing on Aug. 9, 1768, about a visit to London, says :—'I saw nothing there but the ruins of loo, Lady Hertford's cribbage, and Lord Bottetourt, like patience on a monument, smiling in grief. He is

---

[1] 'A principal officer of his majesty's Court, next under the Comptroller.' Johnson's *Dictionary*.

totally ruined and quite charmed. Yet I heartily pity him. To Virginia he cannot be indifferent; he must turn their heads somehow or other. If his graces do not captivate them, he will enrage them to fury, for I take all his *douceur* to be enamelled on iron.' *Letters*, v. 116. On Aug. 14, Walpole wrote :—' There is a disagreeable affair at home, resulting from the disquiets in America. Virginia, though not the most mutinous, contains the best heads and the principal *boutes-feux*[1]. It was thought necessary that the Governor should reside there. It was known that Sir Jeffery Amherst [the governor] would not like that. . . . At the same time, Lord Bottetourt, a court favourite, yet ruined in fortune, was thought of by his friend, Lord Hillsborough. This was mentioned to Sir Jeffery with the offer of a pension. He boggled at the word *pension*; but neither cared to go to his government, nor seemed to dislike giving it up.' *Ib.* p. 120. Walpole in his *Memoirs of George III*, iii. 151, describes Bottetourt as 'of the Bedchamber and a kind of second-rate favourite. He had engaged in an adventure with a company of copper-workers at Warmley. They broke. In order to cover his estate from the creditors he begged a privy seal, to incorporate the Company, as private estates would not then be answerable. The King granted his request, but Lord Chatham, aware of the deception, honestly refused to affix the Seal to the Patent.' In the end 'he did acquiesce in resigning the Seal for a short time, that, being put into commission, it might be set to the grant.' (See also the *Chatham Corres.* iii. 306–322.) Such was the swindler who on the eve of the outbreak with America was sent there as Lieutenant and Governor-General of Virginia. 'Whom,' asked Burke, 'have they selected in these perilous times to soothe the animosity, and reconcile the differences that now unhappily subsist between our colonies and the mother-country ? I need not name the man; everybody knows him as a projector, as one who by wild and chimerical schemes has not only so embarrassed his own affairs as to render his stay in this country impracticable, but brought irretrievable ruin upon many others.' *Parl. Hist.* xvi. 723. He died in Virginia on Nov. 9, 1770, 'greatly lamented by the whole colony.' *Ann. Reg.* xiii. 191. Junius described him as 'a cringing, bowing, fawning, sword-bearing courtier who had ruined himself by an enterprise, which would have ruined thousands if it had succeeded.' *Letters of Junius*, ed. 1812, iii. 109. He it is, I believe, whom Churchill introduces in the following couplet :—

> 'Dashwood is pious, Berkley fixed as fate,
> Sandwich (Thank Heav'n) first Minister of State.'
>
> *Poems*, ed. 1766, ii. 118.

I have little doubt that 'the affair' which these three Lords were 'conducting' was connected with the printing of the Rolls of Parliament, and the Journals of the House of Lords. Nichols says that in

---

[1] Boute-feux, Incendiaries.

1767 William Bowyer was made printer, being 'principally indebted for the appointment to the Earl of Marchmont.' *Lit. Anec.* iii. 39. In a curious inscription written by Bowyer under his own bust in Stationers' Hall it is stated, that 'he was appointed to print the Journals of the House of Lords, at near LXX Years of age, by the patronage of a noble Peer.' *Ib.* p. 293. In the *Journals of the House of Lords*, xxxi. 509, there is an order on March 9, 1767, to leave to a Sub-committee, to which these three Lords belonged, the question of printing the Rolls and the Journals. *Ib.* p. 429.

Note 4. Gibbon describing his student days at Lausanne, says of the writings of Cicero :—'The most perfect editions, that of Olivet, which may adorn the shelves of the rich, that of Ernesti, which should lie on the table of the learned, were not within my reach.' Gibbon's *Misc. Works*, i. 89.

Note 5. A new edition of Hume's *Essays and Treatises* in 2 vols. quarto was published by A. Millar, London, and A. Kincaid and A. Donaldson, Edinburgh, in 1768. A quarto edition of his *History* in 8 vols. was published in 1770.

Note 6. See *ante*, p. 64, *n.* 9.

Note 7. This paper, I have little doubt, is one quoted in Burton's *Hume*, ii. 340. Voltaire is only once mentioned. It begins :—

'Heads of an Indictment laid by J. J. Rousseau, philosopher, against D. Hume, Esq.

'1. That the said David Hume, to the great scandal of philosophy, and not having the fitness of things before his eyes, did concert a plan with Mess. Tronchin, Voltaire and D'Alembert to ruin the said J. J. Rousseau for ever, by bringing him over to England, and there settling him to his heart's content.

'2. That the said David Hume did, with a malicious and traitorous intent, procure, or cause to be procured, by himself, or somebody else, one pension of the yearly value of £100 or thereabouts, to be paid to the said J. J. Rousseau, on account of his being a philosopher, either privately or publicly, as to him the said J. J. Rousseau should seem meet.

'3. That the said David Hume did, one night after he left Paris, put the said J. J. Rousseau in bodily fear, by talking in his sleep; although the said J. J. Rousseau doth not know whether the said David Hume was really asleep, or whether he shammed Abraham[1], or what he meant.'

Dr. Burton adds that this paper 'has the appearance of having been written by a Scottish lawyer.'

Note 8. Dr. Burton thinks that this letter only reached Hume through the press. At all events there is no trace of it among his manuscripts. *Life of Hume*, ii. 358. Rousseau had accused Voltaire of having written a letter against him, which was published as Voltaire's at

---

[1] '*To sham Abram*: to feign sickness, a phrase in use among sailors.' Murray's *New Eng. Dict.*

London, under the title of *Lettre au docteur Jean-Jacques Pansophe.*
The author was M. Bordes, of Lyons. *Œuvres de Voltaire,* liii. 497.
An English translation, published by Payne, is in the list of publications in the *Gent. Mag.* for April, 1766, p. 192. See also *Ib.* p. 563.
Hume himself at first had no doubt of its authenticity. On May 16,
1766, some weeks before Rousseau's outbreak against him, he wrote
to the Countess de Boufflers :—'You have probably seen Voltaire's
letter to our exotic philosopher. I fancy it will rouse him from his
lethargy. These two gladiators are very well matched ; it is like the
combat of Dares and Entellus in Virgil [*Æneid.* v. 362-484]. The
sprightliness and grace, and irony and pleasantry of the one will be
a good contrast to the force and vehemence of the other.' *Private
Corres.* p. 171. Rousseau, after charging Voltaire with being the
author of the letter, continues :—'Le noble objet de ce spirituel
ouvrage est de m'attirer le mépris et la haine de ceux chez qui je me
suis réfugié.' *Œuvres de Rousseau,* ed. 1782, xxiv. 368. Voltaire
replied to this accusation in a letter addressed to Hume, dated
'Ferney, 24 Octobre.' He says :—'Il m'a fait l'honneur de me mettre
au nombre de ses ennemis et de ses persécuteurs. Intimement
persuadé qu'on doit lui élever une statue . . . il pense que la
moitié de l'univers est occupée à dresser cette statue sur son piédestal,
et l'autre moitié à la renverser.' *Œuvres de Voltaire,* liii. 497. See
ante, p. 90, for another extract from this letter. Grimm, writing
on Nov. 1, 1766, says :—'M. de Voltaire a fait imprimer une petite
lettre adressée à M. Hume, où il a, pour ainsi dire, donné le coup de
grace à ce pauvre Jean-Jacques. Cette lettre a eu beaucoup de
succès à Paris, et elle a peutêtre fait plus de tort à M. Rousseau que
la brochure de M. Hume.' *Corres. Lit.* v. 211. An English translation was published by S. Bladon in Paternoster Row, 1766. It is
curious in all the translations to find *Jean Jacques* turned into *John
James.* 'The great soul of John James' reads as comically as 'la
grande âme de Jean-Jacques' reads naturally.

We find no more mention of Rousseau in Hume's letters to Strahan.
On Oct. 8 of this year (1767) he wrote to Adam Smith :—'Thus
you see, he is a composition of whim, affectation, wickedness, vanity,
añd inquietude, with a very small, if any, ingredient of madness. He
is always complaining of his health ; yet I have scarce ever seen a
more robust little man of his years. . . . The ruling qualities above
mentioned, together with ingratitude, ferocity, and lying,—I need not
mention eloquence and invention—form the whole of the composition.' Burton's *Hume,* ii. 377. When we consider the judgments,
wide as the poles asunder, which Hume passed on Rousseau, we are
the more ready to allow that, as regards him at all events, Dr.
Carlyle was right when he said :—'David Hume, like Adam Smith,
had no discernment at all of characters.' Dr. A. Carlyle's *Auto.*
p. 278.

LETTER XXXIII.

An Application to Lord Hertford.

[1767.]

DEAR STRAHAN

It was not possible for me to get an Opportunity last Night of speaking to Lord Hertford[1]; I shall try if I can be more fortunate this Evening; and I shall as soon as possible, give you Information: A Moment will be sufficient, as I have only to put him in Mind of his Engagements—Yours

D. H.

Sunday Forenoon.

Note 1. Dr. Alexander Carlyle gives us a glimpse of Hume as an Under-Secretary of State. He met him at a dinner where there were some people connected with the Court. He says :—' The conversation was lively and agreeable, but we were much amused with observing how much the thoughts and conversation of all those in the least connected were taken up with every trifling circumstance that related to the Court. . . . It was truly amusing to observe how much David Hume's strong and capacious mind was filled with infantine anecdotes of nurses and children.' Carlyle's *Auto.* p. 518.

Fox wrote of Hume :—' He was an excellent man, and of great powers of mind ; but his partiality to kings and princes is intolerable : Nay, it is in my opinion quite ridiculous ; and is more like the foolish admiration which women and children sometimes have for Kings than the opinion, right or wrong, of a philosopher.' *Edinburgh Review*, No. xxiv, p. 277.

LETTER XXXIV.

Applications to Lord Hertford and General Conway.

DEAR STRAHAN

I have been so happy as to prevail in my Applications both to Lord Hertford and to General Conway[1]: I doubt not but Charles Townsend[2] will be favourable to you. Pray, are you thinking of this new Dress in which you promis'd to put me? Shall I pretend to rival Cicero in Garb and Accoutrements[3].

Yours

D. H.

Monday Forenoon.

Note 1. Hume took advantage of his position to pay a compliment to an old friend. Writing to Dr. Blair on May 27, 1767 he says:—
' Tell Robertson that the Compliment at the End of General Conway's Letter to him was of my composing without any Orders from him. He smild when he read it; but said it was very proper and sign'd it. These are not bad Puffs from Ministers of State, as the silly World goes.' *M.S.R.S.E.* Robertson earlier in the year had asked Hume to use his influence with General Conway about an appointment to some military chaplaincy. Stewart's *Life of Robertson*, ed. 1811, p. 355.

Note 2. Charles Townshend was Chancellor of the Exchequer when this letter was written, and, to use Burke's words, still 'lord of the ascendant.' (Payne's *Burke*, i. 146.) He died in office on Sept. 4, 1767.

Note 3. Hume is referring to the proposed new editions of his works. See *ante*, p. 106.

LETTER XXXV.

An Apology for not keeping an Engagement.

[1767 ?]

Mr. Hume asks Mr. Strahan ten thousand Pardons: When Mr. Strahan was so kind to ask him to dine with him on Monday, he was already engagd several days before, but had forgot it. Meeting yesterday with the Gentleman, he put him in mind of it, and insisted that the prior Engagement was to him So that he hopes Mr. Strahan will be so good as to excuse him.

Sunday.

LETTER XXXVI.

Hume in Edinburgh: Tempests brewing in Public Affairs.

DEAR SIR

I never enjoyed myself better, nor was in better spirits, than since I came down here[1]. I live as I please, spend my time according to my fancy, keep a plentiful table for myself and my friends[2], amuse myself with

reading and society, and find the generality of the people
disposed to respect me more on account of my having
been well receiv'd in greater and more renowned places [3]:
But tho' all this makes my time slide away easily, it is
impossible for me to forget that a man who is in his 59th
Year has not many more years to live [4], and that it is time
for him, if he has common Sense, to have done with all
Ambition.   My Ambition was always moderate and confind
entirely to Letters [5]; *but it has been my Misfortune to write*
in the Language of the most stupid and factious Barbarians
in the World [6]; and it is long since I have renounced all
desire of their Approbation, which indeed coud no longer
give me either pleasure or Vanity.

As to my Notion of public Affairs, I think there are
very dangerous Tempests brewing, and the Scene thickens
every moment [7].   The Government has, no doubt, great
Resources, if they employ them with Prudence and Vigour
and Unanimity.   But have we any reason to think they
will do so?   The Parliament will certainly be * * *
by the Populace every day next winter [8].   If they bear
it, they degrade * * * and draw on * * * .   If they
punish, they will still more enrage the Faction, and give
a Pretence for the Cry that Liberty is violated [9].   Are we
sure, that the popular Discontent may not reach the Army,
who have a Pretence for Discontents of their own [10].   The
General in chief is a weak man, and fond of low popularity [11]:
It is true, you have a very honest Chancellor [12] and a very
courageous Chief Justice [13], who will be a great Ressource
in difficult times.   But is it certain that Lord Bute will
abstain from tampering and trying some more of his pretty
Experiments [14]?   What if he take it in his head to open the
Door to Pitt and his Myrmidons, who will, no doubt, chain
the King for ever, and render him a mere Cypher [15].   Our
Government has become an absolute Chimera: So much

* [MS. torn.]

I

Liberty is incompatible with human Society: And it will
be happy, if we can escape from it, without falling into
a military Government, such as Algiers or Tunis [16]. The
Matter will only be worse, if there be no shooting or
hanging next Winter [17]: This Frenzy of the people, so
epidemical and so much without a Cause, admits only
of one Remedy, which however is a dangerous one, and
requires more vigour than has appeard in any minister
of late [18]. I have a very good Opinion of the Duke of
Grafton but his Youth deprives him of Experience and
still more of Authority [19]. I dare [not ve]nture to play the
Prophet, but think you are in great Danger. I see * * *
low: Have the People sense enough to see their Danger,
and to withdraw from that precarious Security. If they
coud see it in time, and catch the Alarm, it woud be a
great Ressource to Government: But this is more than
can reasonably be expected from them.

You say I am of a disponding Character: On the
contrary, I am of a very sanguine Disposition. Notwithstanding my Age, I hope to see a public Bankruptcy [20], the
total Revolt of America [21], the Expulsion of the English
from the East Indies [22], the Diminution of London to less
than a half [23], and the Restoration of the Government to
the King [24], Nobility, and Gentry of this Realm. To adorn
the Scene, I hope also that some hundreds of Patriots [25]
will make their Exit at Tyburn, and improve English
Elóquence by their dying Speeches [26]. I think, indeed,
that no body of common Sense coud at present take the
Road of Faction and Popularity, who woud not upon
occasion have joind Catiline's Conspiracy [27]; and I have
no better opinion of the Gentleman you call my Friend [28].

Pray have you seen Lord Stormont since he came
home [29]? Did he enquire after you?

I think, if you throw off the Errata as it is printed, it will
do very well. It is not long for 8 Volumes [30]; and they

are not all Errors of the Press.   You mention nothing
of the small Edition of my Essays, whence I conclude it is
not going forward[31].   I am Dear S^ir Yours sincerely and
beg the continuation of your Friendship, tho' it shoud be
our Lot not to pass much of our time together.   I wish
much to see you possessd of some Farms in this Country[32],
where there is great Unanimity at present, and a Desire to
support Government[33].

D. H.

EDINBURGH, 25 *of Oct.*, 1769.

Note 1.   By Conway's resignation (Jan. 20, 1768), Hume lost his
office.   'I returned to Edinburgh in 1769,' he writes in his *Autobiography*, 'very opulent, for I possessed a revenue of £1000 a year,
healthy, and though somewhat stricken in years, with the prospect
of enjoying long my ease, and of seeing the increase of my reputation.'   He had stayed on in London till the summer of 1769.   Writing
on Dec. 23, 1768 to the Countess de Boufflers to apologise for not
paying a visit to Paris, he said :—'The truth is, I have, and ever had,
a prodigious reluctance to change my place of abode.'   *Private Corres.*
p. 263.   On March 28, 1769, he wrote to Dr. Blair at Edinburgh :—'I
intend to visit you soon, and for good and all.   Indeed I know not
what detains me here, except that it is so much a matter of indifference
where I live ; and I am amused with looking on the scene, which
really begins to be interesting.'   Burton's *Hume*, ii. 424.   It was during
this stay in London that he called on Boswell in Half-Moon Street.
Piccadilly.   'I am really the *great man* now,' wrote Boswell to the
Rev. W. J. Temple, on May 14, 1768.   'I have had David Hume in the
forenoon, and Mr. Johnson in the afternoon of the same day visiting
me. . . . David Hume came on purpose the other day to tell me that
the Duke of Bedford was very fond of my book, and had recommended it to the Duchess.   David is really amiable ; I always regret
to him his unlucky principles, and he smiles at my faith ; but I have
a hope which he has not, or pretends not to have.   So who has the
best of it, my reverend friend ?'   *Letters of Boswell*, p. 151.   On Aug. 20,
1769, Hume wrote to Adam Smith from Edinburgh :—'I am glad to
have come within sight of you, and to have a view of Kirkaldy from my
windows ; but as I wish also to be within speaking terms of you, I
wish we could concert measures for that purpose.   I am mortally
sick at sea, and regard with horror and a kind of hydrophobia the
great gulf [The Firth of Forth] that lies between us.'   Burton's *Hume*,
ii. 429.   In Humphry Clinker (letter of Aug. 8), Matthew Bramble's
sufferings are described in his sail across this 'great gulf' of seven
miles.   'I am much of the honest Highlander's mind (said he) after

he had made such a passage as this: his friend told him he was much indebted to Providence. "Certainly (said Donald), but by my saul, mon, I'se ne'er trouble Providence again, so long as the brig of Stirling stands."'

Note 2. On Oct. 16, 1769, nine days earlier than the date of the letter in the text, Hume had written to Sir Gilbert Elliot:—'I live still, and must for a twelvemonth, in my old house in James's Court, which is very cheerful, and even elegant, but too small to display my great talents for cookery, the science to which I intend to addict the remaining years of my life! I have just now lying on the table before me a receipt for making *soupe à la reine*, copied with my own hand; for beef and cabbage (a charming dish), and old mutton and old claret nobody excels me. I make also sheep-head broth in a manner that Mr. Keith speaks of it for eight days after; and the Duc de Nivernois[1] would bind himself apprentice to my lass[2] to learn it.' Stewart's *Robertson*, p. 361. Gibbon wrote to Holroyd at Edinburgh on Aug. 7, 1773:—'You tell me of a long list of dukes, lords, and chieftains of renown to whom you are introduced; were I with you, I should prefer one *David* to them all. When you are at Edinburgh, I hope you will not fail to visit the stye of that fattest of Epicurus's hogs, and inform yourself whether there remains no hope of its recovering the use of its right paw.' Gibbon's *Misc. Works*, ii. 110.

Boswell writing on June 19, 1775, says:—'On Thursday I supped at Mr. Hume's, where we had the young Parisian, Lord Kames, and Dr. Robertson, an excellent supper, three sorts of ice-creams. What think you of the northern Epicurus style?. I can recollect no conversation. Our writers here are really not prompt on all occasions, as those of London.' *Letters of Boswell*, p. 203. The 'three sorts of ice-creams' were in those days a great luxury; for Lord Cockburn, writing of Edinburgh twenty or thirty years later, says:—'Ice, either for cooling or eating, was utterly unknown, except in a few houses of the highest class.' Hume's old claret would not have been so costly as in England, for in Scotland claret was exempted from duty till about 1780. Cockburn's *Memorials*, p. 35. On April 17, 1775, Hume wrote to the Countess de Boufflers:—'I have been always, and still am, very temperate. The only debauches I ever was guilty of were those of study; and even these were moderate; for I was always very careful of my health by using exercise.' *Private Corres.*, p. 282.

The house in James's Court he had bought in 1762. On July 5 of that year he wrote to Elliot:—'I have hitherto been a wanderer on the face of the earth, without any abiding city: But I have now at last purchased a house which I am repairing; though I cannot say that I have

---

[1] The Duc de Nivernois had been ambassador in England in 1762. Walpole's *Letters*, iv. 17. Walpole calls him ' a namby-pamby kind of pedant, with a peevish *petite santé*.' *Ib.* v. 131.

[2] 'Formerly a common name in Scotland for a cook-maid.' Note by Stewart.

yet fixed any property in the earth, but only in the air : For it is the third storey of James's Court, and it cost me 500 pounds.   It is somewhat dear, but I shall be exceedingly well lodged.'   Stewart's *Robertson*, p. 360.   During his residence in France, more than once, in the midst of all his good fortune and his grand society, he regretted his snug quarters.   From Fontainebleau, where he suffered, he says, more from flattery than Lewis XIV ever had in any three weeks of his life, he wrote to Dr. Ferguson :—' Yet I am sensible that I set out too late, and that I am misplaced ; and I wish twice or thrice a day, for my easy chair and my retreat in James's Court.'   Burton's *Hume*, ii. 173.   Dr. Blair was his tenant for part of this time.   Hume wrote to him in the spring of 1764 :—' I am glad to find that you are my tenant.   You have got an excellent house for its size.   It was perfectly clear of vermin when I left it, and I hope you will find it so. . . . Never put a fire in the south room with the red paper.   It is so warm of itself that all last winter, which was a very severe one, I lay with a single blanket ; and frequently upon coming in at midnight, starving with cold, have sat down and read for an hour, as if I had had a stove in the room.   The fires of your neighbours will save you the expense of a fire in that room[1].'   *M. S. R. S. E.*   On Dec. 28, 1765, writing to Blair, he said :—' If you leave my House as you thought you would, Nairne may have it for 35 pounds as we agreed.'   *M. S. R. S. E.*   This perhaps was the rent for the house furnished, as Hume had left it when he started for Paris.   In his will he bequeathed the life-rent of it to his sister, ' or in case that house be sold at the time of my decease, twenty pounds a year during the whole course of her life.'   Hume's *Philosophical Works*, ed. 1854, i. xxx. Blair in a letter dated May 13 [1766], says that he is on the point of leaving.   *M. S. R. S. E.*

By a house in Edinburgh, it must be remembered, a single story, or half a story, was commonly meant.   In one single building there were generally many freeholds separately held.   Sir John Pringle, writing to Hume from London on Nov. 2, 1773, about an Edinburgh house, says :—' I will not answer for the clearness [of my reply], as I apprehend some danger in misunderstanding one another from the different terms in use here and in Scotland at present.   When I left it, we had luckily neither parlours, nor first and second floors to confound us.'   *Ib.*

Dr. Robert Chambers, in his *Traditions of Edinburgh*, ed. 1825, i. 219, says that ' till the building of the New Town James's Court was inhabited by a select set of gentlemen.   They kept a clerk to record their names and their proceedings, had a scavenger of their own, clubbed in many public measures, and had balls and assemblies among themselves.'   Hume's flat was on the northern side of the

---

[1] Perhaps it was these fires which caused the conflagration by which this most interesting house was burnt down in 1857.

Court, where the houses were built on so steep a slope, that he who from the south had entered on a level with the pavement found on going to the windows at the north that he was looking down from the fourth story.   Below him he could have seen the topmost branches of a fine row of trees. 'How well,' says Lord Cockburn, 'the ridge of the old town was set off by a bank of elms that ran along the front of James's Court, and stretched eastward over the ground now partly occupied by the Bank of Scotland.' *Memorials*, p. 292. They and many another stately group fell before 'the Huns,' who in Edinburgh in the early part of the present century 'massacred every town tree that came in a mason's way.' *Ib.* p. 291.

Boswell, when Johnson visited him in 1773, was living on the ground floor of the same house, on a level with the Court. 'Boswell,' wrote Johnson to Mrs. Thrale, 'has very handsome and spacious rooms; level with the ground on one side of the house, and on the other four stories high.' *Piozzi Letters*, i. 109. Dr. Burton is mistaken in thinking that the flat in which Johnson was received was the very one which had been occupied by Hume. He quotes a paper, apparently undated, drawn up by Hume for defending an action brought against him by a builder for repairs. In this it is stated that 'at Whitsuntide last, Mr. Boswell, advocate, left Mr. Hume's house in James's Court; and Lady Wallace, dowager, came to it.' The document goes on to say that the Boswells had lived two years in the house. If Boswell lived two years in this flat it must have been later on, for Hume left it for St. Andrew's Square little more than a year before Johnson's visit. Dr. Burton says :—' I have ascertained that by ascending the western of the two stairs facing the entry of James's Court to the height of three stories, we arrive at the door of David Hume's house, which, of the two doors on that landing place, is the one towards the left.' *Life of Hume*, ii. 137. It has been suggested to me that Dr. Burton was misled by Hume's statement that he lived 'in the third story,' and that he should have counted the stories from the outside. My correspondent says :—' If you enter from the Mound, that is from the north side, then the house is on the third story, as stories in Scotland are not reckoned from the pavement flat, but from the one immediately above it.' I feel convinced however that Hume did not live on the pavement flat. In the first place, we have Dr. Burton's positive statement, which was, he says, founded on 'information communicated by Joseph Grant, Esq.' In the second place, Hume, in the letter to Elliot quoted above, says that his house 'is the third story.' As he did not say on which side of the Court it stood, he could never have expected his correspondent to know that it was one of those houses in which the third story was also the sixth. In the third place, in the list of occupants in 1773, given in Chambers's *Traditions of Edinburgh*, ed. 1825, i. 220, it is stated that while Boswell occupied the floor level with the pavement, Dr. Gregory Grant lived on the fourth floor. Now Dr. Blair when Hume's tenant wrote to him on Oct. 8, 1765 :—' I have got two rooms in Dr. Grant's house above me for Mr. Percy's accommodation [1].' *M. S. R. S. E.* Of course Dr. Grant's house would have been above him, had he been living on the pavement level ; but it seems likely that he meant the flat just above. In 1773 the third floor, according to Chambers's list, was occupied by Alexander Wallace, Esq., Banker. It was to this floor that, when ' Mr. Boswell, the advocate, left in Whitsuntide, Lady Wallace, dowager, came.' Whether she was related to the banker I do not know. It is possible that Hume's tenant was not Johnson's biographer, but his cousin, Claude James Boswell, also an advocate, afterwards Lord Balmuto. If, however, it was James Boswell, then his two years' tenancy must have fallen between the end of 1773 and the summer of 1776. It is strange nevertheless that if he ever lived in Hume's old house he should have made no mention of it.

The two stories of this house in a few years saw a remarkable set of inmates and visitors. Round about Hume, and Boswell, and Blair the best society of Edinburgh gathered. Adam Smith had his chamber in Hume's flat [2]; Benjamin Franklin was his guest for several weeks together [3]; it was here that a shelter was offered to Rousseau [4]. It was here that Paoli visited Boswell in 1771 [5], and that Johnson held his levées in 1773 [6]. Some memorial surely should be raised to tell both citizen and stranger of the past glories of this long-neglected Court.

Note 3. Hume enjoyed also the advantage of having been sought by a man of ' the decorum and piety of Lord Hertford.' Writing on Sept. 1, 1763, soon after his appointment as his Lordship's Secretary, he says :—' Elliot said to me that my situation was, taking all its circumstances, the most wonderful event in the world. I was now a person clean and white as the driven snow ; and that were I to be proposed for the see of Lambeth no objection could henceforth be made to me.' Burton's *Hume,* ii. 159.

Note 4. Gibbon, in his fifty-second year, wrote :—' This day may *possibly* be my last ; but the laws of probability, so true in general, so fallacious in particular, still allow about fifteen years [7].' He lived about five more. Gibbon's *Misc. Works,* i. 274.

Note 5. Hume writing of his twenty-fourth year, says in his *Auto-biography* :—' I resolved to make a very rigid frugality supply my deficiency of fortune, to maintain unimpaired my independency, and

---

[1] Mr. Percy, the son of the Earl of Northumberland, was his pupil.

[2] *Post,* Letter of Feb. 11, 1776, note 1.

[3] Dr. A. Carlyle's *Autobiography,* p. 437.

[4] *Ante,* p. 76, n. 5.   [5] Chambers's *Traditions of Edinburgh,* i. 221.

[6] Boswell's *Johnson,* v. 395.

[7] According to the tables drawn up by Dr. William Ogle on the basis of the death-rates of 1871-80 the laws of probability allow a man of Gibbon's age about eighteen years. Whitaker's *Almanack,* p. 346.

to regard every object as contemptible except the improvement of my talents in literature.'

Note 6.   Hume just two years earlier, wrote to dissuade Gibbon from composing in French :—'Let the French triumph in the present diffusion of their tongue.   Our solid and increasing establishments in America, where we need less dread the inundation of Barbarians, promise a superior stability and duration to the English language.' Gibbon's *Misc. Works*, i. 204.   Franklin, writing to Hume from Coventry on Sept. 27, 1760, says :—' I hope with you that we shall always in America make the best English of this Island our standard, and I believe it will be so.   I assure you it often gives me pleasure to reflect how greatly the *audience* (if I may so term it) of a good English writer will, in another century or two, be increased by the increase of English people in our colonies.' *Life of Franklin*, ed. by J. Bigelow, i. 412.   Franklin's reflections would have been far less pleasurable could he have foreseen the meanness of this vast audience of the future.   He was honest enough to think that each man has some right to enjoy the fruits of his own labour. . He would have been the last man to rob English writers of their fairly-earned reward by refusing them a copy-right.   Once, when upholding in Congress a law of libel, he said that he was willing to give up his right of throwing dirt at other people, would other people give up their right of throwing dirt at him.   In like manner he would have urged the Americans to give up their right of robbing Englishmen, when he saw that Englishmen were willing to give up their right of robbing Americans.   I speak with some feeling, for I have learnt that Messrs. Harper of New York are 'reprinting' my edition of Boswell's *Life of Johnson*.

Note 7.   Wilkes had withdrawn to France in 1763.   By not appearing to the indictments which were laid against him, towards the end of 1764, he was outlawed.   ' An exile from his country, distrest in his circumstances, and in a great measure abandoned by his friends, he seemed not only totally ruined, but also nearly forgotten.' *Ann. Reg.* 1769, i. 58.   Had the pardon for which in 1766 he sued from the prime-minister, the Duke of Grafton, been granted, he might have sunk altogether into oblivion.   Had he been offered the bribe of a pension or a place, he would have ceased to be ' a Wilkite ' many years earlier than he did.   He was however treated, not only with neglect, but with some indignity.   In December, 1767, he published a letter to the Duke of Grafton in which he accused him and Chatham of being the tools of Bute.   The public attention and pity were once more roused.   ' They began to think his suffering out of measure, and to reflect that he was at any rate a victim to the popular cause.' *Ib.* p. 59.   In defiance of his sentence of outlawry, he returned to England on the dissolution of Parliament, and in March, 1768, stood for the City of London.   He was unsuccessful, rather, it seems, through the cowardice than the ill-will of the electors.   He at once set up for

the County of Middlesex, and was returned by a great majority. The
Londoners flocked to Brentford to hear the declaration of the poll.
'There has not been so great a defection of the inhabitants from
London and Westminster to ten miles distance in one day, since the
Lifeguardman's prophecy of the earthquake which was to destroy
both those cities in the year 1750.' *Ib.* 1768, i. 86. Strahan, describing
these transactions in a letter to Sir Andrew Mitchell, dated April 1,
1768, says :—' During the continuance [of the poll for London] he
appeared every day on the hustings, though he was more than once
arrested there at the instance of his private creditors. But he found
bail for his appearance, braved it out to the last, and was attended by
a considerable mob every day. When he found the poll going
against him, he publicly gave out he would stand for Middlesex.
There he was likely to stand a better chance, an incredible number
of petty freeholders of that County from Wapping, and its environs,
immediately declared for him, and on the day of election, he carried
it with ease, and with very little disturbance at Brentford ; though
the whole road thither was lined with a mob who insulted every one
who would not join in the Cry of *Wilkes and Liberty*. This success immediately reached London, and occasioned such an intoxication in
the mob—men, women, and children—that they spread themselves
from Hyde Park Corner to Wapping, and broke everybody's windows who refused to illuminate their houses ; among the rest, those
of the Mansion House of the Lord Mayor, who happened that night
to sleep in the Country, were quite demolished ; and though a party
of soldiers were at length sent for by the Mayoress from the Tower,
they, when they came (so general was the infatuation) seemed more
disposed to assist the mob than to disperse them. You will not
easily believe it, but it is true, that the Dukes of Grafton and
Northumberland, and many others of the first nobility, nay some of
the Royal Family itself (viz. the Princess Amelia and the Dukes of
Gloucester and Cumberland) were mean enough to submit to illuminate their windows upon this infamous occasion, in obedience to
the orders of a paltry Mob, which a dozen of their footmen might
easily have dispersed. If you ask me why was not Wilkes secured
on his arrival, and before he had acquired his present consequence ?
—the answer is plain, the Ministry were part of them timid, and
part of them secretly his friends. The outlawry, says the present
Attorney General [De Grey] cannot be defended, because of some
informalities in the passing of it ; and his predecessor [Norton] who
did pass it, is in opposition. The Duke of Grafton, though then in
Town, is now at Newmarket, the Chancellor at Bath, the rest
electioneering in different parts of the country, or skulking in town ;
but not one of them disposed to prevent this insult to their Master
or to issue orders for a party of the Guards (and a small one would
have been sufficient) to clear the streets.
'The next night, the same illuminations were again insisted on,

and the same insolence, with the same impunity, was repeated.'
M. S. R. S. E.
'It is really on extraordinary event,' wrote Dr. Franklin on
April 16, 'to see an outlaw and exile, of bad personal character, not
worth a farthing, come over from France, set himself up as a candidate for the capital of the kingdom, miss his election only by being
too late in his application, and immediately carrying it for the principal county. The mob (spirited up by numbers of different ballads
sung or roared in every street) requiring gentlemen and ladies of all
ranks, as they passed in their carriages, to shout for Wilkes and
liberty, marking the same words on all coaches with chalk, and No.
45 on every door; which extends a vast way along the roads in the
country.' Franklin's *Memoirs* (ed. 1833), iii. 306. Wilkes, after being
allowed his liberty for nearly three months, was committed to the
King's Bench on his outlawry. The mob carried him off in triumph
on his way to prison, taking the horses out of his carriage and
drawing it themselves. He gave himself up the same day to the
marshal. *Ann. Reg.* 1768, i. 100. On May 10, at a riot in St. George's
Fields, before his prison gates five or six people were shot dead by
the soldiers, and about fifteen wounded. *Ib.* p. 108. On June 8
Wilkes's outlawry was reversed; *Ib.* p. 121; but on June 18 judgment was pronounced on him for the charges of which, in February
1764, he had been convicted in his absence; namely the republication
of the *North Briton*, No. 45, and the publication of the *Essay on
Woman*. He was sentenced to two fines of five hundred pounds
each and to two terms of imprisonment of ten and twelve months
each. *Ib.* p. 127. When two of the soldiers who had fired on
the crowd were put on their trial, the anger of the people was
roused by the alleged mockery of justice. They were still more
angered by 'a letter of a Secretary of State recommending an
effectual and early use of the military power; and by another from
the Secretary at War, thanking the soldiers for their alacrity, and
promising them protection; and these words being attended with
pecuniary rewards publicly given, the populace were actuated with
the highest degree of fury and resentment.' *Ib.* 1769, i. 62. Meanwhile 'the disorders in the Colonies increased to such a degree as to
grow every day more alarming. . . . Moreover it was said that the
weakness of Government had encouraged the neighbouring States to
treat us with contempt and indifference.' *Ib.* p. 63.

London during the first six months of 1768 was, to quote Dr. Franklin's words, 'a daily scene of lawless riot. Mobs patrolling the streets
at noon-day, some knocking all down that will not roar for Wilkes
and liberty; . . . coal-heavers and porters pulling down the houses
of coal-merchants that refuse to give them more wages; sawyers
destroying saw-mills; sailors unrigging all the outward-bound ships,
and suffering none to sail till merchants agree to raise their pay;
watermen destroying private boats and threatening bridges; soldiers

firing among the mobs, and killing men, women, and children.'
Franklin's *Memoirs*, 1818, iii. 307. 'We have independent mobs,'
wrote Horace Walpole on May 12, 'that have nothing to do with
Wilkes, and who only take advantage of so favourable a season. The
dearness of provisions incites, the hope of increase of wages allures,
and drink puts them in motion. . . . I cannot bear to have the name
of Liberty profaned to the destruction of the cause; for frantic
tumults only lead to that terrible corrective, Arbitrary Power,—
which cowards call out for as protection, and knaves are so ready to
grant.' *Letters*, v. 99. The *Annual Register* for this year describes
among other riots one on April 18, in which three persons were
killed by shots, and several dangerously wounded (i. 96); a second,
on the 25th, in which 'several lives were lost' (*ib.* p. 99); a third, on
May 10—the one before Wilkes's prison, mentioned above; a fourth,
on May 25, in which 'many lives were lost' (*ib.* p. 114); a fifth, on
June 2, in which two captains of ships were so beaten that their
lives were despaired of (*ib.* p. 119); a sixth, on June 4, in which 'the
coal-heavers and sailors had a terrible battle, when many were
wounded on both sides' (*ib.* p. 120); a seventh, on June 7, 'another
great fray, in which several sailors lost their lives' (*ib.* p. 121); and
an eighth, on June 13, a fight between the coal-heavers and the
military, 'wherein several were hurt on both sides' (*ib.* p. 124). In
the end nine coal-heavers were hanged, and for a time there was
peace. *Ib.* pp. 137, 139. The High Sheriff of Hertford, at the summer assizes, 'sent a turtle for the table of the judges, with burgundy
instead of the common present of claret, and gave for a reason, that
in these licentious times he could not treat His Majesty's chief
ministers of justice with too much respect.' *Ib.* p. 153.

On Feb. 3, 1769, Wilkes was expelled the House of Commons, and
declared incapable of being elected. On Feb. 16 he was a second
time, and on March 16 a third time, elected without opposition; his
election in each case was declared void. On April 13, being elected
for the fourth time by a great majority, the poll taken for him was
declared null and void, and the seat was given to his opponent. *Parl.
Hist.* xvi. 437, 546. There was much less rioting in 1769. Nevertheless on March 22 the King issued a Proclamation, in which it was
stated that 'disorderly persons had in a most daring and audacious
manner assaulted several merchants and others, coming to our
palace at St. James's, and had committed many acts of violence and
outrage before the gates of our palace.' *Ann. Reg.* 1769, i. 229. Less
than a month before the date of Hume's letter, some riotous
weavers, armed with guns and pistols, attacked a party of soldiers
who had been sent against them. Two weavers and one soldier
were killed and several were wounded. *Ib.* p. 136. Five of the
weavers were hanged. *Ib.* pp. 159, 162. Even the Lord Mayor's Feast
was troubled. Of all the Ministers and great officers of state invited,
Lord Chancellor Camden alone attended; and in the procession

only 'five aldermen appeared without dread of popular disgrace.' *Ib.* p. 149.

The Middlesex election had roused the whole country. 'The remotest counties,' says Burke, 'caught the alarm.... The nation was in a great ferment during the whole summer—the like had scarcely been ever remembered.' *Ann. Reg.* 1770, i. 56, 58. Horace Walpole, on his return to London from France, wrote on Oct. 13:— 'I arrived the night before last; and do not find any reason to change my opinion on the state of this country. It approaches by fast strides to some great crisis, and to me never wore so serious an air, except in the Rebellion.' *Letters,* v. 196.

Note 8. Sir James Macdonald wrote to Hume on May 18, 1765 :— 'The silk-weavers got a bill passed in the House of Commons to prevent more effectually the importation of foreign silks, which the Duke of Bedford threw out in the House of Lords. The next day above ten thousand of these people came down to the House, desiring redress, with drums beating and colours flying. They attacked the Duke of Bedford in his chariot, and threw so large a stone at him that, if he had not put up his hand and saved his head by having his thumb cut to the bone, he must have been killed. He behaved with great resolution and got free of them, since which time he has remained blockaded in his own house, and defended by the troops. Yesterday the same number of weavers assembled again at the House of Lords, where the horse and foot guards were to secure the entry for the Peers. The mob were ranged before the soldiers, and their colours were playing in the faces of his Majesty's troops. The degree of security with which these people commit felony seems to me the most formidable circumstance in the whole.... It is really serious to see the legislature of this country intimidated by such a rabble, and to see the House of Lords send for Justice Fielding, to hear him prove for how many reasons he ought not to do his duty. The Duke of Bedford is still in danger of his life if he goes out of his house.' *Letters of Eminent Persons to David Hume,* p. 55.

Note 9. Boswell records the following conversation on April 10, 1783 :—'BOSWELL. "This has been a very factious reign, owing to the too great indulgence of Government." JOHNSON. "*I* think so, Sir. What at first was lenity, grew timidity. Yet this is reasoning *a posteriori,* and may not be just. Supposing a few had at first been punished, I believe faction would have been crushed; but it might have been said that it was a sanguinary reign. A man cannot tell *a priori* what will be best for Government to do.' Boswell's *Johnson,* iv. 200.

Note 10. Their 'pretence' had some foundation. Dr. Brocklesby, Physician to the Army, the friend of Johnson and Burke, in his *Œconomical and Medical Observations* reviewed in the *Gent. Mag.* for 1763, pp. 602, 634, says 'that more than eight times as many soldiers fall by fever as by battle.' The military hospitals 'sweep off the men like a perpetual pestilence. . . . A cruel parsimony frequently devotes many lives to destruction. . . . Soldiers frequently contract inveterate rheumatisms and lose the use of their limbs merely for want of an addition to their clothing. . . . As it is frequently fit that the sick should be kept upon half diet, his unexpended pay should always come into his own pocket, which at present is seldom the case. He might then be able to procure shoes and stockings, the want of which frequently occasions a relapse in weakly men.' Dr. Franklin, describing on May 14, 1768, the riot in St. George's Fields in which the soldiers shot six people dead, continues :—'Several of the soldiers are imprisoned. If they are not hanged, it is feared there will be more and greater mobs; and if they are, that no soldier will assist in suppressing any mob hereafter. The prospect either way is gloomy. It is said the English soldiers [English as distinguished from the Scotch] cannot be confided in to act against these mobs, being suspected as rather inclined to favour and join them.' The soldiers who had fired on the mob belonged to a Scotch regiment. Franklin's *Memoirs* (ed. 1833), iii. 310.

Note 11. The Marquis of Granby was Commander in Chief from Aug. 1766 to Jan. 1770. His popularity is shown by the number of taverns that still bear his sign. 'It was cruel,' wrote Lord Chesterfield on his appointment, 'to put a boy [he was 45 years old] over the head of old Ligonier.' *Letters to his Son*, iv. 248. Junius, who had attacked him in his life-time, after his death wrote :—'His mistakes in public conduct did not arise from want of sentiment or want of judgment, but in general from the difficulty of saying No to the bad people who surrounded him.' *Chatham Corres.* iii. 478. Horace Walpole writing of the division on the address of Thanks on Jan. 9, 1770, says :—'The most serious part is the defection of Lord Granby [the Commander-in-Chief]; for though he has sunk his character by so many changes, a schism in the army would be very unpleasant, especially as there are men bad enough to look towards rougher divisions than parliamentary.' *Letters*, v. 214.

Note 12. Charles Pratt, first Earl Camden, was Lord Chancellor from July, 1766, till his dismissal by the Duke of Grafton in Jan., 1770. In the *London Chronicle* of Oct. 26, 1769 (the day after the date of Hume's letter), the following paragraph appeared :—'Yesterday the Lord Chancellor was *done* at Jonathan's upon the ratio of sixty to forty guineas that he resigns before Christmas; and at night his Lordship was *done* at Arthur's upon the ratio of three to one that he resigns before Saturday se'nnight.'

Note 13. Hume wrote of Lord Mansfield on July 5, 1768 :—'Lord Mansfield said to me that it was impossible for him to condemn Wilkes to the pillory, because the Attorney-General did not demand it. Yesterday he represented to the Spanish Ambassador that moderate sentence as a refinement in politics, which reduced the scoundrel the sooner to obscurity. It would be a strange cause which he could not find plausible reasons to justify.' Burton's *Hume*, ii. 415. Horace Walpole, writing on Nov. 13, 1766, says:—'Lord Mansfield was reduced to make a speech *against prerogative*—yes, yes ; and then was so cowed by Lord Camden, and the very sight of Lord Chatham, that he explained away half he had said.' *Letters*, v. 28. On Dec. 18, 1770, Walpole wrote :—'If we having nothing else to do after the holidays, we are to amuse ourselves with worrying Lord Mansfield, who between irregularities in his Court, timidity, and want of judgment, has lowered himself to be the object of hatred to many, and of contempt to everybody.' *Ib.* p. 270. In the *Memoirs of George III*, iv. 187, Walpole speaks of his 'pusillanimity' and 'abject spirits.' Strahan writing to Hume on Jan 13, 1770, after mentioning that Mansfield's nephew, Lord Stormont, had called on him, continues :—'I took that opportunity of lamenting his Uncle's want of courage ; which if joined to his great abilities might at this juncture be of such eminent service to this country. He said nobody acted more strictly up to the plan of conduct he prescribed to himself. I replied, I was no judge of that ; but I was certain his allowing Wilkes to insult him upon the Bench, and his deigning to vindicate himself against the accusations of that scoundrel, could not be consistent with any plan whatever. At least to me it was wholly incomprehensible. There was no answering this. And I chose not to push the matter further. You will probably think I pushed it too far. Perhaps I might, but it came naturally into the conversation.' *M.S.R.S.E.*

Note 14. Lord Bute's training and character suited an experimenter. Johnson described him as 'a theoretical statesman—a book-minister.' Boswell's *Johnson*, ii. 353. Lord Shelburne wrote of him:—'He panted for the Treasury, having a notion that the King and he understood it from what they had read about revenue and funds while they were at Kew.' Fitzmaurice's *Shelburne*, i. 141. His 'project of Government,' as Burke termed it, is described in *Thoughts on the Cause of the Present Discontents*, Payne's *Burke*, i. 12-14. Though he resigned office in April, 1763, his *influence* was long felt and perhaps still longer dreaded. Mr. Grenville, the Prime Minister, on May 22, 1765, in the name of the Cabinet offered to the King certain points as indispensably necessary for carrying on the public business. The first of these was 'that the King's Ministers should be authorised to declare that Lord Bute is to have nothing to do in His Majesty's Councils or Government, in any manner or shape whatever.' *Grenville Papers*, iii. 41. To this the King assented. *Ib.* p. 185. In the following November Jenkinson (afterwards first Earl of Liverpool) ' owned to Mr. Grenville that the intercourse in writing between His Majesty and Lord Bute always continued, telling him that he knew that the King wrote him a journal every day of what passed, and as minute a one as if, said he, "your boy at school was directed by you to write his journal to you."' *Ib.* p. 220. Hume wrote on Aug. 13, 1767, when he was still an Under-Secretary of State :—'I am told that Lord Townshend openly ascribes his own promotion [to the Lord-Lieutenancy of Ireland] entirely to the friendship of Lord Bute. Charles Fitzroy lately in a great meeting proposed Lord Bute's health in a bumper. It will be a surprise to you certainly if that noble Lord should again come into fashion, and openly avow his share of influence, and be openly courted by all the world.' Burton's *Hume*, ii. 407.

Strahan, at the end of his letter of April 1, 1768, after saying that he thinks that the banishment of Lord Bute from England is probable, continues :—'The case of this nobleman is really singular ; divested of power, he retains all the odium of Prime Minister. Having long since most injudiciously pushed into office, and as injudiciously retired from the political theatre, he hath ever since exercised the power of recommending, or rather nominating every succeeding Ministry. These have by turns spurned at and renounced their maker, and what is truly remarkable, though he has had no influence in their Councils, though he has all along never dared to interpose, even so far as occasionally to serve an humble retainer or dependant, yet, being well known to have named the MEN, he has made himself in the public opinion ultimately responsible for their *measures*; and will ere long, if I am not mistaken, be made the scapegoat of all their misconduct; so that in the end, his master's favour, of which he appears to have little known how to avail himself, will cost him dear.' *M. S. R. S. E.*

It was on March 2, 1770, that Lord Chatham, in the House of Lords, 'spoke of the secret influence of an invisible power ; of a favourite, who notwithstanding he was abroad was at this moment as potent as ever ; who had ruined every plan for the public good, and betrayed every man who had taken a responsible office. . . . There is,' he added, 'something behind the throne greater than the King himself.' *Parl. Hist.* xvi. 842–3.

Note 15. Hume wrote on March 28, 1769:—'I am well assured that Lord Chatham will, after the holidays, creep out from his retreat and appear on the scene.

    "Depositis novus exuviis, nitidusque juventa,
      Volvitur ad solem et linguis micat ore trisulcis."

I know not if I cite Virgil exactly[1], but I am sure I apply him right. The villain is to thunder against the violation of the Bill of Rights in not allowing the county of Middlesex the choice of its member ! Think of the impudence of that fellow, and his quackery—and his cunning—and his audaciousness ; and judge of the influence he will have over such a deluded multitude.' Burton's *Hume*, ii. 422.

[1] ' Quum positis novus exuviis nitidusque juventa
      Volvitur, aut catulos tectis aut ova relinquens,
      Arduus ad solem, et linguis micat ore trisulcis.'
                                    Georgics, iii. 437.

Horace Walpole wrote on March 24, 1769:—'If the Scotch who cannot rest in patience without persecuting Wilkes, and who have neither known how to quiet or to quell him, prompt new violence, the nation will call out for Lord Chatham and Lord Temple. . . . For a little more power men risk what they possess, and never discover that the most absolute are those which reign in the hearts of the people.   Were Cardinal Richelieu, Cromwell, or Lewis XI more despotic than Mr. Pitt at the end of the last reign?   And then he had the comfort of going to bed every night without the fear of being assassinated[1].'   *Letters*, v. 149.   On July 9, 1769, Burke wrote to the Marquis of Rockingham :—'The Court alone can profit by any move-ments of Lord Chatham, and he is always their resource, when they are run hard.'   Burke's *Corres.* i. 179.   On Oct. 29 (four days after the date of Hume's letter) he wrote to the same Lord :—'Though, according to Lord Camden's phrase, Lord Chatham has had a wonder-ful resurrection to health, his resurrection to credit and consequence, and to the power of doing mischief (without which his resurrection will be incomplete), must be owing to your Lordship and your friends.'   *Ib.* p. 202.

Johnson in a paragraph which was struck out of his *Taxation no Tyranny* by 'men in power' suggests that KING WILLIAM may be sought for by the Whigs of America, if they erect a monarchy. Boswell's *Johnson*, ii. 314.   See *post*, Letters of Jan. 25, 1770; March 25, 1771, and Oct. 26, 1775, for Hume's attacks on Lord Chatham.

Note 16.   Burke, in *Present Discontents* (p. 45), written at the end of 1769, says :—'Good men look upon this distracted scene with sorrow and indignation.   Their hands are tied behind them.   They are de-spoiled of all the power which might enable them to reconcile the strength of Government with the rights of the people.   They stand in a most distressing alternative.   But in the election among evils they hope better things from temporary confusion than from estab-lished servitude.   In the meantime, the voice of law is not to be heard.   Fierce licentiousness begets violent restraints.   The military arm is the sole reliance; and then, call your constitution what you please, it is the sword that governs.   The civil power, like every other that calls in the aid of an ally stronger than itself, perishes by the assistance it receives.'

Horace Walpole wrote on Jan. 1, 1770 :—'Is the Crown to be forced to be absolute!   Is Cæsar to enslave us, because he conquered Gaul! . . . Is eloquence to talk or write us out of ourselves! or is Catiline to save us, *but so as by fire*! . . . Despotism, or unbounded licentiousness, can endear no nation to any honest man.   The French can adore the monarch that starves them, and banditti are often attached to their chief; but no good Briton can love any constitution

[1] Burke, in the *Ann. Reg.* for 1761 (i. 47), had said that ' under Mr. Pitt for the first time administration and popularity were seen united.'

that does not secure the tranquillity and peace of mind of all.' *Letters*,
v. 213. See *post*, Letter of Nov. 13, 1775.

Note 17.   The 'shooting' and the 'hanging,' fortunately for
liberty, were not sure to be on the same side.   Professor Dicey points
out that 'the position of a soldier may be, both in theory and practice,
a difficult one.   He may, as it has been well said [1], be liable to be shot
by a court-martial if he disobeys an order, and to be hanged by a judge
and jury if he obeys it.' *Law of the Constitution*, ed. 1886, p. 311.   Hume,
in the midst of the riots of the previous year, writing to a French
lady, had expressed himself with much more calmness than he now
did :—'London, 24th May, 1768.   There have been this spring in
London a good many French gentlemen, who have seen the nation
in a strange situation, and have admired at our oddity.   The elections
have put us into a ferment ; and the riots of the populace have been
frequent ; but as these mutinies were founded on nothing, and had no
connexion with any higher order of the state, they have done but
little mischief, and seem now entirely dispersed.' *Private Corres.* p.
262.   Dr. Blair wrote to Hume from Edinburgh on March 11, 1769 :—
'John [Bull] seems to have lost altogether the little sense he had ;
and I do suspect blood must be drawn from him before he settles.
We look on the distant scene with calmness ; *procul a Jove, procul a
fulmine* ; but to live in the midst of it I would really think disagreeable.' *M. S. R. S. E.*

Note 18.   Burke describes how 'the nation had been in a great
ferment during the whole summer—the like had scarcely been ever
remembered.'   After giving the opinions of each party he continues :—
'The minds of all men were occupied on the one side and the other
with these considerations, and great expectations were formed concerning the manner in which these great points would be handled
in the Speech from the Throne.   The Speech began by taking notice
of a distemper that had broke out among the horned cattle. . . . No
notice whatsoever was taken of the great domestic movements, which
had brought on, or followed, the petitions.   The public were much
surprised at the silence concerning the petitions, and at the solemn
mention of the horned cattle, which filled the place of that important
business.   It became even a subject of too general ridicule.' *Ann.
Reg.* 1770, pp. 58–9.

Johnson in *The False Alarm*, published in Jan. 1770, while he
attacks those 'who have been so industrious to spread suspicion and
incite fury from one end of the kingdom to the other,' and calls the
disturbances 'this tempest of outrage,' yet proposes no rash remedies.   'He cannot favour the opposition,' he says, 'for he thinks it
wicked, and cannot fear it, for he thinks it weak. . . . Nothing is
necessary at this alarming crisis but to consider the alarm as false.
To make concessions is to encourage encroachment.   Let the Court

---

[1] Professor Dicey is perhaps quoting Lord Hervey's words.   See Memoirs of
Lord Hervey, ii. 135, 142.

despise the faction, and the disappointed people will soon deride it.'
Works, vi. 156, 178.

Note 19. The Duke was thirty-four years old. Horace Walpole
wrote on June 16, 1768:—'What can one say of the Duke of Grafton,
but that his whole conduct is childish, insolent, inconstant, and
absurd—nay, ruinous ? Because we are not in confusion enough, he
makes everything as bad as possible, neglecting on one hand, and
taking no precaution on the other. I neither see how it is possible
for him to remain Minister, nor whom to put in his place. No
government, no police, London and Middlesex distracted, the
Colonies in rebellion, Ireland ready to be so, and France arrogant
and on the point of being hostile ! . . . the Duke of Grafton, like an
apprentice, thinking the world should be postponed to a whore
and a horse-race.' *Letters*, v. 106. Junius, in his Letter of April 10,
1769, describes the Duke as 'a singular instance of youth without
spirit.' Hume had written on July 22 of the year before, when the
Duke was in power:—' I fancy the Ministry will remain ; though
surely their late remissness, or ignorance, or pusillanimity, ought to
make them ashamed to show their faces, were it even at Newmarket.'
Burton's *Hume*, ii. 417. When the Duke resigned Walpole wrote :—
' A very bad temper ; no conduct, and obstinacy always ill-placed,
have put an end to his Grace's administration.' *Letters*, v. 223.

Note 20. It is probable that a man who boasted of his ' rigid
frugality' and enjoyed his opulence had before this sold out the
stock, for the rise of which he had been so anxious (*ante*, p. 42).
In his last illness 'he maintained that the national debt must be
the ruin of Britain.' Burton's *Hume*, ii. 497. Thirty-three years
earlier, in 1737, so prosperous had been the country that Sir John
Barnard brought in a bill to reduce the interest of the National
Debt from four to three per cent. Sir Robert Walpole opposed
it, chiefly through 'fear of disobliging the moneyed men in the
House of Commons.' Though the Bill at first was supported by
a great majority (220 to 157), yet Walpole 'by making use of all
his oratory to persuade and all his Exchequer knowledge to puzzle '
got it thrown out by a majority nearly as great. The Debt at that
time amounted to almost fifty million pounds. Lord Hervey's
Memoirs, ii. 325–330.

Note 21. March, 1765. Stamp Act passed. *Ann. Reg.* 1765, i. 38.
March, 1766. Stamp Act repealed. *Ib.* 1766, i. 46.
June, 1767. Tea duties established. *Parl. Hist.* xvi. 376.
Sept. 1768. Convention met at Boston. *Ann. Reg.* 1768, i. 73.
Sept. 1768. Troops sent from England to support the Govern-
ment arrived on the day the Convention broke up. *Ib.* p. 74.
March, 1770. ' Terrible engagement between the soldiery and the
towns-people of Boston ; four persons killed on the spot.' *Ib.* 1770,
i. 99.
Dec. 1773. Tea thrown into the sea at Boston. *Ib.* 1774, i. 49.

Sept. 1774.   General Congress met at Philadelphia. *Ib.* 1775, i. 23.
April, 1775.   'First blood drawn at Lexington.' *Ib.* i. 126.
June, 1775.   Battle of Bunker's Hill. *Ib.* i. 134.

Horace Walpole on Aug. 4, 1768, after describing a riot at Wapping, continues :—'Well! but we have a worse riot, though a little farther off. Boston—not in Lincolnshire, though we have had a riot even there—but in New England, is almost in rebellion, and two regiments are ordered thither. Letters are come in that say the other provinces disapprove; and even the soberer persons there. In truth it is believed in the City that this tumult will be easily got the better of.' *Letters,* v. 114.

Note 22.   Burke, after telling of the peace made with Hyder Ali on April 3, 1769, continues :—'The consequences of this unfortunate war in the Carnatic were not confined to the East Indies; the alarm was caught at home, where the distance of the object and the uncertain knowledge of the danger, having full room to operate upon the imagination, multiplied the fears of the people concerned in a most amazing degree. India stock fell above 60 per cent. in a few days.' *Ann. Reg.* 1769, i. 52.   It was not till nearly a month after the date of Hume's letter that certain news of the peace was received. *Gent. Mag.* 1769, p. 557.   Horace Walpole wrote on July 19, 1769:—'The East India Company is all faction and gaming. Such fortunes are made and lost every day as are past belief. Our history will appear a gigantic lie hereafter, when we are shrunk again to our own little island. People trudge to the other end of the town to vote who shall govern empires at the other end of the world.' *Letters,* v. 177.

Note 23.   Hume wished for the diminution of London because he dreaded its power, exerted as it was at this time against the combination of Court and Parliament. 'The Common-Council was,' to use Johnson's phrase, 'too inflammable.' Boswell's *Johnson,* ij. 164.   Johnson in 1775 'owned that London was too large; but added, "It is nonsense to say the head is too big for the body. It would be as much too big, though the body were ever so large; that is to say, though the country were ever so extensive. It has no similarity to a head connected with a body."' *Ib.* ii. 356.   In 1778 'he laughed at querulous declamations against the age, on account of luxury—increase of London,' etc. *Ib.* iii. 226.   A line in Horace Walpole's Letter of July 19, 1769 (*Letters,* v. 177), shows why the power of London had so often been dreaded. 'London,' he says, 'for the first time in its life, has not dictated to England.'

Note 24.   'Hall, the author of *Crazy Tales,* said he could not bear David Hume for being such a monarchical dog. "Is it not shocking," said he, "that a fellow who does not believe in God should believe in a King?"' *Boswelliana,* p. 210.   '"Sir," said Dr. Johnson, "Hume is a Tory by chance, as being a Scotchman; but not upon a principle of duty, for he has no principle. If he is anything, he is a Hobbist."' Boswell's *Johnson,* v. 272.

Note 25. Hume wrote to the Countess de Boufflers on June 19, 1767:—'You know that ministerial falls are very light accidents in this country; a fallen minister immediately rises a patriot, and perhaps mounts up to greater consideration than before.' *Private Corres.* p. 246. Lord Hervey writing of the year 1727 says:—'Both Whigs and Tories were subdivided into two parties; the Tories into Jacobites and what were called Hanover Tories; the Whigs into patriots and courtiers, which was in plain English "Whigs in place" and "Whigs out of place."' Lord Hervey's *Memoirs,* i. 5. Johnson in the fourth edition of his *Dictionary,* published in 1773, introduced a second definition of *patriot:*—'It is sometimes used for a factious disturber of the government.' In 1775 'he suddenly uttered, in a strong determined tone, an apophthegm at which many will start:— "Patriotism is the last refuge of a scoundrel."' Boswell's *Johnson,* ii. 348.

Note 26. Had Hume's wish been gratified, he would scarcely have been satisfied with the result; for according to Johnson, 'Mr. Wilkes and the freeholders of Middlesex might all sink into non-existence without any other effect, than that there would be room made for a new rabble and a new retailer of sedition and obscenity. The cause of our country would suffer little; the rabble, whencesoever they come, will be always patriots, and always supporters of the Bill of Rights.' Johnson's *Works,* vi. 169.

Hume had expressed wishes fully as violent before. Thus on July 22, 1768, he wrote to Elliot:—'O! how I long to see America and the East Indies revolted, totally and finally—the revenue reduced to half,—public credit fully discredited by bankruptcy,—the third of London in ruins, and the rascally mob subdued. I think I am not too old to despair of being witness to all these blessings.' Burton's *Hume,* ii. 417. On Oct. 16, 1769, he wrote:—'I am delighted to see the daily and hourly progress of madness, and folly, and wickedness in England. The consummation of these qualities are the true ingredients for making a fine narrative in history, especially if followed by some signal and ruinous convulsion,—as I hope will soon be the case with that pernicious people!' *Ib.* p. 431.

Lord North would have laughed at Hume's violence: 'On Nov. 13, 1770, in his speech on the Address he said:—'Can any mortal, who does not read the *Persian Tales* as a true history, believe that because we have little political squabbles among ourselves the people will throw off at once their allegiance, their interest and their honour, abandon their lawful sovereign and offer their necks to a foreign yoke? This surely is the raving of a madman or the dream of an idiot. He that has sense to feed himself, or reason to distinguish rags and straw in a cell of Bedlam from the trappings of royalty, can never draw so monstrous a conclusion.' *Parl. Hist.* xvi. 1050. How different from Hume's were Horace Walpole's feelings as he viewed the troubled scene. Less than a fortnight later he wrote :—'I sit on the beach and contemplate the storm, but have not that apathy of finding that

"Suave mari magno turbantibus aequora ventis[1]," etc.

I love the constitution I am used to, and wish to leave it behind me ; and Roman as my inclinations are, I do not desire to see a Caesar on the stage, for the pleasure of having another Brutus; especially as Caesars are more prolific than Brutuses.' *Letters*, v. 201.

Note 27.   In the debate of March 19, 1770, on the Remonstrance from the City, 'Lord Barington said it was so far from being an act of the City of London, that it could not properly be said to be the act of the poor people to whom it was once read, but of a set of Catilines only, who had no view but to draw all men from law and allegiance.   Mr. Beckford, the Lord Mayor, was stung by this keen reproach ; and to recriminate said that there were people out of the City who were ready to cut throats, and had an army at hand for that purpose.' *Parl. Hist.* xvi. 899.

Note 28.   Who this friend was I have not been able to ascertain.

Note 29.   When Lord Stormont, in 1779, was made Secretary of State, Horace Walpole wrote :—'He has a fair character, and is a friend of General Conway; but he is a Scot and Lord Mansfield's nephew, which the people mind much more than his character.' *Letters*, vii. 266.   His 'return home' was perhaps from a visit to Italy in 1768.   On May 12 of that year Horace Walpole wrote to Sir Horace Mann at Florence:—'I am much obliged to Lord Stormont for his kind thoughts, and am glad you are together.   You will be a comfort to him, and it must be very much so to you at this time, to have a rational man to talk with instead of old fools and young ones, boys and travelling governors.' *Ib.* v. 100.

Note 30.   An edition of Hume's *History* in 8 vols. 4to. was published by Cadell in 1770.

Note 31.   An edition in 4 vols. small 8vo. was published by T. Cadell, London, and A. Kincaid and A. Donaldson, Edinburgh, in 1770.

Note 32.   Sir Gilbert Elliot wrote from Minto on July 11, 1768, to Hume at London :—'Farming, I find, is very expensive—day's wages now at a shilling.'   Burton's *Hume*, ii. 416.   'In 1756,' says Ramsay of Ochtertyre, 'a labourer's wages were generally sixpence a day in summer.'   *Scotland and Scotsmen*, ii. 211.

Note 33.   'April 25, 1768.   Extract of a letter from Edinburgh :— "A number of apprentice boys, amounting to several hundreds, assembled here, and carried on their shoulders a figure which they called Mr. Wilkes.   After parading the streets, and shouting *Wilkes and Liberty*, they carried him to the Grassmarket, where they chaired the mock hero on the stone where the common gallows is usually fixed at executions.   After making a fire they committed the effigy

---

[1] Lucretius, ii. 1.

to the flames."' *Ann. Reg.* 1768, i. 99. Burke, after mentioning how
few Addresses in support of the Ministers were obtained in England
in the summer of 1769, continues :—'It was invidiously observed
that Scotland was much more ready in expressing the most perfect
satisfaction in the conduct and character of the Ministers. Addresses,
which filled the Gazette for several weeks, came from every town
and from almost every village in that part of the kingdom.' *Ib.*
1770, i. 57.

LETTER XXXVII.

The Opening of the Session of 1770.

DEAR STRAHAN

I am extremely oblig'd to you for your account of
the Debate in the house of Peers [1]: It is very judicious
and accurate and impartial, as usual. I now begin to
entertain strong hopes, that the King will weather this
Tempest [2], and that the Infamy of Calumny, Faction,
Madness and Disorder will at last fall on those heads, who
merit it. The Ministry are much better advis'd not to give
nor even to take Provocation [3], than they seem to have
been by the Paper of Ruffheads [4] which you sent me last
Autumn. And as every obnoxious Person is turnd out [5],
the King's Resolution is visible to support his Ministry, and
men will either acquiesce or return to the ordinary,
parliamentary Arts of Opposition [6]. I apprehend, however,
that before the Session ends, this abandon'd Faction, not to
be foild without hopes, will have recourse to the violence
of the Mob, in expectation of provoking the Ministry
to commit some Imprudence: Their greatest Imprudence
woud be remissness on that Occasion. Open Violence
gives such a palpable Reason for the severe Execution of
the Laws, a thing much wanted, that it ought immediately
to be laid hold of, and it will have a very salutary Effect [7].

The part which Chatham acts, after all the Favours and

Distinctions which he has receivd from the Crown, is infamous, like himself [8].

I send you enclos'd an answer to one of Cadells. It is open, that you may read it, as the matter concerns you, no less than him.

I am Dear S[ir] Yours sincerely

DAVID HUME.

EDINBURGH, 25 *Jan.*, 1770.

Note 1. The Session opened on Jan. 9, 1770. 'The debates,' wrote Burke, 'were carried on with a warmth and acrimony of expression before unknown in that assembly.' *Ann. Reg.* 1770, i. 60. Strahan, who was a spectator in the House of Lords on the opening night, sent Hume a long report of the Debate. See *Letters of Eminent Persons to David Hume*, p. 91.

Note 2. Horace Walpole, writing on Jan. 10 of the victory of the Ministers in both Houses, said :—' Where so many caldrons full of passions are boiling, they are not extinguished by one wet sheet of votes.' *Letters*, v. 214.

Note 3. 'Burke on the Address had attacked the House itself, and hinted that the majority was so guilty that they did not dare to take notice of the insults offered to them, and the reproaches cast on them. On the Report he added that he was conscious he had deserved to be sent to the Tower for what he had said ; but knew the House did not dare to send him thither. Sir George Saville used the same language. Lord North took notice of it, but said he supposed Sir George had spoken in warmth. "No," replied Saville coolly, " I spoke what has been my constant opinion; I thought so last night, I thought the same this morning. I look on this House as sitting illegally after their illegal act [of voting Luttrell representative for Middlesex]. They have betrayed their trust. I will add no epithets," continued he, "because epithets only weaken; therefore I will not say they have betrayed their country corruptly, flagitiously, and scandalously ; but I do say they have betrayed their country; and I stand here to receive the punishment for having said so." Mr. Conway, sensible of the weight of such an attack from a man so respectable, alarmed at the consequences that would probably attend the punishment of him . . . took up the matter with temper, wisdom, and art. . . . Had the Ministers dared to send Saville to the Tower, the Cavendishes and the most virtuous and respectable of his friends would have started up, would have avowed his language, and would have demanded to share his imprisonment. A dozen or twenty such confessors in the heat of a tumultuous capital would have been no indifferent spectacle ; the great northern counties were devoted to them. Then, indeed, the moment was serious. Fortunately there were none but subordinate Ministers in the House of Commons, not one of whom chose to cast so decisive a die[1]. The House sat silent under its ignominy—a punishment well suited to its demerits ; and the sword was not called in to decide a contest in which Liberty and the Constitution would probably have been the victims.' Walpole's *Memoirs of George III*, iv. 38. Burke began his reply to Lord North by saying :—' The noble lord who spoke last, after extending his right leg a full yard before his left, rolling his flaming eyes, and moving his ponderous frame, has at length opened his mouth. I was all attention. After these portents I expected something still more awful and tremendous. I expected that the Tower would have been threatened in articulated thunder; but I have heard only a feeble remonstrance against violence and passion ; when I expected the powers of destruction to "cry havoc, and let slip the dogs of war," an overblown bladder has burst, and nobody has been hurt by the crack.' *Parl. Hist.* xvi. 720.

Note 4. Owen Ruffhead is best known by his *Life of Pope*. Johnson speaking of it said :—' He knew nothing of Pope and nothing of poetry.' Boswell's *Johnson*, ii. 166. In a letter to Strahan, dated Parade, Hot Wells, Aug. 24, 1769, Ruffhead writes :—' As to the Pamphlet, I heartily wish you had corrected the inaccuracies you pointed out to me. . . . I think it would be advisable to advertise it as a second edition, but leave it wholly to you.' *Barker MSS.* He had lately been appointed one of the Chief Secretaries to the Treasury. He died on Oct. 25, 1769. *Gent. Mag.*, 1769, p. 511.

Note 5. Horace Walpole, writing on Jan. 18 of the dismissal of the Ministers, says :—' Nothing proves the badness of generals like an ill use of a great victory. Ours have not hurt their own success by neglecting to pursue it, but by pursuing it too far. Lord Huntingdon was turned out the next day, not for having joined the enemy, but merely for having absented himself.' After recounting some of the dismissals or resignations, Walpole continues :—' You may imagine how these events have raised the spirits and animosity of the Opposition.' *Letters*, v. 216. Burke in the *Ann. Reg.*, 1770, i. 63, under the date of Jan. 17, says :—' The whole of administration seemed to be falling to pieces. A violent panic prevailed.' On the 28th the Duke of Grafton resigned, and was succeeded as First Minister by Lord North. ' He is,' wrote Walpole on Jan. 30, ' much more able, more active, more assiduous, more resolute, and more fitted to deal with mankind.' *Letters*, v. 223.

Note 6. Johnson on April 14, 1775, said to Boswell, speaking of Lord North's Ministry :—' You must have observed, Sir, that administration is feeble and timid, and cannot act with that authority and resolution which is necessary. Were I in power I would turn out every man who dared to oppose me. Government has the

---

[1] Lord North was there, as Chancellor of the Exchequer—in a month's time to be Prime Minister.

distribution of offices that it may be enabled to maintain its authority.'   Boswell's *Johnson*, ii. 355.

Note 7. Hume wrote from Edinburgh on April 5, 1770 :—'I am sorry to inform you that all we statesmen in this town condemn loudly the conduct of you statesmen in London, especially in allowing those insolent rascals, the mayor and sheriffs, to escape with impunity.   We were much disappointed not to find them impeached, and a bill of pains and penalties passed upon them. The tumults which might have ensued in London we thought rather an advantage ; as it would give Government an opportunity of chastising that abominable rabble.'   Burton's *Hume*, ii. 435.

Note 8.   'Praise enough
      To fill th' ambition of a private man,
      That Chatham's language was his mother tongue,
      And Wolfe's great name compatriot with his own.
      Farewell those honours, and farewell with them
      The hope of such hereafter. They have fall'n
      Each in his field of glory; one in arms
      And one in council. Wolfe upon the lap
      Of smiling victory that moment won,
      And Chatham, heart-sick of his country's shame.'
                          Cowper's *Poems*, ed. 1786, ii. 57.

Burke in the *Ann. Reg.* for 1770, i. 66, speaking of this time, says :— 'The Earl of Chatham now seemed disposed to recover that almost boundless popularity which he once possessed, and which, in consequence of a subsequent conduct, he had in a great measure lost.' See *ante*, p. 127, *n.* 15. In the debate on the Address Chatham had said :—' The English people are loud in their complaints ; they proclaim with one voice the injuries they have received ; they demand redress, and depend upon it, my Lords, that one way or other they will have redress. They will never return to a state of tranquillity until they are redressed ; nor ought they.' *Parl. Hist.* xvi. 652. On Jan. 22 he went still further :—'If the breach in the constitution be effectually repaired, the people will of themselves return to a state of tranquillity. If not—may discord prevail for ever !' *Ib.* p. 748.

LETTER XXXVIII.

The City Address : the 'detestable' Edition of the History.

DEAR STRAHAN

Tho' I have renouncd the World, I cannot forbear being rouzd with Indignation at the Audaciousness, Impudence, and Wickedness of your City Address[1].   To

punish it as it deserves woud certainly produce a Fray;
but what signifies a Fray, in comparison of losing all
Authority to Government.   There must necessarily be
a Struggle between the Mob and the Constitution; and it
cannot come on at a more favourable time nor in a more
favourable Cause.   I wish therefore, (I cannot say I hope)
that vigorous Measures will be taken; an impeachment
immediately voted of the Mayor and his two Sherriffs for
high Crimes and Misdeamenours, and the Habeas Corpus
suspended till next meeting of Parliament[2].   Good God!
what abandon'd Madmen there are in England!

You have suspended my Chronicle on account of
Sir Gilberts vacating his seat[3].   I am of a Club[4] here
that get down News papers and Pamphlets from London
regularly: So that you wont need to send me the Chronicle
any more.   Please only to let me know the Charge of it,
together with other Articles I owe you.

I am sorry to hear that Dr. Armstrong has printed his
Tragedy among his Miscellanies[5].   It is certainly one
of the worst pieces I ever saw; and totally unworthy of
his other Productions.   I shoud have endeavourd to dissuade him from printing it, had he been a man advisable.
But I knew, that he keeps an Anger against Garrick
for above twenty Years for refusing to bring it on the
Stage; and he never since woud allow him to be so much
as a tolerable Actor[6].   I thought therefore it was wiser not
to meddle in the Affair.

I have had a Letter from Mr. Cadell, which is very
obliging: I agree to the reprinting in any form you and
he please, and I believe ten volumes in large Octavo will
be best.   But I find, that I have been cutting a great way
before the point, and that I am scarce ever likely to see an
End of that detestable Edition[7].   I really have no reason
to believe seriously, that the half of it is yet sold, or that the
Book has at present any sale at all worth speaking of:

Such a habit you and he have got during seven Years past
of deceiving me by false Intelligence, that I am determind
never to believe a word either of you says on that head [8].
For Instance you both told me when I left London, that
there remaind not 700 Copies : He has since wrote me that
before the meeting of Parliament he had disposd of 200 of
these : In his last Letter he says, that the Sale still continues rapid. I must therefore suppose that before the
month of May next, there woud not be 300 in your Warehouses, which is a little enough Number (or too little) for a
Book which woud take near a twelvemonth in reprinting.
But he speaks still of a distant Period for beginning the
new Edition. You see, therefore, that these Stories are
totally inconsistent. I need only say, that I have a Copy
corrected, and I believe considerably improvd at your
Service, whenever you please to call for it. I am no-
wise impatient to have another Edition : I only show you
that I had taken my Measures, in consequence of the
Intelligence conveyd to me ; and I shall add, that, if the
Book has really any Sale, it woud probably be the Interest
of the Proprietors to run the Risque of losing some of that
odious Edition rather than encumber the Market any
longer with it. But of this you are the best Judges.

I am Dear Strahan Yours sincerely

DAVID HUME.

EDINBURGH, 13 *March*, 1770.

Note 1. On July 5, 1769, the City presented a petition to the King,
'to which he made no answer, and immediately turned about to the
Danish Minister, and delivered the petition to the Lord in Waiting.'
Ann. Reg. 1769, i. 113. On March 14, 1770, the City, indignant at
receiving no answer, presented 'a Remonstrance and Petition praying
for the dissolution of Parliament and the removal of evil Ministers.'
Ann. Reg. 1770, i. 79, 80. Horace Walpole, writing to Mann the next
day, says :—'The manifesto on which all seems to turn is the Remonstrance from the City. You will have seen it in the public
papers, and certainly never saw a bolder declaration both against
King and Parliament. Sixteen aldermen have protested against it,

but could not stop it. The King, after some delay, received it yesterday on his throne. . . . The crisis is now tremendous. Should the House of Commons, or both Houses, fall on the Remonstrance, as it in a manner dares them to do, it is much to be apprehended that not only the Lord Mayor and Sheriffs will uphold their act, but that many lords and members will avow them, and demand to be included in the same sentence. The Tower, crammed with such proud criminals, will be a formidable scene indeed. The petitioning counties will certainly turn remonstrants. An association among them is threatened, and a general refusal by the party of paying the land-tax. In short rebellion is in prospect and in everybody's mouth. . . . It is not yet, I hope, too late for wisdom and temper to step in. I sigh when I hear any other language. The English may be soothed—I never read that.they were to be frightened.' *Letters,* v. 229.

In a debate on May 4 Lord Chatham made a remarkable contribution to English history. ' My Lords,' he said, ' when I mentioned the Livery of London, I thought I saw a smile of ridicule upon some faces. . . . The Livery of London, my Lords, were respectable at the time of Caesar's invasion.' *Parl. Hist.* xvi. 968.

Note 2. Horace Walpole wrote on March 20 (*Letters,* v. 230, where the date March 16 is wrong):—' Sir T. Clavering moved to address the King. . . . The House, you may imagine, was full of resentment, and at eleven at night the Address was carried by 271 to 108. . . . The great point is still in suspense—what to do with the offenders. The wisest, because the most temperate method that I have heard suggested is, to address the King to order a prosecution by the Attorney-General. Two others that have been mentioned are big with every mischief—the Tower or expulsion. Think of the three first magistrates of the City [1] in prison, or of a new election for London ! I pray for temper, but what can one expect when such provocation is given ? . . . March 23. Lord North's temper and prudence has prevailed over much rash counsel ; and will, I hope, at last defeat the madness of both sides.'

Note 3. Sir Gilbert Elliot, third Baronet and father of the first Earl of Minto, was Hume's correspondent for many years. He is described in *Scotland and Scotsmen of the Eighteenth Century,* i. 364. Boswell, when considering the English accent which a Scotch gentleman should aim at attaining, says :—' I would give as an instance of what I mean to recommend to my countrymen the pronunciation of the late Sir Gilbert Elliot.' Boswell's *Johnson,* ii. 160.

In Elliot's MS. Journal for 1770 is the following entry :—' Feb. 3, Went to Court . . . Lord North made me the offer of the Treasurership of the Navy ; said the King wished I might accept, as many persons·were doubtful. Though hazardous, I did accept on the spot.' Walpole's *Memoirs· of George III,* iv. 87, *n.* 1. By his appointment

---

[1] The Lord Mayor and the two Sheriffs.

he vacated his seat for Roxburgh, but a new writ being ordered on March 8, he was re-elected. *Parl. Hist.* xvi. 452. No doubt Hume's *Chronicle* had been franked by Elliot. Till his re-election he lost his privilege, but I am surprised that he could not frank as a Minister.

Note 4. I am afraid that this cannot be the famous Poker Club, ' of which Andrew Crosbie was chosen Assassin, in case any officer of that sort should be needed; but David Hume was added as his Assessor, without whose assent nothing should be done, so that between *plus* and *minus* there was likely to be no bloodshed.' Dr. A. Carlyle's *Auto.* p. 420. These ' Poker men ' met, I think, only for conviviality.

Note 5. Dr. Armstrong's *Miscellanies* were published in 1770, in 2 vols. 12mo. His tragedy was *The Forced Marriage.* Churchill attacked him in the last lines that he wrote. Speaking of the Muses he says :—

> ' Let them with Armstrong, taking leave of sense,
> Read musty lectures on *Benevolence,*
> Or con the pages of his gaping *Day,*
> Where all his former fame was thrown away,
> Where all but barren labour was forgot ;
> And the vain stiffness of a *Letter'd* Scott.'
>
> Churchill's *Poems,* ed. 1766, ii. 329.

Note 6. See Boswell's *Johnson,* i. 75, *n.* 2, for the anger of ' Mr. Hawkins, the Poetry Professor,' against Garrick. A much better poet, W. J. Mickle, the author of the *Ballad of Cumnor Hall,* ' inserted in the *Lusiad* an angry note against Garrick, who had rejected a tragedy o his.' Shortly afterwards he saw him act for the first time. The play was *Lear.* ' During the first three acts he said not a word. In a fine passage of the fourth he fetched a deep sigh, and turning to a friend, " I wish," said he, " the note was out of my book." ' Bishop Horne's *Essays,* ed. 1808, p. 38. See also Boswell's *Johnson,* v. 349, *n.* 1.

Note 7. The ' detestable edition ' was that of 1763 in 8 vols. 8vo. When it came out, Hume showed no dissatisfaction with it. On March 12, 1763, he wrote to Elliot :—' In this new edition I have corrected several mistakes and oversights, which had chiefly proceeded from the plaguy prejudices of Whiggism, with which I was too much infected when I began this work.' Burton's *Hume,* ii. 144. On Sept. 3, 1764, he wrote to Millar that he thought the edition very correct. *Ib.* p. 232. Six years later his tone was changed. On June 21, 1770, he wrote of it to Strahan :—' I suppose you will not find one book in the English language of that size and price so ill printed.' Mr. Fortescue, of the British Museum, informs me, that ' it is printed in a small worn-out-looking type on a yellow thin blotting-paper ; it is bad, but not so strikingly bad as Hume's language implies.' His discontent would not have shown itself—perhaps would not have been felt—had the edition been a small one or been

rapidly sold. He was never weary of correcting his own writings. ' I
am,' he wrote to Strahan (*post*, Letter of March 25, 1771), 'perhaps
the only author you ever knew, who gratuitously employed great industry in correcting a work, of which he has fully alienated the
property.' His last corrections he made less than a fortnight before
his death (*post*, Letter of Aug. 12, 1776). Millar, whom Johnson
praised as 'the Maecenas of the age' (Boswell's *Johnson*, i. 278,
n. 1), in his 'rapaciousness' had printed so large a number of
copies of this edition of 1763 that they were not all sold ten years
later (*post*, Letter of March 19, 1773). He deceived Hume not only
as to the number printed, but also sold. In this concealment, though
not apparently in any actual deception, he induced Cadell and
Strahan to share (*post*, *ib*.). He overreached himself, for Hume
would write no more. ' That abominable edition,' he writes (*post*,
Letter of Jan. 30, 1773), 'has been one cause why I have thrown my
pen aside for ever.' Soon after it was brought out he had begun to
prepare for its successor, but he grew angry in his impatience long
before his publishers were willing to print an octavo edition. On
April 24, 1764, Millar had written to him :—'I have just reprinted the
Tudors in small 4to., and I believe I shall like the Stewarts in that size soon.'
M. S. R. S. E. To this Hume, replying in a letter dated ' Paris, April
[? May] 23, expressed his displeasure at the news :—' You were in
the wrong to make any edition without informing me ; because I left
in Scotland a copy very fully corrected, with a few alterations[1], which
ought to have been followed. I shall write to my sister to send it
you, and I desire you may follow it in all future editions, if there be
any such.' He goes on to mention one important alteration, and
adds :—' I have some scruple of inserting it on your account, till the
sale of the other editions be pretty considerably advanced.' Burton's
Hume, ii. 201. It must have been, I suppose, this same scruple which
kept him from making all these corrections in the fine edition in
8 vols. quarto which was published in 1770. That some corrections
were made is shown *post* in his Letter of June 21, 1770.

On Nov. 26, 1764, Millar wrote to him :—' The sale of the Stewarts
has been more than the others. They came out first, and the rest
some years after, which was the cause ; but there are above 2500
complete sets sold in 4to. of the lowest sale [?] vols. [?], but upwards
of 3000 of the Stewarts ; of the 8vo. history near 2000, and of the 8vo.
Essays, 400. They were only published in May last. I was asked
the question [how many editions had been published] at St. James's
the other day, when I said I considered your Works as Classics;
that I never numbered the editions as I did in books we wished to
puff. This I said before many clergy.' *M. S. R. S. E.*[2] Hume, who

[1] By 'corrections' he seems to mean *changes in words*, and by 'alterations'
changes in statements. Millar does not seem to have made any use of this corrected
volume. See *ante*, p. 85.
[2] Dr. Blair, writing to Strahan on April 10, 1778, about his Sermons, says :—

a year and a-half before had complained of 'the languishing sale' (Burton's *Hume*, ii. 148), was so much pleased with the news, false as it undoubtedly was, that he told Millar that he would write the continuation. On Oct. 19, 1767, he wrote to him :—'I intend to give up all my leisure time to the correction of my History, and to contrive more leisure than I have possessed since I came into public office. I had run over four volumes; but I shall give them a second perusal, and employ the same, or greater accuracy, in correcting the other four.' *Ib.* p. 409. On Feb. 21, 1770, he wrote to Elliot :—'I am running over again the last edition of my History, in order to correct it still further. I either soften or expunge many villainous, seditious Whig strokes, which had crept into it. I wish that my indignation at the present madness, encouraged by lies, calumnies, imposture, and every infamous act usual among popular leaders, may not throw me into the opposite extreme. I am however sensible that the first editions were too full of those foolish English prejudices, which all nations and all ages disavow.' *Ib.* p. 434.

It must be allowed that Hume's expectations of the sale of a work in eight volumes octavo were by no means low. He wrote to Millar on Oct. 8, 1766 :—'I own that the quick sale of my Philosophy surprizes me as much as the slow sale of my History. You have scarce dispos'd of 2000 copies in three years.' *M.S.R.S.E.* The population of England and Wales is about three and a-half times as large as it was when Hume wrote this. It is as if an historian of the present day should expect to sell 2,300 copies of an equally extensive work every year.

Note 8. See *post*, Letters of March 15, 19, 24, 1773.

LETTER XXXIX.

Lord Home: End of the Session: Lady Grant.

EDINBURGH, 22 *May*, 1770.

DEAR SIR

A few days ago, Lord Home[1] told me, that, in consequence of a new Arrangement of his Affairs, he shou'd stand in need of a large Sum of Money, which he propos'd to bring from England at lower than legal Interest[2]; and he hop'd his Friend, Strahan, woud be able to assist him on that Occasion. I said, that, tho' Mr. Strahan was a

---

[1] In some late publications you have a way of saying on the title-page, *A New Edition*; but I would much prefer your going on with the succession of editions, which certainly tends to buoy up a volume of Sermons.' *Rosebery MSS.*

rich Man, yet he had such great Enterprizes in hand, that I did not believe he had much ready Money to lend. My Lord replyed, that he expected more your good Offices than your Money, and that he was too well acquainted with the Opinion, entertained by the World of his Situation, to hope for borrowing Money at low Interest upon his own Security: But that Mr. Hay of Drumelzier and Mr. Gavin of Langtoun propos'd to bind with him [3]: Upon which he took my Promise, that I shoud write to you upon the Subject. It is certain that Mr. Hay is a Man of above 4000 pounds a year clear, and Mr. Gavin above 5000; and both of them frugal Men, so that there cannot be better Security in Britain; and that they intend to bind with him, My Lord's Writer [4], who is a man of Character, assur'd me. I think, therefore, that the Scheme is far from being *inadmissible.* I wish really, (as you no doubt do yourself) that you coud assist him on the Occasion; but in all cases, I must beg the favour of you to write me an ostensible Letter, which may satisfy him that I have not neglected his Request.

I find, that your great Reluctance to write me on a certain Subject [5] proceeds from your Unwillingness to retract every thing that you have been telling me these seven Years: But your Silence tells me the Truth more strongly than any thing you can say. Besides, I know not why you shoud have a Reluctance to retract. What you told me was for a good End, in order to excite my Industry, which might be of Advantage both to myself and the Proprietors of the former Volumes. And if there has been any Misconduct with regard to the Octavo Edition, you are entirely innocent of it. So that I see not any Reason why I may not now be told the Truth; especially as you see, that I am fully determind never to continue my History, and have indeed put it entirely out of my power by retiring to this Country, for

the rest of my Life. However, this is as you think proper:
Only, it is needless for Mr. Cadel to give me Accounts,
which are presently refuted by the Event. I say this without the least resentment against him, who is a very obliging,
and I believe a very honest man.

Nothing coud be more agreeable than your political
Intelligence. I have always said, without Flattery, that
you may give Instructions to Statesmen. We are very
happy, that this Session is got over without any notable
disaster[6]. Government has, I believe, gain'd Strength;
tho' not much Authority nor Character by its long suffering
and forbearance. But the Request of the Country Gentlemen, who joind them, was a very plausible Motive[7];
besides, I am told, that their Lawyers, particularly Lord
Mansfield[8], deserted them on this Occasion. But these
are Matters that very little concern me ; and except from
Indignation at so much abominable Insolence, Calumny,
Lyes, and Folly, I know not why I shoud trouble my
head about them : These Objects too, being at a distance,
affect me the less. We are happily in this Country united
as in a national Cause[9], which indeed it has become, in
some measure, by the Virulence of this detestable Faction.

We expect to see Lady Grant soon in this Country ; and
I suppose, that I must pay my Respects to her Ladyship.
I intend to give her *her Ladyship* very often, that she may
at least have some Pennyworths for her Money[10].

I suppose the Edition of my Essays in Twelves[11] is now
finishd or nearly so. As soon as it is finishd, pray, put
Mr. Cadel in mind to send me six Copies in any Parcel to
Balfour or Kincaid.

I am Dear Strahan Yours sincerely

DAVID HUME.

P.S.—Please to tell Mr. Cadel that if a Volume of the
Dictionaire de Commerce[12] comes over for me from Paris, he
pay a Guinea for it, which I shall refund him.

L

Note 1. Hume in his *Autobiography* says :—' My father's family is a branch of the Earl of Home's or Hume's.' The common ancestor 'lived,' he writes, 'in the time of James the First and Second of Scotland.' Burton's *Hume*, i. 3. A cousinship that is separated by a gulf of three hundred years is remote, but in Scotland counts for something, and, no doubt, had its influence on Hume. The Earl about whom he wrote is described in the peerage as the Rev. Alexander, ninth Earl. He was one of the witnesses to Hume's will.

Note 2. 'A statute passed in 1545 limited the rate of interest to 10 per cent. per annum ; in 1624 the rate was lowered to 8 per cent. ; in 1660 to 6 per cent., and in 1713 to 5 per cent.' *Penny Cyclo.* ed. 1838, xii. 506. Adam Smith in the *Wealth of Nations*, published in 1776, says :—' In a country such as Great Britain, where money is lent to government at three per cent., and to private people upon good security at four and four and a half, the present legal rent, five per cent., is perhaps as proper as any.' Ed. 1811, ii. 121. This passage must have been written some time before publication, for in the spring of 1776 government could not have raised a loan on such easy terms, the Three per Cents. having fallen to 86. *Gent. Mag.* 1776, p. 96. By the spring of 1779, Lord North, according to Horace Walpole, ' was happy to get money on the loan under eight per cent.' *Letters*, vii. 181.

Note 3. They would become sureties with him.

Note 4. Writer to the Signet, who answers to the Attorney or Solicitor in England.

Note 5. See *ante*, p. 139.

Note 6. Parliament rose on May 19. *Parl. Hist.* xvi. 1028. Horace Walpole wrote to Mann on May 24 :—' Not only the session is at an end, but I think the Middlesex election too, which my Lord Chatham has heated and heated so often over that there is scarce a spark of fire left. . . . Thus has the winter, which set out with such big black clouds, concluded with a prospect of more serenity than we have seen for some time. . . . Disunion has appeared between all parts of the Opposition, and unless experience teaches them to unite more heartily during the summer, or the Court commits any extravagance, or Ireland or America furnishes new troubles, you may compose yourself to tranquillity in your representing ermine [Mann was the English representative at Florence], and take as good a nap as any monarch in Europe.' *Letters*, v. 238.

Burke wrote on Aug. 15, 1770 :—' As to our affairs, they remain as they have been ; the people in general dissatisfied ; the government feeble, hated, and insulted ; but a dread of pushing things to a dangerous extreme, while we are seeking for a remedy to distempers which all confess, brings many to the support, and most to a sort of ill-humoured acquiescence in the present Court scheme of administration.' Burke's *Corres.* i. 230.

Note 7. Horace Walpole, writing on March 23, 1770, about the City Remonstrance (*ante*, p. 139, *n*. 1), says :—' The House, you may be sure, resented the insult offered to them, and the majorities have been very great; yet has there been no personal punishment or censure, or dubbing of martyrs. The Country Gentlemen have even declared that they will support the Court in no violence. This is very happy at a time when the first overt act of violence on either side may entail long bloodshed upon us.' *Letters*, v. 231. See also Walpole's *Memoirs of George III*, iv. 107. On May 23, the day after the date of Hume's letter, ' Beckford, the Lord Mayor, to the astonishment of the whole Court added a few words' to an Address presented to the King by the City. *Ib.* p. 154.

Note 8. Junius, in his Letter to Lord Mansfield of Nov. 14, 1770, speaking of the debate on the Middlesex Election, says :—' As a Lord of Parliament you were repeatedly called upon to condemn or defend the new law declared by the House of Commons. You affected to have scruples, and every expedient was attempted to remove them. The question was proposed and urged to you in a thousand different shapes. Your prudence still supplied you with evasion ; your resolution was invincible. For my own part, I am not anxious to penetrate this solemn secret. I care not to whose wisdom it is entrusted, nor how soon you carry it with you to your grave.' Horace Walpole says ' that Lord Mansfield, being called upon for his opinion on Luttrell's case in the Middlesex election, declared his opinion should go to the grave with him, having never told it but to one of the Royal Family ; and being afterwards asked to which of them, he named the Duke of Cumberland—a conduct and confidence so absurd and weak, that no wonder he was long afterwards taunted both with his reserve, and with his choice of such a bosom-friend.' The Duke of Cumberland was the King's brother, Henry Frederick. *Memoirs of George III*, iv. 102. Walpole, describing on Aug. 31, 1770, the dearth of news, says :—' We have lived these two months upon the poor Duke of Cumberland, whom the newspapers, in so many letters, call *The Royal Idiot.*' *Letters*, v. 254.

Note 9. Boswell, in his account of the dinner at the Messieurs Dilly's, where Johnson met Wilkes, says :—' Amidst some patriotic groans, somebody said, " Poor old England is lost." JOHNSON. " Sir, it is not so much to be lamented that Old England is lost, as that the Scotch have found it." WILKES. " Had Lord Bute governed Scotland only, I should not have taken the trouble to write his eulogy, and dedicate *Mortimer* to him."' Boswell adds as a note to Johnson's saying :—' It would not become me to expatiate on this strong and pointed remark, in which a very great deal of meaning is condensed.' Boswell's *Johnson*, iii. 78. It was this finding of England, and the anger raised by it in the English, that made the King's cause a national cause to the Scotch. The Scotchman, John Stuart, Earl of Bute, was the head of the *King's Friends*. Burke, speaking in 1769 to

Earl Temple about the union of parties, said that 'he believed no union could be formed of any effect or credit, which was not compacted upon this great principle—"that the King's men should be utterly destroyed as a corps."' Burke's *Corres.* i. 216. 'They are,' he says in the *Present Discontents*, 'only known to their Sovereign by kissing his hand for the offices, pensions, and grants, into which they have deceived his benignity. May no storm ever come which will put the firmness of their attachment to the proof; and which, in the midst of confusions and terrors and sufferings, may demonstrate the eternal difference between a true and severe friend to the Monarchy, and a slippery sycophant of the Court! *Quantum infido scurrae distabit amicus.*' Payne's Burke's Select Works, i. 51. Lord Bute uses the designation 'the King's friends' in a letter to George Grenville, dated March 25, 1763. 'I do not know,' writes the editor of the *Grenville Papers* (ii. 33), 'whether Lord Bute invented it, but this is the first time I find it used in this correspondence.'

Churchill, in his *Prophecy of Famine*, gives expression to the national feeling in England when he says :—

> 'To that rare soil where virtues clust'ring grow,
> What mighty blessings doth not England owe ?
> What *waggon-loads* of courage, wealth, and sense
> Doth each revolving day import from thence ?
> To us she gives, disinterested friend,
> Faith without fraud, and Stuarts without end.'
>
> Churchill's *Poems* (ed. 1766), i. 102.

'What a nation is Scotland,' wrote Horace Walpole at the end of the Gordon Riots (*Letters*, vii. 400), 'in every reign engendering traitors to the State, and false and pernicious to the Kings that favour it the most.' The burning of Wilkes's effigy by the Apprentices of Edinburgh is a strong sign of the popular feeling. The votes of the Scotch members in the House of Commons give no sure indication, for at this time 'there were probably not above 1500 or 2000 county electors in all Scotland ; a body not too large to be held, hope included, in Government's hand. The election of either the town or the county member was a matter of such utter indifference to the people, that they often only knew of it by the ringing of a bell, or by seeing it mentioned next day in a newspaper.' Cockburn's *Life of Lord Jeffrey*, i. 75. The borough members were elected by the town-councils. 'By the constitution of all the Royal Burghs in Scotland (above 60 in number) each town-council elected its successor ; which in practice meant that they all elected themselves. The system of self-election was universal.' Cockburn's *Memorials of His Time*, p. 319. Cockburn believes that 'the first example of popular election in Scotland' was that of the Police Commissioners of Edinburgh. The date is not given, but it was in the early part of the present century. *Ib.* p. 199. 'In 1816 a meeting was held to petition Parliament against the continuance of the property and income tax. This was the first respectable meeting

held in Edinburgh, within the memory of man, for the avowed purpose of controlling Government on a political matter.' *Ib.* p. 302.
In 1826, Sir Walter Scott, writing to Sir R. Dundas, said :—'The
whole burgher class of Scotland are gradually preparing for radical
reform—I mean the middling and respectable classes ; and when a
burgh reform comes, which perhaps cannot be long delayed, Ministers will not return a member for Scotland from the towns. The
gentry will abide longer by sound principles ; for they are needy and
desire advancement for their sons, and appointments, and so on.'
Lockhart's *Scott,* ed. 1839, viii. 297.

Adam Smith, while asserting that 'the spirit of party prevails less
in Scotland than in England,' finds the explanation in its 'distance
from the capital, from the principal seat of the great scramble of
faction and ambition, which makes them enter less into the views of
any of the contending parties, and renders them more indifferent and
impartial spectators of the conduct of all.' *Wealth of Nations,* ed. 1811,
iii. 444. See *ante,* p. 61.

Note 10. Sir Archibald Grant of Monymusk, the second baronet,
married for his fourth wife Mrs. Millar, widow of Andrew Millar,
Esq., of London. Burke's *Peerage and Baronetage.* She was the
widow of the rich bookseller from whose 'rapaciousness' Hume complained that he was suffering. Dr. Alexander Carlyle had met her
and Millar at Harrogate in 1773. He describes how 'all the baronets
and great squires' there paid him civility, so as to get the loan of his
newspapers. 'Yet when he appeared in the morning in his old well-
worn suit of clothes, they could not help calling him Peter Pamphlet ;
for the generous patron of Scotch authors, with his city wife and her
niece, were sufficiently ridiculous when they came into good company. It was observed, however, that she did not allow him to go
down to the well with her in the chariot in his morning dress, though
she owned him at dinner-time, as he paid the extraordinaries.' Dr.
A. Carlyle's *Autobiography,* p. 434. The 'extraordinaries' were the
wine &c. not included in the 'ordinary,' which was only fixed at a
shilling a head ; though, says Carlyle, 'we had two haunches of
venison twice a week during the season. Breakfast cost gentlemen
only twopence apiece for their muffins, as it was the fashion for
ladies to furnish tea and sugar.' She was not Lady Grant when
Hume wrote, for she was not married till the next day *(Gent. Mag.*
1770, p. 239). Sir Archibald Grant was born in 1696. From the
letters which this aged bridegroom wrote to Strahan on his way
home I get the following extracts :—

'Barnaby Moor, Saturday, 26th May, 1770, 7 p.m.,
and to stay all night : 148 miles from London.

' At 4 this afternoon we past the Trent. I promised to write from
north side of it. . . . Weather hath been propitious. Roads and fields
delightfull. Blossoms of fruit, hedges and whins, all which I introduced into the Hanbery (?), regalled the sight and smell. . . . Much

improvement of the comons going forward; tho' shamefull there is not more, when we want both money and wood—little of this last where we have past.'

'Minto House, Edinburgh, 1st June, 1770.

'Faction exists here with equal zeal, tho' not equal importance or consequences.'

'Monymusk [Aberdeenshire], 22nd June, 1770.

'No notion here of factions.' *Barker MSS.*

Note 11. The edition of 1770, in four volumes, was not in 'twelves' (duodecimo), but in small octavo.

Note 12. Grimm, on June 15, 1770, mentioning 'l'immense *Dictionnaire du Commerce* promis par l'Abbé Morellet,' adds, 'qui ne se fera vraisemblablement jamais.' The editor says in a note :—'La conjecture de Grimm s'est vérifiée. Il n'a paru du *Dictionnaire du Commerce* promis par Morellet que le prospectus, qui forme 1 vol. in 8°.' *Corres. Lit.* vi. 492.

LETTER XL.

Cadell disbelieved: Sir Archibald Grant's Plantations.

EDINBURGH, 5 *June*, 1770.

DEAR SIR

Even according to Mr. Cadel's present account, which I have not the least Reason to give any Credit to, you have copies enow [1] to serve you for many Years' Sale ; and I give over all thoughts of any new Edition. Only, if such a thing shoud happen, I think it proper to inform you, that I have a Copy by me, corrected in many places, especially in the four first Volumes [2]. This shall be sent you on demand either by myself, if alive, or by my Brother or Heirs; and I wish that no Edition be made without following it. I shall never make any more Enquiries about the Matter: I did not even make any Enquiries at this time; but receiving from Mr. Cadel some inconsistent Accounts, which he had sent me voluntarily of himself, I took Occasion to mention them to you. As he finds his Credit runs very low with me in that particular (tho' I believe him a very honest man) he may spare himself the trouble of saying any thing farther concerning it. I wish Millar had savd the Expence of this Magnificent Quarto Edition[3], which can serve to no purpose but to discredit the Octavo; and make the sale, if possible, still more slow.

There is a notable[4] Error of the Press in this last Quarto of my Essays, which confounds and perplexes the Sense; and being so easily corrected, I wish you woud give orders for that purpose. It is Vol 2. p. 395. l. 1. for *useful* read *usual*[5]. A boy with his pen in half an hour coud go thro all the Copies. It is the very first Line of the third Appendix. I beg of you not to forget this Request. I have writ to Cadel to the same purpose. It is in the second page of Sheet E. e. e.[6]

I have seen Lady Grant. I am told, that she and Sir Archibald hold as much *amorous play and dalliance*[7], as ever Adam and Eve did in paradise; and they make every body in love with the marryd State. It will be a curious Experiment whether his sly Flattery or her tenacious Avarice will get the better: I conjecture, that the contest is begun already. I took occasion to mention to her Sir Archibald's extensive and noble Plantations[8]; but she told me, that she thought that Planting was his Folly, and that people ought to take care, lest their concern for Posterity shoud hurt themselves[9]. Thus she will check the poor man in the only laudable thing he has ever done[10].

I wish you woud be so good as to send me an account of the Debt I owe you, which, tho' it be but a trifle, I coud wish to pay[11].

The Madness and wickedness of the English (for do not say, the Scum of London) appear astonishing, even after all the Experience we have had. It must end fatally either to the King or Constitution or to both[12].

You say nothing to me of the new Edition of my Essays in 12°, and of my desire to have six copies of it whenever

it is finishd.   Perhaps, you have stopd short in that work,
and I think you much in the right in so doing.

I am Dear Strahan Yours sincerely

DAVID HUME.

———————

Note 1.   See *ante*, p. 8, for Hume's distinction between *enough*
and *enow*.

Note 2.   See *ante*, p. 97, *n.* 17.

Note 3.   See *ante*, p. 141, *n.* 7.

Note 4.   *Notable* as applied to men was still struggling between
the two meanings of *remarkable, memorable, observable*, and *careful,
bustling*. 'I expressed,' writes Northcote, 'to Sir Joshua my curiosity
to see Dr. Goldsmith.   Soon afterwards Goldsmith came to dine
with him, and immediately on my entering the room, Sir Joshua,
with a designed abruptness, said to me, " This is Dr. Goldsmith ;
pray why did you wish to see him ? "   I was much confused by
the suddenness of the question, and answered in my hurry ; " Because
he is a notable man."   This, in one sense of the word, was so very
contrary to the character and conduct of Goldsmith, that Sir Joshua
burst into a hearty laugh, and said that Goldsmith should in future
always be called the notable man.   What I meant to say was,
that he was a man of note or eminence.'   Northcote's *Life of
Reynolds*, i. 249.

Gibbon describes his great-grandmother as ' an active and notable
woman.'   *Misc. Works*, i. 15.   In *The Spectator*, No. 150, in the
description of the men of business in Charles the Second's reign,
we read :—' I have heard my father say, that a broad-brimmed hat,
short hair, and unfolded handkerchief were in his time absolutely
necessary to denote a NOTABLE MAN.'   While in this meaning the
word has dropped quite out of use, in the other also it was, I believe,
uncommon, till it was brought into favour some thirty years ago by
writers of the School of Mr. Carlyle and Mr. Ruskin.

Note 5.   The Third Appendix—the Fourth according to Hume's
subsequent arrangement—begins :—' Nothing is more usual than for
philosophers to encroach upon the province of grammarians.'   Hume's
Phil. Works, ed. 1854, iv. 382.

Note 6.   Each sheet of a book is distinguished by a letter, or
signature as it is technically called.   J, V, and W are not used.
When the end of the Alphabet is reached, the letters are doubled,
and, if that does not suffice, are trebled.   In a quarto, with only
eight pages to each sheet, the Alphabet is soon run through.   E. e. e·
is found on p. 393.

Note 7.   ' Youthful dalliance.'   *Paradise Lost*, iv. 338.

Note 8.   Johnson in his *Journey to the Hebrides* says :—' It may be
doubted whether before the Union any man between Edinburgh
and England had ever set a tree.   Of this improvidence no other

account can be given than that it probably began in times of tumult, and continued because it had begun.' *Works*, ix. 8.   Sir Archibald's country, being on the borders of the Aberdeenshire Highlands, would have remained insecure even longer than the district south of Edinburgh.   'The love of planting,' says Sir Walter Scott, 'which has become almost a passion, is much to be ascribed to Johnson's sarcasms.' *Croker Corres.* ii. 34.   Sir Archibald had done his planting before Johnson visited Scotland.   There were, however, earlier sarcasms than Johnson's.   Wilkes, in 1762, in *The North Briton*, No. 13, had said that 'in that country Judas had sooner found the grace of repentance than a tree to hang himself on' (*ante*, p. 61). Churchill, in 1763, in *The Prophecy of Famine*, describes how in Scotland,

'Far as the eye could reach no tree was seen,
Earth clad in russet scorned the lively green.'
                              Churchill's *Works*, ed. 1766, i. 111.

Note 9.   Addison, in *The Spectator*, No. 583, after recommending planting 'to men of estates, not only as a pleasing amusement, but as it is a kind of virtuous employment,' continues :—' I know when a man talks of posterity in matters of this nature, he is looked upon with an eye of ridicule by the cunning and selfish part of mankind. Most people are of the humour of an old fellow of a college, who, when he was pressed by the society to come into something that might redound to the good of their successors, grew very peevish. "We are always doing (says he) something for posterity, but I would fain see posterity do something for us."'

Note 10.   He had served on the Committee of the House of Commons which in 1729 examined into the state of the gaols.   Hogarth's picture of the Examination of Bambridge was painted for him, and his portrait, no doubt, is given among the Committee men. *Anecdotes of William Hogarth*, ed. 1833, p. 350.

Note 11.   Very likely the debt for the *Chronicle* (*ante*, p. 138).

Note 12.   Horace Walpole wrote to Mann ten days later :—' This is a slight summer letter, but you will not be sorry it is so short, when the dearth of events is the cause.   Last year I did not know but we might have a Battle of Edgehill by this time.   At present, my Lord Chatham could as soon raise money as raise the people ; and Wilkes will not much longer have more power of doing either.... You could not have a better opportunity for taking a trip to England.' *Letters*, v. 242.

LETTER XLI.

Complaints of the 1763 Edition of the History.

DEAR SIR

I am not in the least angry with Mr. Cadel: On the contrary, were I to go to the press with any new work (which it is utterly impossible I ever shoud) he is one of the first persons I shoud apply to for publishing it. But, pray, recollect, that a few weeks before I came down, he told me in your house of his regret that he shoud ever have been forced by Mr. Millar to deceive me ; but that now I might entirely depend upon the Truth of his Information ; there were less than 700 of the 8ᵛᵒ Edition upon hand. But after a twelvemonth's rapid sale, as he pretends, he acknowledges nine hundred and fifty, and I question not but there is above double the Number.

There has been a strange Fatality to depress the reputation of that book: First the Extravagance of Baillie Hamilton [1], then the Rapaciousness of Mr. Millar: But this last is most incurable. I suppose you will not find one Book in the English Language of that Size and Price so ill printed [2], and now since the publication of the Quarto, however small the Sale of the Quarto may be, it shows, by its corrections and additions, the Imperfection of the 8ᵛᵒ so visibly, that it must be totally discredited. Had it been thought proper to let me know the real State of the 8ᵛᵒ Edition, I never shoud have consented to the printing of the Quarto. I suppose the Proprietors will at last be oblig'd to destroy all that remains of the 8ᵛᵒ; I mean, if there appear any hopes of the Sale's ever reviving. If Mr. Millar had been alive, his own Interest, as well as the Shame for his Miscarriage, woud have brought him to that Resolution. There remains only the former Motive with the Proprietors.

I return the Sheet of the Essays which is very elegantly printed[3].   The numerous Editions of that work, which is much less calculated for public Sale, may convince you of the Propriety of moderate Editions.   I hope Mr. Cadel will send me down six copies as soon as the Edition is finishd, that I may have the Satisfaction of seeing one of my Works without Disgust.

I am Dear S[ir] Yours sincerely

DAVID HUME.

EDINBURGH, 21 *June*, 1770.

Note 1.   Gavin Hamilton had been a partner in the firm of Hamilton, Balfour and Neill which in 1754 brought out the first volume of Hume's *History*.   Hamilton wrote to Strahan on Aug. 26, 1762, to say that he had 'parted business with Mr. Balfour.   I am not to concern myself any further in bookselling, but the paper mill is become my sole property.   I have likewise gone out of the printing house; but whether Mr. Balfour will continue with Mr. Neill or not I cannot guess.... It is agreed betwixt us that the matter be kept a secret for some time, and my name is to continue in trade.' *Barker MSS.*

Note 2.   See *ante*, p. 141, *n.* 7.

Note 3.   The edition of 1770 in 4 vols. 8vo. is a beautiful piece of printing.

LETTER XLII.

The Historical Age: Dr. Henry's History.

[*Aug.* 1770.]

DEAR STRAHAN

I believe this is the historical Age[1] and this the historical Nation[2]:   I know no less than eight Histories upon the Stocks in this Country; all which have different Degrees of Merit, from the Life of Christ, the most sublime of the whole, as I presume from the Subject, to Dr. Robertson's American History, which lies in the other Extremity[3].

You will very soon be visited by one, who carries with him a Work, that has really Merit: It is Dr. Henry, the Author of the History of England, writ on a new Plan[4]:

He has given to the World a Sheet or two, containing his Idea[5], which he will probably communicate to you. I have perus'd all his Work, and have a very good Opinion of it. It contains a great deal of Good Sense and Learning, convey'd in a perspicuous, natural, and correct Expression. The only discouraging Circumstance is its Size: This Specimen contains two Quartos, and yet gives us only the History of Great Britain from the Invasion of Julius Cæsar to that of the Saxons: One is apt to think that the whole, spun out to the same Length, must contain at least a hundred Volumes: And unhappily, the beginning of the Work will be for a long time very uninteresting, which may not prepossess the World in its favour. The Performance however has very considerable Merit; and I coud wish that you and Mr. Cadel may usher it in to the Public[6]. I wish that Dr. Robertson's Success may not have renderd the Author too sanguine in his pecuniary Expectations[7]: I dare advise nothing on that head, of which you are the better Judge. I shoud only think, that some Plan, which woud reserve to the Author the Chance of profiting by his good Success and yet not expose the Booksellers to too much hazard, might be the most suitable. You know, that I have been always very reservd in my Recommendations; and that when an Author, tho much connected with me, has producd a Work, which I coud not entirely approve of, I rather pretended total Ignorance of the Matter, than abuse my Credit with you. Dr. Henry is not personally much known to me, as he has been but lately settled in this Town, but I cannot refuse doing Justice to his Work: He has likewise personally a very good Character in the World, which renders it so far safe to have dealings with him[8]. For the same Reason, I wish for his Sake that he may conclude with you[9]. You see I am a good Casuist, and can distinguish Cases very nicely. It is certainly a wrong thing to deceive any body, much more a Friend; but yet the Difference must still be allowd infinite between deceiving a man for his Good and for his Injury [10].

I am Dear S[ir] Yours sincerely

DAVID HUME.

Note 1. See *ante*, p. 15, *n.* 2.

Note 2. Hume is speaking only of the Scotch.

Note 3. Among these Histories were Robertson's *History of America* and Henry's *History of Great Britain*, and probably Sir John Dalrymple's *Memoirs of Great Britain and Ireland*, Monboddo's *Origin and Progress of Language*, and Kames's *Sketches of the History of Man*. Lord Hailes's *Annals of Scotland* may have been begun by this time (see Boswell's *Johnson*, ii. 278), and also Adam Ferguson's *History of the Roman Republic* (see Gibbon's *Misc. Works*, ii. 163) and Watson's *History of Philip II*. Burke, speaking of this last book in a debate on Nov. 6, 1776, said :—'I have been reading a work given us by a country that is perpetually employed in productions of merit.' *Parl. Hist.* xviii. 1443.

Boswell writing of the spring of 1768 says :—' Dr. Johnson's prejudice against Scotland appeared remarkably strong at this time. When I talked of our advancement in literature, "Sir," said he, "you have learnt a little from us, and you think yourselves very great men. Hume would never have written History, had not Voltaire written it before him. He is an echo of Voltaire." BOSWELL. "But, Sir, we have Lord Kames." JOHNSON. "You *have* Lord Kames. Keep him; ha, ha, ha! We don't envy you him. Do you ever see Dr. Robertson?" BOSWELL. "Yes, Sir." JOHNSON. "Does the dog talk of me?" BOSWELL. "Indeed, Sir, he does, and loves you." Thinking that I now had him in a corner, and being solicitous for the literary fame of my country, I pressed him for his opinion on the merit of Dr. Robertson's *History of Scotland*. But to my surprise he escaped.—"Sir, I love Robertson, and I won't talk of his book."' Boswell's *Johnson*, ii. 53. The *Life of Christ* was perhaps *The History of Christ*, by Thomas Brown, published in London in 1777.

Note 4. 'I have heard,' said Dr. Johnson on April 29, 1778, 'Henry's *History of Britain* well spoken of. I am told it is carried on in separate divisions, as the civil, the military, the religious history. I wish much to have one branch well done, and that is the history of manners, of common life.' Boswell's *Johnson*, iii. 333.

Note 5. Boswell writing to Temple on June 19, 1770, says that he has just received the Prospectus of the *History*. 'Mr. Henry,' he continues, 'argues strongly for his extensive plan; but will it not be too much like the *Dictionary of Arts and Sciences* in an historical form? Mr. Hume, when I spoke to him of it, before I saw the plan, seemed to think it would be much of the nature of a book published a few years ago, Anderson's *History of Commerce*. . . . I am to consider the plan at leisure, and give Mr. Henry my opinion.' *Letters of Boswell*, p. 166.

Note 6. Henry was injured by Gilbert Stuart, the malignant editor of the *Edinburgh Magazine and Review*, who 'had vowed that he would crush his work,' and refused to insert a review of it by Hume, because it was laudatory. Had he rejected it for its hypocrisy, he might have had some justification. Hume, joining Robertson with Henry, and pointing out that they were both ministers of religion, continues :—'These illustrious examples, if any thing, must make the infidel abashed of his vain cavils, and put a stop to that torrent of vice, profaneness and immorality, by which the age is so unhappily distinguished. . . . One in particular [Blair], with the same hand by which he turns over the sublime pages of Homer and Virgil, Demosthenes and Cicero, is not ashamed to open with reverence the sacred volumes ; and with the same voice by which, from the pulpit, he strikes vice with consternation, he deigns to dictate to his pupils the most useful lessons of rhetoric, poetry, and polite literature.' Burton's *Hume*, ii. 470-1.

Note 7. 'Dr. Robertson said, "Henry erred in not selling his first volume at a moderate price to the booksellers, that they might have pushed him on till he had got reputation. I sold my *History of Scotland* at a moderate price, as a work by which the booksellers might either gain or not; and Cadell has told me that Millar and he have got six thousand pounds by it. I afterwards received a much higher price for my writings. An author should sell his first work for what the booksellers will give, till it shall appear whether he is an author of merit, or, which is the same thing as to purchase money, an author who pleases the public."' Boswell's *Johnson*, iii. 333. I have seen a MS. letter from Robertson to Strahan, dated May 27, 1768, in which he says :—'I do agree to accept from Mr. Millar, Bookseller in Pall Mall, or, in case of his declining it, from yourself, of the sum of £3400 for the copyright of my *History of Charles V.* in three volumes quarto, and of your engagement to pay me £400 more iñ case of a second edition. The terms of payment to be afterwards settled.' *Barker MSS.* It is of this *History* that Southey is speaking when he mentions 'the thousand and one omissions for which Robertson ought to be called rogue, as long as his volumes last.' *Life and Correspondence of Southey*, ii. 318.

Note 8. Lord Cockburn in his *Memorials*, p. 51, gives an interesting account of Dr. Henry's peaceful death. 'He wrote to Sir H. Moncreiff that he was dying, and thus invited him for the last time— "Come out here directly. I have got something to do this week, I have got to die."'

Note 9. The *History* was published by Cadell. The first volume appeared in 1771, and the fifth, which brought the narrative to the accession of Henry VII, in 1785. The author died in 1790, leaving a

sixth volume (down to the accession of Edward VI) almost completed.
It was published in 1793. The work went through many editions,
and was translated into French. Knight's *Cyclo. of Biog.* and
Lowndes' *Bibl. Manual.*

Note 10.   See *post*, Letter of March 24, 1773.

LETTER XLIII.

Dr. Henry's Introduction to Strahan.

DEAR SIR

This Letter will be deliverd to you by Dr. Henry,
concerning whom and whose work, I have wrote you by
the Post: I have rather chosen that Method of conveying
my Sentiments than by a Letter of Recommendation, which
are often understood to be formal things and carry less
weight with them.   You will there see, that my Esteem
of Dr. Henry and his Performance are very sincere and
cordial.

I am Dear Sir
Your most obedient and most humble Servant
DAVID HUME.

EDINBURGH, 10 *of August*, 1770.

LETTER XLIV.

A new Edition of the Philosophical Pieces.

Mr. Hume's Compliments to Mr. Strahan.   Wishes him
a good New Year: He has receivd the six Copies of his
philosophical Pieces[1], for which he thanks him: They
are very elegantly printed, and correctly, tho' there are
some few unavoidable Errors.   He has sent him an Errata,
which he desires Mr. Strahan to annex if not inconvenient.

EDINBURGH, 5 *of Jan'*, 1771.

Note 1.   Copies, no doubt, of his *Essays and Treatises* of the edition
of 1770.

LETTER XLV.

The Ohio Scheme: Threat of War with Spain.

DEAR SIR

I am very glad to have heard from you, and have sent you my Letter to. Lord Hertford [1] under a flying Seal [2]. I wish you good Success in your Project; tho' I cannot easily imagine how an Estate on the Ohio can ever turn to great Account. The Navigation down the Mississipi is indeed expeditious and safe, except at the Mouth; but the return is commonly so slow, by the violence of the Current, that the Communication of that Country with the rest of the World, will always be under great Obstructions, and be carry'd on under considerable Disadvantages. But these Matters you have undoubtedly weighd and calculated, from better Information than I have had access to [3].

There was an Error in the page in the Errata I sent you, which I have corrected and I return you the Copy. I own, that this quick Sale of my philosophical Writings is as unexpected as the slow Sale of my historical, which are so much better calculated for common Readers [4]. But this proves only, that factious prejudices are more prevalent in England than religious ones. I shall read over several times this new Edition; and send you a corrected Copy by some safe hand. With regard to the History, I only desire to hear from you three or four Months before you put it to the Press.

Dr. Henry's History is undoubtedly liable to the Objection you mention. It will be of enormous Size; and he himself, tho' a laborious Man, never expects to finish it. I think also the Price he demanded exorbitant [5]. It is however writ with Perspicuity and Propriety of Style, as

I told you; but neither sprightly nor elegant[6]; and it is judicious, but not curious: There is danger of its appearing prolix to ordinary Readers: The Subject of his next Volume will be still more uninteresting than that of his first[7].

I am totally detachd from all concern about public Affairs; and care not though all the Ministry were at the Devil[8]. This Spanish War[9] is so enormously absurd, unjust, and unreasonable that I think it never had its parralel. If we be savd from it, it will not be owing to our own prudence, but to the determind Resolution of the King of France[10], who acts a very laudable part: But his Brother of Spain is as freakish and as obstinate as a Mule[11]; and our Ministry are more afraid of the despicable London Mob than of all Europe[12]: Had they punishd that insolent Rascal, Beckford[13], as he deserved; we shoud have been in no danger of a Spanish War[14]; or rather of a general War: For Hostilities never continue limited between two Nations; but soon draw in all their Neighbours: In which case, France begins with declaring a public Bankruptcy[15]; and we make it[16] the third Year of the War. An Event which is indeed inevitable[17]; but might have been delay'd, had it not been for this Quarrel about Falkland Island. You think we shall have peace: I am glad to hear it; but cannot allow myself to think, that any Chance will save Men so infatuated as our Ministry[18]. It is a pleasure however that the Wilkites[19] and the Bill of Rights-men[20] are fallen into total and deservd Contempt[21]. Their Noise is more troublesome and odious than all the Cannon that will be fird on the Atlantic.

I am here employ'd in building a small House[22]: I mean a large House for an Author: For it is nearly as large as Mr. Millar's in Pall-mall[23]. It is situated in our new Square[24]; where I hope to receive you, on your first Excursion to this Country. I beg my Compliments to

M

Sir John Pringle [25] :   I think you are not likely to send us any thing worth reading this Winter.

I am Dear Strahan Yours sincerely

DAVID HUME.

EDINBURGH, 21 *of Jan.*, 1771.

Note 1.   The Earl of Hertford at this time was Lord Chamberlain.

Note 2.   Hume, in one of his French letters, says :—'Je vous adresse cette lettre à cachet volant, sous l'enveloppe de M. de Montigny.' Hume's *Private Corres.* p. 223.   Littré defines *cachet volant* as *cachet qui n'adhère qu'au pli supérieur d'une lettre sans la fermer.*   Hume's enclosed letter had his seal fixed on the upper side.   After Strahan had read the letter he would close it by dropping some wax on the lower side, and bringing the two sides together with the seal uppermost.   Envelopes were not generally used in England till the introduction of Penny Postage in 1840.

Note 3.   Strahan replied on March 1 :—' I was favoured with yours, inclosing your very genteel letter to Lord Hertford, which I delivered to his Lordship.   He received me very politely; and I found no difficulty in impressing him with a just notion of the importance of the subject I wanted to talk to him about.   He was as fond of it, or rather more so, than I was, and for his own sake will do what lies in his power to forward it.   The project is no less than the forming a new government upon the Ohio.   The country is by much the best and mildest in all our portion of America, and being situated at no great distance from any of our Colonies, will, when once settled, fill very fast from the overflowings of them all.   The land carriage is by no means so great an obstacle as you seem to imagine, it being already, by means of other rivers in different parts of the country, so much shortened as to be considerably lower already than it is in the internal provinces of England.—The policy, however, of such a settlement respecting the Mother Country, is not yet decided; and the affair is still under consideration.   I expect it will soon be determined one way or other, and I have some reason to think it will end as we wish it to do, as every objection that hath yet been offered to the scheme can be most satisfactorily answered.   Meanwhile, it is not proper to say anything about it; but if it succeeds, I shall give you a very particular detail of the whole matter, and how I came to have any concern in it.—Lord Hertford is very fond of the idea of having a large tract of country in America, and is otherwise very attentive to the improvement of his fortune, having, I am well assured, profited greatly by the late increase of the price of stocks.' *M. S. R. S. E.*

Smollett gives the following account of an earlier attempt to form a company for settling this country :—' The tract of country lying along the Ohio is so fertile, pleasant, and inviting, and the Indians, called

Twightees, who inhabit those delightful plains were so well-disposed
towards a close alliance with the English, that as far back as the year
1716 Mr. Spottiswood, Governor of Virginia, proposed a plan for
erecting a company to settle such lands upon this river as should be
ceded to them by treaty with the natives.' The scheme dropped
through, but 'it was revived immediately after the Peace of Aix-la-
Chapelle [1748] when certain merchants of London, who traded to
Maryland and Virginia, petitioned the Government on this subject,
and were indulged not only with a grant of a great tract of ground to
the southward of Pennsylvania, which they promised to settle, but
also with an exclusive privilege of trading with the Indians on the
banks of the River Ohio.' The French, who had pushed their posts
down the river, began to harass the English traders. George
Washington, then holding the rank of Major, was sent with a letter
to the Commander of one of the French forts, ordering him 'to depart in peace.' The summons was not complied with. A border
warfare went on, which was only brought to an end by the expulsion
of the French from all the northern part of the American Continent.
History of England, ed. 1800, iii. 375-8. Johnson's description of the
conquered country is curious :—'Large tracts of America were added
by the last war to the British dominions. . . . They, at best, are only
the barren parts of the continent, the refuse of the earlier adven-
turers, which the French, who came last, had taken only as better
than nothing.' *Works*, vi. 202. In writing this, he was thinking no
doubt chiefly of Canada, which elsewhere he had described as 'a
region of desolate sterility.' *Ib.* p. 129.

After the peace a fresh company was formed, of which I have
obtained much information from the kindness of Dr. Israel W.
Andrews, President of Marietta College, Ohio. In 1769, Thomas
Walpole, Benjamin Franklin and others petitioned the King for the
right to purchase 2,400,000 acres (a district about as big as Kent,
Surrey and Sussex) between the Ohio River and the Alleghany
Mountains. Walpole was a London banker, and the Company and
the grant were often called by his name. The Company called itself
the Grant Company, and the colony was to be called Vandalia. The
Privy Council referred the petition to the Lords Commissioners for
Trade and Plantations, who two years after sent in an adverse report
by their President, Lord Hillsborough. Franklin made an elaborate
reply, which was read in Council on July 1, 1772. The petition was
at once granted, and Lord Hillsborough resigned. Horace Walpole
wrote on July 23, 1772 :—'We have had the only perfect summer I
ever remember; hot, fine, and still very warm without a drop of
rain. . . . Not a cloud even in the political sky, except a caprice of
Lord Hillsborough, who is to quit his American Seals, because he
will not reconcile himself to a plan of settlement on the Ohio, which
all the world approves.' *Letters*, v. 401. Franklin, writing to his son
on Aug. 17, says :—'You will hear it said among you, I suppose, that

the interest of the Ohio planters has ousted Lord Hillsborough; but the truth is, what I wrote you long since, that all his brother-ministers disliked him extremely, and wished for a fair occasion of tripping up his heels; so seeing that he made a point of defeating our scheme, they made another of supporting it, on purpose to mortify him, which they knew his pride could not bear.' *Memoirs of Franklin*, ed. 1833, iii. 320. It took time to arrange the details, but at length the price of the land was agreed upon, the plan of government marked out, and the patent made ready for the seals, when the Revolution broke out, and the whole project came to an end. In the Journal of the Continental Congress for May 1, 1782, there is the report of a Committee on a petition of some of the members of the Company. The Committee recommended that in case these lands should be ceded to the United States—they were claimed by Virginia—and the purchasers who remained loyal to the States should relinquish all claims to them, Congress should reimburse them for their outlay. These lands however never became a part of the public domain, but remained in the possession of Virginia. There is nothing to show that any remuneration was made even to those who became American citizens. The English shareholders undoubtedly lost whatever they had expended.

Note 4. Hume, no doubt, compared the sale of his *History* with that of Robertson's *Scotland*, which went through six editions in twelve years. His constant discontent is contemptible when we call to mind his boast, when speaking of his *History*, that the copy-money given him by the booksellers much exceeded anything formerly known in England (*ante*, *Autobiography*). They of course would not have paid him so well, had not his works had a great sale. For the two volumes of his *History* from Julius Cæsar to Henry VII he was to receive £1400. For the *Lives of the Poets* Johnson by his contract was paid £200, though another hundred was added by the booksellers.

Note 5. Strahan wrote to Hume on March 1 of this year:—'The price Dr. Henry expected for his *History* was in my estimation so much beyond its value that I carefully avoided making him any offer at all.' *M. S. R. S. E.*

Note 6. Boswell says of it:—'The language will not, as far as I think, be so flowing and elegant as that of some writers to whom our taste is habituated; but it seems to be distinct, and sufficiently expressive.' *Letters of Boswell*, p. 166.

Note 7. The first volume of Dr. Henry's *History* begins with the invasion of Britain by Julius Cæsar and ends with the arrival of the Saxons; the second volume ends with the landing of William the Conqueror. Hume more than once shows his disgust at having to write the wars of the Saxons. 'What instruction or entertainment can it give the reader,' he asks, 'to hear a long beadroll of barbarous names, Egric, Annas, Ethelbert, Ethelwald, Aldulf, Elfwold, Beorne,

Ethelred, Ethelbert, who successively murdered, expelled, or in-
herited from each other, and obscurely filled the throne of that
kingdom [East Anglia]?'   *History of England*, ed. 1802, i. 47.   Nevertheless he said that 'the *Life of Harold* was the portion of his
History which he thought the best; and on the style of which he had
bestowed most pains.'   *Caldwell Papers*, i. 39.

Note 8.   'The Ministry is dissolved.   I prayed with Francis and
gave thanks.'   Such is Johnson's pious entry in his Journal, when
nearly twelve years later Lord North's Ministry came to an end.
Boswell's *Johnson*, iv. 139.   It lasted from Feb. 10, 1770 to March 20,
1782.

Note 9.   There was only a threat of war.   In 1765 Commodore
Byron had taken formal possession of Falkland's Islands in the
name of his Britannic Majesty.   A settlement was made at Port
Egmont in West Falkland in Jan. 1766.   The French in Feb. 1764
had established themselves on East Falkland.   Two years later they
ceded their settlement to the Spanish.   In Nov. 1769 Captain Hunt
of the Tamar frigate warned off the coast a Spanish schooner which
was taking a survey of the islands.   The Governor of the Spanish
settlement gave a like warning to the English captain.   In Feb. 1770
two Spanish frigates with troops on board arrived, and warnings
were again interchanged by the commanders.   Captain Hunt at
once sailed with the news for England, where he arrived on June 3.
Only a few days later, five Spanish frigates, carrying a train of artillery,
appeared before Port Egmont.   The English had only a sloop of
16 guns.   A few shots were fired, but resistance was seen to be
impossible : a flag of truce was hung out, and articles of capitulation
signed.   The English were to depart with drums beating and colours
flying, and to carry off all their stores; but their departure by the
terms of the capitulation was delayed a few weeks.   'The most
degrading of all the circumstances attending this transaction, and
particularly a new, and to all appearance, wanton insult to the British
flag was, that for the better security of this limitation the sloop was
deprived of her rudder.'   The news of this reached London on
Sept. 24.   *Ann. Reg.* 1771, i. 4–12; *Gent. Mag.* 1770, p. 439; Johnson's
Works, vi. 185–192.

Horace Walpole wrote to Mann on Oct. 4, 1770 :—'Seeing such
accounts of press-gangs in the papers, and such falling of Stocks,
you will wonder that in my last I did not drop a military syllable. . . .
England that lives in the north of Europe, and Spain that dwells in
the south, are vehemently angry with one another about a morsel of
rock that lies somewhere at the very bottom of America—for modern
nations are too neighbourly to quarrel about anything that lies so
near them as in the same quarter of the globe.   Pray, mind; we
dethrone Nabobs in the most north-east corner of the Indies; the
Czarina sends a fleet from the Pole to besiege Constantinople; and
Spain huffs and we arm for one of the extremities of the southern

hemisphere. It takes a twelvemonth for any one of us to arrive
at our object, and almost another twelvemonth before we can learn
what we have been about. Your patriarchs, who lived eight or nine
hundred years, could afford to wait eighteen or twenty months for
the post coming in, but it is too ridiculous in our post-diluvian
circumstances. By next century, I suppose, we shall fight for the
Dog Star and the Great Bear. The Stocks begin to recover a little
from their panic. . . . Oct. 6. I still know nothing of the war. Vast
preparations everywhere go on, yet nobody thinks it will ripen. . . .
Seamen flock in apace ; the first squadron will consist of sixteen
ships of the line.' Walpole's *Letters*, v. 259-261.

When Parliament met, 40,000 seamen were voted and a large addition to the army,' while the land-tax was raised to four shillings
in the pound. *Ann. Reg.* 1771, i. 40-1. By the end of November
all hope of avoiding a war was nearly given up, and our ambassador
at Madrid was ordered to withdraw. *Ib.* p. 45. Happily for peace,
the navies both of England and of Spain were in a wretched
condition (Walpole's *Memoirs of George III*, iv. 204-5) ; while France
was almost powerless through want of money (*Ib.* p. 213). ' Desolation and confusion reign all over France,' wrote Walpole on
Dec. 29. ' They are almost bankrupts, and quite famished.' *Letters*,
v. 275. It was the overthrow of the French ministry, as was
commonly believed, which secured peace. On Jan. 1, 1771, Walpole
describes its fall in terms that almost startle the reader. ' The
general persuasion is that the *French Revolution* will produce peace
—I mean in Europe—not amongst themselves.' *Ib.* p. 276. ' What
effect,' writes Johnson, ' the revolution of the French Court had upon
the Spanish counsels, I pretend not to be informed. Choiseul had
always professed pacific dispositions ; nor is it certain, however it
may be suspected, that he talked in different strains to different
parties.' *Works*, vi. 194. Burke says that ' Choiseul hurried on
war,' and that it was thought that the tottering state of his power
led to peace. *Ann. Reg.* 1771, p. 45. Walpole believed that it was
only as a last desperate resource that he urged war. ' He had found
that his disgrace was determined ; he had no support but the King
of Spain. . . . Despair decided. Could he obtain his master's consent
to declare war, he himself might be necessary. . . . He marched forty
thousand men to the coast opposite to England, and by that rash
step brought on his own fall.' Walpole's *Memoirs of George III*,
iv. 243. Writing to Mann on the evening of Jan. 22, 1771, the
day after the date of Hume's letter, Walpole says :—' I had sealed
my letter, as you will perceive ; and break it open again in a great
hurry, to tell you the Peace was signed last night, and declared
in the House of Commons to-day.' *Letters*, v. 281. On Feb. 22 he
wrote :—' This treaty is an epoch ; and puts a total end to all our
preceding histories. Long quiet is never probable, nor shall I guess
who will disturb it ; but whatever happens must be thoroughly new

matter; though some of the actors perhaps may not be so. Both
Lord Chatham and Wilkes are at the end of their reckoning, and
the Opposition can do nothing without fresh fuel.' *Ib.* p. 282.

Johnson's *Falkland's Islands* was written at the request of the
Ministry to justify the peace. He ridiculed the notion of going to
war for 'a bleak and gloomy solitude, an island thrown aside from
human use, stormy in winter and barren in summer; an island
which not the southern savages have dignified with habitation.'
Johnson's *Works*, vi. 198. One of his finest pieces of writing is
the passage in which he describes the horrors of war. *Ib.* p. 199, and
Boswell's *Johnson*, ii. 134.

Note 10. 'Dec. 29, 1770. It is now said that on the very morning
of the Duke's disgrace the King reproached him, and said, "Monsieur,
je vous avais dit que je ne voulais pas la guerre."' Horace Walpole
to Mann. *Letters*, v. 275.

Note 11. 'King Carlos,' writes Horace Walpole on Nov. 18, 1771,
'hates us ever since Naples.' *Letters*, v. 349. When he was King of
the two Sicilies, an English fleet, in the year 1742, had threatened
Naples with bombardment, unless within an hour the King signed a
treaty of neutrality in the War of the Succession to the House of
Austria. *Œuvres de Voltaire*, xix. 80. In the summer of 1770 a satire
was published on him in London, so 'ludicrous and ironic' that some
Spaniards resolved to murder the printer, and were with difficulty
prevented by their Ambassador, who told them they would infallibly
be hanged. They said they could not die in a better cause. The
Ambassador was inexpressibly hurt, and told our Ministers he did
not know how to write the account to his Court; but wished the
insult might not cause a war.' Walpole's *Memoirs of George III*, iv.
169. The King is described in this satire as an idiot, who, when the
weather stopped his hunting, was amused by winding up three or
four dozen watches, till his mental faculties were fatigued by the
operation. He then took to lashing a horse that was worked on the
tapestry of the room till he fell on the ground worn out with the
effort. *Ib.* p. 372.

Note 12. Burke wrote to the Marquis of Rockingham on Sept. 8,
1770 :—'They [the Court party] are well acquainted with the difference between the Bill of Rights (*post*, p. 171, *n.* 20) and your Lordship's friends, and they are very insolently rejoiced at it. They
respect and fear that wretched knot beyond anything you can readily
imagine, and far more than any part, or than all the other parts
of the Opposition. The reason is plain ; there is a vast resemblance
of character between them. They feel that if they had equal spirit
and industry they would in the same situation act the very same
part. It is their idea of a perfect Opposition.' Burke's *Corres.* i. 237.
Johnson a few months later wrote :—'To fancy that our government
can be subverted by the rabble whom its lenity has pampered into
impudence is to fear that a city may be drowned by the overflowings

of its kennels.' *Works*, vi. 213. Later on he more than once accused
Lord North's Ministry of cowardice. In March, 1776, when talking
to Boswell about the bill for a Scotch militia, 'he said :—" I am glad
that Parliament has had the spirit to throw it out. You wanted
to take advantage of the timidity of our scoundrels" (meaning, I
suppose, the Ministry).' Boswell's *Johnson*, iii. 1. At another time
he described them as 'a bunch of imbecility.' *Ib.* iv. 139. See also
ib. iv. 200.

Note 13. See *ante*, p. 139, *n.* 1, for the Remonstrance of the City of
London presented by Lord Mayor Beckford and Sheriffs on March
14, 1770, and p. 147, *n.* 7, for the unwillingness of Parliament to support Government in any personal punishment of the Remonstrants.
On May 23 (*ante, ib.*) the City had presented a second Address
to the King. The answer which they received was a repetition of
the King's dissatisfaction with the former Address. Whereupon
Beckford, 'to the amazement of the Court, and with a boldness and
freedom perhaps peculiar to himself, made an immediate and spirited
reply, which he concluded in the following words :—" Whoever has
already dared, or shall hereafter endeavour by false insinuations and
suggestions, to alienate your Majesty's affections from your loyal
subjects in general, and from the City of London in particular, and to
withdraw your confidence to, and regard for, your people, is an
enemy to your Majesty's person and family, a violator of the public
peace, and a betrayer of our happy constitution as it was established
at the glorious and necessary Revolution." ' *Ann. Reg.* 1770, i. 203 ;
1771, i. 15. In a note on Boswell's *Johnson*, iii. 201, I have examined
the statement by Horne Tooke that 'Beckford got so confused that
he scarcely knew what he had said,' and that Tooke thereupon wrote
and sent to the newspapers the speech which was published. I had
not noticed the following passage in the *Ann. Reg.* for 1771, i. 15,
which, written as it no doubt was by Burke, no friendly witness,·
conclusively proves that Tooke lied. 'This answer was variously
judged. Those who paid a high regard to the decorums of the Court
declared it indecent and unprecedented to reply to any answer of
thé King. But in the City his spirit was infinitely applauded. Both
parties concurred in admiring the manner in which he delivered himself.' Lord Chatham wrote to Beckford on May 25 :—' In the fulness
of the heart the mouth speaks ; and the overflowing of mine gives
motion to a weak hand, to tell you how truly I respect and love the
spirit which your Lordship displayed on Wednesday. The *spirit of
Old England* spoke that never-to-be-forgotten day. . . . Adieu then
for the present (to call you by the most honourable of titles) *true
Lord Mayor of London* ; that is, *first* magistrate of the *first* city of the
world ! I mean to tell you only a plain truth, when I say, your
Lordship's mayoralty will be revered till the constitution is destroyed
and forgotten.' *Chatham Corres.* iii. 462. Beckford died a month
later—on June 21. *Ann. Reg.* 1770, i. 119. Horace Walpole wrote

on July 26 :—'Instead of Wilkes having been so, it looks as if Beckford had been the firebrand of politics, for the flame has gone out
entirely since his death,

> " And corn grows now where Troy town stood : "

both country gentlemen and farmers are thinking of their harvest,
not of politics and remonstrances.' *Letters*, v. 252. ' " Where," asked
Johnson, "did Beckford and Trecothick learn English? . . . That
Beckford could speak it with a spirit of honest resolution even to his
Majesty, as ' his faithful Lord-Mayor of London,' is commemorated
by the noble monument erected to him in Guildhall." '   Boswell's
Johnson, iii. 201.

Note 14. 'There was perhaps never much danger of war or of
refusal, but what danger there was, proceeded from the faction.
Foreign nations, unacquainted with the insolence of common councils,
and unaccustomed to the howl of plebeian patriotism, when they
heard of rabbles and riots, of petitions and remonstrances, of discontent in Surrey, Derbyshire, and Yorkshire, when they saw the
chain of subordination broken, and the legislature threatened and
defied, naturally imagined that such a government had little leisure
for Falkland's Islands; they supposed that the English when they
returned ejected from Port Egmont, would find Wilkes invested with
the protectorate ; or see the mayor of London, what the French have
formerly seen their mayors of the palace, the commander of the
army and tutor of the king; that they would be called to tell their
tale before the common council ; and that the world was to expect
war or peace from a vote of the subscribers to the Bill of Rights.'
Falkland's Island. Johnson's *Works*, vi. 213. Horace Walpole wrote
on March 23, 1771 :—' France luckily has little leisure to join with
King Carlos or King Brass Crosby [the Lord Mayor]—their confusions and King Lewis's weakness seem to increase every day.'
Letters, v. 287.

Note 15. Wilkes had written to Earl Temple from Paris so early
as Aug. 29, 1763 :—' The distress in the provinces is risen to a great
height. Paris is as gay as usual. The five last years the Government have been at the expense of several public shows in the
city, &c. for the people. The most sensible men here think that
this country is on the eve of a great revolution.' *Grenville Papers*,
ii. 100. Strahan wrote to Hume on March 1, 1771 :—' Luckily for
this nation, the situation of France is such, that we may reasonably
hope to be able to avoid a war for some time to come. Indeed, if
we are not much misinformed, the popular discontents there are
becoming very serious. Perhaps they may come exaggerated to us ;
but this I am certain of, that their finances are in such disorder
that it requires not only the utmost sagacity and ability, but some
very bold political stroke, to put them upon a tolerable footing.'
M.S.R.S.E.

On June 20, Horace Walpole writing about France says (*Letters*,

v. 307):—'Their politics, some way or other, must end seriously, either in despotism, a civil war, or assassination. Methinks it is playing deep for the power of tyranny. Charles Fox is more moderate; he only games for an hundred thousand pounds that he has not.' On July 30 he wrote from Paris (*ib.* pp. 317-319):— 'The distress here is incredible, especially at Court. The King's tradesmen are ruined, his servants starving, and even angels and archangels cannot get their pensions and salaries, but sing, "Woe! woe! woe!" instead of Hosannas. ... The Comptroller-General dispenses bankruptcy by retail, and will fall, because he cannot even by these means be useful enough. They are striking off nine millions from *la caisse militaire,* five from the marine, and one from the *affaires étrangères*; yet all this will not extricate them. You never saw a great nation in so disgraceful a position. Their next prospect is not better; it rests on an *imbécile* [Lewis XVI] both in mind and body.'

Note 16. Hume, I think, has in his mind the French idiom *faire banqueroute.*

Note 17. Hume in October 1769 had hoped to live to see a public bankruptcy in England. He should have become more cheerful as it seemed so close at hand, but he is as discontented as ever. Burke describes the causes which the year before 'concurred, notwithstanding the vast weight of our debts and taxes, to make a war in general not wholly unacceptable.' *Ann. Reg.* 1771, i. 14. The Three per Cent. Consols, which at the beginning of 1770 had been at 86, by the end of the year had fallen to 78. *Gent. Mag.* 1770, pp. 48, 592. On Jan. 28, 1771, they had risen to 84 (*ib.* 1771, p. 48), and on March 1 to nearly 89 (*ib.* p. 144, where Feb. 1 is evidently a misprint for March 1).

Note 18. Strahan replying to Hume on March 1, said:—'You seem much out of humour with the Ministry. Upon my word, as far as I am able to judge, they have acted pretty well of late; though I must own their timidity regarding our domestic incendiaries is altogether inexcusable. However, bating this great fault (and *great* I allow it is), Lord North in particular has acted his part very well; he speaks with courage and firmness in the House, and with temper too. In short, I think he gains ground in the public opinion every day. I firmly believe he means well. And I wish the present Ministry to stand their ground, purely because they are the *present Ministry*; for, as I told your friend Lord Hertford when I had the honour to wait upon him, the King has changed his Ministers so very often since his Accession, that another change would be almost equal to a dethronement.' *M. S. R. S. E.*

Note 19. George III told Lord Eldon that at a Levee 'he asked Wilkes after his friend Serjeant Glynne. "*My* friend, Sir!" says Wilkes to the King; "he is no friend of mine." "Why," said the King, "he *was* your friend and your counsel in all your trials."

"Sir," rejoined Wilkes, "he *was* my *counsel*—one *must* have a counsel; but he was no *friend*; he loves sedition and licentiousness which I never delighted in. In fact, Sir, he was a Wilkite, which I never was." The King said the confidence and humour of the man made him forget at the moment his impudence.' Twiss's *Life of Lord Eldon*, ed. 1844, ii. 356.

Note 20. The Society of the Supporters of the Bill of Rights met for the first time at the London Tavern on Feb. 20, 1769. Its objects were 'to raise an effectual barrier against such oppression [as Mr. Wilkes had suffered], to rescue him from his present incumbrances, and to render him easy and independent.' By the end of the following year 'the accounts of the Society stood thus :—

'Debts of Mr. Wilkes discharged, upwards of   -   £12,000.
Election expenses   -   -   -   -   -   £2,973.
Two fines   -   -   -   -   -   -   -   £1,000.
To Mr. Wilkes for his support   -   -   -   £1,000.
Debts compounded   -   -   -   -   -   £6,621.'

When this result was obtained 'a considerable party in the Society thought the object of its institution was accomplished. Mr. Wilkes and his friends thought otherwise. The Society had not, they said, made him *easy and independent*, according to the original engagement. . . . Many seceded, and at length the Society dissolved.' Almon's *Memoirs of Wilkes*, iv. 7-14. Burke wrote on Aug. 15, 1770 :—' I am glad that you find some entertainment in the *Thoughts* [*on the Cause of the Present Discontents*]. They have had in general (I flatter myself) the approbation of the most thinking part of the people. . . . The party which is most displeased is a rotten subdivision of a faction amongst ourselves, who have done us infinite mischief by the violence, rashness, and often wickedness of their measures. I mean the Bill of Rights people.' Burke's *Corres.* i. 229.

Note 21. 'Jan. 15, 1771. Wilkes and Parson Horne [afterwards Horne Tooke] write against each other; Alderman Sawbridge is dying [this is a mistake, as he was Lord Mayor in 1775-6]; and in short Lord Chatham, like Widdrington in Chevy Chace, is left almost alone to fight it out upon his stumps.' Walpole's *Letters*, v. 278. 'Feb. 22. Both Lord Chatham and Wilkes are at the end of their reckoning, and the Opposition can do nothing without fresh fuel. . . . For eight months to come, I should think we shall have little to talk of, you and I, but distant wars and distant majesties. For my part, I reckon the volume quite shut in which I took any interest. The succeeding world is young, new, and half unknown to me.' *Ib.* pp. 282, 4.

Note 22. On Oct. 2, 1770, Hume had written :—' I am engaged in the building a house, which is the second great operation of human life; for the taking a wife is the first, which I hope will come in time.' Burton's *Hume*, ii. 436.

Note 23. Hume wrote to Millar on Oct. 21, 1766 :—' I hope to be

often merry with you and Mrs. Millar in your House in Pall Mall.'
M. S. R. S. E.

Note 24. St. Andrew's Square.

Note 25. When Boswell was taking Johnson to his father's house, 'I was very anxious,' he writes, 'that all should be well ; and begged of my friend to avoid three topics, as to which they differed very widely; Whiggism, Presbyterianism, and—Sir John Pringle. He said courteously, "I shall certainly not talk on subjects which I am told are disagreeable to a gentleman under whose roof I am ; especially I shall not do so to *your father.*"' Boswell's *Johnson*, v. 376. A quarrel nevertheless took place. 'In the course of their altercation Whiggism and Presbyterianism, Toryism and Episcopacy were terribly buffeted. My worthy hereditary friend Sir John Pringle never having been mentioned happily escaped without a bruise.' *Ib.* p. 384. See also *ib.* iii. 65, and *post*, Letter of May 2, 1776.

LETTER XLVI.

The 'detested Edition' : Lord North: the National Debt : Dalrymple's History.

DEAR Sir

You will have a Copy of my philosophical Pieces corrected in a few weeks by a safe hand, who will deliver them to Miss Elliot[1]. She will inform you by a Penny post Letter[2] of their Arrival. I have perusd them carefully five times over; yet the Corrections I make are not of Importance. Such is the Advantage of frequent Impressions!

It vexes me to the last Degree, that, by reason of this detested Edition of my History, I shoud have so distant or no prospect of ever giving a correct Edition of that Work[3]. I assure you, if Mr. Millar were now alive, I shoud be tempted to go over to Dublin[4], and to publish there an Edition, which I hope woud entirely discredit the present one. But as you are entirely innocent in the Conduct of this Affair, I scruple to take that Resolution. The worst of it is, that Affairs have been so manag'd as to leave me in entire Ignorance of the State of the Sale ; tho' I am now confident, that, as you see evidently I am resolv'd never to

engage again with the public, you will no longer have any
Scruple to tell me the whole Truth of the Matter.

But to leave this Subject, which is so very vexatious, and
to talk of public affairs; I am much inclind to have the
same good opinion of Lord North, which you express [5]:
His taking the Helm in such a Storm [6], and conducting it
so prudently, prepossesses one much in his favour : I am
also assurd, that he was the last in the Ministry who
woud give up the Resolution of punishing that insolent
Fellow, Beckford and the City of London [7]. But to me,
his Conduct of the Spanish Affair appears rash, insolent
and unjust. The publication of the Spanish Papers confirms me farther in that Opinion. It appears, that the
Spaniards had never abandond the Settlement, made by
the French, which was prior to ours [8]; and consequently
that their right was in every respect undisputable. And as
the Court of Spain offerd from the first to disavow the
Governor of Buenos Ayros [9], if we woud disavow Hunt [10],
to run the Danger of a War which woud have thrown all
Europe, and almost the whole Globe into a Ferment, must
be regarded as an unpardonable Temerity. We were
savd from that Disaster by nothing but the extreme Love
of Tranquillity in the French King [11], an Incident which no
Human Prudence coud forsee. But what must we think
of the Effrontery of the Patriots, who rail at Lord North
for Tameness and Pusillanimity ? They did not probably
know the secret, otherwise they woud have exclaimd with
better Reason against his Rashness and Imprudence.

I wish I coud have the same Idea with you of the
Prosperity of our public Affairs. But when I reflect, that,
from 1740 to 1761, during the Course of no more than
21 Years, while a most pacific Monarch sat on the Throne
of France [12], the Nation ran in Debt about a hundred
Millions [13]; that the wise and virtuous Minister, Pitt, could
contract more Incumbrances, in six months of an unneces-

sary War, than we have been able to discharge during eight Years of Peace [14]; and that we persevere in the same frantic Maxims; I can forsee nothing but certain and speedy Ruin either to the Nation or to the public Creditors [15]. The last, tho' a great Calamity, woud be a small one in comparison; but I cannot see how it can be brought about, while these Creditors fill all the chief Offices and are the Men of greatest Authority in the Nation [16]. In other Respects the Kingdom may be thriving: The Improvement of our Agriculture [17] is a good Circumstance; tho' I believe our Manufactures do not advance; and all depends on our Union with America, which, in the Nature of things, cannot long subsist [18]. But all this is nothing in comparison of the continual Encrease of our Debts, in every idle War, into which, it seems, the Mob of London [19] are to push every Minister. But these are all other Peoples Concerns; and I know not why I shoud trouble my head about them.

I maintaind and still maintain that Henry's History has merit [20]; tho' I own'd and still own, that the Length of the Undertaking is a great Objection to its Success; perhaps an insuperable one. But what shall we say to Sir John Dalrymple's new History [21], of which, I see, you are one of the publishers? He has writ down that he has been offerd 2000 pounds for the Property of it: I hope you are not the Purchasers; tho' indeed I know not but you might be a Gainer by it: The ranting, bouncing Style of that Performance may perhaps take with the Multitude [22]. This however I am certain of, that there is not one new Circumstance of the least Importance from the beginning to the End of the Work [23]. But really I doubt much of his Veracity in his Account of the Offer: I shoud be much obligd to you for your Information on that head. Never let the Bargain made by Dr. Robertson be thought extravagant [24], if this be true. I shoud add a great Number of Cyphers to bring up the Knight's Performance to an equal Value with that of the Doctor.

I very much regret with you Sir Andrew Mitchels Death [25]: He was a worthy, well-bred, agreeable man. If the Prince, at whose Court he resided, us'd him ill of late Years, he richly deserves the Epithet you give him [26]. Sir Andrew's chief Fault was his too great Attatchment to that prince.

I am Dear S[ir] Yours sincerely

DAVID HUME.

EDINBURGH, 11 *of March*, 1771.

Note 1.   See *ante*, p. 94, *n*. 8.

Note 2.   The Penny Post was not so extensive as it had once been.   In 1710, for instance, 'any letter, or parcel not exceeding one pound weight or ten pounds value, was conveyed for one penny to and from all parts within the Bills of Mortality, to most towns within ten, and to some within twenty miles round London, not conveniently served by the General Post.'   Chamberlayne's *Present State of Great Britain*, 1710, p. 281.   In 1765 'the port of every letter or packet [weight not mentioned] within the Cities of London or Westminster, the Borough of Southwark and their Suburbs, was one penny upon putting in the same; and a second penny upon the delivery of such as are directed to any place beyond the said Cities, Borough and Suburbs, and within the district of the Penny-Post Delivery.'   *Court and City Register*, 1765, p. 133.   In 1801 the postage was raised to twopence, and from that time we find mention of the Twopenny Post.   The term 'Suburbs' had a very limited signification; for it was not till 1831 that the limits of this delivery were extended to all places within three miles of the General Post Office.   *Ninth Report of the Commissioners of the Post Office*, 1837, p. 4.

The general postage of the country was gradually raised.   In 1710 a letter of a single sheet was conveyed 80 miles for twopence; an ounce weight of letters for eightpence.   Above 80 miles for threepence, and an ounce for one shilling.   In every 24 hours the post went 120 miles.   Chamberlayne's *Present State*, p. 281.   By a scale established in 1764 these charges of twopence and threepence were raised to threepence and fourpence.   To Edinburgh and Dublin the charge was sixpence; to New York, one shilling; to the West Indies, eighteen-pence.   *Court and City Register* for 1765, pp. 131–133. The postage was still further raised in 1784, 1797, 1801, 1805, and 1812, when it reached its maximum.   From that year a letter carried over

80 miles was charged ninepence; over 300 miles, thirteen-pence. *Penny Cyclo.* xviii. 455.

Note 3. Strahan in his letter of March 1 had in vain said:—'The octavo edition of your History must undoubtedly soon be cleared; of which I shall be sure to give you timely notice.' Hume refused to be convinced, or even comforted.

Note 4. In the proceedings in the House of Lords on the question of Literary Property, Lord Camden, on Feb. 22, 1774, arguing against a perpetuity, in fact almost against any copyright whatever, said :— 'It was not for gain that Bacon, Newton, Milton, Locke instructed and delighted the world; it would be unworthy such men to traffic with a dirty bookseller for so much a sheet of a letter-press. . . . Knowledge and science are not things to be bound in such cobweb chains; when once the bird is out of the cage . . . *volat irrevocabile*— Ireland, Scotland, America, will afford her shelter.' *Parl. Hist.* xvii. 1000. How Scotland afforded her shelter I do not understand, for that country must have come under the Copyright Act of the eighth of Queen Anne. In fact in it provision is made for a Court of Arbitration composed of Englishmen and Scotchmen (*post*, Letter lxxiii). Ireland, I believe, was not included till the Act of 41 Geo. III. c. 107, in which protection is granted for books printed 'in any part of the United Kingdom, or British European dominions.' Provision is made at the same time for the delivery 'of two copies of all books entered at Stationers' Hall, for the use of the libraries of Trinity College and the King's Inns, Dublin.' *Statutes at Large*, xliii. 316, 320. Up to that time an Irish bookseller could reprint for the Irish market a book published in Great Britain. In one respect he was at a disadvantage. Dean Swift writing to B. Motte, a London bookseller, on May 25, 1736, said :—'One thing I know, that the cruel oppressions of this kingdom by England are not to be borne. You send what books you please hither, and the booksellers here can send nothing to you that is written here. As this is absolute oppression, if I were a bookseller in this town, I would use all the safe means to reprint London books, and run them to any town in England that I could, because whoever offends not the laws of God, or the country he lives in, commits no sin.' Swift's *Works* (ed. 1803), xx. 17[1].

Gibbon, writing of the first volume of the *Decline and Fall*, published in 1776, says :—'The first impression was exhausted in a few days; a second and third edition were scarcely adequate to the demand; and the bookseller's property was twice invaded by the pirates of Dublin.' *Misc. Works*, i. 223.

---

[1] Mr. Justice Willes, in the case of Millar *v.* Taylor (*post*, Letter lxxiii, *n.* 1), said :—'In the case of Motte *v.* Falkner, 28th November, 1735, an injunction was granted for printing Pope's and Swift's *Miscellanies*. Many of these pieces were published in 1701, 1702, 1708.' Burrow's *Reports*, iv. 2325.

Hume having sold the copyright of his *History* to London book-sellers could not publish a rival edition in Great Britain. In Ireland however he was outside the reach of the Act. There he could reprint his work with such great improvements, that 'it would discredit the present edition.' It would be smuggled into England to the great injury of Strahan and Cadell. The following undated letter to William Mure, most likely written in 1756 on the publi-cation of the second volume of the *History of Great Britain under the Stuarts*, shows that Hume and his publishers were intending at that time to bring out a Dublin edition :—'The first Quality of an Historian is to be true and impartial ; the next to be interesting. If you do not say that I have done both Parties justice, and if Mrs. Mure be not sorry for poor King Charles, I shall burn all my Papers, and return to Philosophy. ... We shall make a Dublin Edition ; and it were a Pity to put the Irish farther wrong than they are already. I shall also be so sanguine as to hope for a second Edition, when I may cor[rect][1]. You know my Docility.' *M. S. R. S. E.*

Note 5. Strahan had written :—' One word of politics more, and I have done. You seem to think we are in a much worse way than we really are. I admit the inexcusable timidity of the Ministry, in suffering so many and so great insults which no Government ought to overlook. But notwithstanding all our follies and all our misconduct the nation in general is actually in a thriving condition. The Opposition is melting away to nothing, and every day falling more and more into contempt. Wilkes is hardly ever heard of but in a way very little to his credit. The boldest of his adherents are either tired out and have deserted him, or they are no more. In short a steady, able, honest Minister (and such I hope Lord North may prove to be) may yet support this country long in honour and credit. Wealth pours in upon us from a thousand channels, particularly the East Indies, which adds perhaps too much to our luxury, and that may at length prove fatal. But this is a poison which operates slowly, and many events may occur to check its progress, without endangering the general welfare and security of the State.' *M. S. R. S. E.*

On Oct. 27, 1775, Hume writing of the disturbances in America, said :—' Tell him [Lord Home] that Lord North, though in appear-ance a worthy gentleman, has not a head for these great operations.' Burton's *Hume*, ii. 479. Gibbon, in describing the eight sessions in which he sat in Parliament, says :—' The cause of government was ably vindicated by Lord North, a statesman of spotless integrity, a consummate master of debate, who could wield with equal dex-terity the arms of reason and of ridicule.' *Misc. Works*, i. 221. Johnson described his Ministry as 'neither stable nor grateful to

---

[1] The MS. is here imperfect.

their friends,' and as 'feeble and timid.' Boswell's *Johnson*, ii. 348, 355.

Note 6. In the latter half of January, 1770, the Lord Chancellor Camden had been dismissed, the new Lord Chancellor Yorke had died suddenly—by his own hand it was commonly believed—the Speaker of the House of Commons had died two days later, the popular Commander in Chief Lord Granby had resigned, and his resignation had been followed by many others ; and at last the Prime Minister himself, the Duke of Grafton, 'in a very extraordinary moment indeed, in the midst of his own measures, in the midst of a session and undefeated,' resigned also. 'It was impossible,' wrote Horace Walpole, 'to choose a more distressful moment than he selected for quitting; and had the scale turned on Wednesday [Jan. 31, when the Opposition had flattered themselves with victory in a division], I do not know where we should have been. The House of Commons contradicting itself, a reversal of the Middlesex election, a dissolution of Parliament, or the King driven to refuse it in the face of a majority! I protest I think some fatal event must have happened.... The people are perfectly quiet, and seem to have delegated all their anger to their representatives—*a proof that their representatives had instructed their constituents to be angry.* ... Yet I am far from thinking this Administration solidly seated. Any violence, or new provocation, may dislodge it at once. When they could reduce a majority of an hundred and sixteen to forty in three weeks, their hold seems to be very slippery.' *Letters*, v. 223, 225. See *ante*, p. 136, *n.* 5.

Note 7. In the Debate of March 15, 1770, on the Remonstrance of the City, 'Lord North spoke in a very high style. ... Speaking of the Lord Mayor, he called him "that worthy magistrate, if I may still call him *worthy* after this action of his."' *Parl. Hist.* xvi. 876. General Conway made a strong speech 'against lenity' (*ib.* p. 888); but 'the danger of still increasing the public ill-humour and discontent by taking violent measures against so respectable a body as the Corporation and Citizens of London' (*Ann. Reg.* 1770, i. 81) deterred the Ministers. See *ante*, p. 147, *n.* 7, and p. 185.

Note 8. See *ante*, p. 165, *n.* 9.

Note 9. The Spanish Ambassador 'owned that he had from Madrid received intelligence that the English had been forcibly expelled from Falkland's Islands by Buccarelli, the Governor of Buenos Ayres, without any particular orders from the King of Spain. But being asked whether in his Master's name he disavowed Buccarelli's violence, he refused to answer without direction.' Johnson's *Works*, vi. 192.

Note 10. Captain Hunt of the Tamar (*ante*, p. 165, *n.* 9). The Spanish Ambassador 'proposed a convention for the accommodation of differences by mutual concessions, in which the warning given to the Spaniards by Hunt should be disavowed on one side, and the violence used by Buccarelli on the other.   This offer was considered as little less than a new insult, and Grimaldi [the Spanish Minister at Madrid] was told that injury required reparation.' *Ib.* p. 193.

Note 11. See *ante*, p. 167, *n.* 10.

Note 12. Lewis XV.

Note 13. In 1736 the debt of England amounted to about 50 millions; in 1748, at the Peace of Aix-la-Chapelle, to 78 millions; in 1756, to 75 millions; in 1763, at the Peace of Paris, to 139 millions. In the next twelve years it was reduced by somewhat more than 10 millions.   In Lord North's administration it rose from 129 to 268 millions.   *Penny Cyclo.* xvi. 100.   See *ante*, p. 130, *n.* 20.

Note 14. Lord Chatham, in the House of Lords on Nov. 22, 1770, said :—'My Lords, while I had the honour of serving his Majesty I never ventured to look at the Treasury but at a distance; it is a business I am unfit for, and to which I never could have submitted.' *Parl. Hist.* xvi. 1106.

Note 15. Burke, in his Speech on American Taxation on April 19, 1774, said :—'Do you forget that, in the very last year, you stood on the precipice of general bankruptcy? . . . The monopoly of the most lucrative trades, and the possession of imperial revenues, had brought you to the verge of beggary and ruin.' Payne's *Burke*, i. 103.   In a note which Hume, shortly before his death, added to the third Appendix in his *History* (v. 475), he says :—' It is curious to observe that the minister in the war begun in the year 1754 was in some periods allowed to lavish in two months as great a sum as was granted by Parliament to Queen Elizabeth in forty-five years.   The extreme frivolous object of the late war, and the great importance of hers, set this matter in still a stronger light.   Money too we may observe was in most particulars of the same value in both periods.   She paid eightpence a day to every foot soldier.   But our late delusions have much exceeded anything known in history, not even excepting those of the Crusades.   For I suppose there is no mathematical, still less an arithmetical demonstration, that the road to the Holy Land was not the road to Paradise, as there is that the endless increase of national debts is the direct road to national ruin.   But having now completely reached that goal, it is needless at present to reflect on the past.   It will be found in the present year, 1776, that all the revenues of this island north of Trent and west of Reading are mortgaged or anticipated for ever.   Could the small remainder be in a worse condition, were those provinces seized by Austria and Prussia?   There is only this difference, that some event might happen in Europe which would oblige these great monarchs to disgorge their acquisitions. But no imagination can figure a situation which will induce our creditors to relinquish their claims, or the public to seize their revenues.   So egregious indeed has been our folly, that we have even lost all title to compassion in the numberless calamities that are awaiting us.'   'The late war' with 'its extreme frivolous objects' of the great Tory historian, was the war by which, according to the great Whig historian, 'the first Englishman of his time had made England the first country in the world.' Macaulay's *Essays*, ed. 1874, ii. 195.

Note 16. See *post*, Letter of Aug. 19, 1771.

Note 17. The *Annual Register* for this year under the title of *Useful Projects* has six entries about agriculture. Arthur Young's first work, *A Six Weeks' Tour through the Southern Counties*, was published in 1768. At this time he and Burke were corresponding about growing carrots, fattening pigs, etc. Burke's *Corres.* i. 248, 257, 262.

Note 18. A passage in Burke's *Speech on Conciliation with America*, spoken on March 22, 1775, shows that even by that date few people saw what was clear to Hume now. After considering three ways of dealing with 'the stubborn spirit' of the Colonists, Burke continues : —'Another has indeed been started, that of giving up the Colonies ; but it met so slight a reception, that I do not think myself obliged to dwell a great while upon it. It is nothing but a little sally of anger ; like the frowardness of peevish children, who, when they cannot get all they would have, are resolved to take nothing.' Payne's *Burke*, i. 187.

Note 19. The 'mob of London' with Hume means the large majority of the Common Council and of the citizens in general.

Note 20. See *ante*, p. 155.

Note 21. *Memoirs of Great Britain and Ireland*; the first volume of which was published in 1771, the second in 1773, and the third, under the title of Vol. ii. parts 3 and 4, in 1788.

Note 22. ' "This Dalrymple," said Dr. Johnson, "seems to be an honest fellow ; for he tells equally what makes against both sides. But nothing can be poorer than his mode of writing, it is the mere bouncing of a schoolboy. Great He! but greater She ! and such stuff."' Boswell's *Johnson*, ii. 210. At another time he attacked 'the foppery of Dalrymple.' *Ib.* p. 237. See also *ib.* v. 402-404 for Johnson's unceremonious treatment of the Baronet and imitation of his style.

Note 23. Hume judged the work more kindly when it was attacked by the Whigs. 'Have you seen Sir John Dalrymple ?' he wrote on April 10, 1773. 'It is strange what a rage is against him on account of the most commendable action in his life. His collection is curious ; but introduces no new light into the civil, whatever it may into the biographical and anecdotical history of the times.' Burton's *Hume*, ii. 467. Horace Walpole, who was angry with Dalrymple for his attack on Algernon Sidney, wrote on March 2, 1773 :—'Need I tell you that Sir John Dalrymple, the accuser of bribery, was turned out of his place of Solicitor of the Customs for taking bribes from brewers ?' *Letters*, v. 441. On May 15 he wrote :—'There are two answers to Sir John Dalrymple, but not very good. The best answer is what he made himself to George Onslow, whom he told on warning [sic] him for traducing the immortal Sidney, that he had other papers which would have washed him as white as snow. With this Sir John has been publicly reproached in print and has not gainsaid it.' *Ib.* p. 462.

Note 24. See *ante*, p. 14, *n.* 1.

Note 25. Sir Andrew Mitchell, the English Minister at Berlin, died in that town on Jan. 28, 1771. *Ann. Reg.* 1771, i. 176. Boswell, when on his travels, writing to him on Dec. 26, 1764, says :—' My most intimate friend, the friend of my youth, and the comfort of my being, is a Mr. Temple [the grandfather of the present Bishop of London].' After asking Mitchell to get Temple employment he continues :— ' Sir, I beg and entreat of you to give me your interest. You are the only man in Britain, except my Sovereign, whom I would ask a favour of. . . . If you can aid me, you will most truly oblige a worthy fellow, *for such I am.' Letters of Boswell*, p. 56. Voltaire, writing from Lausanne on Jan. 5, 1758, says :—' Le roi de Prusse, en parlant à M. Mitchel, ministre d'Angleterre, de la belle entreprise de la flotte anglaise sur nos côtes, lui dit :—" Eh bien ! que faites-vous à présent ?" " Nous laissons faire Dieu," répondit Mitchel, " Je ne vous connaissais pas cet allié," dit le roi. " C'est le seul à qui nous ne payons pas de subsides," répliqua Mitchel. " Aussi," dit le roi, " c'est le seul qui ne vous assiste pas." ' *Œuvres de Voltaire*, L. 1. ' La belle entreprise ' was the disastrous expedition against Rochefort in September, 1757. Smollett's *History of England*, ed. 1800, iv. 88.

Note 26. What ' the epithet ' was is seen in the following extract from Strahan's letter :—' Poor Sir Andrew Mitchel !—my last Letter which was a very long one and in which I pressed his coming home very earnestly, was written the day after he died—Alas ! little did I then think I was addressing myself to his Shade. I wish most heartily he had come to Britain, and enjoyed himself a few Years ; for I have reason to think he was not very happy at Berlin for some years past. You know the Character of the Hero of that Country who perhaps has not his Equal in Europe—mayhap there never existed a greater Scoundrel.' *M. S. R. S. E.*

Mitchell, a little more than a year before his death, makes the following complaint of a slight put on him by the King :—

' Berlin, Dec. 23, 1769.

' Happening last Thursday morning, at the public levee, to stand near the French minister, the King of Prussia passed by me without speaking to me, which I the more particularly take notice of, as it is the first, and indeed the only time that this Monarch, during my very long mission at this Court, has behaved to me in this manner.' Bisset's *Memoirs of Sir A. Mitchell*, ii. 389. A year later he writes :— ' Dec. 29, 1770. Last Wednesday the King of Prussia, at his public levee, after kindly enquiring concerning the state of my health, asked me abruptly, Shall we have peace or war ?' *Ib.* p. 391. This was Mitchell's last despatch. Mr. Carlyle, writing of the year 1756,

says :—'One wise thing the English have done : sent an Excellency
Mitchell, a man of loyalty, of sense and honesty, to be their Resident
at Berlin.   This is the noteworthy, not yet much noted, Sir Andrew
Mitchell ; by far the best Excellency England ever had in that
Court.   An Aberdeen Scotchman, creditable to his Country : hard-
headed, sagacious ; sceptical of shows ; but capable of recognising
substances withal, and of standing loyal to them, stubbornly if needful ; who grew to a great mutual regard with Friedrich, and well
deserved to do so ; constantly about him, during the next seven
years ; and whose Letters are among the perennially valuable Documents on Friedrich's History.'   *History of Friedrich II*, ed. 1864,
iv. 537.

LETTER XLVII.

*The Art of Printing : Revised Editions : Dr. Johnson's
Pamphlet : The Earl of Chatham : Sir John Dalrymple.*

DEAR S[IR]

This will be deliver'd to you, along with a corrected
Copy of my philosophical Pieces by Dr. Robertson.   I
remind you to send me six Copies, as usual.   This is the
last time I shall probably take the pains of correcting that
work, which is now brought to as great a degree of accuracy
as I can attain ; and is probably much more labour'd[1] (I
know not with what degree of success) than any other
production in our Language[2]. This power, which Printing
gives us, of continually improving and correcting our
Works in successive Editions, appears to me the Chief
Advantage of that Art.   For as to the dispersing of Books,
that Circumstance does perhaps as much harm as good[3] :
Since Nonsense flies with greater Celerity, and makes
greater Impression than Reason ; though indeed no particular Species of Nonsense is so durable.   But the several
Forms of Nonsense never cease succeeding one another ;
and Men are always under the Dominion of some one
or other[4], though nothing was ever equal in Absurdity and
Wickedness to our present Patriotism[5].

I long much for an Opportunity of bringing my History

to the same degree of Accuracy. Since I was settled here, I have, from time to time, given Attention to that Object; though the Distance and Uncertainty of the new Edition threw a damp on my Industry: But I shall now apply seriously to the Task; and you may expect the Copy about August[6]. I beseech you do not make this Edition too numerous, like the last. I have heard you frequently say, that no Bookseller woud find profit in making an Edition which woud take more than three Years in selling. Look back, therefore, and learn from Mr. Millar's Books what has been the Sale for the last six Years; and if you make the usual Allowance for a Diminution during the ensuing three, from the Number of Copies already sold, I am persuaded you will find 1500, a number large enough, if not too large[7]: Be not over-sanguine. An Error on the one hand is more easily corrected than one on the other. I am perhaps the only Author you ever knew, who gratutiously (sic) employ'd great Industry in correcting a Work, of which he has fully alienated the Property; and it were hard to deny me an Opportunity of exercising my Talents; especially as this practice turns so much to the Advantage of the Bookseller.

I have another Proposal to make you in the same View. I have found by Experience that nothing excites an Author's Attention so much as the receiving the Proofs from the Press, as the Sheets are gradually thrown off. Now I have had an Opportunity of passing the last four Volumes of my History more than once through this Scrutiny, the most severe of any: The first four Volumes[8] have only been once reviewd by me in this manner. I shall send you the whole Copy[9] about the time above mention'd, and the last four Volumes you may throw off at your Leizure: But the Sheets of the first four, I shoud wish to receive by the Post five times a week. They will make about 250 Sheet and might be finishd in thirty weeks[10]. For this

Purpose I shall apply to Mr. Fraser, my former Collegue in the Secretary's Office, who will supply you with Franks, and such as are not confind to the usual Weight of two Ounces [11]. The corrected Copies I shall send under his Cover; and you will only have to send for them to the Secretary's Office, the same as if I were in London. Mr. Fraser is as regular as an astronomical Clock, and will never dissappoint you. I am almost as regular; and you may give Orders to your People to be the same.

This Affair, therefore, being, I presume, settled to mutual Satisfaction, I come to give you thanks for the Perusal of Mr. Johnson's Pamphlet [12], which is a good one, and very diverting from the Peculiarity and Enormity of the Style [13]. One sees he speaks from the Heart, and is movd with a cordial Indignation against these Ruffians. There is, however, one material Circumstance, which either he did not know, or did not think fit to mention; namely, that the French had regularly settled Falkland Island full three Years before us, and upon Remonstrances from the Court of Madrid, gave up their Right and Colony to the Spaniards, who never had abandond that Settlement [14]. Their Right, therefore, was prior and preferable to ours. For as to our ridiculous Right from the first Dicovery [*sic*], allowing the Facts to be true; will any one say, that a Sailor's seeing a Montain from the Top mast head [15], conveys a Title to a whole Territory, and a Title so durable, that even tho' it be neglected for two Centuries, it still remains with the Nation. Our Ministry, therefore, have acted a Part most unjust, most insolent, and most imprudent; and which the Spaniards will deservedly remember long against us. But this Conduct proceeds entirely from the Timidity of our Ministry, who dread more the contemptible Populace of London [16] than the whole House of Bourbon. I am curious to see how they will get out of the present Scrape [17]; though their past Measures prognosticate nothing good for the future. I say still, had they punishd Beckford[18], disfranchisd the City[19], and restord the Negative to the Court of Aldermen[20], they woud have prevented the present and many future Frays: But still it is not too late; though it may very soon become so.

When I blame the Insolence of our Ministry with regard to Spain, I must at the same time confess, that we do right to swagger and bounce and bully on the present Occasion: For we have not many Years to do so, before we fall into total Impotence and Languor[21]. You see, that a much greater and more illustrious People, namely the French[22], seem to be totally annihilated in the midst of Europe[23]; and we, instead of regarding this Event as a great Calamity, are such Fools as to rejoice at it[24]. We see not that the same Catastrophe or a much worse one is awaiting us at no distant Period. The monarchical Government of France (which must be replac'd[25]) will enable them to throw off *their* Debts[26]; ours must for ever hang on our Shoulders, and weigh us down like a Mill-stone[27].

I think that Mr Johnson is a great deal too favourable to Pitt, in comparing him to Cardinal Richelieu[28]. The Cardinal had certainly great Talents besides his Audacity: The other is totally destitute of Literature, Sense, or the Knowledge of any one Branch of public Business. What other Talent indeed has he, but that of reciting with tolerable Action and great Impudence a long Discourse in which there is neither Argument, Order, Instruction, Propriety or even Grammar[29]. Not to mention, that the Cardinal, with his inveterate Enmities[30], was also capable of Friendship: While our Cut-throat[31] never felt either the one Sentiment or the other[32]. The Event of both Administrations was suitable. France made a Figure during near a Century and a half upon the Foundations laid by the one[33]: England—as above; if I be not much mistaken, as I wish to be[34].

I was pretty sure that Sir John Dalrymple was an *Historian*[35], with regard to the Price offerd him for his Book. So then, his Pride is interested in being esteem'd as good a Writer as Dr. Robertson! I am diverted with conjecturing what will be the Fate of this strange Book: Will it run a few Years? Or fall at once *dead born from the Press*[36]? I think the last Event more probable, notwithstanding the Precedent of Mrs. Macaulay[37], and notwithstanding the Antitheses and Rant and Whiggery of which it is full. After you have offerd him 750 pounds, my Pride, in case I shoud write another Volume, woud make me demand the Equivalent of a parliamentary Subsidy[38]; I think without Vanity, my Book will at least be equal in Value to Falkland Island[39].

But I have writ you a Letter as long as an Essay; and for fear of making it a Treatise, I shall conclude by telling you, that I am with great Sincerity

Dear S[ir] Your most obedient humble Servant

DAVID HUME[40].

EDINBURGH, 25 *of March*, 1771.

Note 1. Johnson describes Savage's *Wanderer* as 'a poem diligently *laboured* and successfully finished.' *Works*, viii. 131. 'JOHNSON. "It appears to me that I labour when I say a good thing." BOSWELL. "You are loud, Sir; but it is not an effort of mind."' Boswell's *Johnson*, v. 77.

Note 2. Pope surpassed even Hume in unwearying industry of revision. 'He examined,' says Johnson, 'lines and words with minute and punctilious observation, and retouched every part with indefatigable diligence, till he had left nothing to be forgiven. . . . His declaration that his care for his works ceased at their publication was not strictly true. His parental attachment never abandoned them; what he found amiss in the first edition he silently corrected in those that followed.' Johnson's *Works*, viii. 323. Lord Lyttelton, too, was by no means inferior to Hume. So many corrections did he make in his *History of Henry II* that 'his ambitious accuracy is known to have cost him at least a thousand pounds. He began to print in 1755. Three volumes appeared in 1764, and the conclusion in 1771.' To the third edition 'is appended, what the world had hardly seen before, a list of errors in nineteen pages.' *Ib.* p. 492.

Note 3. 'The mass of every people,' said Johnson, 'must be barbarous where there is no printing, and consequently knowledge is not generally diffused. Knowledge is diffused among our people by the newspapers.' Boswell's *Johnson*, ii. 170.

Note 4. See *post*, Letter of Jan. 2, 1772, where Hume says :—'The people never tire of folly, but they tire of the same folly.' Horace Walpole has the same thought. Thus he writes :—'Dec. 16, 1764. It is idle to endeavour to cure the world of any folly, unless we could cure it of being foolish.' *Letters*, iv. 303. 'Feb. 7, 1772. I begin to think that folly is matter, and cannot be annihilated. Destroy its form, it takes another. The Reformation was only a re-formation. It is happy when attempts to serve or enlighten mankind do not produce more prejudice to them. What are the consequences of the writings of the philosophers, and of the struggles of the Parliaments in France? Despotism! Lawyers have been found to support it, and priests will not be wanting. Methinks it would be a good text for the gallows, "upon this hang all the law and the prophets."' *Ib.* v. 374. 'Sept. 9, 1773. I have had another letter from you [Sir Horace Mann], with the total demolition of the Jesuits. . . . Well! but here is a large vacuum in the mass of folly,—what will replace it? I ask upon a maxim of mine, *that it is idle to cure men of a folly, unless one could cure them of being foolish.*' *Ib.* p. 502.

Hume, speaking of the Lutherans, says :—'The quick and surprising progress of this bold sect may justly in part be ascribed to the late invention of printing and revival of learning. Not that reason bore any considerable share in opening men's eyes with regard to the impostures of the Romish Church; for of all branches of literature philosophy had as yet, and till long afterwards, made the most inconsiderable progress; neither is there any instance that argument has ever been able to free the people from that enormous load of absurdity with which superstition has everywhere overwhelmed them.' *History of England* (ed. 1802), iv. 37.

Note 5. See *ante*, p. 132, *n.* 25.

Note 6. Strahan must have at last convinced Hume that 'the detested edition' would not last much longer. On July 23 he sent him word that 'a new type was casting for the *History.*' *M.S.R.S.E.*

Note 7. Gibbon, writing of his *Decline and Fall*, says :—'So moderate were our hopes that the original impression had been stinted to five hundred, till the number was doubled by the prophetic taste of Mr. Strahan. The first impression was exhausted in a few days.' *Misc. Works*, i. 222. Each of the ten editions of the *Rambler* published in Johnson's lifetime consisted, according to Hawkins, of 1250 copies. Boswell's *Johnson*, i. 213, *n.* 1.

Note 8. See *ante*, p. 150.

Note 9. *Copy* is generally used of manuscript for printing, but here it is used of the corrected printed edition.

Note 10. An octavo sheet consists of sixteen pages. He wished to receive rather more than eight sheets (128 pages) a week. There were at this time five posts a week between London and Edinburgh, on Monday, Tuesday, Thursday, Friday, and Saturday, To Oxford there was a post every day but Sunday; to Brighton, on Monday, Wednesday, and Saturday; to France, on Tuesday and Friday; to Flanders, on Tuesday and Friday; to Spain and Portugal, on Tuesday. *Court and City Register* for 1765, pp. 130-2. 'Within my recollection,' writes Sir Walter Scott, 'the London post was brought north in a small mail-cart; and men are yet alive [in 1824], who recollect when it came down with only one single letter for Edinburgh, addressed to the Manager of the British Linen Company.' Scott's *Works*, ed. 1860, xxxvi. 77. In 1710 there were posts from London to Scotland every Tuesday, Thursday, and Saturday. Chamberlayne's *Present State of Great Britain*, p. 280.

Note 11. Mason asked Horace Walpole on Sept 9, 1772, to forward to him some letters of Gray. 'Send them to Mr. Fraser at Lord Suffolk's office [Lord Suffolk was a Secretary of State] to be forwarded to me; you may be assured of their coming safe, for Fraser is punctuality and care itself.' *Letters*, v. 406. On Nov. 23, 1773, he wrote :—'Any pacquet how large soever will be sent me from Fraser.' *Ib.* vi. 14. Hume found Fraser much less obliging than he had expected (*post*, Letter of Jan. 2, 1772). I have seen a letter franked by Hume, when he was Under-Secretary; 'Free, Da: Hume,' being inscribed on the outside.

In the *Gent. Mag.* for April 1764, p. 182, are given Heads of the Act for preventing frauds in franking. Before a Parliamentary Committee it had appeared that the postage of freed letters amounted, one year with another, to £170,000, and that the clerks in the Office of the Secretaries of State had made from £800 to £1200 a year each,—one in particular had made £1700 by franking newspapers, etc. By the new Act the privilege of Members of either House was confined to the Session and to forty days before and after it. The weight of the packet was not to exceed two ounces, the whole of the address was to be in the member's writing, and to be attested by his signature.

Before this regulation was made the signature only was required, as is shown in Hume's letter of Feb. 15, 1757 (*ante*, p. 17), where he tells Strahan to send covers already directed to certain members to be franked. In the signature which people of importance and important people still write on the envelopes of their letters, we have, I believe, a trace of the old privilege of franking.

A member of Parliament not only sent, but also received his letters free of postage. Hume at one time used to address letters to the Admiralty, to be forwarded thence to Strahan. Strahan wrote back : —'When you write, you may as well send it by the mail, for the porters at Lord Sandwich's office require as much for bringing a letter to me from thence as the postage comes to.' *M. S. R. S. E.*

Later on the maximum weight was reduced to one ounce, at which it remained till 1840, when franking was abolished. It was stated that the *official* franks 'had been used to free a great coat, a bundle of baby-linen and a piano-forte.' *Life of Sir Rowland Hill*, i. 241. How troublesome to an unhappy Under-Secretary of State this privilege of unlimited franking might become, is shown in the following curious extract from a letter which I had the honour to receive from Mr. Justice Stephen soon after the publication of my *Life of Sir Rowland Hill.*

> 'Judges' Lodgings, Lancaster Assizes,
> Northern Circuit, Jan. 17, 1881.

'. . . I may tell you as a small point which may interest you that my father used to look upon the penny postage as an unspeakable deliverance. He had (as Under-Secretary of State for the Colonies) the curse of an unlimited power of franking. As he was good-natured all his friends and all his most distant acquaintances sent him endless letters to frank. As he was also extremely conscientious he always wrote the whole address with his own hand and signed his name in the corner according to law. He once told me that he had made a calculation that at about the busiest time of a most laborious life he spent as much time in addressing letters in this way as would have kept him at work six hours a day for the whole month of February in every year. I well remember as a child seeing him sit down to direct a great pile of 20 or 30 letters with which he had as much to do as you or I.'

Note 12. *Thoughts on the late Transactions respecting Falkland's Islands.*

Note 13. 'The conversation now turned upon Mr. David Hume's style. JOHNSON: "Why, Sir, his style is not English ; the structure of his sentences is French. Now the French structure and the English structure may, in the nature of things, be equally good. But if you allow that the English language is established, he is wrong. My name might originally have been Nicholson as well as Johnson ; but were you to call me Nicholson now, you would call me very absurdly." ' Boswell's *Johnson*, i. 439.

Note 14. See *ante*, p. 165, *n.* 9.

Note 15. 'In the fatal voyage of Cavendish (1592) Captain Davis . . . . as he was driven by violence of weather about the Straits of Magellan, is supposed to have been the first who saw the lands now called Falkland's Islands, but his distress permitted him not to make any observation.' Johnson's *Works*, vi. 181.

Note 16. Lord North, two days after the date of Hume's letter, was in great danger from this populace. Horace Walpole wrote on March 30, 1771 :—'A prodigious mob came from the City with the Lord Mayor on Wednesday. . . . The two Foxes [Charles Fox was at this time a Junior Lord of the Admiralty] were assaulted and dragged out of their chariot, and escaped with difficulty. Lord North was attacked with still more inveteracy; his chariot was torn to pieces, and several spectators say there was a moment in which they thought he must be destroyed. . . . . The Ministers are more moderate than their party who demand extremities. Young Charles Fox, the meteor of these days and barely twenty-two, is at the head of these strong measures. . . . The King was excessively hissed yesterday as he went to the House.' *Letters,* v. 292. Mr. Calcraft, describing to Lord Chatham the debate that followed, said:—'Lord North disclaimed going out [of office], though he wished much for ease and retirement. He added, that nothing but the King or the mob, who were near destroying him to-day, could remove him; he would weather out the storm; but his pathetic manner and tears rather confirmed than removed my suspicions of his very anxious, perplexed situation.' *Chatham Corresp.* iv. 138.

Note 17. 'The present scrape' was 'a ridiculous contest with a set of printers' (to use Burke's words, *Ann. Reg.* 1771, i. 62) into which the Government and the House of Commons had recklessly plunged. Burke, in writing the history of this affair, begins by re-marking on the licentiousness of the periodical publications at this time. Both political parties were equally guilty of 'the most gross, the most shameful, and the most scandalous abuse. . . . Distinction of character seemed at an end; and that powerful incentive to all public and private virtue, of establishing a fair fame and of gaining popular applause, which to noble minds is the highest of all rewards, seemed now to be totally cut off, and no longer to be hoped for.' *Ib.* p. 60. He agrees with Horace Walpole, who finds the chief source of this evil in 'the spirit of the Court, which aimed at despotism, and the daring attempts of Lord Mansfield to stifle the liberty of the press. His innovations had given such an alarm that scarce a jury would find the rankest satire libellous.' *Memoirs of George III,* iv. 167. 'While an evil so destructive to all virtue was either over-looked or encouraged' (*Ann. Reg.* p. 60), the House of Commons suddenly made an attempt to enforce their standing order against the publication of their debates.

On Feb. 22 Horace Walpole had written to Mann:—'For eight months to come I should think we shall have little to talk of, you and I, but distant wars and distant majesties' (*ante*, p. 171, *n.* 21). On March 22, just one month later, he writes:—'I was in too great a hurry when I announced peaceable times, and half took leave of you as a correspondent. The horizon is overcast again already; the wind is got to the north-east and by Wilkes; and without a figure the House of Commons and the City of London are at open war. It is more surprising that Wilkes is not the aggressor—at least Folly put new crackers into his hand. Two cousins, both George Onslow by name, the son and nephew of the old Speaker, took offence at seeing the debates and speeches of the House printed, and the more as they had both been much abused. They complain, and the

House issues warrants for seizing the printers, and addresses the
King to issue a proclamation for apprehending them.   Out comes a
Proclamation, and no great seal to it. .The City declares no man shall
be apprehended contrary to law within their jurisdiction.   The
printers are seized ; Wilkes, as sitting Alderman, releases one ; the
Lord Mayor, Wilkes, and another Alderman deliver another, and
commit the messenger of the House of Commons to prison.   The
House summons the Lord Mayor to appear before them and answer
for his conduct, but as he is laid up with the gout allow him to come
on Monday last, or to-day, Friday.   He gets out of bed and goes on
Monday.   Thousands of handbills are dispersed to invite the mob to
escort him, but not an hundred attend. . . . He is too ill to stay, and
is allowed to retire.   Wilkes is summoned too ; writes a refusal to
the Speaker, unless he is admitted to his seat.   The Speaker will
not receive his letter, nor the House hear it, though read, and again
order him to attend.'   Walpole's *Letters*, v. 286.   ' March 26.   The die
is cast.   The army of the House of Commons has marched into the
City, and made a prisoner ; but as yet no blood is spilt ; though I own
I expected to hear there was this morning when I waked.   Last
night, when I went to bed at half an hour after twelve, I had just
been told that all the avenues to the House were blockaded, and had
beaten back the peace-officers, who had been summoned, for it was
toute autre chose yesterday, when the Lord Mayor went to the House
from what it had been the first day.   He was now escorted by a
prodigious multitude, who hissed and insulted the members of both
Houses. . . . Well! what think you now ?   When so many men
have ambition to be martyrs, will the storm easily subside ?   Oh ! Sir
Robert, my father, would this have happened in your days ?   I can
remember when on the Convention [with Spain, in 1739] Sir William
Windham, no fool for that time, laboured to be sent to the Tower,
and my father told him in plain terms he knew his meaning and
would not indulge it. . . . My father's maxim, *Quieta non movere*,
was very well in those ignorant days.   The science of government
is better understood now—so, to be sure, *whatever is, is right.'*
Ib. pp. 291-2.

Lord Chatham wrote on March 21, 1771 :—' The storm thickens
admirably well, and these wretches called Ministers will be sick
enough of their folly (not forgetting iniquity) before the whole business is over.   If I mistake not it will prove very pregnant, and one
distress generate another ; for they have brought themselves and
their Master where ordinary inability never arrives, and nothing but
first rate geniuses in incapacity can reach ; I mean a situation wherein there is nothing they can do which is not a fault.'   *Chatham Corresp.*
iv. 119.   Mr. Calcraft wrote to Chatham on March 24 :—' The Ministers avow Wilkes too dangerous to meddle with.   He is to do what
he pleases; we are to submit.   So his Majesty orders ; he will have
" nothing more to do with that devil Wilkes." '   *Ib.* p. 122.   The

difficulty was evaded in the most ignominious manner. The House ordered Wilkes to appear on April 8, and then 'adjourned itself to the ninth.' *Ann. Reg.* 1771, i. 70.

The Lord Mayor and Alderman Oliver were sent to the Tower, where they remained till the prorogation of Parliament on May 8. On their release 'the City was grandly illuminated.' *Ann. Reg.* 1771, i. 104. A Committee of the House had meanwhile inquired into the obstructions to the execution of the orders. It recommended the consideration of the expediency of the House ordering that Miller, the printer of the *Evening Post*, should be taken into custody. The report was received with a roar of laughter. *Parl. Hist.* xvii. 202, 211. Nothing was done, and the freedom of the newspaper press was secured. The *Post* had been Squire Western's paper. ' " Sister," cries the Squire, " I have often warned you not to talk the Court gibberish to me. I tell you, I don't understand the lingo ; but I can read a Journal or the *London Evening Post*. Perhaps indeed there may be now and tan a verse which I can't make much of, because half the letters are left out ; yet I know very well what is meant by that, and that our affairs don't go so well as they should do, because of bribery and corruption.' *Tom Jones*, Bk. vi. ch. 2. Burke notices the abandonment of this half-disguise in his account of the licentiousness of the press. The attacks were made without 'the usual cautions of drawing characters, and leaving it to the sagacity of the reader to trace out the resemblance.' *Ann. Reg.*, 1771, i. 60.

Note 18. See *ante*, p. 138.

Note 19. I cannot find that any one went so far as to propose to disfranchise the City. General Conway in the Debate on March 15, 1770, said :—' If the Livery of London are daring enough to censure this House, shall it be said that a British House of Commons has been afraid to censure the Livery of London ? ' *Parl. Hist.* xvi. 891.

Note 20. ' Had the negative been restored the Remonstrance to the King in March 1770 would never have been voted ; for at the Court of Common Council 3 Aldermen and 109 Commoners voted for it, and 15 Aldermen and 61 Commoners against it.' *Gent. Mag.* 1770, p. 109.

Note 21. Hume twenty-five years earlier, in 1746, had written :— ' I think the present times are so calamitous, and our future prospect so dismal, that it is a misfortune to have any concern in public affairs which one cannot redress, and where it is difficult to arrive at a proper degree of insensibility or philosophy, as long as one is in the scene. You know my sentiments were always a little gloomy on that head. . . I shall not be much disappointed if this prove the last Parliament worthy the name we shall ever have in Britain.' Burton's *Hume*, i. 224. He had more reason for his gloominess now. Lord Chatham, writing on March 24, 1771, one day earlier than the date of Hume's letter, said :—' The scene is unexampled, and England devoted to ruin; Bengal news calamitous.' *Chatham Corresp.* iv. 125. Eleven years later, a few weeks before the fall of Lord North's Ministry, the City of London in an Address to the King 'used these stunning and memorable words :—" Your armies are captured; the wonted superiority of your navies is annihilated, your dominions are lost."' Walpole's *Journal of the Reign of George III*, ii. 483. A few months later (Aug. 4, 1782) Johnson wrote :—' Perhaps no nation not absolutely conquered has declined so much in so short a time. We seem to be sinking.' Boswell's *Johnson*, iv. 139, *n*. 4. Horace Walpole, writing on May 13, 1780, says (*Letters*, vii. 364), ' It is my opinion that the vigour of this country is worn out and is not likely to revive. I think it is pretty much the same case with Europe.... Is not the universal inactivity of all religions a symptom of decrepitude ?'

Note 22. See *ante*, p. 50, *n*. 3, and p. 56, *n*. 8, for Hume's preference of the French. 'What I gained by being in France,' said Johnson, ' was learning to be better satisfied with my own country.' Boswell's *Johnson*, iii. 352.

Note 23. See *ante*, p. 169, *n*. 15, for the hopeless confusion of the French finances.

Note 24. Hume, in a remarkable passage in his *History*, describes the hatred which existed between the English and French. ' The fatal pretensions of Edward III,' he says, ' left the seeds of great animosity in both countries, especially among the English. For it is remarkable that this latter nation, though they were commonly the aggressors, and by their success and situation were enabled to commit the most cruel injuries on the other, have always retained a stronger tincture of national antipathy ; nor is their hatred retaliated on them to an equal degree by the French. That country lies in the middle of Europe, has been successively engaged in hostilities with all its neighbours, the popular prejudices have been diverted into many channels, and among a people of softer manners they never rose to a great height against any particular nation.' *History of England*, ed. 1802, ii. 398.

Horace Walpole, on his return from France in Sept. 1771, describing the state of things under the new Chancellor, Maupeou, says :— ' For the misery of his people, and for the danger of his successors (if he escapes himself) the King, I think, will triumph over his country. . . . The Chancellor is very able, very enterprising, and after being the most servile flatterer proves the most inhuman tyrant. Everybody is pillaged, and numbers ruined. The army is much reduced, and if corruption does not prevent it, their finances will soon be in good order. The besotted old *Bien-aimé* [Lewis XV] neither desires this increase of power, nor feels for the sufferings it occasions; but shudders for his own life, and yet lets Abigail [Mme. Dubarry], who has still less sense than himself, plunge him into all these difficulties and shame. This street-walker has just received the homage of Europe. The holy Nuncio, and every Ambassador but he of Spain, have waited on her, and brought gold, frankincense and myrrh. . . . This prospect is by no means unfavourable to *us*. France and Spain on cool terms; the army no longer the favourite object,—perhaps disgusted—certainly dispirited; . . . the *Vive le Roi* certainly extinguished for the present; . . . a government dissolved and not resettled; and to crown all, a divided and rival Ministry.' *Letters*, v. 332–334.

Note 25.   Through the weakness of Lewis XV the monarchical government existed little more than in form.   The *Roi* was almost as much extinguished as the *Vive le Roi*.   But with 'a Dauphin more unpromising[1]' to follow, Hume's *must* was rather an article of faith than of reason.   Dr. John Moore, who visited Paris in 1772, was struck by the loyalty of the French.   '*Roi*,' he says, ' is a word which conveys to the minds of Frenchmen the ideas of benevolence, gratitude, and love ; as well as those of power, grandeur and happiness.   They flock to Versailles every Sunday, behold him with unsated curiosity, and gaze on him with as much satisfaction the twentieth time as the first. . . . They repeat with fond applause every saying of his which seems to indicate the smallest approach to wit, or even bears the mark of ordinary sagacity. . . . When they hear of the freedom of debate in Parliament, of the liberties taken in writing or speaking of the conduct of the King, or measures of government, and the forms to be observed before those who venture on the most daring abuse of either can be brought to punishment, they seem filled with indignation, and say with an air of triumph, "C'est bien autrement chez nous.   Si le Roi de France avait affaire à ces Messieurs-là, il leur apprendrait à vivre." '   *View of Society in France*, i. 36, 37, 43.

Note 26.   One method of throwing off their debts is described by Horace Walpole in his letter of Sept. 7 of this year :—' The worst part is that by the most horrid oppression and injustice their finances will very soon be in good order—unless some bankrupt turns Ravaillac [the murderer of Henry IV of France], which will not surprise me.'   *Letters*, v. 330.

Note 27.   Walpole wrote on Feb. 25, 1779 :—' It was but yesterday Lord North could tell the House he had got the money on the loan, and is happy to get it under eight per cent.'   *Letters*, vii. 181.   The poor-rate also was beginning to weigh the country down like another mill-stone.   An able writer in the *Gent. Mag.* for Aug. 1769 (p. 373), in a paper entitled *A College of Labour*, says :—' It is a melancholy truth, that notwithstanding the heavy load of other taxes the poor's rate within half a century past has increased throughout the kingdom in a quadruple ratio to what it was ever formerly known to increase in the same period of time ; and that it now equals, if it does not surpass, the whole revenue upon land.'

Note 28.   ' This surely is a sufficient answer to the feudal gabble of a man, who is every day lessening that splendour of character which

---

[1] Walpole's *Letters*, v. 333.

once illuminated the kingdom, then dazzled, and afterwards inflamed it; and for whom it will be happy if the nation shall at last dismiss him to nameless obscurity, with that equipoise of blame and praise which Corneille allows to Richelieu, a man who, I think, had much of his merit and many of his faults:—

> "Chacun parle à son gré de ce grand Cardinal;
> Mais, pour moi, je n'en dirai rien :
> Il m'a fait trop de bien pour en dire du mal;
> Il m'a fait trop de mal pour en dire du bien." '

Johnson's *Works*, vi. 197.

Corneille's lines are well rendered by the saying of 'Old Andrew Fairservice, that there were many things ower bad for blessing, and ower gude for banning like Rob Roy.' Scott's *Works*, ed. 1860, viii. 380.

Note 29. Burke, writing on July 9, 1769, about a visit of Lord Chatham to St. James's, says :—' It is not yet known whether he was sent for, or went of his own mere motion. . . . If he was not sent for, it was only humbly to lay a reprimand at the feet of his most gracious master, and to talk some significant, pompous, creeping, explanatory, ambiguous matter in the true Chathamic style, and that's all.' Burke's *Corresp.* i. 173.

Boswell, writing on June 19, 1775, says :—' On Wednesday last I dined at Sir Alexander Dick's. Mr. Hume was there. He said Mr. Pitt was an instance that in this country eloquence alone, without any other talents or fortune, will raise a man to the highest office.' *Letters of Boswell*, p. 203. Much of Hume's violence against Chatham was, I suspect, due to wounded vanity. Lord Charlemont says in his *Memoirs*, i. 236 :—' Nothing ever gave Hume more real vexation than the strictures made upon his *History* in the House of Lords by the great Lord Chatham. Soon after that speech I met Hume, and ironically wished him joy of the high honour that had been done him. "Zounds, man," said he, with more peevishness than I had ever seen him express; "he's a Goth! he's a Vandal!"' I have not found any other mention of Chatham's speech.

Note 30. ' Richelieu, grand, sublime, implacable ennemi.' Voltaire, *La Henriade*, vii. 340.

Note 31. When Hume writes of Chatham as 'our cut-throat,' we recall the splendid passage in which Burke has enshrined his memory. 'Another scene was opened, and other actors appeared on the stage. The state, in the condition I have described it, was delivered into the hands of Lord Chatham—a great and celebrated name; a name that keeps the name of this country respectable in every other on the globe. It may be truly called,

> Clarum et venerabile nomen
> Gentibus, et multum nostrae quod proderat urbi.[1]

Sir, the venerable age of this great man, his merited rank, his

[1] Lucan, ix. 202.

superior eloquence, his splendid qualities, his eminent services, the
vast space he fills in the eye of mankind ; and more than all the
rest, his fall from power, which, like death, canonizes and sanctifies
a great character, will not suffer me to censure any part of his
conduct.' Burke, *On American Taxation,* April 19, 1774. Payne's
Burke, i. 144. Yet in a note which Burke made more than eighteen
years later he calls Chatham 'that grand artificer of fraud,' and
continues :—' It is pleasant to hear *him* talk of *the great extensive
public,* who never conversed but with a parcel of low toad-eaters.
Alas ! alas ! how different the *real* from the ostensible public man !
Must all this theatrical stuffing and raised heels be necessary for the
character of a great man ?   Oh ! but this does not derogate from
his great splendid side.   God forbid ! '   *Memoirs of Rockingham,*
ii. 195.

Note 32.   Burke, describing on May 25, 1779, 'the very blind
submission' which Lord Chatham had always expected, continues :—' It is true that he very often rewarded such submission
in a very splendid manner, but with very little marks of respect
or regard to the objects of his favour; and as he put confidence
in no man, he had very few feelings of resentment against those who
the most bitterly opposed, or most basely betrayed him.' Burke's
Corresp. ii. 277.

Note 33.   Hume in his *History of England,* ed. 1802, vi. 233, thus
sums up the results of Richelieu's administration :—' The people,
while they lost their liberties, acquired by means of his administration, learning, order, discipline, and renown.   That confused
and inaccurate genius of government of which France partook in
common with other European Kingdoms, he changed into a simple
monarchy.'

Note 34.   'All Mr. Pitt's sentiments were liberal and elevated.
His ruling passion was an unbounded ambition, which, when
supported by great abilities and crowned with great success, make
(*sic*) what the world calls "a great man."   He was haughty, im-
perious, impatient of contradiction, and over-bearing; qualities
which too often accompany, but always clog, great ones. . . . His
eloquence was of every kind, and he excelled in the argumentative
as well as in the declamatory way.   But his invectives were terrible,
and uttered with such energy of diction, and stern dignity of action
and countenance, that he intimidated those who were the most
willing and the best able to encounter him.   Their arms fell out
of their hands, and they shrunk under the ascendant which his
genius gained over theirs.' Character of Mr. Pitt by Lord Chesterfield.   Chesterfield's *Works.*   Appendix to vol. iv. p. 64.

'No man was ever better fitted than Mr. Pitt to be the minister
in a great and powerful nation, or better qualified to carry that
power and greatness to their utmost limits.   There was in all his
designs a magnitude, and even a vastness, which was not easily

comprehended by every mind, and which nothing but success could have made to appear reasonable. . . . Under him for the first time administration and popularity were seen united. Under him Great Britain carried on the most important war in which she ever was engaged, alone and unassisted, with greater splendour and with more success than she had ever enjoyed at the head of the most powerful alliances. Alone this island seemed to balance the rest of Europe.' Burke in the *Ann. Reg.* for 1761, i. 47.

Horace Walpole wrote on May 11, 1778, the day of Chatham's death :—'Well ! with all his defects Lord Chatham will be a capital historic figure, France dreaded his crutch to this very moment.' *Letters*, vii. 60. The House of Lords, by a majority of one, decided not to attend his funeral. *Parl. Hist.* xix. 1233. In the 66 volumes of Voltaire's *Works*, his name, I believe, is not once mentioned. In the copious Index I find only ' Pitt (*André*) : quaker retiré dans les environs de Londres, auquel l'auteur alla rendre visite.'

Note 35. Horace Walpole offered one day to read to Sir Robert in his retirement, 'finding that time hung heavy on his hands. "What," said he, "will you read, child ?" Mr. Walpole considering that his father had long been engaged in public business, proposed to read some history. "No," said he, "don't read history to me ; that can't be true." ' Prior's *Life of Malone*, p. 387. Dalrymple boasted (*ante*, p. 174) that he had been offered £2000 for his History. This letter shows that the amount was only £750.

Note 36. ' All, all but truth, drops dead-born from the press.'

Pope *Epil. to Sat.* ii. 226.

Hume in his *Autobiography* tells how his *Treatise of Human Nature* ' fell dead-born from the press.'

Dalrymple's book passed through several editions.

Note 37. ' Dec. 29, 1763. Have you read Mrs. Macaulay ? I am glad again to have Mr. Gray's opinion to corroborate mine, that it is the most sensible, unaffected, and best history of England that we have had yet.' Horace Walpole to Mason, *Letters*, iv. 157. It was of her that Johnson said, on hearing that she had begun 'to sit hours together at her toilet and even put on rouge :—" It is better she should be reddening her own cheeks than blackening other people's characters." ' Boswell's *Johnson*, iii. 46. See *ib.* i. 447, for Johnson's proposal that that ' sensible, civil, well-behaved fellow-citizen, her footman ' should sit down and dine with them.

Note 38. Hume, while he was engaged on his *History of the Stuarts*, wrote to a friend in the Government for information about 'the old English *subsidies*.' ' I cannot,' he continues, 'satisfy myself on that head ; but I find that all historians and antiquarians are as much at a loss.' Burton's *Hume*, i. 380. In his *History* (ed. 1802, vi. 174) he says :—'In the eighth of Elizabeth a subsidy amounted to £120,000. In the fortieth, it was not above £78,000. It afterwards fell to £70,000, and was continually decreasing.'

Note 39. See *ante*, p. 165, *n.* 9, for Johnson's account of the worthlessness of Falkland's Islands.

Note 40. To this letter Strahan sent the following reply:—

'London, May 25, 1771.

'DEAR SIR,

'. . . The proofs for the first four volumes shall be regularly transmitted to you as you desire; but this had better be done by common franks than by Secretary Fraser. We shall never want above two ounces at a time ; and if they are returned to his office, it will be troublesome to him, as well as to me, to send so great a distance for them. It will be very easy for either you or I to procure a number of covers, half directed—To *David Hume, Esqre. Edinbr.*—and half to *Will. Strahan, King's Printer, London.*—These are neither of them long addresses, and we either of us know a score of members that will readily oblige us. If I am not mistaken this book will be wanted before this edition is finished. But if it is, so much the better, that the Public may know that it is out of print. The impression is to be 1500 and no more, which is of all others the most proper number ; nor is it the interest of the proprietors to print more at a time. . . . The offer of £750 to Sir J[ohn] D[alrymple] turns out to have been more than the real value of it, as the sale of it seems to be already over here. Not above 1000 are yet sold, which was the number first printed, 220 of which arrived here after the second edition was finished. So that will probably stick on hand for a great while to come. If you write another volume, which the best judges of writing are daily enquiring after, you may demand what you please for it. It shall be granted. We cannot indeed afford a sum equal to a Parliamentary subsidy, but you shall not be offered so little as the value of Falkland Islands, which in my mind is a mere trifle. I heartily wish you would seriously think of setting about it. It is the only thing wanting to fill up the measure of your glory as the Great Historian and Philosopher of the Eighteenth Century. But you certainly do not see this matter in the same light I do, otherwise you would not hesitate one moment in continuing a Work, which (imperfect as it is in point of time) will remain for ever the Standard History of this country. I am afraid too, that when you are universally known to have given up all thoughts of this yourself, we shall be pestered with *continuations* from some of our hackney writers, who will be fond of building upon your foundation, and adding their names to one that is like to be as immortal as the language he writes in, or the country he has made the subject of his pen. . . .

'The circumstance you mention about the prior settlement of Falkland Island by the French is not at all known here, as far as I can find, to this moment. However, that matter is now at an end ; at least for the present ; nor do I see the smallest reason to fear our being threatened with a war either with France or Spain soon. If we are weak, so are they ; if we are divided among ourselves, so are

the French; if we are poor, and in debt, so are the French; with this
difference, that we have still some credit left, they have none.   You
know the condition and character of their present King; the Dauphin
[afterwards Lewis XVI] is not much better than a driveller.   Put all
these circumstances together, and I leave it to you to determine
whether or not we are not upon a fair comparison, in a much better
situation than our most formidable enemies.   Add to all this that our
trade is really in a flourishing state, that our Colonies are growing
very considerable without the smallest fear of a separation from us;
and that from all Quarters of the Globe, wealth is daily pouring into
this country, of which you see the most convincing proofs, not only in
this Capital, but over the whole Kingdom, in some degree or another
. . . If the folly and absurdity of the canaille of London doth not receive a check (and a very little matter would effectually do it) it is
impossible to say where it may terminate.   But, in truth, it is more
contemptible than people at a distance can possibly conceive or
believe.   The bustle is chiefly, almost solely, in the newspapers.
Our rascally leaders of sedition are cutting one another's throats.
Wilkes and Horne now entertain the Town with bespattering one
another, and probably before next session they may be totally
extinguished.—Time, steadiness and perseverance in those in power
may of itself do wonders.   In short I look upon the condition of this
country, considering things in an enlarged point of view, and comparing our affairs with those of all the other principal Powers of
Europe, contemplating the resources we actually possess in cases of
extremity, the state of agriculture, which is daily advancing in a
variety of ways, our numerous and most extensive manufactures,
which are by no means on the decline; I say, considering all these
things, I will venture to pronounce the British Empire, still on the
increase in power, riches and consideration.

'I wish you saw things in the same light, and am, whether you do
so or not, with the utmost esteem and attachment

' Dear Sir your faithful and Ob^t Ser^t,

' WILLIAM STRAHAN.'

M. S. R. S. E.

LETTER XLVIII.

*Correcting Books: Warburton and his Gang: Lord North's
Timidity: Powers of Government lost.*

EDINBURGH, 25 *of June*, 1771.

DEAR S^{IR}

I have receivd both your favours, for which I am

oblig'd to you. I shall be able to send off by the Waggon, in less than a Month, a corrected Copy of my History; and shall write you at the time, that you may send for it, if it be not immediatly sent to you. It gives me a sensible pleasure, that I shall now have an Edition of that work, corrected nearly to my mind[1]. I have taken incredible pains on this Edition. It puts me in mind of a saying of Rousseau's, that one half of a man's life is too little to write a Book and the other half to correct it[2]. Most of my Corrections fall upon the Style; tho' there are also several Additions and Amendments in the Subject and in the facts[3].

I have got about a hundred Franks directed to you; and we shall proceed in the manner you desire. I think, however, it will not be amiss to have some of Mr. Fraser's, for large Parcels; and for this purpose you may send him the enclos'd, with twenty Covers, which he will not grudge to frank to you[4]. The rest you may get from your Acquaintance[5] or mine, Lord Beauchamp[6], Mr. Wedderburn[7], Mr. Pulteney[8], Mr. Adam[9], Mr. Stewart of Buckingham Street[10] &c., informing them by a short Note of the reason of your applying to them.

I return you Warburton's Letter[11], which diverted me. He and all his gang, the most scurrillous, arrogant, and impudent Fellows in the world, have been abusing me in their usual Style these twenty Years, and here at last he pretends to speak well of me. It is the only thing from them, that coud ever give me any mortification. We have all heard of the several Schools of Painters and their peculiar manners. It is petulance, and Insolence and abuse, that distinguish the Warburtonian School, even above all other Parsons and Theologians[12]. Johnson is abusive in Company, but falls much short of them in his writings[13]. I remember Lord Mansfield said to me that Warburton was a very opposite man in company to what he is in his Books; then, replyd I, he must be the most agreeable Companion in Europe, for surely he is the most odious Writer [14].

I wish to tempt you into a Discourse of Politics, because I get Information from you. I own, that I am inclind to have a good Opinion of Lord North, but his Insolence to the House of Bourbon [15], and his Timidity towards the London Mob appear unaccountable. Only consider how many Powers of Government are lost in this short Reign [16]. The right of displacing the Judges was given up [17]; General Warrants are lost [18]; the right of Expulsion the same [19]; all the co-ercive Powers of the House of commons abandon'd [20]; all Laws against Libels annihilated [21]; the Authority of Government impair'd by the Impunity granted to the Insolence of Beckford, Crosby, and the common Council [22]: the revenue of the civil List diminishd [23]. For God's sake, is there never to be a stop put to this inundation of the Rabble [24]? We shall have fine work next Elections, if the people above and below continue in the same dispositions, the one insolent and the other timid [25]. For my part, I can account for Lord North's Conduct only by one supposition. He will not expose himself even in the best cause to the Odium of the populace, because he feels that he has no sure hold of the Cabinet, but depends for all his power on some invisible secret Being, call him Oberon, the fairy or any other, whose Caprices can in a moment throw him off, and leave him no Resources either in popularity or authority [26]. In this Light his caution is excusable: He bullies Spain and France [27] and quakes before the Ward of Farringdon without [28]; because, if he shoud be suddenly displaced, he will still retain it in his power to become popular and formidable. But all these Inconveniencies are slight, in comparison of our public Debts, which bring on inevitable Ruin, and with a Certainty which is even beyond geometrical, because it

is arithmetical. I hope you have more Sense than to trust
a shilling to that egregious bubble [2].

I am Dear S[ir] Yours sincerely

DAVID HUME.

Note 1. Strahan had written to Hume on May 25:—'I hope to
make a beautiful edition, as we have got an excellent paper for it,
much better than is generally used, being bespoke on purpose for the
work.' *M.S.R.S.E.* Even with this edition Hume was not satisfied. In the last year of his life he writes:—'I am as anxious of
correctness as if I were writing to Greeks or French; and besides
frequent revisals which I have given my *History* since the last
edition, I shall again run over it very carefully.' *Post*, Letter of Nov.
13, 1775.

Note 2. See *post*, Letters of Sept. 18, 1771, and Nov. 13, 1775,
where Hume repeats this saying.

Note 3. Hume wrote to Sir Gilbert Elliot on Feb. 21, 1770:—'I
am running over again the last edition of my *History*, in order to
correct it still further. I either soften or expunge many villanous,
seditious Whig strokes, which had crept into it. I wish that my
indignation at the present madness, encouraged by lies, calumnies,
imposture, and every infamous act usual among popular leaders,
may not throw me into the opposite extreme. I am, however,
sensible that the first editions were too full of those foolish English
prejudices, which all nations and all ages disavow.' Burton's *Hume*,
ii. 434. Such a passage as this may be illustrated by the following
extract from Mackintosh's brief Character of Hume :—

'Some remains perhaps of a love of singularity, some taint of
sceptical theory affecting his practical sentiments, much tranquillity
of temper and love of order, with the absence of ardent sensibility,
contributed to give Mr. Hume a prejudice against most of the predominant prejudices of his age and country; combined with a
residence in France they led him to prefer the faultless elegance of
our neighbours to the unequal grandeur of English genius, and produced the singular phenomenon of a *History of England* adverse to
our peculiar national feelings, and calculated, not so much to preserve
the vigour, as to repress the excesses of that love of liberty which
distinguishes the history of England from that of the other nations of
Europe.' *Life of Mackintosh*, ii. 169.

Note 4. See *ante*, p. 188, *n*. 11. The covers were the pieces
of paper in which the proofs were to be inclosed. Each cover
would bear Hume's address in Fraser's handwriting, attested by
his signature.

Note 5. Hume in his list of Scotticisms gives 'Friends and acquaintances'; the English form being 'Friends and acquaintance.'

Ante, p. 9. Johnson, I think, never uses the plural form *acquaintances*, though he gives it in his *Dictionary*. It is used by Bacon in *Essay* xviii. ed. 1629, i. 100 :—' What acquaintances they are to seeke.' In the same Essay we find 'those of his acquaintance which are of most worth.'

Note 6. Viscount Beauchamp was the eldest son of the Earl of Hertford, late Ambassador to France (*ante*, p. 40, *n.* 1), and now Lord Chamberlain. Hume, on his going to Paris as Lord Hertford's Secretary in 1763, wrote :—' I find that one view of Lord Hertford in engaging me to go along with him is, that he thinks I may be useful to Lord Beauchamp in his studies.' Burton's *Hume*, ii. 161.

Note 7. Alexander Wedderburne (afterwards Lord Loughborough and Earl of Rosslyn), having deserted his party, had been made Solicitor General on Jan. 23 of this year.

Note 8. Mr. William Pulteney, the second son of Sir James Johnstone, Baronet, was member for Cromartie and Nairn. *Parl. Hist.* xvi. 451. He had been Secretary of the Poker Club, and so was well known to Hume. Dr. A. Carlyle's *Auto.* p. 420, and *ante*, p. 141, *n.* 4. Horace Walpole, writing on Oct. 29, 1767, of the death of General Pulteney, brother of the famous William Pulteney, Earl of Bath, says :—' General Pulteney is dead, having owned himself worth a million, the fruits of his brother's virtues !' After mentioning some bequests Walpole continues :—' All the vast rest, except a few very trifling legacies, he leaves to his cousin Mrs. Pulteney, a very worthy woman, who had risked all by marrying one Johnstone, the third son of a poor Scot, but who is an orator at the India House, and likely to make a figure now in what *house* he pleases.' *Letters*, v. 70. Hume, in a letter to Suard dated Brewer Street, March 10, 1769, shows that 'the poor Scot's third son' could make a generous use of his wealth. He writes :—' Poor Stuart has lost his cause which he had laboured with such assiduity, such integrity, and such capacity. (See *post*, p. 239, *n.* 9.) Never was any sentence more unjust : but the cause had become so complicate, that it had gone beyond the comprehension of almost all our Peers ; and it was in the power of Lord Mansfield, who had shown a violent partiality from the beginning, to twist and turn it as he pleased and to command the plurality of votes. If the event was in one respect disastrous and extraordinary for Stuart, it was in another as fortunate and extraordinary. On rising next morning he found on his table a bond of annuity for 400 pounds a year, sent him by a friend, a man of sense, who had no interest in the cause, but who chose this opportunity to express his esteem and affection for Stuart. The person who has done this noble action is Pulteney ; you may have seen him at Paris with Stuart ; he then bore the name of Johnstone.' *Morrison Autographs*, ii. 318.

Note 9. Robert Adam, Architect to the Board of Works, and Member for Kinross and Clackmannan. *Parl. Hist.* xvi. 451. The Adelphi in the Strand, which by its affected name commemorates the fact that it was built by brothers, was a vast speculation shared between him and some of his brothers. Hume, writing of the great crash in the commercial world in 1772, says :—' Of all the sufferers I am the most concerned for the Adams. But their undertakings were so vast that nothing could support them.... To me the scheme of the Adelphi always appeared so imprudent, that my wonder is how they could have gone on so long.' Burton's *Hume*, ii. 460.

Note 10. Mr. Stewart had been of service to Hume in his search for lodgings for Rousseau. *A Concise Account, etc.* p. 9. He must have held some post which gave the right to use the official frank. There is mention of a John Stewart, Esq., in the *Chatham Corresp.* i. 214–5.

Note 11. 'Aug. 23, 1773. Dr. Gerard told us that an eminent printer was very intimate with Warburton. JOHNSON. "Why, Sir, he has printed some of his works, and perhaps bought the property of some of them. The intimacy is such as one of the professors here may have with one of the carpenters who is repairing the College." "But," said Gerard, "I saw a letter from him to this printer, in which he says that the one half of the clergy of the Church of Scotland are fanatics and the other half infidels." JOHNSON. "Warburton has accustomed himself to write letters just as he speaks, without thinking any more of what he throws out.". . . He told me, when we were by ourselves, that he thought it very wrong in the printer to show Warburton's letter, as it was raising a body of enemies against him. He thought it foolish in Warburton to write so to the printer; and added, "Sir, the worst way of being intimate is by scribbling." ' Boswell's *Johnson*, v. 92.

Note 12. Horace Walpole, writing on Jan. 22, 1764, about Churchill's ' new satire called *The Duellist*,' speaks of the ' charming abuse on that scurrilous mortal, Bishop Warburton.' *Letters*, iv. 171. Churchill describes the Bishop as a man,

> 'Who was so proud that should he meet
> The twelve Apostles in the street,
> He'd turn his nose up at them all,
> And shove his Saviour from the wall;
> Who was so mean (meanness and pride
> Still go together side by side)
> That he would cringe, and creep, be civil,
> And hold a stirrup for the Devil,
> If in a journey to his mind,
> He'd let him mount and ride behind.'
> Churchill's *Poems*, ed. 1766, ii. 79.

Johnson, speaking to George III of the controversy between Lowth and Warburton, said :—' Warburton has most general, most scholastic learning; Lowth is the more correct scholar. I do not know which of them calls names best.' Boswell's *Johnson*, ii. 37. On another occasion Johnson said :—' When I read Warburton first, and observed his force, and his contempt of mankind, I thought he had driven the world before him; but I soon found that was not the case; for Warburton by extending his abuse rendered it ineffectual.' *Ib.* v. 93. Gibbon wrote of him : 'The learning and the abilities of the author [of the *Divine Legation of Moses*] had raised him to a just eminence; but he reigned the dictator and tyrant of the world of literature. The real merit of Warburton was degraded by the pride and presumption with which he pronounced his infallible decrees; in his polemic writings he lashed his antagonists without mercy or moderation, and his servile flatterers (see the base and malignant *Essay on the Delicacy of Friendship* [by Hurd]) exalting the master critic far above Aristotle and Longinus, assaulted every modest dissenter who refused to consult the oracle and to adore the idol.' Gibbon's *Misc. Works*, i. 209. See *ante*, p. 21, *n.* 1.

Note 13. This letter was most likely written in Hume's house in James's Court. Two years later on, Johnson, in the same house though not in the same flat, after scoffing at Hume's scepticism, '" added something much too rough " both as to his head and heart which,' continues Boswell, 'I suppress.' Boswell's *Johnson*, v. 30. Johnson in one or two passages falls not far short of the Warburtonian School. Thus, in his attack on Wilkes, he says :—'The character of the man . . . I have no purpose to delineate. Lampoon itself would disdain to speak ill of him of whom no man speaks well. It is sufficient that he is expelled the House of Commons, and confined in gaol, as being legally convicted of sedition and impiety.' *Works*, vi. 156. Of *Junius* he writes :—"What," says Pope, "must be the priest where a monkey is the god?" What must be the drudge of a party of which the heads are Wilkes and Crosby, Sawbridge and Townsend?' *Ib.* p. 206.

Note 14. Boswell has thus recorded this anecdote in his *Boswelliana*, on the authority of ' Mr. David Hume' :—'Warburton was a prodigious flatterer of Lord Mansfield, and consequently a favourite. David Hume was one day speaking violently against him to his Lordship, who said :—"Upon my word, Mr. Hume, he is quite a different man in conversation from what he is in his books." "Then, my Lord," said Hume, "he must be the most agreeable man in the world." *Boswelliana*, p. 268. Strahan, replying to Hume on July 23, said :—'What his [Warburton's] reasons may be I know not, but I have heard much of his launching out in your praise for some time past, sometimes indeed in my hearing, and with much more seeming cordiality and heartiness than I ever heard him bestow on any other writer. . . . As a companion he is certainly one of the most tractable men I ever saw. So far from being insolent or overbearing, you can hardly get him to contradict you in anything.' *M. S. R. S. E.*

Note 15. By the Opposition Lord North was charged not with insolence to the House of Bourbon but with timidity towards it.

Lord Chatham, writing on Jan. 22, 1771, looks upon the Convention with Spain as 'the most abject and dangerous sacrifice of the rights of England that ever was submitted to.' The following day he writes : —' I still fear that England will prove itself a nation of slaves, in the present consummation of insult and ignominy, heaped upon them by an abandoned and flagitious Court.' *Chatham Corresp.* iv. 77, 82. Burke, in the *Ann. Reg.* for 1771, i. 51, stating the views of the Opposition, says :—' The whole transaction was described as a standing monument of reproach, disgrace, and dishonour, which, after an expense of some millions, settled no contest, asserted no right, exacted no reparation, and afforded no security.' Junius, in his Letter of Jan. 30, 1771, asks, 'Where will the humiliation of this country end ?' and goes on to attack 'the treachery of the King's servants, particularly of Lord North.' Johnson's *Falkland's Islands* is a defence of the Ministry for not having 'snatched with eagerness the first opportunity of rushing into the field, when they were able to obtain by quiet negotiation all the real good that victory could have brought us.' *Works*, vi. 200. 'The honour of the public,' he adds, 'is, indeed, of high importance; but we must remember that we have had to transact with a mighty King and a powerful nation, who have unluckily been taught to think that they have honour to keep or lose, as well as ourselves.' *Ib.* p. 208.

Note 16. On April 14, 1775, Dr. Johnson said :—' Sir, the great misfortune now is that government has too little power. . . . . Our several ministries in this reign have outbid each other in concessions to the people. Lord Bute, though a very honourable man,— a man who meant well,—a man who had his blood full of prerogative, —was a theoretical statesman,—a book-minister,—and thought this country could be governed by the influence of the Crown alone. Then, Sir, he gave up a great deal. He advised the King to agree that the Judges should hold their places for life, instead of losing them at the accession of a new King. Lord Bute, I suppose, thought to make the King popular by this concession, but the people never minded it ; and it was a most impolitic measure. There is no reason why a Judge should hold his office for life, more than any other person in public trust. A Judge may be partial otherwise than to the Crown; we have seen Judges partial to the populace. A Judge may become corrupt, and yet there may not be legal evidence against him. A Judge may become froward from age. A Judge may grow unfit for his office in many ways. It was desirable that there should be a possibility of being delivered from him by a new King. That is now gone by an Act of Parliament *ex gratia* of the Crown. Lord Bute advised the King to give up a very large sum of money, for which nobody thanked him. It was of consequence to the King, but nothing to the public among whom it was divided.' Boswell's *Johnson*, ii. 352.

Note 17. 'At the commencement of the reign of George III the independence of the Judges was still further secured. Although the Statute 12 and 13 Will. III. c. 2, s. 3, enacted that their commission should be no longer " Durante bene placito," but "Quamdiu se bene gesserint," yet, by a most extraordinary interpretation, it was decided at the accession of Queen Anne that their patents terminated at the demise of the Crown ; and the practice had been adopted in the two following reigns. The inconvenience arising from this decision, which necessitated a renewal of the patents of all the judges as the first act of a reign in order to prevent a total failure of justice, had been partially remedied by the statute 6 Anne, c. 7, s. 8, which enacted that all officers, including the Judges, should act upon their former patents for the space of six months after any demise of the Crown, unless sooner removed by the next successor. Now, however, by the express recommendation of George III, full effect was given to the statute of William by an Act of Parliament passed in the first year of his reign, chapter 23, continuing the Judges in their office, notwithstanding the demise of the Crown.' Foss's *Judges of England*, ed. 1864, viii. 198. The Earl of Hardwicke, in his speech on this measure, stated that on the Accession of Anne two Judges were left out ; on the Accession of George I, three Judges ; and on that of George II, one Judge. *Parl. Hist.* xv. 1009. Horace Walpole describes the measure as 'one of Lord Bute's strokes of pedantry. The tenure of the Judges had formerly been a popular topic ; and had been secured as far as was necessary. He thought this trifling addition would be popular now, when nobody thought or cared about it.' *Memoirs of George III*, i. 41.

Note 18. On April 30, 1763, Wilkes, as author of *The North Briton*, No. 45, had been arrested on 'a general warrant directed to four messengers to take up any persons without naming or describing them with any certainty, and to bring them, together with their papers.' Such a warrant as this Chief Justice Pratt (Lord Camden) declared to be 'unconstitutional, illegal, and absolutely void.' 'If it be good,' he said, 'a Secretary of State can delegate and depute any one of the messengers, or any one even from the lowest of the people, to take examinations, to commit or release, and, in fine, to do every act which the highest judicial officers the law knows can do or order.' *Ann. Reg.* 1763, i. 145. 'Johnson would not admit the importance of the question concerning the legality of general warrants. "Such a power," he observed, "must be vested in every government, to answer particular cases of necessity ; and there can be no just complaint but when it is abused, for which those who administer government must be answerable. It is a matter of such indifference, a matter about which the people care so very little, that were a man to be sent over Britain to offer them an exemption from it at a halfpenny a piece, very few would purchase it." This was a specimen of that laxity of talking which I have heard him fairly acknowledge.' Boswell's *Johnson*, ii. 72.

Note 19. Hume is speaking, no doubt, of expulsion from the House of Commons. Yet Wilkes had been expelled on Feb. 3, 1769 (*Parl. Hist.* xvi. 545), and on Feb. 17 he had been declared 'incapable of being elected a member to serve in the present Parliament.' *Ib.* p. 577. He was elected four times, once in March 1768 at the General Election ; and three times after his expulsion, on Feb. 16, March 16, and April 13, 1769 (Almon's *Memoirs of Wilkes,* iv. 4) ; but his seat was given to Colonel Luttrell, who had only received 296 votes against 1143. The *power* of expulsion therefore did not seem lost, even if the *right* were. Hume perhaps saw that such a storm had been raised by the Middlesex election, that no Ministry would ever dare to follow the bad precedent that had been set. He may have been struck too by the fact that Lord Chancellor Camden had declared in the House of Lords his belief, that 'the incapacitating vote was a direct attack upon the first principles of the constitution,' and had gone on to say 'that if, in giving his decision as a Judge, he was to pay any regard to that vote, or any other vote of the House of Commons in opposition to the known and established laws of the land, he should look upon himself as a traitor to his trust.' *Parl. Hist.* xvi. 644. It is true that this speech was followed by his dismissal from office, but he was supported in his statement of the law by the strongly-worded Protest of forty-two dissentient Lords.

The whole aim of Johnson's *False Alarm* was 'intended,' as Boswell says, 'to justify the conduct of Ministry and their majority in the House of Commons, for having virtually assumed it as an axiom, that the expulsion of a Member of Parliament was equivalent to exclusion.' Boswell's *Johnson,* ii. 111. Wilkes for the fifth time was returned for Middlesex in the General Election of November 1774, 'without a shadow of opposition from the Court. . . . The dispute concerning that single seat had produced to them more troubles, vexation, and disgraces, than the contest with the twelve united Colonies of America. It would have been an imprudence of the grossest kind to mix these disputes in the present crisis ; and thus after near fourteen years' struggle it was thought the best way to leave him master of the field.' *Ann. Reg.* 1775, i. 39. Some opposition, it seems, had been intended, for Horace Walpole wrote on the day Parliament met—'St. Parliament's day,' he styles it :— ' Mr. Van is to move for the expulsion of Wilkes ; which will distress, and may produce an odd scene.' *Letters,* vi. 157. On May 3, 1782, on Wilkes's motion all the resolutions of the House respecting the Middlesex election were ordered, by a majority of 115 to 47, 'to be expunged from the Journals of this House, as being subversive of the rights of the whole body of electors of this kingdom.' Fox opposed the motion, as he held that 'it was for the good of the people of England that the House should have a power of expelling any man, whom the representatives of the people of England thought unworthy to sit among them : this was a privilege too valuable to be given up.' *Parl. Hist.* xxii. 1407.

Note 20. Burke in the *Ann. Reg.* for the following year (1772, i. 81) points out the causes by which the House of Commons ' had lost much of its influence with the people and of the respect and reverence with which it was usually regarded. . . . Much of this may be attributed to the ill-judged contest with the printers [*ante*, p. 190, n. 17] and the ridiculous issue of that affair. . . . Many of the Addresses which had been presented to the City Magistrates during their confinement in the Tower were direct libels upon that Assembly, and in other times would have been severely punished as such. . . . The printers, now that the impotency of the House was discovered, laughed at an authority which had been so much dreaded, before it was wantonly brought to a test that exposed its weakness. This discovery being made, the effect naturally followed ; and in the succeeding session the votes of the House, a thing before unknown and contrary to its orders, were printed in the public newspapers without notice or inquiry ; and thus the point in contest was apparently given up by the House.'

Note 21. Horace Walpole states that ' Lord Mansfield's innovations had given such an alarm that scarce à jury would find the rankest satire libellous.' *Memoirs of George III*, iv. 168. Lord Mansfield, in trials for libel, maintained ' that a libel or not a libel was a matter of fact to be decided by the bench, and the question to be left to the jury was only the fact of printing and publishing.' Adolphus's *History of England*, i. 441. By Fox's Libel Bill, which was carried in 1792, it was declared that it was the function of the jury in cases of libel to be judges of law as well as of fact. *Parl. Hist.* xxix. 1537. See Junius's Letter to Lord Mansfield of Nov. 14, 1770, in which he says :—' When you invade the province of the jury in matter of libel, you in effect attack the liberty of the press, and with a single stroke wound two of your greatest enemies.'

Note 22. Strahan, in his next letter, dated July 23, was able to send more comforting news about the citizens. He wrote :—' You see our Lord Mayor, after advertising for a fortnight to invite the whole Livery and all the mob in London to attend him, hath presented another *wise* and *modest* Remonstrance. The papers give you a splendid account of the Cavalcade. But whatever they may tell you, I assure you from ocular demonstration, that it made a most pitiful and paltry figure. A number of people were indeed brought into the streets to gaze at him, and the few Aldermen and Common Council-men that accompanied him, but only about a dozen blackguards followed and holloed him, whose feeble applause was much more than overbalanced by the hisses of the honest spectators, who seemed to be inflamed with just indignation at seeing one of the best and most unexceptionable of Princes teased and abused by a little, pitiful, desperate and abandoned Junto, whom as individuals

P

no reputable man would choose to associate with.' *M. S. R. S. E.*
In Strahan's own paper, *The London Chronicle,* for July 11, 1771,
it is stated that the cavalcade was composed of the Lord Mayor, five
Aldermen, the two Sheriffs, with upwards of one hundred of the
Common Council, in about fifty carriages, and that 'it proceeded
amidst the greatest acclamations of the people.'

Note 23. The King in his speech on opening Parliament on Nov.
15, 1763, announced his intention to apply to the public service the
money arising from the sale of the prizes vested in the Crown, and
of the lands in the islands in the West Indies that were ceded by
the Treaty of Paris. *Parl. Hist.* xv. 1339. The total amount was
upwards of £900,000. In addition, he gave up the hereditary
revenues of the Crown, and accepted instead the fixed sum of
£800,000 a year. According to Blackstone the public was a gainer
by £100,000 a year. In the year 1777 £800,000 being found insufficient
was increased to £900,000. Boswell's *Johnson,* ii. 353, *n.* 4. Burke,
however, in his *Present Discontents,* says that in 1770 the whole
revenue of the Crown was 'certainly not much short of a million,' not
counting the sums that the King drew from his possessions in
Germany. Payne's *Burke,* i. 47. Nevertheless in 1769 application
was made to Parliament for the payment of the debts of the Civil
List, which amounted to over £500,000. *Parl. Hist.* xvi. 602. According to Burke, George II, though during the last fourteen years of
his reign he had received less each year than his grandson, nevertheless at his death left £170,000 to his successor. Payne's *Burke,* i.
68. With all the extravagance of George III's reign there was little
splendour. 'I believe it will be found,' said Burke in 1770, 'that the
picture of royal indigence which our Court has presented until this
year has been truly humiliating. Nor has it been relieved from this
unseemly distress but by means which have hazarded the affection of
the people, and shaken their confidence in Parliament.' *Ib.* p. 47.

Note 24. Johnson had said this same spring in his *Falkland's
Islands* :—'To fancy that our Government can be subverted by the
rabble, whom its lenity has pampered into impudence, is to fear that
a city may be drowned by the overflowings of its kennels.' Johnson's *Works,* vi. 213.

Note 25. It was the people above who were timid, and the people
below who were insolent.

Note 26. Hume is hinting at the Earl of Bute, or the Dowager
Princess of Wales, or both. Strahan replied to him on July 23 :—'It
hath been long said, you know, that somebody behind the curtain
has been a constant check upon the *ostensible* Ministers during this
reign.' *M. S. R. S. E.* On March 2, 1770, Lord Chatham in the
House of Lords attacked 'the secret influence of an invisible power ;'
that 'something behind the throne greater than the King himself;'
that 'favourite, who had betrayed every man who had taken a responsible office. There was no safety, no security against his power and

malignity. He himself had been duped when he least suspected treachery, at a time when the prospect was fair, and when the appearances of confidence were strong.' *Parl. Hist.* xvi. 842-3. On March 25, 1771, Alderman Townsend in the House of Commons said that many who supported the Ministers were 'only solicitous to gratify the ambitious views of one aspiring woman, who, to the dishonour of the British name, is well known to direct the operations of our despicable Ministers. Does any gentleman wish to know to what woman I allude; if he does, I will tell him; it is to the Princess Dowager of Wales.' *Ib.* xvii. 135. Colonel Barré wrote the next day to Lord Chatham :—'It is very extraordinary that this language had no more apparent effect either on the House or the Ministry, than if it had been held concerning the mal-administration of the Duke of Saxe Gotha, or any even pettier Prince of the House of Saxony.' *Chatham Corres.* iv. 134.

Note 27. See *ante*, pp. 161, 173.

Note 28. Wilkes was elected Alderman of the Ward of Farringdon Without on Jan. 27, 1769, while he was still in prison. On his release he was sworn in, on April 24, 1770. Almon's *Memoirs of Wilkes,* iv. 1, 15. Horace Walpole wrote on May 6 :—'I don't know whether Wilkes is subdued by his imprisonment, or waits for the rising of Parliament, to take the field; or whether his dignity of Alderman has dulled him into prudence, and the love of feasting; but hitherto he has done nothing but go to City-banquets and sermons, and sit at Guildhall as a sober magistrate.' *Letters,* v. 235. On June 24, 1771, he was elected Sheriff. 'Being suspected of partiality to the French, he ordered that no French wine should be given at his entertainments.' Almon's *Wilkes,* iv. 172, and *Ann. Reg.* 1771, i. 149. Dr. Johnson lived in Wilkes's Ward, but not being a Freeman of the City he had no vote. Horace Walpole wrote on July 6, a few days after Wilkes's election as Sheriff :—'Does there not seem to be a fatality attending the Court whenever they meddle with that man? Does not he always rise higher for their attempting to overwhelm him? What instance is there of such a demagogue, subsisting and maintaining a war against a King, Ministers, Courts of Law, a whole Legislature, and all Scotland, for nine years together? Massaniello did not, I think, last five days. Wilkes, in prison, is chosen Member of Parliament, and then Alderman of London. His colleagues betray him, desert him, expose him, and he becomes Sheriff of London. I believe, if he were to be hanged, he would be made King of England —I don't think King of Great Britain (the Scots hate him too much).' *Letters,* v. 313. Strahan's letter to Hume of July 23 is in the beginning so curiously like Walpole's, that it can scarcely be doubted that both men are repeating words they have heard. He says :—'With regard to Wilkes, there seems to be a *Fatality* attending the Ministry whenever they meddle with him. In the late election for Sheriffs they should have taken no part at all. . . . Monday and

Tuesday the election was plainly going against Wilkes, and he would most certainly have lost it. But the miscarriage and consequent publication of Mr. R.'s [1] letter had precisely the effect I apprehended, and set the London mob in a flame.' *M. S. R. S. E.*

Sir John Pringle, writing to Hume on Feb. 25, 1776, tells an amusing story of the election for Chamberlain of the City, for which Wilkes was the unsuccessful candidate. He says:—'One of Hopkins's party upbraided Mr. Wilkes by telling him, that he had made his *friends* upon polling go home, and after changing their *coats* return to the Hall, and vote a second time. "My friends do so!" replies Wilkes; "Impossible! My friends have only *one coat* to their back." ' *M. S. R. S. E.*

Junius, in his letter of April 3, 1770, mocks at 'the blustering promises of Lord North,' and tells how he had taken fright at the very moment when Welbore Ellis, set on by him, was going to move to prosecute the Lord Mayor and Sheriffs. 'All their magnanimous threats ended in a ridiculous vote of censure, and a still more ridiculous address to the King. This shameful desertion so afflicted the generous mind of George the Third, that he was obliged to live upon potatoes for three weeks, to keep off a malignant fever. Poor man! *quis talia fando temperet a lacrymis!*'

Note 29.   The three per cents. Consols, on the day on which Hume wrote, were at 81⅝. *Gent. Mag.* 1771, p. 288.

LETTER XLIX.

New Edition of the History.

EDINBURGH, 22 *of July*, 1771.

DEAR Sᴵᴿ

On Saturday last, the 20ᵗʰ of the Month, I deliverd to the Newcastle Waggon [1] the eight corrected Volumes of my History, directed to Mr. Cadell.   I chose to direct the parcel to him rather than to you, because his Shop was easier found [2], and the Waggoner told me, that he often carry'd up Parcels to him.   Please to tell Mr. Cadel, that he may call for it, if it be not deliverd to him about three

---

[1] Mr. R. was Mr. Robinson, 'the Secretary of a Public Office.' A letter in which he canvassed for Aldermen Plumbe and Kirkman was delivered by mistake to the wrong person. 'Its publication won a great many votes for Aldermen Wilkes and Bull.' *London Chronicle*, June 29, 1771.

Weeks hence. You will see that I have made many considerable Improvements, most of them in the Style; but
some also in the matter. I fancy you might be able to send
me a proof Sheet about a month hence; and I shoud have
been here ready to receive it; But I am assurd that Lady
Aylesbury[3] and Mr. Conway are to be with the Duke of
Argyle this Summer; which will oblige me to leave the
Town for a fortnight and go to Inverara[4]. But I shall
fix to you precisely the day when I shall be ready to receive the first proof Sheet; and you may depend upon my
punctuality afterwards. Mean-while, you may proceed to
print the last four Volumes at your own convenience. You
told me that you proposd to make this new Octavo Edition
in ten Volumes[5]. Each four of the Quarto must therefore
be divided into five[6], and you may cast them accordingly.
I woud have you mind nothing but to finish the Chapter
with each Volume, without forgetting the Index[7]. You
may send me down the Quarto Sheet with the Proof
Sheet; and where it contains any Note that is to be
printed at the End I shall return it by the Post[8]. I hope
the Sale of the Quarto is pretty well advancd: For
this new Edition may a little discredit it. I know not
whether the former purchasers may complain of my
frequent Corrections; but I cannot help it, and they run
mostly upon Trifles; at least they will be esteemd such by
the Generality of Readers, who little attend to the extreme
Accuracy of Style. It is one great advantage that results
from the Art of printing, that an Author may correct his
works, as long as he lives[9]. But I have now done with
mine for ever, and never shall any more review them,
except in a cursory manner[10]. I expect for my pains six
Copies, over and above the six that are due me by Agreement[11]. I believe I coud have writ more than a Volume
with much less trouble than I have bestow'd on these. If
you have leizure to peruse the Sheets, and to mark on the

Margin any Corrections that occur to you, it will be an Addition to the many Obligations of the same kind, which I owe to you[12]. But this I cannot expect, considering the many Avocations which you have, unless it prove an Amusement to you in this dead time of the Year. I fancy this Edition will not be publishd till after the new Year[13]. As soon as the new Edition of my philosophical Pieces is printed[14], I shall be obligd to you to have six Copies of it. It is a great Relief to my Spirits, that I have at last a near Prospect of being fairly rid of that abominable Octavo Edition of my History.

I am Dear S^ir Your most obedient humble Servant

DAVID HUME.

Note I. Smollett in *Roderick Random* (ch. viii) describing his hero's journey from Scotland to London in 1739, says :—'There is no such convenience as a waggon in this country, and my finances were too weak to support the expense of hiring a horse ; I determined therefore to set out with the carriers, who transport goods from one place to another on horseback ; and this I accordingly put in execution, on the first day of November, 1739, sitting upon a pack-saddle between two baskets ; one of which contained my goods in a knap-sack. By the time we arrived at Newcastle upon Tyne, I was so fatigued with the tediousness of the carriage, and benumbed with the coldness of the weather, that I resolved to travel the rest of my journey on foot.' After having walked many days he hears one evening at a small town 'that the waggon from Newcastle for London had halted there two nights ago, and that it would be an easy matter to overtake it, if not the next day, at farthest the day after the next.' (Ch. x.) By walking at a great pace all the next day he caught it up in the evening. It seems likely that when the waggon began to go beyond Newcastle to Edinburgh it still kept its old name of the Newcastle Waggon. Churchill in 1763, in *The Prophecy of Famine*, speaking of Scotland, says :—

'What *waggon-loads* of courage, wealth and sense
Doth each revolving day import from thence.'

Poems, ed. 1766, i. 102.

Hume, on Nov. 22, 1762, directing Millar to send him some books, says :—'Be so good as to *embark* three copies in any parcel you send to Edinburgh. The peace will now make the intercourse of trade more open between us.' Burton's *Hume*, ii. 140. Now that there was peace with France and Spain, there was no longer any dread of

foreign cruisers. Johnson, even in time of peace, did not care to
have anything sent to him by sea. He wrote to Boswell on Jan. 29,
1774 :—'If anything is too bulky for the post, let me have it by the
carrier. I do not like trusting winds and waves.' Boswell's *Johnson*,
ii. 272. Boswell writing on Dec. 2 had told him that next week his
box should be sent him by sea. *Ib.* p. 270. It did not arrive till the
very end of January. *Ib.* p. 272. An undergraduate of Queen's
College, Oxford, was charged in the year 1778 two guineas for the
conveyance of his box by carrier from a Cumberland village north of
Carlisle to Oxford. *Letters of Radcliffe and James*, p. 46.

Note 2. Cadell's shop was in the Strand ; Strahan's printing-
house was in New Street, Fetter Lane ; where his descendants, the
Messrs. Spottiswoode, still carry on the business.

Note 3. General Conway, Horace Walpole's cousin and correspondent, 'married Catherine Campbell, Dowager Countess of Aylesbury, daughter of John, Duke of Argyle, by his wife, Mary Bellenden
the beauty, and was the father by Lady Aylesbury of an only child,
Mrs. Damer the sculptor, to whom Walpole left Strawberry Hill.'
Walpole's *Letters*, i. 38, *n.* 1.

Note 4. Inverary, the Duke of Argyle's castle, where Johnson
and Boswell dined two years later. Boswell's *Johnson*, v. 355.

Note 5. It was published in eight volumes.

Note 6. As the quarto edition had been in eight volumes, four of
its volumes would form five of the proposed edition.

Note 7. Strahan was not, for the sake of uniformity in size, to give
part of a chapter in one volume, and part in another ; and he was not
to forget that in the last volume room must be left for the Index.
Hume, like an honest man, made sometimes, if not always, his own
Index. On Sept. 3, 1757, he wrote :—' I have finished the Index to
the new collection of my pieces ; this Index cost me more trouble
than I was aware of when I began it.' Burton's *Hume*, ii. 36. See
ante, p. 17, *n.* 1.

Note 8. The quarto sheet was the copy corrected by Hume, from
which the new edition was to be printed. It sometimes happened
that it contained a foot-note which in the new edition was to be
printed among the notes at the end of each volume. In that case
Hume, after correcting his proof-sheet, would return also the quarto
sheet.

Note 9. See *ante*, p. 182.

Note 10. See *ante*, p. 202, *n.* 1.

Note 11. See *post*, Letter of March 15, 1773. Johnson for ' a very
few corrections in the *Lives of the Poets* was presented with a hundred
guineas' (Boswell's *Johnson*, iv. 35, *n.* 3) ; but this must be looked
upon as a kind of ' conscience money ' on the part of the booksellers,
who had made a great sum by their bargain with him.

Note 12. Dr. Beattie says that ' Mr. Strahan was eminently
skilled in composition and the English language, excelled in the

epistolary style, had corrected (as he told me himself) the phrase-
ology of both Mr. Hume and Dr. Robertson.' Forbes's *Life of
Beattie*, ed. 1824, p. 341.
　　Note 13.　It was not published till 1773.
　　Note 14.　See *post*, second Letter of June 3, 1772.

LETTER L.

The Principles of Penal Law: Landholders versus Stockholders.

Dear Sir

　　I have now the Prospect of being settled, so as to be
able to attend the Correction of the Proof Sheets.　If you
can, therefore, contrive to send me one which will arrive
on Saturday Sennight the 31 of August, you shall have it
returnd by Course of Post; and I shall never after fail to
return one every post, which will be five times a week.　I
am oblig'd to you for humouring me in this particular.

　　I have receiv'd a Present of a new Book, from the
Author, *The Principles of penal Law*[1].　The Direction of it
seems to be writ in your hand; and Cadel is one of the
Publishers.　If the Author does not propose to keep
his Name a Secret, I shoud be glad to know it:　For the
Book is very ingenious and judicious.　In all cases, if you
know the Author, make him my Compliments and give
him my Thanks.　I did not imagine, however, that so
ingenious a Man woud in this age have had so much weak
Superstition, as appears in many passages[2].　But these
perhaps were inserted only from Decency and Prudence:
And so the World goes on, in perpetually deceiving themselves and one another[3].

　　I am always oblig'd to you for your political Speculations:
But I cannot agree with you, that, if matters came to a
fair and open Strugle between the Land-holders and the
Stock-holders, the latter woud be able to reduce the former

to any Composition[4]. The Authority of the Land-holders is solidly establishd over their Tenants and Neighbours: But what Stock-holder has any Influence even over his next Neighbour in his own Street? And if public Credit fall, as it must by the least Touch[5], he woud be reduc'd to instant Poverty, and have authority no-where. My only apprehensions are, with regard to the public, that this open Struggle will never happen, and that these two Orders of Men are so involvd with each other by Connexions and Interest, that the public Force will be allowd to go to total Decay, before the violent Remedy, which is the only one, will be ventur'd on[6]. But this Event will depend much on Accidents of Men and times; and the Decision will not probably be very distant: The first War will put the Matter to a tryal, I fancy about the third or fourth Year of it, if we exert ourselves with our usual Frenzy[7]. You may judge, from our late Treatment of the House of Bourbon, whether we can regard the present Peace as very durable.

I am Dear S^{ir} Yours sincerely

DAVID HUME.

EDINBURGH, 19*th of Augst.*, 1771[*].

Note 1. The author was William Eden, afterwards first Lord Auckland. Nichols's *Literary Anecdotes*, iii. 119. A second edition was published this same year.

Note 2. Horace Walpole speaks of Eden as 'that superlative jackass' (*Letters*, vii. 426), and as 'a most wicked coxcomb,' who 'had not sense or judgment enough to cloak his folly' (*Ib.* viii. 204). I have not done more than glance through the book. The superstitious passages I failed to discover, but I came on much that would not have been unworthy of Bentham or Romilly.

Note 3. Hume was not unwilling at times to assist in this universal deception. In 1764 he was consulted about a young man, whom, says his correspondent, 'to speak plain language I believe to be a sort of disciple of your own ;' but whose hope of advancement lay in his taking orders in the English Church. Hume wrote back :— 'What ! do you know that Lord Bute is again all-powerful, or rather that he was always so, but is now acknowledged for such by all the

world? Let this be a new motive for Mr. V— to adhere to the
ecclesiastical profession, in which he may have so good a patron ; for
civil employments for men of letters can scarcely be found; all is
occupied by men of business, or by parliamentary interest. It is
putting too great a respect on the vulgar and on their superstitions
to pique one's self on sincerity with regard to them. Did ever one
make it a point of honour to speak truth to children or madmen? If
the thing were worthy being treated gravely, I should tell him that
the Pythian oracle, with the approbation of Xenophon, advised every,
one to worship the gods—νομω πολεως [1].   I wish it were still in my
power to be a hypocrite in this particular.   The common duties of
society usually require it ; and the ecclesiastical profession only adds
a little more to an innocent dissimulation or rather simulation, without which it is impossible to pass through the world.   Am I a liar,
because I order my servant to say, I am not at home, when I do not
desire to see company?'   Burton's *Hume,* ii. 185–7.

Johnson recognises 'the universal conspiracy of mankind against
themselves;' but though he may have yielded at times to the temptation of deceiving himself, he would never deceive others.   As regards
children and servants he was wide as the poles asunder from Hume.
'Accustom your children,' said he, 'constantly to a strict attention to
truth, even in the most minute particulars.   If a thing happened at
one window, and they, when relating it, say that it happened at
another, do not let it pass, but instantly check them; you do not
know where deviation from truth will end.'   Boswell's *Johnson,* iii.
228.   'He would not allow his servant to say he was not at home
when he really was.   "A servant's strict regard for truth (said he)
must be weakened by such a practice.   A philosopher may know
that it is merely a form of denial ; but few servants are such nice
distinguishers.   If I accustom a servant to tell a lie for *me,* have I not
reason to apprehend that he will tell many lies for *himself?"'   Ib.* i.
436.   See *post,* Letter of March 24, 1773.

Note 4.   Strahan, in his letter of July 23, had said :—' But supposing what you seem to apprehend to be unavoidable, if matters come
to a public bankruptcy, it will not so materially effect the general
prosperity of the nation as you and many others imagine. . . . But
not to enter further into the consequences of an event, of which
history affords no precedent, I think I may venture to say that the
Stockholders will not tamely submit to be the only sufferers.   The
Debt is in fact a Debt upon the lands of Great Britain, these are the
real Security, supported by the faith of the Legislature.   It is impossible to conceive that the public creditors would suffer the land-
holders to enjoy their full property, and undiminished by taxes too,
whilst they were robbed of their all.'   *M. S. R. S. E.*

Hume, in a note on his Essay *Of Public Credit,* published nineteen
years earlier, had said :—'I have heard it has been computed that all

[1] *Memorabilia,* i. 3. 1.

the creditors of the public, natives and foreigners, amount only to 17,000. These make a figure at present on their income; but in case of a public bankruptcy would in an instant become the lowest, as well as the most wretched of the people. The dignity and authority of the landed gentry and nobility is much better rooted; and would render the contention very unequal, if ever we come to that extremity. One would incline to assign to this event a very near period, such as half a century, had not our fathers' prophecies of this kind been already found fallacious, by the duration of our public credit so much beyond all reasonable expectation. When the astrologers in France were every year foretelling the death of Henry IV, *These fellows*, says he, *must be right at last.* We shall therefore be more cautious than to assign any precise date; and shall content ourselves with pointing out the event in general.' Hume's *Phil. Works*, ed. 1854, iii. 398. It was between the land-holders and the stock-holders that the struggle would lie, if it ever took place, because the land tax was at this time the chief war tax. It had been raised from three shillings to four shillings in the pound only eight months before on the threat of a war with Spain. *Parl. Hist.* xvi. 1330. Lord Macaulay, in describing the origin of the land-tax, says:—'The rate was, in time of war, four shillings in the pound. In time of peace, before the reign of George the Third, only two or three shillings were usually granted; and during a short part of the prudent and gentle administration of Walpole, the Government asked for only one shilling. But, after the disastrous year in which England drew the sword against her American Colonies, the rate was never less than four shillings.' *History of England*, ed. 1874, vi. 325. A passage in Lord Sheffield's speech on April 2, 1798, on Pitt's Bill for the Redemption of the Land Tax shows his fear, that if the struggle of which Hume speaks were to take place, the land-holders would be the sufferers. He says:—'This was such a favourite tax that, he understood, as soon as it was sold, there was an intention of laying a new land-tax. Unfortunately for the country, those whose odious task it was to propose taxes did not always extend their knowledge beyond the bills of mortality. They were too much in the hands of monied men, who were so full of expedients relative to the funds, that they could seldom think of the interior circumstances of the country.' *Parl. Hist.* xxxiii. 1374.

Note 5. Lord North, in his speech on the Budget for 1771, said:— 'Trade flourishes in all parts of the kingdom; the American disputes are settled; and there is nothing to interrupt the peace and prosperity of the nation but the discontents which a desperate faction is fomenting by the basest falsehoods and with the most iniquitous views.' *Parl. Hist.* xvii. 165. In 1772, speaking on the Budget, he said:—'At present there is the fairest prospect of the continuance of peace that I have known in my time. . . . The hypothesis of a ten years' peace is by no means chimerical. The pacific dispositions of the French King, who regulates the motions of our great rival and antagonist, are well known. What then hinders us from cherishing this hope? I know I shall be laughed at for forming any calculation upon so precarious an event. . . . We see some, though no very certain prospect of gradually reducing the national debt.' *Ib.* p. 489.

Note 6. Hume, at the end of chap. xxi. of his *History*, says:—' The first instance of debt contracted upon parliamentary security occurs in this reign [Henry the Sixth's]. The commencement of this pernicious practice deserves to be noted; a practice the more likely to become pernicious, the more a nation advances in opulence and credit. The ruinous effects of it are now become but too apparent, and threaten the very existence of the nation.' Perhaps Johnson had heard this sentence quoted when, 'speaking of the National Debt,' he said to Dr. Maxwell, 'it was an idle dream to suppose that the country could sink under it. Let the public creditors be ever so clamorous, the interest of millions must ever prevail over that of thousands.' Boswell's *Johnson*, ii. 127. (See *ante*, p. 68.)

Adam Smith speaks of 'the enormous debts which at present oppress, and will in the long run probably ruin all the great nations of Europe.' 'The practice of funding,' he continues, 'has gradually enfeebled every nation which has adopted it.' After describing its effects on different nations he asks:—' Is it likely that in Great Britain alone a practice which has brought either weakness or dissolution into every other country should prove altogether innocent?' Further on he adds:—' When national debts have once been accumulated to a certain degree, there is scarce, I believe, a single instance of their having been fairly and completely paid. The liberation of the public revenue, if it has ever been brought about at all, has always been brought about by a bankruptcy; sometimes by an avowed one, but always by a real one, though frequently by a pretended payment.' *Wealth of Nations*, ed. 1811, iii. 392, 418, 420.

Note 7. A statement by Johnson in 1783, when the Debt had been raised by the American War from 129 to 268 millions, shows what a feeling of security there was even then in the stock-holders. He says:—' It is better to have five per cent. out of land than out of money, because it is more secure; but the readiness of transfer and promptness of interest make many people rather choose the funds.' Boswell's *Johnson*, iv. 164.

Lord North on May 1, 1772, speaking of the Stocks, said:—Look back 25 years, and you will find that it is only since that period that they sold for less than their original value.' *Parl. Hist.* xvii. 489. At the time he was speaking they were at 88. *Gent. Mag.* 1772, p. 200. The second Pitt, on April 2, 1798, said 'the present price of three per cents. is about fifty.' *Parl. Hist.* xxxiii. 1367. They were that year as low as 47. The year before, in the alarm of the Mutiny at the Nore, they had fallen to 48 (*Ann. Reg.* 1797, ii. 162), when Hume's forebodings seemed likely to come true.

Note 8. Walter Scott was four days old when Hume wrote this letter. He was born at a short distance from James's Court, on August 15, 1771, in a house belonging to his father, at the head of the College Wynd.

LETTER LI.

Miscarriage of Presentation Copies of the History.

INVERARA, 23 *Augst.*, 1771 [1].

DEAR S[IR]

I own, that I am, at this time, very much out of humour, and with you. Near two Years ago, I wrote to Lady Aylesbury [2], that I had orderd a new Edition of my History and Essays to be sent her : You wrote to me, that they were sent; but she tells me, that she never receiv'd them, and was continually in expectation of them. By what Accident this has happen'd, appears to me totally unaccountable ; and the more so, as I know, that a Copy which I desird to be sent to Lord Hertford came safe to hand. I beseech you to send a Copy immediatly to Mr. Conway in little Warwick Street Charing Cross, and to enquire how the former Mistake happend : For I am certain, that it proceeded not from your Fault, notwith-standing the ill-humour with which I begun my Letter. But I desird, at that time, that a Copy shoud also be sent to Lady Holderness [3]; and I am also suspicious that this Copy has miscarryd by the same Accident ; and the more so, as she never wrote me that she had receivd it, which she woud naturally have done. If you be not sure, that this Copy has been deliverd, please to inform me, that I may enquire ; or rather, send a new Copy, relating the former Accident, and desiring that this Copy be returnd, in case the former Copy was deliver'd. I shall be in Town at the time which I appointed, and ready to receive the Proof Sheets.

I am Dear S^{ir} Your most obedient humble Servant

DAVID HUME.

(Written below in another hand)
Decr. 6th, 1769[4].

Note 1. In Nichols's *Literary History*, i. 141, the following passage occurs in a letter by Daniel Wray, dated Oct. 15, 1771 :—'Have you heard of the Congress at Inverary?... Though fifty beds were made, they were so crowded that even David Hume, for all his great figure as a Philosopher and Historian, or his greater as a fat man, was obliged by the adamantine peg-maker[1] to make one of three in a bed.' Hume also visited Inverary in September, 1775. Burton's *Hume*, ii. 475.

Note 2. See *ante*, p. 215, *n.* 3.

Note 3. The Earl of Holdernesse had been a Secretary of State from 1751 to 1761. Hume wrote from Paris on April 26, 1764 :— 'It is almost out of the memory of man that any British has been here on a footing of familiarity with the good company except my Lord Holdernesse, who had a good stock of acquaintance to begin with, speaks the language like a native, has very insinuating manners, was presented under the character of an old Secretary of State, and spent, as is said, £10,000 this winter to obtain that object of vanity. Him, indeed, I met everywhere in the best company.' Burton's *Hume*, ii. 194. Horace Walpole had written four months earlier to the Earl of Hertford, the English Ambassador at Paris :— 'I have not mentioned Lady Holdernesse's presentation, though I by no means approve it, nor a Dutch woman's lowering the peerage of England. Nothing of that sort could make me more angry, except a commoner's wife taking such a step; for you know I have all the pride of

—A citizen of Rome, while Rome survives[2].'

Letters, iv. 152. The Earl had married 'in Holland a niece of Mr. Van Haaren, with £50,000.' *Gent. Mag.* 1743, p. 612. Walpole wrote to George Montagu from Paris on Sept. 7, 1769 :—'I could certainly buy many things for you here that you would like, the reliques of the last age's magnificence; but since my Lady Holdernesse invaded the Custom House with an hundred and fourteen gowns, in the reign of that two-penny monarch George Grenville, the ports

---

[1] 'Si figit adamantinos
Summis verticibus dira Necessitas
Clavos.' Horace, 3 *Odes*, xxiv. 5.

[2] 'A senator of Rome, while Rome survived.' Addison's *Cato*, Act v. sc. 4.

are so guarded, that not a soul but a smuggler can smuggle anything
into England ; and I suppose you would not care to pay seventy-five
per cent. on second-hand commodities.' *Letters*, v. 184.

Note 4. This entry, which is, I believe, in Strahan's hand, probably gives the date on which the copy of the *History* had been sent
to Lady Holdernesse.

LETTER LII.

The new Edition of the History.

DEAR S^{IR}

I write you in a great hurry ; and can only tell you,
that I like the Paper and Type very much, only I think
that this Size of Type woud have suited better a Duodecimo
than a large Octavo : However it will do very well.

I see the Cause of the Mistake with regard to Lady
Aylesbury's Copy. Some body by Mistake has substituted
Dr. Hunter[1] in her place : But I never thought of making
the Doctor a present, tho I have a great regard for him.
Let Lady Aylesbury's Copy therefore be sent to her at
Little Warwick Street Charing Cross.

I return the Sheet corrected ; and am very sorry, that
you cannot promise me to be regular : I dedicate my
time entirely to it, and coud wish to have a Sheet regularly
every post.

I find that any other Frank except Mr. Frasers[2] will not
suffice, both for the Proof Sheet and the Sheet of the
Quarto ; especially, if you return the corrected Sheet[3],
which I wish, though it be not absolutely necessary.

I am Dear S^{ir} Yours sincerely

DAVID HUME.

EDR., 4 *of Septr.*, 1771.

Note 1. No doubt Dr. William Hunter, Professor of Anatomy in
the Royal Academy, the eldest brother of John Hunter, the surgeon.
Dr. A. Carlyle in his *Auto.*, p. 345, describes seeing him in 1758 at
a Club of Scotch physicians which met at the British Coffee house.

'Hunter was gay and lively to the last degree, and often came in to us at nine o'clock fatigued and jaded. He had had no dinner, but supped on a couple of eggs, and drank his glass of claret; for though we were a punch club, we allowed him a bottle of what he liked best. He repaid us with the brilliancy of his conversation. His toast was, "May no English nobleman venture out of the world without a Scottish physician, as I am sure there are none who venture in." [Horace Walpole, *Letters*, iii. 229, speaks of him as 'the man-midwife.'] ... By his attendance on Lady Esther [Hester] Pitt he had frequent opportunities of seeing the great orator when he was ill of the gout, and thought so ill of his constitution that he said more than once to us, with deep regret, that he did not think the great man's life worth two years' purchase; and yet Mr. Pitt lived for twenty years.' See *post*, Letter of June 12, 1776, for John Hunter.

Note 2. See *ante*, p. 188, *n*. 11.

Note 3. Hume wished to receive by each post a quarto sheet of the old edition from which the new edition was printed, a fresh proof sheet, and also an old proof sheet after the compositors had attended to his last corrections. The weight of the packet would be such that only Mr. Fraser's frank would pass it free through the post.

LETTER LIII.

The Revision of the History a great Amusement.

EDR., 18 *of Septr.*, 1771.

DEAR SIR

I thank you for your Corrections, which are very judicious; and you see that I follow them for the greatest part. I shall be obligd to you for continuing them as far as your Leizure will permit. For tho' I know, that a man might spend his whole Life in correcting one small Volume[1], and yet have inaccuracies in it, I think however that the fewer the better, and it is a great Amusement to me to pick them out gradually in every Edition.

I had a Letter lately from a Bookseller in Lausanne, who tells me, that he intends to publish a Translation of some of my philosophical Pieces; and desires to know the best Edition. If the last in large Octavo be finishd, I shoud point it out to him; and shoud likewise be willing to send

him a Copy of it, if any of our Booksellers have any
Communication with Geneva or Lausanne.   I shoud be
glad to learn from you what answer I can make him.

I am Dear S^{ir} Yours sincerely

DAVID HUME.

P.S.—I wish you coud come up to our Agreement of a
Sheet every post[2].

Note 1.   See *ante*, p. 200.
Note 2.   See *ante*, p. 183.

LETTER LIV.

Dr. Franklin Hume's Guest.

DEAR STRAHAN

Your remarks are always very judicious and just;
and I am much obligd to you.   You see I have adopted all
of them this sheet.   Dr. Franklin left me a few days ago
for the west; but I expect him again in a few days[1].

Yours &c.

D. H.

12 *of Novr.* [1771].

Note 1.   Franklin, writing from London on Jan. 13, 1772, says:—
'I have now been some weeks returned from my journey through
Wales, Ireland, Scotland, and the North of England.'   Franklin's
Works, ed. 1887, iv. 428.   He had visited Edinburgh also in the
autumn of 1759.   See *ib.* iii. 39; Thomson's *Life of Cullen*, i. 139; and
ante, p. 30, *n.* 3.

Hume wrote to Adam Smith on Feb. 13, 1774:—'Pray, what
strange accounts are these we hear of Franklin's conduct?   I am
very slow in believing that he has been guilty in the extreme degree
that is pretended; though I always knew him to be a very factious
man, and faction, next to fanaticism, is of all passions the most
destructive of morality.   How is it supposed he got possession of
these letters?   I hear that Wedderburne's treatment of him before
the Council was most cruel, without being in the least blameable.
What a pity!'   Burton's *Hume*, ii. 471.

Franklin had 'obtained and transmitted to Boston' some letters
'written,' to use his own words, 'by public officers to persons in

Q

public stations on public affairs, and intended to procure public measures.' *Ann. Reg.* 1773, i. 152.   He was accused, altogether falsely he maintained, of having got possession of these letters by treachery.   He used them to show that the Governor and Lieutenant-Governor of Massachusetts Bay were enemies to the Colony.   The Assembly petitioned the King for their removal.   The petition was referred to the Privy Council, before which Franklin was ordered to attend with counsel on Jan. 29.   Wedderburne, the Solicitor-General, attacked him with great severity.   He concluded his invective by saying :—' Amidst these tranquil events here is a man who, with the utmost insensibility of remorse, stands up and avows himself the author of all.   I can compare him only to *Zanga* in Dr. Young's *Revenge* :—

> " Know, then, 'twas I—
> I forged the letter—I dispos'd the picture—
> I hated—I despis'd—and I destroy."

I ask, my Lords, whether the revengeful temper attributed to the bloody African is not surpassed by the coolness and apathy of the wily American.' *Chatham Corresp.* iv. 323.   Franklin was dismissed from his office of Deputy Postmaster-General for the Colonies.

Dr. Priestley says that when Franklin appeared before the Privy Council, ' he was dressed in a suit of Manchester velvet ; and Silas Dean told me, that when they met at Paris to sign the treaty between France and America, he purposely put on that suit.'   Priestley's *Works*, xxv. 395.

LETTER LV.

Variety in Folly: Pitt's Gout: Posterity.

DEAR SIR

I have writ this Post to Fraser [1], whose Conduct has very much dissappointed me.   But if he delays a moment, we can easily do without him.   You need only send me the Proof Sheet under any Frank [2], Dr. Franklin's [3] or Mr. Pulteneys or Mr. Wedderburn's or Lord Beauchamps or Mr. Conway's [4] (Who I hope, by the bye, has receivd the Copy of my History).   The other Sheets, are in a great measure superfluous : Especially as I have a Copy of the Edition, from which this is taken.

I am glad to find, that the abominable Faction in England

is declining[5]. The People never tire of Folly, but they tire of the same Folly[6]: And if their Leaders fall into the Contempt they deserve, it will be very great indeed. I hope that Pitt will have the Gout this whole Session and I pray it may be a hearty and sincere one[7].

I do not think, that you will be able to publish this Season; unless the printing of the four last Volumes be well advancd. But as I have at last been able to get one correct Edition of that work, I am more indifferent. I am sensible, it is an idle Amusement; but still it is an Amusement to think that Posterity will do me more Justice than the present Age[8], whose Suffrage indeed coud not have given me great Vanity.

I wish you saw (as I hope you will) my new House and Situation in St Andrews Square[9]: You woud not wonder that I have abjurd London for ever.

I am Dear S^ir Yours sincerely

DAVID HUME.

2d Jany., 1772.

P.S.—Lord Lyttleton has been so good as to send me the two last Volumes of his Henry II[10]. It woud flatter his Lordship to say that it is truly a Christian Performance[11].

Note 1. See *ante,* p. 188, *n.* 11.

Note 2. If only the proof sheet were sent the packet would not exceed two ounces—the limit of weight for an ordinary frank (*ante, ib.*).

Note 3. Franklin, I conjecture, had the right of franking either as Deputy Postmaster-General for the Colonies, or as Provincial Agent in England for several of the Colonies.

Note 4. For these names, see *ante,* p. 200. It is curious to see Franklin and Wedderburne, who in two years were to be opposed to each other in so memorable a scene, thus brought together.

Note 5. Burke wrote on July 31, 1771:—'As to news, we have little. After a violent ferment in the nation, as remarkable a deadness and vapidity has succeeded. The Court perseveres in the pursuit, and is near to the perfect accomplishment of its project; but when the work is perfected, it may be nearest to its destruction, for the principle is wrong, and the materials are rotten.' Burke's *Corres.* i. 256. In the *Ann. Reg.* for 1772, i. 82, describing the autumn, he says that the general apathy had not yet much pervaded London. 'The citizens said that Government had set its face particularly against the City of London, in a manner that had been unknown since the Revolution. . . . That it had for some time acted, as if they were in an actual state of warfare with her.'

Horace Walpole wrote on Dec. 15 :—'We are so much accustomed to politics, that people do not know how to behave under the present cessation. We can go into the City without being mobbed, and through Brentford without "No. 45" on one's coach-door. Wilkes is almost as dead as Sacheverell, though Sheriff.' *Letters*, v. 359. On Jan. 14, 1772, he wrote :—'The Parliament meets next week. There will, I think, be little to do, unless an attempt to set aside the subscription of the clergy to the Thirty-nine Articles should stir up a storm. Religious disputes are serious ; and yet can one care about shades of nonsense ?' *Ib.* p. 369.

Note 6. See *ante*, p. 187, *n.* 4.

Note 7. Lord Chatham, writing eight days after the date of Hume's letter, mentions 'some sensations which begin to remind me of a winter account of gout to be balanced after a summer of more health than I have known these twenty years.' Chatham *Corres.* iv. 186. Hume's prayer was only partly granted : Chatham was this session troubled with gout, but not so severely as in many other years. *Ib.* pp. 201, 3, 8, 217, 8. Burke in his *Speech on American Taxation*, on April 19, 1774, describing Chatham's second Ministry, says :—'If ever he fell into a fit of the gout, or if any other cause withdrew him from public cares, principles directly the contrary [of his own] were sure to predominate.' Payne's *Burke*, i. 145. In a letter dated Sept. 14, 1775, Burke doubts like Hume whether all Lord Chatham's attacks of gout were sincere. 'Acquainted as I am,' he writes, 'with the astonishing changes of Lord Chatham's constitution (whether natural or political) I am surprised to find that he is again perfectly recovered. But so it is. He will probably play more tricks.' Burke's *Corres.* ii. 63.

Note 8. Hume wrote to Elliot on May 11, 1758 :—'*Vanitas vanitatum, atque omnia vanitas*, says the Preacher ; the great object of us authors, and of you orators and statesmen, is to gain applause ; and you see at what rate it is to be purchased. I fancy there is a future state to give poets, historians, philosophers their due reward, and to distribute to them those recompenses which are so strangely shared out in this life. It is of little consequence that posterity does them justice, if they are for ever to be ignorant of it, and are to remain in perpetual slumber in their literary paradise.' Burton's *Hume*, ii. 44. 'Posterity,' wrote Johnson, 'is always the author's favourite.' *Piozzi Letters*, ii. 14.

Note 9. Hume had not yet moved into his new house. See *post*,
p. 250, *n.* 3.

Note 10. The first three volumes of Lyttelton's *Henry II* appeared
in 1764, and the conclusion in 1771. Lyttelton had begun to print it
in 1755. Johnson's *Works*, viii. 492. It was said that 'it was kept
back several years for fear of Smollett.' Boswell's *Johnson*, iii. 33.
Hume, writing on April 20, 1756, says :—'We hear of Sir George
Lyttelton's *History*, from which the populace expect a great deal;
but I hear it is to be three quarto volumes. " O, magnum, horribilem
et sacrum Libellum[1]." This last epithet of *sacrum* will probably be
applicable to it in more senses than one. However, it cannot well
fail to be readable, which is a great deal for an English book now-a-
days.' Burton's *Hume*, i. 433.

Note 11. 'Lyttelton had, in the pride of juvenile confidence, with
the help of corrupt conversation, entertained doubts of the truth
of Christianity; but he thought the time now come when it was
no longer fit to doubt or believe by chance, and applied himself
seriously to the great question. His studies, being honest, ended
in conviction.' Johnson's *Works*, viii. 490. Horace Walpole, describing on Oct. 19, 1765 the dulness of Parisian society, says :—
'Good folks, they have no time to laugh. There is God and the
King to be pulled down first; and men and women, one and all, are
devoutly employed in the demolition. They think me quite profane
for having any belief left. But this is not my only crime; I have
told them, and am undone by it, that they have taken from us to
admire the two dullest things we had, Whisk (whist) and Richardson.
—It is very true, and they want nothing but George Grenville to
make their conversations, or rather dissertations, the most tiresome
upon earth. For Lord Lyttelton, if he would come hither, and turn
free-thinker once more, he would be reckoned the most agreeable
man in France—next to Mr. Hume, who is the only thing in the
world that they believe implicitly; which they must do, for I
defy them to understand any language that he speaks.' *Letters*,
iv. 425.

Hume wrote to Adam Smith on July 14, 1767 :—'Have you read
Lord Lyttelton? Do you not admire his Whiggery and his Piety;
Qualities so useful both for this World and the next?' *M.S.R.S.E.*
Hume could hardly have meant that Whiggery was good for the
next world; for Johnson 'always said that the first Whig was the
devil'; and Boswell, after mentioning the altercation that passed
between that stout old Whig, his father, and the Tory Johnson,
continues :—'I must observe, in justice to my friend's political
principles, and my own, that they have met in a place where there is
no room for Whiggism.' Boswell's *Johnson*, iii. 326, v. 385.

---

[1]   ' Dii magni, horribilem et sacrum libellum.' Catullus, xiv. 12.
          ' Gods! an horrible and deadly volume!' Ellis.

LETTER LVI.

Hume's Suppressed Essays.

DEAR SIR

I have called on Dr. Millar and he on me; but have never met with him, because tho' this place be not large [1], I live in a manner out of Town, and am very seldom in it [2]. My Sister [3] also has been dangerously ill of late, which has kept me more out of Company. But I am told by a Friend, that Dr. Millar said to him, there was a Bookseller in London, who had advertisd a new Book, containing, among other things, two of my suppress'd Essays. These I suppose are two Essays of mine, one on Suicide another on the Immortality of the Soul, which were printed by Andrew Millar about seventeen Years ago, and which from my abundant Prudence I suppress'd and woud not now wish to have revivd. I know not if you were acquainted with this Transaction. It was this: I intended to print four Dissertations, the natural History of Religion, on the Passions, on Tragedy, and on the metaphisical Principles of Geometry. I sent them up to Mr. Millar; but before the last was printed, I happend to meet with Lord Stanhope [4], who was in this Country, and he convincd me, that either there was some Defect in the Argument or in its perspicuity; I forget which; and I wrote to Mr. Millar, that I woud not print that Essay [5]; but upon his remonstrating that the other Essays woud not make a Volume, I sent him up these two, which I had never intended to have publishd. They were printed; but it was no sooner done than I repented; and Mr. Millar and I agreed to suppress them at common Charges, and I wrote a new Essay on the Standard of Taste, to supply their place. Mr. Millar assurd me very earnestly that all the Copies were suppress'd, except one which he sent to Sir Andrew Mitchel [6], in whose Custody I thought it safe. But I have

since found that there either was some Infidelity or
Negligence in the case; For on Mr. Morehead's Death [7],
there was found a Copy, which his Nephew deliverd up
to me. But there have other Copies got abroad; and from
one of these, some rascally Bookseller is, it seems, printing
this Edition [8]. I am not extremely alarmd at this Event,
but if threatening him woud prevent it, I woud willingly
employ that means. I am afraid all will be in vain; but if
you know him, be as good as try what can be done; and
also learn from what hand he had the Copy. I believe an
Injunction in Chancery might be got against him; but
then I must acknowledge myself the Author and this
Expedient woud make a Noise and render the Affair more
public. In a post or two, I may perhaps get you more
particular Intelligence of the Booksellers Name.

I am extremely obligd to you for the Pains you take
about correcting my Sheets; and you see that I almost
always profit by it.

Yours sincerely
David Hume.

Jany. 25, 1772.

Note 1.   Robert Chambers, in his *Traditions of Edinburgh*, ed. 1825,
i. 21, speaking of this time says, on the authority of ' an ancient native
of Edinburgh, that people all knew each other by sight. The appearance of a new face upon the streets was at once remarked, and
numbers busied themselves in finding out who and what the stranger
was.'

Note 2.   He had not yet moved into his new house, which was outside the town. See *post*, p. 250, *n.* 3.   Perhaps he spent most of his
time there looking after the workmen.   On Oct 2, 1770, he had written
that he could not leave Edinburgh, as he was building a house. ' By
being present, I have already prevented two capital mistakes which
the mason was falling into; and I shall be apprehensive of his falling
into more, were I to be at a distance.' Burton's *Hume*, ii. 436.

Note 3.   Hume writing to a friend in 1753 says :—' About seven
months ago I got a house of my own, and completed a regular family;
consisting of a head, viz. myself, and two inferior members, a maid
and a cat. My sister has since joined me, and keeps me company.
With frugality I can reach, I find, cleanliness, warmth, light, plenty,

and contentment. What would you have more? Independence? I
have it in a supreme degree. Honour? that is not altogether wanting. Grace? that will come in time. A wife? that is none of the
indispensable requisites of life. Books? that *is* one of them; and I
have more than I can use.' Burton's *Hume*, i. 377.

Note 4. Philip, second Earl Stanhope. 'He had great talents, but
fitter for speculation than for practical objects of action. He made
himself one of the best—Lalande used to say the best—mathe-
maticians in England of his day, and was likewise deeply skilled in
other branches of science and philosophy. The Greek language was
as familiar to him as the English; he was said to know every line of
Homer by heart. In public life, on the contrary, he was shy, un-
gainly, and embarrassed. So plain was he in his dress and deport-
ment, that on going down to the House of Lords to take his seat,
after a long absence on the Continent, the door-keeper could not
believe he was a peer, and pushed him aside, saying, " Honest man,
you have no business in this place." "I am sorry, indeed," replied
the Earl, "if honest men have no business here."' Mahon's *History
of England*, ed. 1838, iii. 242. Horace Walpole wrote on March 4,
1745 :—'Earl Stanhope has at last lifted up his eyes from Euclid, and
directed them to matrimony.' *Letters*, i. 344.

Note 5. This Essay must have been destroyed by Hume.

Note 6. See *ante*, p. 181, *n.* 25. Hume wrote to Millar on May 27,
1756:—' I have no objection to Mr. Mitchels having a copy of the
Dissertations.' *M.S.R.S.E.*

Note 7. The death of William Morehead, Esq., in Cavendish
Square, on June 12, 1766, is recorded in the *Gent. Mag.* for that year,
p. 295. He may have been the man mentioned by Hume.

Note 8. Hume wrote to Millar on June 12, 1755:—'There are
four short Dissertations which I have kept some years by me, in
order to polish them as much as possible. One of them is that
which Allan Ramsay mentioned to you. [*The Natural History of
Religion.*] Another, *of the Passions*; a third, *of Tragedy*; a fourth,
Some Considerations previous to Geometry and Natural Philosophy.'
Burton's *Hume*, i. 421. ' In 1783,' says Dr. Burton, *Ib.* ii. 13, 'a work
was published in London called *Essays on Suicide and the Immortality
of the Soul, ascribed to the late David Hume, Esq., never before published;
with remarks intended as an antidote to the poison contained in these
performances, by the Editor.* The editor and his antidote are now both
forgotten; but the style of Hume and his method of thinking were at
once recognised in these Essays, and they have been incorporated
with the general edition of his works. . . . That Hume wrote these
Essays, and intended to publish them, is thus an incident in his life
which ought not to be passed over; but it is also part of his history
that he repented of the act at the last available moment, and suppressed the publication.' Dr. Burton says that 'many copies of the
first edition bear marks of having been mutilated. ·In a copy which

I possess,' he adds, 'after p. 200, the end of the third Dissertation, there are four strips of paper, the remains of half a sheet, cut away. This occurs in signature K, and signature L begins with the fourth dissertation.' (For *signature* see *ante*, p. 152, *n.* 6.) On April 23, 1764, Hume wrote to Millar from Paris:—'I never see Mr. Wilkes here but at chapel, where he is a most regular, and devout, and edifying, and pious attendant; I take him to be entirely regenerate. He told me last Sunday, that you had given him a copy of my Dissertations, with the two which I had suppressed; and that he, foreseeing danger from the sale of his library, had wrote to you to find out that copy, and to tear out the two obnoxious dissertations. Pray how stands that fact? It was imprudent in you to intrust him with that copy: it was very prudent in him to use that precaution. Yet I do not naturally suspect you of imprudence, nor him of prudence. I must hear a little farther before I pronounce.' Millar wrote back on June 5:—'I take Mr. Wilkes to be the same man he was,—acting a part. He has forgot the story of the *two* Dissertations. The fact is, upon importunity, I lent to him the only copy I preserved, and for years never could recollect he had it, till his books came to be sold; upon this I went immediately to the gentleman that directed the sale, told him the fact, and reclaimed the two Dissertations which were my property. Mr. Coates, who was the person, immediately delivered me the volume; and so soon as I got home, I tore them out and burnt them, that I might not lend them to any for the future. Two days after, Mr. Coates sent me a note for the volume, as Mr. Wilkes had desired it should be sent him to Paris; I returned the volume, but told him the two Dissertations I had torn out of the volume and burnt, being my property. This is the truth of the matter, and nothing but the truth. It was certainly imprudent for me to lend them to him.' Burton's *Hume*, ii. 202. Wilkes wrote to Earl Temple that Cotes had sold his books in 1764 for £427. *Grenville Papers*, iv. 16. Cotes, who was his agent, seems to have robbed him. *Ib.* p. 3, note.

LETTER LVII.

The Suppressed Essays: A Note to be added to the History.

7 *of Feby.*, 1772.

DEAR SIR

I suppress'd these Essays, not because they coud give any Offence, but because, I thought, they coud neither give Pleasure nor Instruction: They were indeed bad Imitations of the agreeable *Triffling of* Addison [1]. But if any one think otherwise, and chuse to preserve them, I have no Objection.

Pray, recollect: Did not I send you up a Passage to be inserted in the Reign of Henry VIII, and which I desird you to pin upon the Leaf of the Volume? It ought to have been printed in the last Sheet, and is now too late : But it may be added as a Note. Or is the whole an Illusion of mine, founded on my intending to send it you. The Passage contains a short Extract from an Act of Parliament, concerning the Marriage of the King with Jane Seymour, whom the Parliament recommends to him as a Piece of pure Flesh and Blood, very proper to bring him Heirs [2]. If you have not this Passage, I shall send you another Copy of it.

Yours sincerely
DAVID HUME.

Note 1. It is a curious description of *Essays on Suicide and on the Immortality of the Soul* to call them imitations of the agreeable trifling of Addison.

Note 2. The note was added on p. 459 of vol. iv. of this edition. In the edition of 1778 it is given as a footnote on p. 163 of the same volume. It is as follows :—' The parliament, in annulling the King's marriage with Anne Boleyn, gives this as a reason, " For that his highness had chosen to wife the excellent and virtuous lady Jane, who for her convenient years, excellent beauty, and pureness of flesh and blood, would be apt, God willing, to conceive issue by his highness." ' Hume does not give his reference. Much the same was said by Lord Chancellor Audley in his speech on June 8, 1537. *Parl. Hist.* i. 529.

LETTER LVIII.

A Missing Sheet of the History.

DEAR SIR

The Sheet you mention I deliverd with my own Hands on Friday the 31 of Jany to John Balfour[1], who promis'd to send it with his own Letters to the Post house.

It is by his unpardonable Negligence it is lost. I shall rate him about it; but if you do not receive it this post or the next, you will be so good as send me another copy which I shall not entrust to him in returning it.

I am Dear S[ir] Yours most faithfully

D. H.

Feby. 11, 1772.

P.S.—I am very well pleas'd that the Sheet is found; and also, that I did not know it, till I had writ a very scolding Letter to John Balfour for his losing it.

Note 1. John Balfour was an Edinburgh bookseller (*ante*, p. 2, *n.* 2). On July 10, 1780, he wrote to Strahan:—' Bookselling is at so low a pass that I have sometimes had thoughts of giving it up; it is a laborious business, at present without any profit, and it is only the hope of its amending that makes me continue.' *Barker MSS.*

LETTER LIX.

Learned Printers: Princess Dowager: George III and the East India Company.

EDINBURGH, 22 *of Feby.*, 1772.

DEAR S[IR]

As we are drawing near a Conclusion [1], I cannot forbear giving you many and hearty thanks, both for your submitting to so troublesome a Method of printing and for the many useful Corrections you have sent me. I suppose, since the days of Aldus [2], Reuchlin [3], and Stevens [4], there have been no Printers who could have been useful to their Authors in this particular. I shall scarcely ever think of correcting any more; tho' I own that the receiving of the Sheets regularly by the post has been an Amusement and Occupation to me, which I shall have a Difficulty to supply. I fancy I must take to some kind of Composition in its place.

Pray, have you gone any length in printing the other Volumes, or are you now to begin. In this case, you can scarcely publish this Season. But as you have probably a very large fount[5] of this Type, I hope you are pretty well advancd. I need not put you in mind of sending me a dozen Copies of the History, and half a dozen of the philosophical Pieces.

Your Encomium on the Princess Dowager[6] is elegantly written, and contains a very proper and spirited Reprehension of the scurrillous and scoundrel Patriots who had so long abus'd her[7]. I wonder what they will now do for a Pretence to their Sedition.

I have lately heard a Story, extremely to the King's Advantage; which I shoud be glad to find confirmd. I am told, that this parliamentary Enquiry into the Proceedings of the East India Company did not originally proceed from the Ministry, but from the King himself, who was shockd with the Accounts he receivd of the Oppressions exercisd over the poor Natives, and demanded a Remedy[8]. I wish it may be possible to provide any, that will be durable. I trust much in the Integrity of Andrew Stuart[9] (who, they say, will certainly be one of the Supervisors[10]) for the carrying of such a Plan into Execution.

I hear also that there is an Intention of appointing Professor Ferguson[11] Secretary to the Commission. Surely there is not a man of greater Worth in the World[12]. If you have a Vote or Interest, I beseech you, employ it all in his favour, as well for his Advantage as for that of Humanity.

I am Dear S[ir] Faithfully Yours

DAVID HUME.

Note 1. Hume is speaking of only the first four volumes of the reprint of his *History*. See *ante*, p. 183.

Note 2. ' The politest nations of Europe have endeavoured to vie with one another for the reputation of the finest printing.... If we look into the Commonwealths of Holland and Venice, we shall find that in this particular they have made themselves the envy of the greatest monarchies. Elzevir and Aldus are more frequently mentioned than any pensioner of the one or doge of the other.' Addison, *The Spectator*, No. 367.

Note 3. 'Si on demande quel fut dans notre Europe le premier auteur de ce style bouffon et hardi, dans lequel ont écrit Sterne, Swift et Rabelais, il paraît certain que les premiers qui s'étaient signalés dans cette dangereuse carrière avaient été deux Allemands nés au quinzième siècle, Reuchlin et Hutten. Ils publièrent les fameuses *Lettres des gens obscurs*, longtemps avant que Rabelais dédiât son Pantagruel et son Gargantua au cardinal Odet de Châtillon.' *Œuvres de Voltaire*, ed. 1819–25, xlii. 431. I have failed to discover anything that shows that Reuchlin was a printer.

Note 4. 'Eodem anno [MDLIX] vivis exemptus est Robertus Stephanus Parisiensis typographus regius . . . cui non solum Gallia sed universus Christianus orbis plus debet, quam cuiquam fortissimorum belli ducum ob propagatos fineis patria unquam debuit; majusque ex ejus unius industria quam ex tot praeclare bello et pace gestis, ad Franciscum decus et nunquam interitura gloria redundavit.' *Thuanus*, ed. 1620, i. 708. Robert Stephens, or Stephanus, was born at Paris in 1503, died at Geneva in 1559. 'Thuanus asserts that the Christian world was more indebted to him than to all the great conquerors it had produced, and that he contributed more to immortalize the reign of Francis I than all the renowned actions of that prince.' Chalmers, *Biog. Dict.* xxviii. 371.

Note 5. A fount or font of type is 'a complete assortment of types of one sort, with all that is necessary for printing in that kind of letter.' Chambers's *Ety. Dict.* It is not defined in Johnson's *Dictionary.* Strahan had cast a fresh fount for this edition (*ante*, p. 187, *n.* 6).

Note 6. She died on Feb. 8. Her name is given in the Index of Names in the *Gentleman's Magazine* for that year as 'Wales Princess.' Horace Walpole wrote of her on Feb. 12:—'Nothing ever equalled her resolution. She took the air till within four or five days of her death, and never indicated having the least idea of her danger, even to the Princess of Brunswick, though she had sent for her. Although she had convulsions the day before she expired, she rose and dressed to receive the King and Queen, and kept them four hours in indifferent conversation, though almost inarticulate herself; said nothing on her situation, took no leave of them, and expired at six in the morning without a groan. She could not be unapprised of her approaching fate, for she had existed upon cordials alone for ten days.' *Letters*, v. 374. Of Strahan's encomium, which was in the London Chronicle for Feb. 11, I will give a few extracts :—'She is now in a state far superior to mortal praise or blame, where the lying and malignant voice of faction cannot reach her; and it will now be discovered and believed that never was a more amiable, a more innocent, or a more benevolent Princess. That she interfered in the politics of this country and influenced the King in affairs of state, we will venture to say was utterly void of foundation. . . . Though she

constantly read all the public papers, the unmerited abuse with
which they frequently abounded never excited in her the least
emotion of anger or resentment. . . . She was for many years the
very idol of the people of England.'

Note 7. See *ante*, p. 210, *n.* 26, for Alderman Townsend's attack
on her in the House of Commons on March 25, 1771. Horace Wal-
pold wrote on March 15, 1770 :—' As a prelude to what was to follow,
rather as the word of battle, Lord Chatham some days ago declared
to the Lords, that there is a *secret influence* (meaning the Princess)
more mighty than Majesty itself, and which had betrayed or clogged
every succeeding Administration. His own had been sacrificed by
it. In consequence of this denunciation, papers to which the *North
Britons* were milk and honey have been published in terms too
gross to repeat. *The Whisperer* and *The Parliamentary Spy* are their
titles. Every blank wall at this end of the town is scribbled with the
words, *Impeach the King's Mother*; and in truth I think her person in
danger.' *Letters*, v. 229.

Note 8. Horace Walpole wrote to Mann on Feb. 12, 1772 :—' The
East Indies are going to be another spot of contention. Such a scene
of tyranny and plunder has been opened as makes one shudder !
The *heaven-born hero*[1], Lord Clive, seems to be Plutus, the dæmon
who does not give, but engrosses riches. There is a letter from one
of his associates to their Great Mogul, in which *our Christian* expresses himself with singular tenderness for the interests of the
Mahometan religion ! We are Spaniards in our lust for gold, and
Dutch in our delicacy of obtaining it.' *Letters*, v. 375. On March 5 he
wrote :—' We have another scene coming to light, of black dye indeed.
The groans of India have mounted to heaven, where the *heaven-born*
General Lord Clive will certainly be disavowed. Oh ! my dear sir,
we have outdone the Spaniards in Peru ! They were at least
butchers on a religious principle, however diabolical their zeal. We
have murdered, deposed, plundered, usurped—nay, what think you of
the famine in Bengal, in which three millions perished, being caused
by a monopoly of the provisions by the servants of the East India
Company? All this is come out, is coming out—unless the gold that
inspired these horrors can quash them.' *Ib.* p. 378. On March 27 he
added :—' The House of Commons is going to tap the affairs of India,
an endless labyrinth ! We shall lose the East before we know half its
history. It was easier to conquer it than to know what to do with it.
If you or the Pope can tell, pray give us your opinion.' *Ib.* p. 379.

The Select Committee of Enquiry into the East India Company
was not appointed till April 13, 1772. *Ann. Reg.* 1772, i. 103. The
King in his speech of Jan. 21, on opening Parliament, had said :—' The
concerns of this country are so various and extensive as to require

---

[1] According to Horace Walpole (*Memoirs of the Reign of George II*, ed. 1822,
ii. 276), Pitt, in a debate on the army estimates on Dec. 14, 1757, had described
Clive as ' that man, not born for a desk—that heaven-born general.'

the most vigilant and active attention, and some of them, as well from remoteness of place as from other circumstances, are so peculiarly liable to abuses and exposed to danger that the inter-position of the legislature for their protection may become necessary.' *Parl. Hist.* xvii. 233. In the *Correspondence of George III with Lord North* (i. 81) is given the following letter :—'Queen's House, Jan. 6, 1772, 15 min. pt. 5 p.m. Lord North,—The sketch of the Speech meet with my approbation. When the sentences are a little more rounded ... I doubt not but it will make a very good one.' On this the editor remarks :—' The sentences are *rounded*, and almost without meaning.' That so far from being without meaning, one of them was full of the weightiest meaning, implying at it did a parliamentary enquiry of the highest importance, is shown not only by Hume's mention of this enquiry seven weeks before it was appointed, but also by the *Annual Register*, 1772, i. 101, and 1773, i. 67. In the latter Burke says :—' The mal-administration in India, with all its consequences, were [*sic*] suffered to pass without notice or observation ; and we have already seen in the transactions of the year 1772 that, though the affairs of the Company were evidently alluded to at the opening of the session in the speech from the throne, they were nevertheless suffered to lie over till near its close, when a bill was brought in by the deputy-chairman for enlarging the controlling powers of the Company with respect to their servants in India. The bill came to nothing in that session. *But a member, though in the King's service, not connected with Ministry, whether with or without their consent, at length awakened their attention to this object. This gave birth to the Select Committee, which was armed with full powers for all the purposes of enquiry.'* The passage which I have printed in italics is some evidence of the truth of the report which had reached Hume.

Note 9. Andrew Stuart was the author of *Letters to the Right Hon. Lord Mansfield.* In them he attacked that Judge for his conduct in the famous Douglas cause, when it came, on appeal, before the House of Lords.   That this work, which was never on sale, had been written for publication is shown by the following passage in Strahan's letter to Hume of Jan. 25, 1773 :—' The Letters have been in Lord Mansfield's hands this fortnight, but I have not yet heard how he is affected by them. This will appear in due time. They are not yet made public, only distributed among his friends, but will be pub-lished in a few days.' *M. S. R. S. E.* Johnson speaking about them to Boswell on April 27, 1773, said :—' They have not answered the end. They have not been talked of ; I have never heard of them. This is owing to their not being sold. People seldom read a book which is given to them.' Boswell's *Life of Johnson*, ii. 229. Horace Walpole had written about it on Jan. 25 :—' There is a book you will see that makes and intends to make noise enough. . . . Indeed it is admirable, and it must be confessed that a Scot dissects a Scot with ten times more address than Churchill and Junius. They know each other's sore places better than we do.' *Letters*, v. 430. On May 27 he wrote :—' The book will be a great curiosity, for after all the author's heroism, fear or nationality have preponderated, and it will not be published.' *Ib.* p. 466.

Hume, who was as strong against the successful litigant as Boswell was for him, of course sided with Andrew Stuart. ' I was struck,' he wrote on March 28, 1769, 'with a very sensible indignation at the decision of the Douglas cause, though I foresaw it for some time. It was abominable with regard to poor Andrew Stuart, who had conducted that cause with singular ability and integrity; and was at last exposed to reproach which unfortunately never can be wiped off.' Burton's *Hume*, ii. 423. According to Lord Campbell (*Lives of the Chancellors*, ed. 1846, v. 494), Stuart took so ill the attack made on him in court by Thurlow, who was engaged as counsel on the other side, that he sent him a challenge. ' Thurlow wrote back for answer that the desired meeting Mr. Stuart should have, but not till the hearing of the appeal was concluded. . . . They met in Kensington Gardens, and shots were exchanged—happily without effect. Mr. Stuart afterwards declared that Mr. Thurlow advanced and stood up to him like an elephant.' Lord Campbell adds in a note :—' A gentleman still alive, who remembers the duel well, says that Thurlow, on his way to the field of battle, stopped to eat an enormous breakfast at a tavern near Hyde Park Corner.' Dr. Burton (*Life of Hume*, ii. 425) says that it was not with Thurlow but with Wedderburne that Stuart fought. He corrects this statement in *Letters of Eminent Persons to David Hume*, p. 110. Neither he nor Lord Campbell gives any reference. Stuart was member for Lanarkshire in the Parliament elected in Nov. 1774. *Parl. Hist.* xviii. 29. In 1779 he and Gibbon became colleagues as Lords Commissioners of Trade and Plantations. *Ib.* 7, 29.

Note 10. It was not, says Burke, till the year 1767 that the affairs of the East India Company were first introduced into Parliament. *Ann. Reg.* 1773, i. 63. This introduction was regarded as a startling innovation. ' The novelty of an English minister of state venturing to interfere, as an officer of the Crown, in a matter of private property excited in the highest degree the attention of all sorts of people.' *Ib.* 1767, i. 43. By an annual payment by the Company to the Government of £400,000 a year a respite was purchased from state interference. *Ib.* i. 43 [1]. In 1769, in the alarm caused by the news of Hyder Ali's successes in war, India stock had fallen above 60 per cent. in a few days. The Directors, ' to put a stop to the abuses and mismanagements which had so much disgraced the Company's government in India,'

---

[1] The pagination of the *Annual Register* is so clumsy that it is not always easy either to give or to find a reference. In the number from which I am quoting page 43 is found three times. My first reference is to the first page 43, my second to the second, which is separated from it by only eight pages and is distinguished by an asterisk.

appointed three men 'who should be invested with extraordinary powers, and sent to India under the character of Supervisors, with full authority to examine into and rectify the concerns of every department, and a full power of control over all their other servants in India.' *Ann. Reg.* 1769, i. 53. The ship in which they sailed was never heard of. 'The fate of these gentlemen,' wrote Burke, 'was undoubtedly one of the greatest misfortunes that could have befallen the Company.' *Ib.* 1773, i. 66. It was brought to the brink of bankruptcy and ruin, and could not keep up its payment to the government. In their alarm at the appointment of the Parliamentary Committee the Directors resolved to send out new Supervisors. The resolution came too late. In Dec. 1772 a bill was rapidly carried through Parliament restraining the Company for six months from sending out any such Commission of Supervision. *Ib.* p. 73, and *Parl. Hist.* xvii. 651. Before the time had run out the Regulating Act was carried through both Houses, and Warren Hastings was appointed first Governor-General. 'Thus,' writes Burke, 'this memorable revolution was accomplished. From that time the Company is to be considered as wholly in the hands of the ministers of the Crown.' *Ann. Reg.* 1773, i. 105. Andrew Stuart was not named one of the four Councillors who were to assist the Governor-General. But among them was one who was a still bitterer enemy of Lord Mansfield—Philip Francis, the author of the *Letters of Junius*.

Note 11. The Rev. Dr. Adam Ferguson, Professor of Natural Philosophy in the University of Edinburgh. He had been tutor to the family of Lord Bute, and so had influence at Court. Burton's *Hume*, ii. 34, 45. Hume wrote to Adam Smith on Nov. 23 of this year :—' Ferguson has returned, fat and fair, and in good humour, notwithstanding his disappointment, which I am glad of.' *Ib.* p. 461. It was at his house that Scott, a lad of fifteen, saw Burns. Lockhart's *Life of Scott*, ed. 1839, i. 185. Scott in his review of John Home's *Works* records the following anecdote of him :—' Dr. Adam Ferguson went as chaplain to the Black Watch or 42d Highland Regiment, when that corps was first sent to the Continent. As the regiment advanced to the Battle of Fontenoy, the commanding officer, Sir Robert Monro, was astonished to see the chaplain at the head of the column, with a broadsword drawn in his hand. He desired him to go to the rear with the surgeons, a proposal which Adam Ferguson spurned. Sir Robert at length told him that his commission did not entitle him to be present in the post which he had assumed. "D—n my commission," said the warlike chaplain, throwing it towards his Colonel. It may easily be supposed that the matter was only remembered as a good jest ; but the future historian of Rome shared the honours and dangers of that dreadful day, where, according to the account of the French themselves, "the Highland furies rushed in upon them with more violence than ever did a sea driven by a tempest."' *Quarterly Review*, lxxi. 196.

Lord Cockburn in his *Memorials,* p. 49, describes him in his old age as 'a spectacle well worth beholding. His hair was silky and white; his eyes animated and light-blue; his cheeks sprinkled with broken red like autumnal apples, but fresh and healthy; his lips thin and the under one curled.' In middle age he had had a severe paralytic attack, which so reduced his animal vitality that he always wore a good deal of fur. 'His gait and air were noble; his gesture slow; his look full of dignity and composed fire. He looked like a philosopher from Lapland. His palsy ought to have killed him in his fiftieth year; but rigid care enabled him to live uncrippled, either in body or mind, nearly fifty years more. Wine and animal food besought his appetite in vain; but huge messes of milk and vegetables disappeared before him, always in the never failing cloth and fur. . . He always locked the door of his study when he left it, and took the key in his pocket; and no housemaid got in till the accumulation of dust and rubbish made it impossible to put the evil day off any longer; and then woe on the family. He shook hands with us boys one day in summer 1793, on setting off in a strange sort of carriage, and with no companion except his servant James, to visit Italy for a new edition of his history. He was then about seventy-two, and had to pass through a good deal of war; but returned in about a year younger than ever.' He was born in 1724 and died in 1816.

Note 12. Johnson would certainly have charged Hume with joining in what he calls 'the Scotch conspiracy in national falsehood' (Boswell's *Johnson,* ii. 297); and with sharing in that 'national combination, so invidious that their friends cannot defend it,' which is one of the chief means 'which enables them to find, or to make their way to employment, riches, and distinction' (*Works,* ix. 158). No man was better than Hume at magnifying the merits of a countryman. As Ferguson was unsurpassed in the whole world in worth, so 'Wilkie [the author of the *Epigoniad*] was to be the Homer, Blacklock the Pindar, and Home the Shakespeare or something still greater of his country.' Burton's *Hume,* ii. 32.

[William Strahan to David Hume.]

LETTER LX.

Life tolerable only by Labour: the Princess Dowager: Bengal.

Dear Sir

The approbation of those whose praise is real fame is, in the very nature of the thing, extremely desireable. Judge then how very acceptable your last kind letter was to me; in which you acknowledge my small merits in a very generous

and good-natured way, and much above what they have any
title to. . . . The reading a sheet of your *History* every day
with care and precision, though I at first imposed it upon
myself as a task, soon became a most agreeable amusement. . . .

You say the correcting the sheets has been an amusement
to yourself, and an occupation which you will now find a
difficulty to supply. This I can easily believe. And here
let me make one observation, which I dare say has frequently
occurred to yourself, because it is founded on experience and
a knowledge of the human mind.—To render life tolerable,
and to make it glide away with some degree of satisfaction,
it is necessary that a small part at least of almost every day be
employed in some species of *real* or *imaginary business.* To
pass our whole time in amusement and dissipation leaves a
depression upon the spirits infinitely less bearable than perhaps
the hardest labour [1]. The sentence of, *In the sweat of thy face
shalt thou eat bread*, pronounced against Adam after his fall, as
a punishment, is an apparent mistake, which I am not scholar
enough to rectify, but which I hope will not escape future
commentators [2].—My application of this doctrine you will easily
guess, which is no other than to add this to the other motives
I have formerly taken the liberty to urge, to persuade you to
the continuation of your *History*; in which, if you will make
some progress, however trifling, every day, I will venture to
say you will find your *immediate account* in it, in point of ease
and cheerfulness and general flow of spirits. Fame which
in some sense may be considered as a *future reward*, I will
not mention. The various and complicated miseries to which
mankind are subjected, the loss of those who are deservedly
dear to us, the precariousness of our own existence ; in short
the contemplation of every thing around us, demands a constant diversion of our attention to some object or other [3]. As
far as my experience goes I have generally, if not always
found happiness to dwell not with men of much leisure and
retirement, but with those who had a *little less* time than
they had employment for.—But if after all I can't persuade
you to betake yourself to this kind of composition, I am
sincerely sorry for it ; but will not venture, by still further
urging it, which I could easily do, to trespass upon your
patience any longer.

The half dozen of your *Philosophical Pieces* shall soon be sent you; and a dozen of your *History*, as you desire, as soon as it is finished; which will not be for some time, having hitherto made little progress in the four last vols., as almost the whole fount, and a very large one it is, has been occupied in the four first. For to keep them going, it was necessary, not only to have the sheets constantly passing *to* and *fro*, but some *composing*, and some *printing off*, which all together engrossed a vast quantity[4]. However, I will dispatch them as soon as I can.

I am very happy that you approve of what I said of the Pr. Dowager. It was written in a great hurry upon slips of paper just as the *Chronicle* was going to press. The reprehension it contains of our *worthy*[5] Patriots is surely well merited.—But to show you the obstinacy of John Bull, hardly any other newspaper copied it, nor has a sentence in her favour been written in any of them by any other person[6]. Though I am far from being of a desponding disposition, I almost begin to think, that if we go on at home vilifying and abusing all order and government, and abroad spreading famine and pestilence among those whom chance has subjected to our dominion[7], we shall soon become *ripe for destruction*.

What you have heard of the King is very true, so I have taken the hint, and inserted it, as you will see by the enclosed, in to-night's *Chronicle*[8]. I have also taken occasion to do justice to the character of Mr. Stuart[9]. What I say of him *I know* to be true.—And they say he certainly goes to India in that capacity. I have not heard Professor Ferguson named; nor am I acquainted with him, else I should have paid my respects to him at the same time,—and which, if you will enable me, I can with rather more propriety do upon a future occasion. For John Bull would not fail commenting upon two Scotchmen being praised at once in a paper printed by a *Scotchman*.—My vote[10] and any little interest I have, you may be assured shall be employed in behalf of a gentleman so warmly recommended by you. Our operations in Bengal demand a strict and speedy scrutiny. The barbarities committed upon that unhappy people are really unexampled in the history of all civilized nations, that of the Spaniards on the discovery of America [11] only excepted.—You see how little efficacy the purest precepts of Christianity itself have with mankind, when opposed to the *Auri sacra fames* [12].

I beg the continuance of your Friendship, which I prize above many Lacks of Rupees, and am with unalterable Esteem and Attachment,

Dear Sir Your faithful & obedient Serv[t]

WILL. STRAHAN.

LONDON, *Feby.* 27, 1772.

Note 1.   Boswell records an anecdote of a tradesman 'who having acquired a large fortune in London retired from business, and went to live at Worcester.   His mind being without its usual occupation, and having nothing else to supply its place, preyed upon itself, so that existence was a torment to him.   At last he was seized with the stone ; and a friend who found him in one of its severest fits having expressed his concern, " No, no, Sir," said he, " don't pity me ; what I now feel is ease compared with that torture of mind from which it relieves me."'   Boswell's *Johnson*, iii. 176.   See *ib.* ii. 337 for Johnson's story of an 'eminent tallow-chandler' in retirement.

Note 2.   Strahan was like the old lieutenant in *Tom Jones* who, when asked by Tom how the practice of duelling could be reconciled with the precepts of Christianity, replied :—'I remember I once put the case to our chaplain over a bowl of punch, and he confessed there was much difficulty in it ; but he said, he hoped there might be a latitude granted to soldiers in this one instance ; and to be sure, it is our duty to hope so ; for who would bear to live without his honour?   No, no, my dear boy, be a good Christian as long as you live ; but be a man of honour too, and never put up an affront ; not all the books, nor all the parsons in the world shall ever persuade me to that.   I love my religion very well, but I love my honour more. There must be some mistake in the wording of the text, or in the translation, or in the understanding it, or somewhere or other.   But however that be, a man must run the risk, for he must preserve his honour.'   *Tom Jones*, Bk. vii. ch. 13.

Note 3.   Strahan is perhaps repeating the advice which his friend Johnson so often enforced.   'To have the management of the mind is a great art,' he said, and he often showed Boswell how it was to be done.   Boswell's *Johnson*, ii. 440.

Note 4.   As Strahan was to forward to Hume five sheets of proofs every week, there could not have been less than ten sheets, or 160 pages, always 'passing to and fro.'   At the same time there were the perfect sheets which the printers were striking off, as well as those at which the compositors were still at work.

Note 5.   Perhaps Strahan by italicising 'worthy' implies those of the London Aldermen who were among 'the Patriots' ; for *worthy* was the honourable appellation generally applied to them. See *ante*, p. 178, n. 7.

Note 6. The *Gentleman's Magazine* in the number for March, p. 122, praised her in terms not less extravagant than Strahan's. Nay it went farther, and spoke of Frederick Prince of Wales as 'the best of husbands.'

Note 7. See *ante*, p. 238, *n.* 8. Horace Walpole, writing on April 9 of this year about Charles Fox's dissolute life and 'manly reason,' says :—'We beat Rome in eloquence and extravagance ; and Spain in avarice and cruelty ; and, like both, we shall only serve to terrify schoolboys, and for lessons of morality ! " Here stood St. Stephen's Chapel ; here young Catiline spoke ; here was Lord Clive's diamond-house ; this is Leadenhall Street, and this broken column was part of the palace of a company of merchants who were sovereigns of Bengal ! They starved millions in India by monopolies and plunder, and almost raised a famine at home by the luxury occasioned by their opulence, and by that opulence raising the price of everything, till the poor could not purchase bread." Conquest, usurpation, wealth, luxury, famine—one knows how little farther the genealogy has to go !' Walpole's *Letters*, v. 381.

Note 8. 'We are assured that a parliamentary enquiry into the conduct of the East India Company in Bengal was originally proposed by his Majesty himself, who was greatly shocked with the accounts he received of the oppressions exercised over the poor natives. It is indeed abundantly notorious that the behaviour of our countrymen in that extensive and once rich and populous region has been for some years past so cruel and barbarous as to call aloud to Heaven itself for a most speedy and effectual remedy.' *London Chronicle*, Feb. 27, 1772.

Note 9. 'We hear that all parties who have any influence in the conduct of our India affairs are unanimous in their choice of Andrew Stuart, Esq. of Berkeley-square to be one of the Supervisors. A Gentleman every way well qualified for that most important office ; as he possesses &c.' *Ib.* We may be reminded by Strahan's puff of his countrymen of what Johnson says in his *Life of Mallet* :—' It was remarked of Mallet that he was the only Scot whom Scotchmen did not commend.' *Works*, viii. 464.

Note 10. Strahan must be speaking of his vote at the India House, for he was not in Parliament till November, 1774.

Note 11. 'In the same year, in a year hitherto disastrous to mankind, by the Portuguese was discovered the passage of the Indies, and by the Spaniards the coast of America.' Johnson's *Works*, vi. 233.

Note 12. Virgil, *Æneid*, iii. 57.

'Gold-hunger cursed.' Morris.

LETTER LXI.

The Licentiousness of Patriots.

Dear S[ir]

If the Press has not got further than the 160th page of the sixth Volume, Line penult., there is a Passage which I shoud desire to have restord. It is this : *The full prosecution of this noble Principle into all its natural Consequences has, at last, through many contests, produced that singular* and happy *Government which we enjoy at present*[1].

I own that I was so disgusted with the Licentiousness of our odious Patriots, that I have struck out the words, *and happy*, in this new Edition ; but as the English Government is certainly happy, though probably not calculated for Duration, by reason of its excessive Liberty, I believe it will be as well to restore them : But if that Sheet be already printed, it is not worth while to attend to the matter. I am as well pleas'd that this Instance of Spleen and Indignation shoud remain.

I am Dear S[ir] Yours sincerely

DAVID HUME.

EDINBURGH, 3 *of March*, 1772.

Note 1. The passage was restored, and 'Government' remained 'happy.' See Hume's *History*, ed. 1802, vi. 144. In the preceding sentence he had been describing the declaratory bill against monopolies passed in the year 1624. He continues :—'It was there supposed that every subject of England had entire power to dispose of his own actions, provided he did no injury to any of his fellow-subjects ; and that no prerogative of the King, no power of any magistrate, nothing but the authority alone of laws could restrain that unlimited freedom. The full prosecution &c.'

LETTER LXII.

The proposed Continuation of the History.

Dear S[r]

I am much oblig'd to you for your Attention in returning me the Proof Sheets: But I never doubted of your Exactness in following my Corrections which were also, in part, your own[1]. I had unfortunately bespoke most of the Smith Work of my new house; but I still found a small Job to give Mr. Richardson, who seems to me a clever young Fellow. I remove in little more than two Months. If I find my Time lie heavy on my hands, I may, for my Amusement, undertake a reign or two after the Revolution[2]: But I believe, in case of my composing any more, I had better write something that has no Reference to the Affairs of these factious Barbarians[3].

I am Dear S[ir] Yours sincerely
D. H.

5 *of March*, 1772.

Note 1. Strahan, no doubt thinking of Hume's suspicions of him—his ' want of faith' as he called it—had returned him the proof sheets of his *History*, so that he might see that all his corrections had been followed.

Note 2. Gibbon on Aug. 7, 1773, wrote to his friend Holroyd at Edinburgh :—' You tell me of a long list of dukes, lords, and chieftains of renown to whom you are introduced ; were I with you, I should prefer one *David* to them all. When you are at Edinburgh, I hope you will not fail to visit the sty of that fattest of Epicurus's hogs, and inform yourself whether there remains no hope of its recovering the use of its right paw.' Gibbon's *Misc. Works*, ii. 110. See *post*, p. 253, for Hume's resolution to write no more.

Note 3. Hume's abuse of the English recalls a passage in Boswell's *Life of Johnson*, iii. 170, where Boswell says :—' I ventured to mention [to Dr. Johnson] a person who was as violent a Scotsman as he was an Englishman ; and literally had the same contempt for an Englishman compared with a Scotsman that he had for a Scotsman compared with an Englishman ; and that he would say of

Dr. Johnson, "Damned rascal! to talk as he does of the Scotch."
This seemed for a moment "to give him pause." It perhaps presented his extreme prejudice against the Scotch in a point of view
somewhat new to him, by the effect of *contrast.*'

LETTER LXIII.

Captain Brydone: Hume's House in St. Andrew's Square.

DEAR SⁱR

You will please to send this Letter to Mr. Cadel,
which I have left open for your Perusal.

There is a Friend of mine, Capⁿ Braiden, who has writ,
in the form of Letters, his Travels thro Sicily and Malta [1] :
They are very curious and agreeable; and I as well as
others of his Friends have advisd him to publish them;
and I also advisd him, to carry them to you. If you read
them I hope we shall agree in Opinion. I conjecture
they may make one Volume a little less than a Volume of
the Spectator [2].

I am Dear Sⁱʳ Yours sincerely

DAVID HUME.

St. Andrews Square [3], 3 *of June*, 1772.

Note 1. Captain Patrick Brydone published in the spring of 1773
(*Gent. Mag.* 1773, p. 242) his *Tour through Sicily and Malta, in a Series
of Letters to William Beckford, Esq. of Somerly in Suffolk.* Boswell
(*Life of Johnson*, ii. 468) mentions ' an antimosaical remark introduced
into Captain Brydone's entertaining tour, I hope heedlessly, from a
kind of vanity which is too common in those who have not sufficiently
studied the most important of all subjects.' Brydone had met at
Catania a Canon, Recupero by name, who had measured in a draw-
well 'the strata of lavas, with earth to a considerable thickness over
the surface of each stratum. Recupero has made use of this as
an argument to prove the great antiquity of the eruptions of his mountain [Etna]. For if it requires two thousand years or upwards to
form but a scanty soil on the surface of a lava, there must have been
more than that space of time betwixt each of the eruptions which
have formed these strata. . . He tells me he is exceedingly em-

barrassed by these discoveries in writing the history of the mountain;—that Moses hangs like a dead weight upon him, and blunts all
his zeal for enquiry; for that really he has not the conscience to
make his mountain so young as that prophet makes the world. What
do you think of these sentiments from a Roman Catholic divine?
The bishop, who is strenuously orthodox—for it is an excellent see—
has already warned him to be upon his guard, and not to pretend to
be a better natural historian than Moses.' Brydone's *Tour*, ed. 1790,
i. 141. Johnson remarked on this passage:—'Shall all the accumulated evidence of the history of the world, shall the authority of what
is unquestionably the most ancient writing be overturned by an
uncertain remark such as this?' Boswell's *Johnson*, ii. 468. At
another time he said:—'If Brydone were more attentive to his
Bible he would be a good traveller.' *Ib.* iii. 356.

Cowper, writing to Joseph Hill on April 20, 1777, says:—'Thanks
for a turbot, a lobster, and Captain Brydone; a gentleman who relates his travels so agreeably that he deserves always to travel with
an agreeable companion.' Cowper's *Works*, xv. 38.

Horace Walpole, describing on Oct. 10, 1780 an evening that he
had spent at a lady's house, says:—'Lord and Lady North were
there, *en cour plénière*, with . . . . and Brydone, the Sicilian traveller,
who having wriggled himself into Bushy [Lord North's house] will,
I suppose, soon be an envoy, like so many other Scots.' *Letters*, vii.
451. Mr. Scott of Gala describes a conversation which he had with
Sir Walter Scott in the autumn of 1831, who had come to London on
his way to the Mediterranean. '"I paid a visit," said Sir Walter, "to
my friend Whittaker [the bookseller] to ask him for some book of
travels likely to be of use to me on my expedition to the Mediterranean. Here's old Brydone accordingly, still as good a companion
as any he could recommend. Brydone was sadly failed during his
latter years. Did you ever hear of his remark on his own works?"
"Never." "Why his family usually read a little for his amusement of an evening; and on one occasion he was asked if he would
like to hear some of his travels to Sicily. He assented, and seemed
to listen with much pleasure for some time, but he was too far gone
to continue his attention long, and starting up from a doze exclaimed,
"That's really a very amusing book, and contains many curious
anecdotes. I wonder if they are all true."' Lockhart's *Life of Scott*,
ed. 1839, x. 109.

Note 2. Almost all the editions of *The Spectator* were in eight
volumes, octavo.

Note 3. Hume had moved from James's Court in the Old Town to
his new house in the New Town. 'I charge you,' he wrote to a
friend, 'not to think of settling in London, till you have first seen our
New Town, which exceeds anything you have seen in any part of the
world.' Burton's *Hume*, ii. 462. Samuel Rogers, who visited Edinburgh in July, 1789, made the following entry in his Journal:—'July 16,

1789. Adam Smith said that Edinburgh deserved little notice ; that
the old town had given Scotland a bad name; that he was anxious
to move into the new town. . . . He said that in Paris as well as in
Edinburgh the houses were piled one upon another.' *Early Life of
Samuel Rogers*, p. 92. The new town was laid out on the plan of ' the
ingenious architect,' Mr. Craig, nephew of the poet Thomson. Boswell's *Johnson*, iii. 360. Hume was one of the earliest settlers. His
house, which he had been nearly two years in building (*ante*, p. 171,
n. 22), looks northward into St. Andrew's Square and westward into
St. David Street, or as he wrote it St. David's Street.   Dr. J. H. Burton says that the street got its name from the daughter of Chief
Baron Ord, ' a witty young lady, who chalked on the wall of Hume's
house the words "St. David Street." The allusion was very obvious.   Hume's "lass" [maid-servant], judging that it was not
meant in honour or reverence, ran into the house much excited,
to tell her master how he was made game of. " Never mind, lassie,"
he said ; " many a better man has been made a saint of before." ' Burton's *Hume*, ii. 436. I have noticed that his earlier letters written
from his new house he dates ' St. Andrew's Square.' This address
he gives in his letter of Sept. 20, 1775 (Burton's *Hume*, ii. 475) ; but
on Oct. 27 of the same year he writes ' St. David's Street ' (*ib.* p. 478).
It is likely that Miss Ord had christened the street in the interval.
Hume's adoption of the new name shows that he was pleased with it.
Perhaps his is the only instance of a man who preferred to name his
house, not after the fashionable square into which the front of it
looked, but after a side street.   In the codicil to his will, dated August
7, 1776, he shows his kindness for the young lady :—' I leave to Mrs.
Anne Ord, daughter of the late Chief Baron, ten guineas to buy a
Ring, as a Memorial of my Friendship and Attachment to so amiable
and accomplished a Person.' *M. S. R. S. E.* The Court of Exchequer
of Scotland, of which the Judges were the High Treasurer of Great
Britain, with a Chief Baron and four other Barons, was established by
the 6th Anne, cap. 26. *Penny Cyclo.* x. 110.   Lord Cockburn in his
Memorials, pp. 295-300, describing the introduction into Scotland in
the year 1816 of a Jury Court in civil cases, says :—' One great outcry
against this Court at first was excited by our being required to adopt
the English *unanimity* of juries. We had been accustomed to it for
above a century in the Exchequer, which was an English Court. But
its sittings were solely in Edinburgh, and its verdicts were of a penal
nature.' Writing of the year 1830 he says (*ib.* p. 466) :—' Nobody
could dream of making judicial work out of our Exchequer sufficient
to give occupation even to a single judge.'

(Letter enclosed to Mr. Cadell.)

LETTER LXIV.

The new Editions of the Essays and History.

EDINBURGH, 3 *of June*, 1772.

DEAR S[r]

I have receivd a Copy of the new Edition of my Essays[1] and the four first Volumes of my History, with both which I am very well pleasd with regard to the Paper and Print. I have carefully perusd the Essays, and find them very correct, with fewer Errors of the Press, than I almost ever saw in any book ; and I give you, as well as Mr. Strahan, thanks for the care that has been taken of them. The four Volumes of History passd thro' my own hands ; so that nothing needs be said of them. I fancy the other Volumes will not be finishd ; so as to be publish'd this Season ; but they will be ready early in the Winter[2].

I am Dear S[ir] Your most obedient humble Servant

DAVID HUME.

Note 1. Of this edition I cannot find any mention in any catalogue. Strahan in his letter of Feb. 27 of this year (*ante*, p. 244) speaks of it as nearly ready.

Note 2. By 'the other Volumes' Hume means the last four volumes of his History. The whole work was ready for publication in the following March.

LETTER LXV.

Dr. Percy offended by a Passage in the History.

EDINBURGH, 16 *of Jany.*, 1773.

Dear Sir

You have been guilty of a small Indiscretion in allowing a Copy of my new Edition to go out before the

Publication: For I had a Letter yesterday from Mr. Piercy[1], complaining tho' in obliging terms, of the Note with regard to the old Earl of Northumberland Household book; as if it were a Satyre on that particular Nobleman, which was by no means my Intention: I only meant to paint the manners of the Age[2]. I reply'd to him, that I fancy'd it was too late to correct my Expressions; for that the Work was probably in the hands of the public. I hope it is; or at least beg it may be soon. I know I have no right to demand any account of your Sales: I only entreat you to tell me precisely, as far as you can, the time of your publication; and also when you can send off the Copies for me. You told me in a former Letter that you heard I was continuing my History: I beg of you to believe that such an extravagant and absurd Idea never once enterd into my head.

I am very sincerly Yours

D. H.

Note 1. Dr. Thomas Percy, afterwards Dean of Carlisle and Bishop of Dromore, the author of *Reliques of Ancient English Poetry*. He spelt his name Percy, and not Piercy. He wrote to Hume:—'The name is not, nor ever was, properly written Piercy.' *M. S. R. S. E.* Hume however keeps to his own way of spelling. Mr. H. B. Wheatley in the Preface to his edition of the *Reliques* says (p. lxxi): —'Percy's father and grandfather were grocers, spelt their name Piercy, and knew nothing of any connection with the noble house of Northumberland.' The Bishop boasted however of being the heir male of the ancient Percies. Boswell had examined the proofs of this claim, and says, ' Both as a lawyer accustomed to the consideration of evidence, and as a genealogist versed in the study of pedigrees, I am fully satisfied.' Boswell's *Johnson*, iii. 271. Percy, for the honour of his line, some years later on withstood Johnson, as he now withstood Hume. Johnson had praised Pennant's *Tour in Scotland*. 'Percy,' says Boswell, 'could not sit quietly and hear a man praised who had spoken disrespectfully of Alnwick Castle and the Duke's pleasure grounds, especially as he thought meanly of his travels.' The result was an explosion, in which Johnson cried out,—' Hold, Sir ! Don't talk of rudeness; remember, Sir, you told me (puffing hard with passion struggling for a vent) I was short-sighted. We have done with civility. We are to be as rude as we please.' *Ib.*

Note 2. Hume at the end of his chapter on the reign of Henry VII says :—' It must be acknowledged, in spite of those who declaim so violently against refinement in the arts, or what they are pleased to call luxury, that as much as an industrious tradesman is both a better man and a better citizen than one of those idle retainers who formerly depended on the great families ; so much is the life of a modern nobleman more laudable than that of an ancient baron.' *History of England*, ed. 1802, iii. 400. As a note he added (p. 460) the extract from the Household Book of the fifth Earl of Northumberland. Dr. Percy, in a letter to Hume dated Jan 5, 1772 [an error for 1773], complaining that he called 'the management of the Earl's family niggardly,' maintains that 'what might appear extremely penurious now, might at that time have been exceedingly liberal.' To prove this he proposes to examine the accounts of other households, and begs Hume 'to suspend his asperities till the next edition.' Hume, as is shown by his next letter to Strahan, overcome by Percy's 'very obliging manner' and wishful to avoid giving the family 'great offence,' has the note reprinted. What was struck out besides *niggardly* I do not know. Enough however remains to have stirred up the Percy blood, had any great quantity of it flowed in the veins of the modern Percies. 'My Lord,' he writes, 'passes the year in three country seats, all in Yorkshire ; but he has furniture only for one. He carries everything along with him, beds, tables, chairs, kitchen utensils, all which we may conclude were so coarse that they could not be spoilt by the carriage. Yet seventeen carts and one waggon suffices for the whole. . . . It is amusing to observe the pompous and even royal style assumed by this Tartar chief: he does not give any orders, though only for the right making of mustard, but it is introduced with this preamble, *It seemeth good to us and our council.*' *Ib.* p. 463. In the Errata to the edition of 1773 Hume still further 'suspends his asperities ;' but in the last edition, in two instances, he shows that it was merely a suspense. He writes :—' After the words *this time*, read, it was Henry Algernon Percy, fifth earl of Northumberland, a nobleman no less distinguished by his personal merit than by the greatness of his family, one of the noblest in Europe.' This correction is omitted in the edition of 1778. In the description given on p. 462 of the linen in the Earl's household he had said :—' This linen was made into eight table-cloths for my lord's table, and one table-cloth for the knights. This last, I suppose, was washed only once a month.' In the Errata he says 'dele these words.' They are nevertheless allowed to stand in the edition of 1778. It was not by accident that this was done, for some of the corrections in the same passage were made in the later edition.

LETTER LXVI.

Brydone's Travels: Hume's Continuators: Tristram
Shandy: Andrew Stuart.

EDINBURGH, 30 *Jany*, 1773.

Dear S[IR]

I find you must reprint all that Note about the Northumberland House-hold Book. The Alterations I make are very little material; but being requir'd in a very obliging manner by Dr. Piercy, and, I suppose, by the Family[1], I could not now refuse them, without giving them great Offence, which I wish to avoid.

I have likewise sent you one Addition to the Errata. The Passage at present is Nonsense, tho' I find it has escap'd me in three Editions, notwithstanding it was printed right at first[2]. Be so good as to insert it in its proper place; as I suppose the Errata is not printed.

I never, that I remember, mention'd to Cap[n] Braidon any particular Sum which he might expect[3], as I receivd his Manuscript in Parcels and coud form no Estimate of its Bulk. His Journey over Mount Etna is the most curious part of it; and I wish it be not anticipated by a late German Work which is translated, but I have not read it[4]. I recommended to Mr. Braidon to obliterate some Levities, too much in the Shandean Style[5], which he promis'd to do. I do hope with these Corrections, it will be thought a good readable Book and curious[6].

Considering the Treatment I have met with[7], it woud have been very silly for me at my Years to continue writing any more; and still more blameable to warp my Principles and Sentiments in conformity to the Prejudices of a stupid, factious Nation, with whom I am heartily dis-gusted[8]. I wish my Continuators[9] good Success; tho' I

believe they have sence enough not to care whether they
meet with it or not. Macpherson has Style and Spirit; but
is hot-headed, and consequently without Judgement[10].
The Knight[11] has Spirit, but no Style, and still less Judgement than the other. I shoud think Dr. Douglas[12], if he
woud undertake it, a better hand than either. Or what
think you of Andrew Stuart[13]? For as to any Englishman, that Nation is so sunk in Stupidity and Barbarism
and Faction that you may as well think of Lapland[14] for
an Author. The best Book, that has been writ by any
Englishman these thirty Years (for Dr. Franklyn is an
American) is Tristram Shandy, bad as it is[15]. A Remark
which may astonish you; but which you will find true on
Reflection[16].

I admire very much this Work of Andrew Stuart[17];
tho I was at first exceedingly alarmd at the Imprudence
of the Attempt. I am less so, after perusing it; tho still
it appears imprudent, according to the vulgar Rule of
estimating these Matters.

I woud have you publish this new Edition as soon as it
is ready; and rather submit to some Loss than allow the
Book to be any longer discredited by that abominable
Edition[18], which has given you and me so much Vexation,
and has been one Cause why I have thrown my Pen aside
for ever.

Believe me ever Yours

D. H.[19]

Note 1. The Duke of Northumberland had little concern in the
matter, for he was not a Percy, but a Smithson. He had married the
great-grand-daughter of the eleventh and last Earl of Northumberland. . Horace Walpole wrote on Feb. 25, 1750 :—' Sir Hugh Smithson and Sir Charles Windham are Earls of Northumberland and
Egremont, with vast estates; the former title, revived for the blood
of Percy, has the misfortune of being coupled with the blood of a man
that either let or drove coaches—such was Sir Hugh's grandfather ! '
Letters, ii. 196. The name of Sir Hugh Smithson I have often read
on the list of benefactors to the poor in the parish church of Totten-

ham High Cross. The district in that parish ridiculously called Northumberland Park, for there neither is nor ever was a park, takes its name from a house which belonged to the Smithsons.

Note 2. This passage is, I think, the following, in which Hume describes Lewis XIV's liberality in rewarding literary merit :—' Besides pensions conferred on learned men throughout all Europe, his academies were directed by rules and supported by salaries: A generosity which does great honour to his memory ; and in the eyes of all the *ingenuous* part of mankind will be esteemed an atonement for many of the errors of his reign.' Ed. 1773, viii. 330. *Ingenuous* is a misprint for *ingenious*. In the first edition I find *ingenious*, but in the quarto edition of 1770 *ingenuous*.

Note 3. Strahan had written to Hume on Jan. 25 :—'I have at length agreed, but after much difficulty with Capt. Brydon. You had raised his Expectations so very high, and so much beyond the real Worth of the Book, which will hardly make two Octavo Volumes very loosely printed, that he could not be satisfied with the very utmost the Size and Nature of the Book would admit of. You spoil all young Authors by leading them to expect Prices only due to Veterans in Literature, and Men of established Reputation.' *M. S. R. S. E.*

Note 4. *Travels through Sicily and part of Italy, by Baron Riedesel.* Translated from the German by John Forster. London, 1773.

Note 5. Johnson the year before, speaking of a book of travels, had said that it was an imitation of Sterne. Boswell's *Johnson,* ii. 175.

Note 6. As an example of Brydone's style I will quote the following story:—' Do you remember old Huet—the greatest of all originals? One day, as he passed the statue of Jupiter in the Capitol, he pulled off his hat, and made him a bow. A Jacobite gentleman who observed it asked him, why he paid so much respect to that old gentleman. "For the same reason," replied Huet, "that you pay so much to the Pretender. Besides," added he, "I think there is rather a greater probability that his turn will come round again than that of your hero. I shall therefore endeavour to keep well with him, and hope he will never forget that I took notice of him in the time of his adversity." ' Vol. i. p. 158.

Note 7. He had been appointed to high offices, and had retired on a pension of £400 a year, with a request from the King that he would continue his *History* (*ante*, p. 55). He had been paid for it, as he boasted, at a higher rate than any previous writer (*ante*, p. 33, *n.* 2), and for its continuation he was told that the booksellers were ready to give him whatever sum he chose to name (*ante*, p. 54). These unmanly complaints are in striking contrast with Johnson's contentment. 'I asked him,' writes Boswell, ' if he was not dissatisfied with having so small a share of wealth, and none of those distinctions in the state which are the objects of ambition. He had only a pension of three hundred a year. Why was he not in such circumstances as to keep his coach? Why had he not some considerable office?

S

JOHNSON. " Sir, I have never complained of the world ; nor do I think that I have reason to complain. It is rather to be wondered at that I have so much." ' Boswell's *Johnson*, iv. 116.

Note 8. Three years later Hume wrote to Gibbon, on reading the first volume of the *Decline and Fall*:—' Whether I consider the dignity of your style, the depth of your matter, or the extensiveness of your learning, I must regard the work as equally the object of esteem ; and I own, that if I had not previously had the happiness of your personal acquaintance, such a performance from an Englishman in our age would have given me some surprise. You may smile at this sentiment, but as it seems to me that your countrymen, for almost a whole generation, have given themselves up to barbarous and absurd faction, and have totally neglected all polite letters, I no longer expected any valuable production ever to come from them.' The high position that Hume held among men of learning is shown by what Gibbon has recorded :—' A letter from Mr. Hume overpaid the labour of ten years.' *Misc. Works*, i. 224.

Hume has the less excuse for the outburst in the text against the factiousness of the English, as Strahan in his last letter, dated Jan. 25, had said :—' Our pretended patriots are either asleep or appear to be so. In short Wilkes and Liberty are heard of no more.' *M. S. R. S. E.*

Note 9. Strahan had written to Hume on Jan. 25 :—' After what you now tell me I altogether despair of seeing a continuation of your History from yourself ; but I have some notion it may be done by some other hand ; perhaps Sir John Dalrymple or Mr. Macpherson.' *M. S. R. S. E.* The latter volumes of Smollett's *History* have been so generally taken by the booksellers as a continuation of Hume, that it is commonly believed that he was, as an historian, merely his ' continuator.' He had however published his *Complete History of England from the descent of Julius Cæsar to the Treaty of Aix-la-Chapelle, 1748*, before Hume had done more than bring out the *History of England under the Stuarts*. Hume however had completed his work before Smollett, with the help of William Guthrie, published the five concluding volumes which carried down his *History* to the year 1765. On March 12, 1759, Hume wrote to Dr. Robertson, whose *History of Scotland* had just been published :—' A plague take you ! Here I sat near the historical summit of Parnassus, immediately under Dr. Smollett ; and you have the impudence to squeeze yourself by me, and place yourself directly under his feet.' Burton's *Hume*, ii. 53. This was not Hume's real opinion. He knew his superiority as an historian to Smollett, who in fourteen months had written the history of eighteen centuries. Writing to Millar on April 6, 1758, Hume said : —' I am afraid that the extraordinary run upon Dr. Smollett has a little hurt your sales. But these things are only temporary.' *M. S. R. S. E.*

Note 10. Hume wrote to Adam Smith on April 10, 1773 :—' Have

you seen Macpherson's *Homer*? It is hard to tell whether the attempt
or the execution be worse. I hear he is employed by the booksellers
to continue my History. But, in my opinion, of all men of parts he
has the most anti-historical head in the universe.' Burton's *Hume*,
ii. 467. See *ante*, p. 36, *n.* 1, and *post*, Letter of Nov. 13, 1775.

Note 11. Sir John Dalrymple of Cranston was more than a
knight; he was a baronet. See *ante*, p. 180, *n.* 22, for Johnson's
criticism of his *Memoirs*. He ridiculed his style also when he and
Boswell were on their way to his house, where they had been invited
to dine and spend the night. They had loitered so much that they
could not, they saw, arrive in time for dinner. 'When I talked,' writes
Boswell, 'of the grievous disappointment it must have been to him
that we did not come to the *feast* that he had prepared for us, (for he
told us he had killed a seven-year old sheep on purpose,) my friend got
into a merry mood, and jocularly said, "I dare say, Sir, he has been
very sadly distressed: Nay, we do not know but the consequence
may have been fatal. Let me try to describe his situation in his own
historical style: . . .—"Dinner being ready, he wondered that his
guests were not yet come. His wonder was soon succeeded by impatience. He walked about the room in anxious agitation; sometimes
he looked at his watch, sometimes he looked out at the window with
an eager gaze of expectation, and revolved in his mind the various
accidents of human life. His family beheld him with mute concern.
'Surely (said he with a sigh) they will not fail me.' The mind of man
can bear a certain pressure; but there is a point when it can bear no
more. A rope was in his view; and he died a Roman death."' *Ib.*
v. 403. There is a hit at him in the *Parl. Hist.* xvii. 963, in the
report of the proceedings in the Lords on the question of literary
property on Feb. 7, 1774. He was heard as counsel for the de-
fendants, 'and spoke for two hours and a half, and seemed to exhaust
in this one speech all the knowledge, metaphysical, legal, chemical,
and political he possesses.'

Note 12. Dr. John Douglas, afterwards Bishop of Salisbury, whom
Goldsmith in *Retaliation* describes as 'The scourge of impostors, the
terror of quacks.' See Boswell's *Johnson*, i. 228, 407. In Samuel
Rogers's *Table Talk*, p. 106, it is recorded that 'Hume told Cadell,
the bookseller, that he had a great desire to be introduced to as
many of the persons who had written against him as could be
collected. Accordingly, Dr. Douglas, Dr. Adams, etc., were invited
by Cadell to dine at his house, in order to meet Hume. They came;
and Dr. Price, who was of the party, assured me that they were all
delighted with David.' Dr. Douglas had edited the *Correspondence of
the second Earl of Clarendon and of his brother the Earl of Rochester,
etc.* Hume wrote to Millar on Oct. 27, 1760:—'I am very much
pleased with what you tell me, that the Clarendon Papers have fallen
into Dr. Douglas's hands, especially as Dr. Robertson tells me he
intends to publish them.' Burton's *Hume*, ii. 87.

Note 13. See *ante*, p. 239, *n.* 9. Hume suggests none but Scotchmen. Even Goldsmith is not mentioned, though he was not an Englishman and 'a factious barbarian,' and though his '*History*,' if we may trust Johnson, 'is better than the *verbiage* of Robertson, or the foppery of Dalrymple.' Boswell's *Johnson*, ii. 236.

Note 14. See *ante*, p. 63, for a letter in which Horace Walpole, writing of the Scotch, says :—Do not let us be run down and brazened out of all our virtue, genius, sense, and taste by Laplanders and Bœotians, who never produced one original writer in verse or prose.' *Letters*, vii. 511. At the time when Hume wrote of England that 'you may as well think of Lapland for an author,' there certainly was a dearth of eminent writers who were Englishmen by birth. In the previous ten years had died Churchill, Young, Sterne, Chatterton and Gray. Johnson, Warburton, Blackstone, Horace Walpole, and Lord Chesterfield were living, but the fame of the last two chiefly rests on their Letters which were not as yet published. Cowper, Crabbe, Gibbon, Jeremy Bentham, and Miss Burney had begun to publish before another ten years had run out. Wordsworth and Coleridge, though born, were still too young even 'to lisp in numbers.' Burke, Goldsmith, and R. B. Sheridan, who brought out his first play two years later, must be excluded as they were Irish by origin. Scotland boasted of Hume, Boswell, Adam Smith, Robertson, Beattie, Blair, Henry, Henry Mackenzie, Reid, the Dalrymples, Ferguson, Kames and Monboddo ; but many of these, instead of lasting as 'northern lights,' have turned out to be 'mere farthing candles' (Boswell's *Johnson*, v. 57). Smollett had been dead rather more than a year, Burns was a boy of fourteen, and Scott an infant.

Note 15. Johnson said of Sterne's great work :—'Nothing odd will do long. *Tristram Shandy* did not last.' Boswell's *Johnson*, ii. 449. Horace Walpole spoke of it as 'a very insipid and tedious performance'; 'the dregs of nonsense, which have universally met the contempt they deserve.' *Letters*, iii. 298, 382. Goldsmith in the *Citizen of the World* (Letter 74) called the author 'a bawdy blockhead.' Speaking of him to Johnson, he said he was 'a very dull fellow'; to which Johnson replied, 'Why, no, Sir.' Boswell's *Johnson*, ii. 222. Voltaire looked on Sterne as 'le second Rabelais d'Angleterre'; Swift being the first. *Œuvres de Voltaire*, ed. 1819-25, xxxiv. 513.

Note 16. The exception of Franklin has a somewhat comical effect when we call to mind that in 'these thirty years' had been published *Clarissa* and *Sir Charles Grandison*, *Tom Jones* and *Amelia*, the great *Dictionary*, the *Rambler* and *Rasselas*, Collins's *Odes*, and all Gray's *Poems*. It is highly probable however that Hume, who was a thorough Frenchman in his love of paying pretty compliments, thought that this passage would be shown to Franklin. Strahan had added as a postscript to his last letter, which Hume had just received :—' Dr. Franklin, who sits at my elbow, desires to be affectionately remembered to you and to your worthy sister, who was so kind to him.' *M. S. R. S. E.*

Hume, writing to Adam Smith on April 1, 1776, about the first volume of Gibbon's *Decline and Fall*, said :—'I should never have expected such an excellent work from the pen of an Englishman. It is lamentable to consider how much that nation has declined in literature during our time.' Burton's *Hume*, ii. 487. Voltaire, the year following, in a short criticism on the French translation of *Tristram Shandy*, said :—' Il eût été à désirer que le prédicateur n'eût fait son comique roman que pour apprendre aux Anglais à ne plus se laisser duper par la charlatanerie des romanciers, et qu'il eût pu corriger la nation qui tombe depuis long-temps, abandonne l'étude des Locke et des Newton pour les ouvrages les plus extravagans et les plus frivoles.' *Œuvres de Voltaire*, xlii. 430.

Note 17. Andrew Stuart's *Letters to Lord Mansfield.* See *ante*, p. 239, *n.* 9. Hume on Feb. 24 of this year, advising Adam Smith to buy this work, says :—'They have, they say, met with vast success in London. Andrew has eased his own mind, and no bad effects are to follow. Lord Mansfield is determined absolutely to neglect them.' Burton's *Hume*, ii. 466. ' Dr. Johnson maintained that this publication would not give any uneasiness to the Judge. " For (said he) either he acted honestly, or he meant to do injustice. If he acted honestly, his own consciousness will protect him ; if he meant to do injustice, he will be glad to see the man who attacks him so much vexed ! " ' Boswell's *Johnson*, ii. 475.

Note 18. See *ante*, p. 141, *n.* 7.

Note 19. Hume is so full of his own affairs that he forgets to congratulate Strahan on the following piece of family news in a letter dated Jan. 25 :—' My son George is now Vicar of Islington, with an income of between £300 and £400 a year; a populous and increasing parish, within half an hour's walk of my own house. The purchase however cost a good deal of money, though less than these things usually come to.' *M. S. R. S. E.* It was to George Strahan's vicarage that ' Johnson went sometimes for the benefit of good air.' Boswell's *Johnson*, iv. 271.

LETTER LXVII.

Proposed Continuation of the History.

EDINBURGH,'22 *of Feby.*, 1773.

DEAR SIR

On reviewing your last Letter and recollecting my Answer to it, I am afraid some mistake might arise between us. No doubt, any body, either from their own

Inclination or from your Application, may undertake to write any part of English History they please; and I can have no Objection to it: But that this Work should be publishd as a Continuation of mine, I see liable to considerable Objections; and it is necessary for me to deliberate well upon it. If it be either much better or much worse than mine, it might be improper, for my own credit, to consent to it; and as long as both the Performance and the Author are unknown to me, I cannot without farther deliberation go so far. I beg, therefore, that this Matter may be fully understood between us, and that nothing I have said may be interpreted as my Approbation of a Scheme, which is totally unknown to me.

I desire much to ask you a Question, which, if the Matter depended solely on you, I know you coud answer me in a moment. But as it is, you can easily, by consulting your Partners, be able to give me Satisfaction in it. In short, I wish to know precisely, whether you intend to publish the new Edition this Season or the Season after, or any subsequent Season. It is needless to say any thing about the Index which coud have been ready long ago. I beg it of you, I even conjure you, to give me at last some Answer which I can depend on. I promise you, that this is the last time I shall write to you on the Subject.

I am Dear Sir

Your most humble and most obedient Servant

DAVID HUME.

LETTER LXVIII.

All Faith lost in Cadell and Strahan.

EDINBURGH, 15 *of March*, 1773.

DEAR Sir

The Number of Copies of my History, which I desir'd to have, was twelve. I agreed with Mr. Millar verbally to reserve six on every new Edition; but as I had taken uncommon Pains on this Edition, I proposd twelve, which you very frankly agreed to [1]: I desire one copy to be sent to Lord Beauchamp [2] with my Compliments, and the rest to be shipt off to this Place with the first convenient Opportunity.

You and Mr. Cadel had so much lost all faith with me, that indeed I thought it was impossible for you any longer to deceive me [3]: Yet when you mention'd a new Edition, I own I was so simple as to believe, that all the old one was nearly sold off. This woud have been very blameable in you, if you had proposd any other End than that of seducing me into the continuing of my work, which you thought, and probably with Reason, woud have been for my own Advantage in more respects than one. But however the Consequence is, that I am now at a Loss, and ever shall remain so, what I am to think and believe: And many Questions, interesting to me, which I wishd to ask you, woud, I find, be entirely vain and fruitless; and therefore I shall forbear them, since I can give no manner of credit to the Answers. A very little time will make me totally indifferent about these Matters, which is the State of Mind that I have nearly attain'd already. I only desire that before you begin any new Edition of any of my Writings, you give me Information some time beforehand.

I am Dear S[r] Your most obedient Servant

DAVID HUME.

Note 1. See *ante*, p. 213.
Note 2. See *ante*, p. 203, *n.* 6.
Note 3. See *ante*, pp. 144, 150, 154.

LETTER LXIX.

Dalrymple's Memoirs: Memoirs of King James II.

EDINBURGH, 20 *of March*, 1773.

DEAR SⁱR

I have read twice over all Sir John Dalrymple's new Publication[1], which contains many curious Papers[2]; but it gives me great Satisfaction to find, that there is not one single Mistake in my History, either great or small, which it gives me occasion to correct. I could only wish to have an Opportunity of adding one Note in order to correct a mistake into which Sir John is very anxious to lead his Readers, as if the French Intrigues had had a sensible Influence in the Determinations of the English Parliament[3]: And I believe it is not too late even yet to annex it. I remember Mr. Millar added a similar Note to the last Octavo Edition drawn from K. James's Memoirs[4]; and it was inserted in more than the half of the Copies. I have sent you the Note, which I beg may be printed on a Leaf apart, and annexd to all the Copies afterwards disposd of, and even sent to all the Booksellers that have purchasd any considerable Numbers, as well as joind to my own Copies.

I hear you have given Sir John 2000 pounds for the Property of this Volume, which I scarcely believe[5]. The Book is curious, but far from being agreeable Reading; and the Sale will probably be all at first. I again repeat my Entreaties that this Note may be annexd.

I am Dear SⁱR Very sincerely Yours

DAVID HUME.

Note 1. This letter, though written a day later than Strahan's answer to Hume's letter of the 15th, had not, of course, been received by Strahan when he wrote. I therefore give it before the next letter in the series.

Note 2. This must be the second volume of Dalrymple's *Memoirs of Great Britain and Ireland,* for the first was published in the spring of 1771 (*ante,* p. 174). This work excited great anger among the Whigs. 'I mentioned,' records Boswell on April 3 of this year, 'Sir John Dalrymple's *Memoirs of Great Britain and Ireland,* and his discoveries to the prejudice of Lord Russell and Algernon Sidney. JOHNSON. "Why, Sir, everybody who had just notions of government thought them rascals before. It is well that all mankind now see them to be rascals.... This Dalrymple seems to be an honest fellow; for he tells equally what makes against both sides.' Boswell's *Johnson,* ii. 210.

Hume, in the note mentioned in the next sentence of his letter, says:—'It is amusing to observe the general, and I may say national rage, excited by the late discovery of this secret negotiation [with the French Court]; chiefly on account of Algernon Sidney, whom the blind prejudices of party had exalted into a hero. His ingratitude and breach of faith in applying for the King's pardon, and immediately on his return entering into cabals for rebellion, form a conduct much more criminal than the taking of French gold. Yet the former circumstance was always known, and always disregarded. But everything connected with France is supposed in England to be polluted beyond all possibility of expiation. Even Lord Russell, whose conduct in this negotiation was only factious, and that in an ordinary degree, is imagined to be dishonoured by the same discovery.' *History of England,* ed. 1802, viii. 43.

In a letter to Adam Smith dated April 10, 1773, Hume says :— 'Have you seen Sir John Dalrymple? It is strange what a rage is against him, on account of the most commendable action in his life. His collection is curious; but introduces no new light into the civil, whatever it may into the biographical and anecdotical history of the times.' Burton's *Hume,* ii. 467. Horace Walpole wrote on March 2:—'Need I tell you that Sir John Dalrymple, the accuser of bribery, was turned out of his place of Solicitor of the Customs for taking bribes from brewers?' *Letters,* v. 441. A fortnight later he wrote :—'The town and the newspapers have so fully discussed the book, that I neither listen to the one nor read the other. If it is comfortable to any scoundrel to find himself in better company than he expected, to be sure he has nothing to do but to be introduced by Sir John Dalrymple into History.' *Ib.* p. 451.

Note 3. Hume corrects Dalrymple's mistake in the following words :—'Sir John Dalrymple has given us from Barillon's dispatches in the Secretary's office at Paris a more particular detail of these intrigues.' Hume hereupon gives a list of the men with whom they were carried on, and continues :—'Of these Lord Russel and Lord Hollis alone refused to touch any French money. All the others received presents or bribes from Barillon. But we are to remark that the party view of these men and their well-founded jealousies of the King and Duke engaged them, independently of the money, into the same measures that were suggested to them by the French ambassador. The intrigues of France therefore with the Parliament were a mighty small engine in the political machine.' *History of England*, viii. 43.

Note 4. Hume wrote to Dr. Robertson from Paris on Dec. 1, 1763 :—'I have here met with a prodigious historical curiosity, the *Memoirs of King James II* in fourteen volumes, all wrote with his own hand, and kept in the Scots College. I have looked into it, and have made great discoveries.' Burton's *Hume*, ii. 179. 'These volumes,' adds Dr. Burton, 'were lost during the French Revolution. It is said that an attempt was made to convey them to St. Omers; but having to be committed for some time to the care of a Frenchman, his wife became alarmed lest the regal emblems on the binding might expose the family to danger from the Terrorists. She first cut off the binding and buried the manuscripts, but being still haunted by fears she exhumed and burned them.' Some of these volumes had narrowly escaped destruction a little more than a hundred years earlier, when the London house of the minister of the Grand Duke of Tuscany was sacked in the Revolution of 1688. Macaulay's *History of England*, ed. 1873, iii. 300. The note which Hume had added to his History is given in vol. viii. p. 4 of the edition of 1802.

Note 5. The same statement had been made, but falsely, about Dalrymple's first volume. See *ante*, p. 174. Perhaps the price mentioned is that for the whole work. Dalrymple, when pleading on May 10 of this year at the bar of the House of Commons against the Booksellers' Copyright Bill, said :—'It had been thrown out against him, that after having sold for £2000 the copy of a book, which had the misfortune universally to displease, although it was universally read, he had taken an active part to destroy the value of the very property which he had so disposed of.' *Parl. Hist.* xvii. 1092.

[William Strahan to David Hume[1].]

LETTER LXX.

Strahan's Indignation at Hume's attack on his Truthfulness.

LONDON, *March* 19, 1773.

DEAR SIR

Yours of the 15th I received today, which does not a little surprise me. After having been most unfeignedly attached to

----

[1] Strahan fortunately kept a copy of his answer to Hume, for the original is not preserved among the Hume Papers in the possession of the Royal Society of Edinburgh.

you ever since I had the pleasure of your acquaintance; after having done every thing in my power to oblige you; after having given the most careful attention to your works when under my press, for which I received your repeated ackowledgements; and after having behaved to you in the most open, candid, and ingenuous manner upon every occasion since I became a proprietor in your works; I did not, I could not expect to be told by you, after all, that I was a lying scoundrel, who had constantly deceived you, to whom you could give no manner of credit.

Such it seems, is now your deliberate opinion both of Mr. Cadell and myself. Produce, I call upon you, and have a right so to do, one single instance to support the heavy charge you bring against us; concealing from you, at the desire of the late Mr. Millar, the number of the 8vo. edition of your History alone excepted [1]; which we did purely at his request, having then no interest, nor the least shadow of interest, to deceive you in that or any other particular.

I own that I am quite astonished at the style of your last letter, which is such as should be directed to one of the most worthless of the human race, and to such only.

Do not imagine, however, that I mean to enter into a laboured defence of myself. Far from it. I have nothing to apologize for; nothing have I said or done respecting you, that I now wish unsaid or undone.—Some recent cause of disgust, however groundless, you have conceived; but as my whole conduct respecting you has all along be so more than blameless, this cause, whatever it may be, is to me a perfect mystery.—I told you faithfully, from time to time, how many were left on hand of the 8vo. edition. You told me in a late letter *that we had better submit to some loss, than allow the book to be discredited by that abominable edition* [2].—All proper haste was made to finish and publish it. In my last I told you not above 100 Copies were left; this was so very true, that upon enquiry today, I find they are exactly 76, which we can either destroy, or sell abroad; they are no object [3]. But why do I trouble either you or myself to give you any detail upon this or any other subject; which, as you very politely tell me, *is entirely vain and fruitless, as you can give no manner of credit to my answers.*

Had not Mr. Cadell and I, from the moment we were free

agents[4] and concerned in your works, done everything we could devise for your satisfaction and honour; had we not invariably refused to have any interest in any thing that had a tendency to discredit or displease you; in particular Dr. Beattie's book[5]; had we not on many occasions—But I scorn to instance more particulars—we might have looked for this treatment from you, from which the most blameless conduct on our part has not been able to defend us.

True it is (and this does not depend on my veracity else I would not have mentioned it) that I have said and done every thing in my power to persuade (or, if you please, to *seduce*[6]) you to continue your History, from a full conviction, as you express it in your last, *that it would have been for your own advantage in more respects than one*[7].—Your answer was constantly in the negative; of late, *that such an absurd and extravagant idea never entered your head*[8]; and *that you had thrown your pen aside for ever*[9].—Whether I did well in thus repeatedly obtruding my advice upon you, and you in as repeatedly rejecting it, time only can discover. I know I meant well; that to me is great cause of satisfaction.—And now I cease to trouble you on this head for ever.

I had forgot that you desired 12 copies of this edition. They shall be directly sent you; and as many more as you shall hereafter desire are at your service. Your request respecting future editions of your Works shall be duly attended to. I shall only add, that at no period of my life could I have patiently borne the unmerited treatment you have given me; you will not therefore wonder, that having now, by my own industry, attained to a state of independence, and I will venture to say by a conduct umimpeachable, it should not sit very easy upon my stomach[10].

Some time or other you will perhaps discover with certainty, whether I am or not

Your faithful and Obed^t Servt
W. S.

Note 1. Strahan wrote to Hume on May 14, 1769, in answer to a letter which I have not seen :—' I received your note yesterday. You are in truth the greatest sceptic I ever met with. I have again and again assured you (as I hereby do once more) that you shall most certainly have as many copies of this 4to. edition of your History as you choose to have. Not one of them shall go out of my hands till you are satisfied. The moment the index and titles are printed off the six copies you now ask for shall be sent you. But to send you them before that, would only be a needless incumbrance. If you had a single grain of faith in my promise, you would not only believe this, but believe also, what I have often told you, that everything regarding your Works in future shall be regulated by your own will and directions;—in the manner of printing;—in the number of impressions;—and in everything wherein your interest or fame may be affected. Do learn to put a little confidence in me ; nor imagine that because I was induced to deceive you a little in regard to the number printed of the last 8vo. edition, that I am to make a practice of doing so. In that I was only the mouth of another person, who was afterwards sorry he had occasion to conceal the number of the impression from you.' *M. S. R. S. E.*

Note 2. See *ante*, p. 256.

Note 3. This is perhaps one of the earliest instances that can be found of this use of the word *object*; a use sanctioned, so far as I know, by no correct writer.

Note 4. They had become free agents when Millar in 1767, retiring from business, left Cadell as his successor. Cadell and Strahan were not, I think, partners in business generally, though they undertook many publications in common.

Note 5. Beattie's book is his *Essay on Truth*, in which that amiable poet was supposed to have confuted Hume. The University of Oxford rewarded him by the degree of Doctor of Civil Law, and Reynolds painted him in his Doctor's gown, with his *Essay* under his arm, preceded by the Angel of Truth who is beating down the vices, Envy, Falsehood, etc. These were represented by a group of figures, among whom, it was said, could be discovered the likenesses of Hume and Voltaire. Goldsmith reproached the painter with 'degrading so high a genius as Voltaire before so mean a writer as Dr. Beattie ; for Dr. Beattie and his book together will, in the space of ten years, not be known ever to have been in existence, but your allegorical picture and the fame of Voltaire will live for ever to your disgrace as a flatterer.' Northcote's *Life of Reynolds*, ed. 1819, i. 300.

Sir William Forbes in his *Life of Beattie*, ed. 1824, p. 81, says that he and Mr. Arbuthnot were commissioned by Beattie to sell the manuscript of the *Essay*. They were met by a positive refusal from the bookseller to whom they applied (no doubt Cadell); who offered however to publish it at the author's risk. To this they knew that Beattie would never agree. They thereupon, resorting to a friendly artifice, became themselves the purchasers of the copyright of the first edition, giving fifty guineas for it, but concealing the fact from the author. 'Had it not been,' writes Forbes, 'for this interference of ours, perhaps the *Essay on Truth*, on which all Dr. Beattie's future fortunes hinged, might never have seen the light. It also strongly marks the slender opinion entertained by the booksellers at that period of the value of a work which has since risen into such well-merited celebrity.' Beattie, on receiving a draft for the money, wrote to Forbes on Oct. 26, 1769 :—'The price does really exceed my warmest expectations ; nay I am much afraid that it exceeds the real commercial value of the book; and I am not much surprised that —— [Cadell or Strahan] refuses to have a share in it, considering that he is one of the principal proprietors of Mr. Hume's works, and in consequence of that may have such a personal regard for him as would prevent his being concerned in any work of this nature.' *Ib.* p. 83. In less than four years Beattie's defence of orthodoxy was rewarded by a pension of £200 a year (*ib.* p. 151) ; just half what his antagonist 'the infidel pensioner Hume[1]' received from the same Court. So rapid was the sale of the *Essay* that Cadell and Strahan must have felt that, in refusing it, they had made a great sacrifice to their friendship for Hume. It reached a fourth edition in two years and a half. Forbes's *Beattie*, p. 134. Strahan in 1783, when Hume was no longer living, published Beattie's *Dissertations. Ib.* p. 301.

Note 6. This is the word that Hume had used (*ante*, p. 263).

Note 7. See *ante*, p. 263.

Note 8. See *ante*, p. 253.

Note 9. See *ante*, p. 256.

Note 10. Just one month later Boswell records :—' On Monday, April 19, Dr. Johnson called on me with Mrs. Williams, in Mr. Strahan's coach, and carried me out to dine with Mr. Elphinston [Strahan's brother-in-law] at his academy at Kensington. A printer having acquired a fortune sufficient to keep his coach was a good topic for the credit of literature.' Boswell's *Johnson*, ii. 226.

LETTER LXXI.

An Apology to Strahan.

EDINBURGH, *24th of March*, 1773.

DEAR SIR

If my Letter surprizd you, I assure you yours no less surprizd me ; and gave me no little Concern. You know, that I have frequently accus'd you no less than Mr. Millar and Mr. Cadell, of always representing the fair side of things to me[1] ; and you have frequently remarkd that I was totally incredulous concerning the Representa-

---

[1] Boswell's *Johnson*, ii. 317.

tions you made me. If your End had been to circumvent
me, or take any Advantage of me to my Loss, you would
have been very blamable. But as your Purpose plainly
was and coud be no other, than to put me in good humour
with the Public, and engage me into what must prove
both profitable and amusing to me, I thought the Crime
very venial; as I told you in my Letter: And though I
wishd that the Truth had always been told me, I neither
was disobligd at you nor entertaind in the least a bad
opinion of you [2]. On the contrary, there is no man of
whom I entertain a better, nor whose Friendship I desire
more to preserve, nor indeed any one to whom I have
owd more essential Obligations. You may judge then of
my Uneasyness when I found that I had unwittingly and
unwillingly given you so much Disgust. But how coud
you take it amiss, that I had told you in a Letter what I
had so often told you without offence by words? Your
protracting of this Edition, which you told me two Years
ago was demanded [3], was a sure means of renewing my
former Jealousy.—But I shall not enter into any farther
Detail on this Subject which is needless: But what I
think extremely needful for my own Peace of Mind is to
renew my Professions of that Friendship and Esteem,
which I do and always will bear to you; and to beg of
you very earnestly a Renewal of those Sentiments which
you always professd towards me, and whose Sincerity
I have seen in a hundred Instances. I do not remember
any Incident of my Life, that has given me more real
Concern, than your Misapprehension of me, which, I
hope, a little Reflection without any Explication on my
part woud have sufficd to remove. Sick People and
Children are often to be deceivd for their Good [4]; and I
only suspected you of thinking that peevish Authors, such
as I confess I am, are in the same Predicament. Was the
reproaching you with this Idea, so great an Offence, or

so heavy an Imputation upon your Faith and moral Character? I again beg of you to be assurd of my sincere Sentiments on this head, and entreat the Continuance or rather the Renewal of your Friendship; a Word which I once hop'd woud never have enter'd into our Correspondence⁵.

I am with great Truth & Regard Dear Sⁱʳ

Your most obedient humble Servant

DAVID HUME.

Note 1.   See *ante*, pp. 138, 144, 150, 154.

Note 2.   See *ante*, p. 217, *n.* 3, for the base advice which he gave to a young clergyman. The indifference that Hume shows to truth illustrates, though it does not justify, Lord Shelburne's harsh saying that 'the generality of Scotchmen had no regard tó truth whatever.' Fitzmaurice's *Life of Shelburne*, i. 89. Johnson limited this untruthfulness to their 'disposition to tell lies in favour of each other.' Boswell's *Johnson*, ii. 296. Dr. A. Carlyle, who was a man of great virtue, records without any sign of shame, a lie which he told in the General Assembly of the year 1766, by which the House, which had been disturbed by the sudden death of one of its members, was composed, and went on with its voting. Though he knew that the man was dead, he 'gave out that there were hopes of his recovery.' Carlyle's *Autobiography*, p. 467.

Note 3.   Strahan had written to Hume on March 1, 1771 :—'The octavo edition of your *History* must undoubtedly soon be cleared.' On May 25 of the same year he wrote, speaking of the new edition which he was going to print :—'If I am not mistaken, this book will be wanted before this edition is finished.' *M. S. R. S. E.*

Note 4.   'I deny,' said Johnson, 'the lawfulness of telling a lie to a sick man for fear of alarming him. You have no business with consequences; you are to tell the truth. Besides, you are not sure what effect your telling him that he is in danger may have. It may bring his distemper to a crisis, and that may cure him. Of all lying, I have the greatest abhorrence of this, because I believe it has been frequently practised on myself.' Boswell's *Johnson*, iv. 306. Miss Burney heard George III in one of his attacks of madness say :—'I am nervous, I am not ill, but I am nervous; if you would know what is the matter with me, I am nervous. But I love you both very well, if you would tell me truth. I love Dr. Heberden best, for he has not told me a lie; Sir George [Baker] has told me a lie—a white lie, he says, but I hate a white lie! If you will tell me a lie, let it be a black lie.' Mme. D'Arblay's *Diary*, ed. 1842, iv. 289. See *ante*, p. 217, *n.* 3, for a passage in which Johnson insists on the importance of accustoming children to a strict attention to truth; and *ante*, p. 156, where Hume declares himself 'a good Casuist.'

Note 5. Johnson also had a difference with Strahan, that lasted from March till the end of July, 1778, when he wrote to him :—

'SIR,

'It would be very foolish for us to continue strangers any longer. You can never by persistency make wrong right. If I resented too acrimoniously, I resented only to yourself. Nobody ever saw or heard what I wrote. You saw that my anger was over, for in a day or two I came to your house. I have given you longer time; and I hope you have made so good use of it as to be no longer on evil terms with, Sir,

'Your &c.,

'SAM. JOHNSON.'

'On this,' said Mr. Strahan, 'I called upon him; and he has since dined with me.' Boswell's *Johnson*, iii. 364.

What effect Hume's letter had on Strahan there is nothing to show. There seems however to have been an interruption in their correspondence for ten months.

LETTER LXXII.

Colonel Stuart and the India House.

St. Andrews Square, 25 *of Jany.*, 1774.

DEAR STRAHAN

    I write to you in a great hurry and with great Earnestness : It is to beg your Vote and Interest in the India house for Coll. Stuart, Brother to our Friend, Andrew[1], whose Appointment to command in Bombay is in danger of being over-haul'd by the Court of Proprietors[2]. This woud be a most invidious Measure, very cruel to the Collonel and all his Friends. I know that on Andrew's Account, you woud interest yourself against it; but as he thinks, that my Entreaties woud add something to your Zeal, I hereby join them in the most earnest manner, tho' indeed rather to satisfy him, than that I think they will be any-wise necessary[3].

I am &c.

DAVID HUME.

T

Note 1. See *ante*, p. 239, *n.* 9.

Note 2. The Home Government of the East India Company consisted at this time of a Court of Proprietors, and a Court of Directors elected by the Proprietors. Four Courts of Proprietors, or General Courts, were held regularly in each year. The qualification for a vote in the Court of Proprietors was raised by Lord North's Regulating Act of 1773 from £500 to £1000 of stock. 'According to the Constitution the supreme power was vested in the Court of Proprietors. . . . To act under their ordinances and manage the business of routine was the department reserved for the Court of Directors. . . . Nevertheless all power has centered in the Court of Directors, and the government of the Company has been an oligarchy in fact. So far from meddling too much, the Court of Proprietors have not attended to the common affairs even sufficiently for the business of inspection.' Mill's *Hist. of British India*, ed. 1858, iii. 2, 348.

Note 3. 'Feb. 1, 1774. The following question was at a General Court of Proprietors of East India Stock determined by ballot :— "That it is the opinion of this Court, that it be recommended to the Court of Directors to appoint Col. Robert Gordon Commander-in-Chief of the Forces at the Presidency of Bombay, by rescinding the late appointment of Col. Stuart to that command."

For the question 347 } Majority 155.'
Against it   .   . 192 }

Gent. Mag. 1774, p. 90.

Colonel Stuart therefore lost his appointment ; but the following letter about him from Andrew Stuart to Hume, dated July 10, 1775, seems to show that he was not long in receiving another :—' It is still in the power of a General Court of Proprietors to overturn what has been established by the Court of Directors with so much unanimity. . . . We have every reason to believe that in a Court of Proprietors we should now carry the point by a very splendid majority.' *M. S. R. S. E.* I cannot find that this time any adverse vote was taken in the Court of Proprietors.

LETTER LXXIII.

The Law of Copyright.

[Spring of 1774.]

DEAR SIR

I have writ you an ostensible Letter on the Subject of literary Property, which contains my real Sentiments, so far as it goes. However, I shall tell you the truth ; I do not forsee any such bad Consequences as you mention from laying the Property open[1]. The Italians[2] and French have more pompous[3] Editions of their Classics since the Expiration of the Privileges than any we have of ours: And at least, every Bookseller, who prints a Book, will endeavour to make it as compleat and correct as he can. But when I said, that I thought Lord Mansfield's Decision founded on a vain Subtlely[4], I did not consider the matter in that Light, but only on a simple Consideration of the Act of Q. Anne. The Essay[5] I mentioned is not so considerable as to [be] printed apart; yet any pyrated Edition woud be reckond incompleat that did not contain it.

Yours

D. H.

Note 1. On Feb. 22, 1774, a decision was given in the House of Lords on the question of literary property or copyright, by which, to use the words of the *Annual Register* (xvii. i. 95), ' Near £200,000 worth of what was honestly purchased at public sale, and which was yesterday thought property, is now reduced to nothing. . . . The English booksellers have now no other security in future for any literary purchase they may make but the statute of the 8th of Queen Anne, which secures to the author's assigns an exclusive property for 14 years, to revert again to the author, and vest in him for 14 years more.' Boswell tells how an Edinburgh bookseller, Alexander Donaldson by name, 'had for some years opened a shop in London, and sold his cheap editions of the most popular English books, in defiance of the supposed common-law right of Literary Property.' Boswell's *Johnson*, i. 437. How strictly this copyright had been maintained is shown in the judgment pronounced by Lord Camden, who says :—' Shakespeare's works, which he left carelessly behind him in town when he retired from it, were surely given to the public if ever author's were ; but two prompters, or players behind the scenes, laid hold of them, and the present proprietors pretend to derive that copy from them, for which the author himself never received a farthing.' *Parl. Hist.* xvii. 1000. William Johnston, a retired bookseller, in the evidence which he gave two or three weeks later before a Committee of the House of Commons, said that he had held in whole or in part the copyright of Camden's *Britannia*, Dryden's *Works*, Locke's *Works*, and Steele's *Tatler*, and that, by the threat of filing a bill in Chancery, he had restrained a Coventry bookseller from publishing an edition of *The Pilgrim's Progress*. *Ib.* p. 1082. Lord Camden, who as Chancellor for some years enjoyed an income which was reckoned at £13,000 a year[1], took a very lofty view of the position of authors. 'Glory (he said) is the reward of science, and those who deserve it scorn all meaner views. I speak not of the scribblers for bread, who teaze the press with their wretched productions; fourteen years is too long a privilege for their perishable trash. It was not for gain that Bacon, Newton, Milton, Locke instructed and delighted the world; it would be unworthy such men to traffic with a dirty bookseller for so much a sheet of a letterpress.' *Ib.* p. 1000. Dunning (afterwards Lord Ashburton), 'the great lawyer,' as Johnson called him[2], in his speech for the booksellers had said:—'Authors formerly, when there were few readers, might get but small prices for their labour; that however had not of late years been the case. Hume's *History of England* and Dr. Robertson's *History of Scotland* had been amply paid for. . . . How was this difference to be accounted for? Not from any uncommon generosity in the booksellers, not from any superiority in point of merit in the books, but from the idea of a common-law right prevailing, and from that idea being established by the determination of the Court of King's Bench in the case of Millar *v.* Taylor.' *Ib.* p. 967. I suspect that the Whig ex-Chancellor Camden, when he sneered at those authors 'who traffic with a dirty bookseller,' aimed a blow, which was not too covert to be seen, at the Tory historian, David Hume, and perhaps at the Tory King's-Printer, William Strahan.

The booksellers and authors had been 'hoist with their own petar.' Up to the passing of the statute of Anne they had by common law a perpetual copyright. That Act was passed, not to limit their right, but to give them additional powers for enforcing it. In 'one of the Cases given to the Members in 1709 in support of their application for a bill,' it was stated :—'. . . By common law a bookseller can recover no more costs than he can prove damage : But it is impossible for him to prove the tenth, nay perhaps the hundredth part of the damage he suffers; because a thousand counterfeit copies may be dispersed into as many different hands all over the kingdom, and he not be able to prove the sale of ten. Besides, the defendant is always a pauper; and so the plaintiff must lose his costs of suit. Therefore the only remedy by the common law is to confine a beggar to the Rules of the King's Bench or Fleet; and there he will continue the evil practice with impunity. We therefore pray that confiscation of counterfeit copies be one of the penalties to be inflicted on offenders.' Burrow's *Reports of Cases in the Court of King's Bench,* iv. 2318. In the preamble to the Act we read :—'Whereas printers . . . . have of late frequently taken the liberty of printing . . . . books and other writings, without the consent of the authors or proprietors of such books and writings, to their very great detriment, and too often to the ruin of them and their families: for preventing therefore such

[1] Walpole's *Memoirs of George III,* iv. 45.
[2] Boswell's *Johnson,* iii. 128.

practices for the future, and for the encouragement of learned men to compose and write useful books,' &c. _Statutes at Large_, xii. 82.

Blackstone, in the first edition of the second volume of his _Commentaries_ published in 1766, says :—' But exclusive of such copyright as may subsist by the rules of the common law, the statute 8 Anne c. 19 hath protected by additional penalties the property of authors and their assigns for the term of fourteen years ; and hath directed that, if at the end of that term the author himself be living, the right shall then return to him for another term of the same duration.' ii. 407.

The booksellers do not seem to have made much use of the new Act, but to have had recourse, as before, to the Court of Chancery. William Johnston, in his examination before the Committee, ' being asked why it was not the custom of those who are possessed of copyright to enter them in the books of the Stationers' Company? He said, he could only answer for himself, that he never thought the penalties prescribed by the Act of the eighth of Queen Anne were worth contending for, as a much shorter and more complete relief might be had by filing a bill in Chancery.' _Parl. Hist._ xvii. 1085.

It was not till the year 1769 that in the case of Andrew Millar _v._ Robert Taylor 'the old and often litigated question concerning literary property received a determination in the Court of King's Bench.' Burrows _Reports_, iv. 2303. Taylor had reprinted Thomson's _Seasons_, of which Millar had bought the various copyrights between the years 1727-9. Millar laid his damages at £200. The Jury brought in a special verdict, assessing the damages at one shilling with forty shillings cost. The Lord Chief Justice Mansfield and Justices Willes and Aston held that the perpetual copyright had not been taken away by the Statute of Anne. Justice Yates differed from them. Lord Mansfield prefaced his judgment by a statement which may well excite our wonder. He had now presided over his Court for more than twelve years, yet he was able to say :—' This is the first instance of a _final_ difference of opinion in this Court, since I sat here. Every order, rule, judgment and opinion has _hitherto_ been _unanimous._' 'This,' says the Editor, 'gives weight and dispatch to the decisions, certainty to the law, and infinite satisfaction to the suitors. And the effect is seen by that immense business which flows from all parts into this channel ; and which we who have long known Westminster Hall behold with astonishment.' Burrow's _Reports_, iv. 2395.

By this decision the claim of the booksellers for a perpetual copyright seemed to be established ; but the matter came before the House of Lords in the case of Donaldsons _v._ Becket and others, upon an appeal from a decree of the Court of Chancery founded upon this judgment. _Ib._ p. 2408. There they found to their dismay that the very weapon which their predecessors had forged against their enemies threatened them now with what in their first alarm seemed almost a deadly wound. They at once began to take measures to protect their property. On Feb. 28 they presented a petition to the House of Commons praying for relief. A Committee was appointed to take evidence, and on their report leave to bring in a Copy-right Bill was carried by 54 to 16. Burke was a teller for the majority and Fox for the minority. The smallness of the numbers seems to show great indifference to literature on the part of the members. The Bill was carried through the Commons, the highest total number on any division being 83, and Fox being persistent and violent in his opposition. It was lost in the Lords by 21 to 11. *Parl. Hist.* xvii. 1077, 1089, 1402. Burke, in one of his speeches, said :—'The learned advocate has told us that glory is the only reward sought by the Scotch booksellers; let them have their glory,—let the petitioners have [their] property—we will not quarrel about terms.' *Ib.* p. 1102. Very likely the 'ostensible letter' of which Hume speaks is the one mentioned by Mr. Mansfield, one of the counsel for the London booksellers; who at the bar of the House of Commons, on May 13, said :—'I have by me letters of Mr. Hume, Dr. Robertson, &c., containing the warmest wishes to the petitioners, lamenting the late decision of the House of Peers as fatal to literature, and hoping that the booksellers might get speedy relief.' *Ib.* 1098.

In the Act of Anne there was a provision which I have not seen anywhere noticed. A Court of Arbitration was established in case 'any bookseller shall set a price upon any book as shall be conceived by any person to be too high and unreasonable.' The Court was to be composed of the Archbishop of Canterbury, Lord Chancellor, Bishop of London, the two Chief Justices, Chief Baron, Vice-Chancellors of Oxford and Cambridge, Lord President of the Sessions, Lord Justice General, Lord Chief Baron, and the Rector of the College of Edinburgh. They were to have 'full power to limit and settle the price of books from time to time, according to the best of their judgments, and as to them shall seem just and reasonable.' *Statutes at Large*, xii. 84. This provision was repealed by 12 G. II. c. 36. Burrow's *Reports*, iv. 2390.

Note 2. Baretti in his *Account of Manners and Customs of Italy*, published in 1768, says :—'It is the general custom for our authors to make a present of their works to booksellers, who in return scarcely give a few copies when printed. . . . Our learned stare when they are told that in England there are numerous writers who get their bread by their productions only.' vol. i. p. 236. He was, he said, 'the first man that ever received copy-money in Italy.' Boswell's *Johnson*, iii. 162.

Note 3. *Pompous* still retained the meaning of 'splendid, magnificent, grand'; to adopt Johnson's definition. In his *Rasselas* (Clarendon Press ed. p. 110) he says :—'The most pompous monument of Egyptian greatness . . . are the Pyramids.'

Note 4. Hume must be speaking of the judgment delivered by Lord Mansfield in the Court of King's Bench in the case of Millar *v.* Taylor, for he declined speaking on the appeal; 'it being very unusual, from reasons of delicacy, for a peer to support his own judgment upon an appeal to the House of Lords.' Burrow's *Reports,* iv. 2417. Lord Camden, in attacking the arguments maintained on the side of the booksellers, talks of the 'variety of subtle reasoning and metaphysical refinements, by which they have endeavoured to squeeze out the spirit of the common law from premises in which it could not possibly have existence.' *Parl. Hist.* xvii. 992. He adds :—' I pass over the flimsy supposition of an implied contract between the bookseller who sells, and the public which buys the printed copy; it is a notion as unmeaning in itself as it is void of a legal foundation.' *Ib.* p. 1000. There had been 'subtle reasoning and metaphysical refinements' on both sides. Mr. Justice Aston said :—' It has been ingeniously, metaphysically, and subtilly argued on the part of the Defendant, "That there is a *want of property* in the *thing itself."* ' Burrow's *Reports,* iv. 2336. Mr. Justice Yates had asked :—' Now where are the *indicia* or *distinguishing* marks of ideas ? What distinguishing marks can a man fix upon a set of intellectual ideas, so as to call himself the proprietor of them ? They have *no ear-marks* upon them ; *no tokens* of a particular proprietor.' *Ib.* p. 2366. To this Lord Mansfield replied :—' If the copy belongs to an Author *after* publication, it certainly belonged to him before. But if it does not belong to him after, where is the Common Law to be found which says " there is such a property before " ? All the metaphysical subtilties from the nature of the thing may be *equally* objected to the property before. It is *incorporeal*: It relates to ideas detached from any *physical* existence. There are *no indicia*: Another may have had the same thoughts upon the same subject, and expressed them in the same language *verbatim,*' &c. *Ib.* p. 2397. Johnson, who all along held that there was no such common-law right of literary property as was supposed, nevertheless 'was very angry that the booksellers of London, for whom he uniformly professed much regard, should suffer from an invasion of what they had ever considered to be secure ; and he was loud and violent against Mr. Donaldson. "He is a fellow who takes advantage of the law to injure his brethren ; for, notwithstanding that the statute secures only fourteen years of exclusive right, it has always been understood by *the trade,* that he who buys the copyright of a book from the author obtains a perpetual property ; and upon that belief numberless bargains are made to transfer that property after the expiration of the statutory term." ' Boswell's *Johnson,* i. 437. The London booksellers protected themselves by an 'honorary copyright, which,' wrote Boswell in 1791, 'is still preserved among them by mutual compact.' *Ib.* iii. 370.

Note 5. See *post,* where Hume in his letter of June 8, 1776, says :—'Two posts ago I sent you a Copy of the small Essay which I mentioned.' No doubt this Essay is the one entitled *Of the Origin of Government,* which first appears in the edition of 1777. Hume's *Philosophical Works,* ed. 1854, iii. 34.

LXXIV.

Dr. Wallace's Manuscript: Lord Kames's Sketches.

St. Andrews Square, 2 *of April,* 1774.

DEAR SIR

There is a Subject which I was desird to mention to you, but which I delay'd, till your Application to Parliament were finishd, that you might know on what footing your literary Property was to stand[1]: It is with regard to Dr. Wallace's manuscript, which was certainly finishd for the Press and which I think a very good Book[2]: I told his Son about four or five months ago, before the Decision of the House of Peers, that he ought not to expect above 500 pounds for it; and he has return'd so far to my Sentiments, as to leave the Matter entirely to me; I shoud wish to know, therefore, what you think you cou'd afford. I imagine this Decision will not very much alter the Value of literary Property: For if you coud, by a tacite convention among yourselves[3], make a Property of the Dauphin's Virgil, without a single Line in Virgil's hand, or Ruæus's or the Dauphin's[4], I see not why you may not keep Possession of all your Books as before. However, this Decision throws you into some Uncertainty, and you may be cautious for some time in entering on any considerable Purchase.

Lord Kaims's Sketches[5] have here been published some weeks; and by the Reception it has met with, is not likely to be very popular, according to the prodigiously sanguine Expectations of the Author. But after his Elements of Criticism[6] met with some Success, I shall

never venture to make any Prophecy on that head. I
am glad to hear, that in your Bargain with him, you had a
saving Clause to ensure you against Loss[7]. Cou'd any
such Clause be devis'd with regard to Dr. Wallace's
Book? In the mean time, I ask 500 pounds for it[8]; as
you desire that a positive Demand shoud always be made,
which is indeed but reasonable. It is about half the Size
of Lord Kaims's Sketches; and is better writ.

I am Dear S^{ir} yours sincerely

DAVID HUME.

Note 1. See *ante*, p. 275, *n*. 1. Hume seems to think that as such
feeble opposition had been shown when the Copyright Bill was
brought in, it was certain to be carried. I cannot find what was the
length of time during which the booksellers claimed that the exclusive property in a book should continue. Leave was moved to
bring in a Bill 'for relief of booksellers and others, by vesting the
copies of printed books in the purchasers of such copies from authors
or their assigns, *for a time therein to be limited*.' *Parl. Hist.* xvii. 1086.

Note 2. The Rev. Dr. Robert Wallace published in 1752 *Dissertations on the Populousness of Mankind in Ancient and Modern Times*,
as a reply to Hume's *Essay of the Populousness of Ancient Nations.*
Hume describes it as 'an answer full of politeness, erudition, and
good sense.' *Phil. Works*, ed. 1854, iii. 410. 'Malthus admitted that
Dr. Wallace was the first to point distinctly to the rule, that to find
the limits of the populousness of any given community, we must look
at the quantity of food at its disposal.' Burton's *Hume*, i. 364. He is
mentioned in *Humphry Clinker* (ed. 1792, iii. 6) as one of 'the authors
of the first distinction,' of which Edinburgh that 'hot-bed of genius'
could boast, and in Dr. A. Carlyle's *Autobiography* (p. 239) as having
had a great part in establishing in Scotland the Ministers' Widows'
Fund. By one of the letters of his son, George Wallace, in the
Barker MSS. I learn that the work which he had left finished at his
death was a *Treatise on Taste*. Though a minister of the Scotch
Church he had even written notes on Gallini's *Treatise on Dancing.*
Home's *Works*, i. 17. Ramsay of Ochtertyre says that soon after
Wallace became a preacher somebody 'in a large company of Episco-
palians regretted so genteel a young man should be a Presbyterian
minister. "Oh," said George Home of Argaty; "that puts me in
mind of what I heard a wife say t'other day to her neighbour, on her
regretting that a handsome lad should be made a town-officer—'Have
a little patience; ere seven years he will be as ill-looking as the
worst-favoured of them.'"" So low was their opinion of Presbyterian
accomplishments.' *Scotland and Scotsmen*, ii. 552.

Note 3. For this 'tacit convention,' or 'honorary copyright,' see *ante*, p. 279, *n.* 4. The witnesses against the Copyright Bill complained that 'they were not admitted to the Booksellers' sales.' *Parl. Hist.* xvii. 1093.

Note 4. The title-page of the *Delphine Virgil* is as follows:—*P. Virgilii Maronis Opera. Interpretatione et Notis illustravit Carolus Ruæus, Soc. Jesu. Jussu Christianissimi Regis, ad Usum Serenissimi Delphini.* For Ruæus—Charles De La Rue—see Chalmers's *Biog. Dict.* xxvi. 454. According to Lowndes, *Bibl. Man.*, ed. 1871, p. 2776, the first English edition of the Delphine Virgil was published in 1686. It was frequently reprinted. W. Johnston the bookseller, in his examination before the Committee of the House of Commons (*ante*, p. 275, *n.* 1), 'being asked, whether he did not claim a copyright in some of the editions of the classics *In Usum Delphini*, said, No such right was ever claimed, so as to exclude any other person who chose to print them; that he had purchased the right of printing in part some of those classics, but never supposed that right protected by any law, nor considered it in any other manner than as the purchase of an honorary right, which he explained to be a maxim held by the trade not to reprint upon the first proprietor.' *Parl. Hist.* xvii. 1079. By 'a single line in Virgil's hand' &c. Hume clearly means in his handwriting.

Note 5. *Sketches of the History of Man.* Johnson criticised some statements in it. See Boswell's *Johnson*, iii. 340, 351.

Note 6. 'JOHNSON. "The Scotchman has taken the right method in his *Elements of Criticism*. I do not mean that he has taught us anything; but he has told us old things in a new way." MURPHY. "He seems to have read a great deal of French criticism, and wants to make it his own; as if he had been for years anatomising the heart of man, and peeping into every cranny of it." GOLDSMITH. "It is easier to write that book than to read it."' Boswell's *Johnson*, ii. 89. At an earlier time Johnson had said of it:—'Sir, this book is a pretty essay, and deserves to be held in some estimation, though much of it is chimerical.' *Ib.* i. 393. George Wallace told Boswell thât when Charles Townshend read it, he said:—'This is the work of a dull man grown whimsical.' *Boswelliana*, p. 278.

Lord Cockburn in his *Memorials*, p. 117, describes Kames as 'an indefatigable and speculative, but coarse man. When he tried Matthew Hay, with whom he used to play at chess, for murder, he exclaimed, when the verdict of guilty was returned, "That's checkmate to you, Matthew."' According to Ramsay of Ochtertyre, 'Lord Elibank, Lord Kames, and Mr. David Hume were considered as a literary triumvirate, from whose judgment, in matters of taste and composition, there lay no appeal.' *Scotland and Scotsmen*, i. 319.

Note 7. The *Sketches* sold too well for any loss to be incurred. They passed through several editions.

Note 8. The success not only of himself and Robertson, but of such authors as Blair, Sir John Dalrymple, John Home, Adam Ferguson, and Macpherson, seems to have made Hume think that there was scarcely any limit set to the price that 'the factious barbarians' of the South would pay an author, if only he had the good luck to be born north of the Tweed, and had taken the trouble to 'unscottify' his diction.

[Strahan to Hume.]

LETTER LXXV.

Bargains between Authors and Booksellers.

April 9, 1774[1].

Dᴿ Sɪʀ

I am favoured with yours in regard to Dr. Wallace's book, to which I know not what to say in reply. It may probably be worth the money demanded for it, for anything I know to the contrary, because I have not seen a syllable of it ; but when I consider the subject, the nature of which is not very saleable, and the character of the Author, who though a man of most excellent dispositions, and good abilities, never in his lifetime produced anything that was so received by the public, as could in any manner justify such a price as £500 for a work of his, of the size of a small quarto volume, I cannot hesitate a moment to decline the purchase.—What was got by his *Essay on the Numbers of Mankind* I know not; but his *Characteristics of Great Britain*[2] Mr. Millar and I bought for £30, and I believe we did not make £10 of it. Not that I mean to undervalue the present performance ; but when I have no other guide to go by, it is natural enough to reason from analogy, and to estimate one work by former publications of the same writer. The prices demanded, and indeed given of late for copies[3], hath had a most strange effect upon our present Authors, as every one is abundantly apt to compare his own merit with his contemporaries, of which he cannot be supposed to be an impartial judge.—Mr. G. Wallace carries this idea farther, and asserts what to me is the greatest of all paradoxes, viz. 'That *little* will ever be made by any work for which *much* is not given.'—I wish I could not produce so capital an exception to this rule[4] as Hawkesworth's Voyages ; the

284 . LETTERS OF DAVID HUME. [Letter

event of which purchase, if it does not cure Authors of their delirium, I am sure will have the proper effect upon booksellers[5].—I will not take into the account the present uncertain state of literary property in general. There is no occasion for it. The simple question here is, Is it likely that 2000 of this book will sell in a few years at the price of a guinea bound; because unless that number are likely to be disposed of at that price, it can never bear so large as sum as £500[6].

As for Lord Kaimes's book, neither Mr. Cadell nor I had any hand in the purchase. It was entirely transacted between his Lordship and Mr. Creech[7]. But the *saving clause* removed every objection to our having a concern in it, as we had no trouble about it; but in the present case, to agree to give £500, even with a saving clause, would be undertaking all the trouble attending the publication with a moral certainty of getting nothing for our pains. After all, I wish not, neither does Mr. Cadell, to undervalue any man's performance, so it is better, perhaps, to decline it in our Names altogether, without giving the Reasons above assigned.—Or if you please, as Mr. G. Wallace's expectations from the book were so sanguine that he conceived hopes of getting £2000 for it, we will print it, run all risk of paper, print, etc., and give him half the neat[8] profits: and as in this way, it will be evidently our own interest to promote the sale, he need not doubt our doing everything in our power to promote it[9].

Lord Kaimes's book will be published here next week, and I doubt not but it will sell. It is light summer reading, and not unsuitable to the taste of the present times. It is not the intrinsic merit of any work that ensures the sale; but many other circumstances which men of true judgment and solid learning are apt to overlook[10].

Our Literary Property Bill will be brought in next week, as soon as the parliament reassembles. We hope at least to get something. I wrote to Dr. Robertson for his sentiments above a fortnight ago, but have yet received no answer, which I wonder at[11].

I am ever, with the most sincere Esteem, dear Sir,
Yours etc.

The *Delphin Classics* are of that species of books that will never be pirated, and would indeed never be printed in Britain at all, unless by a large company of booksellers, faithful to one another, by whose joint trade an impression may be sold off in a reasonable time, so as to indemnify them for the expense, with some little profit[12].—For such books we want no protection; nor for large works, voluminous Dictionaries, School books, etc., which no interloper will ever meddle with; but for your light and more saleable productions, of two or three volumes in 12°., the profit on which is sure, and the risk small, the charge of an impression amounting to a small sum.

If your commendations of Henry's *History* are well founded, is not his work an exception to your own general rule, that no good book was ever wrote for money[13]?

Note 1. It is strange that Strahan makes no mention of Goldsmith's death, which had taken place five days earlier. I cannot find any mention of Goldsmith by Hume.

Note 2. *Characteristics of the Present Political State of Great Britain.* London, 1758. *Gent. Mag.* 1758, p. 135.

Note 3. By 'copies' Strahan means 'the copyright of books still in manuscript.' See *ante*, p. 266, *n.* 5, for the £2000 paid to Sir John Dalrymple for his *Memoirs.* Compared with this the £3400 paid to Robertson for his *Charles V* seems moderate (*ante*, p. 14, *n.* 1).

Note 4. Strahan's logic is at fault. It is no exception to the rule laid down by Wallace to show that a work for which much was given produced little. All that he asserted was, that a great gain can only be made by a great outlay. He did not maintain that every great outlay will produce a great gain.

Note 5. Malone says that 'Hawkesworth was introduced by Garrick to Lord Sandwich [the First Lord of the Admiralty], who, thinking to put a few hundred pounds into his pocket, appointed him to revise and publish *Cook's Voyages.* He scarcely did anything to the MS., yet sold it to Cadell and Strahan for £6000.' Prior's *Life of Malone*, p. 441. It had been published the year before in 3 vols. quarto, at a price of three guineas. *Gent. Mag.* 1773, p. 286. Thurlow, in speaking against the Copyright Bill on March 24, 1774, said 'that Hawkesworth's book, which was a mere composition of trash, sold for three guineas by the booksellers' monopolizing.' *Parl. Hist.* xvii. p. 1086. Charles Darwin for the first edition of his *Naturalist's Voyage round the World* 'received payment only in the form of a large number of presentation copies; he seems to have been glad to sell the copyright of the second edition to Mr. Murray for £150.' *Life of Darwin*, ed. 1887, i. 337.

Note 6. Gavin Hamilton, the Edinburgh bookseller, in his letter

about the first volume of Hume's *History*, says:—'The book will sell
at fifteen shillings bound, or ten shillings to booksellers in sheets.'
In a calculation which he makes he reduces the ten shillings to nine,
and then says that there will remain £400 profit to the author and
£200 to the publisher. *Ante*, p. 3. At this same rate a book sold
bound at a guinea would produce £560 profit to the author and
£280 to the publisher. The calculations therefore of Hamilton and
Strahan do not differ much. See Boswell's *Johnson*, ii. 424, for an
interesting letter by Johnson on the book-trade.

Note 7. Lord Cockburn in his *Memorials*, pp. 108, 169, describes
'the famous shop of William Creech, the bookseller. Its position in
the very tideway of all our business made it the natural resort of
lawyers, authors, and all sorts of literary idlers, who were always
buzzing about the convenient hive. All who wished to see a poet or
a stranger, or to hear the public news, the last joke by Erskine, or
yesterday's occurrence in the Parliament-House, or to get the publication of the day or newspapers—all congregated there ; lawyers,
doctors, clergymen, and authors.'

Burns celebrated him in *Verses written at Selkirk*. In the last stanza
but one he says:—

> 'May I be slander's common speech ;
>   A text for infamy to preach ;
> And lastly streekit out to bleach
>   In winter snaw ;
> When I forget thee ! Willie Creech,
>   Tho' far awa.'

Note 8. Johnson defines *neat* in its third meaning as '*pure, un-
adulterated, unmingled* : in the cant of trade.' The only instance
he gives of its use is as applied to liquors. He does not give the
word under its modern spelling, *net*.

Note 9. George Wallace, writing to Strahan on Sept. 23 of this
year, says :—'I have caused a skilful person to make an accurate
computation to assist me in judging of the value of the book. . .
Probably it will swell to 500 pages, and might be decently sold
to gentlemen at a guinea. By the computation each copy costs 3s. 3d.
prime, and if sold to the trade at 15s., an impression consisting of
1000 copies would fetch £580 of profit or thereby, of which I am
told I ought to get about £400. The deuce is in it, if after Kaims's
Elements have come to a *fifth* edition, *three* have sold of Ferguson's
Society, and three of Macpherson's *History*, one shall not sell of this
Treatise.' *Barker MSS.*

Note 10. 'We talked of the uncertainty of profit with which
authors and booksellers engage in the publication of literary works.
JOHNSON. "My judgment I have found is no certain rule as to the sale
of a book."' Boswell's *Johnson*, iv. 121.

Note 11. Dr. Robertson must have written his 'sentiments' soon
after; for Mr. Mansfield at the bar of the House of Commons and

Lord Lyttelton in the House of Lords each said that he had a letter from him. *Parl. Hist.* xvii. 1098, 1400.

Note 12. By such 'a company of booksellers'—eight in number—was Johnson's *Dictionary* published. Boswell's *Johnson*, i. 183. It was a company 'of about forty of the most respectable booksellers in London' who undertook the publication of the *Lives of the Poets. Ib.* iii. 111.

Note 13. I do not know where Hume lays down this general rule. It is the very opposite of Johnson's, that 'no man but a blockhead ever wrote except for money.' Boswell's *Johnson*, iii. 19.

LETTER LXXVI.

Dr. Wight and Dr. Trail: Folly of the War with the Colonies: Dr. Reid and Dr. Beattie.

EDINBURGH, 26 *of Octr.*, 1775.

DEAR S[IR]

I have often regreted the Interruption of our Correspondence[1]: But when you ceas'd to be a speculative Politician and became a practical one[2], I coud no longer expect you woud be so communicative or impartial as formerly on that head; and my object with regard to Authorship, was, for a time, at an End. The Reason of the present Trouble is of a different kind: Dr. Trail[3], the Professor of Divinity at Glasgow, is dead; and Dr. Wight, the present Professor of Church History, is a Candidate for the Office: The Place is filled by a Vote of the Professors: You are understood to have great Influence with Wilson, the Professor of Astronomy[4]: And I interest myself extremely in Dr. Wight's success[5]: These are my Reasons for writing to you. But I must also tell you my Reasons for interesting myself so much in Dr. Wight's Behalf. He is a particular Friend of mine: He is very much connected with all mine and your particular Friends in the Church[6]: He is a very gentleman-like agreeable Man: And above all, he is (without which I shoud not interest myself for him) a very sound and orthodox Divine. The case of Dr. Trail, (his predecessor, as I hope) was somewhat particular with regard to Orthodoxy : He was very laudably a declar'd Enemy to all Heretics, Socinians, Arians, Anti-trinitarians, Arminians, Erastians, Sabellians, Pelagians, Semi-pelagians : In short, of every Sect, whose Name terminated in *ian* [7], except Presbyterian, to whom he had a declar'd and passionate Attachment. He said, that it signify'd nothing to pick out a little straggling Absurdity, here and there, from the System ; while the whole immense Chaos, sufficient to over-whelm Heaven and Earth, still remain'd entire, and must still remain. But in Prosecution of these Views (which one cannot much blame) he mix'd a little of the Acrimony of his own Temper ; and, perhaps undesignedly, sent away all the Students of Divinity very zealous Bigots, which had a very bad Effect on the Clergy of that Neighbourhood [8]. Now, I shall answer for Dr. Wight, that his Pupils shall have all the Orthodoxy, without the Bigotry, instill'd into them by his Predecessor. I believe Dr. Robertson will write you on the same Subject ; and I beg you woud not lose any time in applying to Mr. Wilson, in case he shoud take any other Engagements, tho we do not yet hear of any other Candidate.

I must, before we part, have a little Stroke of Politics with you, notwithstanding my Resolution to the contrary. We hear that some of the Ministers have propos'd in Council, that both Fleet and Army be withdrawn from America, and these Colonists be left entirely to themselves [9]. I wish I had been a Member of His Majesty's Cabinet Council, that I might have seconded this Opinion. I shoud have said, that this Measure only anticipates the necessary Course of Events a few Years ; that a forced and every day more precarious Monopoly of about 6 or 700,000 Pounds a year of Manufactures [10], was not worth contending for ; that we shoud preserve the greater part

of this Trade even if the Ports of America were open to
all Nations; that it was very likely, in our method of
proceeding, that we shoud be disappointed in our Scheme
of conquering the Colonies [11]; and that we ought to think
beforehand how we were to govern them, after they were
conquer'd. Arbitrary Power can extend its oppressive
Arm to the Antipodes; but a limited Government can
never long be upheld at a distance, even where no Dis-
gusts have interven'd [12]: Much less, where such violent
Animosities have taken place. We must, therefore, annul
all the Charters [13]; abolish every democratical Power
in every Colony; repeal the Habeas Corpus Act with
regard to them; invest every Governor with full dis-
cretionary or arbitrary Powers; confiscate the Estates of
all the chief Planters [14]; and hang three fourths of their
Clergy [15]. To execute such Acts of destructive Violence
twenty thousand Men will not be sufficient; nor thirty
thousand to maintain them, in so wide and disjointed a
Territory [16]. And who are to pay so great an Army?
The Colonists cannot at any time, much less after reducing them to such a State of Desolation: We ought
not, and indeed cannot, in the over-loaded or rather over-
whelm'd and totally ruin'd State of our Finances [17]. Let
us, therefore, lay aside all Anger; shake hands, and part
Friends [18]. Or if we retain any anger, let it only be
against ourselves for our past Folly; and against that
wicked Madman, Pitt; who has reducd us to our present
Condition [19]. *Dixi* [20].

But we must not part, without my also saying something as an Author. I have not yet thrown up so much
all Memory of that Character. There is a short Advertisement [21], which I wish I had prefix'd to the second
Volume of the Essays and Treatises in the last Edition. I
send you a Copy of it. Please to enquire at the Warehouse, if any considerable Number of that Edition remain

on hands; and if there do, I beg the favour of you, that you woud throw off an equal Number of this Advertisement, and give out no more Copies without prefixing it to the second volume. It is a compleat Answer to Dr. Reid [22] and to that bigotted silly Fellow, Beattie [23].

I believe that I have formerly mention'd to you, that no new Editions shoud be made of any of my Writings, without mentioning it to me; I shall still have some Corrections to make. By Calculation, or rather Conjecture from former Sales, the last Edition of my History shoud be nearly sold off: Pray inform yourself whether it be not so : And how many remain on hand [24].

I am with great Sincerity Dear Sir

Your affectionate humble Servant

DAVID HUME.

Note 1. This interruption had lasted for more than a year and a-half. When Hume resumed it he was already some way advanced in an illness which at first, he says, gave him no alarm, but which in ten months more was to carry him off.

Note 2. Strahan had been elected for Malmesbury in the Parliament that met on Nov. 29, 1774. *Parl. Hist.* xviii. 24. One cause of the interruption of the correspondence might have been want of time on his side. In one of his earlier letters he said :—'I have borrowed two hours from my pillow to write to you.' *M. S. R. S. E.*

Note 3. Hume, in writing from Paris on June 22, 1764, mentions a Dr. Trail as 'our chaplain'—chaplain to the Embassy, that is tò say. Burton's *Hume*, ii. 204. Horace Walpole mentions the same clergyman in a letter to Conway on Jan. 22, 1756. 'Your brother [Lord Hertford] has got a sixth infanta ; at the christening t'other night Mr. Trail had got through two prayers before anybody found out that the child was not brought down stairs.' *Letters*, ii. 499.

Note 4. Dugald Stewart, in his Life of Thomas Reid (ed. 1811, p. 426), speaking of the appointment of that philosopher to the chair at Glasgow University vacated by Adam Smith, says :—'The Wilsons (both father and son) were formed to attach his heart by the similarity of their scientific pursuits, and an entire sympathy with his views and sentiments.' In a note (p. 528) Stewart adds :—'Alexander Wilson, M.D., and Patrick Wilson were well known over Europe by their observations on the Solar Spots.'

Note 5. Dr. A. Carlyle, writing of Dr. Wight's appointment in 1762 to the chair of Church History at Glasgow, says :—' As he was my near relation, his advancement, in which I had a chief hand, was very pleasing; and as he was the most agreeable of all men, his coming near me promised much enjoyment.' Carlyle's *Auto.* p. 424. See *Ib.* p. 395.

Note 6. 'Hume took much to the company of the younger clergy, not from a wish to bring them over to his opinions, for he never attempted to overturn any man's principles, but they best understood his notions, and could furnish him with literary conversation. Robertson and John Home and Bannatine and I lived all in the country, and came only periodically to the town. Blair and Jardine both lived in it, and suppers being the only fashionable meal at that time, we dined where we best could, and by cadies [errand boys] assembled our friends to meet us in a tavern by nine o'clock; and a fine time it was when we could collect David Hume, Adam Smith, Adam Ferguson, Lord Elibank, and Drs. Blair and Jardine, on an hour's warning. I remember one night that David Hume came rather late to us, and directly pulled a large key from his pocket, which he laid on the table. This, he said, was given him by his maid Peggy (much more like a man than a woman) that she might not sit up for him, for she said, when the honest fellows came in from the country, he never returned home till after one o'clock. This intimacy of the young clergy with David Hume enraged the zealots on the opposite side, who little knew how impossible it was for him, had he been willing, to shake their principles.' Carlyle's *Auto.* p. 274.

Note 7. Hume wrote to his friend, Dr. Clephane, on Sept. 3, 1757: —'I am charmed to find you so punctual a correspondent. I always knew you to be a good friend, though I was afraid that I had lost you, and that you had joined that great multitude who abused me, and reproached me with Paganism, and Jacobitism, and many other wretched *isms*, of which I am only guilty of a part.' Burton's *Hume*, ii. 38.

Note 8. Dr. Traill was unlike the Professor under whom Dr. A. Carlyle studied at Edinburgh ; of whom he writes :—' There was one advantage attending the lectures of a dull professor—viz., that he could form no school, and the students were left entirely to themselves, and naturally formed opinions far more liberal than those they got from the Professor. This was the answer I gave to Patrick, Lord Elibank, when he asked me one day, many years afterwards, what could be the reason that the young clergymen of that period so far surpassed their predecessors of his early days in useful accomplishments and liberality of mind—viz., that the Professor of Theology was dull, and Dutch, and prolix.' Carlyle's *Auto.* p. 56.

Note 9. Parliament had met on Oct. 26. Horace Walpole wrote on Nov. 14 :—' The Parliament grants whatever is asked ; and yet a great alteration has happened in the Administration. The Duke of

Grafton has changed sides, and was turned out last Friday.' After
mentioning other changes he continues:—'The town is impatient to
see whether this change of men implies any change of measures. I
do not see why it should, for none of the new Ministers have ever inclined to the Americans.' *Letters*, vi. 280. There was no yielding in
the King, who on Oct. 15 had written to Lord North:—'Every means
of distressing America must meet with my concurrence, as it tends to
bringing them to feel the necessity of returning to their duty.' *Corres.
of George III with Lord North*, i. 274.

Note 10. Hume is speaking of the trade in English manufactures
only. The elder Pitt, on Jan. 14, 1766, said:—'I will be bold to
affirm, that the profits to Great Britain from the trade of the Colonies
through all its branches is two millions a year. This is the fund that
carried you triumphantly through the last war. The estates that were
rented at £2000 a year threescore years ago are at £3000 at present.
Those estates sold then for from fifteen to eighteen years' purchase;
the same may be now sold for thirty. You owe this to America.'
Parl. Hist. xvi. 105. A writer in the *Gent. Mag.* for 1768, p. 514, who
signs himself F. B. (Benjamin Franklin, I suspect), gives the declared
exports from England, exclusive of Scotland and Ireland, to America
as £2,072,000 a year, and the imports as £1,081,000. He considers
however that the exports really amounted to £3,000,000. It was the
object of the writer to make these as large as possible. (In 1886 the
exports from the United Kingdom amounted to £37,600,000, and the
imports to £81,600,000. Whitaker's *Almanac*, p. 517.)

Great Britain, among other restrictions, would not allow the
Americans to erect steel furnaces, or to export from one province to
another, whether by land or by water, hats or woollen goods of their
own make. She assumed to herself the exclusive right of supplying
them with all goods from Europe. Smith's *Wealth of Nations*, ed.
1811, ii. 424, 426. Sir John Pringle, in a postscript to a letter to Hume,
dated London, July 8, 1775, told him that a sensible man from the
Colonies had complained of the trouble the Americans were put to in
being forced 'at all times (even in time of war) to come with their
cargo of wine taken up in Spain or Portugal to the Isle of Wight, or
other English ports, unload it and put it again on board, before they
could carry it home. The porters at such places could only gain
while the Provincials were unnecessarily the sufferers.' Sir John
had written at the bottom of his letter:—'Burn the enclosed P.S.'
M. S. R. S. E. Adam Smith condemns such a system as this in the
following words:—'To found a great empire for the sole purpose of
raising up a people of customers may at first sight appear a project
fit only for a nation of shopkeepers. It is however a project altogether
unfit for a nation of shopkeepers; but extremely fit for a nation
whose government is influenced by shopkeepers. Such statesmen,
and such statesmen only, are capable of fancying that they will find
some advantage in employing the blood and treasure of their fellow-

citizens to found and maintain such an empire.' *Wealth of Nations*, ii. 471.

Note 11. 'We most carefully distinguish between the effects of the colony trade and those of the monopoly of that trade. The former are always and necessarily beneficial; the latter always and necessarily hurtful. . . . If the colony trade . . . is advantageous to Great Britain, it is not by means of the monopoly, but in spite of the monopoly.' *Wealth of Nations*, ed. 1811, ii. 462, 464. Mr. E. J. Payne in his *History of European Colonies*, p. 127, says :—'The immediate effect of the independence of America was felt in its destroying the Navigation Act, and opening the commerce of the United States to the world. The shipping of the United States increased fivefold in twenty years ; the trade with England increased in the same proportion.'

Note 12. Burke, on March 22 of this year, in his speech on Conciliation with America, had said :—'Three thousand miles of ocean lie between you and them. No contrivance can prevent the effect of this distance in weakening Government. Seas roll, and months pass, between the order and the execution ; and the want of a speedy explanation of a single point is enough to defeat a whole system. You have, indeed, *winged ministers of vengeance*, who carry your bolts in their pounces to the remotest verge of the sea. But there a power steps in, that limits the arrogance of raging passions and furious elements, and says, " *So far shalt thou go, and no farther.*" Who are you, that you should fret and rage, and bite the chains of Nature ? Nothing worse happens to you than does to all nations who have extensive Empire ; and it happens in all the forms into which Empire can be thrown.' Payne's *Burke*, i. 183.

Note 13. The Charter Governments were Connecticut, Rhode Island and Massachusetts. The charter of Massachusetts, which had been adjudged to be forfeited in 1684, was restored by William III with its privileges greatly maimed. Bancroft's *History of the United States*, ed. 1860, ii. 127 ; iii. 80. New Hampshire, New York, New Jersey, North and South Carolina, Georgia and Virginia were Royal Colonies. Maryland and Pennsylvania with Delaware were Proprietary Governments. *Encyclo. Britan.*, ninth ed. xxiii. 730. 'The Charter Colonies in which the Governors were chosen annually by popular election, and the Proprietary Governments had no dependence on the executive government of England, and they transacted their business with it through agents of their own, resident in England.' Payne's *European Colonies*, p. 106. In Massachusetts however, after 1684, the Governor was appointed by the King. Bancroft's *History*, iii. 80.

In a collection of Memorandums found among Hume's papers is entered :—'The Charter Governments in America, almost entirely independent of England.' Burton's *Hume*, i. 127. In his *History*, viii. 330, he says :—'King James recalled the Charters by which the liberties of the Colonies were secured ; and he sent over Governors invested with absolute power.' The Charter of Connecticut was hidden in the hollow of an oak, where it was kept till James's tyranny was overpast. Bancroft's *History*, ii. 432.

Note 14. So devoted were the planters of Virginia to the cause of freedom, that at a meeting of delegates held on August 1, 1775, 'they resolved from the first of the following November not to purchase any more slaves from Africa, the West Indies, or any other place.' *Ann. Reg.* 1775, i. 13. This blow was struck not at the slave-trade, but at British Commerce. It was of men such as these that Johnson said :—' How is it that we hear the loudest yelps for liberty among the drivers of negroes ?' Boswell's *Johnson*, iii. 201. At the same meeting it was resolved that there should be no exportation of tobacco or any other goods to England.

Note 15. Burke, in the *Ann. Reg.* for 1775, i. 16, mentions ' a very ill-timed proclamation ' issued on August 4 of this year by the Governor of Massachusetts Bay, ' for the encouragement of piety and virtue etc.' ' The people of that province had always been .scoffed at for a pharisaical attention to outward forms, and to the appearances of religious piety and virtue. . . . In this proclamation hypocrisy being inserted among the immoralities against which the people were warned, it seemed as if an act of state were turned into a libel on the people ; and this insult exasperated greatly the rage of minds already sufficiently discontented.' The clergy, no doubt, would not only catch the flame but spread it.

The Bishop of Peterborough, preaching before the Society for the Propagation of the Gospel on Feb. 16, 1776, described ' the distresses and persecutions of the American episcopal clergy.' *Gent. Mag.* 1776, p. 171.

Note 16. The King in his speech on opening Parliament on Oct. 26, speaking of the increase in the land forces, said :—' I have also the satisfaction to inform you, that I have received the most friendly offers of foreign assistance.' *Parl. Hist.* xviii. 696. Horace Walpole writing the next day describes this statement as a falsehood. ' They talk of foreign Powers offering them troops ; is *begging* being *offered*? and.if those foreign Powers are not Russia, but little Hesse, etc., are those foreign *Powers* ?' *Letters*, vi. 275. He is partly in error however, as there is no mention of *Powers*. It was from Russia that the King hoped to get troops. Burke ends a letter to the Duke of Richmond, dated Sept. 26, 1775, by saying :—' I beg pardon for this long and unmanaged letter. I am on thorns. I cannot, at my ease, see Russian barbarism let loose to waste the most beautiful object that ever appeared upon this globe.' Burke's *Corres.* ii. 75.

Gibbon wrote to Holroyd on Oct. 14 :—' When the Russians arrive (if they refresh themselves in England or Ireland) will you go and see their camp ? ·We have great hopes of getting a body of these Barbarians. In consequence of some very plain advances King George, with his own hand, wrote a very polite letter to sister Kitty

[Empress Catherine II] requesting her friendly assistance. Full powers and instructions were sent to Gunning [our Ambassador at St. Petersburg] to agree for any force between five and twenty thousand men, *carte blanche* for the terms ; on condition, however, that they should serve, not as auxiliaries, but as mercenaries.' Gibbon's *Misc. Works,* ii. 139. No man knew better than Gibbon the character of these savage mercenaries whom the King hoped to pour in a devastating flood over our settlements. He had investigated the causes of ' the abject slavery' in which the Russians lived. *Ib.* v. 531. Yet in Parliament he gave his constant support to the Ministry. ' I took my seat,' he says, 'at the beginning of the memorable contest between Great Britain and America, and supported with many a sincere and silent vote the rights, though not perhaps the interest, of the mother-country.' *Ib.* i. 220. The Prussians in the wars of Napoleon, after having experienced the French in their country as enemies and the Russians as allies, used to say :—' Better the French as enemies than the Russians as friends.' George III, it should seem, was acting more in sorrow than in anger. In his Speech from the Throne he said :—' When the unhappy and deluded multitude, against whom this force will be directed, shall become sensible of their error, I shall be ready to receive the misled with tenderness and mercy.' *Parl. Hist.* xviii. 696. The Russians, however, were not to be had. On Nov. 3, the King wrote to Lord North :—'The letter of the Empress is a clear refusal, and not in so genteel a manner as I should have thought might have been expected from her. She has not had the civility to answer in her own hand, and has thrown out some expressions that may be civil to a Russian ear, but certainly not to more civilised ones.' George III's *Corres.* i. 282. On Nov. 11, the King mentions a contract with a Lieut.-Colonel Scheither who is to raise troops in Germany at ten pounds per man. ' He need not go far for recruits,' he adds, ' as the moment he acts openly he may have as many Hessians and Brunswickers as he pleases.' *Ib.* p. 292. On Jan. 18, 1776, Gibbon wrote :—' You know we have got eighteen thousand Germans from Hesse, Brunswick, and Hesse Darmstadt. I think our meeting [of Parliament] will be lively; a spirited minority and a desponding majority. The higher people are placed, the more gloomy are their countenances, the more melancholy their language. You may call this cowardice, but I fear it arises from their knowledge (a late knowledge) of the difficulty and magnitude of the business.' Gibbon's *Misc. Works,* ii. 142. Eleven days later he wrote :—' I much fear that our Leaders have not a genius which can act at the distance of three thousand miles. You know that a large draught of Guards are just going to America; poor dear creatures !' *Ib.* p. 143.

Note 17.   The three per cent. consols were at 88 on Oct. 26.   *Gent. Mag.* 1775, p. 504.   See *ante,* p. 179, *n.* 15.

Note 18.   Hume had written twenty-one years earlier:—'Speculative reasoners, during that age [the age of James I], raised many objections to the planting of those remote colonies ; and foretold that, after draining their mother-country of inhabitants, they would soon shake off her yoke, and erect an independent government in America. But time has shown that the views entertained by those who encouraged such generous undertakings were more just and solid. A mild Government and great naval force have preserved, and may still preserve during some time, the dominion of England over her colonies.' *History of England*, vi. 188. In a fine passage in the first edition of this same volume of his History, which he afterwards had the shame of suppressing, he said :—' The seeds of many a noble state have been sown in climates kept desolate by the wild manners of the ancient inhabitants ; and an asylum secured in that solitary world for liberty and science, if ever the spreading of unlimited empire, or the inroad of barbarous nations, should again extinguish them in this turbulent and restless hemisphere.' Burton's *Hume*, ii. 74.

Boswell wrote on June 19 of this year :—' Yesterday I met Mr. Hume. He said it was all over in America ; we *could* not subdue the colonists, and another gun should not be fired, were it not for decency's sake ; he meant in order to keep up an appearance of power. But I think the lives of our fellow-subjects should not be thrown away for such *decency*. He said we may do very well without America, and he was for withdrawing our troops altogether, and letting the Canadians fall upon our colonists. I do not think he makes our *right* to tax at all clear.' *Letters of Boswell*, p. 204.

On Nov. 9 Walpole wrote :—' I think this country undone, almost beyond redemption. Victory in any war but a civil one fascinates mankind with a vision of glory. What should we gain by triumph itself ? Would America laid waste, deluged with blood, plundered, enslaved, replace America flourishing, rich, and free ? Do we want to reign over it, as the Spaniards over Peru, depopulated ? Are desolate regions preferable to commercial cities ? But if the Provincials conquer, are they, like lovers, to kiss and be friends ? Who are the heroes, where are the statesmen, that shall restore us to the position in which we stood two years ago ?' *Letters*, vi. 279.

Adam Smith, who shared most of Hume's thoughts, after showing that ' under the present system of management Great Britain derives nothing but loss from the dominion which she assumes over her colonies,' continues :—' To propose that she should voluntarily give up all authority over her colonies, and leave them to elect their own magistrates, to enact their own laws, and to make peace and war as they might think proper, would be to propose such a measure as never was, and never will be adopted by any nation in the world. . . . The most visionary enthusiasts would scarce be capable of proposing such a measure, with any serious hopes at least of its ever being adopted. If it was adopted however, Great Britain would not only be immediately freed from the whole annual expense of the peace establishments of

the colonies, but might settle with them such a treaty of commerce as
would effectually secure to her a free trade, more advantageous to
the great body of the people, though less so to the merchants, than
the monopoly which she at present enjoys. By thus parting good
friends, the natural affection of the colonies to the mother country,
which perhaps our late dissensions have well-nigh extinguished,
would quickly revive. It might dispose them not only to respect for
whole centuries together that treaty of commerce which they had
concluded with us at parting, but to favour us in war as well as in
trade, and instead of turbulent and factious subjects to become our
most faithful, affectionate, and generous allies.' *Wealth of Nations*, ed.
1811, ii. 475. A few pages further on he continues:—'The persons
who now govern the resolutions of what they call their continental
congress feel in themselves at this moment a degree of importance
which perhaps the greatest subjects in Europe scarce feel. From
shopkeepers, tradesmen, and attorneys they are become statesmen
and legislators, and are employed in contriving a new form of government for an extensive empire, which, they flatter themselves, will
become, and which indeed seems very likely to become, one of the
greatest and most formidable that ever was in the world.' *Ib.* p. 485.

More than five years earlier than the date of Hume's letter, on
May 6, 1770, Horace Walpole had written:—'The tocsin seems to be
sounded to America. I have many visions about that country, and
fancy I see twenty empires and republics forming upon vast scales
over all that continent, which is growing too mighty to be kept
in subjection to half a dozen exhausted nations in Europe. As the
latter sinks and the others rise, they who live between the eras will
be a sort of Noahs, witnesses to the period of the old world and
origin of the new. I entertain myself with the idea of a future senate
in California and Virginia, where their future patriots will harangue
on the austere and incorruptible virtue of the ancient English! will
tell their auditors of our disinterestedness and scorn of bribes and
pensions, and make us blush in our graves at their ridiculous panegyrics. Who knows but even our Indian usurpations and villanies
may become topics of praise to American schoolboys? As I believe
our virtues are extremely like those of our predecessors the Romans,
so I am sure our luxury and extravagance are too.' *Letters*, v. 235.

Patrick Henry had ended his brief but noble speech before the
Convention of Delegates on March 28 of this year, 1775, by saying :—
'It is in vain, Sir, to extenuate the matter. Gentlemen may cry
peace, peace—but there is no peace. The war is actually begun !
The next gale that sweeps from the north will bring to our ears the
clash of resounding arms ! Our brethren are already in the field !
Why stand we here idle ? What is it that gentlemen wish ? What
would they have ? Is life so dear, or peace so sweet, as to be pur-
chased at the price of chains and slavery? Forbid it, Almighty God !
I know not what course others may take; but as for me, give me

liberty or give me death!' *American Orations,* i. 23. A letter written
to Franklin, who had returned to America, by a Mrs. Greene of Warwick, Rhode Island, in the following July, shows by the use of the
one word 'home' how strong was the tie which had bound the
Colonies to the Old Country. She writes:—'Do come and see us,
certain! Don't think of going home [i. e. to England] again. Do sit
down and enjoy the remainder of your days in peace.' *Letters to
Benjamin Franklin,* p. 67.

Note 19. When Hume calls Lord Chatham a madman he is no
doubt referring to the miserable state of health into which that
statesman had fallen eight years earlier. Hume wrote to the
Countess de Boufflers on June 19, 1767:—'You ask the present
state of our politics. Why, in a word, we are all in confusion.
This, you'll say, is telling you nothing new; for when were we
otherwise? But we are in greater confusion than usual; because
of the strange condition of Lord Chatham, who was regarded as
our first minister. The public here, as well as with you, believe
him wholly mad; but I am assured it is not so. He is only fallen
into extreme low spirits and into nervous disorders, which render
him totally unfit for business, make him shun all company, and, as
I am told, set him weeping like a child upon the least accident.
Is not this a melancholy situation for so lofty and vehement a spirit
as his? And is it not even an addition to his unhappiness that
he retains his senses?' Hume's *Private Corres.* p. 243. Horace
Walpole had written on April 5 of the same year:—'There is a
misfortune not so easily to be surmounted, the state of Lord Chatham's health, who now does not only not see the Ministers, but
even does not receive letters. The world, on the report of the
Opposition, believe his head disordered, and there is so far a kind
of colour for this rumour, that he has lately taken Dr. Addington,
a physician in vogue, who originally was a mad doctor.' *Letters,*
v. 45. On Sept. 9 he wrote:—'For Lord Chatham, he is really or
intentionally mad—but I still doubt which of the two.' *Ib.* p. 63.
Junius, in a letter signed Correggio, dated Sept. 16 of this same year,
describes him as 'a lunatic brandishing a crutch, or bawling through
a grate, or writing with desperate charcoal a letter to North America.'
Letters of Junius, ed. 1812, ii. 474.

In charging Chatham with having reduced his country to its
present condition Hume, I believe, is thinking of the effects of the
great war of conquests carried on under his Ministry. 'The fine
inscription on the monument of Lord Chatham in Guildhall records,'
says Lord Macaulay, 'the general opinion of the citizens of London,
that under his administration commerce had been "united with and
made to flourish by war."' *Essays,* ed. 1874, ii. 193. Before long it was
found that commerce can no more be made to flourish by war than by
any other form of robbery. Adam Smith, after stating that 'the last
war, which was undertaken altogether on account of the colonies,

cost Great Britain upwards of ninety millions,' continues :—'The rulers of Great Britain have, for more than a century past, amused the people with the imagination that they possessed a great empire on the west side of the Atlantic.   This empire, however, has hitherto existed in imagination only.   It has hitherto been, not an empire, but the project of an empire; not a gold mine, but the project of a gold mine; a project which has cost, which continues to cost, and which, if pursued in the same way as it has been hitherto, is likely to cost immense expense, without being likely to bring any profit; for the effects of the monopoly of the colony trade, it has been shown, are to the great body of the people mere loss instead of profit.   It is surely now time that our rulers should either realise this golden dream, in which they have been indulging themselves perhaps as well as the people, or that they should awake from it themselves, and endeavour to awaken the people.'   *Wealth of Nations,* ed. 1811, iii. 446-8.   In another passage, speaking of the sums which England had laid out upon the defence of her colonies, he says :— 'The late war [the war in which under Pitt England made her greatest conquests] was altogether a colony quarrel; and the whole expense of it, in whatever part of the world it might have been laid out, whether in Germany or the East Indies, ought justly to be stated to the account of the colonies.   It amounted to more than ninety millions sterling.'   *Ib.* ii. 474.

Burke, in his Speech on American Taxation on April 19, 1774, after describing how by the old and wise policy England had never meddled with the taxation of America, continues :—'This nation never thought of departing from that choice until the period immediately on the close of the last war.   Then a scheme of government new in many things seemed to have been adopted.'   After telling how twenty new regiments were raised, he continues :—'When this huge increase of military establishment was resolved on, a revenue was to be found to support so great a burthen.   Country gentlemen, the great patrons of economy, and the great resisters of a standing armed force, would not have entered with much alacrity into the vote for so large and so expensive an army, if they had been very sure that they were to continue to pay for it.   But hopes of another kind were held out to them; and, in particular, I well remember that Mr. Townshend, in a brilliant harangue on this subject, did dazzle them by playing before their eyes the image of a revenue to be raised in America.'   Payne's *Burke's Select Works,* i. 121.   In an earlier speech, after describing Chatham as 'a being before whom "thrones, dominations, princedoms, virtues, powers (waving his hand all this time over the Treasury Bench, which he sat behind) all veil their faces with their wings,"' apostrophising him, he exclaimed, 'Doom not to perdition that vast public debt, a mass seventy millions of which thou hast employed in rearing a pedestal for thy own statue.' *Chatham Corres.* iii. 145.

In the Protest of some of the Peers on the Cyder Bill (March 30, 1763) mention is made of 'the great load of taxes which have been found necessary in support of a just, prosperous, and glorious war.' *Parl. Hist.* xv. 1314. A tax on the Colonies had not yet been proposed, and it had been found necessary to increase 'the odious excise' by including cyder under it. George Johnstone wrote to Hume on March 22 [1763]:—'We are in a bustle here. I am just going to the House of Commons. The subject is a tax on wine and cyder. . . . Pitt has pay'd Grenville so severely that whenever he now rises there is a general laugh. He imitated his manner so perfectly both in his words and gesture that the original is sure to call the picture to our mind. . . . The Opposition have raised the cry of No excise, and Liberty and the Constitution, and Oh my country against the mode of collecting the cyder duty.' *M.S.R.S.E.* Pitt had attacked the laws of excise as odious. 'Mr. Grenville contended that the tax was unavoidable. . . . "Where," he asked, "can you lay another tax of equal efficiency?" And he repeated several times, "Tell me where you can lay another tax—tell me where?" Upon which Mr. Pitt, in the words of a song at that time popular, replied in a musical tone, "Gentle shepherd, tell me where." The effect on the house was irresistible, and settled on Mr. Grenville the appellation of "the gentle shepherd." ' *Chatham Corres.* ii. 216.

Horace Walpole wrote on Nov. 9, 1775, a fortnight after the date of Hume's letter:—'I probably have little time to be witness to the humiliations that are approaching. Father Paul's *Esto perpetua!* was more the prayer of a good man than of a wise one. Countries are but great families, that rise from obscurity to dignity and then degenerate. This little island, that for many centuries was but a merchant, married *a great fortune* in the last war, got a title, grew insolent and extravagant, despised its original counter, quarrelled with its factors, kicked its plebeian wife out of doors, and thought, by putting on an old red coat, to hector her relations out of the rest of her fortune, which remained in their hands as trustees. Europe, that was jealous of this upstart captain's sudden rise, encouraged him in his folly, in hopes of seeing him quite undone. End of volume the first. The second part is in the press.' *Letters*, vi. 279.

'It must be owned,' writes Lord Macaulay, 'that the expense of the war never entered into Pitt's consideration. Perhaps it would be more correct to say that the cost of his victories increased the pleasure with which he contemplated them. . . . He was proud of the sacrifices and efforts which his eloquence and his success had induced his countrymen to make. The price at which he purchased faithful service and complete victory, though far smaller than that which his son, the most profuse and incapable of war ministers, paid for treachery, defeat, and shame, was long and severely felt by the nation.' Macaulay's *Essays*, ed. 1874, ii. 194.

Note 20. Hume spoke in vain; the nation was not with him,

Burke, writing a month earlier of the ruin of the country, 'which, if I am not quite visionary, is approaching with the greatest rapidity,' continues :—'I am sensible of the shocking indifference and neutrality of a great part of the nation. But a speculative despair is unpardonable, where it is our duty to act. . . . The people are not answerable for their present supine acquiescence ; indeed they are not. God and nature never made them to think or to act without guidance and direction. They have obeyed the only impulse they have received.' Burke's *Corres.* ii. 71-2. On Feb. 2 of the year before, describing 'the supineness of the public,' he had said :—'Any remarkable highway robbery at Hounslow Heath would make more conversation than all the disturbances of America.' *Ib.* i. 453.

Dr. Burton gives a letter by Hume, written a day later than the one in the text, which seems to be in answer to a request to join in one of the Loyal Addresses to the Crown on the revolt of the Colonies. He says :—'Here is Lord Home teasing me for an address from the Merse [Hume's native district], and I have constantly refused him. Besides, I am an American in my principles, and wish we would let them alone to govern or misgovern themselves, as they think proper : the affair is of no consequence, or of little consequence to us. If the County of Renfrew think it indispensably necessary for them to interpose in public matters, I wish they would advise the King, first to punish those insolent rascals in London and Middlesex, who daily insult him and the whole legislature, before he thinks of America. Ask him, how he can expect that a form of government will maintain an authority at three thousand miles' distance, when it cannot make itself be respected, or even be treated with common decency, at home. Tell him, that Lord North, though in appearance a worthy gentleman, has not a head for these great operations ; and that if fifty thousand men and twenty millions of money were intrusted to such a lukewarm coward as Gage, they never could produce any effect. These are objects worthy of the respectable county of Renfrew ; not mauling the poor infatuated Americans in the other hemisphere.' Burton's *Hume,* ii. 478. The General Assembly of the Church of Scotland was far behind Hume in political wisdom. Dr. Blair, writing in the summer of 1776, says of that body :—'We have sent a dutiful and loyal Address. A violent debate was expected upon it. However it did not follow. The factious were afraid to show themselves ; though the words *unnatural and dangerous rebellion* went very ill down with them.' *M. S. R. S. E.*

Horace Walpole, writing from Paris on Oct. 10, about his return to England, says :—'I am not impatient to be in a frantic country that is stabbing itself in every vein. The delirium still lasts ; though, I believe, kept up by the quacks that caused it. Is it credible that five or six of the great *trading* towns have presented addresses against the Americans ? I have no doubt but those addresses are procured by those boobies the country gentlemen, their members, and bought of

the Aldermen; but is it not amazing that the merchants and manu-
facturers do not duck such tools in a horse-pond?' *Letters*, vi. 266.
On Oct. 28, two days after the date of Hume's letter, he wrote from
London :—'At my return I found everything in great confusion.
The Ministers had only provoked and united—not intimidated,
wounded, or divided America.   Errors in or neglect of execution
have rendered everything much worse; and at this instant they are not
sure that the King has a foot of dominion left on that continent... The
Ministers say that it will take sixty thousand men to re-conquer
America.   They will as soon have sixty thousand armies.   Whether
they can get any Russians is not even yet certain. . . Distress and
difficulties increase every day, and genius does not increase in proportion.' *Ib.* p. 277.

Note 21.   Hume here uses *Advertisement* in the same sense as the
French *Avertissement*, which is defined by Littré, *Préface mise à la
tête d'un livre*.   Johnson, in speaking of the *Lives of the Poets*, says :—
'My purpose was only to have allotted to every poet an Advertisement, like those which we find in the French Miscellanies, containing a few dates and a general character.' Boswell's *Johnson*, iv. 35.
In this Advertisement, which is placed at the beginning of *An
Inquiry concerning Human Understanding*, Hume, speaking of his
Treatise of Human Nature, says that 'he had projected it before he
left College,' and that 'sensible of his error in going to the press too
early, he cast the whole anew in the following pieces. . . . Yet several
writers, who have honoured the author's Philosophy with answers,
have taken care to direct all their batteries against that juvenile work,
which the Author never acknowledged, and have affected to triumph
in any advantage which they imagined they had obtained over it; a
practice very contrary to all rules of candour and fair dealing, and a
strong instance of those polemical artifices which a bigoted zeal
thinks itself authorised to employ.   Henceforth the Author desires
that the following Pieces may alone be regarded as containing his
philosophical sentiments and principles.'   In a review of Hume's
Life in the *Ann. Reg.* 1776, ii. 28, Beattie is reproached with obtaining a pension by levelling all his arguments against Hume's
'juvenile production.'

Note 22.   Reid's *Inquiry into the Human Mind* was meant as a
refutation of Hume's philosophy.   Nevertheless in his anxiety not
to misrepresent the meaning of his adversary, and in his reliance on
his candour, he asked leave, through their common friend Dr. Blair,
to submit his reasonings to his examination.   'I wish,' wrote Hume
in reply, 'that the parsons would confine themselves to their old
occupation of worrying one another, and leave philosophers to argue
with temper, moderation, and good manners.'   When however he
had read part of the manuscript, he wrote to the author in terms
of high praise of its philosophy, and added :—'As I was desirous to
be of some use to you, I kept a watchful eye all along over your

style; but it is really so correct, and so good English, that I found not anything worth the remarking. There is only one passage in this chapter, where you make use of the phrase *hinder to do*, instead of *hinder from doing*, which is the English one.' Stewart's *Life of Reid*, pp. 417, 418.

Note 23. Strahan wrote to Hume on June 3, 1776, when the philosopher was near his end:—'Even your enemies relent, and I will venture to say, wish your recovery. Creech of Edinburgh writes me that he had just then (May 29) received a letter from Dr. Beattie in which was the following paragraph:—"I am sincerely sorry to hear of Mr. Hume's bad health. There will be several things in this Edition which I am pretty sure would not offend him, if he were to see them, which I heartily which he may. The Essay is corrected in almost every page—superfluities retrenched—inaccuracies corrected—and many harsh expressions softened." Does not this look like repentance?' Beattie, in his Preface, mentions Hume's 'Advertisement to a new edition of his *Essays*, in which he seems to disown his *Treatise of Human Nature*, and desires that those *Essays*, as then published, may be considered as containing his philosophical sentiments and principles. . . . He certainly merits praise for thus publicly disowning, though late, his *Treatise of Human Nature* . . . In consequence of his Advertisement, I thought it right to mitigate in this edition some of the censures that more especially refer to that work.' Forbes's *Life of Beattie*, ed. 1824, p. 231. Hume perhaps would never have made the idle attempt to have one of his greatest works suppressed, as it were, nearly forty years after its publication, had he foreseen that it would lead to his being partially absolved and publicly praised by Dr. Beattie. When three years after their author's death the *Dialogues on Natural Religion* were published, Beattie felt himself an injured man. In a letter to Mrs. Montagu he says:—' During the last years of Mr. Hume's life his friends gave out that he regretted his having dealt so much in metaphysics, and that he never would write any more. He was at pains to disavow his *Treatise of Human Nature* in an Advertisement which he published about half a year before his death. All this, with what I then heard of his bad health, made my heart relent towards him ; as you would no doubt perceive by the preface to my quarto book. But immediately after his death, I heard that he had left behind him two manuscripts,' etc. Beattie concludes with the following anecdote, which he had from Dr. Gregory:—' Mr. Hume was boasting to the doctor that among his disciples in Edinburgh he had the honour to reckon many of the fair sex. "Now, tell me," said the doctor, "whether, if you had a wife or a daughter, you would wish them to be your disciples. Think well before you answer me ; for I assure you, that whatever your answer is, I will not conceal it." Mr. Hume with a smile, and some hesitation, made this reply:—"No ; I believe scepticism may be too sturdy a virtue for a woman."' *Life of Beattie*, ed. 1824, p. 264. The knowledge that the answer would not be concealed would not have been an inducement to Hume to avow his real sentiments.

A writer in the *Gent. Mag.* for 1777, p. 159, records the following anecdote:—'Of Beattie's *Essay on Truth* Mr. Hume is reported to have said, "Truth! there is no truth in it; it is a horrible large lie in octavo."'

Note 24. Strahan replied that about 400 copies of the *History* were left in stock, and that he intended 'to put it to press again the ensuing summer.' *M.S.R.S.E.* The next edition was published in 1778.

[William Strahan to David Hume.]

LETTER LXXVII.

The War with the Colonies: The Rousing of the British Lion.

'. . . And now a word or two of politics. The increased liberty of the press, which gives you the substance of almost every debate, is the sole cause of my being less *communicative*, and as for my *impartiality*, notwithstanding a little change in my situation, it is noway diminished. But I differ from you, *toto cælo*, with regard to America. I am entirely for coercive methods with those obstinate madmen: And why should we despair of success?—Why should we suffer the Empire to be so dismembered, without the utmost exertions on our part? I see nothing so very formidable in this business, if we become a little more unanimous, and could stop the mouths of domestic traitors, from whence the evil originated[1].—Not that I wish to enslave the Colonists, or to make them one jot less happy than ourselves; but I am for keeping them subordinate to the British Legislature, and their trade in a reasonable degree subservient to the interest of the Mother Country; an advantage she well deserves, but which she must inevitably lose, if they are emancipated as you propose. I am really surprised you are of a different opinion. Very true, things look oddly at present, and the dispute hath hitherto been very ill-managed; but so we always do in the commencement of every war. So we did most remarkably in the last[2]. It is perhaps owing to the nature of our Government, which permits not of those sudden and decisive exertions frequently made by arbitrary Princes, But so soon as the

British Lion is roused, we never fail to fetch up our leeway[3], as the sailors say. And so I hope you will find it in this important case. We had two exceeding long debates in the House last Thursday and Friday. Till $\frac{1}{2}$ after 4 in the Morning the first Day, and $\frac{1}{2}$ after 1 the second. Much was said on both sides, but the Address was at length carried by 278 to 108[4], and I hope this decision will be followed by the most vigorous exertions both by sea and land.—At present I believe we have totally lost America ; but a proper disposition of our fleet, and the troops we shall, even without foreign assistance (except the Hanoverians[5]) be able to send thither, will speedily recover it. Perhaps it may be still a difficult task, but it is worth doing all in our power to accomplish. And a little perseverance on our part will unavoidably throw the Americans into confusion among themselves, even were we to stand upon the defensive, and only block up their ports. They cannot subsist without trade ; they must export their corn, or it is useless, and they must have cloathing for themselves and negroes[6], and a thousand other necessaries and conveniences of life from Europe. Their present anarchy is already, and must every day become more and more intolerable. I have not time just now to launch out into particulars. But the Newspapers will make up the deficiency. Your friend General Conway has declared with the minority. . . . When we have subdued the Colonists, it will require little force to keep them in order ; for all the men of property among them are in their hearts with us, and they will insensibly slide back into their former situation. . . .—*M. S. R. S. E.*

LONDON, *Oct.* 30, 1775.

Note 1. Johnson in his *Taxation no Tyranny*, published in the spring of this year, had said :—' The Americans had no thought of resisting the Stamp Act, till they were encouraged and incited by European intelligence from men whom they thought their friends, but who were friends only to themselves. On the original contrivers of mischief let an insulted nation pour out its vengeance. With whatever design they have inflamed this pernicious contest, they are themselves equally detestable. If they wish success to the colonies, they are traitors to this country ; if they wish their defeat, they are traitors at once to America and England. To them, and them only, must be imputed the interruption of commerce and the miseries of

war, the sorrow of those that shall be ruined and the blood of those
that shall fall.' Johnson's *Works*, vi. 260.

Note 2. 'The war [of 1756] began in every part of the world with
events disastrous to England, and even more shameful than disastrous ... The nation was in a state of angry and sullen despondency, almost unparalleled in history ... At this time appeared
Brown's *Estimate*, a book now remembered only by the allusions in
Cowper's *Table Talk* and in Burke's *Letters on a Regicide Peace*. It
was universally read, admired, and believed. The author fully convinced his readers that they were a race of cowards and scoundrels;
that nothing could save them; that they were on the point of being
enslaved by their enemies, and that they richly deserved their fate.
Such were the speculations to which ready credence was given at
the outset of the most glorious war in which England had ever been
engaged.' Macaulay's *Essays*, ed. 1874, ii. 179.

The following extracts from Lord Chesterfield's *Letters to his
Friends* show the despondency into which at that period had fallen a
man versed in affairs of state :—' Oct. 13, 1756. I wish well to my
species in general, and to my country in particular; and therefore
lament the havock that is already made, and likely to be made, of the
former, and the inevitable ruin which I see approaching by great
strides to the latter.' *Misc. Works*, iv. 211. 'Nov. 26, 1756. I now
quietly behold the storm from the shore, and shall only be involved,
but without particular blame, in the common ruin. That moment,
you perceive, if you combine all circumstances, cannot be very
remote. On the contrary, it is so near, that were Machiavel at the
head of our affairs, he could not retrieve them; and therefore it is very
indifferent to me, what minister shall give us the last *coup de grace*.'
Ib. p. 191. 'Christmas Day, 1757. [After alluding to 'three plans'
which he had suggested.] This, at least, I am sure of, that they are
our last convulsive struggles, for at this rate we cannot possibly live
through the year 1759.' *Ib*. p. 205.

Note 3. This mixed metaphor of the British Lion and leeway
recalls the time of which Ovid sang—
    'Nat lupus inter oves; fulvos vehit unda leones.' *Meta*. i. 304.

Note 4. Horace Walpole, describing the attack on the Court in
this debate, said :—' Mr. Conway in a better speech than ever was
made exposed all their outrages and blunders; and Charles Fox
told Lord North that not Alexander nor Cæsar had ever conquered
so much as he had lost in one campaign. Even his Lordship's
friends, nay the Scotch, taunt him in public with his laziness.' *Letters*,
vi. 278.

Note 5. The King in his Speech from the Throne said that he had
sent Hanoverian troops to Gibraltar and Minorca to replace the
British forces that had been despatched to America. This measure
was attacked as unconstitutional not only by the regular Opposition,
but by several members who called themselves *Independent*; be-

longing, as they did, to that powerful party which in the last two reigns had as strongly opposed the Court as in the present reign they supported it. *Ann. Reg.* 1776, i. 64.

Note 6. Johnson, in his *Taxation no Tyranny*, with his hatred of slavery had written :—' It has been proposed that the slaves should be set free, an act which surely the lovers of liberty cannot but commend. If they are furnished with firearms for defence, and utensils for husbandry, and settled in some simple form of government within the country, they may be more grateful and honest than their masters.' *Works*, vi. 260. In the mouths of the Ministers and their supporters this would have been an idle threat ; for theirs was the party which upheld not only slavery but the slave-trade.

LETTER LXXVIII.

Hume's Anxiety for the Correctness of his Works : the Effects of the Loss of America.

EDINBURGH, 13 *of Novr.*, 1775.

DEAR SᴵR

Your Memory has fail'd you. The last Quarto Edition of my philosophical Pieces in 1768 was in two Volumes, and this Advertisement may be prefixed to the second Volume. There was another Quarto Edition in one Volume six or seven Years before[1] ; but that Edition must be all sold off, as you have made four or five Editions since[2]. Your Correction is certainly just ; and I had evidently been guilty of an Error in my Pen.

I am glad to find there is a Prospect of a new Edition of my History. I was indeed apprehensive, that the blind Rage of Party had entirely obstructed the Sale of it. I am as anxious of Correctness[3] as if I were writing to Greeks or French ; and besides frequent Revisals, which I have given it since the last Edition, I shall again run over it very carefully, and shall send you a corrected Copy. About six Weeks hence, I shall send off by the Waggon the four first Volumes ; and shall direct them to Mr. Cadel's Shop, which will be more easily found than your House[4].

X 2

The other four Volumes shall follow at Leizure. I remember an Author[5], who says, that one half of a man's Life is too little to write a Book; and the other half to correct it. I think, that I am more agreeably employ'd for myself in this manner, and perhaps more profitably for you, than if I were writing such Volumes as Macpherson's History[6], one of the most wretched *Productions* that ever came from your Press.

I am sorry, that I cannot agree with you, in your hopes of subduing and what is more difficult, of governing America[7]. *Think only of the great Kingdom of France which is within a days sailing of the small Island of Corsica; yet has not been able, in eight or nine Years, to subdue and govern it, contrary to Sentiments of the Inhabitants*[8]. *But the worst Effect of the Loss of America, will not be the Detriment to our Manufactures, which will be a mere trifle*[9], *or to our Navigation, which will not be considerable*[10]; *but to the Credit and Reputation of Government, which has already but too little Authority. You will probably see a Scene of Anarchy and Confusion open'd at home, the best Consequence of which is a settled Plan of arbitrary Power*[11]; *the worst, total Ruin and Destruction*[12].

I am extremely oblig'd to you for your Letter to Professor Wilson. I am afraid, however, that all Efforts in favour of Dr. Wight will be in vain. It seems, Dr. Hunter supports a Friend of his; and nothing can be refusd him by the University[13].

I am Dear S[ir] Yours most sincerely

DAVID HUME.

Note 1. There was a quarto edition in one volume in 1758.
Note 2. The editions of 1760, 1764, 1768, 1770, 1772.
Note 3. Hume had written 'careful of correctness,' but had scored 'careful' out. Johnson in his *Dictionary* gives an example from Granville of *anxious* followed not by *for* or *about* but by *of*—'anxious of neglect.' Hume's anxiety was for correctness of style.

Note 4.   See *ante*, p. 215, *n.* 2.

Note 5.   Rousseau, according to Hume's previous statement.   See *ante*, p. 200.

Note 6.   '*The History of Great Britain from the Restoration to the Accession of the House of Hanover.* By James Macpherson, Esq. ; 2 vols. quarto. £2 2s. Cadell.' *Gent. Mag.* 1775, p. 192.   Horace Walpole, writing on April 14, 1775, said :—' For Macpherson, I stopped dead short in the first volume ; never was such a heap of insignificant trash and lies.   One instance shall suffice : in a letter from a spy to James II there is a blank for a name ; a note without the smallest ground to build the conjecture on says, " probably the Earl of Devonshire."   Pretty well !   Yet not content, the honest gentleman says in the index, " The Earl of Devonshire is suspected of favouring the excluded family."   Can you suspect such a worthy person of forgery ? could he forge Ossian ?' *Letters*, vi. 202. Macpherson had published an *Introduction to the History of Great Britain and Ireland,* which soon reached a third edition.   To this work Gibbon pays one of his stately compliments, some years after he had been warned by Hume that the author of *Ossian* was a literary forger.   He says :—' In the dark and doubtful paths of Caledonian antiquity I have chosen for my guides two learned and ingenious Highlanders, whom their birth and education had peculiarly qualified for that office.   See . . . and *Introduction to the History of Great Britain and Ireland*, by James Macpherson, Esq.' *Decline and Fall*, ed. 1807, iv. 244.

Note 7.   Strahan had most people with him in the belief that America would be subdued.   Horace Walpole wrote from Paris on Sept. 6, 1775 :—' You may judge whether they do not stare at all we are doing !   They will not believe me when I tell them that the American War is *fashionable*, for one is forced to use that word to convey to them an idea of the majority.' *Letters*, vi. 248.   Burke wrote on Sept. 24 :—' I confess that from every information which I receive . . . the real fact is, that the generality of the people of England are now led away by the misrepresentations and arts of the Ministry, the Court, and their abettors ; so that the violent measures towards America are fairly adopted and countenanced by a majority of individuals of all ranks, professions, or occupations in this country. . . . I am indeed more and more convinced that it behoves us as honest and honourable men to take the step of a protestation after Parliament has met.   It is unusual.   It would doubtless occasion much speculation.   It would have *some effect* upon the public at large, when they see men of high rank and fortune, of known principles and of undoubted abilities, stepping forwards in so extraordinary a manner to face a torrent, not merely of ministerial or Court power, but also of *almost* general opinion.'   Burke's *Corres.* ii. 68.

Note 8.   Genoa ceded Corsica to France in 1768.   In 1769 Pascal Paoli left the island and sought a refuge in England.   Voltaire in his chapter on Corsica, in his *Siècle de Louis XV*, written at all events as late as 1774, speaks as if the conquest of the country were complete. He says :—'Ainsi donc, en cédant la vaine et fatale souveraineté d'un pays qui lui était à charge, Gênes faisait en effet un bon marché, et le roi de France en faisait un meilleur, puisqu'il était assez puissant pour se faire obéir dans la Corse, pour la policer, pour la peupler, pour l'enrichir, en y faisant fleurir l'agriculture et le commerce . . . Il restait à savoir si les hommes ont le droit de vendre d'autres hommes ; mais c'est une question qu'on n'examina jamais dans aucun traité.' *Œuvres de Voltaire*, xix. 365.

Note 9. See *ante*, p. 288.

Note 10. Hume wrote to Adam Smith on Feb. 8, 1776 :—'The Duke of Buccleugh tells me that you are very zealous in American affairs. My notion is that the matter is not so important as is commonly imagined. If I be mistaken, I shall probably correct my error when I see you, or read you. [*The Wealth of Nations* was on the eve of publication.] Our navigation and general commerce may suffer more than our manufactures.' Burton's *Hume*, ii. 483. See *ante*, p. 292, *n.* 10, for the restrictions placed on American trade in the hope of benefiting the trade of England. By one of 'the principal dispositions of the Navigation Act,' writes Adam Smith, 'all ships, of which the owners, masters, and three-fourths of the mariners are not British subjects are prohibited, upon pain of forfeiting ship and cargo, from trading to the British settlements and plantations.' *Wealth of Nations*, ed. 1811, ii. 252. He considered 'the regulations of this famous act,' though some of them 'may have proceeded from national animosity, as wise as if they had all been dictated by the most deliberate wisdom.' *Ib.* p. 254. If America became free this exclusive navigation would of course at once be lost to England, but Hume had little fear of the consequence. Thirty-three years earlier, in his Essay entitled *Of the Jealousy of Trade*, he had written :—' I shall venture to acknowledge that, not only as a man but as a British subject, I pray for the flourishing commerce of Germany, Spain, Italy, and even France itself.' *Essays and Treatises*, ed. 1770, ii. 111.

Note 11. See *ante*, p. 128, *n.* 16.

Note 12. Horace Walpole, writing a fortnight later to Mason the poet, said :—'What shall I say more ? talk politics ? no ; we think too much alike. England was, Scotland is—indeed by the blunders the latter has made one sees its Irish origin,—but I had rather talk of anything else. I see nothing but ruin, whatever shall happen ; and what idle solicitude is that of childless old people, who are anxious about the first fifty years after their death, and do not reflect that in the eternity to follow, fifty or five hundred years are a moment, and that all countries fall sooner or later.' *Letters*, vi. 284. See *ante*, p. 179, *n.* 15.

Note 13. Dr. William Hunter, the famous physician, had taken his Doctor's degree at Glasgow. Perhaps it was already known that

he intended to make a munificent bequest to the University. Knight's
Biog. Dict. iii. 526. Dr. James Baillie was elected. Dr. Wight succeeded Baillie in 1778. *Caldwell Papers*, ii. 260.

LETTER LXXIX.

*Last Corrections of the History: Smith's Wealth of Nations:
Gibbon's Decline and Fall.*

EDINBURGH, 11 *of Feby.*, 1776.

DEAR S[IR]

Last Monday, I sent to the Newcastle Waggon the
four first Volumes corrected of my History. They are
directed to Mr. Cadell. You will see by the Margins, that
I have not been idle: And as the Corrections have cost
me a great deal of care and Attention, I am anxious that
the Books be safely deliver'd. They may arrive about
three Weeks hence; about which time, if Mr. Cadell does
not receive them, I beg, that he would take the trouble of
enquiring about them; and as soon as they come to hand,
let me know of it by a Line. The other Volumes will be
ready, whenever the Press demands them; of which you
will be so good as to inform me in time.

I hope you will employ one of your most careful Compositors in this Edition: For as it is the last, which, at
my Age and in my State of Health[1], I can hope to see, I
wish to leave it correct. I think that it will not be prudent in you, to make this Edition more numerous than the
former one.

I wonder what Smith means by not publishing[2]. I am
glad to see my Friend Gibbon advertised[3]: I am confident it will be a very good Book; though I am at a Loss
to conceive where he finds materials for a Volume from
Trajan to Constantine[4]. Be so good as to make my
Compliments to him: The Book has not yet arrived here.

I am Dear Sir Very sincerely
Your most obedient humble Servant
DAVID HUME[5].

Note 1. Hume had written to Adam Smith three days earlier:—
'By all accounts you intend to settle with us this spring; yet we
hear no more of it. What is the reason ? Your chamber in my house
is always unoccupied. I am always at home. I expect you to land
here. I have been, am, and shall be probably in an indifferent state
of health. I weighed myself t'other day, and find I have fallen five
complete stones. If you delay much longer, I shall probably disappear altogether.' Burton's *Hume*, ii. 483.

Note 2. In the letter from which the extract in the last note is
taken Hume said:—'I am as lazy a correspondent as you, yet my
anxiety about you makes me write. By all accounts your book has
been printed long ago; yet it has never been so much as advertised.
What is the reason ? If you wait till the fate of America be decided,
you may wait long.' So early as 1770 Smith seems to have thought
of publishing his great work, for Hume wrote to him on Feb. 6 of that
year, hearing that he was going up to London :—'How can you
so much as entertain a thought of publishing a book full of reason,
sense, and learning to those wicked abandoned madmen ?' Burton's
Hume, ii. 433. It is announced in the *London Chronicle* for Saturday,
March 9, 'This day was published elegantly printed in 2 vols. 4to.
price £1 16s. in boards, *An Enquiry into the Nature and Causes of
the Wealth of Nations*. By Adam Smith, LL.D. & F.R.S. Formerly
Professor of Moral Philosophy in the University of Glasgow. Printed
for W. Strahan ; and T. Cadell in the Strand.' Adam Smith, it will be
noticed, here gives the full additions to his name. When seventeen
years earlier he was publishing his *Theory of Moral Sentiments*, he
wrote to Strahan :—'In the titles both of the *Theory* and *Dissertation*
call me simply Adam Smith, without any addition either before or
behind.' Original Letters of Adam Smith, published in the *New York
Evening Post*, April 30, 1887.
    In the *Gentleman's Magazine* the publication of the *Wealth of
Nations* passed unnoticed. In the *Annual Register* (1776, ii. 241) it
is indeed reviewed ; but while sixteen pages are given in the same
number to Watson's *Reign of Philip II*, for it little more than two can
be spared.

Note 3. Gibbon wrote to Holroyd on Jan. 18 of this year:—'We
proceed triumphantly with the *Roman Empire*, and shall certainly
make our appearance before the end of next month.' Gibbon's
Misc. Works, ii. 142. In the *London Chronicle* for Tuesday, Feb. 20, it
is announced as 'published this day, elegantly printed in quarto,
price one guinea in boards.' Horace Walpole had received his copy
before Feb. 14. *Letters*, vi. 307. Writing to Mason on Feb. 18, he
said :—'Lo, there is just appeared a truly classic work ; a history, not
majestic like Livy, nor compressed like Tacitus; not stamped with
character like Clarendon ; perhaps not so deep as Robertson's *Scotland*, but a thousand degrees above his *Charles*; not pointed like
Voltaire, but as accurate as he is inexact; modest as he is *tranchant*,

LXXIX.] *GIBBON'S DECLINE AND FALL.* 313

and sly as Montesquieu without being so *recherché*. The style is as smooth as a Flemish picture, and the muscles are concealed and only for natural uses, not exaggerated like Michael Angelo's to show the painter's skill in anatomy; nor composed of the limbs of clowns of different nations, like Dr. Johnson's heterogeneous monsters. This book is Mr. Gibbon's *History of the Decline and Fall of the Roman Empire*. He is son of a foolish Alderman, is a Member of Parliament, and called a whimsical one, because he votes variously as his opinion leads him; and his first production was in French, in which language he shines too. I know him a little, never suspected the extent of his talents, for he is perfectly modest, or I want penetration, which I know too, but I intend to know him a great deal more.' *Ib.* 310. Five years later Walpole described how Gibbon had quarrelled with him, because he would not give him incense enough about his second volume. He continues :—' I well knew his vanity, even about his ridiculous face and person, but thought he had too much sense to avow it so palpably. The *History* is admirably written . . . but the style is far less sedulously enamelled than the first volume, and there is flattery to the Scots that would choke anything but Scots, who can gobble feathers as readily as thistles. David Hume and Adam Smith are *legislators* and sages, but the homage is intended for his patron, Lord Loughborough. So much for literature and its fops.' *Ib.* vii. 505.

Gibbon, after describing ' a valiant tribe of Caledonia, the Attacotti, who are accused by an eye-witness of delighting in the taste of human flesh,' continues :—' If in the neighbourhood of the commercial and literary town of Glasgow a race of cannibals has really existed, we may contemplate in the period of the Scottish history the opposite extremes of savage and civilised life. Such reflections tend to enlarge the circle of our ideas, and to encourage the pleasing hope that New Zealand may produce in some future age the Hume of the Southern Hemisphere.' *Decline and Fall*, ed. 1807, iv. 249. On p. 122 of the same volume, referring to the *Wealth of Nations*, he says :— ' This I am proud to quote as the work of a sage and a friend.'

Note 4. The first edition was in quarto, each volume containing as much as two volumes of the octavo edition.

Note 5. On March 18 Hume wrote to his brother historian that letter of which Gibbon said that ' it overpaid the labour of ten years.' Gibbon's *Misc. Works*, i. 224. See *ante*, p. 258, *n.* 8.

LETTER LXXX.

Publication of the Wealth of Nations and of the Decline and Fall: the Armament for America.

EDINBURGH, 8 *of April*, 1776.

DEAR SIR

I am employed in finishing the Corrections of the four last Volumes of my History, and these Volumes will probably be sent you by the Waggon next week. You have certainly Occupation enough on the four first till their Arrival. I beg that after the four first are printed off a Copy of the new Edition of them may be sent me by the Waggon, that I may return you the Errata.

I am very much taken with Mr. Gibbon's Roman History which came from your Press, and am glad to hear of its success. There will no Books of Reputation now be printed in London but through your hands and Mr. Cadel's[1]. The Author tells me, that he is already preparing a second Edition. I intended to have given him my Advice with regard to the manner of printing it; but as I am now writing to you, it is the same thing. He ought certainly to print the Number of the Chapter at the head of the Margin, and it woud be better if something of the Contents coud also be added. One is also plagued with his Notes, according to the present Method of printing the Book: When a Note is announced, you turn to the End of the Volume; and there you often find nothing but the Reference to an Authority: All these Authorities ought only to be printed at the Margin or the Bottom of the Page[2]. I desire, that a Copy of my new Edition shoud be sent to Mr. Gibbon, as wishing that a Gentleman, whom I so highly value, shoud peruse me in the form the least imperfect, to which I can bring my work[3].

We heard that yours and Mr. Cadell's Warehouses had been consumed by fire: I intended to have written you on the Occasion, but as I received a Letter from you a few Posts after, in which you mentioned nothing of the Matter, I concluded the Rumor to be false. Dr. Robertson tells me, that there was some Foundation for the Report; but that your Loss was inconsiderable; and that your Copies were insured[4]. I shoud not have been sorry, if some Bales of my Essays had been in the Number; as I think I coud make some Improvements in a new Edition.

Dr. Smith's Performance is another excellent Work that has come from your Press this Winter; but I have ventured to tell him, that it requires too much thought to be as popular as Mr. Gibbon's[5].

If your Ministry have as much Reflection and Combination of thought as to make a successful Expedition on the other Side of the Atlantic with 40,000 men, they will much disappoint my Expectations. They seem to have gone wrong already by the Lateness of their Embarkations[6]. But we shall see, which is the utmost that can be said in most Affairs of this Nature.

I am Dear S^{ir} Yours sincerely

DAVID HUME[7].

Note 1. Gibbon, speaking of the publication of the first volume of his *History*, says:—'After the perilous adventure had been declined by my friend, Mr. Elmsly, I agreed upon easy terms with Mr. Thomas Cadell, a respectable bookseller, and Mr. William Strahan an eminent printer; and they undertook the care and risk of the publication, which derived more credit from the name of the shop than from that of the author. So moderate were our hopes that the original impression had been stinted to five hundred, till the number was doubled by the prophetic taste of Mr. Strahan. . . . I am at a loss how to describe the success of the work, without betraying the vanity of the writer. The first impression was exhausted in a few days ; a second and third edition were scarcely adequate to the demand ; and the bookseller's property was twice invaded by the pirates of Dublin. My book was on every table, and almost on every toilette.' *Misc. Works*, i. 222. The preface to the third edition is dated May 1, 1777. Cadell and Strahan were publishing for Johnson, Blackstone, Hume, Robertson, Adam Smith, and Blair, as well as for Gibbon.

Note 2. Hume's wish that 'something of the contents' should be added at the head of the margin is scarcely reasonable ; as the side marginal entries are numerous, often two or three on a page. In the third edition (perhaps also in the second edition, a copy of which I have not been able to find) his advice about the notes is followed. They are transferred to the foot of each page.

Note 3. Gibbon, in the Journal that he kept when he was serving with the militia, entered on Nov. 2, 1761 :—'I read Hume's *History of England to the Reign of Henry VII*, just published, ingenious but superficial.' *Misc. Works*, i. 139. He was but twenty-four years old when he made this entry. The superficiality was not in any way removed by all Hume's laborious revisions. The author of the *Decline and Fall* would have found still more to condemn, though perhaps still more to admire, than had been discovered by the young officer of militia in his quarters at Devizes.

Note 4. 'March 2. About nine at night a fire broke out in the warehouse of Messieurs Cox and Bigg, Printers, in the Savoy, and notwithstanding every possible effort to stop its progress, the warehouse, the printing-office, and the dwelling-houses of the two partners were in a short time consumed, together with two warehouses filled with books belonging to Mr. Cadell, and Mr. Elmsly of the Strand.' *Ann. Reg.* 1776, i. 124.

Note 5. Hume wrote to Adam Smith on April 1, 1776 :—' Euge ! Belle ! Dear Mr. Smith,—I am much pleased with your performance, and the perusal of it has taken me from a state of great anxiety. It was a work of so much expectation, by yourself, by your friends, and by the public, that I trembled for its appearance, but am now much relieved. Not but that the reading of it necessarily requires so much attention, and the public is disposed to give so little, that I shall still doubt for some time of its being at first very popular.' Burton's *Hume*, ii. 486. Hume's 'trembling' may have been not only that of a friend, but almost of a parent. 'In the *Essays on Political Economy*,' writes Mackintosh, ' it is very evident that Hume was the true master of Smith.' Mackintosh's *Life*, ii. 248.

Boswell, who had arrived in London from Scotland on March 15, and who called on Johnson the next day, records :—'I mentioned Dr. Adam Smith's book on *The Wealth of Nations*, which was just published, and that Sir John Pringle had observed to me, that Dr. Smith, who had never been in trade, could not be expected to write well on that subject any more than a lawyer upon physic. JOHNSON. "He is mistaken, Sir : a man who has never been engaged in trade himself may undoubtedly write well upon trade, and there is nothing which requires more to be illustrated by philosophy than trade does."' Boswell's *Johnson*, ii. 430. On April 28 Boswell wrote to his friend Temple :—' Murphy says he has read thirty pages of Smith's *Wealth*, but says he shall read no more. Smith too is now of our Club. *It has lost its select merit.*' *Letters of Boswell*, p. 233. Boswell, in a note to the *Tour to the Hebrides*, somewhat condescendingly says :—' I value the greatest part of the *Wealth of Nations*.' Boswell's *Johnson*, v. 30, *n.* 3.

Adam Smith wrote to Strahan on Nov. 13, 1776 :—' I have received 300 pounds of the copy money of the first edition of my book. But as I got a good number of copies to make presents of from Mr. Cadell, I do not exactly know what balance may be due to me.' On Oct. 26, 1780, he wrote :—' I had almost forgot I was the author of the inquiry concerning the Wealth of Nations, but some time ago I received a letter from a friend in Denmark telling me that it had been translated into Danish.' Smith goes on to ask Cadell to send three copies of the second edition to Denmark, and continues :—' At our final settlement, I shall debit myself with these three Books. I suspect I am now almost your only customer for my own book. Let me know, however, how matters go on in this respect.' Original Letters of Adam Smith in the *New York Evening Post*, April 30, 1887.

Romilly, writing from London on Aug. 20, 1790, a few weeks after Adam Smith's death, says :—' I have been surprised, and I own a little indignant, to observe how little impression his death has made here. Scarce any notice has been taken of it, while for above a year together, after the death of Dr. Johnson, nothing was to be heard of but panegyrics of him. *Lives, Letters,* and *Anecdotes*, and even at this moment there are two more *Lives* of him about to start into existence.' *Life of Romilly*, ed. 1840, i. 404. One of these *Lives* no doubt was Boswell's, and the other, perhaps, Murphy's. One of Gibbon's correspondents, writing from Madrid in 1792, told him that ' the *Wealth of Nations* had been condemned by the Inquisition, on account of " the lowness of its style and the looseness of the morals which it inculcates." Nevertheless the Court had permitted an extract from it to be published.' Gibbon's *Misc. Works*, ii. 479.

Dugald Stewart, in a note which he added in 1810 to his *Life of Adam Smith* (p. 130), says :—' By way of explanation of what is hinted at in the foot-note, p. 77, I think it proper for me *now* to add, that at the period when this Memoir was read before the Royal Society of Edinburgh, it was not unusual, even among men of some talents and information, to confound studiously the speculative doctrines of Political Economy with those discussions concerning the first principles of Government which happened unfortunately at that time to agitate the public mind. The doctrine of a Free Trade was itself represented as of a revolutionary tendency ; and some who had formerly prided themselves on their intimacy with Mr. Smith, and on their zeal for the propagation of his liberal system, began to call in question the expediency of subjecting to the disputations of philosophers, the arcana of State Policy, and the unfathomable wisdom of the feudal ages.'

Lord Cockburn, in his *Memorials*, p. 45, writing of Edinburgh in the closing years of last century, says :—' The middle aged seemed to me to know little about the founder of the science [of Political Economy], except that he had recently been a Commissioner of Customs, and had written a sensible book. The young, by which I mean the liberal young of Edinburgh, lived upon him. With Hume, Robertson, Millar, Montesquieu, Ferguson, and De Lolme he supplied them with most of their mental food.' Cockburn adds that when Dugald Stewart in the winter of 1801-2 gave his first course of lectures on Political Economy, 'the mere term "Political Economy" made most people start. They thought that it included questions touching the constitution of governments; and not a few hoped to catch Stewart in dangerous propositions. It was not unusual to see a smile on the faces of some when they heard subjects discoursed upon, seemingly beneath the dignity of his Academical Chair. The word *Corn* sounded strangely in the moral class, and *Drawbacks* seemed a profanation of Stewart's voice.' *Ib.* p. 174.

Note 6. See *post*, p. 327, *n.* 14.

Note 7. Strahan must have given Gibbon a copy of a part of this letter, for a long extract from it is published in Gibbon's *Misc. Works*, ii. 161. Answering Hume on April 12, Strahan wrote :—' What you say of Mr. Gibbon's and Dr. Smith's books is exactly just. The former is the most popular work ; but the sale of the latter, though not near so rapid, has been more than I could have expected from a work that requires much thought and reflection (qualities that do not abound among modern readers) to peruse to any purpose [1]. . . . '

If this Ministry cannot land the number of men you mention in America, or very near that number, which from the great difficulty of procuring transports for that purpose, I am afraid they will not ; and if the army there is not able to make a very considerable impression this summer, we shall be in the most awkward and disagreeable situation that can be conceived. *Delay* amounts to *Defeat*; and the expense of a single campaign in the unhappy contest is beyond all conception enormous. Besides, if things do not go well with us there this summer, it will throw us into such confusion at home as nearly to overset (not the Ministry only, that is often of little consequence) but the Government itself. So that our rulers have now much at stake which I hope they will not fail to keep in view. I am hopeful, and upon that hope rests my chief dependence, that the Colonists, tired of the total stoppage of all trade and improvements, and weary of the anarchy under which they now groan, will do half the work for us.' *M. S. R. S. E.*

[1] *The Wealth of Nations* reached its sixth edition by the year 1791, and its ninth by the end of the century. The first two editions were in two volumes qnarto, and the numerous succeeding ones at first in three volumes, and later on in four volumes octavo. It was not till 1839 that an edition in one volume was published. Lowndes's *Bib. Man.* ed. 1871, p. 2417, and *Brit. Mus. Cata.*

LETTER LXXXI.

Hume's Departure for London.

EDINBURGH, 20 *of April*[1], 1776.

DEAR STRAHAN

My Body sets out to-morrow by Post for London[2]; but whether it will arrive there is somewhat uncertain. I shall travel by slow Journies. Last Monday, I sent off by the Waggon, directed to Mr. Cadel, the four last Volumes of my History. I bring up my philosophical Pieces corrected, which will be safe, whether I dye by the Road or not[3].

I am Dear Sir Yours sincerely

DAVID HUME.

Note 1. Hume had finished his far too brief *Autobiography* two days earlier.

Note 2. Sometime in the spring of this year Dr. Black, Hume's physician, sent Adam Smith the following letter :—'I write at present chiefly to acquaint you with the state of your friend David Hume's health, which is so bad that I am quite melancholy upon it, and as I hear that you intend a visit to this country soon, I wish, if possible, to hasten your coming, that he may have the comfort of your company so much the sooner. He has been declining several years, and this in a slow and gradual manner, until about a twelvemonth ago, since which the progress of his disorder has been more rapid. . . . His mother, he says, had precisely the same constitution with himself, and died of this very disorder; which has made him give up any hopes of his getting the better of it. . . . Do not however say much on this subject to any one else; as he does not like to have it spoke of, and has been very shy and slow in acquainting me fully with the state of his health.' Burton's *Hume*, ii. 488. Hume's friends urged him to go to London, partly in the belief that the journey would do him good, and partly to get fresh medical advice. Black however had not thought well of the journey. On April 12, Hume wrote to John Home the dramatist :—'Dr. Black (God bless him) tells me that nothing is so improper for me as leaving my own house, jolting about on the road, or lying in inconvenient inns, and that I shall die with much more tranquillity in St. David [? David's] Street than anywhere else. Besides, where can I expect spiritual assistance so consolatory? When are you to be down? Bring Smith with you.'

Caldwell Papers, i. 35. 'He set out,' he said 'merely to please his friends.' *Works of John Home*, i. 169. Meanwhile Adam Smith had started for Scotland, with Home. At Morpeth 'they would have passed Hume, if they had not seen his servant, Colin, standing at the gate of an inn.' *Ib.* 168. Leaving Smith to continue his journey alone, Home turned back, and accompanied his friend first to London, then to Bath, and afterwards to Edinburgh. They travelled in a post-chaise, by such easy stages that Hume took eleven days in going from Edinburgh to London. On Thursday, April 25, Home records in an interesting diary[1] which he kept of the journey :—'Left Darlington about nine o'clock, and came to Northallerton[2]. The same delightful weather. A shower fell that laid the dust, and made our journey to Boroughbridge more pleasant. Mr. Hume continues very easy, and has a tolerable appetite ; tastes nothing liquid but water, and sups upon an egg. He assured me that he never possessed his faculties more perfectly; that he never was more sensible of the beauties of any classic author than he was at present, nor loved more to read. When I am not in the room with him he reads continually. The post-boys can scarcely be persuaded to drive only five miles an hour, and their horses are of the same way of thinking. The other travellers, as they pass, look into the chaise, and laugh at our slow pace. This evening the post-boy from North Allerton, who had required a good deal of threatening to make him drive as slow as we desired, had no sooner taken his departure to go home than he set off at full speed. "*Pour se dédommager,*" said David.' *Ib.* p. 171. Home says that they arrived in London on Wednesday, April 31 (*sic*). Wednesday was May 1. Hume describing his journey to Dr. Blair, says of Home's turning back to keep him company :—'Never was there a more friendly action, nor better placed ; for what between conversation and gaming (not to mention sometimes squabbling), I did not pass a languid moment.' Burton's *Hume*, ii. 505. The 'gaming' was picquet. 'Mr. David,' writes Home, 'was very keen about his card-playing.' Home's *Works*, i. 169.

Henry Mackenzie describes Home as 'a man of infinite pleasantry as well as great talents, whose conversation, perhaps beyond that of any other of the set, possessed the charm of easy natural attractive humour. His playful vivacity often amused itself in a sort of mock contest with the infantile (if I may use such a phrase when speaking

---

[1] This *Diary* was published by Henry Mackenzie in the Appendix to his *Life of Home*. By a narrow edge of paper left between pages 180 and 181, it is easy to see that there has been a suppression. If the manuscript is still in existence, it would be interesting to see what the passage is that has been suppressed.

[2] Johnson had passed a night here less than three years earlier. Writing to Mrs. Thrale on Aug. 12, 1773, he said :—'We dined at York, and went on to Northallerton, a place of which I know nothing but that it afforded us a lodging on Monday night, and about two hundred and seventy years ago gave birth to Roger Ascham.' *Piozzi Letters*, i. 105.

of such a man) simplicity of David Hume, who himself enjoyed the discovery of the joke which had before excited the laugh of his companions around him.' *Home's Works,* i. 14. He was a good companion for a sick man; for Dr. Robertson used jokingly to say that 'he invested his friends with a sort of supernatural privilege above the ordinary humiliating circumstances of mortality. "He never," said the Doctor, "would allow that a friend was sick till he heard of his death."' *Ib.* p. 7. His kindness is shown in the following anecdote: —'The lady John Home had married not being very remarkable for her personal attractions, David Hume, it is said, asked him "how he could ever think of such a woman?" Home, who was a man of great goodness and simplicity of character, replied, "Ah, David! if I had not, who else would have taken her?"' *Caldwell Papers,* ii. 179.

Sir Walter Scott, who in his fourth year had been taken to Bath for his health, and had stayed there about a year (about 1775), says:— 'My residence at Bath is marked by very pleasing recollections. The venerable John Home was then at the watering-place, and paid much attention to my aunt and to me.' Lockhart's *Scott,* ed. 1839, i. 30.

Note 3. 'Newcastle, Wednesday, 24th April. Mr. Hume not quite so well in the morning—says that he had set out merely to please his friends; that he would go on to please them; that Ferguson and Andrew Stuart (about whom we had been talking) were answerable for shortening his life one week a-piece; for, says he, you will allow Xenophon to be good authority; and he lays it down, that suppose a man is dying, nobody has a right to kill him. He set out in this vein, and continued all the stage in his cheerful and talking humour.' Home's *Works,* i. 169.

LETTER LXXXII.

Hume's Arrival in London.

Brewer Street[1], 2 *of May,* 1776.

DEAR SIR

I arrived here yesterday very much improved by my Journey. I have seen no body but Sir John Pringle, who says that he sees nothing alarming in my Case[2]; and I am willing, and consequently ready to believe him. I intend to call on you this forenoon, and shall leave this in case I miss you. I know not yet what Sir John intends to do with me; so am ignorant how long I shall remain in

London: But wish much to have a Conversation with you; I shall never eat a meal from my own Fireside; but all the Forenoons and Afternoons will be at my Disposal. It will do me Service to drive to your House; so that you need only appoint me by Message or Penny Post[3] an hour any day.

I am Dear S[ir] Yours sincerely

DAVID HUME.

P.S.—I lodge at Mrs. Perkins, a few doors from Miss Elliots[4], and next door to Mr. Forbes the Surgeon. The Afternoons, if equally convenient for you, will rather be more convenient to me, to call on you.

Note 1. Brewer Street, Golden Square, where he had lodged in March, 1769 (*ante*, p. 203, *n*. 8).

Note 2. Hume wrote to Dr. Blair from Bath on May 13:—'You have frequently heard me complain of my physical friends, that they allowed me to die in the midst of them without so much as giving a Greek name to my disorder; a consolation which was the least I had reason to expect from them. Dr. Black, hearing this complaint, told me that I should be satisfied in that particular, and that my disorder was a hemorrhage, a word which it was easy to decompose into αιμος [*sic*] and ρηγνυμι. But Sir John Pringle says, that I have no hemorrhage, but a spincture [*sic*] in the colon, which it will be easy to cure. This disorder, as it both contained two Greek appellations and was remediable, I was much inclined to prefer; when, behold! Dr. Gustard tells me that he sees no symptoms of the former disorder, and as to the latter, he never met with it and scarcely ever heard of it.' Burton's *Hume*, ii. 504. Dr. Norman Moore, the Warden of the College of St. Bartholomew's Hospital, has kindly furnished me with the following note on this passage:—

'Hume seems to have had a cancerous growth in the large intestine, followed by a secondary cancerous growth in the liver.

'The word sphincter is used for a circle of muscular fibres closing an orifice, but as this term is inapplicable to a diseased structure, I think Hume's word *spincture* is written for *stricture*. A new growth (cancer) of the colon would be certain to cause a stricture or narrowing of the intestine, and is frequently followed by one or more tumours in the liver. The natural history of new growths of this kind and the sequence of primary cancer of the intestine and secondary cancer of the liver was imperfectly known in Hume's time; but it is probable that John Hunter had some insight into the matter, for Charles Bernard, in Queen Anne's time, had already noticed the occasional recurrence of cancer after operation; the first step in the observation of the natural history of cancer. Hume's age, the duration of his illness, and the interval between Hunter's observation of the disease in his liver and his death, are all consistent with the opinion that he died of cancer of the intestine, followed by secondary cancer of the liver.'

Note 3. See *ante*, p. 175, *n.* 2.

Note 4. Miss Elliot, I suppose, is the ' Peggy Elliot ' formerly of Lisle Street (*ante*, p. 94, *n.* 8), with whom Hume used to lodge.

LETTER LXXXIII.

The Bath Waters: Journey to Bath: First Lord of the Admiralty at Speen Hill.

BATH, 10 *of May*, 1776.

MY DEAR S^{IR}

I was very sorry not to see you again before I left London, both because I did not see you again and because of the Cause, your being confin'd. I arriv'd here on Wednesday Evening; improv'd, as before, by the Journey; And the short Trial which I have made of the Waters, seems to succeed wonderfully. Dr Gustard[1], with whom I am much taken, says, that he never saw a Case so much what may be calld a Bath Case, and in which he is more assur'd of the Patients Recovery. To tell the Truth, I feel myself already so much reliev'd, that, for the first time these several Months, I have to day begun to open my Mind to the Expectations of seeing a few more Years: But whether this be very desirable at my Age I shall not determine. I have not ventur'd to write any thing to Sir John Pringle till we have made a further Trial.

You have probably or soon will have some Letters directed to me under your Cover[2]. Please direct them to this Place. I hope you will be able to give me the same

Y 2

good Accounts of your Health that I have given you of mine. I believe, I told you, that I had sent to the Newcastle Waggon at Edinburgh, near four Weeks ago, the corrected Copy of the four last Volumes of my History, directed to Mr. Cadell. The great Pains, that these Corrections cost me, make me anxious to hear of their safe Arrival.

When we pass'd by Spine hill [3] near Newbury we found in the Inn Lord Denbigh [4], who was an Acquaintance of my Fellow Traveller [5]. His Lordship inform'd him, that he, Lord Sandwich [6], Lord Mulgrave [7], Mr. Banks [8], and two or three Ladies of Pleasure had pass'd five or six Days there [9], and intended to pass all this Week and the next in the same Place; that their chief object was to enjoy the trouting Season [10]; that they had been very successful; that Lord Sandwich in particular had caught Trouts near twenty Inches long, which gave him incredible Satisfaction; but that for his Part, being a greater Admirer of Sea Fish, in which Bath abounded, and hearing that Friday was the great Market day there for Fish, he commissiond my Friend to send him up by the London Fly [11] a good Cargo of Soles, John Dories, and Pipers [12], which wou'd render their Happiness compleat. I do not remember in all my little or great Knowlege of History [13] (according as you and Dr Johnson can settle between you the Degrees of my Knowlege) such another Instance; and I am sure such a one does not exist: That the first Lord of the Admiralty, who is absolute and uncontrouled Master in his Department, shou'd, at a time when the Fate of the British Empire is in dependance, and in dependance on him, find so much Leizure, Tranquillity, Presence of Mind and Magnanimity, as to have Amusement in trouting during three Weeks near sixty Miles from the scene of Business, and during the most critical Season of the Year. There needs but this single Fact to decide the Fate of the Nation. What an Ornament woud it be in a future History to

open the glorious Events of the ensuing Year with the
Narrative of so singular an Incident[14].

I am Dear Sir Yours sincerely

DAVID HUME.

Note 1. 'Dr. Gusthard was the son of a minister of Edinburgh;
being of good ability and a winning address he had come into very
good business.' Dr. A. Carlyle's *Auto.* p. 534. Hume's employment
of a Scotch physician both in London and Bath calls to mind 'the
pleasant manner' in which Garrick maintained to Boswell the nationality of the Scotch. 'Come, come, don't deny it; they are really
national. Why, now, the Adams are as liberal-minded men as any
in the world; but I don't know how it is, all their workmen are
Scotch. You are, to be sure, wonderfully free from that nationality;
but so it happens that you employ the only Scotch shoe-black in
London.' Boswell's *Johnson*, ii. 325.

Note 2. See *ante*, p. 188, *n.* 11.

Note 3. Clarendon, in his account of the second Battle of Newbury, fought on Oct. 27, 1644, between Charles I and the Earl of
Manchester's army, tells how 'the right wing of the enemy's horse
advanced under the hill of Speen, with one hundred musketeers in
the van, and came into the open field, where a good body of the
King's horse stood, which at first received them in some disorder.'
History of the Rebellion, ed. 1826, iv. 584.

Note 4. Basil, sixth Earl of Denbigh, born 1719. Horace Walpole
wrote on May 19, 1756 :—'My Lord Denbigh is going to marry a
fortune, I forget her name; my Lord Gower asked him how long the
honey-moon would last. He replied, " Don't tell me of the honey-
moon; it is harvest-moon with me."' *Letters*, iii. 13. On Jan. 22, 1761,
Walpole wrote :—'Lord Denbigh is made Master of the harriers,
with two thousand a year. Lord Temple asked it, and Newcastle
and Hardwicke gave into it for fear of Denbigh's brutality in the
House of Lords.' *Ib.* p. 373. For an instance of his brutality, see
ante, p. 106, *n.* 1. It was his father who asked his kinsman, Henry
Fielding the novelist, 'how it was that he spelled his name " Fielding," and not " Feilding," like the head of the house? " I cannot tell,
my Lord," said he, " except it be that my branch of the family were
the first that knew how to spell."' Thackeray's *English Humourists*,
ed. 1858, p. 282.

Note 5. John Home.

Note 6. John, fourth Earl of Sandwich, at this time First Lord of
the Admiralty. See Boswell's *Life of Johnson*, iii. 383, for the murder
of his mistress, Miss Ray, in 1779, by the Rev. Mr. Hackman.

Note 7. Constantine John, second Baron Mulgrave, a junior Lord
of the Admiralty. When a Captain in the Navy he had commanded
an expedition for the discovery of a North-East Passage. Wraxall

(*Memoirs*, ed. 1815, ii. 125) says that 'he possessed two distinct voices; the one strong and hoarse, the other weak and querulous. So extraordinary a circumstance probably gave rise to a story of his having fallen into a ditch in a dark night, and calling for aid in his shrill voice. A countryman coming up was about to assist him; but Lord Mulgrave addressing him in a hoarse voice, the peasant exclaimed, "Oh! if there are two of you in the ditch, you may help each other out of it."'

Note 8.   Perhaps Henry Bankes, M.P. for Corfe Castle, one of the Commissioners of Customs. He died on Sept. 23 of this year. *Gent. Mag.* 1776, p. 436.

Note 9.   Lord Denbigh and Lord Sandwich were each 57 years old.   Mr. Bankes, if this was Henry Bankes, was still older, as his father had been dead 62 years.   Lord Mulgrave was only 32.

Note 10.   They were fishing in
    'The Kennet swift, for silver eels renowned.'
                                    Pope's *Windsor Forest.*
'The trout of the Kennet have long been celebrated for their size and flavour; Fuller speaks of them in his *Worthies*.   The editor of the *Magna Britannia* mentions the trout of the Kennet as being of a prodigious size, and speaks of one 45 inches in length taken at Newbury.' Lysons' *Berkshire*, p. 195.   Fuller speaks of them as follows :—
'Trouts.   This is a pleasant and wholesom Fish, as whose feeding is pure and cleanly, in the swiftest streams, and on the hardest gravell.   Good and great of this kind are found in the River of Kennet, nigh Hungerford, though not so big as that which Gesner affirmes taken in the Leman-lake, being three cubits in length.' Fuller's *Worthies*, ed. 1662, i. 81.

Note 11.   'When I left school,' says Lord Eldon, 'in 1766 to go to Oxford, I came up from Newcastle to London in a coach, then denominated on account of its quick travelling, as travelling was then estimated, a fly; being, as well as I remember, nevertheless three or four days and nights on the road.' *Life of Lord Eldon*, ed. 1846, i. 39. In Chamberlayne's *Present State of Great Britain*, 1710, p. 281, there is the following account of the Flying Coaches as they were in the beginning of the century :—' Besides this excellent Convenience of conveying Letters and Men on Horse-back, there is of late an admirable Commodiousness both for Men and Women of better Quality, to travel from *London* to almost any Town of *England*, and to almost all the Villages near this great City, and that is by Stage-Coaches, wherein one may be transported to any Place, sheltered from foul Weather and foul Ways ; and this is not only at a low Price, as about a Shilling for every five Miles, but with such speed as that the Posts in some Foreign Countries make not more Miles in a Day ; for the Stage-Coaches, called Flying Coaches, make 50 or 60 Miles in a Day, as from *London* to *Oxford* or *Cambridge* ; sometimes 70, 80, and 100 Miles, as Southampton, Bury, Cirencester, Norwich, &c.'

Note 12.   For a description of this fish, see F. Buckland's *Natural History of British Fishes*, p. 104.

Note 13.   Johnson, on April 30, 1773, said that he had not read Hume's *History*. Boswell's *Johnson*, ii. 236.   If Dr. Thomas Campbell's *Diary* can be taken as genuine (see *ib.* ii. 338, *n.* 2), he said on April 5, 1775, that 'he defied any one to produce a classical book written in Scotland since Buchanan.   Robertson, he said, used pretty words, but he liked Hume better; and neither of them would he allow to be more to Clarendon than a rat to a cat.' *Ib.* v. 57, *n.* 3.   Had Hume arrived at Bath a few days earlier he might have met Johnson and Boswell, who had been there on a visit to the Thrales. *Ib.* iii. 45.

Note 14.   Horace Walpole wrote to Mann on April 17:—'You need not be too impatient for events.   The army that was to overrun the Atlantic continent is not half set out yet; but it will be time enough to go into winter-quarters.   What we have heard lately thence is not very promising.   The Congress, that was said to be squabbling, seems to act with harmony and spirit; and Quebec is not thought to be so safe as it was a month ago.   However, that is the business of the Ministers; nobody else troubles his head about the matter.   Few people knew much of America before; and now that all communication is cut off, and the Administration does not think itself bound to chant its own disappointments, or the praises of the enemy, we forget it as much as if Columbus had not routed it out of the ocean.' *Letters*, vi. 327.   On May 17 he wrote:—'As I knew no more than the newspapers would tell you, I did not announce to you the retreat of the King's army from Boston.   Great pains were taken, and no wonder, to soften this disgrace. . . The American war begins to lose its popularity.' *Ib.* p. 336.   Two years later, on May 31, 1778, he wrote to Mason:—'Lord Sandwich has run the gauntlet in the Lords for all the lies he has told all the winter about the fleet, and does not retire; but I am sick of repeating what you must be sick of reading.   An invasion will have some dignity; but to see a great country gambol at the eve of ruin like a puppy on a precipice!   Oh! one cannot buffoon like Lucian when one wants to speak daggers like Tacitus, and couch them in a sentence without descending to details.' *Ib.* vii. 72.

Burke, writing on April 22, 1776, shows that the public could be as careless even as Ministers of the affairs of the nation.   The trial of the Duchess of Kingston for bigamy had been going on.   'All affairs totally suspended with all sorts of people.   We forgot, for a while, war and taxes, and everything else; though the budget will be opened on Wednesday.' Burke's *Corres.* ii. 102.   On May 4 he writes of General Howe's retreat to Halifax:—'In that nook of penury and cold the proud conqueror of America is obliged to look for refuge.' *Ib.* p. 103.   On May 30 he writes:—'The party is at present very high; but it is the glory of the Tories that they always flourish in the decay, and perhaps by the decay, of the glory of their country.

Our session is over, and I can hardly believe by the tranquillity of everything about me that we are a people who have just lost an empire. But it is so. The present nursery revolution, I think, engages as much of our attention. [There had been a change of Governor, Sub-governor, Preceptor, and Sub-preceptor to the Prince of Wales and Prince Frederick].' *Ib.* p. 107.

On Nov. 8, soon after the opening of Parliament, Mr. Luttrell moved an Address to the King for the removal of Lord Sandwich from office. He said 'that the absolute management of the maritime power of the British empire was too important a trust to be committed to a *bon vivant* of Lord Sandwich's levity of disposition and known depravity of conduct, especially now the piping hours of jubilee and dalliance were at end.' Lord Mulgrave defended his chief. 'The British nation,' he said, 'had never known a First Commissioner of the Admiralty equal to the present in capacity and meritorious services.' The motion was negatived without a division. *Parl. Hist.* xviii. 1449-54. The absence of a division is accounted for by 'the partial secession' from the House of a great number of the Opposition. Being over-whelmed in the divisions on which they had ventured, they contented themselves with 'attending the House in the morning upon private business; as soon as a public question was introduced they took a formal leave of the Speaker, and immediately withdrew.' *Ann. Reg.* 1777, i. 48.

Lord Sandwich, according to the reports in the *London Chronicle*, took part in the debates on May 9, 10, and 16. He could easily have gone up to town and returned between the 10th and the 16th. Lord Denbigh was in the House of Lords on the 16th. Boswell this same spring left London for Bath—nearly twice the distance of Speen Hill—on a visit of pleasure on April 26, and was back again by May 1. Boswell's *Johnson*, iii. 45, 51.

LETTER LXXXIV.

The Bath Waters injurious: Complaints of Injustice: Hume's Autobiography: Dialogues on Natural Religion.

BATH, 8 *of June,* 1776.

MY DEAR SᴵᴿR

You will be sorry to hear, that I must retract all the good Accounts, which I gave you of my Health. The Waters, after seeming to agree with me, have sensibly a bad Effect, and I have entirely dropped the Use of them.

I wait only Sir John Pringle's Directions before I leave this place; and I shall, I believe, set out for the North in a few days[1]. If any Letters for me come under your Cover, be so good as to detain them, till I can inform you of my Route.

I am glad to find, that you have been able to set about this New Edition in earnest. I have made it extremely correct; at least I believe that, if I were to live twenty Years longer, I shoud never be able to give it any further Improvements. This is some small Satisfaction to me in my present Situation; and I may add that it is almost the only one that my Writings ever afforded me: For as to any suitable Returns of Approbation from the Public, for the Care, Accuracy, Labour, Disinterestedness, and Courage[2] of my Compositions, they are yet to come. Though, I own to you, I see many Symptoms that they are approaching[3]. But it will happen to me as to many other Writers: Though I have reached a considerable Age, I shall not live to see any Justice done to me[4]. It is not improbable, however, that my Self-conceit and Prepossessions may lead me into this way of thinking[5].

As soon as this Edition is finished, please to send a Copy of all the ten Volumes[6] to Sir John Pringle, the same to Mr. Gibbon[7], a Copy of the History to Mistress Elliott[8] in Brewer Street; six Copies of the whole to me in Edinburgh or to my Brother there in case of my Death[9].

If this Event shall happen, as is probable, before the Publication of this Edition, there is one Request I have to make to you: Before I left Edinburgh, I wrote a small piece (you may believe it woud be but a small one) which I call the History of my own Life[10]: I desire it may be prefixed to this Edition: It will be thought curious and entertaining. · My Brother or Dr. Adam Smith will send it to you, and I shall give them Directions to that Purpose.

I am also to speak to you of another Work more important: Some Years ago, I composed a piece, which woud make a small Volume in Twelves. I call it *Dialogues on natural Religion*: Some of my Friends flatter me, that it is the best thing I ever wrote. I have hitherto forborne to publish it, because I was of late desirous to live quietly, and keep remote from all Clamour: For though it be not more exceptionable than some things I had formerly published; yet you know some of these were thought very exceptionable; and in prudence, perhaps, I ought to have suppressed them. I there introduce a Sceptic, who is indeed refuted, and at last gives up the Argument, nay confesses that he was only amusing himself by all his Cavils [11]; yet before he is silenced, he advances several Topics, which will give Umbrage, and will be deemed very bold and free, as well as much out of the common Road. As soon as I arrive at Edinburgh, I intend to print a small Edition of 500, of which I may give away about 100 in Presents; and shall make you a Present of the Remainder, together with the literary Property of the whole, provided you have no Scruple, in your present Situation, of being the Editor: It is not necessary you shoud prefix your Name to the Title Page. I seriously declare, that after Mr. Millar and You and Mr. Cadell have publickly avowed your Publication of the *Enquiry concerning human Understanding* [12], I know no Reason why you shoud have the least Scruple with regard to these Dialogues. They will be much less obnoxious to the Law [13], and not more exposed to popular Clamour. Whatever your Resolution be, I beg you wou'd keep an entire Silence on this Subject. If I leave them to you by Will, your executing the Desire of a dead Friend, will render the publication still more excusable [14]. Mallet never sufferd any thing by being the Editor of Bolingbroke's Works [15].

Two posts ago, I sent you a Copy of the small Essay
which I mentioned [16].
I am Dear S[ir] with great Regard and Sincerity
Your most obedient humble Servant
DAVID HUME.

Note 1. 'They may say what they will,' wrote Horace Walpole
nearly ten years earlier, 'but it does one ten times more good to
leave Bath than to go to it.' *Letters*, v. 19.
Note 2. Hume's courage had not grown with increase of days and
prosperity, as the following extracts from his letters show. Writing
in 1754 of the first volume of his *History of England under the Stuarts*,
he says :—'A few Christians only (and but a few) think I speak like a
Libertine in religion ; be assured I am tolerably reserved on this head.
Elliot tells me that you had entertained apprehensions of my discretion : what I had done to forfeit with you the character of prudence
I cannot tell, but you will see little or no occasion for any such imputation in this work. I composed it *ad populum*, as well as *ad clerum*,
and thought that scepticism was not in its place in an historical production.' Burton's *Hume*, i. 397. In this very volume of his *History*
(ch. lix), speaking of the trial of Charles I, he says :—'If ever on any
occasion it were laudable to conceal truth from the populace, it must
be confessed that the doctrine of resistance affords such an example ;
and that all speculative reasoners ought to observe, with regard to
this principle, the same cautious silence which the laws in every
species of government have ever prescribed to themselves. Government is instituted in order to restrain the fury and injustice of the
people ; and being always founded on opinion, not on force, it is
dangerous to weaken by these speculations the reverence which the
multitude owe to authority, and to instruct them beforehand that the
case can ever happen when they may be freed from their duty of
allegiance.' Ed. 1802, vii. 148.
In 1761, writing to Dr. Blair about a sermon by a Dr. Campbell in
which he was attacked, he says :—'I could wish your friend had not
denominated me an infidel writer on account of ten or twelve pages
which seem to him to have that tendency, while I have wrote so
many volumes on history, literature, politics, trade, morals, which in
that particular at least are entirely inoffensive. Is a man to be called
a drunkard, because he has been seen fuddled once in his lifetime ?'
Burton's *Hume*, ii. 116. Dr. Burton hereupon quotes the following
anecdote by Lord Charlemont :—'One day that Hume visited me in
London, he came into my room laughing, and apparently well pleased.
"What has put you into this good humour, Hume ?" said I. 'Why
man," replied he, "I have just now had the best thing said to me I
ever heard. I was complaining in a company where I spent the

morning, that I was very ill-treated by the world ; that I had written many volumes, throughout the whole of which there were but a few pages that contained any reprehensible matter, and yet for those few pages I was abused and torn to pieces. "You put me in mind," said an honest fellow in the company, "of an acquaintance of mine, a notary public, who having been condemned to be hanged for forgery, lamented the hardness of his case ; that after having written many thousand inoffensive sheets he should be hanged for one line."' *Memoirs of Charlemont*, ed. 1812, i. 232.

Though Hume wrote his *Dialogues concerning Natural Religion* at least as early as the year 1751 (Burton's *Hume*, i. 328), he had not courage to publish them in the remaining quarter of a century that he lived. To the full violence of the attack made by Johnson on Bolingbroke—about its justice I say nothing—he was himself exposed. Johnson would not have hesitated to say of him :—'Sir, he was a scoundrel and a coward; a scoundrel for charging a blunderbuss against religion and morality; a coward because he had not resolution to fire it off himself, but left half-a-crown to a beggarly Scotchman to draw the trigger after his death.' Boswell's *Johnson*, i. 268. Hume withdrew also from publication at the last moment his *Essays on Suicide and the Immortality of the Soul*, (*ante*, p. 232, *n.* 8).

In 1762 he wrote to Millar :—'I give you full authority to contradict the report that I am writing or intend to write an ecclesiastical history ; I have no such intention ; and I believe never shall. I am beginning to love peace very much, and resolve to be more cautious than formerly in creating myself enemies.' Burton's *Hume*, ii. 130. In an undated letter, believed to be written to Dr. Trail, speaking of his philosophical writings he says :—'I wish I had always confined myself to the more easy parts of erudition.' *M. S. R. S. E.* Yet when Lord Charlemont asked him 'whether he thought that, if his opinions were universally to take place, mankind would not be rendered more unhappy than they now were ; and whether he did not suppose that the curb of religion was necessary to human nature; "The objections," answered he, "are not without weight ; but error never can produce good, and truth ought to take place of all considerations."' *Memoirs of Charlemont*, i. 232.

Landor thus introduces him in his *Dialogue between Alfieri and Metastasio* :—

'METASTASIO. "Hume was thought a free-thinker : was he one ?"

'ALFIERI. "Quite the contrary. A narrow ribbon tied him, neck and heels, to the hinder quarters of a broken throne. If you mean religion, I believe he was addicted to no formulary. His life was indolently and innocently Epicurean."' Landor's *Works*, ed. 1876, v. 132. See *ante*, p. 217, *n.* 3, for his cowardly advice to a young clergyman.

Note 3. In his *Autobiography* he says :—'Though I see many symptoms of my literary reputation's breaking out at last with additional lustre, I knew that I could have but few years to enjoy it.' He speaks of his 'love of literary fame' as his 'ruling-passion.'

Note 4. Sir James Mackintosh, writing in the year 1811, says:— 'Perhaps the name of no man of letters in Great Britain, in the middle of the eighteenth century, was better known throughout Europe than that of Mr. Hume.' Speaking of his philosophical works Mackintosh continues:—'They may be regarded as the cause, either directly or indirectly, of almost all the metaphysical writings in Europe for seventy years; during the whole of that period Mr. Hume filled the schools of Europe with his disciples or his antagonists.' *Life of Mackintosh*, ii. 168.

Note 5. Hume at first wrote:—'It is probable that my Prepossessions lead me into this way of thinking.'

Note 6. The ten volumes are the eight of his *History* and the two of his *Essays*.

Note 7. Gibbon had sent Hume 'the agreeable present' of the first volume of his *Decline and Fall*. Gibbon's *Misc. Works*, i. 224.

Note 8. See *ante*, p. 94, *n.* 8.

Note 9. See *post*, p. 358.

Note 10. Hume had written to Adam Smith on May 3:—' You will find among my papers a very inoffensive paper called "my own Life," which I composed a few days before I left Edinburgh; when I thought, as did all my friends, that my life was despaired of. There can be no objection that the small piece should be sent to Messrs. Strahan and Cadell, and the proprietors of my other works, to be prefixed to any future edition of them.' Burton's *Hume*, ii. 493.

Note 11. ' "Believe me, Demea," replied Cleanthes, "your friend Philo from the beginning has been amusing himself at both our expense; and it must be confessed that the injudicious reasoning of our vulgar theology has given him but too just a handle of ridicule. The total infirmity of human reason, the absolute incomprehensibility of the Divine Nature, the great and universal misery, and still greater wickedness of men; these are strange topics, surely, to be so fondly cherished by orthodox divines and doctors. In ages of stupidity and ignorance, indeed, these principles may safely be espoused; and perhaps no views of things are more proper to promote superstition than such as encourage the blind amazement, the diffidence, and the melancholy of mankind." . . . "I must confess," replied Philo, "that I am less cautious on the subject of Natural Religion than on any other; both because I know that I can never on that head corrupt the principles of any man of common sense; and because no one, I am confident, in whose eyes I appear a man of common sense, will ever mistake my intentions. You, in particular, Cleanthes, with whom I live in unreserved intimacy; you are sensible that notwithstanding the freedom of my conversation, and my love of singular arguments, no one has a deeper sense of religion impressed on his mind, or pays more profound adoration to the Divine Being, as he discovers himself to reason, in the inexplicable contrivance and artifice of nature. A purpose, an intention, a design, strikes everywhere the most careless, the most stupid thinker ; and no man can be so hardened in absurd systems as at all times to reject it." ' Hume's *Philosophical Works*, ed. 1854, ii. 520, 522.

Note 12.   Millar, it should seem, had had no fear of publishing sceptical works. Hume writing to him on May 20, 1757, said :—
' When Bailie Hamilton [the Edinburgh bookseller] was in London, he wrote me that the stop in the sale of my *History* proceeded from some strokes of irreligion, which had raised the cry of the clergy against me. This gave me occasion to remark to you that the Bailie's complaint must have proceeded from his own misconduct ; that the cause he assigned could never have produced that effect ; that it was rather likely to increase the sale according to all past experience ; that you had offered (as I heard) a large sum for Bolingbroke's *Works*, trusting to this consequence.' Burton's *Hume*, ii. 24. It is stated in Knight's *Cyclo. of Biog.* iv. 69, that ' Mallet refused the bookseller's offer of £3000 for Bolingbroke's *Works*, and then published them on his own account.' According to Nichols ' they were published with success very inadequate to our Editor's expectation.' *Lit. Anec.* ii. 370.

Note 13.   Blackstone, only seven years earlier, had said :—' All affronts to Christianity, or endeavours to depreciate its efficacy, are highly deserving of human punishment. . . . About the close of the last century, the civil liberties to which we were then restored being used as a cloak of maliciousness, and the most horrid doctrines subversive of all religion being publicly avowed both in discourse and writings, it was found necessary again for the civil power to interpose, by not admitting those miscreants to the privileges of society who maintained such principles as destroyed all moral obligation. To this end it was enacted by statute 9 & 10 William III. c. 32, that if any person educated in or having made profession of the Christian religion shall by writing, printing, teaching, or advised speaking deny the Christian religion to be true, or the Holy Scriptures to be of divine authority, he shall upon the first offence be rendered incapable to hold any office or place of trust ; and for the second, be rendered incapable of bringing any action, being guardian, executor, legatee, or purchaser of lands, and shall suffer three years' imprisonment without bail.' Blackstone's *Commentaries*, 1st ed. iv. 44. Under the penalties of this bad Act fell those who denied any of the persons of the Trinity to be God. In 1813 an Act was passed to relieve Unitarians from the operations of this statute. *Penny Cyclo.* ed. 1835, iv. 508.

On Sept. 30, 1773, Boswell records :—' I asked Dr. Johnson if it was not strange that government should permit so many infidel writings to pass without censure. JOHNSON. " Sir, it is mighty foolish,

It is for want of knowing their own power. The present family on the throne came to the crown against the will of nine-tenths of the people. Whether those nine-tenths were right or wrong, it is not our business now to inquire. But such being the situation of the Royal Family, they were glad to encourage all who would be their friends. Now you know every bad man is a Whig; every man who has loose notions. The Church was all against this family. They were, as I say, glad to encourage any friends ; and therefore since their accession there is no instance of any man being kept back on account of his bad principles; and hence this inundation of impiety." I observed that Mr. Hume, some of whose writings were very unfavourable to religion, was however a Tory. JOHNSON. "Sir, Hume is a Tory by chance, as being a Scotchman; but not upon a principle of duty; for he has no principle. If he is anything, he is a Hobbist."' Boswell's *Johnson*, v. 271. 'Hobbes's politics,' wrote Hume, 'are fitted only to promote tyranny, and his ethics to encourage licentiousness. Though an enemy to religion, he partakes nothing of the spirit of scepticism ; but is as positive and dogmatical as if human reason, and his reason in particular, could attain a thorough conviction in these subjects.' *Hist. of England*, ed. 1802, vii. 346.

Note 14. Hume, in his will, dated Jan. 4, 1776, after leaving to Adam Smith full power over all his papers except the *Dialogues*, which he desired him to publish, continues :—'Though I can trust to that intimate and sincere friendship, which has ever subsisted between us, for his faithful execution of this part of my will, yet, as a small recompense of his pains in correcting and publishing this work, I leave him two hundred pounds, to be paid immediately after the publication of it.' Hume's *Philosophical Works*, ed. 1854, i. xxxi.

On May 3 of this year, in what he called 'an ostensible letter' which Smith could produce as his justification for whatever course he might take, he wrote to him :—'After reflecting more maturely on that article of my will by which I left you the disposal of all my papers, with a request that you should publish my *Dialogues concerning Natural Religion*, I have become sensible that both on account of the nature of the work and of your situation [1] it may be improper to hurry on that publication. I therefore take the present opportunity of qualifying that friendly request. I am content to leave it entirely to your discretion, at what time you will publish that piece, or whether you will publish it at all.' Later on, seeing Smith's unwillingness to publish the work, he added a codicil to his will dated Aug. 7, in which he says :—'In my later will and disposition I made some destinations with regard to my manuscripts: All these I now retract, and leave my manuscripts to the care of Mr. William Strahan, of London, Member of Parliament, trusting to the friendship that has long subsisted between us for his careful and faithful execution of my

---

[1] Adam Smith was in hopes of receiving some appointment under Government.

intentions. I desire that my *Dialogues concerning Natural Religion* may be printed and published any time within two years after my death.' In 'a new paragraph appended' to the codicil he says:— 'I do ordain that if my *Dialogues*, from whatever cause, be not published within two years and a-half after my death, as also the account of my life, the property shall return to my nephew, David, whose duty in publishing them, as the last request of his uncle, must be approved of by all the world.' Burton's *Hume*, ii. 491–4.

As Adam Smith had been relieved from the trust of publication, he steadily refused to accept payment of the legacy. It was in vain that Hume's brother, 'the sole executor and universal legatee,' 'urged such pleas as this, " My brother, knowing your liberal way of thinking, laid on you something as an equivalent, not imagining you would refuse a small gratuity from the funds it was to come from, as a testimony of his friendship." ' *Ib.* p. 490. There can be no question that had Adam Smith set the wishes of his dead friend before his own delicate sense of honour, he would have accepted the legacy. In the will the bequest follows two of the same amount to Dr. Adam Ferguson and D'Alembert. To neither of these friends, I feel sure, was he so strongly attached as to the author of the *Wealth of Nations*.

Adam Smith three years earlier had made Hume his literary executor. He wrote to him on April 16, 1773 :—'I have left the care of all my literary papers to you.' *M. S. R. S. E.*

Note 15. Hume in his *unostensible* letter to Adam Smith, of the same date as his ostensible one, said :—'I think your scruples groundless. Was Mallet anywise hurt by his publication of Lord Bolingbroke ? He received an office afterwards from the present King and Lord Bute, the most prudish men in the world ; and he always justified himself by his sacred regard to the will of a dead friend.' Burton's *Hume*, ii. 491. On Feb. 8, 1763, Mallet was appointed Keeper of the Book of Entries for Ships in the Port of London. *Gent. Mag.* 1763, p. 98. He was left moreover in the enjoyment of 'a considerable pension' which had been bestowed on him in the previous reign, for the vilest of services. 'He was employed to turn the public vengeance upon Byng, and wrote a letter of accusation under the character of a Plain Man. The paper was with great industry circulated and dispersed.' Johnson's *Works*, viii. 467. Adam Smith, if, as is likely, he had heard of Johnson's stinging sarcasm against Mallet, by which the name of that 'beggarly Scot' chiefly lives, might well have questioned Hume's assertion that the editor of Bolingbroke's *Works* had suffered nothing by their publication.

Note 16. See *ante*, p. 279, *n.* 5.

LETTER LXXXV.

The Cause of Hume's Illness discovered.

My Dear Sᴵᴿ

BATH, 12 *of June*, 1776.

I leave not this Place so soon as I had intended; and shall remain long enough to hear from you. I am sensibly obliged [1] to you for undertaking to execute my Will with regard to my Manuscripts; and I have this same day made a Codicil by which I make you entirely Master of them [2]. It is an idle thing in us to be concerned about any thing that shall happen after our Death; yet this is natural to all Men, and I often regretted that a Piece, for which I had a particular Partiality, should run any hazard of being suppressed after my Decease [3].

The Cause of my Distemper is now fully discovered: It is a Tumour in my Liver, which Mr. John Hunter first felt, and which I myself can now feel: It seems to be about the Bigness of an Egg, and is flat and round. Dr. Gusthart, who had conjectured some such Cause, flatters me, that he now entertains better hopes than ever, of my Recovery; but I infer, that a Disorder, of so long standing, in a vital Part, will not easily be removed in a Person of my Years: It may linger some Years, which would not be very desirable. The Physicians recommend Motion and Exercise and even long Journies [4]: I think, therefore, of setting out for Edinburgh some time next week; and will probably see you in London before the End of the good Season. I am with great Sincerity Dear Sir

Your most obedient humble Servant

DAVID HUME [5].

Note 1. 'Sensibly obliged' is one of Hume's Gallicisms. *Sensibly* even in the sense of *judiciously* or *reasonably* is given by Johnson in his Dictionary as 'low language.'

z

Note 2. Hume must have found reason to substitute for this codicil that of August 7 (*post*, p. 345).

Note 3. In his will he showed his anxiety, not only for the publication of the *Dialogues*, but also for the general suppression of his other manuscripts. In this he was unlike Johnson, who, when he was asked by Boswell 'whether it would be improper to publish his letters after his death,' replied, 'Nay, Sir, when I am dead, you may do as you will.' Boswell's *Johnson*, ii. 60.

Note 4. On June 15 he wrote to Mr. Crawford :—'The true cause of my distemper is now discovered. It lies in my liver, not in my bowels. You ask me how I know thus; I answer, John Hunter, the greatest anatomist in Europe, felt it with his fingers, and I myself can now feel it. The devil's in it if this do not convince you. Even St. Thomas, the infidel apostle, desired no better authority than the testimony of his fingers. . . . They tell me that motion and exercise are my best remedies, and here I believe them, and shall put the recipe in practice. The same remedy wou'd serve you. Will you meet me positively, and as a man of honour, this day month, the 15th July at Coventry, the most central town in England, and let us wander during the autumn throughout every corner of that kingdom and of the principality of Wales?' *Morrison Autographs*, ii. 319.

Note 5. On his way back he sent the following note, written in his own hand and dated Doncaster, June 27:—'Mr. John Hume, *alias* Home, *alias* The Home, *alias* the late Lord Conservator, *alias* the late minister of the Gospel at Athelstaneford, has calculated matters so as to arrive infallibly with his friend in St. David's Street on Wednesday evening. He has asked several of Dr. Blair's friends to dine with him there on Thursday, being the 4th of July, and begs the favour of the Doctor to make one of the number.' Home's *Works*, i. 161. Home had held the office of Conservator of Scots Privileges at Campvere. 'He represented the Dutch ecclesiastical establishment there in the General Assembly of the Church of Scotland, to which that establishment had long had the privilege of sending a member.' *Ib.* pp. 52, 59, 60.

On the day on which the old Epicurean gathered his old friends once more, and perhaps for the last time, round his friendly board in Edinburgh, far away at Philadelphia, on the other side of the broad Atlantic, the curtain had risen on one of the noblest scenes in the great drama of the world. For it was on this very fourth of July that the long-suffering and greatly wronged Colonies put forth their Declaration of Independence:—'We, the Representatives of the United States of America in General Congress assembled, appealing to the Supreme Judge of the world for the rectitude of our intentions, do, in the name, and by the authority of the good people of these Colonies, solemnly publish and declare, that these United Colonies are, and of right ought to be, FREE AND INDEPENDENT STATES. . . . And for the support of this declaration, with a firm reliance on the protection of Divine Providence, we mutually pledge to each other our lives, our fortunes, and our sacred honour.' *Ann. Reg.* 1776, i. 264. The news of this great deed must have reached Hume five or six days before his death. It is reported in the *London Chronicle* of Aug. 17. Upon him it would have come with no surprise. The London politicians had not his foresight. General Conway had written to him so late as June 16:—'I think by the late Quebec news it look's [*sic*] as if your friends, the Americans, did not think their cause worth fighting for; if so, we shall at last have peace on easy terms; and they must take the consequences.' *M. S. R. S. E.*

LETTER LXXXVI.

Return to Edinburgh: A dying Man's Corrections.

EDINBURGH, 27 *of July*, 1776.

DEAR Sᴵᴿ

I arriv'd here about three weeks ago in a very shattered Condition: The Motion of the Chaise, especially during the last days, made me suffer very much; and my Physicians are now of Opinion (which was always my Sentiment) that all Exercise is hurtful to me. I am however in very good Spirits during the Intervals of my Colics; and employ myself in my usual Occupations. As a proof of it, I send you three Leaves of the sixth Volume of my History, which you will please to substitute, instead of the three correspondent Leaves as they stand at present. They contain some Corrections, or rather Omissions, which I think Improvements [1]. You will wonder, that, in my present Situation I employ myself about such Trifles, and you may compare me to the modern Greeks, who, while Constantinople was besieged by the Turks and they themselves were threatened with total Destruction, occupyed themselves entirely in Disputes concerning the Procession of the holy Ghost [2]. Such is the Effect of long Habit! I am Dear Sir

Your most obedient humble Servant

DAVID HUME [3].

Note 1.   On leaves 89-90, 147-8, 251-4 in the edition of 1773, there are long passages which are not found in the edition of 1778. The first is about the meeting of the clergy at St. Andrews; the second, about Philip IV of Spain and the Earl of Bristol; and the third about Charles the First's message to the House of Commons as delivered by Secretary Coke.

Note 2.   In the Council held at Ferrara and Florence in 1438, fifteen years before the capture of Constantinople by the Turks, when the Greek Church sought union with the Latin in the hope of receiving assistance against the common enemy of the faith, 'the single or double procession of the Holy Ghost' was one of the four questions which for nine months was agitated between the two Churches.   'On the substance of the doctrine the controversy was equal and endless; reason is confounded by the procession of a deity; the gospel which lay on the altar was silent. . . . The danger and relief of Constantinople might excuse some prudent and pious dissimulation; and it was insinuated that the obstinate heretics who should resist the consent of the East and West would be abandoned in a hostile land to the revenge or justice of the Roman pontiff. . . . It was agreed (I must entreat the attention of the reader) that the Holy Ghost proceeds from the Father *and* the Son, as from one principle and one substance, that he proceeds *by* the Son, being of the same nature and substance, and that he proceeds from the Father *and* the Son by one *spiration* and production.   It is less difficult to understand the articles of the preliminary treaty; that the Pope should defray all the expenses of the Greeks in their return home; that he should annually maintain two gallies and three hundred soldiers for the defence of Constantinople,' etc.   Gibbon's *Decline and Fall*, ed. 1807, xii. 88-92.   Voltaire, describing the capture of the city, says:—' On s'occupait toujours de controverses, et les Turcs étaient aux portes.'   *Œuvres de Voltaire*, xiv. 408.

Note 3.   Strahan replied on Aug. 1:—'This will be a very correct edition, and I will take care it shall be printed accurately and neatly; and what is very encouraging, your *History* sells better of late years than before; for the late edition will be gone some time before this 'can be finished.   In short, I see clearly, your reputation is gradually rising in the public esteem.—A flattering circumstance this, even in the decline of life; and when by the unalterable course of nature, nothing will soon be left of us but a *Name*.—By the bye, does not this almost universal solicitude to live after we close our eyes to this present scene, mean something[1]?—I hope, I almost believe it

[1] ' It must be so—Plato, thou reason'st well!—
Else whence this pleasing hope, this fond desire,
This longing after immortality?
Or whence this secret dread, and inward horror,
Of falling into nought? why shrinks the soul

does. Else why are we on a variety of occasions, so much interested in what is to pass after our deaths? And do we not, in most of our labours, regard posterity, and look forward to times long posterior to our existence here? You yourself are a living evidence of the truth of what I am now saying.

'I sincerely congratulate you on your retaining your spirits, which people seldom do in the midst of so much pain as you have lately suffered. . . . There is yet little news of importance from 'tother side the Atlantic; but the period cannot be very distant when the fate of America, or rather *our fate* with regard to America must be determined. —I wish, and still hope and expect this foolish quarrel may end happily.' *M. S. R. S. E.*

LETTER LXXXVII.

A further Correction : Hume's Physicians report a cure.

EDINBURGH, 30 *of July*, 1776.

DEAR SⁱR

I must give you the trouble of making a new Correction, which however will be easily done. It is in the second Volume of my philosophical Pieces: That whole Passage from Page 231 till Page 239 line 3 must be thrown into an Appendix under the Title *Of Self-love*[1]: It must be the second Appendix; consequently the second Appendix becomes the third, and the third Appendix, the fourth. In like manner, what is called in Page 239, Part 2 must be Part 1[2], as also that in Page 241 must be Part 2. Let the Printer observe this Alteration with regard to the Appendixes in the Table of the Contents.

I feel myself a good deal better since I am settled here,

Back on herself, and startles at destruction?
'Tis the divinity that stirs within us;
'Tis heaven itself, that points out an hereafter,
And intimates eternity to man.'
                              Addison's *Cato*, v. i.

Gibbon in his *Autobiography*, speaking of an author's regard for 'the fair testimonies of private and public esteem,' says:—' Even his moral sympathy may be gratified by the idea that one day his mind will be familiar to the grandchildren of those who are yet unborn.' Gibbon's *Misc. Works*, i. 273.

and never stir abroad except in a Chair. My Physicians say everywhere that they have cured me, which is very agreeable Intelligence, though somewhat new to me.

I am glad to hear, that you and Dr. Robertson are fully agreed[3]: It gives me pleasure on his account, and I hope, in the Issue, upon yours. I am dear Sir

Yours sincerely

DAVID HUME.

P.S.—The Title of the Section in Page 231 remains the same as before, viz. *Of Benevolence.*

Note 1. See Hume's *Philosophical Works*, ed. 1854, iv. 364.
Note 2. See *ib.* p. 237.
Note 3. The agreement most likely is about the price to be paid for Robertson's *History of America,* which was published the following year.

LETTER LXXXVIII.

The last Correction : Life a Burthen.

EDINBURGH, 12 *of August*, 1776.

DEAR S[IR]

Please to make with your Pen the following Correction. In the second Volume of my philosophical Pieces, p. 245, l. 1, and 2, eraze these words, *that there is such a sentiment in human nature as benevolence*[1].

This, Dear S[ir], is the last Correction I shall probably trouble you with : For Dr. Black has promised me, that all shall be over with me in a very little time[2]: This Promise he makes by his power of Prediction, not that of Prescription. And indeed I consider it as good News: For of late, within these few weeks, my Infirmities have so multiplyed, that Life has become rather a Burthen to me[3]. Adieu, then, my good and old Friend.

DAVID HUME.

Oxford University Press.

HUME'S LAST LETTER TO STRAHAN.

(Page 342.)

P.S.—My Brother will inform you of my Destination with regard to my Manuscripts.

Another Correction.

In the same Page, l. 4, instead of *possession of it* read *sentiment of benevolence* [4].

Note 1. 'Upon the whole then it seems undeniable *that* there is such a sentiment in human nature as benevolence; *that* nothing can bestow more merit on any human creature than the possession of it in an eminent degree; and *that* a part, at least, of its merit arises from its tendency to promote the interests of our species, and bestow happiness on human society.' *Essays and Treatises*, ed. 1770, iv. 30. The correction was made. See *Philosophical Works*, ed. 1854, iv. 243.

Note 2. Writing to his brother on Aug. 6, Hume said :—' Dr. Black says I shall not die of a dropsy, as I imagined, but of inanition and weakness. He cannot however fix with any probability the time, otherwise he would frankly tell me. . . . In spite of Dr. Black's caution, I venture to foretel that I shall be yours cordially and sincerely till the month of October next.' Home's *Works*, i. 65. Dr. Joseph Black, the eminent chemist, was Professor of Medicine and Chemistry in the University of Edinburgh. 'Adam Smith used to say that "no man had less nonsense in his head than Dr. Black."' *Dict. of Nat. Biog.* v. 111. By Black, Smith was attended in his last illness. Stewart's *Life of Adam Smith*, p. 118. Boswell, writing to Temple on June 19, 1775, says :—'I have not begun to read, but my resolution is lively, and I trust I shall have it in my power soon to give you an account of my studies : all that I can say for myself at present is, that I attend, along with John Swinton and others, a course of lectures and experiments by Dr. Black, Professor of Chemistry,—a study which Dr. Johnson recommends much.' *Letters of Boswell*, p. 206. Lord Cockburn describes Black as 'a striking and beautiful person; tall, very thin, and cadaverously pale; his hair carefully powdered, though there was little of it except what was collected into a long thin queue ; his eyes dark, clear, and large, like deep pools of pure water. He wore black speckless clothes, silk stockings and silver buckles. The general frame and air were feeble and slender. The wildest boy respected Black. No lad could be irreverent towards a man so pale, so gentle, so elegant, and so illustrious. So he glided like a spirit, through our rather mischievous sportiveness, unharmed. He died seated, with a bowl of milk on his knee, of which his ceasing to live did not spill a drop.' Cockburn's *Memorials of his Time*, p. 50. See *Quarterly Review*, No. 71, p. 197, for an account of him by Sir Walter Scott. Scott says that he owed his life to him. 'I was,' he writes, 'an

344

uncommonly healthy child, but had nearly died in consequence of my first nurse being ill of a consumption, a circumstance which she chose to conceal, though to do so was murder to both herself and me. She went privately to consult Dr. Black, who put my father on his guard. The woman was dismissed, and I was consigned to a healthy peasant, who is still [in 1808] alive to boast of her *laddie* being what she calls a *grand gentleman.*' Lockhart's *Scott*, i. 19.

Note 3. On Aug. 20 Hume wrote to his old friend the Countess de Boufflers :—' Though I am certainly within a few weeks, dear Madam, and perhaps within a few days of my own death, I could not forbear being struck with the death of the Prince of Conti, so great a loss in every particular. My reflection carried me immediately to your situation in this melancholy incident. What a difference to you in your whole plan of life ! Pray write me some particulars; but in such terms that you need not care in case of decease into whose hands your letter may fall.

' My distemper is a diarrhœa, or disorder in my bowels, which has been gradually undermining me these two years, but within these six months has been visibly hastening me to my end. I see death approach gradually, without any anxiety or regret. I salute you, with great affection and regard, for the last time.—DAVID HUME.' Hume's *Private Corres.*, p. 285.

Adam Smith wrote to Hume on Aug. 22, 1776 :—' You have in a declining state of health, under an exhausting disease, for more than two years together, now looked at the approach, or what you at least believed to be the approach of Death with a steady cheerfulness such as very few men have been able to maintain for a few hours, though otherwise in the most perfect health.' He mentions in a letter of the same date a matter trifling in itself, but one which shows how the habit of 'rigid frugality,' by which Hume in his youth had 'supplied his deficiency of fortune,' clung to him to the end. 'I have this moment,' Smith writes, 'received your Letter of the 15 inst. You had, in order to save me the sum of one penny sterling, sent it by the carrier instead of the Post; and (if you have not mistaken the date) it has lain at his quarters these eight days, and was, I presume, very likely to lie there for ever.' Hume added a postscript to his answer of August 23, written in his nephew's hand :—' It was a strange blunder to send your Letter by the carrier.' *M.S.R.S.E.* See *post*, p. 364, *n.* 4, for this answer.

Note 4. Hume's friends, I am persuaded, would have maintained that there was something not unsuitable to his disposition, in his long train of corrections thus ending with 'the sentiment of benevolence.'

There were among them however those to whom his *Philosophical Pieces* were objects of suspicion and dislike. When, shortly before he died, he took leave of the widow of his old friend, Baron Mure, 'and gave her as a parting present a complete copy of his *History*, she

thanked him, and added in her native dialect, which both she and the
historian spoke in great purity, "O David, that's a book you may weel
be proud o'; but before ye dee, ye should burn a' your wee bookies."
To which, raising himself on his couch, he replied with some vehemence, half offended, half in joke, "What for should I burn a' my
wee bookies?" But feeling too weak for further discussion, he shook
her hand and bade her farewell.' *Caldwell Papers,* i. 40.

[John Home of Ninewells to William Strahan.]

LETTER LXXXIX.

Hume's Will : Disposition about his unpublished Works.

SIR

My brother died on the 25th of August (as you would
probably see by the newspapers[1]) and in a codicill to his latter
will and testament of the 7th of August, has the following
clauses. 'In my latter will and disposition I made some
destinations with regard to my manuscripts. All these I now
retract; and leave my manuscripts to the care of Mr. William
Strahan of London, member of Parliament: trusting to the
friendship that has long subsisted betwixt us, for his careful and
faithful execution of my intentions. I desire that my Dialogues
concerning natural religion may be printed and published any
time within two years after my death; to which he may add, if
he thinks proper, the two essays formerly printed but not
published. My account of my own life, I desire may be prefixed to the first edition of my works, printed after my Death,
which will probably be the one at present in the press. I desire
that my brother may supress all my other manuscripts.' On
the bottom of the same codicill is the following clause: 'I also
ordain that if my dialogues from whatever cause, be not published within two years and a half of my death, as also the
account of my life, the property shall return to my Nephew,
David, whose duty in publishing them as the last request of his
uncle, must be approved of by all the World. Day and date as
above.—DAVID HUME.'

In consequence of which, and in execution of his intentions, that shall be always sacred to me, I have packed up in a round white iron box, a manuscript copy of the Dialogues, and of his life within it, directed for you, as also the two essays, with the same direction, and one in my brother's hand below the first cover [2], both of which will go with the fly [3] from this to-morrow morning ; and which you will please take the trouble to cause enquire for : and beg you will take the further trouble of leting me know, of their haveing comed safe to hand, by directing for me att Ninewells by Berwick, where I shall be for two months ; and when you have taken your resolution for the publication (as I hope you soon will and as it was the last request of your friend in so earnest a manner) shall be glad to know of it ; and when the new edition of his whole works now in the press is published, my brother expected six copys, would be sent me, as presents to some of his most intimate friends. ·Mr Adam Smith with my brothers approbation, is to write a small addition to his life [4], narrating the time and manner of his death, and as he is to be at London begining of winter, will give it you: and is to advise with you, whether that addition is to be made or not.

As the manuscripts were very tight when put in the box, they cannot be taken out the same way, without injureing them : therefore there will be a necessity of knocking of the bottom and pushing them forwards.

I am Sir

Your most humble Ser[t]

JOHN HOME [5].

ST. ANDREWS, EDINBRUGH (sic), Sepbr. 2d, 1776.

Note 1. In the *Gentleman's Magazine* for Sept. 1776 (p. 435) Hume's death has the briefest notice possible :—' Aug. 25, David Hume, Esq. ; Edinburgh.'

Note 2. The two Essays were no doubt those *On Suicide* and *The Immortality of the Soul*, which Hume had printed but suppressed in 1755 (*ante*, pp. 230, 233). Strahan, *post*, p. 355, *n.* 1, describes them as 'the two Essays that were formerly printed but not published.' They had been 'sealed up' and directed by Hume to Strahan (*post*, p. 363). 'The one in my brother's hand below the first cover ' was most likely a duplicate of the *Essay on the Origin of Government*, of which Strahan had already received a copy (*ante*, p. 331).

Note 3. See *ante*, p. 326, *n.* 11.

Note 4. See *ante*, end of *Autobiography*.

Note 5. Dr. Burton thus writes of John Home :—'There was apparently but one point in which the two brothers differed ; and it was a subject on which Hume seems to have been at war with all his clan. The Laird of Ninewells, notwithstanding all the lustre that had now gathered round the name of *Hume,* would not adopt it in place of that of *Home,* which his fathers had borne. He was a simple, single-hearted man, moderate in all his views and wishes, and neither ambitious of distinction nor of wealth. He passed his life as a retired country gentleman ; and while Europe was full of his brother's name, he was so averse to notoriety, that he is known to have objected to the domestic events of births, marriages, and deaths in his family obtaining the usual publicity through the newspapers.' Dr. Burton adds in a foot-note :—'An early acquaintance with this characteristic might have saved me some fruitless investigations.' Burton's *Hume,* ii. 398.

On his brother's marriage in 1751, Hume wrote to one of their female-relations :—'Our friend at last plucked up a resolution, and has ventured on that dangerous encounter. He went off on Monday morning ; and this is the first action of his life wherein he has engaged himself, without being able to compute exactly the consequences. But what arithmetic will serve to fix the proportion between good and bad wives, and rate the different classes of each ? Sir Isaac Newton himself, who could measure the courses of the planets, and weigh the earth as in a pair of scales,—even he had not algebra enough to reduce that amiable part of our species to a just equation ; and they are the only heavenly bodies whose orbits are as yet uncertain.' Home's *Works,* i. 104.

The Laird of Ninewells seems to have clung to the Scotch spelling of his correspondent's name as much as he did to Home. He addresses this letter to 'William Strachan, Esq., Member of Parliament, att the Strand, London.'

[Adam Smith to William Strahan.]

LETTER XC.

Hume's Life and Dialogues on Natural Religion.

MY DEAR STRAHAN,

By a codicil to the will of our late most valuable friend Mr. Hume the care of his manuscripts is left to you. Both from his will and from his conversation I understand that there are only two which he meant should be published, an account of his own life, and Dialogues concerning natural religion. The latter, tho' finely written, I could have wished had remained in manuscript to be communicated only to a few people. When you read the work you will see my reasons without my giving you the trouble of reading them in a Letter. But he has ordered it otherwise. In case of their not being published within three years after his decease he has left the property of them to his nephew. Upon my objecting to this clause as unnecessary and improper, he wrote [to] me by his Nephew's hand in the following terms. 'There is no man in whom I have a greater confidence than Mr. Strahan; yet have I left the property of that manuscript to my nephew David in case by any accident they [it] should not be published within three years after my decease. The only accident I could foresee was one to Mr. Strahan's life; and without this clause my nephew would [could] have had no right to publish it. Be so good as to inform Mr. Strahan of this circumstance.' Thus far his letter which was dated on the 23ᵈ of August. He dyed on the 25 at 4 o'clock afternoon. I once had persuaded him to leave it entirely to my discretion either to publish them at what time I thought proper, or not to publish them at all. Had he continued of this mind the manuscript should have been most carefully preserved and upon my decease restored to his family: but it never should have been published in my lifetime. When you have read it you will perhaps think it not unreasonable to consult some prudent friend about what you ought to do.

I propose to add to his Life a very well authenticated account of his behaviour during his last illness. I must however beg that his Life and those Dialogues may not be published together, as you resolved for many reasons to have no concern in the publication of the [those] Dialogues. His Life I think ought to be prefixed to the next edition of his former works, upon which he has made many very proper corrections chiefly in what concerns the Language. If this Edition is published while I am [you are] at London, I shall revise the sheets, and authenticate its being according to his last corrections. I promised him that I would do so.

If my mother's health will permit me to leave her, I shall be in London by the beginning of November. I shall write to Mr. Home to take my lodgings, as soon as I return to Fife, which will be on Monday or Tuesday next. The Duke of Buccleugh [1] leaves this on Sunday.   Direct for me at Kirkaldy, Fifeshire, where I shall remain all the rest of the season.

I ever am, my dear Strahan,
Most faithfully yours
ADAM SMITH.

Dalkeith House, 5 *Sept.*, 1776.

Let me hear from you soon [2].

Note 1.   Hume, writing to Adam Smith on April 12, 1759, says :— ' Charles Townsend, who passes for the cleverest fellow in England, is so taken with the performance [Smith's *Theory of Moral Sentiments*], that he said to Oswald he would put the Duke of Buccleugh under the author's care, and would make it worth his while to accept of that charge.' Stewart's *Life of Adam Smith*, ed. 1811, p. 58.   In the beginning of 1764 Adam Smith accepted the charge of accompanying the young nobleman on his travels. *Ib.* p. 63.   He returned in October 1766. *Ib.* p. 73.   He was now staying at the Duke's house at Dalkeith.

Note 2.   The draft of this letter so far as the end of the last paragraph but one is among the Hume papers belonging to the Royal Society.   The letter itself, which is in the possession of Mr. W. C. Ford of Washington, United States, was published, with some other of Adam Smith's letters, in the *New York Evening Post* of April 30, 1887.   I have to thank my friend Professor Thorold Rogers for drawing my attention to this publication.   The few words in which the letter as printed differs from the draft I have enclosed in brackets. Strahan had written to John Home from Wincklo, near Ringwood; on Sept. 9, 1776, when he had not seen the manuscript:—' You will see [in my letters to your brother] that I there promise to fulfil his intentions most exactly; a promise I shall most assuredly perform.' On Sept. 16 he replied to Adam Smith from Southampton :—' All that I can say just now is that I shall do nothing precipitately. . . . I will give the *Dialogues* a very attentive perusal before I consult anybody. I own I did not expect to hear they were so very exceptionable, as in one of his late letters to me he tells me *there is nothing in them worse than what I have already published*, or words to that effect. . . . You see by his leaving the *Dialogues* ultimately to his nephew, in case of any accident to me, his extreme solicitude that they should not be suppressed.' *M. S. R. S. E.*

[William Strahan to Adam Smith.]

LETTER XCI.

Proposed Publication of a Selection of Hume's Letters.

DEAR SIR

I received yours of the 13th inclosing the Addition to Mr. Hume's Life; which I like exceedingly[1]. But as the whole put together is very short, and will not make a Volume, even of the *smallest size,* I have been advised by some very good judges to annex some of his Letters to me on political subjects. —What think you of this?—I will do nothing without your advice and approbation; nor would I, for the world, publish any letter of his, but such as, in your opinion, would do him honour. —Mr. Gibbon thinks such as I have shown him would have that tendency.—Now, if you approve of this, in any manner, you may perhaps add greatly to the collection from your own cabinets, and those of Mr. John Home, Dr. Robertson, and others of your mutual friends[2], which you may pick up before your return hither.—But if you wholly disapprove of this scheme, say nothing of it, here let it drop, for without your concurrence, I will not publish *a single word* of his. *M. S. R. S. E.*

LONDON, *Novr.* 26, 1776.

Note 1. Adam Smith wrote to Strahan on Nov. 13 :—'The enclosed is the small addition which I propose to make to the account which our late invaluable friend left of his own life.' *New York Evening Post,* April 30, 1887.

Note 2. In a note on Boswell's *Life of Johnson,* iii. 103, I have shown that Burke and Goldsmith, as well as Boswell's correspondent Sir Alexander Dick, use *mutual friend* instead of *common friend.*

[Adam Smith to William Strahan.]

LETTER XCII.

Hume's Injunction about his Papers.

DEAR SIR

It always gives me great uneasiness whenever I am obliged to give an opinion contrary to the inclination of my friend. I am sensible that many of Mr Humes letters would do him great honour and that you would publish none but such as would. But what in this case ought principally to be considered is the will of the Dead. Mr Humes constant injunction was to burn all his Papers, except the Dialogues and the account of his own life [1]. This injunction was even inserted in the body of his will [2]. I know he always disliked the thought of his letters ever being published. He had been in long and intimate correspondence with a relation of his own who dyed a few years ago. When that Gentlemans health began to decline he was extremely anxious to get back his letters, least the heir should think of publishing them. They were accordingly returned and burnt as soon as returned. If a collection of Mr. Humes letters, besides, was to receive the public approbation, as yours certainly would, the Curls [3] of the times would immediately set about rummaging the cabinets of all those who had ever received a scrap of paper from him. Many things would be published not fit to see the light to the great mortification of all those who wish well to his memory [4]. Nothing has contributed so much to sink the value of Swifts works as the undistinguished publication of his letters [5] ; and be assured that your publication, however select, would soon be followed by an undistinguished one. I should, therefore, be sorry to see any beginning given to the publication of his letters. His life will not make a volume ; but it will make a small pamphlet. I shall certainly be in London by the tenth of January at furthest. I have a little business at Edinburgh which may detain me a few days about Christmass, otherwise I should be with you by the

new year.   I have a great deal more to say to you ; but the post
is just going.   I shall write to Mr. Cadell by next post.

I ever am Dear Sir

Most affectionately yours

ADAM SMITH.

KIRKALDY*, 2 *Dec.*, 1776.   .

Note 1.   Hume writing to Millar so early as July 21, 1757, said :—
'I must beg the Favor of you, that you would burn all my Letters,
which do not treat of Business ; that is, I may say all of them. . . . I
own to you, that it would be very disagreeable to me, if by any
accident these Letters should fall into idle People's hands, and be
honoured with a publication.'   *M. S. R. S. E.*

Note 2.   'To my friend Dr. Adam Smith, late Professor of Moral
Philosophy in Glasgow, I leave all my manuscripts without exception, desiring him to publish my *Dialogues on Natural Religion*, which
are comprehended in this present bequest ; but to publish no other
papers which he suspects not to have been written within these five
years, but to destroy them all at his leisure.'   Hume's *Philosophical
Works*, ed. 1854, i. xxxi.   It is clear that this desire that his papers
should be destroyed did not apply to his letters ; for there was no
reason why he should have exempted from destruction those written
in the last five years.   In the codicil to his will, dated Aug. 7, he
says :—'I desire that my brother may suppress all my other manuscripts' except the *Dialogues* and the two *Essays (ante*, p. 346, *n.* 2).
There can be no doubt, however, that he would not have sanctioned
the publication of his letters.

Note 3.   'One of the passages of Pope's life which seems to
deserve some inquiry was a publication of letters between him and
many of his friends, which falling into the hands of Curll, a rapacious
bookseller of no good fame, were by him printed and sold.'   Johnson's
Works, viii. 281.

Note 4.   It is not impossible that some of his letters may have
contained loose writing.   In one to Lord Advocate Dundas, dated Nov.
26, 1754, referring to the expulsion from the Advocates' Library of three
French works for their indecency (*ante, Autobiography*), he says :—
'By the bye, *Bussi Rabutin* contains no bawdy at all, though if it did,
I see not that it would be a whit the worse.   For I know not a more
agreeable subject both for books and conversation, if executed with
decency and ingenuity.   I can presume, without intending the least
offence, that as the glass circulates at your Lordship's table, this topic
of conversation will sometimes steal in, provided always there be no
ministers present.   And even some of these reverend gentlemen
I have seen not to dislike the subject.'   *Arniston Memoirs*, ed. 1887,
p. 158.

Note 5.   'Of Swift's general habits of thinking, if his letters can be supposed to afford any evidence, he was not a man to be either loved or envied. He seems to have wasted life in discontent, by the rage of neglected pride, and the languishment of unsatisfied desire. He is querulous and fastidious, arrogant and malignant; he scarcely speaks of himself but with indignant lamentations, or of others but with insolent superiority when he is gay, and with angry contempt when he is gloomy. From the letters that pass between him and Pope it might be inferred that they, with Arbuthnot and Gay, had engrossed all the understanding and virtue of mankind; that their merits filled the world; or that there was no hope of more. They show the age involved in darkness, and shade the picture with sullen emulation.' Johnson's *Works*, viii. 225. Cowper writing on April 20, 1777, says :—'I once thought Swift's letters the best that could be written; but I like Gray's better. His humour, or his wit, or whatever it is to be called, is never ill-natured or offensive, and yet, I think, equally poignant with the Dean's.' Cowper's *Works*, xv. 38.

Note 6. Adam Smith was born at Kirkaldy on June 5, 1723. After his return from France in 1766 he settled there, living in great retirement for nearly ten years. ' At length (in the beginning of 1776) he accounted to the world for his long retreat, by the publication of his *Inquiry into the Nature and Causes of the Wealth of Nations.*' Dugald Stewart's *Life of Adam Smith*, ed. 1811, i. 75. Writing to Hume from Kirkaldy on June 7, 1767, he says :—' My Business here is Study, in which I have been very deeply engaged for about a Month past. My Amusements are long solitary walks by the sea-side. You may judge how I spend my time. I feel myself, however, extremely happy, comfortable, and contented. I never was perhaps more so in my life.' *M. S. R. S. E.* Hume, on his return to Edinburgh in 1769, wrote to him from his house in James's Court :—' I am glad to have come within sight of you, and to have a view of Kirkaldy from my windows.' Burton's *Hume*, ii. 429.

In 1778 Smith was appointed a Commissioner of Customs, and removed to Edinburgh, where he spent the last twelve years of his life. Stewart's *Life*, p. 105.

Thirty-eight years after he had left the quiet little town, another great Scotchman, Thomas Carlyle, came to pass two years there as schoolmaster. His description enables us to picture to ourselves the scene of Adam Smith's sea-side walks. ' The beach of Kirkcaldy in summer twilights, a mile of the smoothest sand, with one long wave coming on gently, steadily, and breaking in gradual explosion into harmless melodious white, at your hand all the way; the break of it rushing along like a mane of foam, beautifully sounding and advancing, ran from south to north, from the West Burn to Kirkcaldy harbour, through the whole mile's distance. This was a favourite scene, beautiful to me still, in the far away.' *Reminiscences by T. Carlyle*, i. 104. Little perhaps of this beauty caught the eye of the absent-minded philosopher; who ' when walking in the street had a manner of talking and laughing to himself, which often excited the surprise of the passengers. He used himself to mention the ejaculation of an old market-woman, "Hegh, Sirs !" shaking her head as she uttered it ; to which her companion answered, having echoed the compassionate sigh, "and he is well put on, too !" expressing their surprise that a decided lunatic, who from his dress appeared to be a gentleman, should be permitted to walk abroad.' *Quarterly Review*, No. 71, p. 200. In this *Review*, which is by Scott, some other curious stories are told of the same nature.

[Draft of a Letter from Adam Smith to William Strahan.]

LETTER XCIII.

Hume's Life to be published separately from the Dialogues.

[*Dec.* 1776.]

You certainly judge right in publishing the new Edition of Mr. Hume's works before you publish the dialogues. They might prevent the sale of this Edition ; and it is not impossible that they may hereafter [affect] occasion the sale of another. I am still uneasy about the clamour which I foresee they will excite, and could [1]. . . . I am much obliged to you for so readily agreeing to print the Life together with my addition separate from the Dialogues. I even flatter myself that this arrangement will contribute not only to my quiet, but to your interest. The clamour against the Dialogues, if published first, might for some time hurt the sale of the new edition of his works ; and when the clamour has a little subsided the dialogues may hereafter occasion a quicker sale of another edition.

M. S. R. S. E.

Note 1. The whole of the above paragraph is scored through. I do not know whether this letter was sent.

[David Hume, the nephew of the historian, to William Strahan.]

LETTER XCIV.

Information asked for about the proposed Publication of Hume's Manuscripts.

GLASGOW, *Jany. 30th*, 1777.

SIR,

Presuming upon my connection with a Gentleman whose memory must undoubtedly be very dear to you, as to everyone who had the Happiness of his intimate Acquaintance, I take the liberty of addressing you. You already perceive, that I speak of the late Mr. David Hume ; to whom I had the singular Felicity and Advantage of being Nephew.

I have never been able to learn, so fully and distinctly as I desire, your intention with regard to the Publication of those Manuscripts and Essays which he left behind him, and committed to your care. On this head, I am naturally very much interested : I hope, therefore, that you will excuse me, if I request it of you as the friend of my Uncle, that you would communicate to me all the information with regard to the extent, the time and manner of Publication, which consistently with your own convenience you can. A few Lines, in compliance with this Request, will be regarded as a great favour, and afford me the utmost Satisfaction[1].

I am Sir, your most obed^t most Humble Servt

DAVID HUME[2].

Directⁿ at Professor Millar's[3], College—Glasgow.

Note 1. Strahan replied on Feb. 13 :—' As for Mr. Hume's *Dialogues on Natural Religion,* I am not yet determined whether I shall publish them or not. I have all possible regard to the will of the deceased : But as that can be as well fulfilled by you as by me, and as the publication will probably make some noise in the world, and its tendency be considered in different lights by different men, I am inclined to think it had better be made by you. From you some will conclude it comes with propriety as done *in obedience to the last request of your Uncle*; as he himself expresses it; from me it might be suspected to proceed from motives of interest. But in this matter I hope you will do me the justice to believe I put interest wholly out of the question. However, you shall not, at any rate, be kept long in suspense, as you shall soon have my final resolution. The *two Essays* that were formerly printed, but not published, I think with all your Uncle's other friends whom I know, should never appear again in print.' *M. S. R. S. E.*   For these two Essays, see *ante*, p. 230, and p. 346, *n.* 2.

Note 2. 'David Hume [the nephew of the historian] was born on 27th February, 1757, and died on 27th July, 1838. He was successively sheriff of the counties of Berwick and Linlithgow. He was professor of Scots law in the University of Edinburgh, and a principal Clerk of Session. He resigned these offices on his being appointed a Baron of the Scottish Exchequer. His works are of great authority in the practical departments of the law. While he taught in the University, his students zealously collected notes of his lectures; and as he refused to permit any version of them to be published, the well-preserved collections of these notes have been considered valuable treasuries of legal wisdom. In 1790 he published *Commentaries on the law of Scotland respecting trials for crimes*; and in 1797 *Commentaries on the law of Scotland respecting the description and punishment of crimes.* . . . Few literary reputations have been more unlike each other than those of the two David Humes, uncle and nephew. The former hated legal details and the jargon of technical phraseology; to the latter they were the breath of his literary life. . . . On one point only did they agree—their political opinions. . . . Baron Hume was a supporter of all those parts of the criminal law of Scotland,—in his day not a few,—which put the subject at the mercy of the Crown and of the Judges.'   Burton's *Hume*, ii. 401. ' I remember,' wrote Sir Walter Scott in 1826, 'the late Lord Melville defending, in a manner that defied refutation, the Scots law against sedition, and I have lived to see these repealed by what our friend Baron Hume calls "a bill for the better encouragement of sedition and treason." It will last my day probably ; at least I shall be too old to be shot, and have only the honourable chance of being hanged for *incivisme*.' Lockhart's *Life of Scott*, viii. 297. For an instance of the cruel severity of the Scotch law of sedition, see Boswell's *Johnson*, iv. 125, *n.* 2. Lord Cockburn in his *Memorials*, p. 163, while he admits the usefulness of Hume's *Commentaries* ' for ordinary practice,' denies that ' it is a great work of original thought. . . . The proceedings of the savage old Scotch Privy Council are held up by him as judicial precedents, even in political cases.' As an enlightened exposition of law 'there is no book that has worse stood the test of time. There is scarcely one of his favourite points that the legislature, with the cordial assent of the public and of lawyers, has not put down.' In the Speculative Society, about the year 1799, 'Hume tried to bear down the younger members, who led by Brougham, Jeffrey, Horner,

... were as defying in their Whiggism as their opponents in their Toryism. .... Being supposed to have applied some offensive imputation to the junior party, it was arranged (by lot, I believe) that Jeffrey should require an explanation. This was given; but still they were bound over to keep the peace.' *Ib.* p. 74.

Scott when a student at Edinburgh attended Hume's classes, and 'copied over his lectures twice with his own hand.' He could 'never sufficiently admire,' he says, 'the penetration and clearness of conception' which they exhibited. He speaks of Hume 'as an architect to the law of Scotland.' The second copy of the lectures, 'being fairly finished and bound into volumes was presented by Scott to his father. The old gentleman was highly gratified with this performance, not only as a satisfactory proof of his son's assiduous attention to the law professor, but inasmuch as the lectures afforded himself "very pleasant reading for leisure hours." [He was a Writer to the Signet].' Lockhart's *Life of Scott,* i. 81, 249.

Hume ten days before his death wrote to his nephew:—' I doubt not but my name would have procured you friends and credit in the course of your life, especially if my brother had allowed you to carry it, for who will know it in the present disguise? But as he is totally obstinate on this head, I believe we had better let him alone. I have frequently told him, that it is lucky for him he sees few things in a wrong light, for where he does he is totally incurable.' Burton's *Hume,* ii. 509. The nephew, as the signature to his letter shows, unlike the Feildings, Earls of Denbigh, who were of the same family as Fielding the novelist, was not slow in throwing off the disguise, and in becoming known as a Hume instead of remaining insignificant as a Home. See *ante,* p. 9, *n.* 10.

Note 3. Professor John Millar, in whose house David Hume was living in his student days at Glasgow, was the author of some historical works. 'Let me venture strongly to recommend to you the books of Professor Millar,' wrote Mackintosh to Professor Smyth of Cambridge, — 'his excellent treatise *On Ranks,* and even his tedious and unequal work *On the English Government,* which contains at least an excellent half-volume of original matter.' Mackintosh's *Life,* i. 412.

Dr. J. H. Burton gives an interesting but mutilated letter, written by Hume to his nephew on Dec. 8, 1775. He writes:—' Mr. Millar complains only of one thing, which [is not the] usual complaint of tutors against their pupils; to wit, that he is afraid you [apply too] close, and may hurt your health by too assiduous study.... When I was [of your] age, I was inclined to give in to excesses of the same kind; and I remember [an anecdote] told me by a friend, the present Lord Pitfour. A man was riding with [great] violence, and running his horse quite out of wind. He stopt a moment to [ask when] he might reach a particular place. In two hours, replied the countryman, [if you] will go slower; in four if you be in such a hurry.'

Millar, it should seem, had been trying to give his pupil's mind something of a Whiggish cast, for Hume continues :—' I cannot but agree with Mr. Millar, that the republican form of government is by far the best. The ancient republics were somewhat ferocious and torn by bloody factions; but they were still much preferable to the monarchies or [aristocracies] which seem to have been quite intolerable. Modern manners have corrected this abuse ; and all the republics in Europe, without exception, are so well governed that one is at a loss to which we should give the preference. But what is this general subject of speculation to our purpose ? ' After a passage which is greatly mutilated Hume continues :—' [One] great advantage of a commonwealth over our mixed monarchy is, that it [would consid]erably abridge our liberty; which is growing to such an extreme as to be incom[patible wi]th all. Such fools are they who perpetually cry out for liberty; [and think to] augment it by shaking off the monarchy.' Burton's *Hume,* ii. 481.

It was Professor Millar who was Sir Walter Scott's authority for the famous, but untrue story, of the 'classical dialogue between the two great teachers of philosophy,' Dr. Johnson and Adam Smith. Boswell's *Johnson,* v. 369, *n.* 5.

[John Home to William Strahan.]

LETTER XCV.

Copies of the History asked for: the Dialogues: Hume's sentiments with regard to Futurity.

EDINBURGH, *Feby.* 17*th,* 1777.

SIR

＜   It is a considerable time since Mr. Adam Smith left this, for London, and carryed along with him, the adition he proposed to make, to my brothers account of himself[1], all by his own destination, to be prefixed to the edition of his works in the press, which if it be in the forwardness you intended, may perhaps be now finished, and since you was so obliging, as beside the 6 copys destined to be given to his particular friends by himself you wrote me that I might have as many more, as I choiced, you will please send 3 copys more, along with the 6, by the wagon, directed for me at St Andrews square ; one of these copys, was desired by the author verbally, to be given to one

he had personal obligations to, a little before his death, the
other 2 copys, is at the request of my son and my brothers
nameson, to be given to two persons he is under particular
tyes to.

The request I am further to make, I am not so well entitled
to, which is, that when you do me [the] favour of writeing me,
with the above packet you will please let me know your intentions with regard to the printing of the Dialogues concerning
natural religion, and if you have comed to a determination,
when it may be executed : as you make no difficulty, that they
shall be in proper time ; the anxiety my brother showed by all
his settlements, that it should be published ; I hope you will
admit of as some apology for intermedleing, with what is left
altogether at your disposal from the confidence that was placed
in you.

You was desirous to know, if my brother had got your letter
immediately before his decease.   I can inform you that he
did, and it is now in my possession ; but tho he possesed his
facultys, and understanding and cool head, to the last, he was
scarce in condition to answer it, nor the quesion you put to
him : but so far as I can judge, his sentiments with regard to
futurity were the same, as when he was in perfect health and
was never more at ease in his mind, at any one period of his life ;
and happyly his bodyly uneasyness was not very distressing ;
and if you will allow me to add from myself, a regard to the
estimation of others after we are gone, is implanted in our
frame as a great motive for good conduct and I hope will always
have an effect on that of

Sir Your most humble Ser^{vt}

JOHN HOME [2].

Note 1.   Adam Smith had sent the account by post (*ante*, p. 350).

Note 2.   Strahan's letter to the dying philosopher is preserved
among the Hume Papers at Edinburgh, and is printed in Burton's
Hume, ii. 512.   It is as follows :—

'MY DEAR SIR,

'Last Friday I received your affectionate farewell, and therefore melancholy letter, which disabled me from sending an immediate
answer to it, as I now do, in hopes this may yet find you, not much

oppressed with pain, in the land of the living. I need not tell you, that your corrections are all duly attended to, as every particular shall be that you desire or order. Nor shall I now trouble you with a long letter.

Only permit me to ask you a question or two, to which I am prompted, you will believe me, not from a foolish or fruitless curiosity, but from an earnest desire to learn the sentiments of a man, who had spent a long life in philosophic inquiries, and who, upon the extreme verge of it, seems, even in that awful and critical period, to possess all the powers of his mind in their full vigour and in unabated tranquillity.

I am more particularly led to give you this trouble, from a passage in one of your late letters, wherein you say, *It is an idle thing in us to be concerned about anything that shall happen after our death; yet this,* you added, *is natural to all men.* Now I would eagerly ask, if it is *natural to all men,* to be interested in futurity, does not this strongly indicate that our existence will be protracted beyond this life ?

Do you *now* believe, or suspect, that all the powers and faculties of your own mind, which you have cultivated with so much care and success, will cease and be extinguished with your vital breath ?

Our soul, or immaterial part of us, some say, is able, when on the brink of dissolution, to take a glimpse of futurity; and for that reason I earnestly wish to have your *last thoughts* on this important subject.

I know you will kindly excuse this singular application; and believe that I wish you, living or dying, every happiness that our nature is capable of enjoying, either here or hereafter; being, with the most sincere esteem and affection, my dear sir, faithfully yours.

London, August 19, 1776.'

See *ante,* note at end of *Autobiography* for what Johnson said on Boswell's assertion that he ' had reason to believe that the thought of annihilation gave Hume no pain.' See also *ante,* p. 115 *n.* 1, for Boswell's regret for Hume's ' unlucky principles.'

[John Home to William Strahan.]

LETTER XCVI.

The separate Publication of Hume's Life.

SIR

I wrote you about 10 days ago, and tho I have had no return, I expect it has comed safe to hand, and that you will take the trouble of writing me at your leisure.

Since which I have been informed, that your intention was, to make a seperate publication of my brothers life, with Mr. Smiths addition, which I could scarce have given faith to; if Mr. Smith had not told me, that you proposed it to him, and to add some of his letters, in order to make a volume, and to which he expressly refused to consent, and I hope the report is only founded on that, as it is a project so expressly against the clause in the codicil of his will with regard to it, which I sent you transcribed and is in these words. ' My account of my own life I desire may be prefixed to the first Edition of my works, printed after my death, which will probably be the one at present in the press. I desire that my brother may suppress all my other manuscripts.' This last clause impowers me, as far as I can, to prevent the publication of anything more from him, particularly his private letters, which is at all times unfit to be published : and tho he had made no destination, in which way his life was to be published, it was unfit it should be in a seperate pamphlet, as it would look more like the work of any other person than himself, to prevent which it seemed principally to [be] wrote, and if prefixed to his works, would appear to be genuine.

As my brother always entertained the most favourable oppinion of you, and showed it by the confidence he placed in you by his last deeds, I am confident nothing will be done by you, to make him have a different oppinion if he were alive ; and that it is so, it will be a favour done, to asure Sir

your most humble Servt
JOHN HOME.

EDINR., *Feby. 25th,* 1777 ¹.

Note 1.   Strahan wrote to John Home on March 3, to defend himself for making a separate publication of *Hume's Life* :—' Your
brother,' he writes, 'only desires it may be prefixed to the first
edition of his *Works* printed after his death.   So it shall.'   He points
out that the purchasers of former editions ought to have the right of
buying it separately.   As regards the Letters which he had proposed
to publish, he had consulted Adam Smith, 'who judged this to be
highly improper;' and so he had instantly dropped all thoughts of
it.   'Dr. Smith,' he says, 'so far from objecting to the separate publication, has written a few lines by way of Preface to the *Life*.'

He adds that he had declined to publish the *Dialogues on Natural
Religion*; but that he thought 'they might be published with more
propriety by Home's son, *in obedience to the last request of his Uncle*, as
David Hume himself expressed it.'   He goes on to say:—'The two
Essays formerly printed, but at that time suppressed, I am clearly of
opinion, and so are [sic] every one of your Brother's friends whom I
know, should never more see the light.   I hope you will concur in
this sentiment, and think no more of them; for besides that the
subjects of them are singularly unpopular, we do not think them
equal to his other Works.'   *M.S.R.S.E.*

[John Home to William Strahan.]

LETTER XCVII.

David Hume the Nephew: the Publication of the Dialogues.

SIR
        I was favoured with yours of the 3^d instant, to which you
should have had a return sooner, if I had not thought it necessary to write my son at Glasgow, and to wait his return, as he
was very materially concerned in the purport of yours; and tho
a young man, only just past 20, is able to come to a sound and
rational determination, which tho not yet absolutely fixed upon,
seems to be contrary to my oppinion, which contrariety is
perhaps partly owing to the difference betwixt old age and
young and to different tempers.

My oppinion was that he should delay the publication of the
dialogues on Natural Religion till the end of the two years, after
this that he had a title by his uncles settlement upon your not
publication of them[1]; otherways it carried the appearance of
being too forward, and of more than he was called upon in duty;

and if a clamour rose against it, he would have a difficult task to support himself, almost in the commencement of his man-hood. What weighs with him is, that his publishing as early as he had the power, would look more like obedience, than a voluntary deed, and of judgement; and as such exculpate him in the eyes of the world; as well as that the publick being in expectation of the publication would receive it much better than some time after, when it might be almost forgotten. As it is a question of great importance, and the young man will not be here from Glasgow, till near two months after this, he will advise with his uncles², and his own friends, and will then inform you, whether he accepts of your offer of the immediate surrender of your title; and in which case may possibly desire from you a more formal resignation, if such is requisite, after what you have wrote me³.

We will be both obliged to you, of takeing the charge of keeping the copy sent you, as well as of the printed Essays, tho I am possesed of the original of the first, which it seems has not been correctly copyed being taken in a hurry, and among the last things done by my brothers orders, and some-what under his eye⁴.

I received from Mr. Balfour⁵ the 20 copys of the life you ordered, long before your letter, and am much obliged to you for your attention as to that point, but cannot but be still of oppinion, that its being desired by my brother, to be prefixed, excluded every other prior mode of publication, and left no other, in the power of any other person, whatever reasons might weigh with them. but since Mr. Smith saw it in a different light, I submit, and am more difident as to my own oppinion⁶.

As I never saw the printed Essays, being sealed up and directed by himself for you and consequently cannot judge of their merit, but as they were totaly left to your disposal and judgement, and no earnestness being shown that they should see the light, I am satisfied they be suppressed, since it is your oppinion, and am obliged to you, for asking my concurrence, as a favour no way entitled to by Sir

Your most humble Servᵗ

JOHN HOME.

Note 1. See *ante*, p. 345.

Note 2. His uncles on the mother's side, for Hume had only one brother. His only sister died unmarried.

Note 3. The *Dialogues* were not published till 1779, so that the young man, it should seem, yielded to his father's advice. For the publication of the *Essays* see *ante*, p. 232, *n.* 8.

Note 4. This copy, thus hurriedly taken, is the one mentioned in the following letter :—

'EDINBURGH, 15 *of Aug.* 1776.

'MY DEAR SMITH,

'I have ordered a new Copy of my *Dialogues* to be made besides that which will be sent to Mr. Strahan, and to be kept by my Nephew. If you will permit me, I shall order a third Copy to be made, and consigned to your (sic). It will bind you to nothing, but will serve as a Security. On revising them (which I have not done these 15 Years) I find that nothing can be more cautiously and more artfully written. You had certainly forgotten them. Will you permit me to leave you the Property of the Copy, in case they should not be published in five years after my Decease ? Be so good as to write me an answer soon. My State of Health does not permit me to wait Months for it.

'Yours affectionately,

'DAVID HUME.'

M.S.R.S.E.

It was this letter, for which the dying man required a speedy answer, that, to save Adam Smith 'the sum of one penny sterling,' he sent by the carrier (*ante*, p. 344, *n.* 3).

Dr. Blair wrote to Strahan on Aug. 3, 1779 :—' As to D. Hume's *Dialogues*, I am surprised that though they have now been published for some time, they have made so little noise. They are exceedingly elegant. They bring together some of his most exceptionable reasonings, but the principles themselves were all in his former works.' *Rosebery MSS.*

Note 5. See *ante*, p. 2, *n.* 2.

Note 6. Hume's *Autobiography* was published separately this year in a small duodecimo volume, with Adam Smith's Letter as a Supplement. It is mentioned in the *Gent. Mag.* for March.

The writer of the two following curious letters was James Hutton, the Secretary to the Society of Moravians. He was the son of a Dr. Hutton, a clergyman of the Church of England who resigned his Church preferment on account of a scruple about taking the oaths. 'James was bred a bookseller, and opened a shop by Temple Bar, whence he went to Moravia, to fetch himself a wife of that nation and religion ; but this is not the age for booksellers to make fortunes by the sale of Bibles, Prayer Books, &c. ; and as Mr. Hutton would do little else, that business would not do; and he betook himself to one which it seems did, that of a Moravian Leader.' Thicknesse's *Memoirs*, i. 26, quoted in Nichols's *Lit. Anec.* viii. 447. 'He was,' says Nichols, *Ib.* iii. 436, 'highly esteemed by the two first characters for rank and virtue in the British nation.' 'The two first characters,' of course, were George III. and Queen Charlotte. Nichols quotes a letter by George Steevens, which appeared in the *St. James's Chronicle* on Dec. 17, 1776, dated 'Q——'s Palace,' and signed 'Current Report.' It says :—' Politicians from this place inform us that a new Favourite has lately engrossed the K——'s attention. . . . It is no less a person than the old deaf Moravian, James Hutton, who was formerly a bookseller, and lived near Temple Bar, famous for his refusing to sell Tom Brown's *Works* and Clarke *On the Trinity*. . . . I am sure that a conversation between the King and Hutton must be exceedingly entertaining. Hutton is so deaf that a speaking trumpet will scarce make him hear; and the King talks so fast that an ordinary converser cannot possibly keep pace with him. Hutton's asthma makes him subject to frequent pauses and interruptions.'

According to Mme. D'Arblay, 'Hutton considered all mankind as his brethren, and himself therefore as every one's equal; alike in his readiness to serve them, and in the frankness with which he demanded their services in return. His desire to make acquaintance with everybody to whom any species of celebrity was attached was insatiable, and was dauntless. He approached them without fear, and accosted them without introduction. But the genuine kindness of his smile made way for him wherever there was heart and observation. . . . So coarse was his large, brown, slouching surtout ; so rough and blowsy was the old mop-like wig that wrapt up his head, that but for the perfectly serene mildness of his features, and the venerability of his hoary eye-brows, he might at all times have passed for some constable or watchman, who had mistaken the day for the night, and was prowling into the mansions of gentlemen instead of public-houses, to take a survey that all was in order.' His sect, she adds, was looked upon 'as dark and mystic.' One day, on visiting her father's house, he said he had just come from the King, to whom he had spoken with praise of Dr. Burney [Mme. D'Arblay's father] and of Dr. Burney's *Tours*. "Openly and plainly, as one honest man should talk to another, I said it outright to my Sovereign Lord the King—who is as honest a man himself as any in his own three kingdoms. God bless him!" Mrs. Burney said that the Doctor was very happy to have had a friend to speak of him so favourably before the King. "Madam," cried the good man with warmth, "I will speak of him before my God! And that is doing much more."' *Memoirs of Dr. Burney*, i. 251, 291.

Hannah More says that 'at the royal breakfast-table, to which he had the honour of being occasionally admitted, the King said to him one morning, "Hutton, is it true that you Moravians marry without any previous knowledge of each other?" "Yes, may it please your Majesty," returned Hutton. "Our marriages are quite royal."' *Memoirs of H. More*, i. 318. According to Boswell, 'there was much agreeable intercourse' between Hutton and Johnson. Boswell's *Johnson*, iv. 410. 'One of Hutton's female missionaries for North America replied to Dr. Johnson, who asked her if she was not fearful of her health in those cold countries, "Why, Sir, I am *devoted* to the service of my Saviour; and whether that may be best and most usefully carried on here, or on the coast of Labrador, 'tis Mr. Hutton's business to settle. I will do my part either in a brick-house or a snow-house, with equal alacrity, for you know 'tis the same thing with regard to my own soul."' Piozzi's *British Synonomy*, ii. 120.

It was Hutton who arranged the meeting in 1740 between John Wesley and Count Zinzendorf, the head of the Moravians, when an attempt was made at a reconciliation between the Methodists and the Moravians. The two great leaders met in Gray's Inn Walks, and conversed in Latin, but conversed in vain. Hutton was one of those men, says Southey, 'who made Wesley perceive that all errors of opinion were not necessarily injurious to the individual by whom they were entertained; but that men who went by different ways might meet in heaven.' *Life of Wesley*, ed. 1846, i. 299, 304. Southey gives some extracts from a *Moravian Hymn-Book* printed for James Hutton in 1746. 'The most characteristic parts are,' he says, 'too shocking to be inserted.' The following lines he gives 'as a specimen of their silliness that may be read without offence :'—

'What is now to children the dearest thing here?—
To be the Lamb's lambkins and chickens most dear.
Such lambkins are nourish'd with food which is best,
Such children sit safely and warm in the nest.

.   .   .   .

'And when Satan at an hour
Comes our chickens to devour,
Let the chicken's angels say,
These are Christ's chicks,—go thy way.' *Ib.* p. 482.

In his old age Hutton had the happiness, wrote Miss Burney, 'to fall into the hands of two ladies of fortune and fashion, who live very much at their ease together, and who call him father, and treat him with the tenderness of children. How singularly he merits this singular happy fortune! so good, so active, so noble as he is in all exertions for the benefit of others, and so utterly inattentive to his own interest.' Mme. D'Arblay's *Diary*, v. 267.

[James Hutton to William Strahan.]

LETTER XCVIII.

Request to show some of Hume's Letters to the King.

DEAREST BILLY

I was last night at the Q' house [1] in company with the *Two* [2]. I mentioned to Him that I had seen a strange L^{r} [3] of David's expressing strange wishes and Hopes, it was that L^{r} of 1769 where there was a string of cruel wishes [4]. in another there was mention made of his wishes to have all the American Charters destroyd etc. [5]

I told Him that I hoped I should once be able to shew him even the Originals. If I went too far—you need take no notice. If *you will*, I can shew them to Him.

You could oblige me if you would send by your Servant this Evening or to morrow morning a Cover [6] thus frank'd

To Mr Meser
Fulneck
Leeds

to Mr Wollin's House No 45 Fetter Lane, who wants to send a Packet thither.   No 45 is the second House from New Street.

I think to go tomorrow morning to Kew [7] if fair.   but I can shew those L^{rs} of David H. if you choose it, next Wednesday.

Yr obliged HUTTON.

- *Nov.* 1, 1776.

Note 1.   The Queen's House was Buckingham House, which had been bought by George III for Queen Charlotte.   Horace Walpole wrote on May 25, 1762 :—' The King and Queen are settled for good and all at Buckingham House, and are stripping the other palaces to furnish it.' *Letters*, iii. 508.   It was there that Johnson had his interview with the King.   Boswell's *Johnson*, ii. 33.   That the King was there on the day on which Hutton says that he saw him is proved by one of his letters to Lord North, with its date curiously minute according to his custom :—' Queen's House, October 31st, 1776, 2 min. pt. 5 p.m.' *George III's Corres.* ii. 37.   The old house, which has been pulled down for the new palace, ' with its little wilderness full of blackbirds and nightingales,' is described in Dodsley's *London and its Environs*, ii. 39, and the *Gent. Mag.* 1762, p. 221.

Note 2. The King and Queen.
Note 3. Letter.
Note 4. See *ante*, p. 112.
Note 5. See *ante*, p. 289. Hutton had misread the letter.
Note 6. See *ante*, p. 188, *n.* 11.
Note 7. Miss Burney in her *Diary* thus describes the Court life at Kew:—'July 28, 1786. As there are no early prayers, the Queen rises later; and as there is no form or ceremony here of any sort, her dress is plain, and the hour for the second toilette extremely uncertain. The Royal Family are here always in so very retired a way, that they live as the simplest country gentlefolks.' Mme. D'Arblay's *Diary*, iii. 37. It was here that the King was tended in his attack of madness in 1788. *Ib.* iv. 334. It was in the Gardens that, one day walking with his medical attendants, he caught sight of Miss Burney, and, on her running away, gave her chase. When he came up to her, he kissed her on the cheek, and presently pulling a paper out of his pocket-book showed her the list of the state officers whom he intended to appoint. 'I shall be much better served (he said); and when once I get away, I shall rule with a rod of iron.' *Ib.* iv. 407.

[James Hutton to William Strahan.]

LETTER XCIX.

Hume's Letters shown to the King and Queen.

Here are the Original Letters of David Hume to Mr Strahan, mark'd A. B. C. D. E. F. G. H.
a sensible L^r (copy) of Strahan to Hume. I.
L^r from Hume's Brother. K.
a character of the Princess Dowager by Strahan. L.
Hutton perhaps will recieve them again next Wednesday or Thursday.
I. and *L.* need not be return'd [1].

the above Lines I sent with the inclosed Papers to Kew. they were read on Monday Evening [2] and were return'd to me yesterday. I know not as yet what was thought [3], but *L* is left behind. the Fog hinders me from bringing them this morning. I learnt that both of the Personages had read them. the K. was out and the Q. I believe writing to her Brothers [4], or I should

have seen and spoken with one or other of them—I had only
five words with Him, but as others were present, He could not
enter into the Matter.   I am glad they have read and kept *L.*
you see by the above they know who wrote it.

    Novr. 6, 1776⁵.

    Note 1.   For letter marked A see *ante*, p. 112 (Letter xxxvi).

„	„	B	„	p. 143.
„	„	C	„	p. 287.
„	„	D	„	p. 319.
„	„	E	„	p. 328.
„	„	F	„	p. 337.
„	„	G	„	p. 339.
„	„	I	„	p. 359, *n.* 2.
„	„	K	„	p. 345.

    For L, the character of the Princess Dowager, see *ante*, p. 237, *n.* 6.
    That part of the Letter marked C which deals with the American
War, with the omission of the attack on Pitt, is published in the
London Chronicle of June 14, 1777.   Strahan, no doubt, had had it
inserted.   'It may perhaps contribute,' it is stated, 'to open the eyes
of the nation, which so many have conspired to blind.'
    Note 2.   Monday was November 4.
    Note 3.   At '21 min. pt. 4 p.m.' of the day on which the letters
were read the King wrote to Lord North :—'Nothing can have been
better planned, nor with more alacity executed, than the taking of the
city of New York, and I trust the rebell army will soon be dispersed.'
George III's Corres. ii. 39.   Hume's advice, 'let us therefore lay aside
all anger, shake hands, and part friends,' moved him no more than
Old John of Gaunt's dying words moved Richard.
    Note 4.   The Princes of Mecklenburg-Strelitz.
    Note 5.   It is pleasant to contrast with the letter of the simple
Moravian one written by 'the Great Commoner' to the King, three
weeks before he was made Earl of Chatham.
    'SIRE,
    'Penetrated with the deepest sense of your Majesty's boundless
goodness to me, and with a heart overflowing with duty and zeal for
the honour and the happiness of the most gracious and benign
Sovereign, I shall hasten to London as fast as I possibly can ; wishing
that I could change infirmity into wings of expectation, the sooner to
be permitted to lay at your Majesty's feet the poor but sincere offering of the little services of

                       'Your Majesty's
                          Most dutiful subject,
                             and devoted servant,
                                 'WILLIAM PITT.'

Chatham Corres. ii. 438.

INDEX.

THE END.

Lately Published,
Crown 8vo., pp. xxiv, 710, price 9s.

A TREATISE

OF

HUMAN NATURE

BY

DAVID HUME

REPRINTED FROM THE ORIGINAL EDITION

AND EDITED

WITH AN ANALYTICAL INDEX

BY L. A. SELBY-BIGGE, M.A.

FELLOW AND LECTURER OF UNIVERSITY COLLEGE

Oxford

AT THE CLARENDON PRESS

LONDON: HENRY FROWDE

OXFORD UNIVERSITY PRESS WAREHOUSE, AMEN CORNER, E.C.

𝕮𝖑𝖆𝖗𝖊𝖓𝖉𝖔𝖓 𝕻𝖗𝖊𝖘𝖘, 𝕺𝖝𝖋𝖔𝖗𝖉.

A SELECTION OF

BOOKS

PUBLISHED FOR THE UNIVERSITY BY

HENRY FROWDE,

AT THE OXFORD UNIVERSITY PRESS WAREHOUSE,

AMEN CORNER, LONDON.

ALSO TO BE HAD AT THE

CLARENDON PRESS DEPOSITORY, OXFORD.

[*Every book is bound in cloth, unless otherwise described.*]

LEXICONS, GRAMMARS, ORIENTAL WORKS, &c.

ANGLO-SAXON.—*An Anglo-Saxon Dictionary*, based on the
MS. Collections of the late Joseph Bosworth, D.D., Professor of Anglo-Saxon,
Oxford. Edited and enlarged by Prof. T. N. Toller, M.A. (To be completed
in four parts.) Parts I–III. A—SAR. 4to. 15s. each.

ARABIC.—*A Practical Arabic Grammar.* Part I. Compiled
by A. O. Green, Brigade Major, Royal Engineers, Author of ' Modern Arabic
Stories.' Second Edition, Enlarged and Revised. Crown 8vo. 7s. 6d.

CHINESE.—*A Handbook of the Chinese Language.* By James
Summers. 1863. 8vo. half bound, 1l. 8s.

—— *A Record of Buddhistic Kingdoms*, by the Chinese Monk
FÂ-HIEN. Translated and annotated by James Legge, M.A., LL.D. Crown
4to. cloth back, 10s. 6d.

ENGLISH.—*A New English Dictionary, on Historical Prin-
ciples:* founded mainly on the materials collected by the Philological Society.
Edited by James A. H. Murray, LL.D., with the assistance of many Scholars
and men of Science. Vol. I. A and B. Imperial 4to. half Morocco,
2l. 12s. 6d.

  Part IV, Section II, C—CASS. Beginning of Vol. II, 5s.

B

ENGLISH.—*An Etymological Dictionary of the English Language.* By W. W. Skeat, Litt.D. *Second Edition.* 1884. 4to. 2*l.* 4*s.*

——Supplement to the First Edition of the above. 4to. 2*s.* 6*d.*

—— *A Concise Etymological Dictionary of the English Language.* By W. W. Skeat, Litt.D. *Third Edition.* 1887. Crown 8vo. 5*s.* 6*d.*

GREEK.—*A Greek-English Lexicon,* by Henry George Liddell, D.D., and Robert Scott, D.D. Seventh Edition, Revised and Augmented throughout. 1883. 4to. 1*l.* 16*s.*

—— *A Greek-English Lexicon,* abridged from Liddell and Scott's 4to. edition, chiefly for the use of Schools. Twenty-first Edition. 1884. Square 12mo. 7*s.* 6*d.*

—— *A copious Greek-English Vocabulary,* compiled from the best authorities. 1850. 24mo. 3*s.*

—— *A Practical Introduction to Greek Accentuation,* by H. W. Chandler, M.A. Second Edition. 1881. 8vo. 10*s.* 6*d.*

HEBREW.—*The Book of Hebrew Roots,* by Abu 'l-Walîd Marwân ibn Janâh, otherwise called Rabbî Yônâh. Now first edited, with an Appendix, by Ad. Neubauer. 1875. 4to. 2*l.* 7*s.* 6*d.*

—— *A Treatise on the use of the Tenses in Hebrew.* By S. R. Driver, D.D. Second Edition. 1881. Extra fcap. 8vo. 7*s.* 6*d.*

—— *Hebrew Accentuation of Psalms, Proverbs, and Job.* By William Wickes, D.D. 1881. Demy 8vo. 5*s.*

—— *A Treatise on the Accentuation of the twenty-one so-called Prose Books of the Old Testament.* By William Wickes, D.D. 1887. Demy 8vo. 10*s.* 6*d.*

ICELANDIC.—*An Icelandic-English Dictionary,* based on the MS. collections of the late Richard Cleasby. Enlarged and completed by G. Vigfússon, M.A. With an Introduction, and Life of Richard Cleasby, by G. Webbe Dasent, D.C.L. 1874. 4to. 3*l.* 7*s.*

—— *A List of English Words the Etymology of which is illustrated by comparison with Icelandic.* Prepared in the form of an APPENDIX to the above. By W. W. Skeat, Litt.D. 1876. stitched, 2*s.*

—— *An Icelandic Primer,* with Grammar, Notes, and Glossary. By Henry Sweet, M.A. Extra fcap. 8vo. 3*s.* 6*d.*

—— *An Icelandic Prose Reader,* with Notes, Grammar and Glossary, by Dr. Gudbrand Vigfússon and F. York Powell, M.A. 1879. Extra fcap. 8vo. 10*s.* 6*d.*

LATIN.—*A Latin Dictionary,* founded on Andrews' edition of Freund's Latin Dictionary, revised, enlarged, and in great part rewritten by Charlton T. Lewis, Ph.D., and Charles Short, LL.D. 1879. 4to. 1*l.* 5*s.*

MELANESIAN.—*The Melanesian Languages.* By R. H. Codrington, D.D., of the Melanesian Mission. 8vo. 18*s.*

SANSKRIT.—*A Practical Grammar of the Sanskrit Language,* arranged with reference to the Classical Languages of Europe, for the use of English Students, by Sir M. Monier-Williams, M.A. Fourth Edition. 8vo. 15*s.*

—— *A Sanskrit-English Dictionary,* Etymologically and Philologically arranged, with special reference to Greek, Latin, German, Anglo-Saxon, English, and other cognate Indo-European Languages. By Sir M. Monier-Williams, M.A. 1888. 4to. 4*l.* 14*s.* 6*d.*

—— *Nalopákhyánam.* Story of Nala, an Episode of the Mahá-Bhárata: the Sanskrit text, with a copious Vocabulary, and an improved version of Dean Milman's Translation, by Sir M. Monier-Williams, M.A. Second Edition, Revised and Improved. 1879. 8vo. 15*s.*

—— *Sakuntalá.* A Sanskrit Drama, in Seven Acts. Edited by Sir M. Monier-Williams, M.A. Second Edition, 1876. 8vo. 21*s.*

SYRIAC.—*Thesaurus Syriacus:* collegerunt Quatremère, Bernstein, Lorsbach, Arnoldi, Agrell, Field, Roediger: edidit R. Payne Smith, S.T.P. Fasc. I–VI. 1868–83. sm. fol. each, 1*l.* 1*s.* Fasc. VII. 1*l.* 11*s.* 6*d.*

Vol. I, containing Fasc. I–V, sm. fol. 5*l.* 5*s.*

—— *The Book of Kalīlah and Dimnah.* Translated from Arabic into Syriac. Edited by W. Wright, LL.D. 1884. 8vo. 21*s.*

GREEK CLASSICS, &c.

Aristophanes: A Complete Concordance to the Comedies and Fragments. By Henry Dunbar, M.D. 4to. 1*l.* 1*s.*

Aristotle: The Politics, with Introductions, Notes, etc., by W. L. Newman, M.A., Fellow of Balliol College, Oxford. Vols. I. and II. Medium 8vo. 28*s.*

Aristotle: The Politics, translated into English, with Introduction, Marginal Analysis, Notes, and Indices, by B. Jowett, M.A. Medium 8vo. 2 vols. 21*s.*

Catalogus Codicum Graecorum Sinaiticorum. Scripsit V. Gardthausen Lipsiensis. With six pages of Facsimiles. 8vo. *linen,* 25*s.*

Heracliti Ephesii Reliquiae. Recensuit I. Bywater, M.A. Appendicis loco additae sunt Diogenis Laertii Vita Heracliti, Particulae Hippocratei De Diaeta Libri Primi, Epistolae Heracliteae. 1877. 8vo. 6*s.*

Herculanensium Voluminum Partes II. 1824. 8vo. 10*s.*

Fragmenta Herculanensia. A Descriptive Catalogue of the
Oxford copies of the Herculanean Rolls, together with the texts of several
papyri, accompanied by facsimiles. Edited by Walter Scott, M.A., Fellow
of Merton College, Oxford. Royal 8vo. *cloth*, 21*s.*

Homer: A Complete Concordance to the Odyssey and
Hymns of Homer; to which is added a Concordance to the Parallel Passages
in the Iliad, Odyssey, and Hymns. By Henry Dunbar, M.D. 1880. 4to. 1*l.* 1*s.*

—— *Scholia Graeca in Iliadem.* Edited by Professor W.
Dindorf, after a new collation of the Venetian MSS. by D. B. Monro, M.A.,
Provost of Oriel College. 4 vols. 8vo. 2*l.* 10*s.* Vols. V and VI. *In the Press.*

—— *Scholia Graeca in Odysseam.* Edidit Guil. Dindorfius.
Tomi II. 1855. 8vo. 15*s.* 6*d.*

Plato: Apology, with a revised Text and English Notes, and
a Digest of Platonic Idioms, by James Riddell, M.A. 1878. 8vo. 8*s.* 6*d.*

—— *Philebus,* with a revised Text and English Notes, by
Edward Poste, M.A. 1860. 8vo. 7*s.* 6*d.*

—— *Sophistes and Politicus,* with a revised Text and English
Notes, by L. Campbell, M.A. 1867. 8vo. 18*s.*

—— *Theaetetus,* with a revised Text and English Notes,
by L. Campbell, M.A. Second Edition. 8vo. 10*s.* 6*d.*

—— *The Dialogues,* translated into English, with Analyses
and Introductions, by B. Jowett, M.A. A new Edition in 5 volumes, medium
8vo. 1875. 3*l.* 10*s.*

—— *The Republic,* translated into English, with an Analysis
and Introduction, by B. Jowett, M.A. Medium 8vo. 12*s.* 6*d.*

Thucydides: Translated into English, with Introduction,
Marginal Analysis, Notes, and Indices. By B. Jowett, M.A. 2 vols. 1881.
Medium 8vo. 1*l.* 12*s.*

THE HOLY SCRIPTURES, &c.

STUDIA BIBLICA.—Essays in Biblical Archæology and Criticism, and kindred subjects. By Members of the University of Oxford. 8vo.
10*s.* 6*d.*

ENGLISH.—*The Holy Bible in the earliest English Versions,*
made from the Latin Vulgate by John Wycliffe and his followers: edited by
the Rev. J. Forshall and Sir F. Madden. 4 vols. 1850. Royal 4to. 3*l.* 3*s.*

[Also reprinted from the above, with Introduction and Glossary by W. W. Skeat, Litt. D.

ENGLISH.—*The Books of Job, Psalms, Proverbs, Ecclesiastes, and the Song of Solomon:* according to the Wycliffite Version made by Nicholas de Hereford, about A.D. 1381, and Revised by John Purvey, about A.D. 1388. Extra fcap. 8vo. 3*s.* 6*d.*

—— *The New Testament in English,* according to the Version by John Wycliffe, about A.D. 1380, and Revised by John Purvey, about A.D. 1388. Extra fcap. 8vo. 6*s.*]

—— *The Holy Bible:* an exact reprint, page for page, of the Authorised Version published in the year 1611. Demy 4to. half bound, 1*l.* 1*s.*

—— *The Psalter, or Psalms of David, and certain Canticles,* with a Translation and Exposition in English, by Richard Rolle of Hampole. Edited by H. R. Bramley, M.A., Fellow of S. M. Magdalen College, Oxford. With an Introduction and Glossary. Demy 8vo. 1*l.* 1*s.*

—— *Lectures on the Book of Job.* Delivered in Westminster Abbey by the Very Rev. George Granville Bradley, D.D., Dean of Westminster. Crown 8vo. 7*s.* 6*d.*

—— *Lectures on Ecclesiastes.* By the same Author. Crown 8vo. 4*s.* 6*d.*

GOTHIC.—*The Gospel of St. Mark in Gothic,* according to the translation made by Wulfila in the Fourth Century. Edited with a Grammatical Introduction and Glossarial Index by W. W. Skeat, Litt. D. Extra fcap. 8vo. 4*s.*

GREEK.—*Vetus Testamentum* ex Versione Septuaginta Interpretum secundum exemplar Vaticanum Romae editum. Accedit potior varietas Codicis Alexandrini. Tomi III. Editio Altera. 18mo. 18*s.* The volumes may be had separately, price 6*s.* each.

—— *Origenis Hexaplorum* quae supersunt; sive, Veterum Interpretum Graecorum in totum Vetus Testamentum Fragmenta. Edidit Fridericus Field, A.M. 2 vols. 1875. 4to. 5*l.* 5*s.*

—— *The Book of Wisdom:* the Greek Text, the Latin Vulgate, and the Authorised English Version; with an Introduction, Critical Apparatus, and a Commentary. By William J. Deane, M.A. Small 4to. 12*s.* 6*d.*

—— *Novum Testamentum Graece.* Antiquissimorum Codicum Textus in ordine parallelo dispositi. Accedit collatio Codicis Sinaitici. Edidit E. H. Hansell, S.T.B. Tomi III. 1864. 8vo. 24*s.*

—— *Novum Testamentum Graece.* Accedunt parallela S. Scripturae loca, etc. Edidit Carolus Lloyd, S.T.P.R. 18mo. 3*s.*

On writing paper, with wide margin, 10*s.*

6   CLARENDON PRESS, OXFORD.

GREEK.—*Novum Testamentum Graece* juxta Exemplar Millia-
num. 18mo. 2s. 6d. On writing paper, with wide margin, 9s.

—— *Evangelia Sacra Graece.* Fcap. 8vo. limp, 1s. 6d.

—— *The Greek Testament,* with the Readings adopted by
the Revisers of the Authorised Version:—

(1) Pica type, with Marginal References. Demy 8vo. 10s. 6d.
(2) Long Primer type. Fcap. 8vo. 4s. 6d.
(3) The same, on writing paper, with wide margin, 15s.

—— *The Parallel New Testament,* Greek and English ; being
the Authorised Version, 1611 ; the Revised Version, 1881 ; and the Greek
Text followed in the Revised Version. 8vo. 12s. 6d.

The Revised Version is the joint property of the Universities of Oxford and Cambridge.

—— *Canon Muratorianus:* the earliest Catalogue of the
Books of the New Testament. Edited with Notes and a Facsimile of the
MS. in the Ambrosian Library at Milan, by S. P. Tregelles, LL.D. 1867.
4to. 10s. 6d.

—— *Outlines of Textual Criticism applied to the New Testament.* By C. E. Hammond, M.A. Fourth Edition. Extra fcap. 8vo. 3s. 6d.

HEBREW, etc.—*Notes on the Hebrew Text of the Book of
Genesis.* With Two Appendices. By G. J. Spurrell, M.A. Crown 8vo.
10s. 6d.

—— *The Psalms in Hebrew without points.* 1879. Crown
8vo. Price reduced to 2s., in stiff cover.

—— *A Commentary on the Book of Proverbs.* Attributed
to Abraham Ibn Ezra. Edited from a MS. in the Bodleian Library by
S. R. Driver, M.A. Crown 8vo. paper covers, 3s. 6d.

—— *The Book of Tobit.* A Chaldee Text, from a unique
MS. in the Bodleian Library; with other Rabbinical Texts, English Translations, and the Itala. Edited by Ad. Neubauer, M.A. 1878. Crown 8vo. 6s.

—— *Horae Hebraicae et Talmudicae,* a J. Lightfoot. A new
Edition, by R. Gandell, M.A. 4 vols. 1859. 8vo. 1l. 1s.

LATIN.—*Libri Psalmorum* Versio antiqua Latina, cum Para-
phrasi Anglo-Saxonica. Edidit B. Thorpe, F.A.S. 1835. 8vo. 10s. 6d.

—— *Old-Latin Biblical Texts: No. I.* The Gospel according
to St. Matthew from the St. Germain MS. (g₁). Edited with Introduction
and Appendices by John Wordsworth, D.D. Small 4to., stiff covers, 6s.

—— *Old-Latin Biblical Texts: No. II.* Portions of the Gospels
according to St. Mark and St. Matthew, from the Bobbio MS. (k), &c.
Edited by John Wordsworth, D.D., W. Sanday, M.A., D.D., and H. J. White,
M.A. Small 4to., stiff covers, 21s.

LATIN.—*Old-Latin Biblical Texts: No. III.* The Four Gospels, from the Munich MS. (q), now numbered Lat. 6224 in the Royal Library at Munich. With a Fragment from St. John in the Hof-Bibliothek at Vienna (Cod. Lat. 502). Edited, with the aid of Tischendorf's transcript (under the direction of the Bishop of Salisbury), by H. J. White, M.A. Small 4to. stiff covers, 12s. 6d.

OLD-FRENCH.—*Libri Psalmorum* Versio antiqua Gallica e Cod. MS. in Bibl. Bodleiana adservato, una cum Versione Metrica aliisque Monumentis pervetustis. Nunc primum descripsit et edidit Franciscus Michel, Phil. Doc. 1860. 8vo. 10s. 6d.

FATHERS OF THE CHURCH, &c.

St. Athanasius: Historical Writings, according to the Benedictine Text. With an Introduction by William Bright, D.D. 1881. Crown 8vo. 10s. 6d.

—— *Orations against the Arians.* With an Account of his Life by William Bright, D.D. 1873. Crown 8vo. 9s.

St. Augustine: Select Anti-Pelagian Treatises, and the Acts of the Second Council of Orange. With an Introduction by William Bright, D.D. Crown 8vo. 9s.

Canons of the First Four General Councils of Nicaea, Constantinople, Ephesus, and Chalcedon. 1877. Crown 8vo. 2s. 6d.

—— *Notes on the Canons of the First Four General Councils.* · By William Bright, D.D. 1882. Crown 8vo. 5s. 6d.

Cyrilli Archiepiscopi Alexandrini in XII Prophetas. Edidit P. E. Pusey, A.M. Tomi II. 1868. 8vo. cloth, 2l. 2s.

—— *in D. Joannis Evangelium.* Accedunt Fragmenta varia necnon Tractatus ad Tiberium Diaconum duo. Edidit post Aubertum P. E. Pusey, A.M. Tomi III. 1872. 8vo. 2l. 5s.

—— *Commentarii in Lucae Evangelium* quae supersunt Syriace. E MSS. apud Mus. Britan. edidit R. Payne Smith, A.M. 1858. 4to. 1l. 2s.

—— Translated by R. Payne Smith, M.A. 2 vols. 1859. 8vo. 14s.

Ephraemi Syri, Rabulae Episcopi Edesseni, Balaei, aliorumque Opera Selecta. E Codd. Syriacis MSS. in Museo Britannico et Bibliotheca Bodleiana asservatis primus edidit J. J. Overbeck. 1865. 8vo. 1l. 1s.

Eusebius' Ecclesiastical History, according to the text of
Burton, with an Introduction by William Bright, D.D. 1881. Crown 8vo.
8*s*. 6*d*.

Irenaeus : The Third Book of St. Irenaeus, Bishop of Lyons,
against Heresies. With short Notes and a Glossary by H. Deane, B.D.
1874. Crown 8vo. 5*s*. 6*d*.

Patrum Apostolicorum, S. Clementis Romani, S. Ignatii,
S. Polycarpi, quae supersunt. Edidit Guil. Jacobson, S.T.P.R. Tomi II.
Fourth Edition, 1863. 8vo. 1*l*. 1*s*.

Socrates' Ecclesiastical History, according to the Text of
Hussey, with an Introduction by William Bright, D.D. 1878. Crown 8vo.
7*s*. 6*d*.

ECCLESIASTICAL HISTORY, BIOGRAPHY, &c.

Ancient Liturgy of the Church of England, according to the
uses of Sarum, York, Hereford, and Bangor, and the Roman Liturgy arranged
in parallel columns, with preface and notes. By William Maskell, M.A.
Third Edition. 1882. 8vo. 15*s*.

Baedae Historia Ecclesiastica. Edited, with English Notes,
by G. H. Moberly, M.A. 1881. Crown 8vo. 10*s*. 6*d*.

Bright (W.). Chapters of Early English Church History.
1878. 8vo. 12*s*.

Burnet's History of the Reformation of the Church of England.
A new Edition. Carefully revised, and the Records collated with the originals,
by N. Pocock, M.A. 7 vols. 1865. 8vo. *Price reduced to* 1*l*. 10*s*.

Councils and Ecclesiastical Documents relating to Great Britain
and Ireland. Edited, after Spelman and Wilkins, by A. W. Haddan, B.D.,
and W. Stubbs, M.A. Vols. I. and III. 1869–71. Medium 8vo. each 1*l*. 1*s*.

   Vol. II. Part I. 1873. Medium 8vo. 10*s*. 6*d*.

   Vol. II. Part II. 1878. Church of Ireland; Memorials of St. Patrick.
   Stiff covers, 3*s*. 6*d*.

*Hamilton (John, Archbishop of St. Andrews), The Catechism
of.* Edited, with Introduction and Glossary, by Thomas Graves Law. With
a Preface by the Right Hon. W. E. Gladstone. 8vo. 12*s*. 6*d*.

Hammond (C. E.). Liturgies, Eastern and Western. Edited,
with Introduction, Notes, and Liturgical Glossary. 1878. Crown 8vo. 10*s*. 6*d*.

   An Appendix to the above. 1879. Crown 8vo. paper covers, 1*s*. 6*d*.

John, Bishop of Ephesus. The Third Part of his Ecclesiastical History. [In Syriac.] Now first edited by William Cureton, M.A.
1853. 4to. 1*l*. 12*s*.

—— Translated by R. Payne Smith, M.A. 1860. 8vo. 10*s*.

Leofric Missal, The, as used in the Cathedral of Exeter
during the Episcopate of its first Bishop, A.D. 1050-1072; together with some
Account of the Red Book of Derby, the Missal of Robert of Jumièges, and a
few other early MS. Service Books of the English Church. Edited, with Introduction and Notes, by F. E. Warren, B.D. 4to. half morocco, 35*s.*

Monumenta Ritualia Ecclesiae Anglicanae. The occasional
Offices of the Church of England according to the old use of Salisbury, the
Prymer in English, and other prayers and forms, with dissertations and notes.
By William Maskell, M.A. Second Edition. 1882. 3 vols. 8vo. 2*l.* 10*s.*

Records of the Reformation. The Divorce, 1527-1533. Mostly
now for the first time printed from MSS. in the British Museum and other
libraries. Collected and arranged by N. Pocock, M.A. 1870. 2 vols. 8vo.
1*l.* 16*s.*

Shirley (W. W.). *Some Account of the Church in the Apostolic
Age.* Second Edition, 1874. Fcap. 8vo. 3*s.* 6*d.*

Stubbs (W.). *Registrum Sacrum Anglicanum.* An attempt
to exhibit the course of Episcopal Succession in England. 1858. Small 4to.
8*s.* 6*d.*

Warren (F. E.). *Liturgy and Ritual of the Celtic Church.*
1881. 8vo. 14*s.*

ENGLISH THEOLOGY.

Bampton Lectures, 1886. *The Christian Platonists of Alex-
andria.* By Charles Bigg, D.D. 8vo. 10*s.* 6*d.*

Butler's Works, with an Index to the Analogy. 2 vols. 1874.
8vo. 11*s.*

Also separately,

Sermons, 5*s.* 6*d.*   *Analogy of Religion,* 5*s.* 6*d.*

Greswell's Harmonia Evangelica. Fifth Edition. 8vo. 9*s.* 6*d.*

Heurtley's Harmonia Symbolica: Creeds of the Western
Church. 1858. 8vo. 6*s.* 6*d.*

Homilies appointed to be read in Churches. Edited by
J. Griffiths, M.A.' 1859. 8vo. 7*s.* 6*d.*

Hooker's Works, with his life by Walton, arranged by John
Keble, M.A. Seventh Edition. *Revised by R. W. Church, M.A., D.C.L.,
Dean of St. Paul's, and F. Paget, D.D.* 3 vols. medium 8vo. 36*s.*

Hooker's Works, the text as arranged by John Keble, M.A.
2 vols. 1875. 8vo. 11*s.*

Jewel's Works. Edited by R. W. Jelf, D.D. 8 vols. 1848.
8vo. 1*l.* 10*s.*

Pearson's Exposition of the Creed. Revised and corrected by
E. Burton, D.D. Sixth Edition, 1877. 8vo. 10s. 6d.

Waterland's Review of the Doctrine of the Eucharist, with
a Preface by the late Bishop of London. Crown 8vo. 6s. 6d.

—— *Works,* with Life, by Bp. Van Mildert. A new Edition,
with copious Indexes. 6 vols. 1856. 8vo. 2l. 11s.

Wheatly's Illustration of the Book of Common Prayer. A new
Edition, 1846. 8vo. 5s.

Wyclif. A Catalogue of the Original Works of John Wyclif,
by W. W. Shirley, D.D. 1865. 8vo. 3s. 6d.

—— *Select English Works.* By T. Arnold, M.A. 3 vols.
1869–1871. 8vo. 1l. 1s.

—— *Trialogus.* With the Supplement now first edited.
By Gotthard Lechler. 1869. 8vo. 7s.

HISTORICAL AND DOCUMENTARY WORKS.

British Barrows, a Record of the Examination of Sepulchral
Mounds in various parts of England. By William Greenwell, M.A., F.S.A.
Together with Description of Figures of Skulls, General Remarks on Pre-
historic Crania, and an Appendix by George Rolleston, M.D., F.R.S. 1877.
Medium 8vo. 25s.

Clarendon's History of the Rebellion and Civil Wars in
England. Re-edited from a fresh Collation of the Original MS. in the
Bodleian Library, with Marginal Dates, and Occasional Notes, by W. Dunn
Macray, M.A., F.S.A. In six volumes, crown 8vo. *cloth,* 2l. 5s.

Clarendon's History of the Rebellion and Civil Wars in
England. Also his Life, written by himself, in which is included a Con-
tinuation of his History of the Grand Rebellion. With copious Indexes.
In one volume, royal 8vo. 1842. 1l. 2s.

Clinton's Epitome of the Fasti Hellenici. 1851. 8vo. 6s. 6d.

—— *Epitome of the Fasti Romani.* 1854. 8vo. 7s.

Corpvs Poeticvm Boreale. The Poetry of the Old Northern
Tongue, from the Earliest Times to the Thirteenth Century. Edited, clas-
sified, and translated, with Introduction, Excursus, and Notes, by Gudbrand
Vigfússon, M.A., and F. York Powell, M.A. 2 vols. 1883. 8vo. 42s.

Earle (J., M.A.). A Handbook to the Land-Charters, and
other Saxonic Documents. Crown 8vo. *cloth,* 16s.

Freeman (E. A.). *History of the Norman Conquest of England;* its Causes and Results. In Six Volumes. 8vo. 5*l.* 9*s.* 6*d.*

—— *The Reign of William Rufus and the Accession of* Henry the First. 2 vols. 8vo. 1*l.* 16*s.*

Gascoigne's Theological Dictionary ("Liber Veritatum"): Selected Passages, illustrating the condition of Church and State, 1403-1458. With an Introduction by James E. Thorold Rogers, M.A. Small 4to. 10*s.* 6*d.*

Johnson (Samuel, LL.D.), Boswell's Life of; including Boswell's Journal of a Tour to the Hebrides, and Johnson's Diary of a Journey into North Wales. Edited by G. Birkbeck Hill, D.C.L. In six volumes, medium 8vo. With Portraits and Facsimiles of Handwriting. Half bound, 3*l.* 3*s.* (See p. 21.)

Magna Carta, a careful Reprint. Edited by W. Stubbs, D.D. 1879. 4to. stitched, 1*s.*

Passio et Miracula Beati Olaui. Edited from a Twelfth-Century MS. in the Library of Corpus Christi College, Oxford, by Frederick Metcalfe, M.A. Small 4to. stiff covers, 6*s.*

Protests of the Lords, including those which have been expunged, from 1624 to 1874; with Historical Introductions. Edited by James E. Thorold Rogers, M.A. 1875. 3 vols. 8vo. 2*l.* 2*s.*

Rogers (J. E. T.). *History of Agriculture and Prices in* England, A.D. 1259-1793.

Vols. I—VI (1259-1702). 8vo. 7*l.* 2*s.*

—— *The First Nine Years of the Bank of England.* 8vo. 8*s.* 6*d.*

Stubbs (W., D.D.). *Seventeen Lectures on the Study of* *Medieval and Modern History,* &c., delivered at Oxford 1867-1884. Crown 8vo. 8*s.* 6*d.*

Sturlunga Saga, including the Islendinga Saga of Lawman Sturla Thordsson and other works. Edited by Dr. Gudbrand Vigfússon. In 2 vols. 1878. 8vo. 2*l.* 2*s.*

York Plays. The Plays performed by the Crafts or Mysteries of York on the day of Corpus Christi in the 14th, 15th, and 16th centuries. Now first printed from the unique MS. in the Library of Lord Ashburnham. Edited with Introduction and Glossary by Lucy Toulmin Smith. 8vo. 21*s.*

Manuscript Materials relating to the History of Oxford. Arranged by F. Madan, M.A. 8vo. 7*s.* 6*d.*

Statutes of the University of Oxford, codified in the year 1636 under the authority of Archbishop Laud. Edited by the late J. Griffiths, D.D., with an Introduction on the History of the Laudian Code, by C. L. Shadwell, M.A., B.C.L. 4to. 1*l.* 1*s.*

Statutes made for the University of Oxford, and for the Colleges and Halls therein, by the University of Oxford Commissioners. 1882. 8vo. 12s. 6d.

Statutes supplementary to the above, approved by the Queen in Council, 1882-1888. 8vo. 2s. 6d.

Statuta Universitatis Oxoniensis. 1888. 8vo. 5s.

The Oxford University Calendar for the year 1888. Crown 8vo. 4s. 6d.

The present Edition includes all Class Lists and other University distinctions for the eight years ending with 1887.

Also, supplementary to the above, price 5s. (pp. 606),

The Honours Register of the University of Oxford. A complete Record of University Honours, Officers, Distinctions, and Class Lists; of the Heads of Colleges, &c., &c., from the Thirteenth Century to 1883.

The Examination Statutes for the Degrees of B.A., B. Mus., *B.C.L., and B.M.* Revised to the end of Michaelmas Term, 1887. 8vo. sewed, 1s.

The Student's Handbook to the University and Colleges of Oxford. Ninth Edition. Crown 8vo. 2s. 6d.

MATHEMATICS, PHYSICAL SCIENCE, &c.

Acland (H. W., M.D., F.R.S.). *Synopsis of the Pathological Series in the Oxford Museum.* 1867. 8vo. 2s. 6d.

Annals of Botany. Edited by Isaac Bayley Balfour, M.A., M.D., F.R.S., Sydney H. Vines, D.Sc., F.R.S., and William Gilson Farlow, M.D., Professor of Cryptogamic Botany in Harvard University, Cambridge, Mass., U.S.A., and other Botanists. Royal 8vo. Vol. I., half morocco, 1l. 16s.

Vol. II. No. 1. *Just Published.*

Burdon-Sanderson (J., M.D., F.R.SS. L. and E.). *Transla-* *tions of Foreign Biological Memoirs.* I. Memoirs on the Physiology of Nerve, of Muscle, and of the Electrical Organ. Medium 8vo. 21s.

De Bary (Dr. A.). *Comparative Anatomy of the Vegetative Organs of the Phanerogams and Ferns.* Translated and Annotated by F. O. Bower, M.A., F.L.S., and D. H. Scott, M.A., Ph.D., F.L.S. With 241 woodcuts and an Index. Royal 8vo., half morocco, 1l. 2s. 6d.

CLARENDON PRESS, OXFORD. 13

De Bary (Dr. A.) Comparative Morphology and Biology of the
Fungi Mycetozoa and Bacteria. Authorised English Translation by Henry
E. F. Garnsey, M.A. Revised by Isaac Bayley Balfour, M.A., M.D., F.R.S.
With 198 Woodcuts. Royal 8vo., half morocco, 1l. 2s. 6d.

—— *Lectures on Bacteria.* Second improved edition. Authorised translation by H. E. F. Garnsey, M.A. Revised by Isaac Bayley
Balfour, M.A., M.D., F.R.S. With 20 Woodcuts. Crown 8vo. 6s.

Goebel (Dr. K.). Outlines of Classification and Special Mor-
phology of Plants. A New Edition of Sachs' Text Book of Botany, Book II.
English Translation by H. E. F. Garnsey, M.A. Revised by I. Bayley Balfour,
M.A., M.D., F.R.S. With 407 Woodcuts. Royal 8vo. half morocco, 21s.

Müller (J.). On certain Variations in the Vocal Organs of
the Passeres that have hitherto escaped notice. Translated by F. J. Bell, B.A.,
and edited, with an Appendix, by A. H. Garrod, M.A., F.R.S. With Plates.
1878. 4to. paper covers, 7s. 6d.

Price (Bartholomew, M.A., F.R.S.). Treatise on Infinitesimal
Calculus.

Vol. I. Differential Calculus. Second Edition. 8vo. 14s. 6d.

Vol. II. Integral Calculus, Calculus of Variations, and Differential Equations.
Second Edition, 1865. 8vo. 18s.

Vol. III. Statics, including Attractions; Dynamics of a Material Particle.
Second Edition, 1868. 8vo. 16s.

Vol. IV. Dynamics of Material Systems; together with a chapter on Theoretical Dynamics, by W. F. Donkin, M.A., F.R.S. 1862. 8vo. 16s.

Pritchard (C., D.D., F.R.S.). Uranometria Nova Oxoniensis.
A Photometric determination of the magnitudes of all Stars visible to the naked
eye, from the Pole to ten degrees south of the Equator. 1885. Royal 8vo.
s.6d.

—— *Astronomical Observations* made at the University
Observatory, Oxford, under the direction of C. Pritchard, D.D. No. 1.
1878. Royal 8vo. paper covers, 3s. 6d.

Rigaud's Correspondence of Scientific Men of the 17th Century,
with Table of Contents by A. de Morgan, and Index by the Rev. J. Rigaud,
M.A. 2 vols. 1841–1862. 8vo. 18s. 6d.

Rolleston (George, M.D., F.R.S.). Forms of Animal Life.
A Manual of Comparative Anatomy, with descriptions of selected types.
Second Edition. Revised and enlarged by W. Hatchett Jackson, M.A.
Medium, 8vo. cloth extra, 1l. 16s.

—— *Scientific Papers and Addresses.* Arranged and Edited
by William Turner, M.B., F.R.S. With a Biographical Sketch by Edward
Tylor, F.R.S. With Portrait, Plates, and Woodcuts. 2 vols. 8vo. 1l. 4s.

Sachs (Julius von). Lectures on the Physiology of Plants.
Translated by H. Marshall Ward, M.A. With 445 Woodcuts. Royal 8vo.
half morocco, 1l. 11s. 6d.

14 CLARENDON PRESS, OXFORD.

Westwood (J. O., M.A., F.R.S.). Thesaurus Entomologicus
Hopeianus, or a Description of the rarest Insects in the Collection given to
the University by the Rev. William Hope. With 40 Plates. 1874. Small
folio, half morocco, 7*l.* 10*s.*

𝕿𝖍𝖊 𝕾𝖆𝖈𝖗𝖊𝖉 𝕭𝖔𝖔𝖐𝖘 𝖔𝖋 𝖙𝖍𝖊 𝕰𝖆𝖘𝖙.

TRANSLATED BY VARIOUS ORIENTAL SCHOLARS, AND EDITED BY
F. MAX MÜLLER.

[Demy 8vo. cloth.]

Vol. I. The Upanishads. Translated by F. Max Müller.
Part I. The *Kh*ândogya-upanishad, The Talavakâra-upanishad, The Aitareya-
âra*n*yaka, The Kaushîtaki-brâhma*n*a-upanishad, and The Vâ*g*asaneyi-sa*m*hitâ-
upanishad. 10*s. 6d.*

Vol. II. The Sacred Laws of the Âryas, as taught in the
Schools of Âpastamba, Gautama, Vâsish*th*a, and Baudhâyana. Translated by
Prof. Georg Bühler. Part I. Âpastamba and Gautama. 10*s. 6d.*

Vol. III. The Sacred Books of China. The Texts of Confucianism. Translated by James Legge. Part I. The Shû King, The Religious portions of the Shih King, and The Hsiâo King. 12*s. 6d.*

Vol. IV. The Zend-Avesta. Translated by James Darme-
steter. Part I. The Vendîdâd. 10*s. 6d.*

Vol. V. The Pahlavi Texts. Translated by E. W. West.
Part I. The Bundahi*s*, Bahman Ya*s*t, and Shâyast lâ-shâyast. 12*s. 6d.*

Vols. VI and IX. The Qur'ân. Parts I and II. Translated
by E. H. Palmer. 21*s.*

Vol. VII. The Institutes of Vish*n*u. Translated by Julius
Jolly. 10*s. 6d.*

Vol. VIII. The Bhagavadgîtâ, with The Sanatsu*g*âtîya, and
The Anugîtâ. Translated by Kâshinâth Trimbak Telang. 10*s. 6d.*

Vol. X. The Dhammapada, translated from Pâli by F. Max
Müller; and The Sutta-Nipâta, translated from Pâli by V. Fausböll; being
Canonical Books of the Buddhists. 10*s. 6d.*

Vol. XI. Buddhist Suttas. Translated from Pâli by T. W.
Rhys Davids. 1. The Mahâparinibbâna Suttanta ; 2. The Dhamma-*k*akka-
ppavattana Sutta; 3. The Tevig*g*a Suttanta; 4. The Akankheyya Sutta;
5. The *K*etokhila Sutta ; 6. The Mahâ-sudassana Suttanta ; 7. The Sabbâsava
Sutta. 10*s*. 6*d*.

Vol. XII. The *S*atapatha-Brâhma*n*a, according to the Text
of the Mâdhyandina School. Translated by Julius Eggeling. Part I.
Books I and II. 12*s*. 6*d*.

Vol. XIII. Vinaya Texts. Translated from the Pâli by
T. W. Rhys Davids and Hermann Oldenberg. Part I. The Pâtimokkha.
The Mahâvagga, I-IV. 10*s*. 6*d*.

Vol. XIV. The Sacred Laws of the Âryas, as taught in the
Schools of Âpastamba, Gautama, Vâsish*th*a and Baudhâyana. Translated
by Georg Bühler. Part II. Vâsish*th*a and Baudhâyana. 10*s*. 6*d*.

Vol. XV. The Upanishads. Translated by F. Max Müller.
Part II. The Ka*th*a-upanishad, The Mu*nd*aka-upanishad, The Taittirîyaka-
upanishad, The Br*i*hadâra*n*yaka-upanishad, The *S*veta*s*vatara-upanishad, The
Pra*s*na-upanishad, and The Maitrâya*n*a-Brâhma*n*a-upanishad. 10*s*. 6*d*.

Vol. XVI. The Sacred Books of China. The Texts of
Confucianism. Translated by James Legge. Part II. The Yî King.
10*s*. 6*d*.

Vol. XVII. Vinaya Texts. Translated from the Pâli by
T. W. Rhys Davids and Hermann Oldenberg. Part II. The Mahâvagga,
V-X. The *K*ullavagga, I-III. 10*s*. 6*d*.

Vol. XVIII. Pahlavi Texts. Translated by E. W. West.
Part II. The Dâ*d*istân-î Dînîk and The Epistles of Mânû*sk*îhar. 12*s*. 6*d*.

Vol. XIX. The Fo-sho-hing-tsan-king. A Life of Buddha
by A*s*vaghosha Bodhisattva, translated from Sanskrit into Chinese by
Dharmaraksha, A.D. 420, and from Chinese into English by Samuel Beal.
10*s*. 6*d*.

Vol. XX. Vinaya Texts. Translated from the Pâli by T. W.
Rhys Davids and Hermann Oldenberg. Part III. The *K*ullavagga, IV-XII.
10*s*. 6*d*.

Vol. XXI. The Saddharma-pu*nd*arîka; or, the Lotus of the
True Law. Translated by H. Kern. 12*s*. 6*d*.

Vol. XXII. *G*aina-Sûtras. Translated from Prâkrit by Hermann Jacobi. Part I. The Â*k*ârânga-Sûtra. The Kalpa-Sûtra. 10*s*. 6*d*.

Vol. XXIII.   The Zend-Avesta.   Translated by James Dar-
mesteter. Part II. The Sîrôzahs, Yasts, and Nyâyis.   10s. 6d.

Vol. XXIV.   Pahlavi Texts.   Translated by E. W. West.
Part III.   Dînâ-î Maînôg-î Khirad, Sîkand-gûmânîk, and Sad-Dar.
10s. 6d.

Second Series.

Vol. XXV.   Manu.   Translated by Georg Bühler.   21s.

Vol. XXVI.   The Satapatha-Brâhmana.   Translated by
Julius Eggeling. Part II.   12s. 6d.

Vols. XXVII and XXVIII.   The Sacred Books of China.
The Texts of Confucianism.   Translated by James Legge.   Parts III and IV.
The Lî Kî, or Collection of Treatises on the Rules of Propriety, or Ceremonial
Usages.   25s.

Vols. XXIX and XXX.   The Grihya-Sûtras, Rules of Vedic
Domestic Ceremonies.   Translated by Hermann Oldenberg.

Part I (Vol. XXIX), 12s. 6d.   *Just Published.*
Part II (Vol. XXX).   *In the Press.*

Vol. XXXI.   The Zend-Avesta.   Part III.   The Yasna,
Visparad, Âfrînagân, and Gâhs.   Translated by L. H. Mills.   12s. 6d.

The following Volumes are in the Press:—

Vol. XXXII.   Vedic Hymns.   Translated by F. Max Müller.
Part I.

Vol. XXXIII.   Nârada, and some Minor Law-books.
Translated by Julius Jolly.   [*Preparing.*]

Vol. XXXIV.   The Vedânta-Sûtras, with Sankara's Commentary.   Translated by G. Thibaut.   [*Preparing.*]

*** *The Second Series will consist of Twenty-Four Volumes.*

Clarendon Press Series.

I. ENGLISH, &c.

An Elementary English Grammar and Exercise Book. By O. W. Tancock, M.A. Second Edition. Extra fcap. 8vo. 1*s*. 6*d*.

An English Grammar and Reading Book, for Lower Forms in Classical Schools. By O. W. Tancock, M.A. Fourth Edition. Extra fcap. 8vo. 3*s*. 6*d*.

Typical Selections from the best English Writers, with Introductory Notices. Second Edition. In 2 vols. Extra fcap. 8vo. 3*s*. 6*d*. each.
Vol. I. Latimer to Berkeley.   Vol. II. Pope to Macaulay.

Shairp (*J. C., LL.D.*). *Aspects of Poetry;* being Lectures delivered at Oxford. Crown 8vo. 10*s*. 6*d*.

A Book for the Beginner in Anglo-Saxon. By John Earle, M.A. Third Edition. Extra fcap. 8vo. 2*s*. 6*d*.

An Anglo-Saxon Reader. In Prose and Verse. With Grammatical Introduction, Notes, and Glossary. By Henry Sweet, M.A. Fourth Edition, Revised and Enlarged. Extra fcap. 8vo. 8*s*. 6*d*.

A Second Anglo-Saxon Reader. By the same Author. Extra fcap. 8vo. 4*s*. 6*d*.

An Anglo-Saxon Primer, with Grammar, Notes, and Glossary. By the same Author. Second Edition. Extra fcap. 8vo. 2*s*. 6*d*.

Old English Reading Primers; edited by Henry Sweet, M.A.
I.   Selected Homilies of Ælfric. Extra fcap. 8vo., stiff covers, 1*s*. 6*d*.
II. Extracts from Alfred's Orosius. Extra fcap. 8vo., stiff covers, 1*s*. 6*d*.

First Middle English Primer, with Grammar and Glossary. By the same Author. Extra fcap. 8vo. 2*s*.

Second Middle English Primer. Extracts from Chaucer, with Grammar and Glossary. By the same Author. Extra fcap. 8vo. 2*s*.

A Concise Dictionary of Middle English, from A.D. 1150 to 1580. By A. L. Mayhew, M.A., and W. W. Skeat, Litt.D. Crown 8vo. half roan, 7*s*. 6*d*.

A Handbook of Phonetics, including a Popular Exposition of the Principles of Spelling Reform. By H. Sweet, M.A. Ext. fcap. 8vo. 4*s*. 6*d*.

C

Elementarbuch des Gesprochenen Englisch. Grammatik,
Texte und Glossar. Von Henry Sweet. *Second Edition.* Extra fcap. 8vo.,
stiff covers, 2s. 6d.

History of English Sounds from the earliest Period. With
full Word-Lists. By Henry Sweet, M.A. Demy 8vo. 14s.

Principles of English Etymology. First Series. *The Native
Element.* By W. W. Skeat, Litt.D. Crown 8vo. 9s.

The Philology of the English Tongue. By J. Earle, M.A.
Fourth Edition. Extra fcap. 8vo. 7s. 6d.

An Icelandic Primer, with Grammar, Notes, and Glossary.
By Henry Sweet, M.A. Extra fcap. 8vo. 3s. 6d.

An Icelandic Prose Reader, with Notes, Grammar, and Glossary.
By G. Vigfússon, M.A., and F. York Powell, M.A. Ext. fcap. 8vo. 10s. 6d.

The Ormulum; with the Notes and Glossary of Dr. R. M.
White. Edited by R. Holt, M.A. 1878. 2 vols. Extra fcap. 8vo. 21s.

Specimens of Early English. A New and Revised Edition.
With Introduction, Notes, and Glossarial Index.

> Part I. By R. Morris, LL.D. From Old English Homilies to King Horn
> (A.D. 1150 to A.D. 1300). Second Edition. Extra fcap. 8vo. 9s.

> Part II. By R. Morris, LL.D., and W. W. Skeat, Litt.D. From Robert
> of Gloucester to Gower (A.D. 1298 to A.D. 1393). Third Edition.
> Extra fcap. 8vo. 7s. 6d.

Specimens of English Literature, from the ' Ploughmans
Crede' to the ' Shepheardes Calender' (A.D. 1394 to A.D. 1579). With Intro-
duction, Notes, and Glossarial Index. By W. W. Skeat, Litt.D. Fourth
Edition. Extra fcap. 8vo. 7s. 6d.

The Vision of William concerning Piers the Plowman, in three
Parallel Texts; together with *Richard the Redeless.* By William Langland
(about 1362–1399 A.D.). Edited from numerous Manuscripts, with Preface,
Notes, and a Glossary, by W. W. Skeat, Litt.D. 2 vols. 8vo. 31s. 6d.

The Vision of William concerning Piers the Plowman, by
William Langland. Edited, with Notes, by W. W. Skeat, Litt.D. Fourth
Edition Extra fcap. 8vo. 4s. 6d.

Chaucer. I. *The Prologue to the Canterbury Tales;* the
Knightes Tale; The Nonne Prestes Tale. Edited by R. Morris, LL.D.
Sixty-sixth thousand. Extra fcap. 8vo. 2s. 6d.

—— II. *The Prioresses Tale; Sir Thopas; The Monkes
Tale ; The Clerkes Tale ; The Squieres Tale*, &c. Edited by W. W. Skeat,
Litt.D. Third Edition. Extra fcap. 8vo. 4s. 6d.

Chaucer. III. *The Tale of the Man of Lawe ;* The Pardoneres
Tale; The Second Nonnes Tale; The Chanouns Yemannes Tale. By the
same Editor. *New Edition, Revised.* Extra fcap. 8vo. 4*s.* 6*d.*

—— IV. *Minor Poems.* By the same Editor. Extra fcap.
8vo. *Just ready.*

Gamelyn, The Tale of. Edited with Notes, Glossary, &c., by
W. W. Skeat, Litt.D. Extra fcap. 8vo. Stiff covers, 1*s.* 6*d.*

Minot (Laurence). Poems. Edited, with Introduction and
Notes, by Joseph Hall, M.A., Head Master of the Hulme Grammar School,
Manchester. Extra fcap. 8vo. 4*s.* 6*d.*

Spenser's Faery Queene. Books I and II. Designed chiefly
for the use of Schools. With Introduction and Notes by G. W. Kitchin, D.D.,
and Glossary by A. L. Mayhew, M.A. Extra fcap. 8vo. 2*s.* 6*d.* each.

Hooker. Ecclesiastical Polity, Book I. Edited by R. W.
Church, M.A. Second Edition. Extra fcap. 8vo. 2*s.*

OLD ENGLISH DRAMA.

The Pilgrimage to Parnassus with *The Two Parts of the
Return from Parnassus.* Three Comedies performed in St. John's College,
Cambridge, A.D. MDXCVII–MDCI. Edited from MSS. by the Rev. W. D.
Macray, M.A., F.S.A. Medium 8vo. Bevelled Boards, Gilt top, 8*s.* 6*d.*

*Marlowe and Greene. Marlowe's Tragical History of Dr·
Faustus,* and *Greene's Honourable History of Friar Bacon and Friar Bungay·*
Edited by A. W. Ward, M.A. *New and Enlarged Edition.* Extra fcap.
8vo. 6*s.* 6*d.*

Marlowe. Edward II. With Introduction, Notes, &c. By
O. W. Tancock, M.A. Extra fcap. 8vo. Paper covers, 2*s.* Cloth 3*s.*

SHAKESPEARE.

Shakespeare. Select Plays. Edited by W. G. Clark, M.A.,
and W. Aldis Wright, M.A. Extra fcap. 8vo. stiff covers.

The Merchant of Venice. 1*s.*   Macbeth. 1*s.* 6*d.*

Richard the Second. 1*s.* 6*d.*   Hamlet. 2*s.*

Edited by W. Aldis Wright, M.A.

The Tempest. 1*s.* 6*d.*   Midsummer Night's Dream. 1*s.* 6*d.*
As You Like It. 1*s.* 6*d.*   Coriolanus. 2*s.* 6*d.*
Julius Cæsar. 2*s.*   Henry the Fifth. 2*s.*
Richard the Third. 2*s.* 6*d.*   Twelfth Night. 1*s.* 6*d.*
King Lear. 1*s.* 6*d.*   King John. 1*s.* 6*d.*

Shakespeare as a Dramatic Artist; a popular Illustration of
the Principles of Scientific Criticism. By R. G. Moulton, M.A. Crown 8vo. 5*s.*

Bacon. I. *Advancement of Learning.* Edited by W. Aldis Wright, M.A. Third Edition. Extra fcap. 8vo. 4*s.* 6*d.*

—— II. *The Essays.* With Introduction and Notes. By S. H. Reynolds, M.A., late Fellow of Brasenose College.' *In Preparation.*

Milton. I. *Areopagitica.* With Introduction and Notes. By John W. Hales, M.A. Third Edition. Extra fcap. 8vo. 3*s.*

—— II. *Poems.* Edited by R. C. Browne, M.A. 2 vols. Fifth Edition. Extra fcap. 8vo. 6*s.* 6*d.* Sold separately, Vol. I. 4*s.*; Vol. II. 3*s.*

In paper covers :—

Lycidas, 3*d.*   L'Allegro, 3*d.*   Il Penseroso, 4*d.*   Comus, 6*d.*

—— III. *Paradise Lost.* Book I. Edited by H. C. Beeching. Extra fcap. 8vo. stiff cover, 1*s.* 6*d.*; in white Parchment, 3*s.* 6*d.*

—— IV. *Samson Agonistes.* Edited with Introduction and Notes by John Churton Collins. Extra fcap. 8vo. stiff covers, 1*s.*

Bunyan. I. *The Pilgrim's Progress, Grace Abounding, Relation of the Imprisonment of Mr. John Bunyan.* Edited, with Biographical Introduction and Notes, by E. Venables, M.A. 1879. Extra fcap. 8vo. 5*s.* In ornamental Parchment, 6*s.*

—— II. *Holy War, &c.* Edited by E. Venables, M.A. In the Press.

Clarendon. *History of the Rebellion.* Book VI. Edited by T. Arnold, M.A. Extra fcap. 8vo. 4*s.* 6*d.*

Dryden. *Select Poems.* Stanzas on the Death of Oliver Cromwell; Astræa Redux; Annus Mirabilis; Absalom and Achitophel; Religio Laici; The Hind and the Panther. Edited by W. D. Christie, M.A. Second Edition. Extra fcap. 8vo. 3*s.* 6*d.*

Locke's Conduct of the Understanding. Edited, with Introduction, Notes, &c., by T. Fowler, D.D. Second Edition. Extra fcap. 8vo. 2*s.*

Addison. *Selections from Papers in the Spectator.* With Notes. By T. Arnold, M.A. Extra fcap. 8vo. 4*s.* 6*d.* In ornamental Parchment, 6*s.*

Steele. *Selections from the Tatler, Spectator, and Guardian.* Edited by Austin Dobson. Extra fcap. 8vo. 4*s.* 6*d.* In white Parchment, 7*s.* 6*d.*

Pope. With Introduction and Notes. By Mark Pattison, B.D.

—— I. *Essay on Man.* Extra fcap. 8vo. 1*s.* 6*d.*

—— II. *Satires and Epistles.* Extra fcap. 8vo. 2*s.*

Parnell. *The Hermit.* Paper covers, 2*d.*

Gray. *Selected Poems.* Edited by Edmund Gosse. Extra fcap. 8vo. Stiff covers, 1*s.* 6*d.* In white Parchment, 3*s.*

—— *Elegy and Ode on Eton College.* Paper covers, 2*d.*

Goldsmith. Selected Poems. Edited, with Introduction and Notes, by Austin Dobson. Extra fcap. 8vo. 3s. 6d. In white Parchment, 4s. 6d.

—— *The Traveller.* With Notes by G. Birkbeck Hill, D.C.L. Extra fcap. 8vo. Paper covers, 1s.

—— *The Deserted Village.* Paper covers, 2d.

Johnson. I. *Rasselas.* Edited, with Introduction and Notes, by G. Birkbeck Hill, D.C.L. Extra fcap. 8vo. Bevelled boards, 3s. 6d. In white Parchment, 4s. 6d.

—— II. *Rasselas; Lives of Dryden and Pope.* Edited by Alfred Milnes, M.A. (London). Extra fcap. 8vo. 4s. 6d. *Lives of Dryden and Pope.* Stiff covers, 2s. 6d.

—— III. *Life of Milton.* Edited, with Notes, etc., by C. H. Firth, M.A. Extra fcap. 8vo. *cloth,* 2s. 6d. *Stiff cover,* 1s. 6d.

—— IV. *Vanity of Human Wishes.* With Notes, by E. J. Payne, M.A. Paper covers, 4d.

—— V. *Wit and Wisdom of Samuel Johnson.* Edited by G. Birkbeck Hill, D.C.L. Crown 8vo. 7s. 6d.

—— VI. *Boswell's Life of Johnson. With the Journal of a Tour to the Hebrides.* Edited, with copious Notes, Appendices, and Index, by G. Birkbeck Hill, D.C.L., Pembroke College. With Portraits and Facsimiles. 6 vols. Medium 8vo. *Half bound,* 3l. 3s.

Cowper. Edited, with Life, Introductions, and Notes, by H. T. Griffith, B.A.

—— I. *The Didactic Poems of* 1782, with Selections from the Minor Pieces, A.D. 1779–1783. Extra fcap. 8vo. 3s.

—— II. *The Task, with Tirocinium,* and Selections from the Minor Poems. A.D. 1784–1799. Second Edition. Extra fcap. 8vo. 3s.

Burke. Select Works. Edited, with Introduction and Notes, by E. J. Payne, M.A.

—— I. *Thoughts on the Present Discontents; the two Speeches on America.* Second Edition. Extra fcap. 8vo. 4s. 6d.

—— II. *Reflections on the French Revolution.* Second Edition. Extra fcap. 8vo. 5s.

—— III. *Four Letters on the Proposals for Peace with the Regicide Directory of France.* Second Edition. Extra fcap. 8vo. 5s.

Keats. Hyperion, Book I. With Notes by W. T. Arnold, B.A. Paper covers, 4d.

Byron. Childe Harold. Edited, with Introduction and Notes, by H. F. Tozer, M.A. Extra fcap. 8vo. 3s. 6d. In white Parchment, 5s.

Scott. Lay of the Last Minstrel. Edited with Preface and
Notes by W. Minto, M.A. With Map. Extra fcap. 8vo. Stiff covers, 2*s.*
Ornamental Parchment, 3*s. 6d.*

—— *Lay of the Last Minstrel.* Introduction and Canto I,
with Preface and Notes, by the same Editor. 6*d.*

II. LATIN.

Rudimenta Latina. Comprising Accidence, and Exercises of
a very Elementary Character, for the use of Beginners. By John Barrow
Allen, M.A. Extra fcap. 8vo. 2*s.*

An Elementary Latin Grammar. By the same Author.
Fifty-Seventh Thousand. Extra fcap. 8vo. 2*s.6d.*

A First Latin Exercise Book. By the same Author. Fourth
Edition. Extra fcap. 8vo. 2*s. 6d.*

A Second Latin Exercise Book. By the same Author. Extra
fcap. 8vo. 3*s. 6d.*

> A Key to First and Second Latin Exercise Books, in one volume, price 5*s.*
> Supplied to *Teachers only* on application to the Secretary of the Clarendon Press.

Reddenda Minora, or Easy Passages, Latin and Greek, for
Unseen Translation. For the use of Lower Forms. Composed and selected
by C. S. Jerram, M.A. Extra fcap. 8vo. 1*s. 6d.*

Anglice Reddenda, or Extracts, Latin and Greek, for
Unseen Translation. By C. S. Jerram, M.A. Third Edition, Revised and
Enlarged. Extra fcap. 8vo. 2*s. 6d.*

Anglice Reddenda. Second Series. By the same Author.
Extra fcap. 8vo. 3*s.*

Passages for Translation into Latin. For the use of Passmen
and others. Selected by J. Y. Sargent, M.A. Seventh Edition. Extra fcap.
8vo. 2*s. 6d.*

Exercises in Latin Prose Composition; with Introduction,
Notes and Passages of Graduated Difficulty for Translation into Latin. By
G. G. Ramsay, M.A., LL.D. Second Edition. Extra fcap. 8vo. 4*s. 6d.*

Hints and Helps for Latin Elegiacs. By H. Lee-Warner, M.A.
Extra fcap. 8vo. 3*s. 6d.*

First Latin Reader. By T. J. Nunns, M.A. Third Edition.
Extra fcap. 8vo. 2*s.*

Caesar. The Commentaries (for Schools). With Notes and
Maps. By Charles E. Moberly, M.A.

> *The Gallic War.* Second Edition. Extra fcap. 8vo. 4*s. 6d.*
> *The Gallic War.* Books I, II. Extra fcap. 8vo. 2*s.*
> *The Civil War.* Extra fcap. 8vo. 3*s. 6d.*
> *The Civil War.* Book I. Second Edition. Extra fcap. 8vo. 2*s.*

Cicero. *Speeches against Catilina.* By E. A. Upcott, M.A., Assistant Master in Wellington College. In one or two Parts. Extra fcap. 8vo. 2*s.* 6*d.*

—— *Selection of interesting and descriptive passages.* With Notes. By Henry Walford, M.A. In three Parts. Extra fcap. 8vo. 4*s.* 6*d.*

Each Part separately, limp, 1*s.* 6*d.*

Part I. Anecdotes from Grecian and Roman History. Third Edition.
Part II. Omens and Dreams: Beauties of Nature. Third Edition.
Part III. Rome's Rule of her Provinces. Third Edition.

—— *De Senectute.* Edited, with Introduction and Notes, by L. Huxley, M.A. In one or two Parts. Extra fcap. 8vo. 2*s.*

—— *Selected Letters* (for Schools). With Notes. By the late C. E. Prichard, M.A., and E. R. Bernard, M.A. Second Edition. Extra fcap. 8vo. 3*s.*

—— *Select Orations* (for Schools). In Verrem I. De Imperio Gn. Pompeii. Pro Archia. Philippica IX. With Introduction and Notes by J. R. King, M.A. Second Edition. Extra fcap. 8vo. 2*s.* 6*d.*

—— *In Q. Caecilium Divinatio,* and *In C. Verrem Actio Prima.* With Introduction and Notes, by J. R. King, M.A. Extra fcap. 8vo. limp, 1*s.* 6*d.*

—— *Speeches against Catilina.* With Introduction and Notes, by E. A. Upcott, M.A. In one or two Parts. Extra fcap. 8vo. 2*s.* 6*d.*

Cornelius Nepos. With English Notes. By Oscar Browning, M.A. Third Edition. Revised by W. R. Inge, M.A. (In one or two Parts.) Extra fcap. 8vo. 3*s.*

Horace. *Selected Odes.* With Notes for the use of a Fifth Form. By E. C. Wickham, M.A. In one or two Parts. Extra fcap. 8vo. *cloth,* 2*s.*

Livy. *Selections* (for Schools). With Notes and Maps. By H. Lee-Warner, M.A. Extra fcap. 8vo. In Parts, limp, each 1*s.* 6*d.*

Part I. The Caudine Disaster. Part II. Hannibal's Campaign in Italy. Part III. The Macedonian War.

—— Books V–VII. With Introduction and Notes. By A. R. Cluer, B.A. Second Edition. Revised by P. E. Matheson, M.A. (In one or two Parts.) Extra fcap. 8vo. 5*s.*

—— Books XXI, XXII, and XXIII. With Introduction and Notes. By M. T. Tatham, M.A. Extra fcap. 8vo. 4*s.* 6*d.*

—— Book XXII. By the same Editor. Extra fcap. 8vo. 2*s.* 6*d.*

Ovid. Selections for the use of Schools. With Introductions and Notes, and an Appendix on the Roman Calendar. By W. Ramsay, M.A. Edited by G. G. Ramsay, M.A. Third Edition. Extra fcap. 8vo. 5*s.* 6*d.*

Ovid. Tristia. Book I. The Text revised, with an Introduction and Notes. By S. G. Owen, B.A. Extra fcap. 8vo. 3*s*. 6*d*.

Plautus. Captivi. Edited by W. M. Lindsay, M.A. Extra fcap. 8vo. (In one or two Parts.) 2*s*. 6*d*.

—— *The Trinummus.* With Notes and Introductions. (Intended for the Higher Forms of Public Schools.) By C. E. Freeman, M.A., and A. Sloman, M.A. Extra fcap. 8vo. 3*s*.

Pliny. Selected Letters (for Schools). With Notes. By the late C. E. Prichard, M.A., and E. R. Bernard, M.A. Extra fcap. 8vo. 3*s*.

Sallust. With Introduction and Notes. By W. W. Capes, M.A. Extra fcap. 8vo. 4*s*. 6*d*.

Tacitus. The Annals. Books I–IV. Edited, with Introduction and Notes (for the use of Schools and Junior Students), by H. Furneaux, M.A. Extra fcap. 8vo. 5*s*.

—— *The Annals.* Book I. With Introduction and Notes, by the same Editor. Extra fcap. 8vo. limp, 2*s*.

Terence. Andria. With Notes and Introductions. By C. E. Freeman, M.A., and A. Sloman, M.A. Extra fcap. 8vo. 3*s*.

—— *Adelphi.* With Notes and Introductions. (Intended for the Higher Forms of Public Schools.) By A. Sloman, M.A. Extra fcap. 8vo. 3*s*.

—— *Phormio.* With Notes and Introductions. By A. Sloman, M.A. Extra fcap. 8vo. 3*s*. .

Tibullus and Propertius. Selections. Edited by G. G. Ramsay, M.A. Extra fcap. 8vo. (In one or two vols.) 6*s*.

Virgil. With Introduction and Notes. By T. L. Papillon, M.A. Two vols. Crown 8vo. 10*s*. 6*d*. The Text separately, 4*s*. 6*d*.

—— *Bucolics.* Edited by C. S. Jerram, M.A. In one or two Parts. Extra fcap. 8vo. 2*s*. 6*d*.

—— *Aeneid* I. With Introduction and Notes, by C. S. Jerram, M.A. Extra fcap. 8vo. limp, 1*s*. 6*d*.

—— *Aeneid* IX. Edited, with Introduction and Notes, by A. E. Haigh, M.A., late Fellow of Hertford College, Oxford. Extra fcap. 8vo. limp, 1*s*. 6*d*. In two Parts, 2*s*.

Avianus, The Fables of. Edited, with Prolegomena, Critical Apparatus, Commentary, etc. By Robinson Ellis, M.A., LL.D. Demy 8vo. 8*s*. 6*d*.

Catulli Veronensis Liber. Iterum recognovit, apparatum criticum prolegomena appendices addidit, Robinson Ellis, A.M. 1878. Demy 8vo. 16*s*.

—— *A Commentary on Catullus.* By Robinson Ellis, M.A. 1876. Demy 8vo. 16*s*.

Catulli Veronensis Carmina Selecta, secundum recognitionem
Robinson Ellis, A.M. Extra fcap. 8vo. 3s. 6d.

Cicero de Oratore. With Introduction and Notes. By A. S.
Wilkins, Litt. D.
Book I. Second Edition. 1888. 8vo. 7s. 6d.   Book II. 1881. 8vo. 5s.

—— *Philippic Orations.* With Notes. By J. R. King, M.A.
Second Edition. 1879. 8vo. 10s. 6d.

—— *Select Letters.* With English Introductions, Notes, and
Appendices. By Albert Watson, M.A. Third Edition. Demy 8vo. 18s.

—— *Select Letters.* Text. By the same Editor. Second
Edition. Extra fcap. 8vo. 4s.

—— *pro Cluentio.* With Introduction and Notes. By W.
Ramsay, M.A. Edited by G. G. Ramsay, M.A. 2nd Ed. Ext. fcap. 8vo. 3s. 6d.

Horace. With a Commentary. Volume I. The Odes, Carmen
Seculare, and Epodes. By Edward C. Wickham, M.A. Second Edition.
1877. Demy 8vo. 12s.

—— A reprint of the above, in a size suitable for the use
of Schools. In one or two Parts. Extra fcap. 8vo. 6s.

Livy, Book I. With Introduction, Historical Examination,
and Notes. By J. R. Seeley, M.A. Second Edition. 1881. 8vo. 6s.

Ovid. P. Ovidii Nasonis Ibis. Ex Novis Codicibus edidit,
Scholia Vetera Commentarium cum Prolegomenis Appendice Indice addidit,
R. Ellis, A.M. 8vo. 10s. 6d.

Persius. The Satires. With a Translation and Commentary.
By John Conington, M.A. Edited by Henry Nettleship, M.A. Second
Edition. 1874. 8vo. 7s. 6d.

Juvenal. XIII Satires. Edited, with Introduction and
Notes, by C. H. Pearson, M.A., and Herbert A. Strong, M.A., LL.D., Professor
of Latin in Liverpool University College, Victoria University. In two Parts.
Crown 8vo. Complete, 6s.
Also separately, Part I. Introduction, Text, etc., 3s.   Part II. Notes, 3s. 6d.

Tacitus. The Annals. Books I-VI. Edited, with Introduction and Notes, by H. Furneaux, M.A. 8vo. 18s.

---

*King (J. E., M.A.) and C. Cookson, M.A. The Principles of
Sound and Inflexion*, as illustrated in the Greek and Latin Languages. 1888.
8vo. 18s.

Nettleship (H., M.A.). Lectures and Essays on Subjects connected with Latin Scholarship and Literature. Crown 8vo. 7s. 6d.

—— *The Roman Satura.* 8vo. sewed, 1s.

—— *Ancient Lives of Vergil.* 8vo. sewed, 2s.

Papillon (*T. L., M.A.*). *A Manual of Comparative Philology.*
Third Edition, Revised and Corrected. 1882. Crown 8vo. 6s.

Pinder (*North, M.A.*). *Selections from the less known Latin*
Poets. 1869. 8vo. 15s.

Sellar (*W. Y., M.A.*). *Roman Poets of the Augustan Age.*
VIRGIL. New Edition. 1883. Crown 8vo. 9s.

—— *Roman Poets of the Republic.* New Edition, Revised
and Enlarged. 1881. 8vo. 14s.

Wordsworth (*J., M.A.*). *Fragments and Specimens of Early*
Latin. With Introductions and Notes. 1874. 8vo. 18s.

III. GREEK.

A Greek Primer, for the use of beginners in that Language.
By Charles Wordsworth, D.C.L. Seventh Edition. Extra fcap. 8vo. 1s. 6d.

A Greek Testament Primer. An Easy Grammar and Read-
ing Book for the use of Students beginning Greek. By the Rev. E. Miller,
M.A. Extra fcap. 8vo. 3s. 6d.

Easy Greek Reader. By Evelyn Abbott, M.A. In one or
two Parts. Extra fcap. 8vo. 3s.

Graecae Grammaticae Rudimenta in usum Scholarum. Auc-
tore Carolo Wordsworth, D.C.L. Nineteenth Edition, 1882. 12mo. 4s.

A Greek-English Lexicon, abridged from Liddell and Scott's
4to. edition, chiefly for the use of Schools. Twenty-first Edition. 1886.
Square 12mo. 7s. 6d.

Greek Verbs, Irregular and Defective. By W. Veitch. Fourth
Edition. Crown 8vo. 10s. 6d.

The Elements of Greek Accentuation (for Schools): abridged
from his larger work by H. W. Chandler, M.A. Extra fcap. 8vo. 2s. 6d.

A SERIES OF GRADUATED GREEK READERS:—

First Greek Reader. By W. G. Rushbrooke, M.L. Second
Edition. Extra fcap. 8vo. 2s. 6d.

Second Greek Reader. By A. M. Bell, M.A. Extra fcap.
8vo. 3s. 6d.

Fourth Greek Reader; being Specimens of Greek Dialects.
With Introductions, etc. By W. W. Merry, D.D. Extra fcap. 8vo. 4s. 6d.

Fifth Greek Reader. Selections from Greek Epic and
Dramatic Poetry, with Introductions and Notes. By Evelyn Abbott, M.A.
Extra fcap. 8vo. 4s. 6d.

The Golden Treasury of Ancient Greek Poetry: being a Collection of the finest passages in the Greek Classic Poets, with Introductory
Notices and Notes. By R. S. Wright, M.A. Extra fcap. 8vo. 8s. 6d.

A Golden Treasury of Greek Prose, being a Collection of the finest passages in the principal Greek Prose Writers, with Introductory Notices and Notes. By R. S. Wright, M.A., and J. E. L. Shadwell, M.A. Extra fcap. 8vo. 4*s.* 6*d.*

Aeschylus. Prometheus Bound (for Schools). With Introduction and Notes, by A. O. Prickard, M.A. Second Edition. Extra fcap. 8vo. 2*s.*

—— *Agamemnon.* With Introduction and Notes, by Arthur Sidgwick, M.A. Third Edition. In one or two parts. Extra fcap. 8vo. 3*s.*

—— *Choephoroi.* With Introduction and Notes by the same Editor. Extra fcap. 8vo. 3*s.*

—— *Eumenides.* With Introduction and Notes, by the same Editor. In one or two Parts. Extra fcap. 8vo. 3*s.*

Aristophanes. In Single Plays. Edited, with English Notes, Introductions, &c., by W. W. Merry, D.D. Extra fcap. 8vo.
 I. The Clouds, Second Edition, 2*s.*
 II. The Acharnians, Third Edition., In one or two parts, 3*s.*
 III. The Frogs, Second Edition. In one or two parts, 3*s.*
 IV. The Knights. In one or two parts, 3*s.*

Cebes. Tabula. With Introduction and Notes. By C. S. Jerram, M.A. Extra fcap. 8vo. 2*s.* 6*d.*

Demosthenes. Orations against Philip. With Introduction and Notes, by Evelyn Abbott, M.A., and P. E. Matheson, M.A. Vol. I. Philippic I. Olynthiacs I–III. In one or two Parts. Extra fcap. 8vo. 3*s.*

Euripides. Alcestis (for Schools). By C. S. Jerram, M.A. Extra fcap. 8vo. 2*s.* 6*d.*

—— *Hecuba.* With Notes by C. H. Russell. *In the Press.*

—— *Helena.* Edited, with Introduction, Notes, etc., for Upper and Middle Forms. By C. S. Jerram, M.A. Extra fcap. 8vo. 3*s.*

—— *Heracleidae.* Edited with Introduction and Notes by C. S. Jerram, M.A. Extra fcap. 8vo. 3*s.*

—— *Iphigenia in Tauris.* Edited, with Introduction, Notes, etc., for Upper and Middle Forms. By C. S. Jerram, M.A. Extra fcap. 8vo. cloth, 3*s.*

—— *Medea.* By C. B. Heberden, M.A. In one or two Parts. Extra fcap. 8vo. 2*s.*

Herodotus, Book IX. Edited, with Notes, by Evelyn Abbott, M.A. In one or two Parts. Extra fcap. 8vo. 3*s.*

Herodotus, Selections from. Edited, with Introduction, Notes, and a Map, by W. W. Merry, D.D. Extra fcap. 8vo. 2*s.* 6*d.*

Homer. Odyssey, Books I–XII (for Schools). By W. W. Merry, D.D. Fortieth Thousand. (In one or two Parts.) Extra fcap. 8vo. 5s. Books I, and II, *separately,* each 1s. 6d.

—— *Odyssey,* Books XIII–XXIV (for Schools). By the same Editor. Second Edition. Extra fcap. 8vo. 5s.

—— *Iliad,* Book I (for Schools). By D. B. Monro, M.A. Second Edition. Extra fcap. 8vo. 2s.

—— *Iliad,* Books I–XII (for Schools). With an Introduction, a brief Homeric Grammar, and Notes. By D. B. Monro, M.A. Second Edition. Extra fcap. 8vo. 6s.

—— *Iliad,* Books VI and XXI. With Introduction and Notes. By Herbert Hailstone, M.A. Extra fcap. 8vo. 1s. 6d. each.

Lucian. Vera Historia (for Schools). By C. S. Jerram, M.A. Second Edition. Extra fcap. 8vo. 1s. 6d.

Lysias. Epitaphios. Edited, with Introduction and Notes, by F. J. Snell, B.A. (In one or two Parts.) Extra fcap. 8vo. 2s.

Plato. Meno. With Introduction and Notes. By St. George Stock, M.A., Pembroke College. (In one or two Parts.) Extra fcap. 8vo. 2s. 6d.

Plato. The Apology. With Introduction and Notes. By St. George Stock, M.A. (In one or two Parts.) Extra fcap. 8vo. 2s. 6d.

Sophocles. For the use of Schools. Edited with Introductions and English Notes By Lewis Campbell, M.A., and Evelyn Abbott, M.A. *New and Revised Edition.* 2 Vols. Extra fcap. 8vo. 10s. 6d.
Sold separately, Vol. I, Text, 4s. 6d. ; Vol. II, Explanatory Notes, 6s.

Sophocles. In Single Plays, with English Notes, &c. By Lewis Campbell. M.A., and Evelyn Abbott, M.A. Extra fcap. 8vo. limp.
Oedipus Tyrannus, Philoctetes. New and Revised Edition, 2s. each.
Oedipus Coloneus,   Antigone, 1s. 9d. each.
Ajax,   Electra,   Trachiniae, 2s. each.

—— *Oedipus Rex:* Dindorf's Text, with Notes by the present Bishop of St. David's. Extra fcap. 8vo. limp, 1s. 6d.

Theocritus (for Schools). With Notes. By H. Kynaston, D.D. (late Snow). Third Edition. Extra fcap 8vo. 4s. 6d.

Xenophon. Easy Selections (for Junior Classes). With a Vocabulary, Notes, and Map. By J. S. Phillpotts, B.C.L., and C. S. Jerram, M.A. Third Edition. Extra fcap. 8vo. 3s. 6d.

—— *Selections* (for Schools). With Notes and Maps. By J. S. Phillpotts. B.C.L. Fourth Edition. Extra fcap. 8vo. 3s. 6d.

—— *Anabasis,* Book I. Edited for the use of Junior Classes and Private Students. With Introduction, Notes, etc. By J. Marshall, M.A., Rector of the Royal High School, Edinburgh. Extra fcap. 8vo. 2s. 6d.

Xenophon. *Anabasis*, Book II. With Notes and Map. By
C. S. Jerram, M.A. Extra fcap. 8vo. 2*s.*

—— *Anabasis*, Book III. Edited with Introduction, Analysis,
Notes, etc., by J. Marshall, M.A. Extra fcap. 8vo. 2*s.* 6*d.*

—— *Cyropaedia*, Book I. With Introduction and Notes by
C. Bigg, D.D. Extra fcap. 8vo. 2*s.*

—— *Cyropaedia*, Books IV and V. With Introduction and
Notes by C. Bigg, D.D. Extra fcap. 8vo. 2*s.* 6*d.*

—— *Hellenica*, Books I, II. With Introductions and Notes
by G. E. Underhill, M.A., Fellow and Tutor of Magdalen College. Extra
fcap. 8vo. *cloth*, 3*s.*

Aristotle's Politics. With an Introduction, Essays, and Notes.
By W. L. Newman, M.A., Fellow of Balliol College. Vols. I and II.
Medium 8vo. 28*s.*

Aristotle. On the History of the Process by which the Aristo-
telian Writings arrived at their present form. An Essay by Richard Shute,
M.A., late Student of Christ Church; with a Brief Memoir of the Author.
8vo. 7*s.* 6*d.*

Aristotelian Studies. I. On the Structure of the Seventh
Book of the Nicomachean Ethics. By J. C. Wilson, M.A. 8vo. stiff, 5*s.*

Aristotelis Ethica Nicomachea, ex recensione Immanuelis
Bekkeri. Crown 8vo. 5*s.*

Demosthenes and Aeschines. The Orations of Demosthenes
and Æschines on the Crown. With Introductory Essays and Notes. By
G. A. Simcox, M.A., and W. H. Simcox, M.A. 1872. 8vo. 12*s.*

Head (Barclay V.). *Historia Numorum: A Manual of Greek
Numismatics.* Royal 8vo. half-bound. 2*l.* 2*s.*

Hicks (E. L., M.A.). *A Manual of Greek Historical Inscrip-
tions.* Demy 8vo. 10*s.* 6*d.*

Homer. *Odyssey*, Books I–XII. Edited with English Notes,
Appendices, etc. By W. W. Merry, D.D., and the late James Riddell, M.A.
1886. Second Edition. Demy 8vo. 16*s.*

Homer. A Grammar of the Homeric Dialect. By D. B. Monro,
M.A. Demy 8vo. 10*s.* 6*d.*

Polybius. Selections from Polybius. Edited by J. L. Strachan-
Davidson, M.A., Fellow and Tutor of Balliol College. With three Maps.
Medium 8vo. buckram, 21*s.*

Sophocles. The Plays and Fragments. With English Notes
and Introductions, by Lewis Campbell, M.A. 2 vols.

    Vol. I. Oedipus Tyrannus. Oedipus Coloneus. Antigone. 8vo. 16*s*

    Vol. II. Ajax. Electra. Trachiniae. Philoctetes. Fragments. 8vo, 16*s.*

IV. FRENCH AND ITALIAN.

Brachet's Etymological Dictionary of the French Language.
Translated by G. W. Kitchin, D.D. Third Edition. Crown 8vo. 7*s.* 6*d.*

—— *Historical Grammar of the French Language.* Translated by G. W. Kitchin, D.D. Fourth Edition. Extra fcap. 8vo. 3*s.* 6*d.*

Works by GEORGE SAINTSBURY, M.A.

Primer of French Literature. Extra fcap. 8vo. 2*s.*

Short History of French Literature. Crown 8vo. 10*s.* 6*d.*

Specimens of French Literature, from Villon to Hugo. Crown 8vo. 9*s.*

_____

MASTERPIECES OF THE FRENCH DRAMA.

Corneille's Horace. Edited, with Introduction and Notes, by George Saintsbury, M.A. Extra fcap. 8vo. 2*s.* 6*d.*

Molière's Les Précieuses Ridicules. Edited, with Introduction and Notes, by Andrew Lang, M.A. Extra fcap. 8vo. 1*s.* 6*d.*

Racine's Esther. Edited, with Introduction and Notes, by George Saintsbury, M.A. Extra fcap. 8vo. 2*s.*

Beaumarchais' Le Barbier de Séville. Edited, with Introduction and Notes, by Austin Dobson. Extra fcap. 8vo. 2*s.* 6*d.*

Voltaire's Mérope. Edited, with Introduction and Notes, by George Saintsbury. Extra fcap. 8vo. cloth, 2*s.*

Musset's On ne badine pas avec l'Amour, and *Fantasio.* Edited, with Prolegomena, Notes, etc., by Walter Herries Pollock. Extra fcap. 8vo. 2*s.*

The above six Plays may be had in ornamental case, and bound in Imitation Parchment, price 12*s.* 6*d.*

_____

Perrault's Popular Tales. Edited from the Original Editions, with Introduction, etc., by Andrew Lang, M.A. Extra fcap. 8vo., paper boards, 5*s.* 6*d.*

Sainte-Beuve. Selections from the Causeries du Lundi. Edited by George Saintsbury, M.A. Extra fcap. 8vo. 2*s.*

Quinet's Lettres à sa Mère. Selected and edited by George Saintsbury, M.A. Extra fcap. 8vo. 2*s.*

Gautier, Théophile. Scenes of Travel. Selected and Edited by George Saintsbury, M.A. Extra fcap. 8vo. 2*s.*

L'Éloquence de la Chaire et de la Tribune Françaises. Edited by Paul Blouët, B.A. Vol. I. Sacred Oratory. Extra fcap. 8vo. 2*s.* 6*d.*

Corneille's Cinna. With Notes, Glossary, etc. Extra fcap. 8vo.
cloth, 2*s.* Stiff covers, 1*s.* 6*d.*

Louis XIV and his Contemporaries; as described in Extracts
from the best Memoirs of the Seventeenth Century. With English Notes,
Genealogical Tables, &c. Extra fcap. 8vo. 2*s.* 6*d.*

Maistre, Xavier de. Voyage autour de ma Chambre. Ourika,
by *Madame de Duras;* Le Vieux Tailleur, by *MM. Erckmann-Chatrian;*
La Veillée de Vincennes, by *Alfred de Vigny;* Les Jumeaux de l'Hôtel
Corneille, by *Edmond About;* Mésaventures d'un Écolier, by *Rodolphe Töpffer.*
Third Edition, Revised and Corrected. Extra fcap. 8vo. 2*s.* 6*d.*

—— *Voyage autour de ma Chambre.* Limp, 1*s.* 6*d.*

Molière's Les Fourberies de Scapin, and *Racine's Athalie.*
With Voltaire's Life of Molière. Extra fcap. 8vo. 2*s.* 6*d.*

Molière's Les Fourberies de Scapin. With Voltaire's Life of
Molière. Extra fcap. 8vo. stiff covers, 1*s.* 6*d.*

Molière's Les Femmes Savantes. With Notes, Glossary, etc.
Extra fcap. 8vo. *cloth,* 2*s.* Stiff covers, 1*s.* 6*d.*

Racine's Andromaque, and *Corneille's Le Menteur.* With
Louis Racine's Life of his Father. Extra fcap. 8vo. 2*s.* 6*d.*

Regnard's Le Joueur, and *Brueys and Palaprat's Le Grondeur.*
Extra fcap. 8vo. 2*s.* 6*d.*

*Sévigné, Madame de, and her chief Contemporaries, Selections
from the Correspondence of.* Intended more especially for Girls' Schools.
Extra fcap. 8vo. 3*s.*

Dante. Selections from the Inferno. With Introduction and
Notes. By H. B. Cotterill, B.A. Extra fcap. 8vo. 4*s.* 6*d.*

Tasso. La Gerusalemme Liberata. Cantos i, ii. With Introduction and Notes. By the same Editor. Extra fcap. 8vo. 2*s.* 6*d.*

V. GERMAN.

Scherer (W.). A History of German Literature. Translated
from the Third German Edition by Mrs. F. Conybeare. Edited by F. Max
Müller. 2 vols. 8vo. 21*s.*

Max Müller. The German Classics, from the Fourth to the
Nineteenth Century. With Biographical Notices, Translations into Modern
German, and Notes. By F. Max Müller, M.A. A New Edition, Revised,
Enlarged, and Adapted to Wilhelm Scherer's 'History of German Literature,'
by F. Lichtenstein. 2 vols. crown 8vo. 21*s.* ...

GERMAN COURSE. By HERMANN LANGE.

The Germans at Home; a Practical Introduction to German
Conversation, with an Appendix containing the Essentials of German Grammar.
Third Edition. 8vo. 2s. 6d.

The German Manual; a German Grammar, Reading Book,
and a Handbook of German Conversation. 8vo. 7s. 6d.

Grammar of the German Language. 8vo. 3s. 6d.

German Composition; A Theoretical and Practical Guide to
the Art of Translating English Prose into German. Ed. 2. 8vo. 4s. 6d.

German Spelling; A Synopsis of the Changes which it has
undergone through the Government Regulations of 1880. Paper covers, 6d.

Lessing's Laokoon. With Introduction, English Notes, etc.
By A. Hamann, Phil. Doc., M.A. Extra fcap. 8vo. 4s. 6d.

Schiller's Wilhelm Tell. Translated into English Verse by
E. Massie, M.A. Extra fcap. 8vo. 5s.

GERMAN CLASSICS.

*With Biographical, Historical, and Critical Introductions, Arguments
(to the Dramas), and Complete Commentaries.*

Edited by C. A. BUCHHEIM, Phil. Doc. Professor in King's
College, London.

Lessing:
  (a) *Nathan der Weise.* A Dramatic Poem. 4s. 6d.
  (b) *Minna von Barnhelm.* A Comedy. 3s. 6d.

Goethe:
  (a) *Egmont.* A Tragedy. 3s.
  (b) *Iphigenie auf Tauris.* A Drama. 3s.

Schiller:
  (a) *Wilhelm Tell.* A Drama. Large Edition. With a Map. 3s. 6d.
  (b) *Wilhelm Tell.* School Edition. With a Map. 2s.
  ⁴(c) *Historische Skizzen.* With a Map. 2s. 6d.

Heine:
  (a) *Prosa:* being Selections from his Prose Writings. 4s. 6d.
  (b) *Harzreise.* Cloth, 2s. 6d. ; paper covers, 1s. 6d.

Modern German Reader. A Graduated Collection of Ex-
tracts from Modern German Authors :—
Part I. Prose Extracts. With English Notes, a Grammatical Appendix, and
  a Complete Vocabulary. Fourth Edition. 2s. 6d.
Part II. Extracts in Prose and Poetry. With English Notes and an Index.
  Second Edition. 2s. 6d.

Becker (the Historian):

Friedrich der Grosse. Edited, with Notes, an Historical Introduction, and a Map. 3s. 6d.

Niebuhr:

Griechische Heroen-Geschichten (Tales of Greek Heroes). Edited, with English Notes and a Vocabulary, by Emma S. Buchheim. Second. Revised Edition. *cloth*, 2s.

An Old High German Primer. With Grammar, Notes, and Glossary. By Joseph Wright, Ph.D. Extra fcap. 8vo. 3s. 6d.

A Middle High German Primer. With Grammar, Notes, and Glossary. By Joseph Wright, Ph.D. Extra fcap. 8vo. 3s. 6d.

VI. MATHEMATICS, PHYSICAL SCIENCE, &c.

By LEWIS HENSLEY, M.A.

Figures made Easy: a first Arithmetic Book. Crown 8vo. 6d.

Answers to the Examples in Figures made Easy, together with two thousand additional Examples, with Answers. Crown 8vo. 1s.

The Scholar's Arithmetic. Crown 8vo. 2s. 6d.

Answers to the Examples in the Scholar's Arithmetic. 1s. 6d.

The Scholar's Algebra. Crown 8vo. 2s. 6d.

Aldis (W. S., M.A.). A Text-Book of Algebra: with Answers to the Examples. Crown 8vo. 7s. 6d.

Baynes (R. E., M.A.). Lessons on Thermodynamics. 1878. Crown 8vo. 7s. 6d.

Chambers (G. F., F.R.A.S.). A Handbook of Descriptive Astronomy. Third Edition. 1877. Demy 8vo. 28s.

Clarke (Col. A. R., C.B., R.E.). Geodesy. 1880. 8vo. 12s. 6d.

Cremona (Luigi). Elements of Projective Geometry. Translated by C. Leudesdorf, M.A. 8vo. 12s. 6d.

Donkin. Acoustics. Second Edition. Crown 8vo. 7s. 6d.

Etheridge (R.). Fossils of the British Islands, Stratigraphically arranged. Part I. PALAEOZOIC. 4to. 1l. 10s. *Just ready.*

Euclid Revised. Containing the Essentials of the Elements of Plane Geometry as given by Euclid in his first Six Books. Edited by R. C. J. Nixon, M.A. Crown 8vo.

Sold separately as follows,

Book I. 1s.   Books I, II. 1s. 6d.

Books I–IV. 3s. 6d.   Books V, VI. 3s.

D

Euclid.—Geometry in Space. Containing parts of Euclid's
Eleventh and Twelfth Books. By the same Editor. Crown 8vo. 3s. 6d.

*Galton (Douglas, C.B., F.R.S.). The Construction of Healthy
Dwellings.* Demy 8vo. 10s. 6d.

Hamilton (Sir R. G. C.), and J. Ball. Book-keeping. New
and enlarged Edition. Extra fcap. 8vo. limp cloth, 2s.

Ruled Exercise books adapted to the above may be had, price 2s.

Harcourt (A. G. Vernon, M.A.), and H. G. Madan, M.A.
Exercises in Practical Chemistry. Vol. I. Elementary Exercises. Fourth
Edition. Crown 8vo. 10s. 6d.

Maclaren (Archibald). A System of Physical Education:
Theoretical and Practical. Extra fcap. 8vo. 7s. 6d.

Madan (H. G., M.A.). Tables of Qualitative Analysis.
Large 4to. paper, 4s. 6d.

*Maxwell (J. Clerk, M.A., F.R.S.). A Treatise on Electricity
and Magnetism.* Second Edition. 2 vols. Demy 8vo. 1l. 11s. 6d.

—— *An Elementary Treatise on Electricity.* Edited by
William Garnett, M.A. Demy 8vo. 7s. 6d.

Minchin (G. M., M.A.). A Treatise on Statics with Applications to Physics. Third Edition, Corrected and Enlarged. Vol. I. *Equili-
brium of Coplanar Forces.* 8vo. 9s. Vol. II. *Statics.* 8vo. 16s.

—— *Uniplanar Kinematics of Solids and Fluids.* Crown
8vo. 7s. 6d.

*Phillips (John, M.A., F.R.S.). Geology of Oxford and the
Valley of the Thames.* 1871. 8vo. 21s.

—— *Vesuvius.* 1869. Crown 8vo. 10s. 6d.

*Prestwich (Joseph, M.A., F.R.S.). Geology, Chemical, Physical,
and Stratigraphical.* In two Volumes.

Vol. I. Chemical and Physical. Royal 8vo. 25s.
Vol. II. Stratigraphical and Physical. With a new Geographical Map of
Europe. Royal 8vo. 36s.

Rolleston (George, M.D., F.R.S.). Forms of Animal Life.
A Manual of Comparative Anatomy, with descriptions of selected types.
Second Edition. Revised and enlarged by W. Hatchett Jackson, M.A.
Medium, 8vo. cloth extra, 1l. 16s.

Smyth. A Cycle of Celestial Objects. Observed, Reduced,
and Discussed by Admiral W. H. Smyth, R.N. Revised, condensed, and
greatly enlarged by G. F. Chambers, F.R.A.S. 1881. 8vo. 12s.

*Stewart (Balfour, LL.D., F.R.S.). An Elementary Treatise
on Heat,* with numerous Woodcuts and Diagrams. Fifth Edition. Extra
fcap. 8vo. 7s. 6d.

Vernon-Harcourt (*L. F., M.A.*). *A Treatise on Rivers and Canals*, relating to the Control and Improvement of Rivers, and the Design, Construction, and Development of Canals. 2 vols. (Vol. I, Text. Vol. II, Plates.) 8vo. 21s.

—— *Harbours and Docks;* their Physical Features, History, Construction, Equipment, and Maintenance; with Statistics as to their Commercial Development. 2 vols. 8vo. 25s.

Walker (*James, M.A.*). *The Theory of a Physical Balance.* 8vo. stiff cover, 3s. 6d.

Watson (*H. W., M.A.*). *A Treatise on the Kinetic Theory of Gases.* 1876. 8vo. 3s. 6d.

Watson (*H. W., D. Sc., F.R.S.*), *and S. H. Burbury, M.A.*

I. *A Treatise on the Application of Generalised Coordinates to the Kinetics of a Material System.* 1879. 8vo. 6s.

II. *The Mathematical Theory of Electricity and Magnetism.* Vol. I. Electrostatics. 8vo. 10s. 6d.

Williamson (*A. W., Phil. Doc., F.R.S.*). *Chemistry for Students.* A new Edition, with Solutions. 1873. Extra fcap. 8vo. 8s. 6d.

VII. HISTORY.

Bluntschli (*J. K.*). *The Theory of the State.* By J. K. Bluntschli, late Professor of Political Sciences in the University of Heidelberg. Authorised English Translation from the Sixth German Edition. . Demy 8vo. half bound, 12s. 6d.

Finlay (*George, LL.D.*). *A History of Greece* from its Conquest by the Romans to the present time, B.C. 146 to A.D. 1864. A new Edition, revised throughout, and in part re-written, with considerable additions, by the Author, and edited by H. F. Tozer, M.A. 7 vols. 8vo. 3l. 10s.

Fortescue (*Sir John, Kt.*). *The Governance of England:* otherwise called The Difference between an Absolute and a Limited Monarchy. A Revised Text. Edited, with Introduction, Notes, and Appendices, by Charles Plummer, M.A. 8vo. half bound, 12s. 6d.

Freeman (*E.A., D.C.L.*). *A Short History of the Norman Conquest of England.* Second Edition. Extra fcap. 8vo. 2s. 6d.

George (*H. B., M.A.*). *Genealogical Tables illustrative of Modern History.* Third Edition, Revised and Enlarged. Small 4to. 12s.

Hodgkin (*T.*). *Italy and her Invaders.* Illustrated with Plates and Maps. Vols. I—IV, A.D. 376-553. 8vo. 3l. 8s.

Hughes (*Alfred*). *Geography for Schools.* With Diagrams.
Part I. Practical Geography. Crown 8vo. 2s. 6d.

  Part II. General Geography. *In preparation.*

Kitchin (*G. W., D.D.*). *A History of France.* With numerous
Maps, Plans, and Tables. In Three Volumes. *Second Edition.* Crown 8vo.
each 10s. 6d.

  Vol. I. Down to the Year 1453.

  Vol. II. From 1453-1624.   Vol. III. From 1624-1793.

Lucas (*C. P.*). *Introduction to a Historical Geography of the
British Colonies.* With Eight Maps. Crown 8vo. 4s. 6d.

Payne (*E. J., M.A.*). *A History of the United States of
America.* In the Press.

Ranke (*L. von*). *A History of England,* principally in the
Seventeenth Century. Translated by Resident Members of the University of
Oxford, under the superintendence of G. W. Kitchin, D.D., and C. W. Boase,
M.A. 1875. 6 vols. 8vo. 3l. 3s.

Rawlinson (*George, M.A.*). *A Manual of Ancient History.*
Second Edition. Demy 8vo. 14s.

Ricardo. *Letters of David Ricardo to Thomas Robert Malthus*
(1810-1823). Edited by James Bonar, M.A. Demy 8vo. 10s. 6d.

Rogers (*J. E. Thorold, M.A.*). *The First Nine Years of the
Bank of England.* 8vo. 8s. 6d.

*Select Charters and other Illustrations of English Constitutional
History,* from the Earliest Times to the Reign of Edward I. Arranged and
edited by W. Stubbs, D.D. Fifth Edition. 1883. Crown 8vo. 8s. 6d.

Stubbs (*W., D.D.*). *The Constitutional History of England,*
in its Origin and Development. Library Edition. 3 vols. demy 8vo. 2l. 8s.

  Also in 3 vols. crown 8vo. price 12s. each.

—— *Seventeen Lectures on the Study of Medieval and
Modern History,* &c., delivered at Oxford 1867-1884. Crown 8vo. 8s. 6d.

Wellesley. *A Selection from the Despatches, Treaties, and*
other Papers of the Marquess Wellesley, K.G., during his Government
of India. Edited by S. J. Owen, M.A. 1877. 8vo. 1l. 4s.

Wellington. *A Selection from the Despatches, Treaties, and*
other Papers relating to India of Field-Marshal the Duke of Wellington, K.G.
Edited by S. J. Owen, M.A. 1880. 8vo. 24s.

A History of British India. By S. J. Owen, M.A., Reader
in Indian History in the University of Oxford. In preparation.

VIII. LAW.

Alberici Gentilis, I.C.D., I.C., De Iure Belli Libri Tres.
Edidit T. E. Holland, I.C.D. 1877. Small 4to. half morocco, 21*s.*

Anson (Sir William R., Bart., D.C.L.). Principles of the
English Law of Contract, and of Agency in its Relation to Contract. Fifth
Edition. Demy 8vo. 10*s. 6d.*

—— *Law and Custom of the Constitution.* Part I. Parliament. Demy 8vo. 10*s. 6d.*

Bentham (Jeremy). An Introduction to the Principles of
Morals and Legislation. Crown 8vo. 6*s. 6d.*

Digby (Kenelm E., M.A.). An Introduction to the History of
the Law of Real Property. Third Edition. Demy 8vo. 10*s. 6d.*

Gaii Institutionum Juris Civilis Commentarii Quattuor; or,
Elements of Roman Law by Gaius. With a Translation and Commentary
by Edward Poste, M.A. Second Edition. 1875. 8vo. 18*s.*

Hall (W. E., M.A.). International Law. Second Ed. 8vo. 21*s.*

Holland (T. E., D.C.L.). The Elements of Jurisprudence.
Fourth Edition. Demy 8vo. 10*s. 6d.*

—— *The European Concert in the Eastern Question,* a Collection of Treaties and other Public Acts. Edited, with Introductions and
Notes, by Thomas Erskine Holland, D.C.L. 8vo. 12*s. 6d.*

Imperatoris Iustiniani Institutionum Libri Quattuor; with
Introductions, Commentary, Excursus and Translation. By J. E. Moyle, B.C.L.,
M.A. 2 vols. Demy 8vo. 21*s.*

Justinian, The Institutes of, edited as a recension of the
Institutes of Gaius, by Thomas Erskine Holland, D.C.L. Second Edition,
1881. Extra fcap. 8vo. 5*s.*

Justinian, Select Titles from the Digest of. By T. E. Holland,
D.C.L., and C. L. Shadwell, B.C.L. 8vo. 14*s.*

Also sold in Parts, in paper covers, as follows :—
Part I. Introductory Titles. 2*s. 6d.*   Part II. Family Law. 1*s.*
Part III. Property Law. 2*s. 6d.*   Part IV. Law of Obligations (No. 1). 3*s. 6d.*
Part IV. Law of Obligations (No. 2). 4*s. 6d.*

Lex Aquilia. The Roman Law of Damage to Property :
being a Commentary on the Title of the Digest 'Ad Legem Aquiliam' (ix. 2).
With an Introduction to the Study of the Corpus Iuris Civilis. By Erwin
Grueber, Dr. Jur., M.A. Demy 8vo. 10*s. 6d.*

Markby (W., D.C.L.). Elements of Law considered with reference to Principles of General Jurisprudence. Third Edition. Demy 8vo. 12s.6d.

Stokes (Whitley, D.C.L.).   The Anglo-Indian Codes.
  Vol. I. *Substantive Law.* 8vo. 30s.
  Vol. II. *Adjective Law.* In the Press.

Twiss (Sir Travers, D.C.L.).   The Law of Nations considered as Independent Political Communities.
  Part I. On the Rights and Duties of Nations in time of Peace. A new Edition, Revised and Enlarged. 1884. Demy 8vo. 15s.
  Part II. On the Rights and Duties of Nations in Time of War. Second Edition, Revised. 1875. Demy 8vo. 21s.

IX. MENTAL AND MORAL PHILOSOPHY, &c.

Bacon's Novum Organum. Edited, with English Notes, by G. W. Kitchin, D.D. 1855. 8vo. 9s. 6d.

—— Translated by G. W. Kitchin, D.D. 1855. 8vo. 9s. 6d.

Berkeley. The Works of George Berkeley, D.D., formerly Bishop of Cloyne; including many of his writings hitherto unpublished. With Prefaces, Annotations, and an Account of his Life and Philosophy, by Alexander Campbell Fraser, M.A. 4 vols. 1871. 8vo. 2l. 18s.
  The Life, Letters, &c. 1 vol. 16s.

—— *Selections from.* With an Introduction and Notes. For the use of Students in the Universities. By Alexander Campbell Fraser, LL.D. Third Edition. Crown 8vo. 7s. 6d.

Fowler (T., D.D.). The Elements of Deductive Logic, designed mainly for the use of Junior Students in the Universities. Ninth Edition, with a Collection of Examples. Extra fcap. 8vo. 3s. 6d.

—— *The Elements of Inductive Logic,* designed mainly for the use of Students in the Universities. Fourth Edition. Extra fcap. 8vo. 6s.

—— *and Wilson (J. M., B.D.). The Principles of Morals* (Introductory Chapters). 8vo. *boards,* 3s. 6d.

—— *The Principles of Morals.* Part II. (Being the Body of the Work.) 8vo. 10s. 6d.

Edited by T. FOWLER, D.D.

Bacon. Novum Organum. With Introduction, Notes, &c. 1878. 8vo. 14s.

Locke's Conduct of the Understanding. Second Edition. Extra fcap. 8vo. 2s.

Danson (J. T.). The Wealth of Households. Crown 8vo. 5s.

Green (T. H., M.A.). Prolegomena to Ethics. Edited by
A. C. Bradley, M.A. Demy 8vo. 12s. 6d.

Hegel. The Logic of Hegel; translated from the Encyclo-
paedia of the Philosophical Sciences. With Prolegomena by William
Wallace, M.A. 1874. 8vo. 14s.

Hume's Treatise of Human Nature; reprinted from the
Original Edition, and edited by L. A. Selby-Bigge, M.A., Fellow and
Lecturer of University College. Crown 8vo. 9s.

Lotze's Logic, in Three Books; of Thought, of Investigation,
and of Knowledge. English Translation: Edited by B. Bosanquet, M.A.,
Fellow of University College, Oxford. Second Edition. 2 vols. Crown
8vo. 12s.

—— *Metaphysic,* in Three Books; Ontology, Cosmology,
and Psychology. English Translation; Edited by B. Bosanquet, M.A.
Second Edition. 2 vols. Crown 8vo. 12s.

Martineau (James, D.D.). Types of Ethical Theory. Second
Edition. 2 vols. Crown 8vo. 15s.

—— *A Study of Religion : its Sources and Contents.* 2 vols.
8vo. 24s.

Rogers (J. E. Thorold, M.A.). A Manual of Political Economy,
for the use of Schools. Third Edition. Extra fcap. 8vo. 4s. 6d.

Smith's Wealth of Nations. A new Edition, with Notes, by
J. E. Thorold Rogers, M.A. 2 vols. 8vo. 1880. 21s.

X. FINE ART.

Butler (A. J., M.A., F.S.A.) The Ancient Coptic Churches of
Egypt. 2 vols. 8vo. 30s.

Head (Barclay V.). Historia Numorum. A Manual of Greek
Numismatics. Royal 8vo. half morocco, 42s.

Hullah (John). The Cultivation of the Speaking Voice.
Second Edition. Extra fcap. 8vo. 2s. 6d.

Jackson (T. G., M.A.). Dalmatia, the Quarnero and Istria;
with Cettigne in Montenegro and the Island of Grado. By T. G. Jackson,
M.A., Author of 'Modern Gothic Architecture.' In 3 vols. 8vo. With many
Plates and Illustrations. Half bound, 42s.

Ouseley (Sir F. A. Gore, Bart.). A Treatise on Harmony.
Third Edition. 4to. 10s.

—— *A Treatise on Counterpoint, Canon, and Fugue,* based
upon that of Cherubini. Second Edition. 4to. 16s.

—— *A Treatise on Musical Form and General Composition.*
Second Edition. 4to. 10s.

Robinson (J. C., F.S.A.). A Critical Account of the Drawings
by *Michel Angelo and Raffaello in the University Galleries, Oxford.* 1870.
Crown 8vo. 4s.

Troutbeck (J., M.A.) and R. F. Dale, M.A. A Music Primer
(for Schools). Second Edition. Crown 8vo. 1s. 6d.

Tyrwhitt (R. St. J., M.A.). A Handbook of Pictorial Art.
With coloured Illustrations, Photographs, and a chapter on Perspective by
A. Macdonald. Second Edition. 1875. 8vo. half morocco, 18s.

Upcott (L. E., M.A.). An Introduction to Greek Sculpture.
Crown 8vo. 4s. 6d.

Vaux (W. S. W., M.A.). Catalogue of the Castellani Collec-
tion *of Antiquities in the University Galleries, Oxford.* Crown 8vo. 1s.

The Oxford Bible for Teachers, containing Supplementary
HELPS TO THE STUDY OF THE BIBLE, including Summaries of the several
Books, with copious Explanatory Notes and Tables illustrative of Scripture
History and the characteristics of Bible Lands; with a complete Index of
Subjects, a Concordance, a Dictionary of Proper Names, and a series of Maps.
Prices in various sizes and bindings from 3s. to 2l. 5s.

Helps to the Study of the Bible, taken from the OXFORD
BIBLE FOR TEACHERS, comprising Summaries of the several Books, with
copious Explanatory Notes and Tables illustrative of Scripture History and
the Characteristics of Bible Lands; with a complete Index of Subjects, a Concordance, a Dictionary of Proper Names, and a series of Maps. Crown 8vo.
cloth, 3s. 6d.; 16mo. cloth, 1s.

LONDON: HENRY FROWDE,
OXFORD UNIVERSITY PRESS WAREHOUSE, AMEN CORNER,

OXFORD: CLARENDON PRESS DEPOSITORY,
116 HIGH STREET.

☞ *The* DELEGATES OF THE PRESS *invite suggestions and advice from all persons
interested in education; and will be thankful for hints, &c. addressed to the*
SECRETARY TO THE DELEGATES, *Clarendon Press, Oxford.*

www.ingramcontent.com/pod-product-compliance
Lightning Source LLC
Chambersburg PA
CBHW031816270326
41932CB00008B/440